TAKE YOUR SHAME
AND SHOVE IT

TAKE YOUR SHAME AND SHOVE IT

We Ain't in the Garden of Eden No More

HOWARD ZIEHM

Printed in the United States of America
ISBN 978-1-947352-25-4 (sc)
ISBN 978-1-947352-30-8 (hc)
ISBN 978-1-947352-28-5 (e)

Library of Congress Control Number: 2022908773

2022.05.11

MainSpring Books
5901 W. Century Blvd
Suite 750
Los Angeles, CA, US, 90045

www.mainspringbooks.com

To My Wife Judy

Who Allowed Me To Be Who I Needed To Be

"Some thought he was a little angel, I knew he was a little devil"

David Phillips Highschool classmate
and Westpoint graduate

TABLE OF CONTENTS

INTRODUCTION

As much as sex fascinates us, it also leaves us in fear of its mysterious force. We are the only species that faces this conundrum. Some hide their fears in the rituals or repressive tenets of religion that teach that sex is a sin and should only be done in the dark. Even those who acknowledge that they love sex are challenged to overcome doubts about their adequacy. Men stress about getting an erection and if they are "big" enough to make a woman happy. Conversely women wonder if they are pretty or if their tits and asses are big and shapely enough to attract a man. Men worry about cumming too soon and women wonder if they should feign orgasms while having sex.

As a child I had no idea that there even was something called sex. My only concern was getting to heaven so I could live with little lord Jesus and not have to go to hell and live with the devil in the scorching hot middle of the earth. This was terrifying but true because it said so in a book called the Bible that God wrote. The Bible was said to have the answers to all of life's questions yet when it came to sex its answers were wanting.

Then there was the mysterious glow that came over me when I was in the vicinity of girls. What caused it I had no idea. I didn't even like girls. They were sissies. That it was both pleasant and terrifying at the same time drove me crazy. No one provided me answers and the pressure continued to grow. I suspected the force was coming from something beneath a girls dress so I devised a plan to find out. I had no inkling of the many lairs, both mental and physical, good and bad, that my simple effort to relieve my curiosity would lead me, but even if I had, it wouldn't have mattered, I had to find out. It all began innocently enough at grandma's house when I decided to steal a peek up her dress.

1

WHAT WERE THEY HIDING?

The question made me think that there was something different about them that I wasn't supposed to know. "What were they hiding under their skirts and why do they get to wear soft silk underwear while boys had to wear rough cotton ones?" The secrecy made me think that maybe their sprinklers were somehow different than mine. Many times I would ask my mother, "What do girls sprinklers look like?" She would never give me an answer.

I reasoned that if I could somehow get myself into a position that would allow me to look up grandma's dress the mystery would be solved. So while she was busy in the kitchen at the back of the house, I laid down in the doorway that connected the dinning and living rooms, and pretended to play with my little wood train, driving it back and forth between the jambs. The doorway was the only path between the front of the house and the kitchen. If I were patient enough, she would eventually have to step over me. I figured right. As she approached the doorway, I casually rolled over on my back so I could get a view up her dress as she traversed over my head. But at the moment of truth, she stepped far to the side, passing over my legs rather than over my head. She had done it on purpose! She didn't want me to see what was up there. Whatever it was must be important! Very important!!

I was born on April 7, 1940 in Milwaukee, Wisconsin; meaning, since Wisconsin made lots of cheese, I was a Cheesehead. Along with this appellation came several others: I was an American, a German and a Christian. America stood for everything that was right in the world and the fact that we were having a war with the 'Krauts' meant it was best not to boast about being German. Things would work out if I let God and his son, 'little lord Jesus,' protect me and my family from evil. All we had to do was pray each night and go to church every Sunday to let them know their work was appreciated.

My first conscious recollection was looking up a narrow flight of stairs that led to the second floor flat where I lived with my mother. Because I liked to roam, and had no respect for boundaries, I felt fully justified in opening the little wooden accordion gate that was meant to keep me safely confined upstairs. When I managed to get past it, I suddenly found myself tumbling head over heals down the cascade of stairs until I reached the bottom. My soft boned body was unharmed and I was just a bit startled—unlike my hysterical mother who was now standing at the top of the stairs going berserk. I quickly reasoned that I should join in on the hysteria and began to cry.

For reasons unknown to me, my mother and father didn't live together and though my mother was the foundation of my life, I spent intermittent periods of various lengths living with grandparents, uncles and aunts. Mostly I lived with my father's parents, grandma and grandpa Dittman, who had a large house made of stone in Wauwautosa, a suburb north of Milwaukee. It sat in the middle of the block on raised ground a few steps back from the sidewalk. It's gable roof along with two big blue vases that stood as sentinals outside the front entry door and the fireflies in the backyard that blinked on and off when darkness came, gave it a fairytale like air. My mother would drop by at least once a week to take me to a movie or the zoo and make sure I was happy where I was living. If I said I wanted to move, which was usually if I had been punished for something like drawing little pictures on the wall down by the baseboard, she would arrange to drop me off at one of the other relatives. More often than not, that was her sister, Auntie Ester and her husband Joe Hokinger.

I wasn't unhappy and had no problem with being farmed out. I had a good imagination and was very capable of entertaining myself no matter where I lived. Grandma Dittman discovered this one morning when she entered my room to see why I was making so much noise. She had been downstairs doing her chores when she heard me going: "woo . . . woo . . . woo." Upon entering the room, she saw that I was making believe I was an engineer driving a train. I was standing up behind the headboard of my crib bed holding on to the two decorative pegs that stuck up from its sides as though they were the levers that drove the engine. The puzzled look on her face was not due to the fact that I was driving a choo choo, but that I was wearing one of her silk slips. While she was downstairs, I had quietly snuck down the hall and grabbed it off the top of her bed where it had been left lying and tiptoed back to my bedroom so I could slip into it before returning to my crib bed to play engineer in my fantasy train. It mattered not that the slip was much too large for my small body, I just loved how nice the silk felt against my skin. Too young to be considered a pervert, my little fetish was just shined off as a bit odd.

When the time came for me to be dumped off at Auntie Ester's house about an hour away in Springfield, I had a special opportunity to enjoy my infatuation with trains in a more realistic way. Each evening just before sundown, a long freight train would lumber by in the distance and as soon as I heard its whistle blowing, I would run out on the front lawn waving a white towel my aunt had given me. My hopes were by franticly waving it; I would get the attention of the engineer. It was a joyous thrill when he waved back with a white handkerchief. As the train disappeared around a cove of trees, I wondered where it was going; to what unknown lands did the tracks lead? Auntie Ester was a somewhat skittish woman with light curly reddish hair and Uncle Joe, a tall handsome good-natured man with a warm resonant German accent, never punished me, but they chose not to have children of their own for a reason, and after two weeks or so, I became more than they could handle and I would find myself heading back to the Dittmans who I knew would welcome me with a little present.

Life in the early 40's was sparse. World War II was going at full force and though I had no idea what it was about other than the Germans were bad and us Americans were good, I did understand that to help us win the war; milk, sugar and flour had to be rationed. Meat was hard to come by and we only had it when my grandpa could trap a squirrel or rabbit in the backyard. Roasted squirrel or rabbit was a treat to be relished.

My mother 1943

3

It was a mystery to me where my mother lived, since I only saw her when she came by for a visit. That usually included a visit to the zoo or a movie—preferably a Disney movie. I loved animals and came out of the theatre after seeing Bambi with tear-filled eyes.

Despite the fact that I wasn't under her constant care, I knew she loved me. She insisted that I be properly clothed to protect me from getting colds or Polio. The images of little children encased in iron lungs, large barrel-like apparatus that allowed for only the head of the victim to stick out, was so terrifying that I didn't mind being over-dressed to prevent that fate from happening to me. No matter who I stayed with, instructions were given for them to send me to bed no later than eight o'clock. When she visited and my bedtime came, I would insist she read me my favorite story: 'The Little Engine That Could.' The sound of its determined chugging as it struggled to reach the top of the hill, "I think I can, I think I can," followed by "I knew I could, I knew I could" as it raced down the hill was a comforting thought as I fell asleep.

At times, when she had to leave early, I was told it was because she was going somewhere to look for a new daddy for me. Why this was necessay I had no idea. At those times she always seemed to come to the Dittmans wearing a white body hugging knit dress that molded around all the curves of her body. She had plenty of curves—nice full ones—and I found them attractive, but had no clue why the dress would help her find me a new daddy. She seemed to be happy when she had that dress on and it was none of my business anyway.

The existence of sex was not in my universe. It simply just did not exist. The weird little thing between my legs, called a sprinkler because peepee sprinkled out of it, was only there for that specific purpose. When not sprinkling it was supposed to be covered. Putatively this was because it was a private part and dirty. Any thoughts about where babies came from was explained with the established science of Storkology; that babies were delivered by storks who dropped them atop chimneys much like Santa Claus did with presents at Christmas time. At baby time, a chimney was a very important part of a house.

Grandpa Dittman wasn't as strict as grandma Dittman and sometimes would take me along to the small cabinet-making factory he owned that was not far from the house. There I would use the strips of dovetails as trains and pull them along the floor between the little piles of sawdust I had used to make hills. In the evening, after dinner, he would read stories from the newspaper to my grandmother as they sat around a small table in the kitchen located at the back of the house. Children were *"meant to be seen and not heard,"* so I would pretend to be playing on the floor, but my ears were peeled like a hawk. He always started with stories about the war; how things were progressing. Americans didn't like the Germans because we were fighting them so the word 'German' was always spoken in a muted voice. It was best not to let the neighbors hear us saying that word.

After the war news, grandpa moved to the local crime stories. One in particular about a window peeper who was running around the Milwaukee area enthralled me. He was using old tires to stand on so he could get high enough to peek into a window. There was no mention about what he was peeping at. When I was told to go to bed, I climbed the stairs with the thought of that window peeper in my mind. At the top of the stairs was a small window at the end of the hall where I imagined if the peeper had made a stack of tires high enough; he might be peeking into the house at that very moment. So as soon as I got to the top of the stairs, I would scurry down the dark hall as fast as I could to my bedroom and bury my head under the covers.

My father's brother, uncle Eddie, was a skilled ghost-story teller and would put me on his knee to make the experience more intimate. My favorite, which he told with an eerie timbre to his voice, was about a train whose engineer and passengers were all skeletons. It made my hair stand on end. I actually loved to be scared except when I was put down in the cellar for an hour as punishment for drawing little pictures on the wall. Because there was always the possibility that the window peeper or some other maniac was hiding in the darkness, I stayed at the top of the stairs where a bit of light peeked through the bottom of the door.

Because of the little pictures I drew on the wall, my mother got the idea that I might be a budding artist and entered me in an art contest sponsored by a mail order art school that was frequently advertised in the paper. It was just a scam to buy art lessons, but at least she had my best interests at heart. As did her entering me in singing contests when she heard me enthusiastically singing the song Uncle Remus sang in Disney's, Song of the South:

'Zippity Doo Dah, Zippity Ay; My oh my what a wonderful day'

It was her dream that she might have a future Frank Sinatra on her hands; so I was led down to the Orpheum theatre in downtown Milwaukee in hopes that I would be discovered. On a rainy Saturday, I stood silently with my mother among a group of other contestants in the wings of the theatre's huge stage. When my name was called, my mom nudged me onto the stage. I was overwhelmed. In a timid and trembling voice, I began singing: "Pecos Bill was quite a cowboy down in Texas . . ., the words so quiet I doubt if anyone heard them. The black void that loomed in front of me made me feel like a small mouse. I exited the stage with a life-long case of stage fright and an irrational disdain for Frank Sinatra.

Being that I was an interloper in each of the neighborhoods I resided in, I didn't have many friends. So I was delighted when two older boys about seven or eight who lived a few houses up the street from the Dittmans, invited me to play cowboys and Indians with them. I loved cowboys and Indians and one of my prized possessions was a bow and arrow that my grandfather bought me when they took me to an Indian reservation north of Milwaukee. After donning my little cowboy outfit, including hat, chaffs and vest, I ran up the street to join my new friends. Emulating Roy Rogers, my favorite movie-cowboy, I leapt out from behind some bushes and shot at them with my toy gun, yanking it spastically up and down while making a shooting sound with my voice; khhhk . . . khhhk . . . khhhk. The irritated look on their faces told me they didn't appreciate my stupid gun technique.

I wasn't invited back for cowboys and Indians again, but they did drop by a few days later to ask me to join them on a mission to fight some Germans who were hiding out in a drainage tunnel at the end of the street. I had been playing by myself in front of the house and though fearful of Germans because of the stories I had heard about them when grandpa read the newspaper, I didn't want to miss the opportunity to reestablish my friendship after screwing up during the cowboys and Indians game. My friends claimed it was my patriotic duty to kill Germans. When we arrived at the end of the street, they quickly scampered down a steep embankment to the tunnel's entrance. It looked dark and scary and I hesitated for a moment. *"Well, what are you waiting for?"* they shouted up to me before disappearing into the darkness. Not wanting to appear craven, I edged my way down the embankment, but by the time I got to the opening they were long out of sight. Timidly I entered the tunnel and walked along the shelf that ran alongside its curved wall. About fifty-feet in, a sharp turn led into total blackness and I could only hear distant murmurings coming from my friends. It made the eldritch environment even more frightening. After five steps forward, I abruptly turned and ran back to the entrance. I felt ashamed that I had deserted the mission and stood frozen with fear while I listened to the screams that cascaded out from tunnel as my friends fought the Germans. I was petrified. Then silence prevailed. *"They must have killed the Krauts."* The scowls on their faces when they emerged let me know they were none to happy with my desertion and began to imply that they might have to kill me as well for my treason. I ran home scared out of my wits; an experience I would keep to myself.

The only friend I had of the opposite sex was my cousin Sharon, the daughter of my mother's brother, uncle Wally and his wife Marion. She was my same age and had pretty dark eyes. My mother's parents, Grandma and Grandpa Eckl, lived on the west side of Milwaukee in an attractive house surrounded by verdant vegetation. I enjoyed going to their house for visits, not in the least that Grandma Eckl's white Spitz, Buddy, was always happy to see me and the whole Eckl family spoke with a friendly 'Bavarian' patois. My visits to the Eckls always included a T-bone steak that Grandpa had got through a secret connection which he would pan fry on the little gas stove he kept in his basement. After voraciously devouring it, I would run over to Sharon's house who lived with her parents on the second floor of a two story duplex just around the block. The house sat on the corner of a treeless street. I wasn't allowed in so I had to shout Sharon's name until her mother came to the window so I could ask her down to play. We had always had a good time until the day I came by just after a rain storm that had fallen earlier in the day. Aunt Marion, as was often the case, was in a bad mood and was reluctant to let Sharon come down to play, but because muddy water was trickling down the street next to the curb and I wanted to get busy building little dams to divert the water, I became irritated that she took so long before joining me. We soon became totally engrossed with our project and were well on the way building several dams, when she announced that she had to go number two, a nice way to say she had to go BM. I advised her to just squeeze it back for a few minutes until we were finished. Taking a BM never stopped me from my play. To make me happy, she tried as best she could, but within a minute she had pooped in her panties. My mother was forgiving when I did the same thing, which was fairly often, but Sharon knew her mother was not going to be happy. She tried to sneak back upstairs to clean herself off, but when I heard her mother's angry screams, I knew she had been discovered. The sound of a leather strap hitting her flesh and the screams of pain that followed made me feel guilty. Her mother made it clear that she thought I was a bad influence on her daughter and at age four, I became a persona non-gratis. So ended my first brief encounter with the opposite sex. I would never see Sharon again.

2

A THREE YEAR OLD PERVERT

Of course, I still had my best friend, little Lord Jesus, who I learned about in Sunday school. He was very real and I believed every word of the songs we sang about him; "Jesus loves me yes I know, for the Bible tells me so." My fertile imagination even created a more temporal image of him when I sometimes day dreamed about bounding after him with other little children through a beautiful meadow filled with yellow lilies as though he were the Pied Piper.

My mother rarely said no to me. I had been wrestling for some time with the question: 'Why did boys have to wear cotton underwear and girls get to wear silk?' It made no sense. Who made that rule? Grandma Dittman had begun hiding her slips and I missed the feeling of soft silk against my skin so I was happy as-a-lark when a wee bit of whining got her to buy me some silk panties. And I appreciated her support when a few disapproving looks came my way while I frolicked wearing my silk panties in the wading pool during our visits to Washington Park. She gave the offenders a "back-off" glare that let them know in no uncertain terms to keep their opinions to themselves.

When the time neared for me to begin my first year in school, thinking about how hard it was going to be caused me much anxiety. It shouldn't have been that way since my mother, who never had a college education, had already taught me the ABC's. I was also able to count as high as I could think and knew the name of every state and its capital. I enjoyed learning. Nevertheless, the thought of school terrified me. "Would it be hard? What if I was dumb and couldn't answer the questions?" Once school began, the fear remained. Other than inaudibly responding "here" during roll call, I tried to make myself as invisible as possible by never raising my hand to answer a question.

Only one thing piqued my interest. That was the fact that two of my classmates were twin sisters. Both of them had the same pretty faces, wore their hair the same and always dressed the same, usually in little green and red plaid dresses. They always stayed close to each other as though they were one. I thought about them a lot when I lie in my bed at night. They were surreal. I wanted to touch them but was far too shy to even say hello. When I looked at them, I felt a strange feeling in my BM factory, (our family's name for an anus). If they knew I existed they made no effort to let me know. They were very garrulous and usually surrounded by friends. One day, during a class recess, I finally mustered up the nerve to approach them—not to talk—but to lift up one of their short plaid dresses to see what was underneath. My silly grin was met with a horrified look from the twins and a stern admonishment from the teacher. After that I remained in my dark shell for the rest of the year. It was no surprise that my report card was rife with Dees (a Dee being poor).The teacher likely thought I was retarded.

3

A BRAND NEW DADDY

I was about to make one of the many radical changes that would be a pattern throughout my life. Late one summer day, shortly after the war came to an end, my mother took me to Washington Park where she told me we were going to meet a man she had met and said she liked. His name was Bob—a name I liked because it was simple and common, unlike my name, which was long and rare. He had a nice face and curly black hair. The military uniform he wore and his strong physique gave him a deportment of confidence; someone who couldn't be pushed around. He offered to play catch with me and showed me how to fly a kite so that it would soar high into the sky. I had no idea why my mother wanted me to meet Bob, but I went home feeling that because of him I had had a great day.

A few weeks later my mother asked, "Would you like to have a new daddy?" The way the question was posed led me to believe that it was no big deal to switch daddies so I responded affirmatively. I rarely saw the one I had now anyway, so why not?

A short time later, a foot of snow had covered Wauwatosa with a soft white blanket that was perfect for making snowmen or little igloos. The drifts in front of the Dittman's house were almost three-feet high and I was outside, bundled up in a snow suite and a hat with earflaps, busy at work digging a tunnel into the snow bank that had formed at the foot of the steps that led to the house. Suddenly my mother stormed by without saying a word and slammed the door behind her when she got inside. A few moments later, my father came from the opposite direction and did the same thing. I just continued playing, instinctively knowing to stay away. I could hear the loud argument taking place inside. After ten minutes, everything quieted down and my mother, distraught with tears in her eyes, stormed out of the house. Five minutes later my father did the same, less the tears. Neither of them said anything to me as they passed.

Several weeks later, a warm spring sun was beginning to melt the snow. Before it was gone, I was outside hard at work digging tunnels into the drifts, when a cab pulled up to the curb. I turned to look to see who it was. As the cab waited, my mother jumped out to tell me that the court had just awarded custody of me to my grandparents. "Do you want to live with them or with me?" I had no clue what was going on but without hesitation, I said: "you" and she grabbed me by my hand and without further ado, led me into the waiting cab. A half hour later we were at Milwaukee's Union station boarding a train that I was told was going to take us to where my new daddy lived.

Sixty-five years later, after a few glasses of wine, my mother loosened her tongue during a diner to celebrate her eighty-seventh birthday and divulged a more complete version of the story. She and Bob, my daddy-to-be, had checked into a room at a hotel in Milwaukee, where since it was unlawful for unmarried couples to occupy a room together, they checked in under an alias. The suspicious desk clerk wanted to see proof of marriage, but a haughty show of indignation by my mother, which she was well capable of, made him back down and they were given a key to a room. Once in the room, they wasted little time in getting carried away and unknowingly knocked the phone off the hook that was sitting on a night table next to the bed. In those days, outgoing calls had to be relayed through the desk clerk and when he picked up the open line all he heard was laughing in the background about how they had pulled a fast one to get the room key. The humorless desk clerk, outraged that he had been made a fool, placed a call to the police, which got my mom and Bob thrown in the clink. Later in the day, while in front of a judge, they claimed they were intending to get married and got him to drop the case if they went to a justice of the peace and consummated the deal. Ironically my new life was spawned from the fires of sexual sin.

4

SHOE SHINE BOY AND THIEF

First Lieutenant Bob Ziehm, my new daddy, met my mother and me at the Louisville train station. After hugs and kisses, he drove us to E-Town where we would be living until he could obtain housing on the Fort Knox base. He had been drafted during the war out of Marquette University where he was studying dentistry and played football. After the war ended he accepted the army's offer to help pay to finish school if he stayed in the service. Housing was scarce on the base and the shack that was to be our temporary home in E-Town, was a far cry from what I had been use to at the Dittmans. It was attached to the side of a barn that sat behind the main house. One room was inside the barn and the other was a shed attached to its side that looked across a little dirt yard to a chicken coop. If we went to a movie at night, the surprised cockroaches would scamper into myriad little holes when we returned and turned on the lights. I didn't care. That I now seemed to be part of a regular family made me very happy.

Bob Ziehm began to show me things boys need to know, like how to throw and catch a baseball, how to dry my back with a towel after a bath and how to let my sprinkler peek out through the barn door in my pants and shake it when I was done peeing. Unfortunately, silk panties didn't come with barn doors, so my days of wearing them were over. And he encouraged me to stand up for myself like a man. Skinny as a stick with blond hair so thin that any breeze would blow it all over the place, I didn't appear to be a formidable character, but I had a feisty side. Both he and my mother discovered that fact when they tried to tuck me tightly into bed each night. My mother's obsession with preventing me from catching a cold meant that the covers and sheets had to be tucked in tight. This conflicted with my need to have them loose so my toes could stick straight up. Inevitably, a violent wrestling match over who would get their way pursued. Because they were bigger they won and I wound up pinned inside the covers each night with safety pins; only my head was left protruding as though I were a moth in a cocoon.

The training I got from my bedtime battles helped me win my first childhood fight. A small disagreement found me squaring off with a neighborhood kid on the dirt driveway in front of the barn. He was eleven, four years older than me, but was also skinny. I had no doubt that I could take him. Flailing my arms as though they were a bird's flapping wings, I reined enough blows on my foe until he soon crumbled. From the corner of my eye, I could see my new dad looking on with approval. I walked away feeling like a cocky little shit!

When space on the base became available at a trailer park just a couple of miles from the famous gold depository, we were able to move out of E-Town. By building a screened in porch along side the trailer, my dad doubled its living space and gave me my own bedroom. For Christmas I was given a bicycle and joined in races around the figure eight road that ran through the trailer park. I never won, but not for trying. I pumped my heavy Schwin bike laden with metal fenders, center panel, bell ringer and front light, as fast as my skinny legs could manage, leaving me panting and sweating profusely at the end of each race. The propinquity of the trailer park to a wild wooded area afforded me the opportunity to join friends in building secret hide outs or donning a pack filled with white bread baloney or peanut butter and jelly sandwiches and taking hikes along one of the many dirt trails. I hoped that during one of my hikes I might make some exotic discovery, like Mammoth caves—discovered as my mother had told me, by someone who saw a rabbit run into a little hole. Wild blackberry bushes were quite common in the nearby fields, and I would be greeted with smiles of approval when I came home with a pail full of the delicious ripe berries that I had picked on one of my excursions. My skinny nimble body had no trouble crawling—just like Bre'r Rabbit could do—under the prickly thorns to get at every ripe berry available.

My mother, prone to be overly protective, would sometimes say; "If its too hard you don't have to do it." But I enjoyed working and before I turned seven, I was busy selling pretty lime stone rocks that I had found in the fields or golf balls that I fished out of a shallow pond at the nearby golf course. Since I didn't know how to swim, my mother would not be happy if she knew I was wading into the lake, so when I slipped and wound up drenched from head to toe, despite it being almost dark and cold, I had to find a place where I could take off all my clothes and dry them enough before coming home. If she saw what had happened, I could expect a spanking. I didn't want my adventures to be curtailed so I stayed away until my cloths appeared to be dry.

By seven I had my own shoe shine business. With a self-built cumbersome box that had a footpad mounted on top of a short upright two by four, I congregated near the main PX, which was located at the commercial hub of the fort, with a half-dozen other shoeshine boys. A shine was ten cents and was usually augmented with a tip that ran anywhere from a dime to a quarter. Recruits, who earned only twenty-five dollars a month, were the most generous; and officers the least, rarely tipping more than a nickel. On my best day, when I worked from nine in the morning to ten at night, I took in five bucks. That was a lot of money in an era when a hot dog was ten cents, a hamburger fifteen cents and a coke five cents with a two-cent refund when you returned the bottle.

My newfound sense of stability resulted in a radical improvement in my performance at school. I was one of a few in my second grade class to come home with a report card that showed all "S"s, satisfactory being the highest of the three grades possible.

Just as I was beginning to think my life was secure, I was given an unexpected shock one day as I was pedaling home from school. A car pulled along side of me just after I turned off of Gold Vault Road to begin the last half-mile to the trailer park. The driver slowed down to match my pace and through the open passenger side window called in a plaintive voice: "Howie?" My head exploded in fear when I turned and saw it was my old dad. The thought of him taking me back to Milwaukee sent me into a panic. Without saying a word, I turned my bike around and in standing position, pumped as hard as I could back onto Gold Vault Road and took a right turn that headed up the road to where my new dad worked at the Dental Clinic at the top of the hill. It was about a mile away. My head was down during the entire sprint, not daring to turn to see if my old dad was following me. My heart raced and felt like it would burst as my skinny legs strained to pedal up the last two hundred yards of incline where the clinic sat. Dripping in sweat, I threw my bike down on the ground and ran into the front door of the clinic and past a gauntlet of dental chairs until I came to where my new dad worked at the back of the room. Somewhat humiliated, I told him what had just happened. He had me sit down and left for a few minutes. When he returned he told me that the MP's were going to remove my old dad from the base and I didn't need to worry. I began to relax. He had once told me that we must always obey our leaders and that civilians are only tolerated as long as they behave. On that day, I totally concurred.

Already an entrepreneur at seven years old, I was left in large part to my own means. It was easy for me to develop a secret personality; one that I knew I couldn't confide to anyone, least of all to my stepfather who was very religious. Along with one of my shoeshine buddies, I began shoplifting. When it came time to take a break, we would jaunt around the corner and cavalierly walk into the PX and snitch petty items like candy and some not so petty items, like expensive pocketknives. Being two little white boys, we were above being suspected of evil and were able to steal with impunity.

My friend was much more avaricious than I, but also a lot more sloppy about his vice and his mother eventually discovered his large knife collection in his room. Since he had no way of explaining how he had come by it, he had to confess to the truth. Without a partner, I stopped stealing from the PX; but I had been infected with the petty theft bug and more broadly, the idea that breaking the law is not a big deal as long as you don't get caught. And I knew I was too smart to get caught. My secret life as a little urchin also emboldened me to panhandle if I needed some change to buy a hamburger or a movie ticket and couldn't find enough coke bottles laying around that I could turn in for the two cents refund, I could hit up a few GI's who parted with their money rather easily. Worried that I might be an officer's son, they never refused.

Before coming to Kentucky, I had never met a negro, but as a shoe shine boy I came into contact with many young black recruits who were the most generous tippers when paying for a shoeshine. Despite a minor confrontation I had with a black shoeshine boy, I found their easy-going personalities easy to like. That the stories in Disney's "Song of the South" were told by Uncle Remus, a black man, was one of the main reasons I felt comfortable around them. The confrontation happened when I had decided to stay late to shine shoes and carried my box over to the nearby greyhound bus station where the action was during the evening. The bus station was the turf of the black kids and one of them approached me and demanded a ten-cent protection fee if I wanted to work there. Negroes were known to be good fighters. Joe Lewis, the brown bomber was the heavyweight champ, so rather than take a chance of getting the crap beat out of me, I paid the fee and nothing more came of it.

But even at Fort Knox, Negroes were expected to stay in their place. They even had their own movie theatre, a run down building that showed movies that were no longer in circulation. Of course white people could go there if they wished and when my mother saw that her favorite movie, "Shane," starring Alan Ladd, was playing there, she took me to see it. Shane was a great movie. The classic line near the end of the film "Come back Shane, come back," made me cry. Though we were the only two whites in the audience, nothing was done to make us feel uncomfortable.

Robert Ziehm naturally wanted kids of his own, and with a look of pride on his face, told me that I was soon to have a brother. As is common, a man's first son was considered to be a chip-off-the-old-block, so my new brother was given the name of Robert, or Bobby, as we would fondly call him. The seven years in age that separated my new brother and I was too much for me to see him as a playmate and this was even more so for my next sibling, Nancy, a sister who was born two years later.

Though Nancy would become a thorn in my side, which I will explain in a moment, her arrival answered the question that had been racking my brain for the first nine years of my life. While my mother changed her diaper, I managed a few quick peeks to see what her sprinkler looked like. Quite frankly, I liked hers much better than mine. I had no clue how it worked, but it was neat and simple—just a little slit between her legs. My thing was a monstrosity, a dangling tube with weird looking sacks hanging from it. Why had god given boys such ugly sprinklers?

To accommodate our larger family, we moved a mile away into a complex that had been converted from a drab yellow army hospital into apartments. Each rectangular single story wood frame ward of the hospital was attached at its end to an enclosed ramp system that provided for patients to be wheeled from ward to ward without being exposed to the weather. The ramps were now boarded up and each ward had been divided into three apartments. The twenty-yard wide open space between each ward served as a parking lot and a yard area to play or hang clothes to dry. It wasn't attractive, but it was a lot roomier than the trailer we had lived in for last few years.

Though we weren't rich, I was well provided for with toys including an electric train, an erector set and even a clarinet to stimulate some interest in music. My propensity to prefer roaming in the woods rather than practicing scales was not conducive to learning music, so not much came out of that, but I loved comic strips and comic books and arduously collected every issue of Donald Duck, Mighty Mouse, Little Lulu and Smilin' Jack that I could get my hands on. I went to great lengths to make sure my collection had every issue of Mickey Mouse vs. the Blot. I rarely missed listening to radio dramas like the Shadow and the weekly installments of the Lone Ranger that always ended with the Ranger shouting "Hi Ho Silver" as he rode off into the distance.

My mother's pleasant demeanor seemed to change after she had Nancy. Her doting on her created a sibling rivalry that I found difficult to deal with. Nancy was my mother's version of a chip-off-the-old-block and was not to be aggravated. When she was, whether real or imagined, a good scolding or spanking followed. Nancy did nothing to endear me to her after she quickly learned that just by whining about some putative offense I had made against her, ensured that a tirade would come my way from my mother and possibly a spanking when my father came home. It didn't help to improve the confused feeling I was already having about girls. Though I had not the slightest idea why, I tried to draw their attention to me by showing off on the playground during recesses. That I seemed to have little success, just added to the confusion.

5

DON'T LOOK

When another sister, Christine, came along a year later, my mother's mood went even more sour. It helped somewhat that my father hired a black lady named Mary to help with the extra chores. We all liked Mary and looked forward to eating her mouth-watering Kentucky Fried Chicken, which she prepared every Friday before leaving for the weekend. But my mother had a way of nagging that was grating and it subconsciously began to affect me.

My stepfather was raised in Berlin, Wisconsin where his father owned a Rexall drug store. They were real heartland people and devout Lutherans. His mother was a stern woman who was very proud of her impressive salt-and-pepper-shaker collection and his father, who owned a Rexall drug store, was a quiet man who seemed not to mind being dominated by his wife. When we visited, he was always very nice to me when I stopped into his drug store while exploring the town, always giving me an ice cream cone.

On the other hand, my mother made no attempt to hide the fact that she didn't like Bob Ziehm's family. I struggled to understand why. Maybe they didn't approve of their son marrying a divorcee. At that time, being divorced was frowned upon; a holdover from the Catholic Church threatening eternal damnation to people who were divorced. Though my new dad was more than a decent person, the conservative religious environment in which he had been raised made him very set in his ways. Meals always began with prayers and "Now I lay me down to sleep, I pray the lord my soul to keep" had to be said before I went to bed in case I died during the night. I accepted the prayers as necessary to keep me from going to hell, but I had child-like difficulty in dealing with his insistence on perfect table manners. Putting my elbows on the table could result in a blow from a knife handle flying across the table, which thanks to my quick reflexes I always managed to dodge. Though my mother doted on Nancy, I could count on her to defend me from his rage. I had the sense that she had been a gay blade in her day and maybe her incessant nagging was a reaction to his conservative ways. For his part, he accepted it without retort. She was the mother of his children, which was enough for him. Years later she would tell me she only married Bob Ziehm to find me a father. If that was true, it was her problem not mine.

By no means was it all turmoil at our family. My mother loved animals and I was given a big fluffy St Bernard puppy for my birthday that I named Bolivar. He instantly became my best friend. I took him wherever I could and we became inseparable. Like Mary's little lamb, he would follow me wherever I went, which sadly added one more traumatic event to my life. I was leaving to walk to school and Bolivar had to be chained to prevent him from following me. But he was so strong that he could easily break the chain. When my father came out of the house and the dog refused to obey his commands to sit down, he lost his cool and began beating him. His blows went on for several minutes until Bolivar finally cowered. The memory was indelible in my mind and resulted in me vowing to never hit an animal.

A trauma of a different variety, my first sexual trauama, came a few weeks later. I and three of the other boys my age who lived in the nearby wards, were avid Monopoly players. We were in the middle of a game at Richard Koch's apartment, which was kitty corner in the ward across from the one I lived in. His father, being a Major, entitled him to the privlidged apartment near the front. As the four of us sat on the floor deeply concentrated on the game, I hadn't noticed that Richard's mother had come into the room and was now standing right next to us. When I heard her asking if we would like some lemonade, I looked up to respond. She was only wearing her panties and a bra! I quickly returned my gaze to the monopoly board. The snap shot I had taken of her slender body with long legs and the silky ecru colored panties clinging softly to her lithe body was like an acid etching in my mind. I knew it was wrong for me to see a grown women's body. Only recently my mother had slammed the bathroom door in my face after I had inadvertently opened it when she was on the toilet. So

I kept my eyes turned down and sat silent with a face sanguine with shame. My stupor was broken when I heard Richard say; "It's OK if you look." I glanced up and was greeted by a pretty warm smile that affirmed what he had said. But I still felt guilty even though her demeanor made no doubt that she was comfortable walking around the room in her panties. Looking back; I wonder if she might have enjoyed my embarrassment. At that time, I had no clue what to think.

After she left, we continued playing our game, but I couldn't stop thinking about what I had just seen. As soon as I returned home, thinking I needed to admit my transgression, I told my mother what had happened. She made it clear that what Richard's mother had done was disgusting, but the fact that his father was a Major and mine only a Captain, meant not much could be done about it. Such was life in the army.

6

A REBELLIOUS URCHIN

Army brats don't form lasting friendships because they never know when their dad is going to be transferred to another base and the family will have to pack up and move. Losing friends was a drag, but because moving to new places was exciting, adapting to new situations became easy. My father was assigned to Fort Campbell, Kentucky, home of the 101st Airborne Division. The camp had no on base housing so our family took residence eighty miles away in Evansville, Indiana, where we moved into a comfortable red brick house. Despite the mundane title of "The Refrigerator Capitol of the World," Evansville was a charming city. It was situated on the Ohio River and when the steamer Avalon, an old Mississippi paddleboat, made its annual stop, our whole family paid a small fee to come on board and take a short ride up and down the river.

When I began the fourth grade, because my last name started with Z, I found myself assigned to the obscure last desk of the far right row. The kid sitting in the row next to me was sixteen years old, the result of repeatedly failing to master fourth grade class work. He probably felt weird sitting in a room with a bunch of little kids, but since he never talked, no one knew. I wasn't exactly a genius myself. The urchin I had become at Fort Knox resulted in me being more interested in mischief than schoolwork and my grades quickly plummeted to straight Cee's. I was back to being terrified of school. I had doubts if using an encyclopedia to do a report would be more than I could handle. I did the safe minimum to get by. All my book reports began with: "This book was very interesting" and ended with: "This book was very interesting and everyone should read it."

At lunchtime, rather then eat at the school cafeteria, I would leave with a friend to go four blocks away to a hamburger stand across from the high school. The place was hopping with blaring music and lots of chitchat. After gobbling down a cheeseburger, frenchfries and a coke, to avoid being seen by the truant officer, we would return via an alley that ran parallel to the main drag. Then one day, just to be mean and have a little fun, we trampled down several tomato plants growing in a small backyard garden. An idea that lingered in some remote corner of my brain was telling me that being a bad ass would bring me respect and make girls like me. Ten minutes later, the garden's owner was on the school's grounds asking if anyone could help him identify the punks who had destroyed his tomatoes. From an empty classroom on the third floor, I cowered on my knees and peered over the windowsill, waiting until the guy gave up and went home. Our stupid stunt had made using that alley no longer possible and consequently eating at the hamburger joint as well.

As terrified as I was, no lesson was learned from the experience and I continued to draw attention to my self with obnoxious behavior. In an attempt to calm me down, one of my teachers, who in my eyes looked like a prototypical old maid, the worse fate that could befall a woman, took a seat on a chair in front of the class and then ordered me as punishment for my misbehavior to come up and plant a kiss on her cheek. Other than being humiliating and giving my classmates a good laugh, it did nothing to make me change my ways.

We only stayed in the brick house for a half year, which was a good thing because I had to sneak home from school on various circuitous routes to avoid getting beat up by some older kids who were out to get me. I didn't specifically know why, but if I had bothered to look at the whole picture, I might have recognized that I did lot's of things that probably pissed people off. As much as moving to a new house was good for me, it was even better for Bolivar. Because my father didn't want him in the main house, he was made to stay in the basement of the red brick house on cold and rainy days. I knew he loved the outdoors and it hurt me to see him sent down into the house's dank cellar. Our new one story tract house was in a housing project called Iroquis Gardens on the edge of town. He would have plenty of space to roam.

I had tons of energy and burned it at an incredible rate. It explained why I was so skinny. Whether it was earning a buck for cutting neighbor's lawns or testing myself on the swing set's trapeze bar that my father had bought for us kids, I was always active. I could do a hundred curls and would have done more except that my mother still insisted I go to bed by eight each night. The Woodmare Insane Asylum was only a half-mile away and sometimes on hot days, I would go there to buy a coke out of the machine that was in their basement. The inmates who screamed at me from behind the bars of their rooms on the third floor, didn't frighten me as I walked by. They were locked up. But after I noticed a guy with a shaved head strapped down on a guerney in the basement, it gave me nightmares and I decided the nut house might not be a smart place to visit.

I kept my brain active, not by doing schoolwork; but by assiduously building my stamp and comic book collection. I loved fantasy, and each Saturday I caught a city bus to take me to a local movie house that was running a serial about Superman's battle against the Atom Man. The serial had reached the point where Luther was about to send Superman to *The Empty Doom*. All week long I wondered; "What did the *empty doom* look like." It sounded terrifying. When it was announced that the city bus drivers had gone on strike, I realized I would have no way of getting to the theatre and would miss seeing the *empty doom*. I was in an empty gloom thinking about it. Then, on Saturday morning at eleven O'clock, it was announced on the radio that the strike had ended and bus service would resume immediately. If I sprinted down the street I could catch the bus just in time to get to the theatre before the serial started. That I was soaking wet as I arrived at the bus stop mattered not, seeing the *empty doom* was all that was important. I entered the theatre just as the serial was beginning. To my great disappointment, the *empty doom* didn't deliver. The guy on the guerney was scarier.

Though I was a good Christian as my parents had brought me up to be, I felt comfortable bending the rules from time to time to get what I needed. Knowing I was too smart to get caught stealing, I added to my stamp collection by pilfering many gems right in front of the dealer in downtown Evansville that I often visited. While paging through his inventory books that he had placed in front of me, I would surreptitiously slide issues that were too expensive for me to buy off the page and onto my lap where an open magazine waited to gather them.

That I finally got caught stealing was probably a good thing. I had gone swimming with a friend at the indoor YMCA pool in downtown Evansville. We were walking up the hill that came off the Ohio River to catch a bus, when the aroma of fresh glazed doughnuts in the window of a bakery crossed our noses. My friend nonchalantly said: "Wait a minute" and dashed in and returned seconds later with two doughnuts ringed around his index finger. We had just begun to bite into our sweet purloined treats when a strong hand suddenly gripped our shoulders. The burly baker who owned the shop was none to pleased. He made it clear that he could turn us over to the police but thanks to our sweet little faces, his anger melted and he released his grip and let us go. It was a blessing. I had been pushing my luck and it was time to wise up.

7

A LITTLE WHITE MOUSE

It was time to move again, this time to Fort Meade, Maryland. As a difficult but humane gesture, I parted with my beloved Bolivar. Complaints from a neighbor had forced us to tie him up to a chain in the backyard where he spent his day doing nothing except tugging to break free. No leather collar could hold him and the bull chain that was wrapped around his neck had rubbed it raw. When my mother told me they had found a farmer willing to take him, I said yes without hesitation. The farmer would report a few weeks later that he was happy as could be chasing rabbits.

Once again, because of a lack of housing on the base, we took up residence in a small one story three bedroom cinder block house in a prosaic development called Harandale, located at the north edge of Glen Bernie, a town halfway between Baltimore and Washington DC. It was little more than a traffic stop on Hwy 17. The iconic monuments I saw in Washington DC truly impressed me when my father took our family to the nation's capital for a patriotic visit, but a sight I would witness later in the summer at a local swimming hole would leave a more jolting impression. On a stifling hot day, I had joined some of my young friends to cool off in the waist deep water that had formed at the bend in the creek that ran through the nearby woods. Suddenly two teenage boys showed up to join us and nonchalantly took off their clothes, I was shocked. Going nude was a sin. I had never seen a mature male in the nude so I couldn't help but gawk at one of the boys who was preparing to make a dive off of the boulder that was next to the little waterfall at the deep end of the pool. His sprinkler looked like a little white mouse peeking out of a bush. How odd it looked, surrounded by black curly hair that allowed only its white tip to protrude. I was aware that I would someday have hair down there, but at this point nary a strand could be found anywhere on my body. Their nude bodies made me uncomfortable and I was glad when they left.

There was little to like about Glen Bernie. The school's softball field was on the side of a steep hill and every ball that got past the infield rolled all the way to the bottom and because the Catholics had to eat fish on Fridays, crab cakes were forced upon us at the school lunch counter. I absolutely hated them. I had a hard time understanding why the Catholics had the right to force me to eat fish and foiled the teacher's attempts to make me eat the vile things by stuffing them into my pockets when no one was looking. No one was going to force me to do something I didn't like if I could help it.

Exciting things were taking place in America as the second half of the twentieth century began. Each day when I came home from school, I immediately turned on the new entertainment miracle that my father had splurged to buy for us—a television. It was made by Sylvania and had a fifteen-inch screen with rounded edges on the corners. The picture was black and white and the screen had to be constantly adjusted to keep it from scrolling up or down. I especially loved the cartoons, albeit the only ones that came on during the eight hours of programming, were the same dozen or so episodes of Felix the Cat. On Saturday, my siblings and I watched the 'Howdy Doody Show', starring Clarabell the clown and in the evenings I often joined my parents to watch the George Gobel Talent Show. Because of television, I became enthralled with NBA basketball, which was broadcast each Saturday during the season. George Yardley of the Fort Wayne Pistons seemed never to miss with his deadly two handed set shot. It became my dream to be able to shoot like that and maybe become a pro player myself some day.

Television only offered what was considered to be clean wholesome entertainment, but when it came to the movies, the code was a bit looser, especially when it came to crime or horror. The Hays rating system, named after the postmaster general who headed it, protected the public from hearing dirty words or even seeing fully clothed adults sitting together on a bed. But movie producers were discovering that censorship could be used as an effective advertising ploy. A film released in 1951 called 'The Thing,' ran an advertising campaign that suggested that responsible parents should not allow their children to see the film and those with heart conditions would be smart to avoid it. I knew my parents were responsible, but my powerful sense of curiosity made it mandatory for me to see that film. Along with a friend, we walked several miles into Glen Bernie on a Saturday afternoon so we could sneak into the theatre through its back exit door. We found seats in a row near the front and made sure to keep our feet off the ground so as not to get bitten by the rats that were scurrying everywhere in search of dropped kernels of popcorn. Well into the movie, I was lured half-asleep listening to a group of scientists speculate about what was in the block of ice they had stashed in the adjoining room. But when one of them went to casually open its door to inspect how the block of ice was doing; a thunderous burst of music awoke everyone from their lethargy. I almost toppled backwards over my seat. 'The Thing' was standing right in the middle of the door! The eruption of loud screams in the audience sent all the rats scurrying back to their holes. However, there were no reports of deaths due to heart attacks.

Regardless of 'TheThing' and the excitement of television, six months of Glen Bernie was more than anyone should have to endure and I was delighted to hear that my father was promoted to Major and reassigned to Germany. I left the States as an average student, with little interest in anything other than basketball, comic books and my stamp collection.

8

WHO AM I?

After circling the Frankfurt Germany airport three times, our DC6 had finally been cleared to land. The rises and falls of the air pockets we hit each time we looped around the city shook our stomachs like bowls of Jell-O and as we approached touch down the sound of regurgitators filling up the provided vomit bags was ubiquitous. It had been a tough trip; nineteen hours in a frigid cabin whose walls vibrated like they were agitated by an eggbeater, all made even more unpleasant by the eight year old kid sitting next to me who kept shoving his feet against my side to hog as much of the seat for himself as possible. If it had not been for my mother seeing what was going on, and jumping up out of her seat to loudly tell the kid's mother to make her little brat back off, I wouldn't have gotten a single wink of sleep.

So weary as we were, it was a relief to escape the acrid smell of barf and join my father who was waiting in the terminal for us to deplane. After hugs and kisses, we all piled into our green fast-backed Pontiac, which had been shipped over from the States, and drove for three hours to a little college-town just south of Nuremberg called Erlangen. Because of, "to-the-victor-go-the-spoils," our new home was a small mansion that had been commandeered from a wealthy German family. It sat on the corner of two cobble-stoned streets, in a neighborhood of equally impressive houses. Its large backyard was replete with apple and plum trees and a three-car garage. The house had a big living room and a dinning room that was serviced by a dumb waiter that was used to bring food up from the ample kitchen situated in the basement. A sunroom that was half as large as our entire house in Harandale, and four spacious bedrooms on the second floor, made my new home a far cry from anything I had ever envisioned myself living in.

Six years after the war ended, German labor was still very cheap and my father hired a twenty-six year old German girl, named Eva, to help my mother with work around the house, including cooking our meals and to my relief, taking over my former job; washing the dishes. She spoke perfect English and told us that things were very good for the Germans before they started losing the war. That certainly was not the case now when shabby clothed scavengers combed through our garbage cans each week looking for scraps of left over meat.

Erlangen had not been subjected to any bombing, but Nuremberg, where I began the seventh grade two months after we arrived, was marred by many destroyed buildings scattered throughout the city. The baunhauf, where I would at times need to catch a train back to Erlangen, was repaired just enough to make it functional. However, just across the street, because it served no military purpose and the allies saw no reason to destroy it, the famous Nuremberg castle was left untouched. Even during a war some sanity prevails. The newly constructed American school in Furth, a suburb of Nuremberg, was a three-story building that accommodated all grades from seventh through high school. It had a gymnasium and athletic fields so we could play American sports.

On the first day of school I faced a conundrum. After the teacher went through her usual routines; assigning seats, introducing herself, etc., she began passing out identification cards needed to use the cafeteria. Methodically, after each student had his or her name called, they came to the front of the class to receive their card. When the teacher called out: "Howard Dittman," no one answered. She repeated: "Howard Dittman?" No one came forth. There were only a few kids who had yet to receive a card. I knew my name was Howard, but my last name was Ziehm. I had no clue who this Howard Dittman was. When all the ID's were handed out, I was the only kid who hadn't received one. Deep in my psych I knew something was wrong and I felt embarrassed. The teacher asked what my name was and quietly I told her; "Howard Ziehm."

During the ride back to Erlangen on the school bus, (formerly an army hospital bus) my mind was churning like a popcorn machine. Everything was confusion. The high seat backs that could be folded down to make hospital beds, kept me hidden from the other kids who were sticking their heads out into the aisle and having fun bantering back and forth about their first day at school. I just kept to myself, feeling odd that I was the only one in the class whose name had not been called. As we traveled along the tree lined rustic road, my subconscious brain began to stir up recollections of the name "Dittman." The vague thought that I had once had another dad surfaced momentarily, but then quickly retreated. Why would that be? It made no sense. That evening, still puzzled and feeling shame, I waited until my mother was alone after we finished diner and quietly asked her if I had ever had another daddy. Without knowing what had prompted the question, she confirmed that I did but that he was gone for good. I went to bed wondering how a big chunk of my life had been erased from my memory.

A few days later, I was taken aside and asked by my parents if I wanted to have my name changed legally to Ziehm. Without giving it a second thought, I said yes. Over the next few weeks, the memories of my early life in Wauwautosa slowly bubbled to the surface. My stepfather had told me that when he played football at Marquette, the cheerleaders had come up with a special cheer just for him: "I scream, you scream, we all scream for you Ziehm." I would now venture into the future as a "Ziehm" and hopefully garner a few screams myself.

But in the meantime I was a painfully skinny stick that struggled to gain self esteem. I found myself to be an object of derision, sometimes just embarrassing and other times painful. When a big pimple faced fat kid tackled me while we played football with a few army brat friends in front of my house and plopped his ample ass over my face so he could release a gargantuan fart while I struggled to get my breath; I just had to endure the stench since I wasn't strong enough to push him off. As if that wasn't enough, my pencil thin forearm broke while trying to stop two friends who were having fun by pushing the collapsible hospital bus seat down on top of me as we returned home from school. My skinny forearm cracked but stayed in place. However, I was endowed with good coordination and began working towards my dream of becoming an NBA player by working at the base gym on my basketball game. A deadly two-handed set shot that I developed was enough to allow me to hold my own in the three on three games I played with the troops.

A year after arriving in Germany, my father's joy in being reunited with my mother somehow resulted in another brother being added to the family. I hadn't the slightest idea how that happened. My best guess was it was an answer to a prayer. Needing more room, we moved to an even more impressive confiscated mansion with a big front yard that would give us the extra room needed for the new arrival who was given the name Michael.

Other then our maid Eva, the only Germans I came into contact with was the CG (civilian guard) who rode on the school bus with us and Herr Google, who ran the craft shop at the base's recreation center where he taught me basic woodworking skills. One of the rare exceptions was a young blond boy, slightly older than me, maybe fifteen or so, who was riding his bike past our house. After I invited him into our yard to play croquet, he fell to the ground and began doing push-ups to show me how strong he was. I had vaguely heard of the Hitler Youth but knew little about them other than they were very physically fit. I inferred that he was probably one of them. For that matter, there was virtually no talk of Hitler by anyone. All I knew was that the American army had defeated his army. The only evidence of Hitler came when thinking I might find some letters with rare stamps on their envelopes, I had crawled around the attic of our house where rather than discovering any stamps, I found a Nazi banner hidden at the back of a small hole. A short time later I found a German Lugar buried in the ground in the backyard where I had been digging little canals to float a toy boat in. If I had known more about the war, I might not have been so surprised at the violent reactions that I provoked when I teased a few Germans with childish pranks. While growing up, my favorite comic strip had been the 'Katzenjammer Kids' and I got a big kick out of the pranks that Hans and Fritz, the strip's imps, pulled on the Captain. So when a friend and I entertained ourselves by crouching behind a hedge in a vacant yard adjacent to my house, and used pea shooters to take pot shots at Germans riding past the house on their bicycles, we were surprised when we actually hit one and panic stricken when he threw down his bicycle and bounded over the five foot high hedge and fence as though he were a gazelle. By the time he landed on the ground, my friend and I were scampering up a stack of logs stacked against the fence so we could jump back to safety. My friend succeeded, but the pile collapsed just as I reached the top and the nape of my neck found itself in the clutches of the German's strong hand. One of the peas had just missed his eye and he couldn't be blamed for wanting to haul me away and teach the American brat a lesson. It was only Eva's persuasive pleading that dissuaded him from doing so.

9

BOING!!

Being that we were now a large family, some of our vacations were taken separately; my father traveling to Italy with my brother and a few weeks later, my mother and I taking a similar trip. Witnessing the many marvels of Europe, be it King Ludwig's fairy tale castle in Bavaria, the Coliseum in Rome or the huge dykes that held back the North Sea in Holland, was one of the perks of being an Army brat. But no city made a more profound impression on me than a trip to Paris with just my mother and father while my siblings remained in Erlangen with Eva. There was, of course, the Eiffel Tower, Notre Dame, and the Arc de Triumph that sat at the head of the magnificent Champs Elysee, but the big event was a show we had planned to attend; a show my mother had talked about for years and was extremely excited to see until now.

We were in our hotel room on the last afternoon of our three-day stay and my ears were glued to the serious discussion my parents were having. It was about whether I should be allowed to accompany them as had been originally planned to see the world famous, "Follies Begere." My mother had waxed enthusiastically many times about the Parisian dancing girls who lifted their frilly petticoats and kicked their legs high in the air to expose their long black stockings. But she had just learned that the Follies Begere was no longer the spirited Can Can girls, made famous in the romantic paintings of Toulouse-Lautrec. The dancers were now naked! As they discussed the issue, I heard my mother mumble something about the "low morals of the dirty French." I always considered my mother to be the liberal one in the family, but it was now my conservative religious father arguing the case to let me come along. At fourteen years old, I had yet to see a naked woman, pictures or otherwise. I breathed an excited sigh of relief when my mother eventually backed down and my father won the debate.

Under a brightly lit marquee, men attired in tuxedos and women in fancy evening gowns and furs, exited limousines at the entrance of the Follies. My heart began to pound when I saw the photos in the display box while we stood in line for our tickets: beautiful women wearing nothing but tiny patches between their legs that seemed to be held in place only by some kind of glue. We took our seats in the orchestra section of the large gilded auditorium in a row about three quarters back from the front. The theatre had a balcony and several boxes on the sidewalls as one would see at an opera house. Then the lights dimmed and the murmur quieted. The conductor in the pit just beneath the large stage lifted his arms and with a swift stroke of his baton, brought the orchestra to life with a spirited and sophisticated arrangement. As the music began to build to a crescendo, trapezes carrying incredibly beautiful young women, each naked except for the tiny piece of fabric between their legs, that according to the program was called a cache-sexe, suddenly descended from the rafters.

I was seeing a naked woman for the first time and while being aware of the warm feelings that were beginning to overwhelm me, I studied their bodies to see what makes their anatomy so special. The ladies were all dancers with athletic lithe bodies. Their breasts were small and firm and the curves of their hips and the roundness of their butts and beauty of their faces mesmerized me. But something had happened to me that made analysis irrelevant. My penis had become so hard that I was forced to cover it with my program lest my parents see.

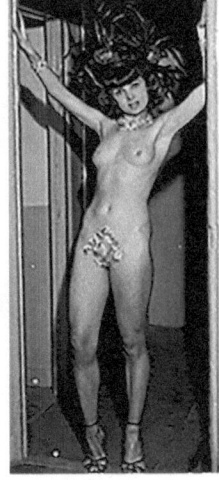

The star of the show was Yvonne Menard. She moved across the stage with sensual grace, cavorting with muscular men who only wore little pouches over their sprinklers. I fantasized about what it must be like to be one of them and was amazed at how nonchalant all the dancers were with their nudity. Yvonne Menard artistically slithered across the men's bodies as though she were the serpent in the Garden of Eden, rubbing her breasts against them in the most teasing of ways. One of the male dancers picked her up and carried her across the stage, one hand on the small or her back and the other on her thigh. Her back arched so that her breasts begged to be touched. My trousers strained to keep the hard little monster beneath from leaping out.

By holding my jacket in my arm, I was able to lap it over the tent that protruded from the front of my pants as we exited the theatre. It gave no indication that it was going to go down anytime soon and quite frankly, I didn't want it to. Back at the hotel, I kept my back to my parents as I slipped into my PJs. The room had one double bed for my parents and a portable that the hotel had provided as a temporary bed for me. Luckily, since it was set up on the far side of the room from where my parent's bed was, I had a modicum of privacy. As my tent was still fully raised, I didn't dare turn towards mom and dad and quickly jumped into my bed as though nothing was happening. They gave no indication that they knew what I was experiencing, or if they did, were not prepared to deal with it. I had no interest in falling asleep. My stiff sprinkler continued to sate me with this new and wonderful pleasure. For fear of being exposed, I didn't dare roll over on my back and lying on my stomach would have been painful, so I laid sideways with my back to my parents and pretended to fall asleep while I replayed the entire performance over and over in my mind. Not knowing about masturbation, meant relief wasn't possible. Besides, I liked how it felt when it was hard. Eventually the sheer lateness of the hour allowed me to doze off. When I awoke the next day, I was pleased that the sight of a naked woman had made my sprinkler hard, but was clueless as to why.

10

NO ONE WOULD WANT TO DO THAT

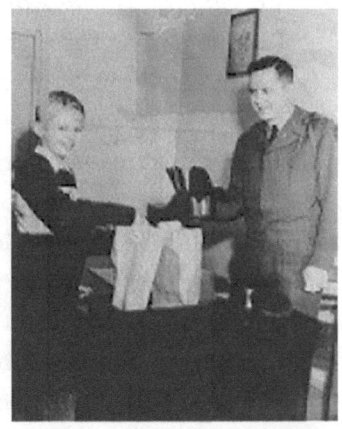

Me and Chaplin Lederman

Shortly after the trip to Paris, my father explained to me that it was time for me to begin my catechism training so I could become a full fledged member of our church. I was delivered into the hands of Chaplin Laederman each Saturday morning so he could guide me through my studies. In his quiet home study, we went over the various intricacies of the Lutheran faith. He was not pushy and I enjoyed my time with him, but found it difficult to understand the trilogy; that god is father, son, and Holy Ghost, all at the same time. Lederman, who held the rank of Captain, calmly explained it was just one of those things that had to be accepted on faith. So that's what I did.

Though the Trilogy that Chaplin Lederman had tried to explain was a bit bizarre and took a bit of a stretch to understand, something that was told to me during a break by one of my eighth grade classmates was ridiculous: "Men put their things into girl's wee wees to make babies." Unlike the trilogy, which was God's work, this was just stupid and I told him so: "No way! Who would want to do that?" The kid insisted that he was right and when the bell rang to return to class, the discussion was ended. But he seemed so sure of himself that my curiosity led me to the library a day later to see if I could find some clarification. Though I was a mediocre student at best, I had gotten over my fear of libraries and was now quite capable of finding my way around the book stacks. This was a good thing, because it would have been impossible for me to ask the librarian if there were any books about boys putting their pee pees inside of girls wee wees. A small book titled, *"Everything You Should Know About Sex,"* sounded just what I was looking for, and I began paging through it as soon as I pulled it off the shelf. The book was laid out in a style that would appeal to a young person's eye. The pages were uncluttered and handled the subject of sex in a question and answer style. The questions were printed in light blue ink, which made the book not to appear too academic. Simple diagrams were included to help the reader understand the physiology of what was being discussed. After a few flips of its pages, I came to a section that was titled: "How is sperm delivered to the egg?" I had to read the answer twice before I accepted that I had read it correctly: "The penis becomes hard and erect so that it may naturally fit into the vagina." A little diagram showed how the penis fits into the uterus. It was just weird. I had experienced a nice hard penis when I was at the Follies Bergere, but I had no idea that it had gotten hard so it could slip inside a girl's vagina. The book went on to explain how seamen filled with little sperms comes out of the tip of the penis during an orgasm and they swim up the uterus like tiny fish where they fertilize the female's eggs. Girls had eggs ? ? And what was an orgasm ? ?

We never talked about sex at home, so I figured my parents were just uncomfortable discussing it. My father had once made a passing remark that it was something that would be discussed at school. I had no plans to discuss the revelation I had just discovered and left the library that day with the thought that the whole thing sounded revolting. Other than mentioning it to my best friend, Willie DeQuire, (pronounced de queer) I just kept it to myself.

Willie, a black Sergeants son, and I played basketball together at the base gym and shinned shoes each Friday in the barracks where the young troops were more than happy to pay a buck for a spit shine so they could head out to the haufbrau houses for a night of drinking and still be ready for inspection the next morning. Even though he could dribble on his knees like the legendary Harlem Globetrotter, Marcus Haynes, I didn't think he knew any more about sex than I did. So it surprised me when he told me he knew how to have an orgasm and would prove it if I came over to his house when his parents weren't home.

The next day, he called for me to come by and see the demonstration. As a Sergeant, his father didn't warrant the luxurious kind of house I lived in, but his modest two-story house was still quite nice. When I arrived the door was open and he shouted for me to come up to the bathroom on the second floor. I found him lying stretched out on his back in a tub filled with warm water. Without a word of introduction, he made a fist around his brown penis and began stroking it up and down. Within a couple of minutes it became very stiff and the skin that covered its tip retreated, leaving only the pinkish head exposed. Indifferent to my presence, his strokes became more aggressive. Suddenly a white fluid gushed out of his pee hole like a volcanic explosion. Willie just grinned at me with a look of satisfaction and made no effort to get out of the way of the white fluid that was now floating across the top of the water and over his chest. He didn't moan and groan, but his wide grin left no doubt that it had felt good.

Physically, I was one-or-two steps behind all my friends. Tall, dark and handsome aptly described, Mike Walsh, an artillery Captain's son who was my same age. He was very proud of the fact that when he stood on the diving board at the base swimming pool, his penis and balls made a nice bulge in his tight swimming suit. Unlike me, he had a full crop of pubic hair growing around it. I was yet to sprout even one strand. Girls were attracted to him and I was uncomfortable with the fact that my blond skinny body didn't seem to engender any interest at all. He was as confident around girls as I was terrified.

Regardless of the fact that my sisters seemed to mostly enjoy causing trouble for me, I liked girls and harbored a deep desire to be noticed by them; sometimes doing silly things like throwing a paper wad at them or tugging at their hair. I had a big crush on one of my classmates, Mary Alice Beaudry, a pretty girl from Georgia with sandy blond hair. But believing that there was no way that she could like me; I never made any effort to talk to her. Better safe than sorry. So while riding home on the bus from school, I was surprised to have my shoulder tapped by the person sitting behind me so they could give me a little folded note that had been passed forward from someone sitting in the rear. When I opened it, I got a little heartthrob when I discovered it was from Mary Alice, informing me that she was going to have a party and I was invited.

When I turned to nod to her that I was flattered at being asked, she beckoned for me to come to the rear because she had something she wanted to tell me. Of course I did her beckoning and while feeling like the awkward teenager that I was, bent over so she could whisper into my ear with her soft southern voice to tell me that my friend Willie wasn't being invited since he was a Negro. "The girls were afraid that he might try to kiss them." When I quietly asked if Willie had ever attempted to kiss any of them she responded: "No, but that's just the way we feel." As his best friend, she, and the other girls thought: "It would be best if you explained it to him." I was too unsophisticated to know that this was going to hurt Willie's feelings and not questioning how the girls felt, I obediently agreed. It was common knowledge among white people that Negroes liked white women since it was a status symbol. It was also common knowledge that only fat and ugly white women liked Negroes because they couldn't do any better. Willie was bright and articulate and would someday become a dentist. He didn't graciously receive the news when I told him in euphemistic terms, that he was a pariah. "He had never done anything offensive, so why were they afraid?" he wanted to know. I didn't have an answer. Our friendship ended that day and of course I knew why.

Mary Alice's dad was a Colonel and their commandeered house even had a swimming pool like the movie stars in Hollywood had. There were seven or eight kids at the party and other than Larry, a slightly pudgy kid who came wearing a brief silky blue swimsuit, we all made small talk while sitting around the pool and enjoying some party snacks. When Mary Alice suggested we move to a den in the basement, Larry, who almost seemed to be posing while standing on the diving board, showed little interest in joining us and seemed content to remain outside while we retreated to the den. Larry was a friend of mine and I thought him to be a bit weird, but no one, including me, had the slightest inkling that he may have had issues that he was wrestling with. We had even less of an idea of what they could be.

The dimly lit wood-paneled den was very cozy. Several large pillows were scattered around the shag carpet that covered the floor. A wet bar sat against one wall and a ping-pong table sat in the middle. No one seemed interested in playing games, least of all Mary Alice, who took my hand and led me like a lamb to sit next to her on one of the pillows. My ears suddenly became very hot. I had no idea what was expected of me. It was said that girls matured faster than boys and there was little doubt that in this case it was certainly true. I wasn't sure what to do next and was happy when she took the lead. She snuggled against me in a position that left me no choice but to place my arm around her shoulder. The incredible sweet feeling that filled my body was intoxicating. My eyes were drawn sideward by a magnetic like force to her small breasts that looked like two soft little pillows beneath her angora sweater. They begged to be touched. Unsure if she would be offended if I followed through on my urge, I slowly let my hand dangle as low as possible over her shoulder as we continued to snuggle. Slowly her body adjusted so that the tips of my fingers lightly touched her lovely breasts. The sweet ache in my anus ran all the way up my spine to the base of my head. Not wanting to risk ending the sweet feeling that had overwhelmed me, I didn't dare go any further without her invitation. We both sat silent, wondering what the other was thinking until the warm spell was abruptly broken when her mother called down to invite us upstairs for milk and cookies.

11

BACK TO THE GOOD OLD USA

The thought of my hand atop Mary Alice's pert breast was a memory to be cherished, unlike the bad taste that had been left in my mouth because I had not stood up for my friend Willie. But both memories were to be erased when my father announced that we would shortly be returning to the United States. He had been assigned to Fort Ord, California, just outside of Monterey, California! California was the land of sunshine and movie stars! I almost gave myself an anxiety attack worrying that I might die before we got back. I would be leaving Germany with an outstanding two-handed set shot and the realization that I loved it when my dick was hard. That I was at best an average student, having struggled to earn a Cee in Algebra I, was a non-issue.

Forty-foot waves smashed against the bow of the Navy Transport that was returning us to the States. Six days of heaving up and down resulted in everyone, including the ship's doctor, to succumb to seasickness. Crew members were lying in the passageways too sick to stand up. I stumbled over one of them on my way to get a breath of fresh air, hoping not to barf on the way. In the ship's mess, where we had been invited to join the Captain and some of his officers for dinner, he had no sooner finished remarking that it was one of the roughest passages in his memory, when the ship listed violently to starboard, causing my mother to fall backward off her chair. I began to doubt if I would ever see America again, but in the early summer of 1955, our rugged Navy Transport docked at a pier in New York's harbor, just a few slips away from the luxurious Queen Elizabeth.

While waiting for our forty-nine Pontiac to be unloaded from the ships cargo bay, we used the time to tour New York, including a trip to the top of the symbol of American might, the Empire State building. It felt good to be home and to be an American. As soon as our 49 Pontiac was in our possession, we all piled in to begin the long trek across the country. Stuffed in the backseat next to the curbside window, my gangly teenage body struggled to make itself comfortable among my smaller siblings. To my dismay, Nancy sat besides me and frequently complained that I was crowding her, which brought on automatic threats from my mother that I was going to get a spanking if I didn't stop. Traversing the country on two lane black top highways made progress slow and tempers heated. For entertainment we read Burma Shave signs spaced a hundred yards apart: The Wolf—Is Shaved—So Neat and Trim—Red Riding Hood—Is Chasing Him—Burma Shave

But everyone's mood changed to happy excitement as we arrived at Fort Ord. The huge base was situated just north of a trio of small towns that hug the graceful arc of Monterey Bay. Seaside, the northern most, was little more than a bunch of large sand dunes and sat adjacent to the fort. Monterey, once the capital of the state, had a plethora of historic Spanish buildings and Steinbeck's famous Cannery Row that made it an international tourist draw. At the tip of the peninsula was Pacific Grove, a blue-collar-town, that because of its location, sat mired in unrelenting foggy weather caused by two ocean currents that collided off the spectacularly scenic seventeen-mile drive in Pebble Beach. On the other side of the peninsula was Carmel, a storybook Hansel and Gretel town that enjoyed more sunshine because it was largely sheltered from the fog by Carmel hill. Its charming cottages, art galleries and fine restaurants were immersed in a forest of eighty-foot high pine trees and windswept moss covered Cyprus trees. From its beach at the end of Ocean Avenue, was a spectacular view across the breaking white-capped waves to the craggy cliffs of Point Lobos. No more need to be said than this was the environment that had inspired the likes of John Steinbeck, Robert Louis Stevenson, Frank Lloyd Wright and naturalist John Muir.

Being military people meant that we would be provided a less-than-inspirational single story three-bedroom cement block house on the base. The project sat at the border between Seaside and Fort Ord. A high chain link fence separated the military from the civilian community. Our small yard consisted of a few tuffs of scruffy grass bordered by a succulent called ice plant. It was all that could grow in this sandy and chilly windswept area. Fog persisted until ten AM each morning and returned back at three PM each afternoon. Until my body developed immunity to the bites of the voracious denizens of the sand, the eponymous sand fleas, I had to endure several months of living with itchy red spots all over my body.

While waiting for school to begin, I worked on my basketball game, playing three on three games at the base gym, which had, much to my delight, a main court with glass backboards. Rather than walk the three miles to the gym, I decided to give hitch hiking a try. By adding a bit of showmanship to my solicitations along with my innocent non-threatening clean-cut face, it rarely took me more than five minutes to catch a lift. It was a skill that I would often employ over the next couple of decades.

The U. S. government paid MUHS, as the highschool was commonly known, to educate all the army brats whose parents worked at military facilities on the peninsula. That included the Army language school at the Presidio, the Naval Post Graduate School in Monterey and of course, Fort Ord. When the new school year began, I was among a busload of army brats from the latter being delivered to the school. It was the largest school I had ever attended, over twenty-five hundred students. But like all of Monterey, it had a friendly vibe. For the most part, the buildings were Spanish style structures set tier like on the side of a hill. At the base of the hill were athletic fields and a football stadium that had an oval running track around it. A few outdoor basketball courts and the school gymnasium, that included an outdoor swimming pool, were just south of the football field.

12

AN IRRATIONAL EPIPHANY

My father insisted that I enroll in college prep courses. I had no special academic talent or ambition and still harbored dreams that my two-hand set shot was where my future lied. But my father was the boss, and in the fifties, the sure fire American formula to happiness was to go to college, get a good job and have a family. So as an obedient, church going son, I did as my father had ordered and found myself sitting on the first day of school in a college required Geometry class. The teacher's name was Mr. Poskus. He was medium height, stocky build, and notwithstanding his wire rimmed glasses and hoary hair cut in a flat top, had a pleasant demeanor. There were approximately thirty of us who were in attendance and Mr. Poskus began reading from a list of those who had registered to take his class.

As he went down his list and checked off each name after it was acknowledged by: "here," he called out: "Gary Cunningham?" No one answered and Mr. Poskus looked a bit puzzled that Cunningham was not in attendance. Cunningham had taken Algebra I from Poskus the year before.

"Maybe he's dropped the class" one of the other students suggested.

"Why would he do that? He's the smartest guy in the class?" Poskus retorted.

I sat inconspicuously somewhere in the middle of the room and had no clue who Cunningham was. For that matter, I didn't know anyone. But as everyone chuckled over Poskus's quip, I thought to myself: "I'm the smartest guy in this class." That I had barely managed to pass *algebra I* should have made it abundantly clear that my thought was beyond irrational. There was no justification for this naïve self-proclamation. It was as though a little man in my head had suddenly flicked a switch and some lights came on. It was crazy. Cunningham could have been another Einstein. But the epiphany proved to be true. I proceeded to breeze through the class, scoring the top grade on every test I took. Memorizing axioms, theorems and formulas wasn't work to me, it was fun, an adventure into the unknown like discovering a cave in the woods. I augmented my school studies by reading books by and about Einstein and texts on subjects like analytical geometry and college algebra or Eddington's "The Nature of the Universe." I began to imagine myself as being a brilliant scientist someday.

The fact that I had the ability to easily comprehend what to some was abstruse, made me a bit cocky, or maybe some would say, arrogant. Poskus required all his students to write their name in full on the top right hand side of the page. I didn't have time for this and just wrote "Z." When someone asked why I wasn't required to properly write my full name, Poskus retorted: "because he's Z." Math was a world where I could hide my insecurity and inferiority complex. It was a little closet where I felt safe; I was top dog.

At six feet two and one hundred thirty three pounds, I was too skinny for the varsity basketball team, but my gifted shooting ability caught the eye of coach Clark, a former Little All American from Michigan, and I earned a spot on the first string of the lightweight basketball team. But as the season progressed I found myself sitting on the bench. When it came to organized sports my brain had a wiring problem. Left to run free in pick up games, I excelled, but when put in an organized environment with set plays, I became too mental and froze. The fear of making a mistake overwhelmed me. The graceful arc that was key to the success of my set shot came out of my hands like a line drive clunker. I was resolved to fix the problem when the season ended and didn't lose heart that I had a future playing basketball.

I was well aware that I had three distinct personas: the athlete, the science nerd and one that was a closely held secret—the sex fanatic—not the kind that had sex, but the kind that liked the feeling of a hard dick. I continued to work on the first two, playing pickup games at the base gymnasium and reading all the science and math books I could get my hands on, but the third was still in an infantile stage and I struggled to develop it. The sight of a nude female body and the gratifying sensual reaction it aroused in my body, or put more succinctly; how good it made me feel when my dick was hard, had been wetted in France. Since then, I had only been able to replace that stimulation by going to the Monterey public library and drool over the pictures of topless African women that I was able to find in National Geographic Magazines. I was so innocent looking that the librarians just assumed I was fascinated by culture and geography.

13

EEEK! THEY PULLED THEMSELVES APART

"Mom . . . Nancy and Christine are pulling themselves apart!" I had been working in my bedroom on my stamp collection and the girls, possibly knowing what a confused nerd I was, decided to have a little fun with me. Patiently waiting for me to leave my room, they left their bedroom door wide open, knowing that as I walked by I would peek in. When I did, the two of them were already lying on their backs with their panties pulled down and their legs spread so I would have a clear view of their vaginas, which they were pulling wide open. Not taking time for a momentary further glance, I ran down the hall to protest to my mother: "Mom . . . Nancy and Christine are pulling their sprinklers apart!" I could hear them laughing their heads off. My mother screamed: "If you do anything so filthy again you're both going to get a spanking." I had run away so quickly that I barely saw what they had done. I had no clue that a vagina had a labia and absolutely no idea that it could be pulled apart. It was horrifying.

Rather than being concerned that I was a sexual retard when it came to the female anatomy, my mother made matters worse by complaining to my father about why I was maturing so slowly. I already had a complex about my own body and she was making it worse. Once again, my father surprised me by coming to my support, saying it wasn't anything to worry about. I knew my mother didn't really understand the sexual needs of a boy. Off hand remarks that "they (the family) were all going to have a good laugh when I brought my first girl friend home," or remarks to my sister when referring to men to: "treat them like old shoes," made me feel isolated. And then there was her incessant nagging at my stepfather, which seemed to be getting worse.

When my father was promoted to Lt. Colonel, it gave him enough money to make a down payment on a new three-bedroom house in Seaside. It sat just outside the Fort Ord reservation two miles up a long sand hill from the Pacific Coast Highway on an oxymoronic named treeless street called Yosemite. The view of Monterey Bay all the way out to Pacific Grove was spectacular except that it could rarely be seen because of the fog and heavy mist that always hung over the area.

As soon as we moved in my father built a large loft in the two-car garage so he could store his footlockers filled with collectable items such as professional documents pertaining to his occupation, model trains that he hoped to have fun with after he retired and other unknown memorabilia. I speculated that among the unknowns was something that might please my "third" personality. The deck of playing cards that I had seen him purchase from the souvenir shop in the lobby of the Follies Bergere might just be in one of those footlockers. They could be real "dick" hardners.

On the first opportunity when I found myself home alone, I rummaged through a drawer in my parent's bedroom where I found a ring of keys, some of them of the small paddle lock type. In the garage, I took a ladder and climbed up onto the loft that only had about four feet of headroom. After scurrying around on my hands and knees, I was delighted to find that the keys did indeed open the footlockers and after a few false alarms, I opened one to discover the sought after deck of cards right on top. A quick peek inside the deck was enough to make my heart begin to thump.

It was too risky to stay up in the loft, so after taking out the deck of cards and relocking the foot locker, I climbed down and replaced the ring of keys in the bed room drawer and then went into the house's small bathroom, where after locking the door behind me and pulling my pants and underwear below my knees, plopped down atop the toilet seat and began to savor each card. They were all in color and had a different naked women posing on each one. All were very arty in ways that accented each woman's curves without showing the genitals. Some had round and full breasts, some small and firm and some perky and some hanging. They all had beautiful faces and firm fleshy butts. My dick could have supported a twenty-pound weight if one had been hanging from it. I massaged it with my hand, but unlike Willie de Quire, no sperm came out. When I heard my parents pull up in the driveway, I pulled my pants up and quickly hid the cards in my bedroom and hustled to the living room where I turned on the television and took a seat on the couch. When they walked in I was watching "Howdy Doody" and greeted them with an angelic smile.

14

SWING THOSE HIPS

In 1956 when Snooky Lanson failed miserably at his attempt to sing the current hit song: *You Ain't Nothin' but a Hound Dog*; it was the first sign of a rebellion that was about to overtake not only America, but the entire western world. Snooky was one of a quartet of singers who performed on a weekly television program sponsored by Lucky Strike cigarettes called *Your Hit Parade*. I was a big fan of the show and watched it each week. Hearing Snooky sing Eddie Fisher's *"Oh my PaPa"* or Gisele MacKenzie sing Doris Day's, *"How much is that Doggy in the Window,"* was to hear pop music at its best. But when, without warning, a couple of songs by a southern boy from Tennessee named Elvis Presley, made the top ten, disaster struck. Ed Sullivan wasted no time in debuting Presley on his iconic variety show where his handsome face, sexy long black sideburns and close-to-lewd hip gyrations, brought hysterical reactions from teenagers across the country as he sang and played his guitar. A few weeks later after Presley hit the top of the charts again with *'I'm All Shook Up,'* The Rock and Roll era had begun and along with it, the sexual revolution. It was embarrassing to watch tight jointed Snooky try to imitate Elvis and evidently the entire country felt the same. *'Your Hit Parade's'* days were numbered. Rock and Roll was like looking at pictures of naked women, it made me feel sexy and I loved it. It spoke to the new generation, one that wanted to explore the limits. Almost all of us teens wanted to join in on the fun. My friend, Dave Phillips, the son of the nearby Army Language School's commanding general, gave me a demonstration in the school hallway during a class break on how to be loose and cool and gyrate like Elvis. The rock rage came on like a juggernaut. New performers and bands came on the radio every day. Buddy Holly with; *'That'll be the day;'* the Everly Brothers; *'Wake up Little Suzie.'* Chuck Berry's lilting lyric, "Long distance information down in Memphis Tennessee," and Bobby Darin's humorous: "Splish Splash I was taking a bath," were almost mutinous in their overt sexuality. Bo Diddley's pounding rhythm and songs like *'Cherry Pie'* and *'Lavender Blue'* or instrumentals like *'Wipe Out'* or *'Green Onions'* that made you want to gyrate your hips, sent chills through my spine. I had no idea what having sex felt like and had yet to even have an orgasm, but somehow the sweet twangy sounds of electric guitars and provocative lyrics sung with lusty voices to a pounding beat provided all the vicarious thrills I needed until the time came when I could experience the real thing.

I spent the summer working as a bus boy and dishwasher at the base's main cafeteria, a job that left me soaked in sweat each day when I left to go home. On my break I would hang out with the elderly black shoeshine man at the Greyhound bus station and was rewarded when he invited me to join him and his cousins to go to San Francisco to watch the Giants play my favorite team, the Milwaukee Braves. Packed in his cousin's old jalopy, we dodged in and out of traffic at eighty miles an hour. The white people we passed on the road were probably just as horrified by a white boy sitting with all those Negroes as they were at the crazy driving antics. In the first inning, my baseball hero, Warren Spahn, struck out the side, including Willie Mays on three pitches. But the biggest thrill of the summer was the discovery that a couple of magazine stores in Seaside carried a nice selection of girlie magazines.

No store owner was going to tolerate a fifteen year old, who actually looked like a twelve year old, standing in front of his news rack paging through girlie magazines, so I had to do my browsing surreptitiously. Nonchalantly walking into the store, I drifted over to the magazine section where I would select a large family magazine like Life or Post and when my peripheral vision saw that the store's clerk wasn't looking, slip a naughty magazine between its pages and then kneel down in front of the bottom tier so I could pretend to be reading something wholesome rather than the filth that the laws and mores of society said I should'nt be looking at.

American cheesecake magazines still couldn't show sex organs or nipples, so the models had to wear pasties and diaphanous bikini panties that had an opaque patch covering what was between their legs. But what they showed was more than enough for me. Beauty Parade, Gala, Black Silk Stockings and Cabaret featured girls in skimpy panties and nylons, garter belts and high heels. Photos of pretty girls daring enough to wear the scandalous new and highly controversial French bikini bathing suit began to appear in some of the commercial magazines like Life. The bikini's waistband was just barely below the belly button, but at least it was going down in the right direction. The magazine that excited me the most was Cabaret. It featured layouts of some of the top strippers in the country like the 4D girl, Tempest Storm, and the sensual blond beauty, Lili St Cyr. Her layout was photographed at a club that she was performing at in Los Angeles and I dreamt of the day when I could go to clubs like that. Something about strippers made me nuts. There were also a few nudist camp magazines on the racks, but I found them to have no erotic value whatsoever. Naked people playing volleyball were not a turn on. I needed a little sleaze to excite me.

Because I couldn't diddle myself in the store or buy the magazines, I had no choice but to rekindle my old shoplifting skills so I could bring the magazines home. Not once did anyone suspect that the angelic baby faced kid looking at good clean family fare was actuality sliding filthy girlie magazines down the front of his pants with the intent of removing them free-of-charge from the premises. Once I had my purloined smut at home, I stashed them behind the row of math and science books I kept on a shelf in a linen closet just outside the bathroom. The collection soon grew to an impressive size and each night after dinner I would spend countless hours either standing in front of the closet or sitting in the bathroom, pretending to study my science and math books when in actuality I was just enjoying a nice after-dinner-hard-on.

Fragile shoots

I had no doubts in my mind about my masculinity and athleticism, even making the varsity basketball team during my junior year, but I couldn't escape the fact that I was rail thin and still without a single strand of pubic, chest or facial hair. In the showers during P. E., or especially after basketball practice, my physical shortcomings stood in stark contrast to most of Fragile shoots my teammates who were the sons of Italian fishermen and were all blessed with the hirsute qualities that are identified with manhood. They all had hairy bodies, ample pubic hair and beards. That I lacked all these attributes and was frighteningly skinny, made me stand out like a sore thumb and earned me the debasing moniker "fragile," which got shortened to "frage." I hated that name with a passion, but there was nothing I could do about it; even though it was somewhat mitigated by the fact that in the classroom I was at the top of the pecking order with the moniker: "Z."

15

THIS CAN'T BE

Notwithstanding that I was a little pervert and a thief, I continued to dutifully go to church each Sunday morning with my parents and earnestly listen to the sermons.

However, when a new Chaplain who had just been assigned to the base to tend to its Lutheran flock, fulminated in his drawn out southern drawl: "I once knew a man who knew all about science and mathematics and all that kind of stuff . . . but he did not know the real wisdom. . . . He did not know G . . . odddd. the source of all true wisdom." He went on with his diatribe making the same point over and over. I found myself feeling like I was being attacked. I knew math and science, or was at least trying to, and didn't understand why that should be a negative as the minister was implying. I accepted God as a fact. There was not even a hint of doubt in my mind about his existence. I accepted the fact that everyone believed in God and didn't question anything; Adam and Eve, Noah's Ark, Christ walking on water and rising from the dead. I believed it all; but I didn't see why knowledge of math and science needed to be trivialized to enforce the obvious and universal truths stated in the bible; which was written by God. I left church that day with a bad feeling.

As every budding scientist, I dreamt of becoming another Einstein. My dreams of being a professional basketball player were beginning to look unrealistic. Again I had started the year on the first string and because I couldn't relax during a game, wound up on the bench by the end of the season. More and more I was beginning to realize how gifted I was with math and science. What could be better than to be the most revered genius in the world? Another Einstein? But then while reading an autobiography of my hero, I came across a sentence that jolted me. Einstein said at the age of four he had doubts about God's existence and decided to conduct a little experiment. He uttered aloud, "I do not believe in God" and when lightning didn't strike him down for uttering this heresy, he reasoned that his hypothesis was correct . . . **Huh? . . . Einstein didn't believe in God? . . .** I read the sentence again to make sure I had understood the words correctly. I had! Einstein didn't believe in God. I was at a loss at how to accept this.

The next day I mentioned to Bill Roy, a classmate and fellow nerd who was also hoping to have a career in science someday; "Did you know that Einstein doesn't believe in God?" His abrupt reply startled me: "Good Man!" Whoa! . . . First Einstein and now Bill Roy! In less than two days I had discovered two people who challenged what I thought was the most fundamental basis of human existence: that we were all created by God; the one true God; the Christian God. I mulled the jolt that had been dealt to my whole mental psyche for a few hours and brought it up again when I went to my algebra II class that was also taught by my favorite teacher, Mr Poskus. **Yikes!** He agreed with Einstein and Roy. I didn't know what to think. Were they all wrong or had my parents guided me down a false path? Why would they do that? Maybe Einstein's "lightning argument" was wrong. It did seem a bit shallow. I wasn't ready or strong enough to defenestrate sixteen years of indoctrination so I opted to take the expedient way out. I became an agnostic. That was a safe bet. If there was a God I could still go to heaven because I hadn't totally rejected him.

16

SO THIS IS WHY WE LIKE GIRLS

Sequin

So that's what its all about!! I was home alone and since I knew my parents would be gone for several hours, was on the living room couch rather than in the bathroom, paging through my girlie books. I had straddled the edge of the pillows with one leg on the couch and the knee of my other leg on the floor so I could tease my hard dick by rocking back and forth against the edge of the cushion as I turned the pages. I was really turned on by some pictures in Cabaret Magazine of a stripper named Geraldine "Sequin" Gardner. She was on her haunches wearing only a G-string panty and pasties. The panty's fringes hung provocatively over the curves of her hips and buns. Her black nylons held up by a satin garter belt made me think I was getting a peek into her bedroom. She had her back arched so her breasts stood up firmly and she had her hands placed lovingly atop them as though they were a prized possession that she loved to show off. I could only fantasize what it would be like if those were my hands. Her hair was dark black and her bangs that covered half her fore head, made her dark eyes and pouting lips peek out as though they were personally teasing me. The rocking back and forth was starting to make my dick sore from the incessant rubbing, when suddenly a spasm shot through my groin that left me practically helpless. A big gob of sperm was gushing out of my penis. It felt wonderful beyond description. Wow! The crotch of my pants was soaking wet and I barely moved for five minutes. When I recuperated, I began turning the pages once more and within minutes I was hard again and repeated the experience with little effort. I had heard it said that masturbation caused warts or that it was like sticking a hot iron in the face of Jesus, but I didn't care. I wasn't even sure I liked Jesus anymore. It felt so good I knew I was going to do it again; and again; and again. I was going to be a jack-off junkie!! An addiction I had no intention of kicking! I told no one about my new experience, nor did I have any idea or interest of how to repeat it with girls in the flesh. Teenagers rarely had sex anyway. Magazines were more than enough. And I couldn't imagine many girls would want to go out with someone known as "frage," so I made no attempt to socialize with them; although I did leave my typing class every day with a big boner caused by admiring the full round ass that filled the blue jeans of the girl sitting in front of me. To keep from embarrassing myself for that indiscretion, I had to cover my crotch with my books when it was time to get up and leave the class.

To say I knew little about sex would be an understatement and the idea that deviant sex even existed was light years beyond my comprehension. That would change one night when I got off from the job I had directing cars to open spaces at the annual Monterey County fair. Each evening my father was to come by at 11PM when the fair closed to take me home. But on the final night he didn't show up, and after I waited until midnight, I decided to hitch a ride back to Seaside. I had never hitched at night before and though the fog hanging over Freemont Ave made for an eldritch atmosphere, I bravely stuck my thumb out. Within a minute a car stopped and I opened the door of the old model two door Dodge that had pulled over to offer me a ride. I told the middle aged guy sitting behind the wheel where I was headed and he nonchalantly told me to hop in.

As we slowly drove down Freemont, I wondered why my father hadn't shown up. It was not like him to leave me to be out so late by myself. My ride had only driven about a quarter of a mile down Freemont when the driver asked: "What have you been doing?"

"Working in the parking lot, parking cars." I quietly retorted, not wanting to seem unfriendly, but not looking to get into a spirited conversation either.

After we drove a couple of blocks further down Freemont he asked; "That doesn't give you too much time to look at girls does it?"

I thought the question unusual, but without looking at him mumbled: "It doesn't really interfere all that much."

I kept my eyes forward as we drove through the thick fog; the passing lights on the lampposts the only indication that we were moving.

"Do you like to look at girls?"

Not having any idea why he cared but not wanting to be unfriendly, I quietly answered: "Yeah I guess so."

My eyes remained straight ahead, focused on the road: "Does it get hard when you look at girls?"

The weird question caught me off guard: "Yeah sometimes."

I could tell he was liking what I was telling him but had not the slightest clue why. "Do you like it to get hard?"

I didn't know where he was going with the questions but since I would be hopping off in about a mile I continued to answer in a near inaudible voice.

"Yeah, I guess so," preferring to tell a lie in this strange situation. "If I feel it would it get hard?"

All I could think of to say was: "Uh . . . I don't know."

We had just passed Broadway Ave where the Del Rey Theatre stood on the southwest corner. Because of the late hour it was closed and empty as was the little magazine store next to it where I sometimes pilfered girlie magazines. The neighborhood wasn't a ghetto but nonetheless rough. The questions were making me feel strange. Then, without warning, the guy hung a sharp right off Fremont and onto an unlit and uninhabited dirt road.

Turning to me with a plaintive smile: "Why don't we go down here and find out?"

The dim light that was my brain suddenly turned on. I had heard of homosexuals but the idea seemed so bizarre that I thought maybe there were ten or so in the whole world. Now I was sitting next to one! Panic-stricken, I grabbed the handle of the car door and flung it open so I could jump out. The creep, also a bit shocked, slowed down. The darkness made it impossible for me to see where I was about to jump, but I didn't care and a split second later I was tumbling across the shoulder of the dirt road into some tall grass along the edge. It cushioned my fall and feeling no injury, I sprang back to my feet and ran terrified as hell back down the road towards Freemont. Not turning to see if the guy had turned around to follow me, I ran a mile up Freemont until I came to Old Grove Avenue, the street that led up the hill to my house. Mustering all the energy I could, I ran the half mile up the hill until I came to Yosemite Street. Only then did I know that the guy was nowhere to be seen and it was safe enough for me to walk the final half block to my house. Sweat was pouring off of me as I stood at the front door and since I didn't have a key, banged away. After a minute, my father opened it to let me in. He had fallen asleep and apologized. I was too embarrassed to say what had just happened. I went straight to bed, my heart still pounding from the long run. There was no need to tell anyone the story lest they put restrictions on me. My freedom was important.

However, the other little secret I was keeping didn't fare so well. My long forays in the bathroom and in front of the closet had made my father's suspicious, and it only took a little browsing for him to discover the secret cache of girly books that I thought were cleverly secreted behind my science books. I had just moseyed back to my closet after dinner to indulge myself with a bit of arousal, when I found myself standing dumbfounded as I realized that my entire collection had been removed. A confrontation was obviously in the works and I had no idea how I was going to deal with it. But when I returned to the living room, nothing was said; not even a knowing look. For three weeks that was to be the case, until just as suddenly as my collection had disappeared; it reappeared. Every magazine was once again sitting secreted behind my science and math books as though nothing had happened. This of course made me happy, but also confused. I left the magazines untouched and walked back out to the living room not knowing what to suspect. My quandary was quickly answered when my father sidled up to me after I had sat down on the couch and began watching The George Gobel Variety Hour, to quietly whisper in my ear: "We don't need that kind of thing around here." He left it at that. I couldn't help but wonder why it had taken him three weeks to return the collection. I had my suspicions.

I had no intention of giving up my illicitly earned source of joy and found a place up in the garage loft behind the footlockers. It was not as convenient as the bathroom, but I could still find plenty of opportunities when I was home alone to hoist myself up on the loft and cuddle up with the sparsely clad ladies in the magazines as though we were on an intimate date, stroking myself until I shot a load or two.

17

NERD BY DAY, PERV BY NIGHT

Mr. Poskus asked me to stay for a bit after Algebra 2 class and asked if I had heard of MIT. I had never heard of the school, but Poskus, who had attended Tufts University in Boston, described it as the most prestigious science school in the world. He suggested that I consider it as a choice for college. The idea held great appeal for me, a conquest of the highest order. My ego swelled as I thought about the possibilities and I became cocky enough to believe I could win admission to the school if I put my mind to it. I began to buckle down in my other college prep courses such as English, which I was only garnering B's in, to raise my over-all grade point average.

As the school's "future Einstein" I began receiving various awards like being selected to attend Boys State and a science award from Bauch and Lomb. My reputation as "Z" had spread around the school and Mr Glasser, my chemistry teacher, also granted me special status when I told him I wanted to build a small cyclotron to enter into the State science fair. I had obtained plans from its inventor, Nobel laureate E. O. Lawrence, and felt confident I could pull it off. Glasser, whose thick glasses made his eyes appear to bulge out, giving him a batrachian appearance, allowed me to spend my class time in a small auxiliary lab at the side of the classroom to work on my project. He also agreed to allow Gary Cunningham to act as my assistant. Obviously, if I was successful, he would reap rewards as well. But it soon became apparent to me and Cunningham, that we didn't have the funds to buy the various components we would need and our time in the side room lab degenerated into having a contest shooting wadded up paper balls into a waste paper basket ten feet away at the end of the room.

I couldn't really blame my fellow nerd, Bill Roy, for taking umbrage at the fact that I was getting the recognition that he felt should have been his as the school's elite science student, and my arrogance and his jealousy led him to begin mocking me as a pinhead, which I interpreted to be a reference to the fact that I had a small head size. The size of my head had never before been an issue, but added to my other moniker, fragile, and lack of pubic hair, effected me more than it should have and caused me to sink even deeper into the social abyss that I was already in.

The only women in my life were my mother, whose constant nagging at my father was driving me crazy, and my sisters, who seemed to enjoy messing with me. A minor pushing confrontation with Nancy in the back seat of our car during a family trip to Yosemite National Park, resulted in my mother's insistence that I be given a spanking. At sixteen, the humiliation of being bent over my father's knee was far more painful than any blows from the belt. I left the tent feeling like a geek.

My mind was like a ping-pong ball in an air-mix machine. My mother's nagging, my physical inferiority complex, my fear of girls, questions about God, fear of choking during basketball games and my need to steal girlie magazines to use as stimulation to engender orgasms, were just some of the issues I was dealing with. I had endless energy and burned much of it off on the basketball court or by walking twenty-seven holes on the Fort Ord Golf Course, a sport my mother recommended I take up just to get me out of her hair. As an army dependant, I could play unlimited rounds for five bucks a month. Unfortunately, all those bouncing balls knocking against each other began to take a toll.

The first manifestation came at 2AM in the morning when my father startled me in the hallway and asked me what I was doing. "There's an alligator in the hallway," I told him, well aware that what I was saying sounded weird, but nevertheless was absolutely true. As we continued to speak, my dream began to disintegrate and I became slightly embarrassed that I had been discovered sleepwalking and having such a strange hallucination. He led me back to bed where I slept soundly for the rest of the night. The next morning, I only had a vague recollection of what had transpired. I hoped it was a one-time thing and didn't think much more about it.

That was not to be the case. While attending the California Boys State Convention, I found a stranger in my bunk at 2AM. I was at the convention, thanks to the Monterey Chapter of The American Legion, to get a hands-on experience of how democracy works. It was a mystery to me why I had been selected, since I had never shown any interest in running for one of the school offices, but I knew if I wanted to get into MIT, it would not be in my interest to turn down any honor that was bestowed upon me. When I arrived in Sacramento, where the convention was being held, I joined nearly a thousand other male students from every high school in the state in one of the large open barns that were usually reserved to house cows and pigs during the State fair. We were expected to form communities where everyone could run for an office, or at least accept an assignment to some type of governmental position. Some kids came prepared with elaborate campaigns to win the high offices, like, attorney general, secretary of state and governor. My inferiority complex made the thought of standing in front of everyone to give a speech too horrifying for me to even think about, so I gladly accepted a mundane position as a Sheriff's deputy.

The convention lasted for three days. On the second day we all gathered to listen to the ambitious guys, all my age, deliver speeches from the podium about why they deserved to be elected to the high offices. One kid, who was running for Governor, was almost crying as he told everyone in a plaintive voice how much it would mean to his mother if he won the election. We should vote for him to make her happy. I knew I was a chicken shit, but I would never have been able to prostrate myself like that.

After listening to the speeches, we all returned to our bunks and the lights were dimmed so we could have a good nights rest. Around 1 AM, I was still awake and decided to climb down from the top tier of my bunk and take a stroll around the barn. After a half-hour of peregrinations around the rows of hundreds of symmetrically arranged beds, I headed back to my bunk to turn in for the rest of the evening. The repetitive layout of the bunks caused me to lose my bearings and I became lost. Relieved when I eventually managed to find my bunk, I began to climb up into it, but as I placed my hands atop the bed, I discovered that someone had taken my spot. I gently aroused him.

"I think you're in my bed."

Half asleep he looked at me in disbelief. "No, I don't think so, I've been here all night." "Are you sure this is your bed?" I asked.

"Yeah, I'm pretty sure." "OK"

I quietly wandered away leaving the poor kid to wonder what in the hell had just happened. After several similar scenarios, I somehow found my bunk, climbed in and went back to sleep. The next morning when I woke up I realized that I had gone sleep walking.

18

BITTEN BY A BEAT BUG

The Monterey American Legion was puzzled why I didn't show up to recount what I had learned from my experience, but given my fear of public speaking—another ping-pong ball bouncing around in my head—it was an impossibility. My sphere of comfort was hanging with a few of the school's other budding intellectuals at *The Sancho Panza*, Monterey's bohemian coffee house. It was located just a block from the high school in a Spanish casa built in 1841. Its wood plank floors, stone fireplace and shelves of eclectic books made for a stimulating atmosphere for young minds to think out of the box while they sipped on a cup of espresso, its bitter taste drowned with a heaping tablespoon of sugar. Even though all of us who gathered at the *Sancho Panza* dressed and wore our hair in acceptable conservative styles—I had a buzz cut—we imagined ourselves to be open minded thinkers. Francis Sherwood's father was even rumored to have been a communist, a word that I, and most Americans, found terrifying. I had no idea about politics other than my dad was a Republican, so that's what I was. It was not unusual to hear someone cavalierly saying *"goddamn or Jesus Christ."* It had been drummed into me that taking the name of the lord in vain was a sin, but as a recent convert to agnosticism, I saw no reason to continue to abide by this restraint. I was having a friendly chat with Gary Cunningham and one of my best friends, Tom Rhoads, who I admired in large part because he was super cool, had a perfect flattop, owned his own car and had a beautiful girl friend to boot, when I mustered up the courage to casually throw in a *goddamn*. No one gave it a second thought, but blood instantly rushed to my head as though water was gushing through a hole in a dam that had broken somewhere inside my brain. Within minutes the flush ebbed and I knew I had passed the Einstein lightning test. I was still alive and standing. A link in the Puritanical chain had been broken. Still, I knew better than to use that kind of language too freely, especially around my parents.

There was a conundrum at the Sancho Panza that puzzled me. Its owner was an MIT graduate. "Why would a scientist now be running a coffee house?" Even though I had recently read Jack Kerouac's best selling book, *"On the Road,"* and found the lifestyle he described fascinating, I couldn't comprehend how anyone could go from MIT, a school by now I was in complete awe of and convinced that I would soon attend, now be selling coffee when he could be making incredible scientific discoveries. It made no sense. However, thanks to Mel Soree, our basketball team's best player, I would get a short look at Kerouac's world that I would find inspirational. With seconds left in a game against our archrival, Santa Cruz, Mel drove the lane and scored the winning basket that made MUHS the Central Coast champions. A large fish was thrown on the court by a Santa Cruz fan after the game as an insult to the mostly Italian kids on our squad. But who cared. Our team would now travel to San Francisco to vie for the Northern California championship.

Maybe just to allow me to say I had played in the championship tournament, coach Larsh put me into our opening game in the first quarter. It was being played at the vast and mostly empty Cow Palace. I found myself holding the ball thirty feet from the rim and not knowing what to do with it, tossed up a two handed set shot that miraculously went through the basket. I heard a smattering of oohs in the audience. It would be my one moment of glory. We went on to lose the game and were eliminated from further play.

The team was already booked to stay overnight in a hotel and for reasons unknown, coach Larsh had assigned me to a room with two of the most incompatible roommates that could have been imagined; Sal Mareano, a hulking Italian fisherman's son, and Steve Hover, a gangly kid with modest athletic ability. Despite my unsettling late night hitchhiking experience, I still had doubts that there were more than a handful of homosexuals in the world, but as soon as the door to our room was closed, Sal began chasing

Hover around the room while uttering: "Hover, you're going to give me a blowjob." Sal could break me in two if he wanted, so I could only watch and hope that Hover would find a way to escape. It wasn't looking good. Sal had him pined down on top of the bed, straddling him with his knees and his crotch inches from his face when there was a knock on our door that brought the assault to an end. The team's jock contingent, Mel Soree, Claude Crabbe, Steve Hansen and Sal's brother Mike, were out in the hall in their underwear and wanted Sal to join them for some silly mischief.

The morning after seeing basketball sensation Bill Russell do an unbelievable reverse slam dunk in a University of San Francisco game that Coach Larsh had arranged tickets for our team to attend, he invited several of us, including myself and Dave Phillips, to accompany him on a ride to North Beach to see if we could spot a few of the odd characters known as Beatniks. Thanks to Kerouac, they were recently getting lots of press time. I had no idea that Larsh held a secret passion to become a writer, which would have explained his motivation to visit the area. As we drove down several of the little streets leading off of the triangular junction of Columbus and Broadway Avenues, where "Beats" were rumored to congregate, the few we passed probably found our car full of gawking teenagers with buzz cuts to be as amusing as we found them with their long unkempt mops and beards. Yet I found the area alluring with its little coffee shops, well-stocked bookstores, freewheeling ambiance and doe-eyed girls with long sexy hair that hung to the smalls of their backs.

19

MIT HERE I COME!

Mastering English grammar or having an expansive vocabulary; was not a high priority for me. Why did a scientist need to know how to write? But to improve my chances of getting into MIT, I buckled up and during my senior year got an A in English class and all the other inconsequential college prep courses that I would need to stand a chance. There were some teachers at MUHS who thought the idea of me being accepted to MIT was a fantasy. Their doubt was based on the low grade point average that I had earned as a ninth grader, which would lower my overall GPA. Just in case they were right, I applied to a less prestigious school, the Illinois Institute of Technology. ITT held its entrance exams months before I would take the standard SAT that MIT would be vetting. When the results came back, I learned that I had aced the math and science sections but failed the vocabulary section.

Howard Ziehm

My doubters would have the last laugh if I didn't do something radical to improve my word skills. Over the next three months, I feverishly studied every vocabulary improvement book I could get my hands on like '30 Days to a Better Vocabulary' and 'Readers Digest.' Seeing the number of simple words I didn't know the meaning of made it clear that my vocabulary was indeed, pathetic. After I finished taking the SAT at Cal Poly, I felt my crash learning had been successful and felt confident that I had again aced the math and science sections and had done reasonably well on the vocabulary section. The results would be sent to MIT and all I could do was wait.

"We are happy to inform you that you have been accepted . . ." were the first words I read when I opened the letter from MIT that arrived in the mail four weeks later. I screamed with joy as I ran to tell my parents. Fourteen thousand gifted students in the United States and from around the world had submitted applications and I was one of the nine hundred who had been accepted. Only five, including me, were from California. My ego was bursting.

That my rebellious side overruled my good senses was made manifest a few weeks later when I took the SAT exam again—not for myself, but for Claude Crabbe. Claude needed to post a reasonable score in order to attend the University of Utah who wanted him for their football team. He was a teammate on the basketball squad, held several school track records, was all-league in football and had a ten-inch dick surrounded by lots of hair. Rumor was that he was using it on his beautiful girlfriend, a cheerleader for Pacific Grove high school. We were polar opposites when it came to our attributes and not close friends, but like a puppy wanting to be accepted into the pack, I ignored what the consequences would be if I got caught, and agreed to take the exam for him when he asked. I was supplied with a phony identification card and a ride to the UC Berkeley campus where the exam was being held. Fortunately everything went off without a hitch. I intentionally missed a fair number of questions so not to draw suspicion by making him look too smart. It was a stupid thing to do, but in many ways I was stupid.

Being accepted to MIT made me an instant celebrity at MUHS. Congratulations came from the teachers who believed I had the talent and from the doubters who didn't. The school's paper, The Toreador, did a congratulatory article on me as well as several of my friends who were going to attend prestigious schools. Dave Phillips was accepted to West Point and

Tom Rhoads to UC Berkeley. But neither of those was MIT. I considered myself the crème de la crème. That my father would be shelling out a lot of bucks to pay for my education was just what fathers did. I didn't give it a second thought. It was expected in America, part of our national heritage.

As confident as I was about my intellect, I was equally unconfident about my social skills. When it came to knowing how to talk to girls, I had no clue. Other than carrying schoolmate Sharon Watson's books during Twirp Week, I had no female friends and had not a single date all through high school. In my mind I was an ungainly fragile pinhead. To avoid any discomfort, I had no intention of attending the upcoming graduation ceremony or the party afterwards. Going on stage to accept my diploma was a fearful thought, a hangover from my experience as a child in Milwaukee. And having to find a date, and worse, having to dance with her, was unthinkable. Besides, I didn't have a car.

Suddenly my parents recognized that they had raised a social zombie and to make amends, insisted that I attend the graduation ceremonies. To quickly bring me up to speed, they signed me up for two weeks of dance lessons at the local Arthur Murray Dance School. Because I had passed Driver's Ed and now had a license, my dad said I could use the family car for the evening. It would be the first time I would drive unaccompanied. Every time I thought about having to ask some girl for a date, my stomach churned. Then word came to me via one of the other girls in my class, that Carmen Oleta liked me and hinted that I should ask her out to the prom. I had always found her long dark hair, beautiful eyes and face hauntingly attractive, but up to this point I didn't think she even knew I existed. Our academic interests were very different, hers being the humanities and mine the sciences. She was very smart and had been chosen to be a co-valedictorian at the graduation ceremony. Why would she want to go out with me, a social recluse? Clearly my parents expected me to attend the prom, so I mustered up the courage to ask her to be my date. I couldn't help but being a bit surprised when she accepted my invitation.

Feigning illness, I still managed to dodge the graduation ceremony, reasoning with iconoclastic fervor that it was just a meaningless exercise. But the following night I found myself nervously standing in front of Carmen's house on the west side of Monterey. It was an older middle class home, sitting half way up a long sloping hill that ran down to the bay. After getting control of my nervousness and making sure the white carnation that I was going to give her was still in my hand, I proceeded up the stairs and after a brief pause on the porch, rang the bell. I felt uncomfortable in a suit, but when she opened the door and gave me a smile my nervous jitters subsided. She looked absolutely beautiful in her graduation gown and I felt lucky to be going out with her. I did my best to hold a reasonable conversation while we dined at Neil De'Von's Steak House on Cannery Row and was proud that by carefully counting the two and three step dances I had recently learned, that I didn't step on her toes while we later danced at the party. She seemed to have an innate ability to let me think I was leading her when the truth was just the opposite. The evening had been a joy. When I dropped her off at one in the morning, an hour I had rarely seen, I shyly asked her if she would like to join me the next day for a ride down the coast to Big Sur. Again she thrilled me by saying yes. A small kiss ended the evening.

The stretch of the Pacific Coast highway south of Carmel is one of the most beautiful in the world. Through moss covered Cypress trees that hug the edge of the highway are views of Carmel Bay where waves, fifty feet below, crash against outcrops of craggy rocks. I had driven the road before with coach Larsh who was then my driving education instructor, and because of the many winding turns, rarely went over twenty-five miles an hour. On the way back, coach Larsh took the wheel and said; "Now let me show you some real driving." I sat wide-eyed in the passenger seat as he wheeled around the curves like he was driving a Ferrari at the Leguna Seca racetrack. However, not wanting to take any chance of wrecking the family car or horrifying Carmen, I drove slowly along the coast, inserting a few words of conversation in between nature's awe-inspiring views.

It was a beautiful day. The always-pending fog had yet to come in and warm sunshine basked the coast as we approached Point Lobos State Park. So I asked her if she would like to take a walk. She liked the idea and after parking in a lot near the cliffs, we began to walk down a little sandy path that wended it's way through clumps of ice plants and twisted cypress trees, many made near barren by the unrelenting wind. The soft roar of the nearby crashing waves made for a very romantic atmosphere.

The path was deserted and we took a seat on a log that had been hewn out to make it into a little bench from which to enjoy the view. She offered no resistance when I took her hand and a warm glow enveloped me as I timidly leaned over to kiss her. She responded with the kind of passion I had heard Latin women were famous for. She left no doubt that she wanted a major make-out session. I wasn't ready for it. My neurons were totally overwhelmed and I went comatose. My hands and body became cold as ice and I struggled to move, let alone say anything. She was confused but thankfully remained calm as we continued to sit in silence. I felt like an absolute geek or even worse, a zombie. My whole body remained trance like. There was no point of going on. Quietly we walked back to the car. The fog was now rolling in and turning the sky gray and the air cold. It was a perfect metaphor for how I felt. It made my misery even worse. On the drive back, I attempted a few feeble words to explain what had happened, but since I really had no explanation, I knew they were useless. I would have liked to floor the accelerator to make the trip back to Monterey at Coach Larsh speed, but I couldn't even do that. We just slowly and silently ambled back to her house where I left her off, doubting if I would ever date her again.

That question became more or less moot the following week when I was asked—and when I hesitated—ordered; to take a Sunday ride with the family. Sitting in the back seat with my young siblings made me feel like a big goofy child and I was sulking as we began the drive up the two-lane road that led to Carmel. My father got right to the point.

"You know Carmen is a Catholic don't you?" I had no idea what he was getting at.

"So What?"

"So What! Don't you know that Catholics insist on the children being brought up Catholic?"

Children? I barely knew how children were made let alone thinking about making any or getting married for that matter. My mother's incessant nagging had made me see no joy in family life.

"Who cares?" was all that I could think of saying.

He became livid and though he wasn't a violent man, I sensed he was ready to explode.

"Anyone who marries a Catholic can just call it quits with the family. They worship god in a false way."

He glanced back at me to make the point. I had never overtly challenged his authority, but this conversation was so far removed from reality that I dared to mutter:

"I don't believe in any of that anyway." That did it!

"Why . . . Why . . . anyone who doesn't believe in god ought to be horse whipped!" My mother, who had been sitting silent, came to my rescue.

"Calm down Bob, you can't just beat religion into him" she said in her best nagging voice.

He backed off. I was lucky that she had stood up for me and knew better than to say anything more; but still thought to myself, *"maybe I'll just call it quits with the family."* Of course that was just an idle teenager threat. Who would pay the three grand a year for me to go to a school that had the highest tuition in the country? Because I had been kept ignorant of our family's finances (they saw it as none of my business) I had no understanding of the strain paying for my education was going to be on them.

A month later, wearing a full length tweed coat and the Rolex watch that I had been given as a graduation present, I hugged my mother and shook my father's hand as he reminded me not to forget to go to church, to which I responded with a lie by saying I wouldn't. I turned to walk up the gangway and before entering the cabin of the DC3, turned one more time to wave one final goodbye. I was glad to be getting away. As I strapped myself into the seat, I felt quite full of myself—as though I had the world by the balls.

20

ASSHOLE COEFFICIENTS

Flying across the country gave me some time to think about the new life I was about to begin and the old one I was leaving. My stepfather was a good man, but I understood our relationship was more one of duty rather than love. And I knew my mother had no clue who I was. If anything, I was a reminder of her first failed marriage. I only had a vague idea what a college fraternity was about, but several had made offers for me to stop by their houses during what was called rush week. But only one, Theta Xi, had offered to pick me up at the airport and take me to their house and provide me lodging until classes began; so I wrote back that I was interested in talking to them. I still intended to live in one of the dorms on the campus, but a look couldn't hurt. In the lobby of Boston's Logan airport I spotted a guy holding a sign with my name on it. It put me at ease that someone was there to take care of me. He introduced himself as Tibor Stefansky. After a few welcoming words, we walked out to the parking lot to his car; a neat little red MG!.Wow! He owned his own car and a sports car no less. As we headed into Boston, I learned that he was from Venezuela and studying Chemistry. Tibor was good looking and spoke with a confident air, nothing like the nerdy image I had formed about what an MIT man would look like. I had a bad habit of forming predisposed images. Wind blew through my hair as we flew via the Sumner tunnel under Boston Harbor and out onto Storrow Drive. An esplanade ran between the road and the Charles River. Half way down the drive, Tibor pointed out across the river to MIT's famed dome, shinning majestically in the sun. To think that I would be going to school there was beyond words. I told him I planned to study mathematics and he told me that several other brothers at Theta Xi were also math majors. When I mentioned that I played basketball and intended to try out for the team, he told me that one of the other brothers was a star player on the MIT varsity squad. I was so callow that I had no idea that I was being given a sales pitch to join the fraternity, which needed new members each year to pay the bills, but his attention to me was comforting.

Moments later we had exited Storrow Drive and were slowly ambling down Bay State Road, seemingly looking for a parking space, when one magically appeared directly in front of Theta Xi, complements of a brother standing in it during the entire time it had taken to pick me up from the airport. The fraternity at 66 Bay State Road was one of a continuous line of three storied redbrick townhouses that ran from the beginning of the block to its end. The sidewalks on both sides of the street were alive with a mixture of MIT freshman visiting fraternities and girls moving into the nearby Boston University women's dorm, a multi storied red brick building just up the street.

After helping me carry my bags up the stairs and depositing them in the foyer, I was led into a crowded living room where several of the house's brothers were courting other rushies. After being warmly welcomed by the house's president, Dick McDowell, bespectacled and rail thin and more the image of what I had expected MIT students to look like, I was guided after he learned that I planned on trying out for the basketball team, to an adjoining room to meet the house's jock contingency. Hugh Morrow didn't look like a star varsity player, medium height and with slightly buckteeth, but he was delighted that I was going to try out for the team. I was a bit miffed when he told me he was studying for a degree in Metallurgy. "That's where the big money is. Starting salary for a grad is six hundred a month." I thought to myself for a moment; "Weren't we at MIT to probe the arcane mysteries of the Universe? Making money was not part of the goal." Also present and talking to another rushie, were Manny Penna, a charming Brazilian, purported to be the school's best soccer player and two other brothers, Bruce Craig from Georgia and Ed Priest from Tennessee. It was time to dump my ludicrous idea of what an MIT man looked like. The other rushie, Arnie Aus, was an athletically built Canadian with a full shock of blond hair. He was telling the brothers that he planned to go out for the crew team.

And all these high IQ geniuses were—maybe not in the same way—but as crazy about sex and females as I was. Morrow, Craig and Priest invited Aus and I to leave the crowded fraternity to go outside to play a little Frisby, which I quickly realized was more about impressing the girls on their way to the dorm by making daring catches as we dashed between the cars slowly driving down the street. Craig mentioned that Theta Xi had an annex up the block directly across from the girl's dorm, where if one was so disposed, he could sit in a darkened room with binoculars and spy on the girls across the street who could often be seen running around in their rooms only wearing panties and bras or less. Priest, with a wanton smile on his face, told Aus and I that the house library was reserved for make-out sessions when girls from the local schools came to attend a party.

The conversation that night at dinner was very light hearted. The prior year, the school administration had banned and removed from the racks an issue of Voodoo, the school humor magazine, that ran a piece loaded with sexual double entendres. The front-cover of the issue read: "Give VD to your girl friends." It was confiscated by the school authorities and taken out of circulation. It was explained to me that the cool nerds lived in the fraternities and the nerdy nerds lived in the dorms, where they were referred to as "dorm tools." I was hoping that I had left all the pejoratives that had been attached to me in high school behind, so when McDowell informed me in the morning that the brothers had voted to offer me a chance to pledge the fraternity, I called my parents to see if they would be agreeable to let me join. Despite the fact that it was going to cost them a bit more money, my father overruled my mother's objections and told me to accept the invite.

Each of the new pledges was assigned a desk in a room also occupied by one or two upper classmen who would provide us rookies with a bit of moral guidance and help with our homework when needed. Theta Xi had several brilliant students, one of them, Tony Barlow, though still only in his third year, was already a paid consultant to Texas Instruments. We were each assigned a bunk bed on the house's unheated top floor. An elderly and personable black man, named Schmitty, prepared our meals and his not-as-personable wife, Vera, worked as the house waitress. Schmitty was also a willing sounding board to vent personal problems.

On the first day of school, several pledges, including myself, were being escorted to the school's campus, which was about a mile away. We stood on the south side of the corner of Mass Ave. and Beacon Street, waiting for the light to change so we could cross over and hitch a ride across Harvard Bridge. The locals, who were very proud of their school, were more than happy to help its students by giving them a ride. Pretending to be impatient that the light had yet to change, two of the brothers suggested we make a dash across the street at the first break in traffic. The continuous flow had not broken, but suddenly brother Ed Grabowski yelled: "Now!" All four of us pledges ran out into the middle of the street where cars began honking at us like we were chickens with their heads cut off. From the center of the street, I only had time to get a glimpse of the brothers, still back on the curb and laughing their heads off. It was a silly prank but a valuable lesson. Don't be blindly gullible; a lesson I would retain for the rest of my life.

The rest of the week wasn't as traumatic, but no less exciting. Seeing Norbert Weiner, professor emeritus and inventor of Cybernetics, who looked like a penguin as he waddled down the hall with his head tilted down and cigar in his mouth as though pondering some new exotic theory, was like seeing Einstein. The modern-tiered lecture hall, where my first physics lecture took place was awe-inspiring.

Tony French, the professor who gave the lecture, looked to be no more than thirty years old. As he ran back and forth across the width of the room, knocking small flatbed railroad cars against each other to demonstrate the principle of conservation of momentum, he simultaneously filled up the two long green backboards that ran the entire width of the room, with formulas. When they were filled, he pushed a button that activated a motor to raise the two used boards so the two clean ones behind would be exposed. The modernity elicited oohs and aahs from the hundred students in attendance. Without missing a beat, French continued to write formulas at a breath catching speed and just as the hour long lecture came to an end, he concluded with the tidy formula $F = dp/dt$; or in lay terms, Force equals the rate of change of momentum with respect to time. I felt so lucky to be there. Hustling down the school's long corridors between classes with a slide rule hanging from my belt was a nerd's dream.

At the end of my first week, I was told I had a message from the commanding officer of the Naval ROTC department inviting me to come to his office. I had applied for one of the fifty spots open in the Navy ROTC program, but had not been accepted. I speculated that someone might have dropped out, opening a spot for me. My appointment was at 10AM in the morning and I went to the commander's office to see what he had in mind. When I knocked on his door several times, there was no answer. I waited a few minutes and since I had no more morning classes, headed back to the frat house. As I walked across Harvard Bridge, the cool autumn wind blowing off the Charles River woke me up. Why would I want to commit myself to four years of NROTC classes followed by four more years of military service after graduation? As an army brat, I had already experienced thirteen years of military life. The bohemian side of my nature, still in its inchoate stage, told me to take the officer's absence as an omen and I never called back. It was one of the most important decisions I would ever make.

The workload was overwhelming and near impossible to complete, a fact the school recognized by awarding grades on a class average basis—the highest score on a test getting an A regardless of the percentage of correct answers. Competition was steep. By the end of the first month everyone was ready to blow off some steam. As Theta Xi's president, Dick McDowell, had promised, a party had been planned for Saturday night. Notices had been placed on the bulletin boards of several of the local girl's schools like Radcliff, Smith and Wellsley, inviting them to attend. Being that MIT had only one coed in 1958, this was a major event—a chance to mingle with members of the opposite sex. Boston had a plethora of schools so there were plenty of girls around, but there were also a lot of fraternities that would be throwing parties. We could only hope to draw our fair share. By this time, I knew most of the brothers quite well and Manny Penna, as far as I could tell, was the only brother who had previously had sex and was comfortable around women. By and large, the rest of us were socially inept. We were all pleased that a few girls showed up on Saturday evening and were mingling in the foyer waiting to be approached by one of the brothers. Most seemed to be as nervous as us; possibly because MIT men had a reputation of being animals when it came to party time; a natural result when young men are starved for women. Manny Penna lightened up the mood by playing some lively ragtime music on the upright piano that sat against the wall in the foyer. It was meant to break the ice and get everyone to socialize.

Though no one expected to have sex, a few of the brothers hoped to at least get their hands on a bit of female flesh before the evening was over. This was mostly not accomplished by charm, but by drugging the girl with copious amounts of alcohol so that she would agree to be dragged into the library with little resistance. Naturally it was a two way street. There were always girls from the all female schools who were at the party looking forward to being petted by male hands. Such was the state of dating in the late 50's. Us pledges were forewarned not to turn the lights on if we came into the library in case a brother was managing to have his way with a girl. It could ruin it for both of them. My attempts at conversation with a few of the girls were feeble and drew indifferent responses, so I spent most of the evening talking with several brothers who were equally devoid of social skills.

Among my fellow freshman that had pledged Theta Xi, I was far from the smartest, but within a month I realized that I could handle my classes with the same ease as I had done in high school. Calculus was a total snap and though physics and chemistry gave me some difficulty, I didn't feel any need to grind away on my homework each evening. Consequently, when brothers Bruce Craig, Manny Penna and Ed Priest asked me and two other pledges to join them after dinner in the library for a game of hearts, I accepted their offer. I wanted to be liked; to be with the in crowd, to put the days of being "a fragile pinhead" behind me. The two other pledges were Canadian, Arnie Aus and Gary Matchett from Duluth Minnesota. The games became a nightly routine. It was the first time in my life that I had a social life. I loved the light banter that took place during the games and "shooting the moon" if I got dealt the right cards.

During the card games, Aus, Matchett and I discovered that we shared a need for independence. We wanted not to just be part of the fraternity with all its rules, but to have our own clique. It was a fact that each study room at the frat house had one desk too many. The three of us decided to make a controversial suggestion to the house leadership: allow us to convert a sleeping room on the top floor into a combination study and sleeping room for the three of us to reside. For good reason, freshmen were to live under the watchful eye of an upper classman, but the thought of making the study rooms less crowded had merit and our request was granted.

Within a few days, we had the room set up. Aus and Matchett took desks against the front windows overlooking Bay State Road and I happily put mine against the back-wall. My desk would be next to a little three-foot high refrigerator where I could store the insane amounts of coca cola that I had begun to drink and tape to its door a particularly lascivious page that I had removed from one of my girlie magazines. It was of a slutty looking blond wearing yellow panties with her legs spread wide open. While I studied, a quick glance to the side provided me a nice distraction. Aus and I would sleep in a bunk bed placed against one of the sidewalls and Matchett in a single against the opposite side. A coin flip determined that I would take the top bunk.

The nightly card game destroyed any semblance of a rational study routine. This was not a problem for Matchett, easily the smartest of our trio. He could read a physics or chemistry book like a comic book and do all the problems without blinking an eye. Aus was not as swift as Matchett, but was definitely above average. As I mentioned, Calculus was a breeze for me and after the first month, I didn't even attend class; just cramming the night before the monthly tests which I aced with ease. But Physics and Chemistry were not intuitive. I had to work hard to diagnose a problem. Craig's playful teasing while we played cards about how hairy, (a favorite "in" word at MIT) the concept of chemical mass action was, made me edgy. MIT was not Monterey High. Everyone arrived as the top dog in their high school, but soon learned that at MIT that was not likely to be the case.

Unlike Harvard, just a mile up the river, where no one flunked out their first year, MIT always had several. A morose rumor had it that at least one student would commit suicide during the Christmas break by jumping off the Harvard Bridge into the icy Charles River. The warning bells that should have rang in my head remained silent and instead of becoming a serious student, I began slowly edging towards just the opposite.

A month after we moved into our private room, it had earned the appellation, "The Freshmen from hell." As could have been predicted, we thought of ourselves as special and looked at our fellow pledges with a bit of condescension. One evening while Matchett sat with his feet up on his desk, puffing on his meerschaum pipe while laughing over something he found amusing in the physics text book, "I kid you not," he suddenly turned to Aarne and me and with a twinkle in his eye suggested that we rate each of our fellow pledges with an AH coefficient. He went on to explain that AH was an acronym for asshole, and the coefficient would be defined as the size of the asshole divided by the total man. In other words; if you had a small asshole, your AH coefficient would be nearly zero. If, on the other hand, you were a big asshole, your AH coefficient could approach one. By fiat, the three of us were to have AH coefficients of .00001. He suggested we play some little humiliating prank at the end of each week on the pledge who had the largest AH coefficient. Aus and I loved the idea. Though it was subconscious, I knew that the best way to guard against being bullied was to be a bully, especially when it was just harmless fun.

A pledge from New York named Eric Bender, was the first winner of the AH coefficient sweepstakes. His lack of a sense of humor or any other kind of fun, earned him an AH rating of .9. He was a skinny clean-cut kid whose closely spaced eyes made it natural to give him the moniker, 'Beady Eyes.' On his desk he kept a picture of his parents, their bland expressions reminiscent of the stern farmer and his wife depicted in Grant Wood's classic painting, 'American Gothic.' Late at night, while everyone was sleeping, we crept down the stairs and removed the photograph and took it to the second floor bathroom where after tying wires to it, lowered it into the toilet bowl and left it hanging face-up just above the water line. After closing the lid, we tiptoed back up to our room and hit the sack; chuckling as we dozed off knowing some early morning whizzer would be greeted by stares from 'Beady Eyes's' parents when they opened the lid.

Although some brother's had to feign outrage, the prank earned plenty of snickers from the entire house. Matchett went right to work on the next prank. Despite just being out of high school, he was a fairly accomplished chemist and educated Aarne and me about a chemical called Nitrogen triiodide. It was inert when wet, but became explosive when it dried. It only needed to be touched to go off. In small quantities, it created no more than a loud pop. To get the chemicals he needed for his brew, Gary designed another experiment that required the same ingredients. When the professor looked at the list he asked with a skeptical voice; "You're not making NI3 are you?"

"Of course not, that would be dangerous" Gary answered in his best responsible-citizen voice.

Two weeks later he walked into our room with a test tube half-full of NI3 paste. For just being an obnoxious asshole, Val Silby, a foreign exchange student from Latvia, who to demonstrate his proficiency with English, used helpful servings of; "god damn," "fucking assholes," and "clods" in his speech, had scored a resounding .97 AH rating over the prior week. We knew that pissing him off promised to be priceless. To give the chemical plenty of time to dry, we steeled into the dorm sleeping area early in the afternoon while everyone was either at classes or studying at their desks.

Silby slept in the top bed of one of the bunks against the back wall. After Gary smeared a few dabs under his bed covers, we were about to leave, when as an afterthought, he applied the last few dabs left in the test tube to the top of Silby's bedpost and to the light switch next to the door. Knowing that there would be fireworks that evening, it was hard to concentrate on doing homework. Our ears were kept peeled for Silby coming up the stairs to turn in for the night. Around eleven he entered the sleeping room and because of the already frosty autumn temperatures, quickly hopped atop his bunk and climbed under the blankets. It sounded like someone was making popcorn. "Goddamns, fucks, shits, bastards and assholes" came pouring out of the room as he jumped out of his bunk, totally confused by what was going on. 'Beady Eyes', who had turned in earlier, was also in the room and jumped out of his bed to turn on the light. The switch exploded with a loud bang rewarding us with an unsuspected bonus. We were all on the floor laughing uncontrollably. The next day, as a third year organic chemistry student, brother Ed Grabowski knew exactly what had happened. It didn't take a genius to know that the "Freshmen from Hell" were the perps. The three of us were called into the sleeping room where Grabowski began giving us a stern reprimand. 'Beady Eyes' had come along to revel in our punishment and after telling Grabowski that initially he thought Silby's electric blanket had shorted out, he smugly rested his elbow on the top of Silby's bedpost. He jumped a foot off the ground as the small dab that had yet to be touched went off. Grabowski struggled to keep from breaking up.

Other than Boston's dirty air that caused a big boil on the side of my face, which according to the school's doctor was because my skin had previously only been exposed to the pristine Monterey air, it was an incredible city. There were colleges and bright young people all over the place. There was Harvard, which us MIT nerds facetiously referred to as 'The Little

Out-house Up The River,' Boston University, Boston College, Radcliff, Smith, Wellesley, Tufts, Northeastern and a host of small schools, made it seem as though there was a school on every block. With all that brain power in town there was plenty of need for culture. MIT offered concerts by the likes of The Ray Charles band and poetry readings by T. S. Eliot and the city provided the Boston Symphony and for a lighter evening of orchestral music, The Pops. Near Copley Square, was the Exeter Theatre where one could go to see the best foreign films like Bergman's Seventh Seal or Marcel Camus,' Black Orpheus. They also played short films like Reefer Madness, an educational film produced in the mid 30's to warn against the dangers of marijuana. It was also at the Exeter theatre, that I saw a newsreel where Utah All American, Claude Crabbe, was seen catching a game winning touchdown pass. I smirked to myself as I reflected on the fact that they had me to thank for that feat.

The Red Sox played within hearing distance from the frat house at Fenway Park I saw Ted Williams hit his last home run with a swing so fluid that it would never be erased from my memory. The MTA was only a half block away in Kenmore Square and could drop one off only twenty steps from the ticket booth of the Boston Garden where the Celtics played and I got to watch the incredible Bob Cousy make behind-the-back passes to the likes of Heinson and Bill Russell.

When Smitty wasn't available to cook dinner on the weekends, there was no shortage of great restaurants. Elsie's sandwich shop in Harvard Square, The English Room on Newberry Street, the European in the Italian section of town, or for special occasions, Durgin Park in the Faneuil Hall Market Place, where surly waitresses served inch thick prime rib. But more often then not, the epicurean experiences of a poor college student were just late night coffee breaks at an all night diner in Kenmore square where the servers—all recovering alcoholics—would grab the dougnut or bagel with their hand and slam it down on a chipped worn plate after repeatedly failing because of the shakes to pick it up with tongs.

21

SHE HAD A HEART ON!

The cultural attractions in Boston added greatly to my education, but one on Howard Street, just south of Scolly Square, would change my life. Craig, Penna and Morrow invited Matchett, Aus and I to accompany them to a Saturday night show at the Old Howard burlesque theatre. Boston was a puritanical city, testified to by the fact that "Banned in Boston" was a metaphor for censorship. It still had blue laws that prohibited Sunday shopping or even listening to music on a jukebox on the Sabbath until after one in the afternoon. I had no idea that Boston even had a burlesque theatre and was in an elated mood as I hopped on the MTA at Kenmore Square with my frat brother's to be going to one. We got off at the Scollay Square station fifteen minutes later. My first impression of the area as we came up from the underground station was not good. It was very dark and dank. All I saw were a few sleazy bars and a scattering of derelicts and sots. Then my eyes were drawn down to the middle of the block of one of the side streets where a brightly lit marquee hung over the sidewalk. Like flies being attracted to a light, we hastily rushed down the little side street until I could see written on the marquee in large red letters: "IRMA THE BODY." Irma the Body was one of the strippers often featured in layouts in Cabaret magazine. I had jacked off to her countless times. Wow! Now I was going to see her live!

On the side walls of the foyer leading into the theatre, were large posters of Irma wearing provocative garments that made her appear nearly nude, or at least about to be. Because her large breasts flowed over the top of the corset she wore, her nipples had to be covered by pasties. Posters of other provocatively attired stars who would be appearing in coming weeks, were also on the sidewall. The Old Howard was a showcase of sexual delights. Lest my brothers think I was a pervert, I kept the thrill of being shown this place to myself. The theatre was packed with dirty old men and working class types as well as several other small cliques of college-kids who had come to see naughty entertainment. There were no women in the audience that I could see. The seats near the stage were long gone, but we found good seats half way back in the center of the auditorium that would offer a reasonable view. As we waited for the show to begin, a weathered looking old man, wearing an ill fitting suit, walked up and down the aisle hawking popcorn, candy and novelties from a tray he had hanging from a strap around his neck. His sallow looking skin and worn eyes made me believe he had been working at the theatre for many decades. He claimed that the pen with a picture of a stripper imbedded in its plastic handle and the mini magazine he was hawking, would provide thrills unheard of and could be found nowhere else in the world.

When the lights went down, a six-piece orchestra situated in the pit just below the stage, began playing a jaunty tune. Quickly an attractive young woman in her twenties strutted onto the stage. She wore a flower print dress and high heels, and after a bit of teasing the audience with tawdry smiles, began to slowly remove her clothes, handing each item to a stage hand standing in the wings. "What a neat job that was!" She peeled down to a filmy g-string panty and a see through bra that revealed that her nipples were coverd with pasties. Then, after removing her bra and throwing it to the side, she treated the crowd to few spirited bumps and grinds that the orchrestra enhanced with staccato bursts of music. Each thrust elicited enthusiastic applause and hoots from the crowd.

A busty stripper, who was an expert in using her god-given endowments, followed that act. Once she had discarded her clothes, she sashayed around the stage to give everyone a chance to admire her large breasts. Then, coming to the front of the stage, she began slinging them so the tassels attached to her pasties twirled, first from one direction, then the other. As the guys went wild, she gyrated faster and faster until the tassels were spinning like airplane propellers. Then showing how adroit she was with her tits, she somehow manipulated them so the tassles would spin in opposite directions. My dick was hard as could be, but I didn't want to embarrass myself in front of my brothers, so I forced myself to keep my hands off of my lap and just applauded. I wasn't into hooting and hollering, but the big smile on my face said much the same. The first two striptease acts were followed by a comedy skit, which I assumed was meant to give time for the audience's stiff penises to cool down. The skit began with two forty-year-old vaudeville comedians standing on one side of the stage admiring a pretty young lady on the other side of the stage. Dressed in a print dress and high heels, she pretends to water some fake plastic flowers. One of the comedians, Funkhauser, a short little fat guy with a round face and head topped with a squashed down bowery hat, is getting all worked up looking at the young lady, but admits to his friend Stan, a dapper street-wise hustler, that he is convinced he has no chance of ever meeting her. Stan tells him that's nonsense and convinces him that if he introduces himself to the lady like a gentleman, she will be more than pleased.

Funkhauser, encouraged by the little pep talk, walks across the stage to where the lady is now halfway up a ladder so she can water some high hanging flowers. She gives no indication that she even knows he is standing at the foot of the ladder admiring her until he puts his hand on her butt to give it a little squeeze.

Startled, she turns to look down at him and in an irritated voice asks, "What are you doing?"

"I'm just helping you out." Funkhauser responds.

"You're not helping me out, you're helping yourself out," she protests.

The routine continues; Funkhauser returns back to Stan and almost cries as he tells him how poorly things went. Stan grabs him by the hand and tells Funkhauser he is going to show him how to properly woo a lady. He walks over and gives her a bouquet of flowers for which he is rewarded with a little kiss and gets no complaint when he lightly taps her behind. After they return to their side of the stage, Stan tells Funkhauser to go back and woo her on his own. But his attempts to mimic Stan's suave technique falls flat again and when he puts his hands on her butt, she comes down from the ladder to give him a slap across the face and a stern admonishment: "Funkhauser, stop your funking around!" and then storms off the stage. It was sophomoric third grade humor, but in the late fifties, even alluding to racy language in front of a woman was unheard of.

After two more house girls and another skit, it was feature time. All eyes were raptly focused on the closed stage curtain as the orchestra played to a crescendo. Highlighted by a key light, the curtain slowly rose to reveal standing in the middle of the stage, 'Irma the Body,' dressed in an innocent Little Bo Peep outfit that included a broad brimmed sun hat with a garland of flowers around the rim. Her flouncy dress completely covered her long legs but her thin waist and breasts, bulging over the top of her white bodice, clearly showed that she did indeed have a body. Her long auburn hair and cheeks covered with ample rouge, eyes with long lashes, and lips painted a bright red, made her look garishly sweet and nasty. After giving the audience three or four seconds to take it all in, she suddenly reached down and pulled up the front of her ruffled dress to reveal a gorgeous pair of long legs sheathed in white nylon stockings held up by a lacy garter belt. Her diaphanous g-string panties had a little red heart covering her pussy. She looked down at her crotch and then pointed to the little red heart:

"Look! I got a heart on!"

The whole place howled. I had never heard a woman talk like that. It was hot. Looking up with a big smile on her face to acknowledge the audience's enthusiastic appreciation, she proceeded to do her act. After taking off her dress she hopped onto a bed and writhed like she was going into heat. While on her back, she lifted one of her legs at a forty-five degree angle and reached up to unsnap her garter, symbolic that all restraints were being removed. Then she began to slowly roll the top of her stocking down her thigh, each inch of exposed flesh asking: "would you naughty boys like to see more?" By the time only the toe of the stocking remained attached to her leg, the audience was in an erotic trance and she lowered her leg so by holding the top end with her hand it became stretched like a rubber band on a sling shot. When she released her grip it flew through the air like a bird being freed from a cage. The rest of her act proceeded to show off, with great élan, her well-endowed body, ending as the orchestra played a spirited rendition of the national anthem of burlesque, David Rose's, 'The Stripper.' Irma's hips thrust forward and bumped and grinded with such energy that every guy in the audience felt as though it was his hard dick that was getting a workout.

She was a star for good reason. Her act took over fifteen minutes to perform and was broken into three segments, each making me more and more aroused. A brief intermission gave the sallow looking guy a chance to sell hot dogs, popcorn and more silly souvenirs. The second half of the show, which also ended with Irma, was much shorter but just as exciting. The whole evening lasted almost two hours. Unlike the Follies Bergere, the show wasn't artsy; quite the opposite; it was pure raunch and I loved it. As we left the theatre to go back to the frat house, I had no idea if my frat brothers were as smitten by the show as I was, but I knew I would be coming back to the Old Howard many times and always by myself. What was the point of having a friend sit next to you while you're getting off. I left even smitten by the seediness of Scollay Square; a cleaner environment would have made the show seem sterile.

I had no trouble making the Freshman basketball team and along with practice, card games, a job I took at the school library, visits to the Old

Howard and not to mention my school studies, I had a very busy schedule; maybe too busy. When it came time to take exams I was so far behind that I was forced to cram a whole months of study into one night to catch up.

I always managed to suceed, but on one late night of cramming I became exhausted and crawled up onto my bunk to take a short nap. I asked my two roommates, who continued to study, to wake me up in an hour. I went out like a log. A minute later I was jumping out of my bed and using my pillow to beat something that was under my bed covers. Both Aarne and Gary looked at me in disbelief and wanted to know what the hell I was doing. Sweating and breathing heavily I told them: "There's an alligator in my bed." While they just gaped in disbelief, I realized that I had been sleepwalking. Embarrassed, I apologized and made an effort to convince them it was no big thing. We all had a little laugh. My mother had said it was from over exertion and maybe she was right.

At the end of the first semester I earned B's and C's. Mass action was not as hairy as Bruce Craig had led me to believe, but not getting an A in calculus was a blow. I had paid a price for not attending class where I had missed taking all the short ten-minute quizzes the instructor gave each Friday. When he computed the final grades he averaged the total of the little quizzes, which in my case was zero, with the monthly tests and the final, all of which I had scored well over ninety. Despite having been told that I was the only person in class who understood the concept of a limit, I was now being branded as a B level mathematician. I felt I had been graded unfairly but didn't have the gumption to make a protest. The damage to my psyche that I could never get less than an A in math, was now shattered. It was fuel for the self-doubt that lay just below the surface.

22

IS IT A HE OR A SHE

Over the Christmas break, I recognized how homesick I was and broke my vow to never return home and rejoined my family in Monterey. Two weeks of listening to my mother nag, over things as minor as why I had spent money on Christmas gifts for everyone, had me practically running to the train station to get back to Boston. The boredom of the three-day trip was mitigated by turning my back to the sleeping little old lady sitting next to me and pleasuring myself while I paged through the girlie magazines that I had brought along. I even managed to treat myself to a quick orgasm while sitting in Grand Central Station as I waited to board the train to Boston. My suitcase covered my damp crotch when it came time to walk to the train.

My return to Boston began with enduring the inane ritual called Hell Week. The fraternity brothers doled out a menu of abuses and humiliations that we pledges were to willingly accept to prove that our desire to be full-fledged members knew no bounds. Most of it was the expected cliché's of sleep deprevation, verbal insults and paddling which I took with panache because I didn't want to give anyone an excuse to think of me as weak. I wanted no one to think of me as "fragile." A task that was rumored, but didn't happen, would have been much more terrifying; to go to the Old Howard to ask a stripper to gift him her *merkin*, a fake pubic hair wig used to cover a shaved vagina. Whether any of the girls actually wore them or not was unknown. To be required to ask a girl, even a stripper, such a personal question was for me beyond the pale. When Hell Week came to an end, I had become Delta 576; the five hundred seventy sixth member of the fourth chapter admitted to the Theta Xi national fraternity founded in 1864 at the Rensselaer Polytechnic Institute in Troy, New York. In all honesty, it didn't mean a whole lot to me. I felt a rapport with my two roommates, Aus more than Matchett, and with Bruce Craig, Manny Penna and Hugh Morrow but it ended there. I hoped to join Hugh on the varsity basketball team when the next season began.

Thinking the Nazi banner that I had found while living in Germany would make a neat wall decoration for our room, I had brought it along when I returned. Aus and Matchett were delighted when I showed it to them and we hung it on the sidewall next to the front window. Aus said his father, a Lithuanian, had fought on the German side during the war. A few days later, Dick McDowell made the long trek up the stairs to our room to tell me a girl was on the library phone that would like to speak to me. A girl? When I picked up the phone, the first thing she asked was if I lived in the room with the Nazi banner. I told her I did. She went on to say that she was a resident at the Boston University girl's dorm just up the street and wanted to know why I had that banner in my room. I told her it was just a decoration; a souvenir from when I lived in Germany. She said, as a Jew, she found it very offensive. I had absolutely no clue why it offended her, but didn't feel it was my place to put the fraternity in a bad light with the girls dorm up the street, so agreed to take it down. Two of the house's brothers, Steve Strauss and Bruce Karnoff, were Jews, and had not protested the banner's presence so I was confused why she had a problem with it.

To me, Jews were nothing more than adherents to another religion, not any different than Catholics or Protestants. But since she had made the effort to call me and seemed to be legitimately disturbed, I sensed that there was something I didn't understand. William Shire's twelve-hundred page tome, '*Rise and Fall of the Third Reich*' had just been published and though I had ample class assignments before me, I began to read it. I was shocked to learn of all the atrocities that the Nazis had perpetrated against the Jews during the war, many heinous beyond description. During the two plus years I lived in Germany, not one peep was mentioned about this. I heard nothing in school while in Germany or in Monterey and nothing in the barracks where I shined shoes or from the Germans that I had contact with in Erlangen. Our maid Eva had even said things were very good under

Hitler when the war first began. If my parents knew what had gone on, they never said anything. I don't believe they did. There was no reason to suspect that Shear's book was inaccurate, so I understood why she found the banner appalling. I was about to throw it away when Aus said he would like it, so I gave it to him. Despite his father fighting on the side of the Germans, I doubted if he had a clue about the Nazis either.

I was the only brother in the fraternity to have a collection of Rock and Roll and Show Music classics. Though no one overtly complained when Buddy Holly's, *That'll Be The Day* or Fats Domino's *Going to New Orleans*, or the music of Bernstein's *West Side Story* or Roger and Hammerstein's *Oklahoma* blared from my room when I was home in the afternoon, I got the drift that they found my tastes to be plebian. Rock and Roll was trash and show music was schmaltz. To the contrary, I thought their tastes were stilted. Matchet averred that no worthwhile music had been written since Bach. Bruce Craig loved the classics and especially Bach, but was not so fervent and took it upon himself to introduce me to the classics. I was very open-minded and appreciated his tutelage and quickly found myself a passionate lover of classical music, albeit without shunning my love for pop music.

Whether it be comic books, stamps, pop music or girlie magazines, I had a festish for making collections and I got right to work putting together a collection of classical music L. P.s. Obviously I didn't have the money to carry out this task, so I had to resort to my well honed shoplifting techniques to remove albums I desired from the student store. It was a dangerous and stupid habit that I somehow managed to pursue without getting caught. It probably would have gotten me expelled from the school. Obviously I didn't weigh the consequences of my actions very well. Ironicaly my indifference to getting caught would eventually prove to be a plus. While I was in a pilfering mode, I decided to right what I considered to be a wrong; that being the confiscation of the 1957 edition of Voodoo titled: Give 'V. D. to Your Girl Friend.' My library job afforded me access to the school's rare book collection where a bound copy of the entire year of the magazine was stored. The idea of sexual censorship did not sit well with me and I removed the volume from the darkness of the rare book archive and placed it in the Theta Xi library where it would be freely available. Whether all or any of my brothers saw it that way, was never expressed to me. It was my first act to lift sex from the dark abyss of American repression.

The rebellion that had been swirling in my head over the years was quickly becoming more congealed. "Hang down your head Tom Dooley, Hang down your head and cry" was the eponymous opening line of the hit song by the Kingston Trio. I was so taken by their melodious melodies and resonant harmonies, that I bought a cheap guitar and a songbook so I could learn to play their songs on my own. I had a tin ear and knew so little about music; that it took me three months before I even understood how to tune the instrument or worse, even why it needed to be in tune. Eventually I learned to play well enough to convince two of my brothers at the fraternity to form a trio to enter the annual school talent show. It didn't go well, but it was a first step in the direction I somehow knew I was headed. Folk music was in the forefront of the civil rights movement, and though I wasn't directly involved, it was something I supported. My pilfered record collection soon began to add the calypso music of Harry Belafonte, the African protest music of Miriam Makeba and especially the spine tingling folk music of Joan Baez.

Like a lot of science nerds, I didn't understand why we had to take humanities and didn't appreciate what was being taught. Although Machievelli's caveat that rulers should feign allegance to their subjects dominant religion caught my eye, the intellectual battles waged by Locke and Hobbs skirted over the top of my head when I read their works. I treated them as little more than assignments that had to be passed in order to move on. By now I had abandoned agnosticism and had become a complete atheist. I wouldn't understand that even though St. Augustine and St Augustus were Christians, they had spearheaded great advancements in human reasoning. "Wasn't human reasoning always as it was now?" Only the cynical and witty Voltaire touched me. He was antiestablishment and not afraid to express his mind regardless of the consequences. I was taught not to question authority, so I never offered an opinion during class discussions. However, my ears perked up when brother Craig told me what one of our other brothers had done in a Humanities class. Bruce Karnoff was a third year philosophy major. He wore thick wire rimed glasses that sat on his large Jewish nose that made him look like a Rabbi. He wasn't a jock and didn't strike me as being someone with a sense of humor so I had little contact with him. But after Craig told me what he said during a discussion in an Ethics class, I found myself admiring his boldness and lack of fear to be disrespectful. The professor had finished delineating what he considered was the totality of joyful experiences, when Bruce raised his hand:

"Yes, Mr. Karnoff?

"I think you are forgetting to include the joy of a large burp, a large fart and a large shit!"

For this delightful insight and recognition of the joy of shear animal pleasure, he was asked to leave the class. I couldn't put my finger on it at the time, but there was something about his disrespect that was very 60's. This was the rock and roll age. Authority was to be challenged.

Over the summer, I found myself once again washing dishes. I had written requests for a summer job to over thirty companies, all of them in cities that had a National League baseball team so I could attend games when the Milwaukee Braves were in town, but was rejected on the basis that they only hired students who might come to work for them after they graduated. Being an Army brat, I was not based in any particular city. After a year at MIT, I was only able to get a job because my father was able to pull a few strings to get me work at one of the cafeterias at the Presidio language school.

When I returned to Boston in the fall, I was as anxious to get back to the Old Howard as I was to continue my studies. I was also well on my way to become a disciple of the Kerouac philosphy. Folk music was opening my eyes to injustice. For the most part, I kept my opinions to myself, because when I didn't I was surprised to find how antithetical they could be to my friends. After I read a short book about Castro's revolution that pointed out that it was made possible in large part by Batista's indifference to his subjects well being, Aus, whose family had escaped communism in Latvia, was ready to come to blows with me.

An even bigger controversy occured when a black kid was making the rounds of the fraternities during Rush week. As far as I knew, MIT had no black students and this was the first year they had admitted a black as well as a female, who was surprisingly very attractive. When the black student stopped into Theta Xi, Bruce Karnoff and Dick McDowell befriended him and vehemently argued that we should offer him a bid. Most of the other brothers were less enthusiastic, not willing to object on racial grounds, but rather with excuses that their parents would cut their funding if they discovered that they were in a fraternity with a black. It was agreed that a bid would only be extended with a unanimous vote, which of course didn't happen. High IQ's didn't trump prejudice.

Not many tears were shed when Aus and I announced we were moving out of the fraternity and taking a basement apartment in the historic and artistic Beacon Hill district. Neither of us had much in common with the brothers living in the main house and the three brothers we chumbed with, Craig, Morrow and Penna, lived in the Annex. Being called "stupid shits" by Matchett when we asked his help in solving a homework problem, though compared to him we were, had gotten old as well. Few, if any, were sorry to see that the fourth floor clique had broken up. For better or for worse, I was now free of any supervision.

Beacon Hill was Boston's version of San Francisco's North Beach. Charles Street ran along its base where several coffee houses and small clubs served the hill's hep culture. On the other side of the hill was dreary Scollay Square and my beloved Old Howard Theatre.

Charles street crossed into Cambridge over the Longfellow bridge and exited at the north end of the MIT campus. With my library earnings and some help from my parents, I was able to purchase a new Italian Lambretta motor scooter, which made travel between our apartment and the campus or fraternity very quick and easy. Aus could ride on its back seat so the two of us could continue to take our meals at the fraternity and stay afterwards for a few hands of Hearts or Bridge. On weekends, if we didn't eat out, he showed me how to prepare smelts and I showed him how to make a cherry pie.

I made the varsity basketball squad and began, as usual, on the first string and, as usual, on the bench by the end of the season. Two of my teammates, Dave and Bill, were the yet to be notorious Koch brothers. The school had hired an ex-marine to coach the team which had never had a winning record. My fraternity brother, Hugh Morrow led the team in scoring with a twenty points a game average and Dave Koch proved to be a gifted athlete, but we still ended the season as losers.

Politics never came up so all I knew about the Koch brothers was that they went to prep school at Andover and were studying chemistry as a preparation for working in the family oil business. I only nudged once into the world of politics when Aarne and I were each paid five dollars by two of our Beacon Hill neighbors who were law students at BU who wanted us to vote for their candidate to be president of the Boston's Young Democrats club. Their boy lost because the other guy had bought more votes.

My mind, now bubbling with an olio of contradictions; MIT student, athlete and folky, found justification to become a regular patron of the Old Howard when I heard that one of the school's humanities professors had said that it was the best place to go to see authentic American humor. To become more of a folky bohemian, I let my hair go uncut and because it was all I was genetically capable of, grew a poor excuse of a beard. I topped off my new "beat" look with a long beige canvas raincoat. As the only person at MIT attired like this, it would be safe to say I was the school's first "beat."

As much as I was pleased with my new image, I was to soon discover that many Americans didn't like those who stepped off the line. During thanksgiving break, I joined Aus, and a few of the other brothers, for a short ski trip to Stowe Mountain. I had never skied before so Aus gave me a half hour lesson on the beginners slope before taking me to the top of the intermediate slope and giving me a little push to get me started down the hill. Halfway down, a failed snowplow turn resulted in my head imbedded in a drift while the rest of my body was bent over in an arc much like an ostrich with its head buried in the sand. Despite the inauspicious start, I had become fairly proficient by the end of the day but, because of my library job, had to get back to Boston where since it was only a hundred miles away, I could return by hitchhiking.

Fortifying myself with a hot Toddy to warm up my innards, I walked two blocks to the edge of town and stuck my thumb out to hitch a ride back to Bean Town. There were several hours of daylight left, so I was sure I could catch a few rides and be back before nightfall. It wasn't until the sun began to set and a light snow began to fall, that a car finally stopped. I ran to it and told the driver, a guy in his late twenties, that I was heading to Boston. He told me to jump in. Glad to get out of the cold and just be moving, I didn't bother to ask him how far he was going and was surprised when he left me off at desolate spot about ten miles up the road. The few rays of sunlight that still crept over the western horizon were gone within a few minutes. Then the snow began to come down hard and a fairly brisk wind came up. It was hard to keep my eyes open. Only one car passed every ten minutes . . . if that. The darkness and snow made me nearly invisible. I had noticed a lone light illuminating a side road junction about a quarter mile back towards Stowe, so I walked to it, hoping the illumination would help someone to see me.

I began to suspect that I was the victim of some kind of sick joke. The guy who had given me the ride to nowhere was probably laughing his head off over a few beers with some buddies about the fix he had put some long hair college punk in. I was in trouble. I was already beginning to shiver and my feet were starting to tingle and become numb. Only one car had passed over the last hour. Around midnight I saw a set of headlights coming my way and I stuck my thumb out and wildly gesticulated with my arms. The small truck just sped by, its rear wheels kicking snow up in my face as it did. But then . . . fifty yards down the road, it stopped! I ran like all hell and opened the door to ask the guy if he was heading to Boston. He told me to hop in!

He was an older man who worked for the Boston Globe and was headed into town to pick-up the morning edition. We exchanged pleasantries and recognizing how cold I looked, he pulled into a little all-night diner several miles down the road so we could get a nice cup of hot coffee. A surly overweight waitress, who looked pissed that she was working the late night shift, came over to take our order. Speaking to the man who had just saved me possibly from death:

"And what can I get for you"

He ordered a coffee and some apple pie. After jotting down his request, she momentarily glanced at me with my long straggly hair and dirty canvas raincoat. I could see the disdain in her face. Turning back to my benefactor she asked:

"And what will he . . . or she . . . or whatever it is have?"

I ate my pie and coffee and silently endured the feeling of being unwanted. The old guy picked up the tab and we headed out. Forced to drive at a slow speed because of the blinding snow, we got to Boston around five in the morning. I was a little wiser but no less determined to continue on the track I had set for myself even though I had no clue what it was.

Incredibly, I thought my parents would be impressed with my new rebellious look when they came to pick me up at the Columbus, Georgia bus station where I had just arrived to spend Christmas vacation with them at nearby Fort Benning where my father was now stationed. My "beat" look didn't last long. The next morning I was hauled off to the base barber to have my locks shorn. They also informed me that a date with an officer's daughter had been arranged for me so I could attend a Christmas party. Pleading that I hadn't brought along appropriate clothes fell on deaf ears. My mother took a pair of my father's dress pants and took its forty-inch waist down to thirty-three inches. His legs were much shorter than mine as were the sleeves of his sports jacket, which also had shoulders that were meant to fit a portly figure, not a skinny stick. When I was driven to meet my date, I looked every bit a burlesque comedian; all that was missing was the bowery boy hat. I need not explain that my date was not smitten.

It was the dawn of the jet age. My always-forgiving father, after reminding me to be sure to go to church, sent me back to Boston by jet. Jet travel was so new that the Atlanta airport had yet to smooth out a little hill in the middle of its runway and the plane almost went airborne as it sped across it. My life was about to take a similar desultory path. As quickly as the jet had soared skyward, my grades at school were plunging downward. When I examined my midterm report card, I saw that I had passed everything but excelled in nothing. Because I had played cards on the eve of the finals and then stayed up all night cramming for my chemistry final, I had fallen asleep after only doing two of the problems during the three-hour exam. The professor sensed something was wrong and gave me a grade of E, which allowed me a second chance to take the exam a few weeks later at which time I scored a B. It should have sent a message but it didn't.

When the school year ended, Aus told me he was leaving school for a year to work for IBM Toronto. We had both taken a programming course, studying FORTRAN and his grades were impressive enough for IBM to offer him a job. It was a sweet deal for him. His father was not wealthy and IBM had told him if he did well, they would help pay for the remainder of his education.

23

GET UP AND DANCE

Granted I wasn't a stellar student, but still I would have thought an MIT education would qualify me for something more than a summer job with the campus ground crew cutting grass on the athletic fields. I made the best of it. I enjoyed being outdoors. My supervisor was a little fifty-year-old Italian guy who looked like he just got off the boat from Sicily. During breaks he entertained me with stories about his early sex life when he was still a boy living in Italy. My favorite was the one where he described sitting in a bathtub with only the tip of his dick above water, as though it was a small island. He then placed an ant atop it and excited himself by watching it frantically scurrying around like a shipwrecked sailor trying to find a way off.

I couldn't afford the Myrtle Street apartment on my own, but fortunately Manny Penna, my charming Brazilian fraternity brother who though graduated, was staying in Boston over the summer to work as an assistant for one of his professors, suggested that I share an apartment with him on Beacon Street. The street level apartment was only one room with two six-foot high sash windows that looked out to the sidewalk. We kept them open to give relief from the hot and humid Boston summer. That also enabled Manny to sit on the ledge and flirt with the girls as they passed by. His wavy light brown hair, handsome face, perpetual smile and charming demeanor was too much for many of them to resist, and it was a rare day when I didn't come home from my grass cutting job to find Manny entertaining a few girls in our room. They felt safe and comfortable around him. All it took was a drop of a needle on an LP to play some Brazilian music and he would have them dancing with him in the middle of the room. Most of the girls didn't know how to dance the Samba, Mambo or Cha Cha Cha, but after a minute or two of his easy-going guidance, they were moving like natural born Latinas. Too shy to flirt or dance, I just sat on the edge of the bed with a wan smile, marveling at how much the girls were enjoying themselves.

For two weeks the laughter and frivolity couldn't penetrate the shell of fear that I was encased in. I just sat and watched. Then one afternoon, while Manny and two lovely girls laughed with delight about the fun they were having; I found myself asking the questions: "What is wrong with me? Why am I sitting here?" I had no answer. Nor did I have an answer for "What am I afraid of?" Enough was enough! I got up and started dancing with one of the girls. At first I felt awkward, but quickly realized that the girl liked dancing with me and I liked dancing with her. I was having fun in a way I had never experienced before. Manny was not the kind of guy to be possessive or become jealous and was happy over the next few days to teach me all the steps. Being athletic, I soon became a pretty good dancer. The energetic rhythm of the Samba mixed with the laughter filling our room, made me feel like I was living a scene right out of my favorite movie, 'Black Orpheus.'

The incredible summer was capped off with a three day canoe trip in Canada's Algonquin Park. Arnie Aus had called to ask if I would like to join him and two Lithuanian friends for what sounded like an incredible adventure. I was not one to turn down an adventure and two days later I was on the road thumbing my way to Toronto. When night fell, I tossed my sleeping bag down in a field near the side of the road and cleaned up in the morning at a nearby restaurant or filling station. Despite my last ride almost getting rear-ended when he stopped to pick me up on a clover leaf entry road just after I crossed into Canada at Niagara Falls, I arrived safe and sound a few hours later at Arnie's family's modest house just off of Kings Road on Coady Ave.

The next day, revitalized after a good night's sleep, Aus and I joined his high school chums and we bantered endlessly as we drove north through the bountiful Canadian forests on our way to Algonquin Park. After Aus gave me a quick lesson on the art of canoeing, we paddled out onto the lake to begin enjoying some of the most pristine land in North America. Each evening, the dinners of the fresh fish we had caught and fried on an open fire, were washed down with a few glasses of schnapps. The Aurora Borealis put on an eye-popping display each evening as we lie in our sleeping bags. My job was to gather wood each morning to make a fire to warm the chilly air and cook a breakfast of pancakes and hot coffee before we paddled and portaged ever deeper into the park. No other humans were seen for three days. A melancholy mood hung over all of us as the adventure came to an end and we piled into the car to start the trip back to Toronto. Rather than risking an accident or waking everyone's parents up when we got back, we all concurred that we should sleep under the stars one more night, so Arnie pulled the car off the road, where serrenditously we found a small path that was lit just enough by the light of a waning moon, to allow us to follow it through some overhanging branches to a little grassy lea where we could toss our sleeping bags down on the soft grass.

All fell quickly fast asleep, except for me. I decided to explore the area. I got up and with no idea where it would lead, began walking further down the path. I liked to explore the unknown. The sound of rushing water could be heard in the distance. Even with a full moon, the knee high grass that hugged the narrow path made it hard to see where I was going. I paused when I came to the edge of a cliff and could hear the sound of rushing water far below. The leaves of the copse I was under was blocking the moonlight and it seemed dangerous to go on, so I decided to turn back. Then I realized I was lost. Hopefully I would soon stumble upon something familiar. Instead I found something amazing. There were three bodies lying across the path that were blocking my way. "What were they doing there?" Suddenly, one of them came to life and jumped up. It shook me loose from my sleep walk! I meekly apologized and climbed back into my own bag, feeling embarrassed that I had made a fool of myself. Was this mental curse ever going to end?

I had enough of hitchhiking and returned to Boston the old fashioned way, by Greyhound. Summer was coming to an end and Manny's mother had come to Boston from Brazil to pay him a visit. She was a short woman with a warm round face and treated me as though I were one of her sons. She cooked us some delicious Brazilian dishes capped off with fried bananas for desert. I could see why he was so charming and confident. He had told me that his father had taken him to a whorehouse when he was sixteen so that the prostitute could teach him about sex. Americans were taught that sex was dirty; something that should be done in the dark and only done when you were married and even then only to make babies. I no longer believed any of that, but was still a virgin and had no idea how I would break what I considered a curse.

The summer had passed quickly; faster than it ever had. Dancing, laughing, canoeing and eating fried bananas; I had never enjoyed myself so much. It was time to return to school for my junior year. School had always been something I looked forward to; but this year was different. I didn't want the fun to end. I began classes without my heart being in it.

The fraternity welcomed me back into the fold and gave me a room in the annex. All my favorite brothers, Craig, Penna and Morrow had graduated. Craig, of all things, enlisted in the army. Maybe he needed a break from the intense study that MIT demanded. I would miss watching the NFL football games with him. It had led me to become a loyal and rabid *Packer fan—a cheesehead*—for the rest of my life. There were a few brothers who came by the annex to spend an hour or so, peering out of a dark room into the girl's dorm across the street. Rarely did they see anything and when they did, it was not more than for a blink of the eye. I preferred my thrills to be more guaranteed. I had discovered over the summer, that on Thursday afternoons the dancers at the Old Howard took off their pasties and some of the feature dancers went so far as to pull down their g-strings and flash their pussies. Even the raunchiest American girlie magazines didn't show pussies. There was no way I was about to chance missing those Thursday afternoon shows and accordingly arranged my class schedule so that I would be free to visit the Old Howard on raunch day.

It was obvious that The Old Howard had a mole at the police station. When a vice officer was on his way to make sure nothing salacious was going on, a little red light placed at the front of the runway would light up and the girls would hastily get their pasties back on and tame down their acts. As soon as the light went off, things got hot again. Thank god for a few good bad cops! When possible, I always took a seat in the second row so I could be close to the action and still be hidden by a row of seats so I could subtly massage my hard cock beneath my pants with my palm. I didn't want to offend the strippers incase they resented someone getting off at their expense for free. I was a master at hiding what I was doing so that even someone sitting next to me wouldn't know what was going on. Getting off three times during a show, by skillfully holding back my orgasms, was not a problem. The comedy acts provided plenty of time to recharge. I always used two orgasms on the feature, one during her first act and another when she returned after the intermission. Knowing that my pants would be soaking wet when I walked back onto the street, I made sure to bring a jacket or sweater along so I could drape it across my forearm and hide my indiscretion.

Princess Do May

Big name strippers like the fiery redhead Blaze Starr, the 44D girl, Tempest Storm and Irma the Body always packed the house. Blaze was Louisiana's notorious governor, Huey Long's girl friend. But many of the lesser known acts like Baby Lulu Wilnot or Dolores Del Rio could raise my cock to an erection with the best of them. Princess Do May blew my mind when she stripped down to her native American head dress and then thrust her hips forward so she could slide her g-string to the side and pull her pussy lips apart to expose the pink opening between her legs. My eyes and those of every other guy in the theatre nearly came out of their sockets when she remarked with a cute smile: "Yeah there's a hole there, what did you think you'd find?" At least in my case, I wasn't sure. There were still debates among my friends whether the hole was in the front or on the bottom. Thanks to the Princess, I now knew. The Fascinating Jennifer was my favorite stripper and my heart beat a bit faster when I would see in the Boston Globe that she was scheduled to be the coming weeks feature attraction. For me, her coquettish smile, sexy lingerie, firm body and slinky-on-the-bed movements made her act the ultimate tease. Wearing a common flower-print dress, she looked every bit the girl next door as she sauntered across the stage casting coy glances to the audience. Then stopping for a moment, she would reach to the side of her dress to unhook a clasp and her dress would fall to the floor. The sight of her left standing in high heels, bra, panties and a garter belt that held up the sheer black nylons was mouth watering. Her act was intimate, like secretly watching a woman undressing in her bedroom. Sitting pertly on a divan, she began by removing her nylons and opening her thighs just enough to give flashes of the soft flesh between them. Every movement was slow and erotic. Lying prone on her tummy, she would begin to slowly undulate up and down as though she were having sex. Her buns rose and fell like two soft little mountains of flesh. As her humping became more and more intense, I could feel the cum in my balls begin to rise up my hard shaft so that as she reached her orgasmic crescendo, I reached mine. It felt as though we had just had sex together, even though I was still a virgin.

The Fascinating Jennifer

By chance, after one of her performances, I saw her leaving the theatre wearing an expensive fur coat and escorted by what looked like an Italian mobster. I silently bemoaned the fact that I knew I had no chance of dating such a sexy and sensual woman. I was not the type of guy that could attract a girl like that. Ironically, decades later, I would learn that Sequin was her inspiration to get into stripping.

Over the summer, I had let my hair grow back so that along with the dirty raincoat my "beat" mien would be reestablished. Confused about where I saw myself in the world of science, I changed my major from math to physics to electrical engineering. My outside interests were draining my energy and

I no longer had the drive to spend two hours at basketball practice. When I informed the coach that I wasn't returning for the upcoming season he, despite my disheveled appearance, pleaded for me to come back, saying he was planning on me to play forward for him. I declined. The team went on to do just fine without me, having the first winning season in school history. Dave Koch made the conference allstar team and set the school scoring record.

I wasn't blind to what I was doing to myself. A student in one of my electrical engineering classes, just out of the military, always sat in the front row, alert and posing lots of questions to the instructor. I sat in the back row, fighting to stay awake. His stint in the military had made him more cognizant of the opportunity he was now getting; he knew what life was like without a degree and was at school to train for a career that would result in a comfortable living. Naively, I assumed my financial survival was a given no matter what I did.

The experiment with different majors didn't go well and I returned to mathematics. It required that I take two difficult courses in analysis; 18.21 and 18.22 in MIT parlance. The second depended on knowledge learned in the first. The instructor was a young grad student named E. O. Thorpe. He had a nervous twitch where he would enlarge his eyes much like Superman did when he was using X-ray vision. I found myself subconsciously emulating him. It took me several months of concentrated effort before I was able to overcome the irritating habit. By midterm, the hours that I had put in at the Old Howard had caused me to fall behind in Thorpe's class. It was not a course that I could cram for as I so often had done before. I decided that my best strategy was to flunk it so I could repeat it the next semester. I would be unable to handle 18.22 without being grounded in the concepts learned in 18.21. Thorpe blew that plan all to bits. I was shocked when I got my report card to find that he had given me a low, but passing grade; a Dee.

More surprises were to come. Naively, I expected at least Cees in all my other classes but got an F in linear algebra that I would have liked to blame on the fact that it was taught by a monotonous Chinese grad student who I could barely understand, and a Dee in Russian, which I made little effort to master. The only phrase Russian phrase I could easily regurgitate was: Простите товарчшь учцтель Я саепал грчьчо ошиькч; transalated as; Forgive me comrade teacher, I have made a course mistake. My grade point average was two point two, a hair above straight Dees, which normally would not qualify one for dismissal from the school, but my dirty raincoat and scraggly look had drawn more attention then what my callow little mind had comprehended. I was notified that I would not be welcome back the next semester. Shocked and devastated, I met with the head administrator of the math department to plead my case, but couldn't get him to overturn the decision; being told that I didn't look "like an MIT man."

I knew he was right. I had made my own bed and called my parents, expecting them to be furious. My mother, in particular, had repeatedly complained that the cost of my education was a real drain on the family. I knew from the start that she didn't really understand what going to MIT had meant to me, and now that I had flunked out I couldn't really explain why she was wrong. But my stepfather, who never ceased to surprise me, was consoling rather than mad. I told him I could reapply for admission after I sat out for a semester and got a good recommendation from an employer. He pulled a few strings and got me a job a few miles outside of Boston at Hanscom Airbase. Considering that I was only his stepson, it was incredibly gracious of him.

24

FINALLY!!!

No longer being enrolled at MIT meant I didn't qualify to live at the frat house, but they agreed to let me rent a room on the top floor of the annex anyway. It was small, just large enough for a chair, a small desk and a bed. I cleaned up my appearance so I wouldn't cause a stir at my new job on the military base. Each day I drove my motor scooter the twenty miles to the base, sometimes through snow, taking route 2 out of Harvard square all the way to Lexington where after circling three fourths of the way around a rotary with a monument in its center commemorating Paul Revere, I drove the half-mile to the gate of the Airbase where my I. D was checked before I was allowed to go to work. When I got back home in the evenings, I took most of my meals at the all night cafeteria in Kenmore Square where the rehabilitated alcoholics worked the counter. Life was now to be a bit more austere. The sexual force that drove my passion for strippers was too strong to be cast aside and my passion for folk music and strumming my guitar was like having a good friend. However, I was determined to dig myself out of the hole I had dug for myself. The stigma of being a failure was not an option.

There were already so many American and Russian satellites in space by 1961, that it had become a major task to keep track of them. Satellite location data arrived in analogue form, i. e. degrees and minutes, and needed to be converted into digital form before it could be entered into a computer. The conversion work was all done by hand, tables being provided to make the calculations. This was my new job. It took failing out of school to be rewarded with work that used my brain.

A Master Sergeant, of Italian descent, named Joe, was my boss. He had a personality akin to TV's Sergeant Bilko, friendly with a good sense of humor, but still demanding that the work get done in a timely manner. Eddy, a skinny young Corporal and I were his crew. We did all the computations. After Eddy and I finished our work, it was passed to the girls on the second floor so they could punch out cards that could be fed into to the computer. Hopefully our work would keep all the space junk created by the U. S. and Russia from crashing into each other.

I quickly recognized that there were only a modest number of different conversions to be made, and they were cyclical, so within a week I had them all memorized and the days work was finished in a couple of hours. This made me very popular with Joe and the job became a lot more fun than I had anticipated. With time on our hands, Joe could entertain Eddie and me with abundant jokes and sexual quips. We soon became good friends and sat around most of the day bull shitting. I was even invited to Joe's wedding, a real Italian affair with lots of food, music and dancing and Corporal Eddy asked me to join him and his equally thin, but very attractive young wife, for an evening hot-dog roast at the beach where I brought my guitar along and entertained them with renditions of the Kingston Trio's "Tell Old Bill" and "Tom Dooley."

When my work was finished, I began wandering up to the second floor where the brass resided so I could flirt with the Colonel's cute secretary. I was nearing twenty-one and hoping I could lose my virginity sometime in the near future. She clearly enjoyed the flattery, but it got me nowhere. I had just finished flirting for five minutes and was about to go back downstairs, when by chance, I bumped into another MIT student out in the hall who was at Hanscom working to help pay his way through school. Larry Roven and I shared an interest in folk and pop music and when I told him I didn't know how to do Chubby Checker's new dance, 'The Twist,' he offered to give me a quick lesson. He began to pivot on one foot so his hips, knees, arms and elbows could sling from side to side across his gangly body and I began to mimic the same moves. We were twisting away when a stern cough brought our little dance lesson to an abrupt end. The Colonel, hearing the commotion out in the hall, had peeked out from his office and gave us a look that reminded us that we were on a military base and not in a night club. Larry and I agreed to get together over the weekend to finish the dance lesson and trade some guitar licks.

He lived in an apartment building on Mass. Ave. just south of Harvard Square. Thinking we looked hep, we sat on the steps outside his building for an hour and traded licks. Our meager repertoire was quickly exhausted, so he asked me if I wanted to go along with him to visit a friend of his who was also from MIT. "The guy is a real freak. He likes to do wild things like dance in the street." With nothing better to do than to meet a real freak, I accompanied Larry to an area around Tremont Street and Mass Avenue known as the South End. We were no more than halfway down a little street called Pembroke, when Larry pointed to a small man with semi-long black hair cut in a pageboy style doing a little dance on the sidewalk. It was just as Larry had described. The man danced like a puppet on a string, his arms and legs flapping loosely without any discernible form.

The dancing puppet's name was Bernie Goldhirsh. He was very genial and more than happy to talk about himself, which was warranted, being that he had quite a bit of sucess for a kid his age—he was a month younger than me. After telling us that someone had been murdered last night right in front of his house, he explained how he had come to own two houses on Pembroke. With five hundred dollars in his bank account and another fifteen hundred borrowed from a mafia loan shark, which came with the caveat that his legs would be broken if it wasn't paid back on time, he dressed up in a nice suit and got a bank to give him a mortgage so he could buy the two properties, one of them was the one we were now standing in front of and the other was a half block up the street. Bernie claimed Yuppies were moving in and the area was on the rise. I left with the feeling that I had made a good friend.

Not that I wasn't trying, but getting laid was proving to be impossible. I had my share of dates, including a hip doe-eyed Jewish girl from upscale Newton who I took on the back of my motor scooter to a Pete Seeger concert in Ipswich, and another with a slender raven haired beauty from Charlestown, whose bleach blond sister was dating Clete Boyer, the New York Yankee third baseman. The Jewish girl gave no indication that she was interested in sex and all I got from the Charlestown girl was an introduction to smoking cigarettes, which I did to make myself appear cool in her eyes. After a week of hacking, I remained a virgin, but with a raw throat.

It looked like I was getting close to getting laid when a young waitress my age, who I met at a little bar in Kenmore Square called the Rathskellar, began coming up to my room each evening after she got off of work, for the express purpose of losing her virginity. She was reasonably attractive and very willing. What else could I ask for? But every time I began to push my cock in it would go soft! It was the same anxiety attack that caused my veins to turn to ice when I took Carmen to Point Lobos after the prom. Rather than giving her pleasure, I was giving her self-doubt. Eventually she stopped coming by. Two virgins trying to get laid, was not going to do anyone good.

I was at work killing time in the second floor hallway, talking to Larry Roven, when a guy who worked in the data room came out and approached us. I had seen him around but we had never talked. His name was Paul and he had a problem that he thought maybe I could help him with. His seventeen-year old cousin was coming into town from St Louis for the weekend and he and his girl friend were planning to show her the town. He wanted to know if I would be interested in being her date. He teased me by telling me she was very wild and rumored to have been fucking one of her high school teachers back in St. Louis . . . He had a car and would do the driving; all I had to do was come along. Paul was a few years older than me and his face was slightly pockmarked from prior bouts with acne. It was reasonable to wonder if his cousin suffered from the same plight. Skin conditions often run in the clan, so to speak. He insisted that we would all have a good time. I thought to myself that she was probably more than I cold handle, but what the hell. I told him, "Why not?"

As I heard Paul lumbering up the stairs to tell me they were outside in the car waiting, I had no illusions about what to expect as we hussled back down. His two-door coup was double-parked on Bay State Road where Paul's date was sitting in the front seat. She leaned forward so I could stoop down and climb into the back seat where my date was waiting. I was still in a mild state of shock as Paul made quick introductions: "Howard this is Laura, Laura this is Howard" and nodding to his date, "this is Elaine." Laura was an absolute doll; a younger version of 'The Fascinating Jennifer.' She had a fresh face with lively dark eyes and a sexy smile. The silky dress she wore hung loosely over her curves. Without being asked, she said in a very matter-of-fact voice: "I don't care what we do, as long as it's honest," The look in her eyes and the way she held her mouth told me that she was not suggesting we go out for an ice cream sundae. As I looked at her I was discovering something in myself. I told Paul to take Laura and me to Scollay Square. I had no expectations that I was going to get laid; we were just going to have a wild time; good honest sexual fun; "what could be more honest than the Old Howard?" Paul turned around to give me a look of misgiving, after all she was his cousin and only seventeen, but Laura told him not to worry and just drive. He did as he was told and when we arrived at a dimly lit corner from where the brightly lit Old Howard could be seen a block away, I told him to stop. Elaine leaned forward so I could climb out of the car and reach back to help Laura. The way she readily took my hand told me she was excited. For a moment as we stood next to the car, Paul gave us both one last "Are you sure?" I didn't need to say a word; Laura let him know that she was. I liked her moxie. I told him to pick us back up at the same corner in three hours.

After the coup's bright red taillights disappeared around the corner, Laura and I stood alone: our fresh-faced innocence in sharp contrast to the dissoulute winos wandering nearby. I slipped my hand firmly around hers, so she would know that she was with a guide who knew the area, and led her down the hill to the Old Howard. The guy in the ticket booth probably recognized me since I had been there so often and didn't ask for I. D.s. I doubted if he cared. The envy of all the eyes that were upon us as we walked down the aisle was palpable. We took a couple of seats close to the stage. I wanted her to experience the real thing, as a voyeur and not as a shrinking violet in the back row. She had never been to a burlesque show and there was no doubt that she loved every bit of it; strippers, comedians, even the hot dog vender from whom we bought a couple of dogs with mustard and scarfed them down as we watched a stripper bump and grind and twirl her tassels.

We had an hour to kill after the show ended before Paul came to pick us up, so I took her to a smoke-filled sleazy bar just up the hill that I knew catered primarily to blacks. The place was packed and loud. It was jumping with fun. A few black hookers standing around the bar were working their trade. Their shinny tight mini skirts stretched around their big asses and showed off their big legs that glistened like hot chocolate candy bars melting in the sun. We were the only white people in the joint. Moments after we found a small table near the back of the room, a sexy black waitress with a big smile and bountiful tits busting over the top of her low-cut blouse came to take our order. Like the Old Howard, they didn't give a damn about I. Ds. Playing the role of a man-of-the-world, I ordered us a couple of college-kid drinks, i. e. whisky sours. Nonchalantly, I pulled out a buck and tipped the waitress. I wanted to look as if it was the kind of thing I normally did. In short time, Laura and I were both feeling pretty good, and went to the dance floor where we joined the dozen or so dirty dancing black people to do a little dirty dancing of our own.

At no time were we made to feel unwelcome. With some regret, our good time came to an end when we had to leave to rejoin Paul and Elaine. He was already waiting for us across the street as we left the bar. I'm sure he was wondering what I was doing to his sweet cousin. As soon as we crawled into the back seat, Laura left little doubt what she wanted to do with me. She put my hands over her breasts and began kissing me on my mouth and neck. My hands had no choice but to find their way beneath her silky dress and under her bra so I could feel her hard nipples. Without thinking my hand was into her panties and my fingers became wet with the moistness between her pussy lips. As the aroma of Laura's vaginal juices wafted from the back seat, Ted and his date remained silent as he headed back to my place to drop me off.

But young Laura had no intention of cooling down and when Paul stopped the car so I could get out, she said: "Why don't you take your date home and come back and get me afterwards." It was not a request. It was an order. There was no one else in residency at the annex over the summer, meaning we didn't have to be quiet. We dashed up the stairs to my room, kissing and fondling along the way. As soon as we sat on the bed, she lifted her sexy silky dress up over her head and unsnapped her bra. Any anxiety wanting to bubble up from the recesses of my frightened brain was stymied by the vision of her perfectly shaped teenage breasts and the soft blue panties covering her round shaped-in-heaven buns. I edged her back and spread her legs so I could suck on the inviting wide swath of blue silk that covered her pussy, moving it to the side only when I knew she had been teased enough and desperately needed more intimate contact. She pulled me up onto the bed and engulfed my stiff dick with her mouth.

Before I knew what was happening, she was straddling me and pulling her panties aside so she could guide my cock into her wet crevice. I was inside of her so fast that the dreaded moment of self-doubt had no chance to raise its ugly head. It was incredible. Wonderful! Beyond belief!! I had crossed the Rubicon. We humped on the bed like crazed animals, the springs squeaking like a scene from a Russ Myer movie. Words are not capable, nor should be, of describing the feeling I felt when I reached orgasm. I could tell she felt the same. I had just discovered the passageway to pleasure. For a few moments we both lie silent, completely drained of energy. Paul's voice calling up from the first floor telling Laura it was time to go, broke our reverie. The sweet spell came to an end. I never saw or heard from her again. She returned to St Louis the next day, but blue silk panties would always remain a life long favorite. Back at work, Paul told me he had arrived at my place earlier but decided not to interrupt us until he heard the bed stop squeaking. I had a lot to thank him for.

25

SHE TOUCHED A NEGRO'S HAIR

With a letter in hand from the colonel at Hanscom, stating that I had performed my job meretriciously, I expected to get readmitted to MIT without a problem. I expected wrong. Evidently my disheveled appearance had made a worse impression than I had imagined. I was told that I was not to be welcomed back. Only after groveling before a professor in the math department, was I able to convince him that I truly wanted to continue at MIT. My humbling display softened his heart and he wrote me a letter of recommendation so I could get readmitted. He also was good enough to recommend a list of courses he thought would get me back on track. I knew it was going to be difficult. I would be taking the difficult required course in mathematical analysis, 18.22; that was predicated on the course that I had previously gotten a Dee in. I would have to redo that course on my own and hope to catch up by the end of the term so I could pass the final. I was determined to persevere.

When I realized I had none of the prerequisites to take an advanced course in statistics, that my advisor had recommended to me, I was forced to drop it, but other than that I was doing well academically and even found time to work on improving my guitar skills and of course visits to the Old Howard once in awhile. Still smitten by folk music and wanting to be part of that scene, I let my hair grow long again but abandoned the funky raincoat. There was nothing to be gained by upsetting the school's fashion police.

To me, Joan Baez's earthy three-octave soprano voice accompanied on the guitar by her clever finger picking technique was almost sexual. I was determined to learn how to play like that. Ironically, her father was a professor at MIT and she performed at a club in Harvard Square called the Club 47, but I was not aware of either fact. When I expressed my desire to learn finger picking to Larry Roven, he suggested I get in touch with a teacher named Rolf Cahn whom he had taken lessons from. Hoping he might take me as a student, I gave him a call. Unfortunately, he would only be in Cambridge for a few more days until he completed his gig at the Club 47 but invited me to come by over the weekend and meet with him at a friend's apartment where he was staying while in town.

Rolf was in his mid-forties, had black hair with short bangs hanging over his forehead and mutton chop side-burns. Perched on a nose that looked like a bird's beak was a pair of thick glasses that made his eyes seem to bulge from their sockets. My first impression was that he was homely-as-sin. But being that he spoke to me as though we had been life long friends, I quickly found myself drawn to him. He had the mein of a mentor. He didn't preach; he engaged. We fell into a discussion about social and political issues in a way none of my humanities professors had ever managed to do. Before I left, he sat on a stool and using a nylon strung classic guitar, gave me a demonstration of his virtuosity in flamenco, and then changing to a steel strung guitar, a demonstration of folk and blues techniques. I was snowed. Before I left he made a suggestion; "Why don't you consider coming to California during the summer to take some lessons from me?" Impulsively, I told him I would.

There were still a few months before the school year ended, when my former MUHS classmate, Dave Phillips, called to invite me to come to New York over the spring vacation to join him and his fiancée, Sharon Watson at her Eastside apartment on 65th street. He would soon be graduating from West Point and they had plans to be married soon after. At one time, I knew Sharon had a little crush on me, but had no idea that she and Dave had developed a thing. Marriage was not in my plans, but I was happy for both of them and soon stood on the side of route 2 at the west end of Harvard Square with my thumb out and a guitar strapped over my shoulder, to catch a ride to New York to help them celebrate their engagement.

Keeping to the small back roads, I managed to catch multiple short rides from one small town to the next. Progress was slow but steady. Just outside of Hartford, an old red Ford converted into a hot rod, stopped to pick me up. The driver was a young red headed guy in his mid twenties. He was an animated talker, but because the roar of the modified hot rod engine, hearing was difficult and we had to almost shout to be heard. As we bombed our way over the hilly two lane rural road, he told me he could take me halfway to New York, but had to first make a short stop at a bar to pick up his new girl friend. When he added that she was formerly Miss Switzerland and was now working as a stripper, I thought to myself; "Maybe there is a God after all?!" He told me how proud he was of her. "The last time we were out she gave me the most incredible blow-job I ever had had and you know what else she did?" . . . his head turned towards me for a second as though I might have the answer . . . "While she was performing at the club, she reached out and put her hand on top of the negro's hair who was sitting next to the stage. Is that outrageous or what??"

A half hour later, we pulled off the road onto a little gravel parking area in front of the club on the northside outskirts of Hartford, where his girl friend worked. It was a one-story wood building painted white, that if not for a small flat rectangular backlit sign with a string of red lights around it, would have still looked like the roadside grocery store that it probably once was. He left the engine running and told me to wait while he ran up a little ramp and disappeared into the club. Two short minutes later he came out followed by a gorgeous little trashy blond in a tight silver mini skirt that embraced the curves of her round ass as if it had been painted on. My eyes strained to see if she was wearing anything beneath the translucent white blouse she wore. In fact, she was—a sexy red half bra that barely covered her lush tits! There was only room for two on the front seat, so my red headed benefactor opened the passenger door and told his hot little sexpot to climb in and sit on my lap. With a big smile, she willing obeyed; no doubt enjoying the fact that she was about to give this young beatnik a real thrill by plopping her sexy bottom on his lap. Red's grin left no doubt that it turned him on to share his prize. And of course I had a big smile on my face. His tires spun in the loose gravel as we three smilers peeled back out onto the hilly little black tar road. Was I in a dream . . . my hands on the hips of a real live stripper—Miss Switzerland at that; enjoying her buns bounce up and down on my lap? I let Red and his girl friend do all the talking, being content to enjoy my private thoughts. But my dream ended forty-five minutes later and my ear-to-ear grin dissolved as I watched Red and Miss Switzerland disappear over a hill. They had left me off at a good spot where it would be easy to catch another ride and by days end I was in Manhattan and knocking on the door of Sharon's apartment.

The same round-faced happy girl, who I had known at MUHS, greeted me when she opened the door. Dave came out from a back room to see who was at the door and greeted me with a few of the witty type remarks that he was known for when he wrote a column for our highschool paper, 'The Toreador.' Both of them seemed to be more amused than shocked by the longhaired disheveled folknik with a guitar strung across his shoulder that was standing in front of them. Sharon brought me into the room, where after leaning my guitar case against a wall so it wouldn't be smashed, I was introduced to five of Dave's neat and trimmed fellow cadets, who had also been invited to the celebration. His younger brother, Richard, had also come to New York and was content to stay at the back of the room and just stare at me through his thick glasses with an impish grin. A few beers and some light conversation was enough to put everyone at ease before we took seats around a long table in the dinning room to partake of the great dinner Sharon had prepared. Plans were to head over to the Bronx and take in a Yankee game after we finished eating.

Dave's brother continued to smile at me for no apparent reason. I soon found out why. Seconds after we retired back to the living room for coffee, I was on the floor pinned down by Dave, his brother, and all five cadets bent on shearing my very unmilitary locks. But they hadn't counted on an MIT nerd being able to twist and turn with such vehemence that made getting the shears on my head impossible. Five minutes later the soaking wet attackers were forced to back off and give me the respect I had earned. My long blond locks were still in place as we headed to the Bronx to see the Yankees play.

I had no grade lower than a C when I got my report card. An A on my 18.02 mathematical analysis final had raised my grade point average over the full term to a B. My faith in my innate ability was restored. Even E. O.Thorpe complemented me. When I returned from Berkeley, I would have only a little more than a year left to earn a degree. Jumping into the future for a moment: E. O.Thorpe would leave MIT two years later and send the gambling casinos in Las Vegas into a tailspin. He had worked out a card counting system that turned the odds of winning black jack into his favor. Before they realized what was happening, he had pocketed thousands of dollars in winnings. He was banned from the casinos and to protect themselves from such schemes in the future, began using multiple decks to make card counting much more difficult. Hollywood would eventually make a movie "21" starring Kevin Spacey based on E. O.'s story. He was a fellow rebel!

To arrange transportation to Berkely, I began checking the school's bulletin board to see if anyone driving to San Francisco wanted riders to share gas expenses. I found a Boston University student who fit my needs perfectly. He was graduating at the end of May and was going to Los Angeles to seek his fortune, but was willing to go by way of San Francisco since he had another rider who wanted to be dropped off at Stanford University in Palo Alto. When, in early June, the B. U. student, whose name was Daryl, picked me up at the annex, I discovered that we would be driving across the country in a shinny red Ford convertible. It made the trip a little more exciting. Daryl was a handsome young man who was dressed and coiffed appropriately for one who was looking to begin a career in business. Already in the car was the Stanford student as well as another MIT student who was going only as far as Nebraska. The Stanford student was a short, but attractive, French girl named Arlette. She came accompanied by a French poodle named Sabaccus, who stood two feet tall and had curly black hair that almost covered his eyes. Daryl decided that I, with my long hair and guitar, would fit best in the backseat with Arlette and her dog.

We were an eclectic group in high spirits as we headed out on the Mass Pike. It was a beautiful sunny day and Daryl put the top down so we could all enjoy nature's glory. Daryl planned to drive eight or nine hundred miles a day, stopping only at night to sleep in motels. The MIT student only needed a ride back to Nebraska where his parents lived. He was very quiet and not prone to divulge much about himself. Daryl planned to make the whole trip in four days.

The New England spring air was still a bit nippy and the top was down, so Arlette and I shared a blanket to keep warm. Our propinquity quickly led to conversation and by the time we stopped for the evening, we knew a lot about each other. She would be taking medical classes at Stanford where a serious boy friend was waiting for her. As a French Jew, she was impressed that I was a liberal folky as well as an MIT intellect. When we stopped that night at a roadside motel, I shared a room with Daryl and the Nebraska kid and Arlette shared a room with Sabaccus.

The next day, having a serious boyfriend, didn't prevent Arlette from snuggling next to me and encouraging me to put my arm around her. Sabaccus was happy to enjoy the wind blowing through his hair, but Daryl's eyes kept glancing back at us in the rearview mirror and I suspected that he was envying me, especially since he and the MIT kid exchanged nary a word. I imagined that he probably was use to getting his way with girls and wondering why Arlette hadn't come on to him.

As the sun hung low over the flat cultivated Nebraska plains, the MIT kid directed Daryl through a maze of country roads edged by forests of six-foot high corn stalks until we came to a modest wood frame house sitting alone in the midst and solitude of America's corn belt.

I couldn't help but reflect about what one of the recent Theta Xi pledges from Kansas had told several of us about an experiment he had dreamed up: A female child would be put in a windowless room at birth and not allowed to see humans for her entire life. When she became old enough to give birth, she would be artificially impregnated and after the child was born, food would be withdrawn. The question would be: how long it would take, or if . . . before she ate the baby.

Putting those gruesome thoughts aside, I was glad to see the quiet rider given a sincere, but stolid welcome back home. As the good mid-westerners that they were, we were offered lodging for the night and a hearty farm-fresh meal before we turned in. The house was spotlessly clean and the kid's parents were pleasant but as tacit as their son. If my long hair or a woman traveling without a man displeased them, they didn't say.

After sleeping in a comfortable bed with a large picture of Jesus above its headboard and wiping my ass in the morning with toilet paper that had a picture of Jesus above its dispenser, I joined Daryl and Arlette outside the house the next morning to say good bye to our hosts and continue our trip west. Daryl suggested that Arlette sit in the front with him but, much to my delight, she said she preferred to remain in the back with Sabaccus and me. He seemed irritated that she had rejected his offer, but coolly acquiesced. He had to feel like a chauffer as we headed back onto the highway.

Arlette and I continued to snuggle beneath the blanket while Daryl brooded as the day wore on. She felt comfortable with me. I was no longer a virgin, but still shy and smart enough not to force myself on her. I didn't have to. After lunch, we were on the road again and under the blanket, when she took her hand and put it on my inner thigh. She must have had a PhD in cock teasing, because mine was rock hard within minutes. I didn't need anymore incouragement and my hand soon found its way inside her panties where I found a moist meaty vagina begging to be stimulated by a vibrating finger. My little French whore and I both maintained a calm demeanor so Daryl wouldn't know what was going on—assuming he didn't—and she adroitly extricated my penis from the confines of my underwear so it could be gently stroked just enough to keep it hard without going off. As the day came to an end, I had enjoyed a nice hand job and Daryl had suffered from copious steam blowing out of his ears.

He was soon to endure more psychological pain. We were standing in front of the last motel we would stay at before reaching California, when Arlette announced that she and I would be taking a room together. He was the cool guy from BU with a convertible and I was the shy scraggly nerd beatnik from MIT who was about to get laid. It would be disingenuous if I didn't say that it gave me a perverse thrill to see him seethe. He pompously stated that since we were traveling in his car, he had the responsibility to see that we maintained a proper moral code. We both looked at each other in disbelief. Needless to say his claim was overruled and she and I proceeded that night to release all the passion that had been stored up over the last three days.

I wouldn't have been surprised to find that Daryl had abandoned us in the morning, but probably since he still needed our share of the gas money, he knocked on the door and told us we would be leaving in fifteen minutes. There was little talk between he and us for the last leg of the journey. An hour out of Berkely, Arlette asked me if I would be willing to take Sabaccus for the summer since she wouldn't have much time for him between classes. I loved dogs and had grown fond of the frisky little fellow and though I had no idea where I was going to live—as well as now being a bit pussy whipped—told her yes. The four great days with Arlette had made me in many ways more of a man.

26

NOT JUST SQUARE . . . A CUBE

I had no clue about where I wanted to be dropped off when we reached Berkeley, so I told Daryl to leave me off anywhere in downtown. With my guitar, a backpack with a sleeping bag tied across its top, and Sabaccus dutifully panting by my side, I shed a tear as I stood on the corner of Telegraph and Delaney Avenue waving goodbye to Arlette as she and Daryl drove away. My four-day affair with her was the longest I had ever been with a woman other than my mother. She had left me her boy friend's phone number so we could stay in touch and five bucks to pay for dog food.

Glancing up and down Telegraph Avenue showed the business section to be about four or five blocks long with the entrance to the University just a block to the east. It was early Saturday afternoon and a warm sun was shinning. I had about twenty-five dollars to my name, including the five Arlette had kicked in. Since I didn't intend to call Rolf until Monday, I had two days to get my act together. I was free as a bird and it felt great!

The potpourri of straights, beats, short hairs, long hairs, whites and blacks, who went about doing their business on Telegraph Avenue made me feel at ease. My immediate concern was to find a place to stay before nightfall. I began walking down Telegraph Avenue, lined with little shops, bookstores and coffee houses, hoping I might find a sign advertising a cheap room for rent.

Firm round buns had a magnetic like attraction for me and when I saw a pair filling out the tight blue jeans of an attractive redhead on the other side of the street, I was helpless to resist the urge to cross to the other side. She appeared to be in her mid twenties. Not wanting her to feel as though she were being stalked, I kept a comfortable distance behind as I ogled her rear. However, when she stopped to look at something in a store window, it would have been too obvious if I also stopped, so I found myself suddenly standing right next to her. Overcoming my shyness, I asked her if she knew of any real cheap places to rent.

Her friendliness quickly put me at ease. Her name was Paula and she asked if I was new in town. I told her my story and in amiable Berkeley fashion, she invited me up to her pad that was only a half block away so I could take a shower and have a cup of tea. When I finished cleaning up and having my tea, she took me to meet a friend of hers who managed several apartment houses in the area. Twenty dollars wasn't going to get me a room, but he was willing to let me rent the space underneath one of his rooming houses for ten bucks a month.

The house, on ChanningWay, was only a half block from where Daryl had dropped me off earlier in the day. A coat of peeling brown paint was all that protected the exterior wood of the somewhat dilapidated two-story single-family house that was now being rented out by the room. It had a porch out in front where I could sit and watch the passing traffic. I was told I could share the communal kitchen and bathroom on the first floor. We then walked to the back of the house where he opened a little wood door secured by an unlocked latch and after stooping, we entered the windowless area that was not quite high enough for me to stand erect. After he turned

on a 50-watt pull-string light, I saw that a large forced-air furnace sat in the center and occupied most of the space. A soft fine layer of dust covered the hard dirt floor. When he told me that my pet dog would not be a problem and he would throw in an old rug to put on the ground and a mattress as well; I told him I would take it.

There wasn't much to do in the way of decorating the place and I had an urge to look at some girlie magazines, so I took

Sabaccas and walked up Channing to a magazine store on the corner of Telegraph. I tied my new canine buddy to a signpost and wandered into the store as though I was just looking for something to read. While pretending to browse a Time magazine, I noticed a couple of young guys in front of a rack in the rear intently interested in the magzaines they were browsing. That was a sure sign that I had spotted the hot area. Not wanting to appear too anxious, I slowly migrated to the back of the store, picking up a magazine or two along the way as though I were considering a purchase, until I stood in front of the rack at the rear. Voila! The best selection of girlie magazines I had ever seen: French Frills, Nylon Jungle, Touch, all published by a Hollywood company called Parliament. The magazines were all about sexual teasing, unlike the boring nudist magazines that I had seen while living in Boston that featured pictures of floppy titted old women playing volleyball. The models in these California magazines were cute and naughty. Most wore nylons, garter belts, high heels and sexy panties or corsets. Their breasts and nipples were exposed and a lot of the pictures featured a few good crotch shots of the girls panties that made one drool about what lied beneath. Unlike the air brushed photos in Playboy, these models looked real and had looks on their faces that they wanted sex.

I knew that too much browsing would result in a warning from the cashier to buy something or get out, so after ten minutes I left with a nice boner and rejoined my fury black friend waiting patiently outside. Overjoyed to see me, he hopped up and down like a Mexican jumping bean. I bought him a bag of dog food and myself a hunk of cheese and a baguette of French bread (real beatnik food), from a small market up the street and the two of us returned to our new home to crash. It had been a long day.

A light coat of dust covered Sabacus and me when we awoke the next morning. He had frolicked around on the dirt floor all night trying to find a comfortable spot to sleep. The central heater going on and off during the night did little to contribute to a restful sleep. Nonetheless, I was in good spirits and after shaking the dust out of Sabaccas and going upstairs to wash up, walked to a nearby restaurant I had seen on Telegraph called the Mediterranean Café. It offered a buffet style menu and an open-air patio where Sabaccus would be able to see me after I tied him to a signpost. He tended to be hyper and I didn't want to freak him out.

The café quickly got busy as the locals began to come in and the tables were soon taken. A young curly haired "hep cat," who looked like Plato, asked if he could join me. Of course I said yes. His name was George and he became my first 'beat' friend. He was not a student, but lived in Berkeley just because he liked the scene. In the coming weeks, we would often sit on the curb in front of his nearby apartment and strum away hoping to draw attention from females. He was about as competent on the guitar as I was—just a chord strummer.

But today, he was kind enough to take me on a tour up to the campus. After we crossed Bancroft Avenue and passed beneath the iconic Sather gate, George pointed to a frizzy haired man wearing a white shirt standing nonchalantly next to a pillar on the corner of the terrace that surrounded Sproul Hall. "That's Mario Savio," he told me.

Savio was in the national news accused of being a communist rebel rouser. My first thought at seeing him was: "So that's what a communist looks like." I kind of expected him to have a green tint or something. I didn't have the slightest clue what he was about. My sympathies were to the left, especially when it came to black people, but other than casting my phony ballot at the Boston Young Democrats election, I had little knowledge of American politics.

That evening, Rolf sounded very pleased when I called to let him know I was in town and he gave me directions on how in the morning to get to his place on Fairview Street. After another dusty night, I emerged from my underground hovel and tied Sebastian with a long rope to a tree behind the house. After leaving him a bowl of water, I headed off to Rolf's place. It was about two miles away, just inside the city limits of Oakland. On the way, at the corner of Ashworth and Telegraph, I passed a large supermarket called the Co-op. That name sounded communistic to me and I felt a tinge of fear that I would be corrupted if I went inside; which of course I didn't.

The front door, except for a screen door to keep the flies out, was open when I arrived. I knocked and was greeted with a yell: "Come in." Light poured into the front room through the several French windows that made up the wall facing the street. Rolf was sitting on a wood chair at the back of a disheveled room. He was shirtless and in deep concentration. He held an acoustic guitar on his lap in the classic position. Without getting up he asked me: "Do you think this riff sounds better this way?" and after playing me a slightly different version of the same thing, "or this way?" I had no clue, but told him they both sounded great. It was probably what he wanted to hear. He explained that they were both renditions done by two famous flamenco guitarists, one of which was Segovia and the other whom I had not heard of. As he put his guitar into it's case and leaned it against the wall, I noticed the fingernails on his right hand were very long which I assumed was beneficial to guitar playing. He looked to be in good shape and mentioned that he had done a bit of boxing but was now into martial arts; not what I had expected a musician to be interested in.

After a bit of perfunctory conversation, he asked me if there was much prejudice against Jews at MIT. Surprised by the question, I told him the truth: "No, I wasn't aware of any." Maybe he was unaware that MIT had many Jews, including its most famous professor, Norbert Weiner. I was a bit perplexed why the subject interested him. Even though I had read Shear's book, "Rise and Fall of the Third Reich," it hadn't registered on me how paranoiac the war had left the world's Jewish population—even in America. Oddly, Weiner stated in his autobiography that he grew up hating Jews. But when he was eighteen, he discovered that he had an uncle who was a Rabbi. I would eventually learn that Rolf's family had escaped from Germany at the onset of Hitler's reign. That would have explained his obsession with self-defense. We didn't pursue the subject any further and we began my first lesson.

At the end of the hour, Rolf had me playing a version of "Wildwood Flower" in which the thumb plays the melody while the index finger strums the chords. It wasn't as neat as Joan Baez's finger picking version of the song, but it was as much as I could expect on a first day. I was quite satisfied and thanked Rolf as I put my ax back in its case and prepared to leave. Suddenly a collie came bursting through the door, followed seconds later by the most beautiful girl I had ever laid my eyes on. Debbie Green was tall and slender. Her small boned feminine face was framed by beautiful long brown hair that hung to the small of her back. She didn't exhibit the slightest trace of arrogance or haughtiness, which in my mind she certainly could have, being as beautiful as she was, but instead welcomed me with a warm sincere smile.

Rolf invited me to hang around for a bit and have a cup of tea with he and Debbie. I was told that before coming to Berkeley, the two of them had performed together at the club 47 in Boston. For a reason that I wasn't made aware of, she now was living in an apartment above Coady's bookstore on Telegraph Avenue. I got the sense that Rolf still thought of her as his girl friend. It was a lot for my head to absorb, not the least of which was how a man so homely as Rolf, could appeal to a woman so beautiful as Debbie. But then again, I knew less than nothing about how women's minds worked. Having a week to kill before my next lesson, I spent some time exploring the area. I was sitting on the ledge of the fountain in front of Sproul Hall with my guitar and Sebaccus at my side, when a pretty olive skinned girl with long dark hair began to talk to me. The guitar, dog, long hair and clothing made me look hep, which by no stretch of the imagination was the case, but I faked it quite well and we easily fell into a conversation, she doing most of the talking. I was discovering that Berkeley girls were incredibly friendly and she invited me to come along while she visited a friend. I felt I was making substantial headway into becoming part of the Berkeley beat scene.

After crossing the campus to its north end, we made our way through an attractive residential area replete with abundant trees and homes fronted by large lawns and flower gardens. My new friend told me many of the faculty had homes there, as did a few lucky students who had found guest rooms or cottages for rent. Her friend was one of them and we stepped down a few steps off the sidewalk and entered the open door of his small basement apartment. He was in sandals, faded worn Levis and shirtless. A few strands of his sparse straggly hair covered his high forehead. He showed little joy in seeing her. I was given a brief introduction, which elicited a perfunctory nod. He didn't offer us a seat and just began ranting about something about which I had no clue. I couldn't tell if their relationship was serious or casual and he had given me no reason to like him or want to talk to him, so I just stood with my hands in my pockets and silently observed.

My ears were suddenly jolted. The guy had said a word that should not be used in front of a woman. He said; "Fuck!" Even at the Old Howard the comedians only said, "funking." Every other word that came out of the guy's mouth was; "fuck." "If I gave a fuck . . ." or "The whole fucking thing is a joke." Whoa! . . . It crossed my mind: "Should I hit the guy in the mouth?" but when I saw that my friend wasn't the least bit offended, I calmed down before doing something rash that would have made me the talk of the town: "MIT man slugs Berkeley student for using the word "Fuck."" I began to realize I was in a new culture and had lots to learn. My friend probably realized the same and didn't show any desire to see me again after we parted ways.

An accomplished thief like myself, had no problem snatching a block of cheese and a baguette from the little open air market on Telegraph and a girlie magazine or two from the newsstand, but I knew I couldn't pilfer my way through the summer, so I stopped into the student employment office to see if I could get a gig of some sort. I was told part-time janitorial positions were all that were available. That sounded fine with me. It wouldn't interfere with my guitar lessons and give me lots of free time to practice as well. The next morning I reported to the school employment office where I was told to go to the Harmon Gymnasium facility and check in with the head janitor; a man named Dean.

He was a gregarious good old boy from Tennessee and led me down the hall to show me my duties. I imagined I would be waxing the basketball court or something similar, but instead I was taken downstairs to the locker rooms where the showers and toilets were. Dean took a mop out from a closet and marched me into one of the shower rooms and began to demonstrate. Working the mop back and forth vigorously, I was shown how to wash down the entire floor with a lye solution that would kill any mold that might be forming. We then walked into the large bathroom area just off to the side. It had around fifteen sinks, toilets and urinals. After donning a pair of rubber gloves, Dean reached down into one of the toilet bowls and began cleaning it out with a sponge. Looking up at me intermittently as he scrubbed, he said in a sweet Tennessean drawl: "I want you to take your sponge and pour a little disinfectant in here and then get right down real good with your sponge and wipe under the rim real nice to make sure it's nice and clean. Don't be afraid to get under there reeeeeal good, OK? Then flush the toilet and make sure it looks nice as apple pie and there's no stains left anywhere." He gave me an equally effusive demonstration for the urinals. There were enough showers and toilets to occupy my full four-hour shift, so cleaning up piss, shit and mold was to be my raison d'etre for the foreseeable future.

Sabaccus's enthusiastic welcome always raised my spirits when I returned home from work each night and after feeding him his dinner, I would take a walk with him around the area. Near the end of my first week in town, I was strolling by The Rathskeller, a basement hangout on Telegraph Avenue for the beer drinking frat crowd. It was the only place open and I walked down the stairs to just take a peek. As I suspected, it was just a lot of loud college-kids drinking beer. I turned to go back up and rejoin Sebaccus when I heard someone calling my name. How startled I was to see Tom Rhoads, my friend from MUHS. Since he was working as the bartender at the Rathskeller, we only had time for a brief conversation. He had already been married and divorced and after graduating from UC Berkeley, had decided to stay in town while building a new life. I had once again made a dirty raincoat part of my 'beat' costume, and thinking that I had fallen on hard times and was now a main street hobo, he stuffed a hundred forty bucks into my hand before turning and going back to work. I wouldn't get my first paycheck for another week, so I was more than happy to take the bread. It had been good to see a familiar face, but I was conflicted: "Should I come back to see him again? It might not sit well with the hep crowd that I was trying to impress." I didn't go back.

27

THAT'S IT?

Five minutes before my second lesson with Rolf ended, Roddie once again ran into the room with Debbie close behind. She was just as beautiful as when I had first met her and just as friendly. When we finished my lesson, Rolf invited me to hang out with them. Wow! Not only was I taking lessons from a maestro, I was now becoming part of his "in crowd." As Debbie and I conversed, Rolf momentarily left the room and returned with a small cloth pouch. With a mischievous smile on his face, he cavalierly announced that he and Debbie were going to smoke a joint and asked if I would like to join them. I had heard the word joint used in the cult movie **'Reefer Madness'** and knew it was a marijuana cigarette, but I had never seen or known anyone who used marijuana. The movie referred to the marijuana user, a piano player in a jazz club, as a hop-head. They also said it was more addictive than heroine. I didn't want to appear square, especially with Debbie in the room, and with masked hesitation told him: "sure." While I pondered what I was getting into, Rolf gave a little homily praising the benefits of marijuana over alcohol. As he talked, he simultaneously took a cigarette paper from a flat little red box and holding it lengthwise between his fore and index finger so it formed a little trough, massaged a few leaves into it from a dull green bud that he had carefully plucked out of the cloth pouch. A moment later, a bit of skillful twirling and twisting had transformed the paper into a skinny little cigarette. He looked at his creation admiringly and then twisted the ends a bit so the marijuana wouldn't fall out. Recognizing that I was a tyro, he explained as he wetted the newly rolled cigarette with saliva, that the moisture would assure that it wouldn't burn too quickly.

He then lit the tip of what he referred to as a joint, and put it between his lips so he could inhale as much of its smoke as his lungs would hold. While seeming to hold his breath, he checked the end of the joint to make sure it was still lit, and satisfied that it was, handed it to Debbie who repeated the same routine and then passed it onto me. Foregoing my fear of whether I was about to turn myself into an addict, I took the joint and took a quick puff, blew out the smoke, and then handed it back to Rolf who was anxiously waiting his next turn.

After inhaling again and holding his breath that made opening his mouth impossible, Rolf said through his nose: "Take a deep inhale and hold it in your lungs for a moment to give it a chance to be absorbed."

My first puff hadn't left me with anything that could be called a buzz, so when it was again my turn, I followed his advice; drew a lot of smoke into my lungs and held it.

Nothing happened. After the joint made several rounds between the three of us, Rolf pulled out a little alligator clip from his pouch and clipped it to the tiny stub that was left so we could enjoy the joint to the very last puff. I expected to feel drunk—or something, but there was nothing, not even the little dizzy feeling I felt when I first inhaled a tobacco cigarette. "What was the big deal?" Both Debbie and Rolf were smiling and had become quite giddy. I had no clue why they were so elated.

Cookies and a pot of tea soon followed since they both had become inexplicably hungry. Never knowing a cookie I didn't like, I was happy to partake of the little snack. In the course of the conversation, Rolf asked where I was staying and when I told him: "under a house up near the campus," he offered to let me move into the garden shed behind his house. My dog wouldn't be a problem. I didn't hesitate to accept his offer. Breathing dust all night was neither good for Sabacuss or me.

Over the coming weeks, Rolf educated me with little tidbits of wisdom. "Do gooders cause all the world's problems." he liked to say. After I had indulged smoking pot with Rolf and Debbie several more times, I finally felt a little buzz after the third try. "My god, this is it! What's the big deal?" The version the government promoted in it's documentary, *'Reefer Madness,'* was grossly exaggerated. The films narrator explained that the evils of heroine, cocaine and opium are nothing compared to the evils of marijuana. This had no relation to what I was experiencing. With grass, I felt a little buzzed, but in complete control of my facilities. I could hold a coherent conversation and was left with nothing worse than a hearty appetite. It made me feel creative. I was truly enjoying myself and felt "cool."

The fact that the government documentary had lied was unsettling. Evidence was beginning to come out that lies had been used to justify why we needed to be in Vietnam. Being an army brat, I had always trusted the government. Now I was beginning to have doubts. My draft status was One A, i. e. most eligible, and guys were being called up by the thousands. Because no one in the government knew where I was, made me assume that I need not be concerned.

During one of my strolls with Sabbacus, I got the nerve to just drop in on Debbie to say hello. I had no idea if she would appreciate it or not, but she was so beautiful I couldn't resist. She had said she lived above Coady's bookstore on Telegraph Avenue. Its façade was painted black and an uninviting narrow flight of stairs on the left side led to the only apartment above. When I got to the top, I paused a moment before knocking on the door. No one answered and I was about to give up when I heard a male voice inside say: "Someone's at the door." I thought she lived alone—"maybe I shouldn't have come." Still no one answered and I was about to leave when a young mop haired guy sporting a full black mustache opened the door. After asking if Debbie was at home, he nodded for me to step inside, and then left me standing while he disappeared into a room in the back corner of the apartment. The only light coming into the room was through two small windows on the outer wall. The unpleasant smell of a kitty litter box saturated the air. I was surprised that she was living in such a funky environment, but then who was I to talk.

Several moments later, she came out from her room and greeted me warmly, if not enthusiastically. She introduced me to Charlie, the guy who had let me in. A few minutes later a tall shirtless young guy with a lean frame came out of her bedroom just long enough to be introduced to me as Peter, before retiring back to the bedroom. He struck me as someone who had little going for himself. I only stayed for a couple of uncomfortable moments and left wondering if Peter was Debbie's boy friend or lover or maybe all three of them were lovers. Maybe they thought I was trying to move in on them? And what was her relationship with Rolf? The concept of free love was new to me as was the word "fuck" and I didn't want to make a fool of myself by making assumptions about things I didn't understand.

As the summer wore on, I learned more about Rolf. He had married a white blues singer named, Barbara Dane, while they were living in Detroit. Both were into civil rights issues and in the heat of the McCarthy era they found themselves being accused of being communists; probably because of their involvement with organized labor and folk music. The communist label had been attached to folk music since the days of Woody Guthrie and Pete Seeger. Perhaps to escape to a more liberal leaning environment, they moved briefly to Los Angeles, where they had a son they named Nicky, and then on to Berkeley. Nicky was now eleven and living with Barbara on the other side of town. Though they had been divorced for almost a decade, Rolf still had a good relationship with her and his son who would often drop by. I found him to be a good-natured kid and as one would expect; considering his parents—very hep . . . or at least trying to be.

The garden shed behind Rolf's house was quite comfortable. I had a mattress on the floor at one end and Sabaccus had a soft bed nearby. I bought myself a cheap tape recorder so I could emulate—as I had seen Rolf do—the styles of other musicians that I admired by listening to them on tape and then going back and forth until I could decipher the notes they had played. I was drawn to the blues and within time started to pick up some of the riffs of John Lee Hooker and Lightning Hopkins.

Being that I was around the house all the time, my relationship with Debbie grew warmer and she even offered to teach me how to play **Freight Train** using the finger picking technique of the legendary Elizabeth Cotton. She graciously sat down with me for several hours until I got the idea of how it was done. Not many people knew that she had taught Joan Baez finger picking technique when they were both performing at the Club 47.There was so much to like about her, but in my wildest dreams I knew I had no chance of becoming her boy friend. She told me that she had come west with Rolf but their relationship didn't work out, so she moved in with Charlie and Peter, both whom she knew from Boston. Peter was her current lover. Rolf had remained a father figure as he was becoming for me.

28

JUMP OFF THE DEEP END

Summer vacation was drawing to an end and it would soon be time to return to Boston to complete my education. Out of the blue, Rolf made me a stunning offer. He was thinking of starting a Folk Music club in Berkeley and wanted to know if I would like to join him and Debbie Green as a third partner. He had connections that would put up the money, which he estimated would be about five grand. I was dumbfounded and told him I would seriously think about it.

Over the next few days the project became articulated much more clearly. The club would be modeled after the Club 47 in Boston. Rolf's primary function would be to raise the money and be the club's feature performer on weekends. From time to time, Debbie would accompany him on stage. The two of them would also be in charge of booking the talent. The club would feature a different performer or band on each weekday night. Debbie and I would share the day-to-day management responsibilities and I would also be expected to do the majority of the menial labor tasks. Since I had no experience in managing anything, I wasn't sure what this entailed, but Rolf assured me it would be no problem. It was too good to be true. I told him I would do it.

When my mother heard that I was not planning to return to MIT and instead open a coffee house in Berkeley, she went ballistic: "After we ate tuna fish sandwiches to pay for you to go to MIT for the last three years; you're going back!" I was actually stupid enough to think that she would be pleased. Trying to calm her, I explained I would complete my education at Berkeley. The fact that they had skimped for the last three years to put me through the most expensive school in the country didn't register. I was oblivious to her protestations. Set on having my way, I was going to do this whether my parents liked it or not. She knew full well that I was stubborn, and belatedly acquiesced without giving it her blessing. A few days later Rolf, Debbie and I formed a very informal partnership; each of us a one-third owner.

Rolf was the primary mover and Debbie and I his willing followers. He suggested we call it, **The Cabale**, a word derived from ancient Hebrew that meant a secret society. Both Debbie and I liked its mysterious connotation and promptly agreed. He also dictated that the entire gate from the door would go to the musicians, which of course would include him. The rest of the operating expenses, including a salary for me of twenty-five dollars a week, would come from profits made at a concession stand that would offer non-alcoholic drinks and pastries. Rolf insisted that there be no tables or waitresses since that would be a distraction to the performers. The Cabale would be about the music, not about making money. That concept would appeal to the antiestablishment movement that the folk movement, especially in Berkeley, championed. It also appealed to me.

Within a week, Rolf had found a vacant storefront at 2504 San Pablo Avenue, just south of Dwight Way. It was forty feet wide and one hundred twenty five feet long and was portioned into three rooms; one large where the performances could take place, and two smaller rooms in the rear that could serve as the concession area and a green room. It was in the industrial section of Berkeley, which meant that the club would be a couple of miles from the heart of the city, but Rolf averred that if we had good music, the patrons would come. Two other clubs, The Steppenwolf, owned by Max Scherr, the publisher of the Berkeley Barb and the Blind Lemon, were also on San Pablo; the Lemon just a block north and the Steppenwolf a mile away near University Avenue. Both catered to the beer and wine crowd and wouldn't be competition. The Cabale would be the only club in Berkeley whose sole purpose was to offer live folk music.

Our landlord was in the ice cream manufacturing business and liked the idea of his property becoming a nightspot, especially since we planed to serve ice cream dishes as well as coffee drinks. By agreeing to advance five thousand dollars to pay for remodeling, he became the clubs principle backer. I made no attempt to know the details of the deal, a life long pattern I would regret, and as far as I knew, neither did Debbie. In my case, I was just thrilled to be part of the hep folk scene.

Rolf and Debbie began discussing whom to book for the first month. Berkeley and the nearby communities had an established, although loosely knit, folk scene, and there were plenty of performers to choose from. There were also avid fans of the folk music movement and what it represented politically, who would be happy to assist our effort to make the club a reality. Chief among these was Roy Stafford and his wife Mariam. Roy was an architect and offered to design the club gratis. Within a week he presented us with a simple, but very attractive plan. It was approved by Rolf and rubber-stamped by Debbie and me. The stage, six by eight feet, would sit centered against the north wall. Wooden chairs, painted red, would be placed in rows surrounding the stage. The walls would be painted olive green and the wall opposite the stage would be covered with acoustic tile to subdue any echo from the stage. Paintings, by local artists, spread around the room, would add to the ambiance. A small table at the front door would suffice as the admissions area.

Drinks and snacks would be served across a chest high counter that spanned, except for a small entry space against the wall that allowed performers access to the green room, the width of the second room. At Rolf's insistence, sales of drinks and snacks would only be made during the breaks. The musical performances were not to be disturbed.

I and a few other volunteers, George the Greek among them, supplied the labor to make Roy's plan a reality. I also received word from UC Berkeley that I would be admitted in the fall, with the stipulation that I would have to take a remedial English class, called subject A, that was given only at eight AM in the morning. It was because I had failed to get a passing grade on an essay that was part the school's admissions process. It was humiliating that after three years at MIT, I was being required to take a remedial class meant for incoming freshmen, but I had no choice and had to admit that I had never made much of an effort to improve my writing skills.

As opening night approached, Rolf and Debbie solidified our schedule of performers. Rolf would be the weekend feature on both Friday and Saturday night. Debbie would join him at the end of his sets for a few duets and solos of her own. On Sunday evenings that were expected to be slow, Janet Anderson, a ballad singer who accompanied herself on the zither, would perform. Monday would be Hootenanny night, where amateurs could perform and audition. Steve Talbot, a white Blues man whose day job was a switchman at the railroad yard, would take the stage on Tuesdays. Wednesdays would be for bluegrass aficionados and feature Dave Fredrickson's band and vocalist Toni Brown. Though I had yet to meet Toni, I thought I sensed a tinge of female rivalry from Debbie when her name was mentioned. Al White and Perry Lederman, a singing duo would perform on Thursday. All the energy was so positive I was left with no doubt that the club was going to be a success.

Arlette had wrapped up her studies at Stanford and got in touch with me two weeks prior to the Cabale's grand opening. She was returning to Boston and would be taking Sabaccus back. I was glad to be able to tell her that he was still with me and OK; leaving out the story that I had almost lost him when he got loose from his leash and that only after running up and down the streets, nearly in tears, yelling: "Sabaccus, Sabaccus," did the big hunk of black curly hair come bounding down the street, nearly knocking me over as he jumped on me to show his appreciation. I knew between the club and school, I was in no position to give him a decent life, and was glad to hear that he would now be back in her care. She also had a 1945 Dodge that she was going to give me. So here I was: twenty-one, been laid, owned a club and had a car. Life was good!

29

THE CABALE

It didn't take long to realize that attending my Subject A class at 8AM and then several more classes later in the day and then driving around the bay area in my 45 Dodge to tack the arty calendars that advertised our first month's schedule to telephone poles and construction walls and then clean showers and toilets for four hours at the Harmon Gym, might be more than I could handle. To make matters worse, my inflated intellectual ego got knocked down a notch when I discovered that classes at Berkeley were every bit as intense as those at MIT. It wasn't going to be the breeze that I had expected. Less than two weeks after school began, I was already behind a week. I had little time to do homework and my heart wasn't into it. I was not only wasting my time, but the school's as well. And I questioned where a degree in math was going to take me. The Vietnam War was growing and the thought of sitting in a cubicle designing bombs or some widget for a corporation, didn't seem so cool anymore.

There had to be more to life! I had no clue what it was, but I opted to take the dive and dropped out of school all together. Some inner confidence told me I would always be able to take care of myself even if I didn't have a college degree. Still insensitive to the strain that my parents had been under to provide me an education, I called my mother and asked if she could send me the seven hundred dollars that they would have had to pay for my schooling if I had continued. Probably stunned, she at first agreed, but got in touch with me a day later to tell me that the money wasn't coming and that I was on my own. I knew she was right! It was time to swim on my own and what a swim it would be.

It was actually a blessing. I was now free of any parental obligations. I didn't need my mom to buy me socks and underwear and I also didn't need to pay heed to their moral standards. I was appreciative of what I had received, but I had my own observations about life and I no longer felt it had to be weighed down by theirs.

The Cabale opened on a Friday night in mid September of 1962. The place was packed to the gills with paying customers as well as "in crowd" freebies. Rolf took the stage and genialy welcomed the audience. He was a consummate professional, charming and capable as a musician. His opening set included several folk songs like Wildwood Flower, and some traditional blues like "Nobody Knows You When You're Down and Out." Debbie joined him near the end of his first set. There wasn't a guy in the audience whose eyes weren't riveted on her. She performed very professionally, singing several duets with Rolf, followed by a few solo ballads. They both got a standing ovation as they walked off the stage.

The entire room had become smothered in cigarette smoke and I opened the front doors to allow some of it to escape. The concession area became packed like a sardine can as people lined up to buy refreshments during the break. The two girls behind the counter had all they could do to keep everyone happy. Rolf returned to the stage after a fifteen-minute break to showoff his virtuosity in flamenco. By the end of the evening, it was apparent by the audience's reaction, that Berkeley was thrilled to have a folk club and the success of the Cabale was a given.

We had taken in over two hundred dollars at the door, all of which went to Rolf and a bit to Debbie. After the paying patrons filed out, a small contingent of the Berkeley folk crowd hung around for a little jam session, including my friend George the Greek, Teddy Bernstein from New York, Mark Silber, who worked at Lundberg's guitar store on Dwight Way, and Ken Striker, a competent guitar picker. Several pretty folkie chicks hung around to listen to the music and smoke some weed. Rolf and Debbie left shortly after taking a few tokes, leaving me to lock up when everybody cleared out. I had moved out from Rolf's garden shed and was now sleeping in the green room on a mattress that I kept leaned against the wall until everyone left, which was not until several hours later.

That would become the nightly ritual: a small crowd of insiders hanging around after the club closed to smoke some pot, drink some booze or wine, and play their axes. To establish a pecking order of who was to be most desired by the few chicks that had hung around, there was a constant battle over who would have the axe. Rarely could someone manage to get through a few songs or even a few riffs, before someone else would grab the axe out of their clutches and say: "Hey man, dig this." Many exchanges would take place back and forth during the impromtu jam sessions. I didn't have the nerve to play in front of anyone and was content just to watch and maybe learn a few techniques in the process. After everyone cleared out at two or three in the morning, I would retreat to the green room and topple my mattress to the floor and many times, without getting undressed, crash on top of it until I woke up the next morning around noon. After washing up in the men's room, I would head across the street to The Golden Rose Café and treat myself to a bowl of pork fried rice and eggs, the only breakfast I could afford on my meager twenty five dollar salary. I then returned to the club and did my daily janitorial duties and anxiously awaited the coming evening's performances.

The week's performers didn't disappoint. Steve's Talbott's gravely voice and down home blues guitar style almost made you forget that he was white. Dave Fredrickson's bluegrass band played to a hooting and hollering country crowd, but the big surprise of the first week was our Thursday night act, Perry Lederman and Al White. They were simply dazzling. The audience sat spellbound as Perry accompanied Al's full-bodied voice on guitar as they performed unique renditions of blues, folk and even show tunes like "Summer time" from Porgy and Bess. Using a microphone placed in front of his 1922 Martin guitar strung with silk on steel strings, Perry produced a sound that was a cross between acoustic and electronic. The plastic finger picks he used on his thumb and fingers; produced a brilliant sound that even included riffs of sixteenth notes. When Perry retuned his guitar to an open chord, he began playing an introduction to the blues classic, "John Henry." His hands moved up and down the frets with runs of bass notes followed by a few well-placed harmonics that were spine tingling. After the twelve bar intro was completed, Al began singing in his strong resonant voice: "John Henry . . . was a steel driving man." The whole room reverberated with hair-raising excitement. It was as though you could feel John Henry, out in the hot sun, swinging his heavy sledgehammer with awesome force to drive the spikes into the railroad ties. Word of mouth quickly spread and the following week Al and Perry played to a standing room only audience.

Al was a light skinned African American, handsome and well educated, and married to a beautiful white girl. That would have been shocking anywhere in America except Berkeley. I was not one to express my opinions when it came to social issues, but inwardly I was very proud to be part of this budding revolution that I saw taking place around me.

The Cabale quickly established itself as not only a place for people to come to enjoy music, but also as a place for the hip crowd to hang out, many without paying admission. (hip had slowly replaced hep) They began to use the refreshment room as their own private club while performances were taking place. The hippest of the hip was Bobby Neuwirth. He had dark wavy hair, a face that featured large dark smiling eyes and a mouth that always had a little twist that gave the appearance that he might be slightly inebriated—which he often was. He was a loveable lush and often took the stage when we needed a fill in, capably performing a set of Woody Guthrie's children's songs. He was mostly friendly with the bluegrass crowd and was a magnet for the girls and the envy of every guy, simply because it seemed like he could get laid at will. He knew how to be empathetic and even my partner, Debbie, was enamored by him. The fact that he made the room light up when he walked in made it impossible not to like him.

Bobby Neuwirth

A month after the club opened, Rolf, unceremoniously announced that he was pulling out of the partnership. He told Debbie and I that we would be equal partners and he wanted no remuneration. We would have run of the show. It took me completely by surprise. Though Debbie and I had been running the day-to-day operation of the club, Rolf was the backbone. We were both sad and a bit miffed to see him leave, but since the club's operation was practically on automatic, we felt confident that we could keep it going.

Why had Rolf dropped out so quickly? I knew he had a big ego and when the big crowds that he initially drew began to wane, it was possible that he couldn't handle it. He was certainly a competent musician, but even I could see that his act could only pull a crowd for so long. Bobby Neuwirth, who had been a part of the Cambridge folk scene and was friends with both Rolf and Debbie when they were performing together at the Club 47 and living together in Cambridge, had another theory. After they moved to Berkeley, the romance cooled and she moved out. The Cabale was an attempt to reignite the fire by recreating the exact same environment in which it had flourished. After a month, it was obvious to him that his plan hadn't worked and running a club was not what he had in mind for himself.

I could see that Neuwirth was probably right and that I had been used as just a big dumb lout to help pull it off. So what! At twenty-one, I was now half owner of a successful folk music club. It was also clear to me that I wasn't really an accepted member of the Berkeley folk establishment. It had to bug people that Rolf had picked me to be a partner and I could see why. Nonetheless, the club now belonged to Debbie and me. We decided to make a few changes so it could make money. We put in tables and added a waitress to take orders. Because the in crowd had made the backroom their private hangout, customers felt intimidated when they came in to purchase refreshments, so I tore down the wall that separated it from the performance room. Now they would have to be quiet or at least whisper while someone was on stage. I hadn't consulted our architect, Roy Stafford, and when he saw what I had done, he was very displeased and divorced himself from the club. I could care less. As I said, the folk community had always wondered why I had been involved in the first place. No one had made any attempt to learn who I was. If they had, they might have discovered that I was not the timid mouse that some may have thought.

Chris Stracwitz

Debbie was well respected in the folk community and we had no trouble continuing to book talent, including Rolf's ex wife, Barbara Dane. However, after several months, the local talent pool that we had been relying on to fill our schedule, was beginning to get stale. That changed when a tall, cherubic faced German immigrant, named Chris Strachwitz walked into the club one evening. At first I thought he had just come by to hear some good music and had no way of knowing that when he left that evening, the Cabale would be on the road to become one of the elite folk venues in the country. During the break, he sidled up to me to introduce himself and tell me about a Texan bluesman named Mance Lipscomb, that he was bringing up from Navasota, to record for his record label, Arhoolie, a small company he had recently started and ran from his home in the Berkeley hills. Mance was going to perform at a small folk festival while he was in the bay area, and Chris wanted to know if we might be interested in booking him for a week at the Cabale. Neither Debbie nor I had ever heard of Lipscomb, so Strachwitz suggested that we listen to a few of his songs that he had recorded on a tape he had brought along. Struggling to hide our excitement, as soon as we finished listening to the tape, we told Stachwitz we would be delighted to book him for a solid week.

Mance became an immediate hit the moment he stepped on stage; not only for his music, but also for his humanity. Born in 1895, he was the son of an ex slave father and a Choctaw Indian mother and had worked as a sharecropper, earning, for his entire life, little more than thirty dollars a month. He managed to earn a little extra money by playing local parties on the weekends in his hometown. Despite this hard life, he sang with a soft and melodic voice and accompanied himself on an acoustic guitar that he played with a finger picking style that was all his own. He was a consummate performer, sliding in little bits of humor and stories between his songs. The civil rights movement was in its seminal days and Mance's appearance at the club provided a chance for liberal and well off urban whites to interface with a poor southern black. That he handled it so gracefully, made people comfortable. They could see that the differences between them and him were small and insignificant.

He played to standing room only crowds through out the week, and despite his age, was happy, after we closed, to party with the Cabale in-crowd until two or three in the morning. He didn't smoke grass but he loved downing scotch whiskey, which the cadre of his admirers sitting in front of him, eagerly provided just to keep him playing.

30

UNCLE SAM CALLS

The Vietnam War was proving the government to be a pack of liars. Speculation that the Tonkin Bay incident was fabricated was beginning to make people think twice. Young people were becoming more rebellious. Nobody over thirty was to be trusted. I had always been rebellious, not for any reason that I could sit down and exactly say why, other than I just enjoyed being out on the edge. It was part of me. I began wearing a kaki army jacket and a Castro style army hat. It was my new look. I wasn't a real rebel, just a play rebel . . . And having a good time doing it. I began to chain smoke because that was part of the hip rebellious image. It was uncool to smoke filtered cigarettes. Guys like Neuwirth smoked 'Galois', a strong French unfiltered cigarette and I followed suit. If I need to borrow a fag—the hip name for a cigarette, and could only find a filtered one, I would tear off the filter before smoking it. Drawing raw smoke into my lungs was cool. Being health conscious was square. At first we were only pot smokers, but after Neuwirth introduced 'Green Death,' the name he gave to Rainier Ale, we soon became sots. Rainer ale came in quart sized green bottles and each evening after the club closed, a bottle or two or three got guzzled down and a couple of joints smoked while friendly battles took place over who would play the axe. Even Debbie joined in, which I could see was to please Bobby who she had taken a shine to and even took him home afterwards to have sex. Lucky bastard!

The army notified my father that he was being shipped off to Korea for a year and because it was still a war zone, his family couldn't accompany him. They had moved back to Monterey while he waited for orders to report. Unknown to me, they had driven up to Berkeley to see what my club looked like but were too intimidated by what they perceived was going on inside, to come in. I had had no contact with them after I decided to leave school, so when they sent me a letter, I was a bit surprised. I was even more surprised when I opened it and discovered it was a forwarded letter from the draft board ordering me to report for a pre-induction physical. Needless to say, I was not elated. It would bring to an abrupt end the life I was now living and terminate my involvement with the Cabale. Getting drafted pretty-much meant going to Vietnam. A lot of body bags were starting to come back and the government needed new bodies to replace them.

Fuck that! I wasn't going! I didn't bother showing up for my appointment. A week later, after giving it a little more thought, I realized I might be getting myself into some serious trouble. A lot of guys were splitting to Canada and they were not treated lightly if they returned to the States. Draft dodging could put you in jail. I just had to face the music and show up to take the physical and hope I wouldn't get sent to Vietnam. But before I did, I would at least have a little fun and fuck with their heads. I wrote the draft board a rambling letter explaining how terrified I was about all the killing and massacres that were going on and how frightened I was, but now, I had come to my senses and would fight for my county's freedom if called upon. I would report for a physical if directed.

A few days later they sent me a letter ordering me to report in three weeks to the Army medical facility in downtown Oakland. Bobby Neuwirth was now spending lots of time hanging around Debbie and was at the club the morning the letter arrived. In his devil-may-care confident manner, he told me not to sweat it. "Don't worry man, we'll get you out." His plan was simple. I would just get so fucked up that they would give me a 4F deferment (physically unqualified). He would show me how to do it.

For the next three weeks, under his expert direction as well as some assistance from a few other friends, I stayed plastered day and night on everything I could get my hands on: Green Death, brandy, pot, Bennies. The pot put me to sleep but the Benzedrine kept me awake. Just for good measure I stopped washing, brushing my teeth and taking showers. After three weeks I had become an odoriferous shaggy looking drugged up bum, a garlic infested turd, too disgusting, repulsive and foul smelling to serve our country in its bull shit war in Vietnam—or at least I hoped so.

Looking like something between a zombie and a Benzedrine buzz machine, I boarded a city bus at 7AM at the stop just outside the Cabale, and headed to the Induction Center in Oakland. A bottle of apricot brandy and a little bag with a couple of joints and a few benies, were tucked into the pocket of my dirty old beat raincoat, so I could fuck myself up one last time before I went in. No amount of sunshine could have made the ride pleasant, so it didn't matter that it was a typical gray and cold Bay area day when I stepped off the bus into the shit-hole that is downtown Oakland. The area had plenty of vacant lots and I found one along the way to the Induction Center where I could drug myself up one last time. Just in case the exam went into the afternoon, I hid what was left of my drugs under some bricks. After making sure no prying eyes from one of the winos in the area had seen what I had done, I stumbled off in a stupor to face my pending doom.

The induction center was an inimical looking windowless three-story brick building. A sergeant sat at a little worn wood desk just inside its small entrance door. It felt like entering a prison. After showing him my letter to report, he directed me to climb the stairs to the second floor and follow the yellow idiot line painted on the floor. The line led to a large room filled with nervous looking young kids sitting on metal fold out chairs arranged in several rows. I took an empty seat in the last row. Fifteen minutes later, another sergeant showed up, and told everyone in my row to follow him down the hall where we were then told to strip down to our underwear and stand in line like sheep waiting to be sheared.

One by one we moved from booth to booth, taking various medical tests. The male nurse taking my blood pressure, couldn't believe what he was reading. It was off the charts. After releasing the pressure in the band wrapped around my arm, he pumped it up again, thinking there must be a mistake. After the third try he resigned himself that his reading was accurate and sent me on to the next booth where I was to take a hearing test. There I took a seat at a little table in a shower-sized booth where a young GI placed earphones on me before running the tests. In the confined area, it took only a moment for the stench emanating from my reeking body to fill the space. After the young GI finished my test and removed the earphones, he politely asked if I had taken a bath in awhile. Inaudibly, I muttered that I didn't have a shower where I lived. The poor kid was probably close to passing out by the time I exited.

The final station was a written exam to determine any psychological problems. The answer to each question was a yes or no to be indicated by putting an x in the appropriate box. Do you have a drug problem? I didn't check either box, instead putting a question mark at the margin. Are you homosexual? I checked yes and no and then erased the boxes until there was a little hole in the paper. When the shrink reviewing my answers asked me to explain my responses, I told him I used drugs but didn't see that it was a problem. Regarding the hole in the paper by the homosexuality boxes, I muttered that I wasn't sure if I was or wasn't.

I was to be given a card indicating my draft status before leaving the Induction-center. Most guys were handed a card that classified them as 1A; but when it came my turn to get a classification card, I was told to come back after lunch to be retested. I had no way of knowing if they were suspicious that I had jacked myself up or if I was just nervous. Thankfully, I had come prepared and returned to my hidden stash where I rejacked myself up before returning. My afternoon tests showed no improvement. I was hoping for a 4F, but Uncle Sam didn't want to take any chances on losing a body to fight his war, so he gave me a 1Y, a one-year deferment. I would have to come back in a year and do it all over again. Obviously they already realized that the war was going to go on for a long time.

31

WHAT AN ASSHOLE

Debbie and I were more than generous about granting free passes, and it unfortunately led to abuse. Don't trust anyone over 30 sounded cool, but I quickly learned not to take that adage too seriously. Other than joining a few weekend gatherings at Phil Huffman's house, an amiable supporter of the folk scene, to drink beer and wine, smoke pot and eat copious amounts of the delicious chili made by Midj, his Mexican wife, I didn't socialize much with the local folk crowd.

All the same, I wanted to be liked and availed myself to helping my hip friends out. Neuwirth would ask to borrow my "short," a hot rod term from 40's Chicago black gangster argot meaning, "car" that he liked to use as a way to impress how much hipper he was than anyone else. Soon after, to be, "in," we all had to call cars, "shorts." At least in his case, I felt obliged, being that he helped me avoid the draft. But after Teddy Bernstein, who just hung around the scene without adding anything significant, came back at one A. M to tell me: "Hey man, your 'short' broke down in San Francisco, its parked on Howard and Seventh," I wasn't too happy. I had lent it to him so he could run around Frisco while I was at work.

It was the first sign that a lot of hip people were ass holes and a lot of, so called straights, were more likely to be good reliable friends. Fortunately, one of these, Dave Cleveland, was at the Cabale when Bernstein gave me the bad news about my car. Dave, in his mid thirties with short hair and glasses, had started coming to the Cabale after he got off from work and was always eager to help out with chores if asked. He drove me across the bay to see what was the probem with the car. It was just out of gas! The little fucker couldn't be bothered to put a few bucks of gas into the tank?

The incident woke me up. Not surprisingly, there were cliques at the Cabale and for various reasons; I was not in the mix. I was not a performer and not even a musician. I was someone to use to get into the club for free, or in Teddy's case, to use my car. I was not about to become an "in" group sychophant and along with Dave Cleveland, Sidney Locker, Gordon Hope and at times, ClarenceVan Hook, I formed my own clique. All of us were in our early to late 20's. Sidney was an Englishman, with a little goatee and as would be expected; bad teeth. Gordon, six foot six and married to six foot three Kay, was a graduate of the University of Michigan. Clarence was a mellow spade dude, a professional electrician and a musician, who performed well, but lacked charisma.

Initially we just did goofy things together. Gordon showed up at the Cabale one evening, wearing a black cape slung over his shoulders and tight white Levis with a pair of his wife's bikini panties on top. He looked like a perverted superhero. After I closed down the club, he, along with Cleveland, Sidney and I, jumped in my short and went across the bay to a pool hall on Howard Street. Naïve to the ways of San Francisco, we had no idea why some guy began stalking Gordon every time he bent over to take a shot. Irritated by the interloper, we left and headed to Chinatown to get a bite to eat, but fared no better there when a burly white guy that looked as though he had recently been released from a mental hospital, started stalking us. When we noticed he was holding an open pocketknife in his hand, we tried to duck down some alleys to lose him, but every time we turned around he was still close by. Half panicked that he was bent on wreaking bloody havoc on four silly weirdos from Berkeley, we ran to the car and hightailed it over to Golden Gate Park, where we finished the evening by scampering around the off limit site of the remains of the once magnificent 1915 San Francisco World's Fair. The fifty-foot tall faux Grecian pillars were made eerily beautiful by the light from a full moon and the maze of scaffolds that lie inside were an irresistible playground for a group of young morons who had not a care in the world. At 4AM we were finally exhausted and headed back to Berkeley.

Everything wasn't about mindless adventures. Sidney, in particular, was interested in what makes the mind tick. His long neck and prominent Adam's apple along with a shock of hair that hung down from his forehead and the habit of never appearing anywhere in public, including the beach, without wearing a sports jacket and tie, lent itself well to his image of being an amature psychiatrist. He had a degree in Chemistry that he earned in his native country, England, and an interest in hallucinogenic drugs. Due to him, my interest in psychology was wetted and I began to read works by Carlos Castaneda, Heman Hesse and Wilhelm Reich, one of the principles of the Austrian psychiatric movement who advocated sexual freedom.

Hesse said don't be overly analytical and I liked that. But being that I was an orgasm junky, Reich's Ogone energy theory had particular interest for me. He claimed that neurotic behavior stems from the incomplete release of what he called, Orgone energy. This mysterious energy could only be released through a complete sexual orgasm. He hypothesized that unless the stomach muscles and hips were relaxed, that goal was impossible to reach; a 'stiff' isn't going to be a good fuck. His ideas held sway with me as I noticed that uptight people usually walked with tight hips. Men were afraid to appear effeminate if they let their hips sway and women afraid of being deemed to be sluts. I began walking with my hips loose and quickly found that doing so made me feel very sexual. Being a male slut was cool.

Thinking grass might make me more musically creative, I would smoke a joint while I was alone at night after everyone had cleared out and then tape record some of the riffs I had been working on. By watching the various performers I was learning a lot. In the morning I would play back the tape to see how soulful I sounded. To my great surprise, I was always shocked at how lousy the recording sounded. It was as though I was playing with fingers covered in molasses.

Grass didn't do much for my musical ability, but it made my mind relax and seemed to open it to new ways of thinking. I decided on a little experiment. I would stay high for thirty days and see what happened. For the first three weeks, other than being a stoner, not much changed. I did my chores at the club and had no problem running the show when it was my turn. And of course there were the usual less-than-stellar insights like; "what if our universe is just an atom inside of a much larger atom?" However, near the end of the third week, high as usual, I was standing, mid morning, in front of the club, pondering what my day held, when I felt my mind, encased in a large transparent bubble, exiting my head. It was like a big soap bubble and it rose about two feet into the air before hovering over me. From within the bubble, I peered down at myself and made a disconcerting observation: ***"What an asshole!"***

The bubble quickly reentered my head, bringing my mind back to its traditional position. Upon reflection, I realized that if it had not, and I continued what seemed to be a rather unfavorable self-analysis, my ego would have been destroyed. Maybe I was an asshole? But who wants to know that? Maybe we're all assholes and our egos protect us from being too self-critical? It was a trip that I had no intention of repeating.

32

THE JOY OF EXCITING A WOMAN

I didn't have the sexual charisma that Neuwirth had, but the folk scene and *Free Love* were synonymous and I got my share of pussy. Some girls weren't smitten by my disheveled rebellious noncommittal look, but the ones who availed themselves to me weren't disappointed. I loved eating pussy and after stimulating one girl's clit and vagina for twenty minutes with my tongue, nose and face, leaving her sopping wet before we fucked, remarked; "Who would have ever thought you'd be so good." She made my day!

Unexpected sex was often the best. Debbie was at the club one evening during my shift and whispered to me that one of our waitresses, a girl named Kathy, wanted to fuck me. She was not what I would call, "my ideal girl," and I had made no effort to have sex with her, but she was, nevertheless, very attractive. I didn't have a place to grant her wish, but when Gordon dropped by, I told him my problem and he said I could borrow his bungalow. Debbie agreed to watch the club while I was gone and Kathy and I were soon on our way to Gordon's bungalo. I began by showing her how stiff my dick had become by taking six shirts on clothes hangers out of Gordon's closet and hanging them from my hard rod. She was more than impressed and after removing the shirts, wrapped her legs around my waist and imbedded my penis that was pointing to the ceiling with her wet cunt. I placed my hands on her round ass cheeks so we could run around the room fucking. The walls shook as I banged her against the wall. Gordon's largess wasn't just beneficent; he was peeking through the window and jacking off while we fucked. Unknown to me, it was my first pornography show.

Porno films were only available on the black market and very hard to come by: and then only in black and white 8mm format. I knew of no one who possessed any, although a vague rumor had it that it was possible for a girl to make money in San Francisco if she was willing to do pornography. It was illegal and sounded very sleazy; even dangerous. Despite a lot of the girls at the Cabale being sexually permissive, I knew of none who had made a porn film.

Free love had a price; it came with risks; namely sexual diseases or worse, getting a girl pregnant. Syphilis was unheard of, but getting a dose of the clap (gonorrhea) and crabs, was almost a given. A shot of penicillin took care of the clap and lotions were available at almost every drug store to kill crabs. Ironically, curing crabs could be a turn on. The day after I had sex with a woman a few years older than me, we each discovered we had crabs. Neither of us knew which one had passed it on, but she had dealt with the problem before and knew exactly what to do. After the eggs were killed with the lotion, it was advisable to shave off all the pubic hair to dispense with all the dead eggs and any little rascals that might still be hanging on. I found her shaved pussy to be a real turn on as she found my shaved cock. We were soon back to sucking each other's barren genitals. A shaved pussy was to become a life-long fetish of mine, years before it was adopted by popular culture in the next century. I also took to shaving my own pubes back to the base of my shaft to make deep penetration easier.

In the free-thinking atmosphere of Berkeley, it was no secret that girls liked sex every bit as much as the guys. But beyond dealing with an annoying STD, they had to deal with pregnancy. The pill was not yet available and the most common birth controls were diaphragms—a little rubber barrier inserted in the cervix, and foam gel, which after being shot up the cervix with an applicator, created a barrier. Since the STDs were not fatal, no pressure was put on males to use prophylactics and the burden to avoid pregnancy fell on the females. They were expected to use a diaphram or foam. But if a girl forgot, which happened from time to time, and got pregnant, there was a tough choice to make. Have the baby or get an abortion. Even if they wanted to have the baby, many girls in the scene enjoyed multiple partners and in pre DNA days, proving the identity of the father was very difficult. And in an era when women were grossly discriminated against in the workplace and didn't get paid well, raising a child on their own probably meant a life of poverty.

Religious Luddites refused to allow abortion to become safe and legal. Abortions were provided by underground doctors; some of them quacks or in Mexico. Worse were the gory draconian methods like using a coat hanger. I knew girls who had been put through this nightmare, and it left them scared. No one really knew what the answer was, but free love was here to stay, like it or not.

Golf and sports were too plebian for the beat life, so I gave them up but my addiction to strippers was a different matter. Sadly, burlesque was in its waning days and the only true burlesque theatre in San Francisco, was the President Follies on McAlister Street. The strip clubs in North Beach that served alcohol held no interest for me. The loud hooting and hollering from inebriated idiots made concentrating on the sexuality of the dancer's performance near impossible. The shows were a far cry from those at the Old Howard, they showed exploitation films between acts, but it was all that was available and on occasion I would spend an afternoon there. What there was of the small audience was much different than what I had seen at the Old Howard. It was dead and depressed and even strange. On one of my visits, I had been seated for only a few moments, in an empty row so I could massage my cock, when a large black woman took a seat in the empty row in front of me, but four seats to my left. I thought it was decent of her not to block my view of the stage, but it seemed odd that a fat black woman was attending a burlesque show. I was a babe in the woods when it came to the ways of San Francisco, and when I noticed her turning her head several times to look at me, I didn't think too much about it until she began to edge her way down the row, one seat at a time, until she was sitting in front of me, but just one seat to my left. "What the fuck was going on?" Two minutes later, she placed her large arm across the back of the vacant seat in front of me and then slowly let it migrate down the back of the seat and onto my leg. I liked black chicks, just not big fat ones; so much to her disappointment, I got up and moved. I wasn't quite sure where the whole thing was going and was a long way from wanting to find out.

In November of 1963, the Cabale was to have its first nationally known performer. Thanks to Chris Strachwitz, Lightning Hopkins, king of the

Texas blues men would be at our club for a three-day gig. Lighting, because of his fear of flying, had come to the bay area by train and Chris had gone to the station to pick him up, while Debbie and I and a host of the Berkeley folk crowd, waited nervously at the Cabale to welcome him. Lightning was a big star, having made many records. "Would he be a prima donna?" I wondered. The moment he stepped through the door he put us all at ease with a big smile that flashed his big gold tooth, and then after taking his guitar out of its case and a swig of apricot brandy from the flask he carried in his coat pocket, he took a chair on the stage and began to sing; "Big Boss Man you ain't so big, you just tall that's all," and then threw me a bone: "Howard, you ain't so big, you just tall, that's all."

My head swelled with pride. Like a lot of aspiring white blues guitarists, I was a black wannabe, and being recognized by one of my idols was almost a religious experience. I was a big Hopkins fan. Even while living behind Rolf's house, I was teaching myself a couple of his licks by listening to his music on the little tape machine I had bought, playing the riffs over and over until I unraveled his finger movements. His appearance at the Cabale established us as northern California's premier folk club.

Lightning's songs ranged from epics like the "Galveston Ice Storm" to tragic-humorous love songs like "She's Mine" with its sick, but funny line; "the poor child was deaf, dumb, crippled and blind . . . but she was mine!" Fans of his came from all over the bay area, as far south as San Jose and as far north as Sacramento. Lightning packed the house night after night. The notoriety brought us national recognition and bands from across the country began to play the Cabale.

The notoriety also caught the attention of the bay area's musician's union and they tried to use their muscle to force us to hire only union talent. By and large, our talent was just liberal minded young people who enjoyed folk music. They weren't union and had no interest in becoming union. Nevertheless, the union was adamant that we hire a union piano player each night even though we had no use for a piano player and what we would have to pay for someone to sit around doing nothing, would bankrupt us. A labor confrontation could be fatal. Neither Debbie nor I were business people, but she was at least beautiful, and we decided that she should be the one to meet with the union bosses to see if they could be convinced to back down. The plan worked. She told me after she returned from the meeting, that moments after she walked into the room to face the eight tough cigar-smoking officials, they were calling her dear and sweetheart. By the time she left, they agreed that they would be happy if we just put an upright piano in the club. Feminine beauty had made them more than happy to compromise their principals.

33

SHE LOVED BEING A SLUT

Little did I know, my forays to San Francisco to attend the President Follies and its drab strip-shows, would result in the most exciting sexual experience I would have since "little blue panties" had ended my virginity. Christmas was drawing near and I wondered if Debbie even knew, or cared that I lusted for her. Neuwirth seemed to have a lock on her favors, but then again, he was in a different girl's bedroom almost every night. I had been pondering what kind of gift I should get her for Christmas, and while wandering around San Francisco, passed a lingerie shop that carried the sleazy kinds of panties and lingerie that the models wore in the Parliament girlie magazines. I was strangely wired with some kind of special radar that led me to these places.

In the window was a see-thru red string panty with black lace trim and a little matching see thru bra. The backside barely covered the buns and a little rectangular strip covered the pussy. As I stood outside fantasizing and pondering, a debate took place in my mind. "Would Debbie think I was a sleazy-sicko if I gave those panties to her as a gift? A Christmas gift; no less! But maybe she would think it was kinky and be flattered that I saw her as a sex object. What would Neuwirth think about me buying his girl friend panties? Why should I care? Was there any chance that she would model them for me after she opened the gift-wrapped package?"

Having never been in a shop like this before, I felt a bit embarrassed as I quietly told the saleslady that I wanted to buy the panties in the window. I still looked like a teenager and I wondered what she thought about me as she went to the window and asked me to point them out? My face was flushed, or at least felt like it was. The intimate process of deciding how to adorn a woman's sex organ was exciting. I pointed to the panties that I had in mind and she pulled them out of the window to allow me to hold them. I did my best to mask my juvenile decorum and calmly told her I would take them. She was an older lady, maybe in her mid forties, and I wondered as she was wrapping the panties up, if she had similar sexy panties like that under her dress? I would have liked to ask her, but of course I didn't. The whole thing was a turn on.

Debbie was delighted! Not only did she put the little panties on so I could see how sexy she looked, but got so turned on that we fucked. My speculation that she would be pleased with the gift was borne out. There was something to say for having a naughty mind on the inside combined with a shy personality on the outside. Naughty but nice comes to mind. I now knew that it was not a sin to make a woman feel sexy or to let her know you think she is sexy and likely a whore in the bedroom. It was a big step in conquering my sexual insecurities.

We were not, so-to-speak, about to become an item. I was a wild man, not the kind of guy a girl could see having a future with. While the horses were running at Bay Meadows, each Friday night after I closed the Cabale, I joined Clarence Van Hook at his cousin's house in Emeryville to smoke pot and get jacked up on Bennies. When the sun rose, we picked up some doughnuts and coffee and then sped out to Bay Meadows, talking bullshit about how much money we were going to make. By the end of the day, we would return broke and brain dead after the 'bennie" high had wore off. My entire twenty-five dollar salary from the Cabale had been spent, meaning that I would be eating doughnuts from the Cabale's kitchen for the rest of the week.

When Bay Meadows closed, I along with the boys in my clique, headed to Reno. The old Dodge had finally had its day after conking out right in the middle of the Bay Bridge, so I was now driving a 51 Ford convertible that had to be jump started to get it going. It was a beautiful sunny day, and as soon as the boys pushed me fast enough so I could pop the clutch, we were on our way with nary a care in the world, despite a war raging on the other side of the planet. By late Saturday afternoon, we strolled into Harrah's ready to do some gambling and make some money. Downing a few bennies would keep us awake all night and our minds acute. We were each convinced that we had a winning strategy to beat the house odds. But by Sunday morning, we were all standing outside the casino flat busted; not even money for gas to get back home. Gordon said he heard that Casinos didn't want losers to be hanging around and would hand out mercy money to get them out of town. He was right. We were losers and they did hand out money. The manager handed us five bucks and wished us on our way, but before we could all pile into the car, Clarence grabbed the five bucks and ran back to the tables, saying he had a sure hunch he would win. Ten minutes later we were emptying our pockets of every penny we could find, about three bucks, enough to buy almost ten gallons, and by putting the car in neutral and coasting down all the hills, we managed to eke into Berkeley just in time for me to open the Cabale's doors. Tempting fate gave me a perverse thrill.

Failing at gambling didn't upset me. I wasn't a loser. I never doubted that I would be successful, and despite not yet having a regular girl friend, I would be successful with that some day as well. Some girl would see past my façade, see who I really "thought" I was. By now the Cabale had been open for almost a year and it was already summer. After spending a day at the Sausolito beach with Sidney and Debbie—Sidney wore a sports jacket and tie, even at the beach—I had closed the Cabale for the evening and was not feeling very good. A bee, attracted to the sun tan lotion while I was at the beach, had stung the top of my foot and it was swollen to the size of an Idaho patato. It was all I could do to just hobble around during my shift. All thought of pain went south when Debbie called me at 2 A. M., not to see how I was doing, but to invite me to her apartment to share her bed. "Could it be that she saw more in me than I thought?" She was living on the first floor of a house that was about a mile away on Shattuck Avenue. I told her I could be there in fifteen minutes. There was no way to jump start my car on one foot, so all I could do was hop up the street, which I did as fast as possible. She was a prize and possibly winning her was not to be taken lightly.

A light was on in her living room when I arrived and I hopped up the wooden staircase to her porch and knocked on the door. Sweating profusely from all the hopping, I waited for the door to open. A few seconds later it cracked open a sliver and her eyes darted nervously beyond me as though someone might be watching. She told me in a quiet and hurried nervous voice that I would have to split right away: "Bobby Neuwurth had called and was on his way over!"

Tail between my legs like a spanked puppy, I lumbered back down Dwight Way and returned to the back room of the Cabale to spend the evening by myself. But it was not all bad. The hopping had forced the bee infection out of my fucked up foot and I had just been taught that even in 'free love' Berleley, when it came to sex, there was a pecking order.

34

OFF TO MEXICO

Debbie and I made some modifications to the club and changed its policy of awarding the entire gate to the performers. It allowed both of us to take out modest salaries. My mattress in the green room had become filthy from people stomping on it every night, so it was with great joy that I was now able to move out and share an apartment with Sidney. The two of us rented the entire lower floor or an old two story house on Blake Street, just inside the Oakland border. It was a mixed race working class neighborhood. Living upstairs was an ultra cool spade dude named Doyle Forman. "Spade dude" was the new non-offensive hip term for blacks. His wife was a skinny red headed white woman. Doyle was an artist and very dexterous; he could roll and light a joint with one hand. His wife was a woman of few words, but we often visited each other's apartments and he always offered us a smoke when he came down or we went up. It was the Berkeley way of doing things.

I had given up on Debbie and my new fantasy girl lived just two houses away in the upstairs flat of another house that had been converted into apartments. Judy Galpin was a twenty-year old blond who I fell in love with—at least sexually—the moment I saw her. Her flowing long blond hair and the curves of her body supercharged my libido. I offered her a waitress job at the Cabale and presumed sex would follow. She readily accepted the position, but my callow plan went nowhere. Instead, she seemed to enjoy teasing me, or maybe torture is a better word. I was inwardly pissed after I learned she had already fucked Neuwirth and Teddy Bernstein, the asshole who left my car in San Francisco.

There were enough other girls willing to have sex with me that there was no reason to be unduly upset by Judy Galpin's rejection. The Cabale was booming and we had just booked Mississippi John Hurt, recently rescued from obscurity by John Fahey, a talented local guitarist who sometimes played at the Cabale. The discovery of Hurt had been heralded in Time magazine as well as an appearance on The Tonight Show. His finger-picking technique had been emulated by countless aspiring folk musicians; who previously had only had a few scratchy tracks taken off of a 78rpm record recorded in 1928, as models to develop their own techniques. The Cabale would be his first west coast gig. It had been assumed that Hurt was dead, but Fahey and a friend, Tom Hoskins, had played a wild hunch and traveled to Avalon Mississippi, on the basis that one of Hurt's songs titled *"Avalon, My Home Town."* When they arrived in the small one street town and asked the first person they met if anyone knew John Hurt: the man replied "Yessir, that's him just up the street." Hurt had been a poor sharecropper all his life. He was about to earn five hundred dollars for playing the Cabale for a week.

Patrons and members of the press packed the room on Mississippi John's opening night. With a derby hat perched atop his head, he performed with such panache and composure to the mostly all white audiences, that it was hard to believe that he hadn't been on stage for nearly thirty years; let alone that he likely had little contact with white people. I put him up in an extra room at my house while he was in town and after the Cabale closed, he was happy to sit in my living room surrounded by as many folkies as it could hold, and continue to play into the wee hours until he passed out. Money Road was the name of one of Avalon's two streets, and John Hurt had finally discovered where it led. He loved sipping whiskey and only stopped playing when he died a year later.

Of course, there were talents who passed through the doors of the Cabale whose talents, unfortunately, weren't immediately recognized. Fahey, had recorded himself on his own record label, Tacoma, and was posthumously rated by Rolling Stone as the 35th greatest guitarist of all time. But even more incredible was a white blues singer from Texas who started coming by on Monday night to perform at the hootenanny. She was not a beauty, being a bit overweight and having a troubled complexion, but heads turned when she belted out a blues song. Debbie and I considered hiring Janis Joplin, but the guitarist she used as her accompaniment was weak and distracted from the force of her music. We also had doubts that her repertoire was large enough to fill an evening, so we passed on the idea.

Her bawdy personality made her fun to be around and she often had a good story to relate when she arrived to spice up the evening. She had thumbed a ride at an entry ramp to the bay bridge when a truck driver stopped to pick her up. He didn't open the door so she could climb in, but rather started trash talking to her while she stood outside. When she finally had it with his bullshit and yelled: "Are you going to give me a fucking ride or not?" He pleaded, "Don't go now bitch, I'm about to cum!" Things were never dull when Janice was around. On another occasion someone came running through the front door yelling: "Janis's been run over." She had come across the bay on her motor scooter and had left moments earlier to go back home. We all dashed out and saw her lying in the middle of the intersection. When someone spotted a car a short distance away driving away on San Pablo, we assumed it was a hit and run. After an ambulance arrived, she was whisked away and taken to the hospital where it was determined that she wasn't hurt, but had just toppled over because she was so drunk that she couldn't maintain balance.

Janis was always welcomed at the Cabale and though I had no sexual desire for her, we double dated on one occasion. A garrulous spade-dude who worked in Frisco as a cable car operator, invited she and I to come to his Nob hill apartment for a late night dinner. Janis had performed earlier in the evening at the hootenanny and I just assumed he liked her singing. He had been coming to the Cabale for several weeks and I always enjoyed talking to him, so his offer to enjoy high cuisine was too good to refuse. Janis and I got to his place around one in the morning and were rewarded with a wonderful dinner, good conversation and generous amounts of wine and marijuana. Afterwards, we both were barely able to move, let alone drive home, so while our benefactor cleaned up we zonked out on the comfortable couches in his tastefully decorated living room.

At first I thought the hand that was gently caressing my forehead was part of a dream, but when I opened my eyes and saw the friendly black face of our benefactor gleaming at me, I knew what was happening. Janis's snoring was not mixing well with the mood music that was now playing in the background. The San Francisco gay community was still, by and large, underground, and I was still forming an opinion on how I felt about homosexuality. But I was not as naïve as I once had been and didn't want to hurt the dudes feelings, so I calmly told him that I liked him but it wasn't my thing. There was a moment of discomfort, but he didn't push any further. I went back to sleep and kept the experience to myself. I had come to realize that there were many more gays in the world than I had once thought but still didn't know how to deal with them. Still, he would have been welcomed at the Cabale if he came back but he didn't.

Strachwitz often remarked when he came by the Cabale: "You guys are so crazy." He was right and I think it might have also been one of the reasons he kept coming around. The 60's counter culture credo was that everything establishment was bullshit and being crazy by getting high on grass and booze was a way of making it clear we wanted no part of straight society. And moreover, a hip chick wasn't going to fuck a straight dude, so if you wanted to get laid you better be a little crazy. I had no trouble playing that role. The fact that I had never been busted for shoplifting, made my next crazy move easy.

It began when Sidney and I needed to raise a little cash to pay our rent. We had paid the prior two months by breaking into the basement garage where the landlord stored a dozen or so washers and dryers. Dave Cleveland would come by with his pick-up truck and help us transport several of them down to a second hand dealer on San Pablo Avenue, where we offered to sell them so cheap, that the store owner didn't bother asking questions. But after doing this for a couple of months, we were afraid if we removed any more appliances from the garage, it would become obvious that things were missing. Sidney had been making a little money by dealing lids and there were always plenty of people around the Cabale looking to score. A pound of grass could be purchased for a hundred bucks and then broken down into one-ounce lids, which went for fifteen bucks. It was an easy way to make money, but pounds weren't always available.

One evening, standing inside the front door of the Cabale, was a tall stranger wearing a broad rimmed leather hat, a tan leather fringe jacket, buffalo pants held up by a wide belt with a showy turquoise buckle, high leather boots that came up to his knees, all topped off with several pieces of American Indian jewelry around his neck and on his fingers. It was impossible not to notice him. His name was Chan Laughlin. He claimed that he had just returned from spending time in the Arizona desert living with an Indian tribe who used peyote during their rituals. His cool demeanor gave me the impression that he knew things others didn't. Before he left, he mentioned that he had brought back several peyote cacti if anyone was interested in buying.

'The Psychedelic Experience,' written by Harvard professor Timothy Leary, was creating

Chan Laughlin

a lot of interest among young American's who had become disenchanted with the American government and its war that seemed to have no rational explanation as to why we were involved. Leary's book described experiments he had performed on himself with lysergic acid diethylamide, commonly known as LSD. He praised its ability to open the mind to a colorful altered universe that brought extraordinary insights. He described the experience as a "trip." LSD was not yet available in the underground market, but a peyote trip, although accompanied by acute stomach sickness and vomiting, was said to be in many ways, similar. That was enough to turn me off, but not Sidney, who purchased a half dozen Peyote buttons from Chan and kept them stored in a closet at our house until such time that he was in the right mood to deal with the deleterious side effects.

Chan Lauglin's persona as a daring adventurer; a man who lived with strange Indian tribes and joined them in drug induced ceremonies, fascinated me. A daring devil-may-care man was probably attractive to women. "Don't the movies show that?" I thought to myself. "Isn't that what it's all about? Being desired by women." I didn't feel I had the 'need-to-be-cared-for' appeal that Neuwirth had or the musical talent some other guys had to make woman swoon, but it was a fact that sexy women were attracted to daring men: gangsters, cowboys, race car drivers: men who challenged the limits. I recalled *The Fascinating Jennifer* leaving the Old Howard in the arms of a gangster.

Moreover, I was not attracted to dull girls; I liked wild girls. Maybe I wasn't projecting a wild enough image. I knew a lot of girls interpreted my baby face as a sign that I was sweet, innocent and dull.

I began to speculate that taking a trip down to Mexico to score twenty or so kilos of marijuana would be an adventure of heroic magnitude. It was the kind of wild adventure that would make me an interesting character. The fact that a guy named Billy, known to several people when they hung together in New York, showed up at the Cabale one night with eyes deadened from serving four years in prison in Mexico for smuggling grass, wasn't enough to dissuade my fantasy. "I never got caught, I was too smart!" Putatively, kilos could be purchased for fifteen dollars below the border, meaning I would turn a nice profit once I returned to the states. I would also be admired for supplying my hip friends with abundant amounts of marijuana. But there was more to my plan. Still lusting for the sexy Judy

Galpin, I would invite her to come along. Accompanying a picaresque adventurer like me would be irresistible and she would happily submit to my sexual needs during the trip. Admittedly, it was a dangerous way to overcome the deep seeded inferiority complex that I knew resided inside my psyche, so I put aside any thoughts that warned against the adventure.

To get it rolling, I began grilling Chan Laughlin, who had mentioned in passing that he had previously smuggled grass up from Mexico. He was very cooperative and provided me with explicit directions: "Go to the Hotel Guadalajara where you will find a bunch of cab drivers lined up in front of the hotel. Ask for Jose De La Torres. Once in the cab, tell him you are looking to score some kilos of grass. He will tell you he knows nothing about that. About a block later he will pass you a joint and ask you how much you are looking for and how much you want to pay. Offer him ten bucks for a kilo and negotiate from there."

It sounded so easy. Several people in the community, including Rolf, were willing to front me money in return for some of the merchandise when I got back. What an adventure it was going to be. As I had planned, a free trip to Mexico was enough to entice Judy Galpin to come along, and Sidney convinced me that I should go with a partner in case something went wrong. It was the sensible thing to do.

With five hundred bucks in my pocket, the three of us headed south in my recently purchased, '53 Mercury. The old Ford that needed to be jump started would never do. I cut my hair nice and short and dressed myself to look like a respectable college boy. After crossing the Mexican border, we checked into a motel just south of Tijuana. The three of us shared a single room where Judy made it clear, although nicely, that my largess wasn't going to be rewarded with pussy that night and probably not anytime soon. I didn't let it upset me, having a woman along made the trip more pleasant and knowing she would be watching, bolstered my ego.

We were all in high spirits the next morning after having a hearty breakfast of ranchero eggs at a small restaurante. With the windows rolled down and warm desert air blowing through our hair, it was a pleasure to be alive while we zipped down Mexican highway number one. Just south of Hermosillo, we left the desert and began driving through a hilly jungle. The air turned redolent with the musky smell of Guava trees. There would be little civilization until Mazatlán, a small ocean side city, almost eight hundred kilometers away.

Two hours after refueling at a small one-pump station halfway through the jungle, the car's engine began to sputter. I didn't know shit about cars and neither did Sidney and of course neither did Judy. I just kept driving. The thought of breaking down in the middle of the jungle was not a comforting one and each of us were tense and sitting straight backed in our seats. This was not a place where you could call triple A. The thermometer gauge began to rise and I tried not to think what would happen if we broke down. Putting the car in neutral and coasting down hills, made the temperature guage drop, but as soon as I reengaged the engine, it began to shoot up again. With about fifteen kilometers to go (about ten miles) before we reached Mazatlán, the thermometer was pegged in the red zone and steam was blowing out of the radiator. By some miracle, we limped into the outer edge of town where I spotted a sign than said 'Mechanico.' It pointed to a little dirt road that that led up a hill covered with weeds and dry yellow grass. I was able to nurse the lurching car up the hill until we came to a little hut surrounded by broken down cars and rusting parts. The old Mercury was steaming and hissing like a pot of boiling tea. A young man, who looked to be somewhere in his thirties, emerged from the hut. It was obvious what our problem was and in broken English he told us not to worry. We didn't talk price—we didn't have an option. Since it would take "mucho hora" to fix, he offered to drive us to the nearby beach.

Mazatlán had yet to become a tourist Mecca cloistered with high rises and hotels. It was now serenity personified: the beach a mile long expanse of sand with nary a person in sight and eighty degree water so shallow that one could wade hundreds of yards off shore and still touch bottom. Having faith that the unknown Mexican mechanico was going to make things right, we three American drug smugglers took advantage of the Eden we had been delivered to. Sidney paced along the shore in sports jacket and tie; Judy, ever hyper as I was beginning to recognize as part of her personality, tanned herself in the sun while looking gorgeous as ever; and myself, playing the role of the cool, calm, fearless leader, waded far off shore undaunted by the thought that sharks might be lurking. Late in the day our young mechanico returned to tell us that the car was fixed. He explained in broken English that he had taken parts out of his own car in order to repair mine. The bill came to twenty dollars. "Viva el Mexico!"

Guadalajara, a city of a few hundred thousand in 1963, is situated on a mile high plateau. The elevation keeps temperatures moderate year around. After checking into a hotel room that had three separate beds, we meandered over to the large public square in front of the massive Cathedral de Guadalajara, and took a table at one of the outdoor tourist café's that sat in its shadow. It was Sunday and my plans didn't call for me to rendezvous with Jose until Monday. After just relaxing and absorbing the ambiance, I left my friends and walked the short distance to the Hotel Guadalajara to scope things out. Along the way I made mental notes about the surrounding area so I wouldn't make any unnecessary fuck ups after I had scored. As Chan had said, there were a bunch of taxis in front of the hotel, all parked perpendicularly to the curb. I made no effort to affirm if there was a Jose De La Torres among them, not wanting to give him the opportunity to set up a double deal with the polica where he could get my money and if he turned me in, a reward as well. Because Chan had already dealt with him, there was no reason to believe that he would do this, but better safe than sorry.

I noted a small park located just two blocks from the Hotel Guadalajara that would make a convenient rendezvous point for Sidney to meet me after I made my score. I could be dropped off by Jose at the far side of the park, and then carry my grass-laden suitcases to the other side of the park where he and Judy could be waiting with our car. It was important that Jose didn't know what kind of car I was driving, since there was the outside chance that he could still report me to the polica and get a reward.

I rejoined Sidney and Judy at the patio cafe outside the Cathedral and we spent the rest of the day entertaining ourselves by sipping cappuccinos and tipping the Mariachi bands that roved from table to table. Not wanting to make any kind of a scene, it was necessary to amicably tolerate the relentless onslaught of souvenir hawkers and beggars that visited our table. Most of the beggars could be dismissed rather easily, but one haggard woman, just stood aside our table looking so feeble and needy, that Sidney's heart finally melted and he dug into his pocket and donated a few pesos to the poor soul. As the day wore on, we watched her go around the square, working table after table. The same silent technique she had used on us seemed to always garner a donation. We all laughed, when at the end of the day, we saw her feeble limbs spring to life as she ran across the square to join her husband and children, who had just pulled up in a car to take her home from her day's labor. Considering the tense day I had in front of me, a little humor didn't hurt.

Relying on the cool demeanor I could engender during a math test, I hid my nervousness as I began to prepare for what could be a dangerous adventure. Around noon, wearing a sports coat, white dress shirt and a nice pair of slacks, I had Sidney and Judy drive me to the small park where we would rendezvous when I returned. We drove around the park and decided that the north side seemed to have the least street traffic and the best place to hook back up. I estimated that it would take only a few hours to score, so I told them to be at the park around two in the afternoon. If I wasn't there when they arrived, just wait. I stood in an unoccupied doorway for a few minutes, until the car was well out of sight. When I felt secure that there was little chance that I could be connected to it, I proceeded to the Hotel Guadalajara. Five minutes later, with two empty leather suitcases in my hands, I stood across the street from the old three-story hotel fronted by a white ornate awning that ran the entire length of the block.

Knowing that I had to look a bit strange arriving from across the street carrying suitcases, I did my best to act casual as I asked the first driver I came upon if he knew Jose De La Torres. Without saying a word, he pointed to a cab six spaces away. I got the sense that the question may have been asked before. It would be ridiculous to think that no one knew what Jose was up to. I quickly walked to his cab.

"You're Jose De La Torres" "Si senor."

He immediately took my bags and put them in his trunk while I climbed into the back seat. He had to know that my bags were empty when he picked them up. Getting behind the wheel, he backed out onto the wide boulevard that fronted the hotel. Neither of us said anything. After taking a left turn down the side street that runs next to the hotel Jose spoke:

"Where can I take you senor? "

I reminded myself how Chan had advised me to conduct the conversation—don't be too pushy.

"Oh, I'd just like to take a ride around town."

I wasn't sure how he perceived me. I was clean cut and very young looking; a baby faced high school student. As we ambled through several blocks of traffic, I broached the subject of scoring grass:

"My friend in San Francisco tells me you can find me some kilos." "Oh no, senor, that is illegal, I know nothing about marijuana." After a twenty second pause: "Who is your friend?"

"His name is Chan." I replied.

My stomach began to sink as it appeared that I might have made this whole trip in vain. About a half block further down the street, Jose reached back with his right arm and handed me a lit joint.

"How much do you want, senor?" "I was hoping to get fifty kilos"

"How much do you want to pay?" he asked. "I heard a kilo goes for eight dollars"

"Oh no senor. A kilo is twenty five dollars."

Negotiating was never my forte; I hated bickering over prices. I had about five hundred dollars to score with and after a bit of perfunctory haggling, I agreed to the price; I would still make out quite nicely. He asked to see my money and knowing I had no other choice, I showed it to him. As though he had known the outcome of our negotiations, we were already leaving Guadalajara and heading south on a two-lane highway to a destination unknown to me.

A bit of small talk relaxed both of us as much as that was possible. A half-hour down the highway, he made a left turn onto a narrow dirt road that led into an uncultivated field. Nothing suggesting civilization was visible in the distance. Jose's cab could only bump along over the deep rutted road. Our top speed was no more than fifteen miles an hour. The slow pace meant that the two-hour time period that I had arranged to meet Sidney and Judy had been way too optimistic. Three miles down the road, we came to a couple of barns surrounded by several primitive one story stone houses. Jose stopped the cab and got out, telling me: "Bring your money Senor." We entered the one room house through a portal without a door. The open room was about twenty feet square with ten-foot high walls that had four small rectangular open windows near the top. Its floor was hard dirt. The only illumination was from a few amber rays that the setting sun cast into the room. There appeared to be no electricity or plumbing and no furniture other than the chair in the middle of the room, where an old woman was sitting.

Jose began talking to her in Spanish. She wore a long dress typical of a peasant woman and a shawl of faded material. A young brown skinned man, who appeared to be in his mid twenties, stood next to her. The woman appeared to be at least seventy, her face deeply wrinkled. I assumed she was the young man's mother or grandmother. She and Jose continued to converse several minutes while I stood silently to the side. I found it strange that the old woman was a drug dealer and they probably thought that it was strange that the skinny baby faced American was a drug dealer. Suddenly the conversation ended and Jose signaled for me to follow him back to the cab.

"They didn't have any marijuana now, but there is someone in the next village who has some."

As we drove away, Jose told me the young guy was the woman's husband. I knew some guys liked older women, but this was extreme. Maybe she was just prematurely aged as a result of doing hard farm labor under the unrelenting Mexican sun. My whole plan had become disheveled. There was only about an hour of daylight left and it would be well into the evening when we got back to the city. The huge potholes in the road we now traveled, made the first road look like a super highway. Top speed was no faster than five miles an hour. It took almost five minutes to maneuver the cab across a stream that had no bridge and another five minutes was spent waiting for a stubborn cow to move to the side. Jose didn't have any quit in him, and we kept on. A city cab in the middle of Mexican nowhere made for a strange sight. By the time we got to our destination, the sun had set and the land was shrouded in darkness. Jose told me to wait while he disappeared into the empty void. After five minutes he returned and told me to give him the money. I handed it over and he again disappeared. Sitting alone I was wondering what I had gotten myself into. A minute later, Jose was jumping back into the cab. "They are going out to the fields to get the marijuana. We have to wait till they come back."

The pristine air, unencumbered by city pollution, made the stars twinkle like little diamonds set on black velvet. Other than the fact that I was a little white boy committing a crime in Mexico, it would have been a beautiful sight indeed. Jose and I, two strangers speaking different languages, continued to make small talk. A low, nearly full moon, began to make its way across the sky. It lifted the curtain of darkness enough so that I could see that a barn sat a short distance to our left and a ridge of small hills hovered over us to our right. An hour passed and no one had returned. Once again my stomach began to feel sick. The thought that I could be murdered and no one would find me—maybe forever—crossed my mind.

"Christ, what could Sidney and Judy be thinking? What if they panicked and split?"

Jose didn't make things better when after two hours he suggested: "Maybe they are not coming back, Senor."

It was a very real possibility. Nothing was stopping them from just taking my money and disappearing. What the fuck could or would I do about it. Absolutely nothing! My spirits recovered five minutes later, when, in front of the large lunar globe that had now made its way halfway across the sky, silhouettes of three Mexicans, with what appeared to be large burlap bags slung over their backs, were hurriedly trekking across the crest of the small hill just to the right of our cab. Walt Disney couldn't have framed a better shot. In no time they had descended the hill and were at the back of the cab. As I stood by, Jose helped them transfer the merchandize into the trunk. I wondered why there was no sweet smell of marijuana, but my question was quickly answered when I saw that the grass had been compactly packaged into one-kilo bricks, each about twelve by six by two inches, and wrapped in red cellophane. Evidently they had a packaging machine out in the field. These guys were pros. As soon as my score was safely ensconced in the trunk, we sped off, or bumped off would probably be a better description. Jose was as relieved as I was that the deal was consummated. Five minutes down the road, he made a brief stop, explaining that we should test the merchandize. Opening a corner of one of the packages, he adroitly pulled out a little weed and rolled a joint . . . lit it . . . took a toke and then passed it to me. I liked the way he took good care of his customers. After a few deep draws, I began to feel mellow. It was good shit. Being high made the trip back to town seem a whole lot more enjoyable.

Still paranoiac, I had Jose drop me off several blocks from the park where Sidney and Judy would be waiting for me in the car. He seemed to understand. As soon as he disappeared around the corner, I began lugging my fifty-pound pot-laden suitcases through the dark deserted streets. I prayed to my atheist god that Sidney would be waiting for me. Sweat was pouring off of me as I arrived at the park's edge. My eyes darted around its sparsely lit perimeter. I saw no one. Panic was not an option. Knowing it would look suspicious if a "policia" saw a skinny white guy lugging two heavy suitcases down the street at two in the morning, I had no choice but to do exactly that. I slowly made my way towards the hotel, wondering if Sidney and Judy would even be there when I got back. It wouldn't be unreasonable for them to have concluded that I had been busted or even dead and decide to split.

Lady luck was with me. The desk clerk at the hotel was in a back room or sleeping when I entered the lobby and I quickly slipped down the hall that led to our room. There were shit-eating grins on all faces when Sidney opened the door and saw me standing there. He told me they had waited until ten O'clock before leaving. Judy was elated to see me. Maybe I would finally get in her panties? Neither knew what they would have done if I hadn't made it back. Fortunately that decision was now moot. After showing them the sixteen bricks in my suitcase and rehashing the day, we all crashed from mental exhaustion.

There was still lots of work to be done. The next day, after having a good breakfast, we headed back to the States. The weed had to be stashed under the back seat before crossing the border, and since the beach at Mazatlan was virtually secluded, it seemed a logical place to do the job. I parked the Mercury behind a small sand dune covered by wispy ocean grass to keep it out of view in case someone came down the road. Sidney and Judy served as lookouts while I took out the back seat cushion and stashed the bricks in between its springs. I made sure the little hole Jose had punctured into the one kilo when we had a quick taste, was sealed. Once all the kilos were comfortably stashed and the cushion replaced, I checked to make sure there were no bulges that might draw the suspicion of a trained border agent. It looked good. We all got back in the car and headed towards the border.

There were three options on where to cross; Tijuana, Nogales, and a small crossing in the middle of the desert. I chose Nogales, Arizona. Tijuana was too busy and it would look suspicious if I was crossing at the sparsely populated point in the middle of the dessert; kind of like the three bears of crossing points: one was too hot, one too cold and the other just right.

Judy and Sidney started getting nervous as we approached Nogales. The last thing I needed was to get busted because of their jitters, so I told them it would be better if I dropped them off at the bus station where they could catch a ride to the states. I would make the crossing alone and then reunite with them in Tuscon, Arizona. They loved the idea.

Running a comb through my hair one last time, I made the final approach to the checkpoints. There were two of them, one Mexican, the other U. S. The Mexican side waved me through with a cursory question and I continued the fifty yards to the U. S. checkpoint. That at least meant if I got busted it would be in the good old U. S.A. Staying as cool as I would if I were just stealing a girlie magazine off a news rack, I drove up to the waiting American agent. He began asking me some routine questions:

"Where have you been?" "Just to Guadalajara."

"What were you doing there?" "Just vacationing a few days."

"Are you bringing anything back with you" "No, just a couple of souvenirs."

I had purposely purchased a few common Mexican souvenirs to make my trip look legitimate. They were placed on top of a neatly folded Mexican blanket lying on the back seat. After the routine questions, I stepped out of the car holding the papers he had handed me that needed to get stamped to make my entry official. When I saw him stick his head into the rear seat area to see if anything was under the blanket, my mind momentarily panicked: "Christ, if he gets a whiff of grass I'm fucked."

But by calmly asking: "Where do I take these papers?" I broke his concentration.

He pulled his head out of the car and pointed to the little booth a few yards back, and then walked away from my car. I was home free. I got my papers stamped and slowly rode away as though I hadn't a care in the world. Wow, what a rush. I was too full of myself to have any fear. Over the next fifty years, I would have more than a few nightmares replaying that border crossing. I would never get caught, but would wake up in a sweaty panic before realizing it was only a dream.

Judy and Sidney were waiting for me at the Tucson greyhound bus station when I showed up. They had arrived only a few minutes before I got there. Judy was still nervous. What if we got stopped and the cops found the grass under the seat? She had a point. I called Dave Cleveland and set up an alternate plan. At a large vacant lot a few blocks from the bus station, I removed the kilos from under the back seat and repacked them into my suitcases so I could take them back to the bus station and send them to Berkeley with Cleveland's name as the recipient. Wasn't Greyhound's motto: Leave the driving to us?

I had scored eight kilos of fine Mexican weed but had failed to score even a peek of Judy Galpin's pussy. Such is life. All the pressure now removed, we enjoyed a delightful trip back to Berkeley. However, profits from my adventure were not so delightful. After giving my investors their share, and handing out lots of freebies to my friends, as well as smoking up a whole bunch, there wasn't much left to sell.

A pound of that was lost when I got burned by a spade dude. He asked me to follow him to a two-story apartment building on Shattuck Avenue, where he claimed his partner had the bread to make the deal. After we both parked on the street, I brought the merchandise with me and followed him a short distance to a flight of stairs that led up a narrow passageway to the apartments on the second floor. The dude asked if I would mind waiting while he went upstairs to do the deal. His partner wanted to remain anonymous. It was a reasonable request. Moreover, I knew this dude and spade dudes, especially ones who came to the Cabale, were trustworthy. After all, us folkies were fighting for their civil rights. I watched him bound up the narrow staircase after I handed him the brown bag containing the pound of grass. Decked out in my Castro outfit, I waited outside on the street. Fifteen minutes later, when he still hadn't returned, I started to wonder what was going on. Finally, after another ten minutes, I climbed the stairs to investigate. Looking down the long hall, I knew I had been burned when I saw an open window at the far end. When I got to it I found a fire escape that led to the alley below. The dude had read my little naïve liberal ass like a book and played me like the sucker I was.

There was another dealer in town that carried a gun and would have tracked the guy down and beat the shit out of him or worse. That wasn't who I was or had any intention of becoming. It wasn't a racial thing. The guy was just a thief. I had done my share of stealing so I couldn't be too outraged. Live on the edge of a sword and expect to get cut. But I had learned another lesson; meaningless aphorisms, like all spades are cool or people over thirty are not to be trusted or all long hairs are to be trusted, should be taken with a grain of salt. The money was not worth becoming uptight over and I let the incident slide. It wasn't as though I had nothing going for myself.

35

WHEW! AN LSD SCARE

Begging to be used, the half dozen buttons of dried peyote buttons sat for several months in Sidney's bedroom closet. They finally got their wish. Sidney told me when I got home one evening, that he had ground them up and threw them in a milk shake to mask the bitter taste. The side effects weren't that bad and he described the trip as being colorful.

It was known that the active ingredient in peyote was Mescaline, available, although infrequently, on the underground market. Ingesting it didn't cause any bad side effects. Sidney suggested to Cleveland and me, that if he had the materials he could manufacture Mescaline. It could be very profitable.

Obtaining the raw materials would be a problem. They weren't readily available to the general public. Dave told us not to worry. He could use his position at his daytime job at the UC chemistry lab to procure what we needed. Security at his work was very lax and he doubted there would be any problem pilfering the equipment we would need to set up our lab. That being settled, we agreed to form a partnership and build Berkley's first Mescaline factory.

By weeks end, Sidney had drawn up a list of all the equipment and chemicals that would be needed. For our laboratory, we rented a garage behind a small unobtrusive house on one of the quiet residential streets in Berkeley's south side that was owned by a sweet and unsuspecting little old lady. Over the next two weeks, Cleveland came by each evening with urns, beakers, hoses, Bunsen burners, scales, spatulas and titration gauges. Late in the evening, when the little old lady was asleep, we dug a deep pit next to the garage to make a septic tank to dispose all of our waste products. After the pit was filled with gravel and sod meticulously replaced, its presence was completely concealed.

Using stationary with a UC Berkeley letterhead that Dave had pilfered from his workplace, Sidney, posturing as a University of California researcher, wrote a letter to a chemical supplier in St Louis, requesting the raw materials that we would need. Obviously the package couldn't be sent to the University, so he requested that it be shipped to a San Francisco mailbox address. When the supplier balked at sending the relatively large order to an unregistered lab, Sidney assuaged their concerns by hinting that he was doing special government work. Top secret you know!

Three weeks later, the raw materials arrived and we began production. Each evening, after the little old lady was fast asleep, Sidney, looking every bit the part of Dr. Frankenstein, mixed and cooked the raw materials that should result in copious amounts of Mescaline. There was some concern that the pungent odor of ether, a by product of the cooking process that was wafting all the way out to the street, could expose us. But since we were working late at night that worry was put aside. If our landlady caught whiffs of the smell, she didn't say. For that matter, the ether probably made her sleep more deeply. To avoid her and any questions she might have, we always vacated by four A. M.

The chemistry was not simple. Each attempt met with failure and it began to look like our factory was going to be a bust. However, near the end of the second week, Sidney held up a test tube with a minute amount of material that had precipitated to the bottom. It reminded me of my experiences in Chemistry lab at MIT; was the material on the bottom just an anomaly—some impurity from a dirty test tube—or was it Mescaline? Even if it was, the cost of producing such a small amount was much higher than the product could be sold for. Despite doubts about what the stuff was, Sidney offered to sample it and afterwards claimed it had given him a psychedelic high. His lack of exuberance made me doubtful. Who cared, I was happy to just be a part of America's new rebellious generation.

Though my crazy side adventures might have given the impression that I was losing my interest in operating the Cabale, that couldn't be further from the truth. Despite my deep-seated fear of public speaking that dictated that I introduce the performers from a microphone in the back room, I was proud and excited that the Cabale had become the premier folk club in northern California; on a par with the Ashgrove in Los Angeles. We booked blues legends, Homesick James, Elmo James, Brownie McGee and Sonny Terry, Jessie Fuller, Bukka White and well-known performers from the east coast like Ramblin' Jack Eliot and The Jim Kweskin Jug Band. I built a special augmentation to the stage that allowed it to be enlarged after lowering a bigger surface leaning against the back wall so our flamenco night with Dave Jones could also feature a dancer. Her tapping heels added immeasurably to the drama of the music. The large stage also allowed us to book famous gospel groups like the Staple Singers.

Ralph Gleason devoted his entire column in the San Francisco Chronicle to us when we booked, Elmer Snowden, father of the jazz banjo. He had played with the likes of Duke Ellington and Bessie Smith but had fallen into relative obscurity before playing the Cabale. Gleason's column helped us draw a standing room only crowd for an entire month of weekends. Elmer, in his seventies, was a practiced hustler, and would try to shake me down for a few extra dollars each night after he finished playing. I had to resort to hiding out in the back alley until his plaintive calls; "Howard . . . Howard where are you?" ceased.

Drugs were as much of the scene as was the music, and Sidney's Peyote experience had given him the yen to take the next step into psychedelic nirvana. Several cubes of "Owsley Purple" were now sitting in our refrigerator. The acid was so named after a San Francisco chemist named "Owsley" (a shortened version of his full name, Augustus Owsley Stanley III) who had earned himself a reputation for producing the highest quality LSD available on the street. It came in sugar cubes saturated with doses of the drug, which turned the color of the cubes to light purple, thus "Owsley Purple." It even came with a marketing slogan: "You can trust Owsley Purple."

Timothy Leary's book, The Psychedelic Experience, was a guide on how to use LSD and what you might expect. He said a trip could be very intense and recommended that a first timer not take more than 75 micrograms. He also suggested not tripping alone. Nevertheless, Sidney did just that and took a trip alone while I was working at the Cabale. His description was much more glowing then his peyote trip: the walls moved, there was color everywhere and objects became distorted. It sounded amazing. I couldn't discern any harm that had been done to him.

Ever since coming to Berkeley, I had been experimenting with drugs. I was careful to stay away from the ones that were well known to be addictive, but I was fascinated by the mind adventures and since LSD was not in the addictive category, I told Sidney that I wanted to take a trip. Following Leary's advice to not travel alone, I asked Susan Black, a beautiful and intelligent blond Stanford student who I had known since my days of residing in the backroom of the Cabale. The Berkeley counter culture fascinated her and she frequented the Cabale often on weekends when she didn't have classes. Her tight white skirts and black nylons excited me; enough to entice me after I closed the Cabale to bomb my way down to Palo Alto in my old Dodge at one thirty in the morning to spend the rest of the night in the sack with her. She was as close to a serious affair as I had ever gotten—and even if it was not that far—I felt comfortable around her. I was pleased when she agreed to take an LSD trip with me.

I began making plans for the trip; I wanted to make sure we would feel secure. A trip lasted up to eight hours so we both agreed that she should plan on spending the weekend at my place to give herself time to come down before returning to Palo Alto. Saturday night was Debbie's turn to run the club, so it was agreed that would be the day we would travel together into the psychedelic unknown.

Early in the evening, we sat comfortably next to each other on a mattress lying on the living room floor next to the room's interior wall. Sidney, playing the role of a trip guru, was standing in front of us. The shock of hair that curled over his forehead along with his bucktooth, made his smile more mischievous than normal. After a few words to put our minds at rest, he went to the kitchen and returned with two cubes of Owsley Purple and a glass of water. After a moments-pause and mutually reassuring looks, Susan and I put the cubes in our mouths and washed them down with the water. We had crossed the point of no return. A warm pleasant glow came over me a few minutes later. Susan seemed to be having the same reaction. We looked at each other and laughed. There was no sense of anything ominous. Time became vague and by the end of the first hour—as best as I could tell—there were no cascades of colors or distortions. The two of us just felt very alive and happy; so we headed out of the house to observe the local universe. We held hands and giggled as we headed up Ashby Avenue. The world glowed with euphoria, including the subversive co-op supermarket as we passed it before heading up Telegraph towards the campus.

Then as we arrived at the business stretch of Telegraph, the quarter mile that ended at Sater Gate, something happened. The glowing world of euphoria had changed into a macabre horror show. The faces of the merchants looking out from their shops, impatiently waiting for customers to come in, were distorted. They looked like gargoyles waiting to pounce on helpless prey. People who we passed on the street looked alien, cold and unfriendly. I held Susan's hand tightly. We hadn't spoken a word for several blocks. I was afraid to look at her; terrified that she may have been transformed into something grotesque. And then simultaneously, we looked at each other. We broke into laughter. She looked as beautiful as ever! I told her what I had been going through and she acknowledged that she had been having the same experience. What psychic forces could explain that?

Fatigue began to set in, so we headed back to my place. As we walked along, I began to notice circular rainbows of color around the streetlights. "Wow, do you see that?" I asked Susan. She did. By the time we got back to my pad, my head was a kaleidoscope. We were back on the mattress from where our trip had begun and were conveying to Sidney what we were going through when I noticed that the wall next to me began to have little ripples of colorful waves running across it. They moved quickly as if they were caterpillars with jet packs. I lay down and tried to close my eyes hoping for a respite, but discovered there were no closed eyes while on LSD. The hallucinations just kept going on.

Susan and I were too overwhelmed to be of much help to each other. If not for Sidney, we might have been in trouble. His presence and prior experience helped immensely, assuring both of us that what we were going through was a normal progression. He calmly told us to just maintain our cool.

After several hours, the trip came to an end. I couldn't imagine taking another one or a stronger one anytime soon. Over the next few months, little flashes of the experience would pop up. I was not against taking acid again, but I felt it would be wise to give my brain time to stabilize. I was confident that no permanent alterations to my brain had occurred, but the intensity of the drug meant it needed to be used carefully and infrequently. I only saw Susan a few times after that. We had shared an amazing experience together, but, like most girls, she probably knew that there was little future with me. I was bent on being wild and untamed.

36

CAN'T BE NO GOOD REVEREND WIDOUT SOME PUSSY

Strachwitz's oft repeated German accented mantra; "You guys are crazy . . . crazy," wasn't enough to scare him away from asking me to join him in promoting a big time concert at the three thousand seat Berkeley Community Center. It would feature Jimmy Reed, Reverend Gary Davis and John Hammond, a white bluesman from New York. This was a great opportunity to become seriously involved in the music business. I had just become hip to Jimmy Reed's music and it's distinctive sensual walking base line and Reverend Gary Davis, a blind black man out of New York, was one of the most idolized blues guitarists in the country, recorded multiple times on the Folkways label. Why Chris wanted to include John Hammond, a white kid who was the son of a record company executive, was a mystery to me. He was very accomplished, but being that he was white and clean cut, how could he have soul? It wasn't for me to ask. I was just excited about the offer and told him yes. He would handle all the arrangements; all I had to do was help with the labor; a task a lot of people seemed to think was my forte.

We plastered the bay area with advertising posters and pre sale tickets began to move fairly well. A bit of concern came when we heard a rumor that Jimmy Reed had fallen off the stage at his last concert and had had a concussion. It was only a week until the concert, but his manager assured us that he was recuperating and there would be no problem.

The Reverend had a substantial flock of worshippers in Berkeley, some, like Mark Silber who repaired guitars at Dwight's guitar shop, could play respectable similes of his intricate style. They were all at my house waiting for Strachwitz to arrive from the airport with their idol. While in Berkeley, he was to stay with Sidney and me in a spare bedroom we had. After the concert, he was booked Tuesday thru Thursday at the Cabale. He would be in my care for a fair amount of time and I realized, when Chris helped him out of the car and introduced the two of us, that it would be an unusual task. We were still standing on the front lawn, when he grabbed me firmly by my arm and started demanding: "Liqua, liqua, liqua, can't be no good Reverend widdout da liqua. Pussy pussy pussy. I'm gonna hold you by da arm till I gets some pussy, can't be no good Reverend widdout da pussy." Hiding my laugh, I told him I would see what I could do and guided him into the house where his flock had been patiently waiting.

Reverend Gary Davis

By the end of the day, the Reverend was downing the "liqua" offered to him by his congregation and to their great joy, entertaining them with his guitar. Those who wanted to learn from one of the great masters; studied with bug-eyed intensity every move of his dancing fingers as they ran up and down the guitar's neck. In the early evening, I chased everyone out and put the half conked Reverend to bed so he would have plenty of time to sober up before the concert the next night.

However, by mid morning of the next day, my living room was again packed with his acolytes. When the Reverend got out of bed, he was more than willing to play his guitar in return for free "liqua." He was like a jukebox, put some coins in and it plays, in this case, "liqua" replaced the coins." He liked the attention and seemed able to handle his drinking, so I left the house to take care of some last minute details before the evening's concert. In mid-afternoon, unknown to me, Strachwitz had stopped by to see how the Reverend was faring. He wasn't faring well. He had come outside to get some sun and have a smoke, but when Chris arrived, the Reverend had dropped some of his ashes on the old stuffed chair he was sitting in and it had caught on fire. Chris told me he jumped out of his car and pulled the Reverend, who seemed oblivious to the smoke billowing up around him, to safety. The Reverend thought Chris had gone crazy or something. Safely back in the house, his somewhat stoned admirers, consoled him with a few more swigs of "liqua" and he was soon back playing for them again.

That evening, Reverend Gary Davis opened the show. After Chris led him onto the stage and introduced him to enthusiastic applause, he sat down on a chair and began fumbling with the microphone in front of him. After making redundant adjustments for three or four minutes, he began to incoherently ramble about some perverted sexual fantasy he had. His brain was still addled from all the imbibing he had done all afternoon and the fact that he was blind made him unable to discern the effect he was having on the audience, who sat flummoxed about what was going on.

Meanwhile, outside in the ticket booth, I was stuffed into the small ticket booth next to the entrance with Judy Galpin. Giving her the job was one more attempt to earn her gratitude and get you know what. A few days prior, Debbie had remarked to me that Judy seemed maniac as we watched her violently scrub the counter top in the refreshment room, seemingly indifferent to the fact that she was scraping the skin off her knuckles on the bottom of an overhanging shelf. She asked me what it was I saw in her. Her long blond hair and beautiful body were enough to overshadow any mental defects as far as I was concerned. Anyway, who could really explain the reasons why men are turned on to any particular woman? I had brought along a couple of bottles of Green Death, which I shared with Judy as she sold tickets and in short order we were both pretty soused and indifferent to any one who saw my hands gliding over her sexy body.

As the concert promoter, wasn't it my right? It was sexual harassment, but at the time, that concept had yet to be defined; at least by me.

Jimmy Reed and his band received a rousing ovation as they came on stage. The audience was ready to forgive the Reverend Gary Davis fiasco. It didn't last long. The band began playing a few bars of *"Down in Virginia."* Rather than the bucolic images of *"wind blowing through tall green grass,"* they were treated to music so discordant and out of tune that the audience began yelling: "tune your guitar." Reed seemed unable to recognize that his guitar was not tuned and just kept playing until a near revolt from the audience forced him to stop. His repeated attempts to tune his instrument met with failure. Chris and I surmised, that his prior fall off the stage had impaired him. There was not a happy face to be found when the evening came to an end, despite the fact that the rich white boy, John Hammond, had performed admirably. Years later, in 2011, John Hammond would be inducted into the Blues Hall of Fame, dispelling my silly assumption that a rich white boy couldn't have soul. It was also eventually revealed that Jimmy Reed had suffered from epilepsy since childhood, and his fall the previous week off the stage was due to an unexpected attack.

When I went backstage after the concert was over, I noticed a rotund sweet-faced spade chick having a spirited conversation with him about Jesus and God. As she spoke of heavenly matters, his hands were focused on worldly matters as he irreverently ran them all over her body that made my behavior in the ticket booth look amateurish. Maybe she thought since he was blind, he had to touch her to know where she was, because she didn't seem to mind. She even accompanied him back to the house and into his bedroom where he got the "pussy, pussy, pussy" that he needed to be a good Reverend.

Notwithstanding that we had sold one thousand tickets, my behavior in the booth had not gone unnoticed and Strachwitz and I were no longer welcome to use the Berkeley Community Theatre as a venue. And though Judy Galpin finally let me fuck her a few weeks later after I spent a day painting her apartment, the sex was far from heated. However I did learn one thing from the experience, kissing a woman's ass is not the way to earn her love or her favors. Bobby Neuwurth, who treated most of his women like shit, proved that theory over and over. I was only now beginning to recognize that fawning is not the way to a woman's heart.

Both Strachwitz and I, because of our obsession with traditional blues folk music, had missed the boat with our concert. We were unaware of the power of a revolution in folk music that was underway on the east coast. 'The times they were a changing. Two weeks after our catastrophy, Marianne Pollard, a black woman who frequently promoted concerts in the Bay Area, was on the phone with Manny Greenhill discussing booking Pete Seeger for a small concert in Berkeley. She was told that Seeger was booked: "Why don't you put on Bob Dylan?" whom he also represented. She didn't think Dylan had much of a following on the west coast, but still had her heart set on putting on a concert, so she suggested putting him on at a small auditorium at a local high school. Greenhill laughed, and insisted that if she wanted to book him, it had to be at the large Berkeley Community Center theatre, the same that we had only filled a third. He was persuasive and reluctantly she agreed. The next day, Ralph Gleason put a line at the bottom of his column announcing the Bob Dylan engagement. In three days, all three thousand seats were sold out. Traditional folk music was being supplanted by modern folk music. Performers who sang about present day struggles like those taking place in American ghettos or Vietnam, were, as they should, replacing performers who sang about wrongs of the past.

I was only vaguely acquainted with Dylan and thought of him more as a poet than a musician. I had never been enamored by poetry, even though Seamus Heaney, the eventual Nobel Prize winning Irish poet, packed the house when he played the Cabale and left me with tears in my eyes when he said goodbye, I was years away from appreciating Dylan's significance. The country was in a fever pitch to hear voices that challenged the establishment and the excitement in the air the night Dylan performed in Berkeley was through the roof. Word leaked out that Perry Lederman, who knew Dylan from when they both hung out at Izzy Young's guitar shop in Greenwich Village, was going to bring him by the Cabale after the concert ended. Eyes darted towards the front door every time it opened. When they did show up, Perry introduced us, but after a quick look around he whisked him back out the door and up the street to The Blind Lemon, where they could drink beer and wine. A dozen people dashed out and followed them. When I stopped by, after closing the Cabale, a free for all jam-session was in full bloom. Everyone was plastered and having fun joining Dylan and Perry, as they played non stop twelve bar blues into the night. Even I joined in the fun. Dylan was already well on the way to becoming the voice of the

American civil rights revolution. In simple musical poetry, he expressed the hypocrisy that was making us all so angry.

But I was mired in my own struggle, a need I couldn't verbalize, but knew subconsciously that it dealt with sexuality. I felt no desire to join the mainstream movement that was beginning to take place around me. Truth be told, woman still terrified me.

37

RIDE THE RAILS

"Ride the rails all the way to New York!" How could I say no. Perry Lederman asked me to accompany him to New York, where he hoped to get a record deal with either Folkways or Electra. He planned to travel hobo style, i. e. hopping freights. It was an adventure I couldn't refuse, a chance to fulfill my childhood fantasy. Hopping freights was real Americana; from Steinbeck's "Grapes of Wrath" to Kerouac's "On the Road." Perry had hopped freights before and knew the ropes. We would hitchhike ninety miles north to Roseville, a small town at the base of the Sierras, where trains heading east were assembled, and from that point on, we would travel strictly by rail. We got to Roseville late in the afternoon and were dropped off at a point where the highway was cut into the side of a hill that overlooked the freight yard. After we both donned our backpacks, that had sleeping bags strapped atop, Perry grabbed his guitar case and we scampered across the busy highway and then slid down an embankment that dumped us into the freight yard. Perry warned me that if a yard bull caught us, we could expect a nightstick to be laid aside our heads. So, after scanning the yard and assuring ourselves that it was safe, we gingerly dashed across several rows of empty tracks, towards a line of boxcars that appeared to be in the process of being assembled to leave the yard. A friendly railroad worker was happy to help us out, telling us that as soon as several more cars were added and an engine attached, the train would be moving to Sparks, Nevada. I kept close behind Perry, running along the line of assembled boxcars, looking for one that didn't have its latch sealed. Breaking a seal could put one in jail.

Within minutes we found an unsealed door and slid it back enough to be able to peer inside and make sure the car was void of cargo or hoboes, who might do who knows what. The floor of the car was five feet above ground and after tossing our backpacks in, I gave Perry a foot boost so he could climb inside and then provide me a hand so I could follow. Perry wasted no time in finding a loose scrap of wood left over from a packing crate and placing it on the floor between the door and it's jamb, so in case of a sudden jolt, it couldn't slam shut and trap us inside. I could see that Perry knew his stuff. All the running had left us damp and tired, so using our backpacks as pillows; we lay down on the floor to cool off until the train was ready to roll.

For the next two hours, we lie on the floor in near darkness, while our car jolted back and forth as additional cars were added. Finally, as the sun began to set, we began to roll out. No longer worried that we could be hassled by yard bulls, we peered out the narrow slit left open in the door. Judging by the speed of the cars whizzing by on the adjacent highway, I estimated we were doing about forty-five miles an hour. Within an hour the train began to labor up the steady incline that led across the Sierra Nevada Mountains. Reflected light from a half moon made the distant peaks appear as silhouettes. Monotony and fatigue soon overcame both of us and we fell fast asleep. At some unknown hour, we were awakened by voices up by the engine. The train had made a stop. A peek out of the door revealed that we were taking on fuel and water after the hard climb. The temperature had plunged to near freezing and Perry and I returned to our warm sleeping bags. An hour later we were on the move again, actually rumbling would be more accurate. We were on the downside of the mountain and flying like a bat-out-of-hell going at least sixty or seventy miles an hour.

Bright rays of sunshine came through the crack in the door and nudged us out of our slumber. The train had come to rest in the large freight yard at Sparks, Nevada, just a few miles east of Reno. Sleeping on a hard floor and being bounced around all night had left us both very stiff. Gingerly, Perry got on his stomach and edged his feet out the door until they were close enough to the ground, for him to let go and fall the rest of the way. I passed down the backpacks and his guitar and then climbed out myself. Pointing to tracks near the middle of the yard, a young guy, working nearby switches, told us a train, yet to be assembled, would be heading east late in the afternoon on track seven. It was cool how hospitable railroad workers were to hoboes. It was still early morning and we had lots of time to kill, so we hitched into Reno "America's Biggest Little City in the World."

We had little cash and neither of us had any intention of gambling and leaving Reno destitute. Instead we intended to sate ourselves at the generous buffets provided at rock bottom prices by the casinos, to keep the gamblers near the tables. About two in the afternoon, after pigging out on eggs, sausages and fried chicken, we hitched back to the railroad yard to see if our train had been assembled.

"There it was!" Track seven now had a long row of cars ready to go. Trouble was, only a few of them were boxcars, the others being coal hoppers, gondolas and auto transporters. The few boxcars were all sealed and riding in a filthy coal hopper wasn't an option. The gondolas weren't much better, leaving the auto transporters as the only option. They each had a small platform at their ends, large enough to put down a sleeping bag, but it would mean traveling unprotected from the elements. Acting rashly, we threw our bags on the platform of a transporter that was hooked up behind a refrigerator car. No sooner had we hopped on, a sudden jolt took up the slack between the couplings and we began rolling out of the yard.

The setting western sun painted the small desert hills with a golden rim of light. Unlike the train out of Roseville, this mother began kicking ass. We were situated in the final third of the near hundred-car-long train, and when we went around a long graceful bend in the tracks, I could see that we were being pulled by three powerful diesels. It was exhilarating!

The pleasantly warm desert air turned freezing as the sun dipped behind the hills. But a stroke of serendipity was with us. Exhaust from the continuously running compressors on the refrigerator car poured warm air directly down on the platform where we were sitting. But stops and starts to wait for other trains to clear the track, made progress slow and unpredictable, and by the third day we had only got as far as Green River, Wyoming. At this rate it would be an eternity before we got to New York. Moreover, a friendly yard worker, who was walking by, warned us that aggressive bulls were on the loose. Perry decided it was time to change plans. Slinging our backpacks over our shoulders, and with Perry carrying his guitar, we said goodbye to our train and headed into town. A skin chapping wind whipped across our faces as we trudged across the long steel trestle bridge that ran across the tracks and the river to the outer edge of the small town and its nearby main street.

It was a relief to sit down in a comfortable booth at the little nearby café that sat just a block from the bridge. While I sipped on a cup of piping hot coffee and enjoyed some delicious scrambled eggs, Perry, between bites of toast, engrossed himself in the small local newspaper. He had a smile on his face when he looked up and pointed to what he was looking for—a cheap car. The fact that it was an old Cadillac hearse mattered not—gas was cheap. He phoned the owner who gave us directions to his place, which was only a few blocks from the café. The hearse, when we arrived, was parked in a barren yard cluttered with junk. It looked like it had been sitting there for some time.

The guy wanted five hundred bucks for the old relic, but he was no match for Perry, a Brooklyn Jew, and soon was worked down to let us have it for one hundred fifty. I was thoroughly impressed with Perry's negotiating skills. After paying the guy and getting the papers signed over, we drove a short mile to the mammoth multi-pump gas station on the edge of highway 80, that services all the cross-country truckers. Perry did the pumping, making sure the meter reading fell just between one and two cents, so as to get the extra half-cent of gas for free. By trading turns at the wheel and sleeping in the casket, we arrived in Manhattan two days later.

Perry' s New York friends welcomed him back with enthusiasm. His virtuosity on the guitar had made him quite a legend. One of them was more than happy to let us crash at his loft, just several blocks from Greenwich

Village. The racehorse pace that seemed second nature to New Yorkers was somewhat intimidating to me, so I mostly kept in the background as Perry played court.

The following morning, after Perry dropped off demo tapes with Electra and Folkways records, we stopped in at a nearby studio, where Dylan was recording. I was surprised, and flattered, that he remembered me from the brief introduction I was given in Berkeley.

A scrawny, pimple-faced eighteen-year-old junkie, named, Eddie, was hanging out at the loft when we returned. Perry wanted to say hello to his old friend, Izzy Young, at the Folklore Center and mentioned that we were going to drive into the village. Eddie asked to come along, which was not a problem. Because the hearse was so long, the only place we could find to park was next to a fire hydrant on the corner of Minetta Lane and McDougal, just down from the Folklore Center. Perry averred that New Yorker's were very liberal about parking restrictions. Before visiting the Center, we popped into a drug store on the corner to buy some gum and cigarettes. While Perry and I made our purchases, Eddie wondered down a cramped aisle to the back of the store, apparently to look at some magazines. The Chinaman behind the counter kept a suspicious eye on all of us. It appeared he had no love for the local beatniks, who probably had stolen from him more than once. Perry and I had already left and were walking up the stairs into the Folklore Center, when Eddie came running down the street to join us. Neither of us thought anything of it.

Izzy, in his forties, a bit overweight, slightly balding and bespectacled, was thrilled to see Perry. The two of them were already reminiscing about old times, when Perry was a finger-picking prodigy and Dylan wrote songs in the back room. Suddenly the six Italian street punks, who had been standing outside the drug store when we first pulled up, came running into the store and headed right towards Eddie. Grabbing him by the arm, they began to drag him out onto the street. Edie was resisting and squealing that he hadn't taken anything. I gathered that they were claiming that he had pilfered something from the drug store.

Like the idiot that I still was, I stepped in: "He doesn't have to go anywhere if he doesn't want to."

One of the gang pushed me back: "Stay out of this punk, if you know what's good for you."

The gang, wearing sleeveless wife-beater tee shirts, surrounded Eddy outside on the sidewalk. Evidently they saw themselves as self-appointed enforcers for the neighborhood. There was a lot of tension between the local Italians and the beats, who they considered to be interlopers. Eddie repeated his claims of innocence, even going so far as to empty his pockets. The punks didn't want to hear it and started roughing him up, shoving him to the ground and kicking him several times. It was a scene right out of West Side Story, my favorite musical: except this wasn't about a romance. Perry and I could do nothing but watch as we stood nearby on the sidewalk. It had the makings of a New York street gang fight. After a few kicks to his side, Eddy managed to stumble down the street and out of harm's way.

The gang's leader walked back towards Perry, and after sticking his nose an inch from his face, pushed him in his chest enough to knock him back a few feet. He then moved over to me and just glared. I had given up fist fighting long ago and knife fighting was never in my league. Wrestling with the mantra that a man should be macho, I debated how I should react. Fortunately, because I was quite a bit bigger than the kid, all I got was a sneer. I likely dodged a severe gang beating if I had made a bad choice.

Perry knew how the neighborhood punks thought, and thinking that they probably would be waiting for us when we got back to our hearse, he convinced a cop to accompany us to the corner. Indeed, there they were; lurking around the fire hydrant. The burly cop sized up the situation and began by giving us a stern lecture about being illegally parked by a hydrant. He told Perry he didn't want to see us around there again. This pleased the gang, who snickered and gave us the finger as we drove off. It left me with a good impression about how skillfully that New York cop had handled the whole situation. It was a win-win all the way around. Hats off to him.

Perry returned to Berkeley without a record deal, a trip we made in the hearse in twenty-nine hours by swallowing a bunch of bennies. I felt sorry for him that he had been rejected without much of an explanation, but at least he still owned a hearse. However, on our return, I was to discover I had a more consequential issue to deal with. It had been a year since I had been granted a 1Y deferment. I had begun to think that the draft board had forgotten about me. No such luck. A letter ordered me to report back to the Oakland induction center to be reexamined. The Vietnam War was expanding; more troops being sent into the conflict and more casualties coming out. The government wasn't offering much of a plausible reason for U. S. involvement other than the domino theory—if one Southeast Asian country goes commie; they'll all go commie: one by one. In America, commie was beyond a dirty word, it was the devil incarnate!

Resistance to the draft was growing rapidly. Guys were heading to Canada, skipping out of the country, maybe never able to return. It was better than death or a life without arms or legs or in some cases both. It was better than having a brain that didn't function. To make matters worse, there were news stories showing pictures of young Vietnamese men driving around Saigon on motor scooters as though nothing was going on. Why weren't they in the army? And evidence was mounting that the Tonkin Bay incident, the initial rationale for the war, was a fraud. It all made serving in the military hard to swallow.

Adding to the feeling of being exploited; was the fact that those with political connections seemed to be able to find all sorts of legal means to avoid being drafted. But I wasn't connected, and my only chance was to once again convince them that I was a lost cause. I showed up at the induction center; fucked up and unwashed. Like before, I floated through the tests in a stupor and finally wound up in front of a sergeant who was going over my Q&A test.

"Do you still use marijuana?" he wanted to know.

"Well yeah . . . but I also use LSD sometimes" I mumbled. His eyes lit up.

"You use LSD? . . . WHAT'S IT LIKE??"

His heartfelt interest surprised me.

"It's really cool man. You see all these colors and stuff . . . and the walls move and you see weird shit and stuff . . . It's really cool man."

If I had been able to offer him a cube of Owsley purple right there on the spot, he probably would have taken it. My other answers still reflected my doubts about homosexuality, but that didn't seem to be so much of an issue anymore since gays and straights got shot about the same way. I left the center thinking there was a chance I was going to be classified 1A.

The letter from the draft board arrived a week later. I opened it slowly, afraid of what I was about to see. There it was . . . in bold print. 4F!! I WAS OUT!! Not having to go in the army and be treated like a piece of meat or fucked up in some kind of horrible way was like getting two years added to my life.

I had come to see how society manipulates its citizens. Those in power; political, business and religion, live in their own little world, free to do almost anything they want, and get rich at the same time. I wasn't against war, but it had to be warranted and the burden shared by all. I was no one's pawn, left or right. I saw hatred on both sides of the fence; hatred by the right for those who dodged the draft and hatred by some on the left for the kids who wound up in the military; the ones who weren't smart or lucky enough to have discovered that they were being exploited; kids that had been indoctrinated and caught in an untenable situation; called heroes by people who otherwise wouldn't give them the shit off their toilet paper.

38

BIG MOMMA THORTON ROCKS

Strachwitz stopped by the Cabale and asked me if I wanted to accompany him to Kimball's, a black club in Emeryville, the tough blue-collar town, north of Berkeley. He wanted me to hear Big Momma Thorton. Other than the fact that she was a blues singer, he didn't mention that she was the first to record "Hound Dog" the Lieber and Stoller song later made famous by Elvis Pressley. Chris had called to let the owner of the club know that we were coming, and as owners of a record company and a folk club, we were given VIP treatment and seated at a table just off the stage. While we waited for Big Momma, the club's shake dancer came out from behind a curtain at the back of the stage. She was a sexy looking spade chic with not overly large breasts, but with strong muscular legs. She wore a silver lamé bikini and bra with strands of fringe hanging around the edges. She didn't wear shoes and wasted no time jumping atop our table and straddling Chris's face, where she began gyrating her booty to the beat of the music played by the house band. The fringe tickled Chris's nose and he seemed confused if he should look up or down. The black crowd hooted and hollered with loud appreciation, as Chris's pink white face turned beet red. My eyes bulged out of their sockets while I waited for my turn, which quickly followed. None of the burlesque shows I had attended offered such an intimate experience. I focused on her gyrating crotch and stayed glued there until she jumped off our table and completed her show on the stage. I would have liked to have played with myself, but didn't think it would be a wise thing for a white cat to do in a spade club.

After she left the room, the emcee announced it was time for Big Momma. She was indeed a big woman. Five foot seven and close to two hundred pounds. With one of her large bare arms that protruded from the slit on the side of her moo-moo dress, she grabbed the whole damn microphone, stand and all and bolted out a loud burst of: "You ain't nothin' but a hound dog." The whole place started to rock. Within seconds the dance floor was inundated with couples nasty dancing. There was nothing I had to think about. I went backstage after her performance to ask if she would like to play the Cabale. I knew Debbie would concur. She was slightly nervous about playing a white club, but after I assured her she would be loved, she agreed.

For a full month of Saturdays, she packed the Cabale. The white crowd went crazy over her music, but yet to discover the joy of dancing, stayed in their chairs. So I took it upon myself to loosen things up. I cleared a little space to the side of the stage and then invited a pretty black girl, named Lenore, to dance with me. I was athletic and had no trouble moving my head, shoulders and hips to the music. Lenore and I did the Monkey and the Swim until we were dripping wet. Each week, a few of the less inhibited folkies, joined us; but most just preferred to listen.

That I could dance like a spade, caught the eye of a few girls.

One was the wife of Bobby Neuwirth's best friend, Buzzy Martin. Buzzy was part of the bluegrass crowd and his wife was not a typical long haired folky. But she was a beautiful woman and it caught me totally by surprise when she asked if I would take her and a friend dancing. We had never even talked before. Dancing was a sexual expression and white people had a reputation for being stiff. I had no intention of trying to have sex with her, but that she had found me appealing was a pleasant surprise to me. And telling me afterwards that she had a great time and that I was the first guy from MIT that she liked, was a huge step forward for me.

In April of 1964, Strachwitz recorded: *'Mance Lipscomb Live at the Cabale'* for his Arhoolie label. The engagement came in the midst of the turmoil that would become known as: *'The Free Speech Movement.'* To quell the incipient demonstration, the police had driven a car onto the campus in front of Sproul Hall, but students quickly surrounded it and climbed atop, rendering it incapacitated. Quite a few people from the Cabale were participating. I got the feeling that most were not that clear about what the demonstration was about. It was just cool to go and fuck with the cops. I wasn't very clear myself and had no interest in joining the festivities. The demonstration would go on for several weeks. One of its organizers came to the Cablale to ask me if I thought Mance would agree to join them in a parade down Telegraph Avenue. Knowing Mance, as I now did, I was sure he would agree; even though he would have no idea what the issues were. I told the guy, who I knew was well meaning, that it was not Mance's battle to fight. He was born in 1895 and was now near the end of his life. He should just be allowed to enjoy it as best he could. The guy understood and we left it at that.

The reputation of the Cabale had spread all the way to Philadelphia. It was known as a club that offered a forum for all forms of folk music and the ethnicities that enjoyed them. A black girl named Marsha Hunt, would write in her book, "Hair," that when she came form Philadelphia and walked into the Cabale, she knew: "It was the real thing." I will tell the rest of Marsha's incredible story later in this memoir.

Several months after the Free Speech demonstrations, I was treated to a heart-warming experience that portended hope for the future when it came to civil rights and racial barriers. Being that Lighting Hopkins didn't like to fly, after he finished playing the Cabale, I had driven him down to LA where he was booked to play the famous Ash Grove for a week. Our eight-hour ride together was filled with small talk and sharing sips from the little flask of Apricot brandy that he was never without. It was late in the afternoon by the time we got to LA, and I had a nice little buzz going and Lightning was conked out.

As I passed Dodger center fielder Wally Moon's sports store off to the side of the two lane101 at Cahuenga, I awoke Lightnin' from his slumber so he could give me directions to his cousin's house where he would be staying. It would turn out to be in a predominantly black section of south central LA, known as Watts. His cousin's house was one of the many single story houses with well-kept lawns that lined the street. I parked in front against the curb, and while Lightning took his bags out of the rear seat, I got out to stretch my legs. A white boy with long blond hair was not a common sight in the neighborhood. Suddenly, from down the block, five or six little black kids came running towards us. I thought they were excited to see Lightning but when they began offering me candy bars, I became confused. Lightning just smiled, his big gold tooth gleaming: "They think you're a Beatle," he explained. I couldn't help but marvel how music transcends all racial barriers.

39

A PICARESQUE FOOL DOESN'T IMPRESS ANYONE

Erik Anderson

Debbie had finally given up on Neuwirth, who was spending more time with country singer Toni Brown and going back and forth to New York to hang with Dylan. She had moved on to have a short affair with Cy Koch, a young blond kid who had an infectious smile and was a tremendous guitar and piano player. But that didn't last long. She would later describe him to me as being very weird. I couldn't help being jealous that I wasn't in the loop and became even more envious, when she dumped Koch and moved on to a tall, dark and handsome musician, named Eric Anderson. I had been brought up in an era when "tall, dark and handsome" was every girl's dream man and being that I was blond, still made me feel inferior. Eric had performed regularly at the North Beach café and after performing at one of our Hootenanies, Debbie became smitten by him and insisted that we put him and his group, *'The Snope County Camp Followers'* on the schedule. He was more than likeable, but envy is hard to put aside and it was near impossible for me to appreciate his music, which like Dylan, was contemporary folk.

I began seeing less and less of her and had no idea what she was up to. She was still her usual charming self, so much so, that she had charmed Lenny Bruce to drop by the club and put on an adhoc performance. She, and a few friends had gone to the Hungry I to hear the controversial comedian perform and had been invited to a party afterwards where she got to meet him personally. Like all men, he was attracted to her and showed up the next night at the Cabale after he finished his night's show at the Hungry I. I loved Lenny Bruce. When I read his book, 'How to Talk Dirty and Influence People,' I couldn't put it down. He was known to use heroine, and had been arrested multiple times, not for heroine use, but for using words like "fuck" or "shit" in context like: "What the fuck is this all about" or "who gives a shit?" The harassment only added to his fame.

Only a few stragglers remained when he walked in shortly after midnight. He was half bombed on who knew what, so Debbie quickly took him under her wing and then cajoled him to go on the stage and do a set. Lenny wasn't a performer; he was an event. He was incredible. Ad libbing without any fear of irreverence, he began talking about anything that came into his head. A four by six abstract painting hanging on the wall next to the stage became the focus of his humor. He turned its askew lines and clashing colors into a kaleidoscope of observations about the mental state of the artist and society at large. Everything he said was both brilliant and funny. Very funny! I was laughing so hard I couldn't stay in my chair and wound up on the floor practically hysterical, much like I had done as a kid when I watched Red Skelton or Sid Ceasar. When Ralph Gleason heard of Bruce's unscripted performance in the intimate environs of the Cabale, his next day column bemoaned the fact that he wasn't there. Lenny stayed at Debbie's pad overnight and she didn't say anything about having sex, but rather told me he borrowed her nylons to use as a tourniquet while he shot up in her bathroom.

I was neither laughing or thinking that Debbie was so charming, when a few weeks later she informed me that she had sold her share in the club to my drug smuggling guru, Chan Laughlin. It came as a total surprise. She was moving back to New York to support Eric's career. He had just been signed by Vanguard to do an album. And though I was incapable of admitting it, my reckless drug exploits did not augur a promising future for the Cabale and much less for a woman. Eric was on his way to becoming one of the new wave of social poets. He wasn't Dylan, but he was on the playing field.

Too spaced out to know how insignificant I had become in the Berkeley scene, I was barely shocked, when three weeks later, Carol Peery, a quirky, light skinned, five foot seven, one eyed spade dude from Los Angeles, told me that he and his Jewish girl friend, Elaine, had just purchased Chan's share of the Cabale and were now my new partners. Chan and I had yet to even have a pow wow so the change to another new partner was not a complete surprise. Elaine was Peery's source of money, but there was no doubt he ran the show. That no one seemed to feel obligated to at least tell me they were selling their share, should have upset me, but I was detached from reality and just rolled with it.

Peery's one glass eye had the effect of making it seem as though he was looking everywhere and nowhere at the same time. Nevertheless, his strange, but endearing personality, fit right in at the Cabale. His hand was rarely seen without a cigarette that he held pressed between his ring and fourth finger, so that when he took a drag his entire palm would cover his mouth. That, and the fact that he tilted his head while he inhaled, gave the impression that he was always thinking profound thoughts. It took me a while to realize that the head tilt was so he could aim his good eye at me. Brought up in the rough and tumble streets of LA, he didn't lack for street smarts or confidence, and as usual, I became the club's labor force.

Peery wasted no time in taking over. He wanted to put his stamp on the club and suggested that we change its name to "The Cabale Creamery." Business had begun to wane and we needed something to inject new energy, so if a name change could help, I was all for it. He convinced me that a group he was very close to in Los Angels, 'The Chamber Brothers,' would build our crowds back up. He was right. Their music, perfected during years of singing in the choir of a Mississippian Baptist church, was an amalgam of soul, gospel and folk. Willie and Joe played guitar, George the bass and

Lester the harmonica. Crowds returned to the club and it appeared that my new partnership was going to work out just fine.

Then, on a Tuesday afternoon in December of 1964, while I was at the club doing janitorial work, *'The New Lost City Rambler's'* walked in. I had booked them to play the weekend, so being that they were from New York, I asked why they were in town so early.

"We're booked to play tonight."

I pointed to the schedule calendar posted in the window: "No you're not, you don't start till Friday. I worked this whole thing out with Manny."

Manny Greenhill was their manager and when I had discussed booking the Ramblers with him over the phone, he tried to pawn them off on me for a Tuesday through Thursday gig. I told him I could only pay their guarantee, if they played the weekend. After much debate, he finally agreed and sent me the contract, which I signed and sent back. Mike Seeger took the contract out of his briefcase and handed it to me. It indicated that they were booked Tuesday through Thursday. My dated signature was on the bottom. Seeger told me they had another booking for the weekend.

Greenhill had pulled a fast one. He had agreed to my requested dates over the phone, but being a trusting idiot and shitty businessman, I took him for his word and didn't double check the contract when it arrived in the mail. The Ramblers weren't about to give an inch. Why should they? Because they weren't advertised on the schedule correctly, they played the next three nights to a near empty house. Having to pay their fee erased the gains we had made with the Chamber Brothers. Manny Greenhill was revered in the folk community, having given many artists their starts and supporting liberal political movements, but he was no hero of mine.

Maybe the incident only accelerated the inevitable. Peery approached me a week later and with his head in its typical cocked position, took a long drag from his cigarette before removing his cupped hand away from his mouth to stare at me for a moment with his glass eye before giving me an ultimatum: he and Elaine wanted to buy me out. They would give me fifteen hundred bucks for my share, a thousand now and five hundred three months later. Either I go or they go.

Taking a good look at myself, I knew I wasn't mature enough to run the club on my own. I no longer knew who I was or what my goals were. Debbie was gone, Rolf was gone and after the fiasco at the Berkeley Community

Theatre, I doubted if Strachwitz would want to partner up with me. Even if I wanted to continue with the Cabale, I didn't have the money to buy their half. I had dumped the career that a degree from MIT would have led for a career in the folk music scene and now it was dumping me.

Despite the insanity, I had a lot to be proud of. But unlike Debbie, who was back in New York helping Eric develop his career and unlike Chan Laughlin, who had taken the money that he sold his share of the Cabale for, and morphed himself into Travus T. Hipp (some say the origin of the word hippy), to start another club in Virginia City, Nevada, called the Red Dog Saloon, from which he became a celebrity on Nevada radio that he used to spawn the rave phenomenon; I had no such grandiose plans for myself, and decided to multiply my money with another trip to Mexico.

40

RUBBER GRASS

On a Sunday afternoon, I was approaching San Diego with few thoughts in my head other than how much money I would make after I made my score. Twenty-five hundred bucks seemed reasonable. I had, what I considered to be a foolproof plan to make it impossible to discover the grass I would be bringing across the border. By running it through a sieve, I would clean it of all seeds and twigs and then stash the much reduced volume inside a couple of inner tubes which I would then insert inside the tubeless tires I would be driving on. Any chance of a border agent seeing the stash or getting a whiff would be completely eliminated.

My reverie was interrupted when steam began pouring out from beneath the hood of my Mercury. I motored on and pulled into a Texaco station a few miles down the road, just a few miles short of San Diego. Always the optimist, I hoped I only had a minor problem, but that was not the case. Only one attendant was on duty and was only able to take a quick look under the hood. He told me I had a blown head gasket, and since it was Sunday and he also had to pump gas, the job would take some time. Five hours and eighty bucks later—enough to buy four kilos—I finally crossed the border into Tijuana.

I had hoped to be in Hermosillo by this time, but rather than drive on Mexican highways during the night, I parked my car, and after gulping down a couple of taco's, dropped into one of T. J.'s many stripper bars that were rumored to have the hottest shows in North America. As was my wont, I found a seat at a little table right next to the stage so I wouldn't miss anything. The girls didn't go nude, but they knew how to be raunchy and I was soon mesmerized.

Skin-tight silver mini skirts drove me nuts, and I smiled lasciviously at one girl whose crotch was peeking out just below the hemline. She evidently noticed the effect she was having on me, because when she left the stage, she came directly to my table to ask if I wanted to go upstairs to the balcony with her. I was aware that my baby face branded me as an easy mark, but I wasn't stupid and had no intention of letting her clean me out of my drug money. I could handle myself and mumbled yes. My eyes stayed glued on her swaying ass as I followed her up a flight of stairs to a dark and near empty balcony. She led me to a table near the back, where no sooner had my butt touched the chair, when a couple of drinks were being slapped down on the table by a waitress who magically appeared out of the darkness.

"Would you like to buy me a drink?" my hot stripper friend asked, knowing the answer was yes.

The sexy senorita who had brought me upstairs, began to grind her crotch against my shoulder and shove her cleavage against my face. My brain was now being operated by my dick, and knowing that the waitress would soon be back to sell me more drinks, I stuffed my hand into my pocket so I could quickly give her some Pesos to make her go away and continue to enjoy my hot new grinding friend. It had become irrelevant what the cost of drinks were.

Senorita stripper's crotch was now so close to my nose that I was becoming intoxicated by the alluring perfume she was wearing. She wanted to know my name. I told her: "Howie."

"What's your name?" as if I cared.

"Mimi . . . Mimi for Money" she replied with a little smile on her face. "What a lovely name" I robotically retorted.

While her body continued to grind against me, I tried to maneuver my hand up her mini dress. She was a master at making me feel like I was getting somewhere without actually letting me get anywhere. As the game went on, a steady flow of drinks arrived at our table, forcing me to take momentary breaks from my groping so the waitress could be paid. Becoming a bit more brazen, I got on my knees, and hoping she would spread her legs so I could get to her pussy, began to lick between her thighs. She wouldn't oblige but giggled in such a way that I could see she was enjoying herself, even as she pushed my head away. I also knew that she was working and her job and the charade would continue until I was cleaned out, so after a half hour, I belatedly told her I had to leave.

As I got up from my chair, she surprised the hell out of me: "Why don't you come by at one o'clock when I get off of work?

Smiling, she added: "Sometimes Mimi does it for free."

I was overwhelmed that she found me attractive and told her I would come back. All jacked up and trying to kill time until Mimi got off work, I wandered up and down Main street, dodging the ubiquitous Mexican urchins selling Chiclets and looking into the shops that all sold the same cheap junk. Because of the car problem, I was already down to nine hundred dollars and as my dick began to relax, my mind retook the helm and I wondered how much *Mimi for free* would extract from me by the morning if I shacked up with her. "Hey man, you're in Mexico on business. Don't be a fool!" I went back to my car, jacked off to release the urge, and then drove to the edge of town, where I checked into a small motel.

"Fuck, another car problem?" The thumping sound of a tire going flat broke me out of my ennui as I drove through the monotonous desert just south of Hermosillo.

There was nary a dwelling in sight. After pulling off to the side of the road, I took the jack out from the trunk and after removing the flat tire, went to take out the spare. "Fucking stupid goddamn idiot!" I had failed to make sure the spare was inflated and it was flat. Fortunately I had a hand pump but unfortunately; discovered that no matter how vigorously I pumped, the tire wouldn't inflate. It was tubeless and the inner rim had to be drawn in tightly around the hub before it could hold air. A garage in the States would have put the tire on a machine that would uniformly compress it against the hub, but I wasn't in the States. Where was I going to find a machine out here in the middle of nowhere? I tried standing the tire on edge and using my weight to compress the rim against the hub while at the same time feverishly working the pump with my free hand, but my effort was less than feckless.

I was about to learn a lesson in humility. An old Mexican man, wearing a sombrero that shaded his sun-wrinkled face, came pedaling by on a rickety old bicycle. He stopped a moment to see what I was doing. Seeing my plight, he got off his bike, and without saying a word, took a short rope from the little knapsack that was tied to the back of his bicycle seat. With the rope in hand, he walked over to where I was standing next to my flat spare tire and tied it around its circumference. He then took a small stick that was lying nearby and put it through the loop. After twisting it several times, the rope began to tighten and compress my tire against the rim. A few strokes on the pump and it began to inflate. Man! What ingenuity! Here I was, an American out of MIT, and that simple solution to my problem had alluded me. "Gracias, gracias, mucho gracias" I told him as he rode off without asking anything for saving my ass.

Once in Guadalajara, I checked into a room on the second floor of a modest hotel that was near to where I would again meet up with Jose De La Torres. A short nap reenergized me and I went out on the town in search of another strip joint in hopes of meeting another *'Mimi for Money.'* To my delight, there were many sexy young Mexican girls wearing tight skirts and high heels scurrying around the streets, but to my demise, they were all on the arms of their rotund mothers. I soon realized that because of the Catholic Church's strong influence, abundant places to imbibe alcohol were tolerated, but none that offered strippers. Resigned to that fact, I stopped into one of the joints just to have something to do.

Never more than a college-boy drinker, I was looking bored while sipping a whisky sour, when a young Mexican guy in his mid twenties, came by my table and struck up a conversation with me in English. Since I was on an illicit mission, my radar went up. He told me he had spent time in the States and as we talked, he seemed like an OK guy and I began to relax. We even drank a few shots of Tequila together. That loosened me up quite a bit and when he offered to show me some other clubs, I agreed to follow him. "Maybe he was going to take me to some good strip shows."

But there were none, just clubs that offered drinking and dancing. Since neither of us had a date, we drank and drank and drank. The tasteless Tequila, mixed with orange juice, went down very easily. By the time we got to the third club it was: "fuck the orange juice," and I was downing my tequilas straight. The pleasant buzz pushed my inhibitions to the side and soon I was out on the floor dancing with some of the sexy senoritas that despite dressing hot as hell, were all good Catholic girls.

The next club we hit was too dark to see much, other than I was the only gringo in the place. Shit who cares? High as a kite and with no idea where I was, I shared laughs with my new amigo. I had just finished downing another Tequila, when suddenly my head started swimming. Moments later I was sick-as-a-dog. The room was going round and round and I couldn't maintain my balance. I unsuccessfully tried to grab the table before crashing to the floor. My unknown Mexican friend helped me to my feet. When I regained a bit of composure, he asked me where my hotel was. He called for a cab and accompanied me back. It was a perfect set up to be robbed. After he helped me to my room, I crashed on the bed and became oblivious to the world.

When I came to, I checked my wallet. My drunken stupor hadn't cost me. Nothing was missing or out of place. He could have cleaned me out or done other endless things, most of them bad. Maybe that kind of camaraderie was typical in the Guadalajara club scene, but I couldn't afford to test my luck again. Since my identity and whereabouts had been breached, before hooking up with Jose I relocated to a different hotel. My new Hotel, which was more like a motel, was on the outskirts of central Guadalajara. It's red brick exterior with mortar spilling freely out between the joints, gave it a provincial look. The clean rooms and lobby that had floors of shinny Sautile, was the kind of place a tourist would be inclined to stay. It would appear that I was nothing more than a clean-cut American tourist on vacation. Even better, was that the bathroom window opened out to an atrium landscaped with ferns and tropical plants. The window would provide good ventilation to help remove the scent of marijuana that was sure to be produced while I worked to clean the grass I planned to score. A restaurant on the premises was also convenient.

Jose remembered me from my prior visit and since I was bringing him business, was glad to see me. He remembered that I wasn't one to haggle, and wasted no time manipulating a good deal for himself by telling me grass was a bit scarce and I would have to pay a slightly higher price per kilo than I had before. It didn't matter. I was just happy that the score went much smoother than what had happened on my prior trip. Jose's middleman was a pudgy dark-haired Federale with a mustache, just like you might see in the movies. When we rendezvoused with him outside the city at a little house on the side of the road, he began by asking Jose in Spanish, if I would be willing to smuggle guns into Mexico. That was way out of my league and I turned down the offer. It didn't seem to upset him and we all hopped into Jose's cab and drove to a nearby farm where I bought sixteen kilos of weed, all neatly packaged in cellophane wrapped bricks. Taking my usual paranoiac cautions, I had Jose drop me off a few blocks from my hotel and from there lugged my score back to my room and locked the door so I could start removing seeds and twigs.

Nothing went according to script thereafter. Extracting the seeds and twigs would take three days rather than the one that I had estimated. Even with gloves covering my knuckles to keep them from being rubbed into bloody pulp by the seive's mesh, my hand wound up aching and my fingers cramping. But I had no option than to soldier on. Each day I worked from dawn to midnight. When I woke up, my first task was to wash down all the walls and furniture to remove all the cannabis dust that had settled around the room and any hints of its sweet odor, before the maids came in to change the towels and make my bed. Difficult as it was, by the end of the third day, the sixteen kilos had been reduced to a nice little pile. Through a small slit that I had cut into each of the two inner tubes I had brought along, I carefully spooned every flake inside and then sealed the slits with a rubber patch. Each tube was now puffed up like a soft balloon. After placing the remaining twigs and seeds into a plastic bag and locking them in my leather suitcase, which I planned to discard somewhere along the road before I crossed the border, I was ready to leave town. When I got to Hermosillo I would insert the grass-stuffed tubes inside my tires. From there it was less than a hundred miles from the border so my drive on the unnaturally filled tires would be minimal. Once over the border, I would remove the tires and take the tubes out.

I was quite relaxed when I arrived in Hermosillo, a town that seemed to always be warm and pleasant. After a few trips around its side streets, I found a perfect location to insert the tubes. A garage, located on a sparsely populated side street, was just a block from a place along the curb where I could dismount and remount my tires without raising suspicion.

I hadn't discarded the seeds and twigs yet, so I drove a mile north out of town where I spotted a deep arroyo adjacent to the highway. Quickly pulling over to the side and taking a quick glance to make sure there were no unwanted eyes, I heaved the suitcase as far as I could into the gulch. It tumbled several times before coming to rest near the bottom under a large cactus. It would be unlikely that it would ever be discovered and if it were, I would be long gone from Mexico.

A seemingly innocuous one-story office building sat about twenty-five yards back from the curb where I planned to do my work. The lawn in front of the building was mowed, but yellow from the lack of water. The shades in its front windows were drawn and if anyone was inside, I couldn't tell, but it appeared that no one was at home. It took less than five minutes to remove the first tire and I rolled it to the garage. Several men were busy working just inside its large open entry door. I hadn't counted on anybody, including the manager, being unable to speak a word of English. Without the ability to communicate, it proved impossible for me to explain that I just wanted the inner circumference of the tire pulled to the outside of the hub. They looked at me as though I was loco. *"Esso bueno, esso bueno."* The tire is perfectly good. Why would I want to break the seal? My pleading was futile. The manager was not about to do something he considered to be stupid. He had a point but that didn't do me much good.

Now seriously frustrated, I rolled the tire out of the garage and back to my car where I took out the few tools I had in my trunk and attempted to pop the rim over the hub by myself. I was sweating like a pig as I wrestled with it. The white, 'establishment' dress shirt that I was wearing had become soaking wet. Then I heard a voice: "Do you need some help?" I looked up and saw a man standing above me on the curb. Since there were no students around, I hadn't realized that I was parked in front of a school. The man explained that he was a teacher and had seen my struggles from his office and came out to see if he could be of assistance. After I explained my inability to communicate to the mechanic about what I needed done, without asking further questions, he accompanied me back to the garage and conveyed my request to the mechanic in Spanish. The mechanic shook his head; showing that as far as he was concerned, I was a crazy gringo, but did what was asked. After profusely thanking my benefactor, who luckily didn't ask for a cover story about what I was doing because I didn't have one, he returned to the school and I was back in business. Innovative methods of drug smuggling weren't that common, and the idea of an angelic baby-faced American making smuggling preparations in broad daylight in front of his school, probably never crossed his mind.

In the next hour, I made several trips back and forth to the garage, and soon I had two tires loaded with grass mounted on my front axle. All that remained was to drive north and cross the border. I would do that just before the sun set. It would look more normal; a young tourist returning from a few days of fun in Mexico. On the way out of Hermosillo, I took a quick glance at the arroyo where I had ditched the "never to be discovered" suitcase and was shocked to see a crowd of about twenty Mexicans congregated below. They were excited by the strange discovery someone had just made. I consoled myself that I would be far across the border if by any wild stretch of the imagination, it could somehow be connected to me.

The border crossing at Nogales went without a hitch. Although there was slight bumping in the front tires, there didn't seem to be any major problem and I began to think: "Why take the tubes out and risk exposure if by chance I get stopped for a traffic ticket or have some mishap?" There was no good reason that I could think of and I decided to continue on to Berkeley without a stop.

At ten P. M, a cold damp fog hung over the freeway as I drove through Los Angeles on U. S. 101. I had been smoking cigarettes like a fiend to calm my nerves. My mouth felt rancid and vile and my gums ached. I had been trying to stop smoking for months, even having a bit of success when I smoked an unlit cigarette for three weeks. But I was now back to two or three packs a day. I knew part of the addiction was just a ritual; having something to put into your mouth or to point at someone to create a barrier and keep them at bay, a security blanket of sorts. Suddenly, after a spate of uncontrolled coughing, I had an epiphany: "What the fuck are you doing?" I put the cigarette out and tossed it and the rest of the pack out the window right in the middle of the Hollywood Freeway. My mind was clear and resolved. The wretched habit had just been defenestrated into the smoggy LA night. Smoking a joint was different, it gave you a high, but cigarettes just fucked you up. Goodbye and good riddance!

"Holy fuck!!!" Horrified isn't enough to describe my face. Sidney just smirked and Dave Cleveland didn't know what to say. He had come by at ten in the morning to the cute little house on the north end of Berkeley where Sidney and I now resided, to help remove the tubes from the tires. I had gotten back to town in the wee hours and could do nothing but crash until the morning. We were all looking at a fine dark green powder with a few marble-sized hard balls mixed in. My vision of how the grass would react inside the tire was beyond stupid. No wonder I left MIT. Rather than rotate in sync with the circumference of the tire, the grass resisted movement and was slowly ground up by the rotating wheel. Sixteen kilos was now a small bucket of marijuana sand and a few hard little marijuana marbles. We just looked at each other; it was not a time for words.

The grass was so fine, that if rolled into a joint, it fell out like sand in an hourglass. The only way it could be smoked was in a hashish pipe. But that proved to have problems as well. Not only was it difficult to light, but, because microscopic specs of the inner tube had rubbed off while the grass rotated inside, it had a rubber taste. What a goddamn disaster!

Over the next few days I pondered how I could pedal my 'rubber grass.' While having a cup of coffee at the Mediterranean café, I ran into a New York junkie named Rick who used to come by the Cabale once in awhile. His pock-marked-ashen face endowed him with a certain street-wise wisdom when it came to drugs. He was what could be called a functioning junkie. I mentioned that I was trying to find a way I could market my 'rubber grass.' He offered to come by my pad to take a look at it. As we smoked a bowlful in a little toke pipe, he picked up one of the little balls and rolled it between his fingers.

"Why don't you tell people its Egyptian hash?" he suggested. "Egyptian hash?" I had never heard of it.

"Yeah man, those little round balls look just like Egyptian hash."

Junkies would screw anyone and it took a junkie's mind to come up with such a cool idea. I immediately started spreading the word that I had Egyptian hash for sale. A day later, Greek George told me he had a potential buyer he could introduce me to if I would give him a piece of the action. That was a no brainer and I told him to make arrangements for me to meet the guy.

The next day I arrived at George's apartment an hour before the buyer was due. I needed time to prepare the deception that would aid in making the sale. The buyer would want to have a little taste of the merchandise before making a score, so I took steps to make sure he would be impressed. Even though I no longer smoked cigarettes, I would have a pack of Camels available in my shirt pocket. One of the cigarettes would be a setup in which a pinch of tobacco had been removed from its tip so some good strong pot could be put inside and then covered with a bit of tobacco so the cigarette would look normal again. I placed it back in the pack in a position where I would know exactly where it was. George and I then chatted while we waited for the buyer to arrive.

He was a UC Berkeley student and brought his girlfriend along to impress her how hip he was. We all sat around a coffee table in the living room; George and I on the couch, and the student and his girl friend on the floor. I placed an assortment of various sized balls of Egyptian hash atop the table so they could be inspected. Mimicking the slow cool cadence of Rick the junkie, I pointed to several of the little balls and bragged what great shit it was. He picked up one of the medium sized balls and began inspecting it, remarking that it indeed looked like good Egyptian hash. As I suggested we take a taste and prove his point, I pulled out a single edged razor blade to shave a few flakes from one of the balls onto a sheet of paper. I knew it was what he expected. Taking the spiked cigarette from my pocket, I calmly removed the pinch of tobacco from its tip that covered the loaded potent grass beneath and after folding the paper that I had shaved the flakes of Egyptian hash onto, placed it over the cigarette and with gentle taps of my finger, nudged them down the chute until the valuable hash filled the cigarette. A twist of its tip and a quick moistening in my mouth, made it ready to light.

It was Showtime. A little smile let him know how lucky he was. While my left hand was occupied with the joint, I used the trick I had learned from my former neighbor, Doyle Foreman, and used my free hand to pull a book of matches from my pocket and as though I were a magician, opened its cover and bent one of the matches down against the striking pad and drew it sharply across the pad with my thumb. Their eyes lit up in awe as the match ignited. After taking a quick toke, I passed the spiked joint to my anxious buyer.

"You sure can tell the difference between pot and hash," he remarked as he glanced between me and his girl friend who was looking thoroughly impressed with his streetwise knowledge. He handed her the joint so she could see what he was talking about, and after George took a toke it came back to me for one last draw.

"Yeah man, good shit huh?" I uttered as I began to feel the effects of the imbedded strong pot I was holding in my lungs.

The kid bought the largest ball for a hundred bucks, but the other balls were so small that I was unable to find any other buyers. Someone who had just returned from Boston, where Rolf Cahn was now living, told me that because the chemicals used to bleach cigarette papers were loaded with toxins, Rolf was advocating smoking pot only in pipes. I placed a call to him to tell him about the pot I had for sale. "It was perfect for pipe smoking." I described how it had become pulverized; leaving out that it had a mild rubber taste which I didn't think was that big of a deal. When I told him he could have all sixteen kilos for three hundred bucks, all he wanted to know was how quickly I could get to Boston. I told him I would make the delivery within ten days.

There was not much in Berkeley that I liked anymore. Drawn by the lure of pot and *'free love,'* bikers had moved onto Telegraph Avenue; giving the once friendly street a mean demeanor. Drug use was becoming excessive. I still enjoyed light use of grass to heighten mental awareness, but with the availability of brands like Thai Stick and Panamanian Red, that almost knocked you out after one toke, it was becoming too powerful for my tastes. I had no regrets that I had experimented with LSD, but had done so very carefully, only taking a light 75 microgram dose. Recently, Perry Lederman had been boasting about taking five hundred micrograms a week. That was crazy. He looked like his brain was fried the last time I saw him, so I assumed the rumor was true. It was an ominous portent for the future and, at least for me, Berkeley had lost its luster.

Before leaving, I tried to collect the five hundred bucks Carol Perry still owed me for the Cabale, but business had been slow and it was obvious he had no intention of paying me. So without regret, I took my few belongings, including an electric guitar that I had purchased from Willie Chambers, and split town. A manila envelope full of the rubber grass was stashed in the bottom of the spare tire well, well hidden by the tire resting on top. With a dozen bennies that Clarence Van Hook had given me in my shirt pocket, I passed the co-op on the corner of Ashworth and Telegraph that I still had never entered because of my fear of becoming a commie, and began what I planned to be, a nonstop drive to Boston.

By the second night, the bennies were playing tricks with my mind. Every time I went around a corner or over a small hill, I found myself pumping the brakes to avoid running into one of the trucks that loomed directly in front of me. They were just phantoms, illusions brought on by the bennies doing tricks with my mind. At ten at night, I was wired and jittery as I drove the last few miles of my trip through Rhode Island. The gas gauge was bumping empty, so I pulled off at an exit road hoping to find an open station. I passed beneath a railroad overpass and thought for a moment that I was heading into a forest area, when to my relief, I saw an open gas station nestled among the trees. It was a cold dark damp night and I shivered as I filled my tank. After refueling, not quite sure where the on-ramp was, I headed slowly back up the road. About to reenter the highway just after passing beneath the railroad overpass, my rear window lit up with flashing red lights. It was the fucking cops! "Christ!" Rhode Island was a state known to hand out forty-year sentences for possession of marijuana!

"Shit! Just be calm," I told myself.

Because fumes from the engine leaked into my car, I had been keeping the windows open. The gusts of cold air that shot across my face had helped to keep me awake, but also made me shiver. I just sat quietly while I waited for the cops to arrive. After giving me a once over with a flashlight, the first cop to arrive asked to see my license and then without saying anything, disappeared back to his patrol car. His partner stood silently outside my passenger door. The flashing red lights made it possible for me to see in my rear view mirror that the cop who had left with my license was on his phone checking my I. D.A few minutes later he returned, and after shinning his flashlight in my face, began asking questions.

"Where are you going?"

"Up to Boston. I'm visiting friends there." "Would you mind stepping out of your car?"

I got out, not sure what was going to happen. I had to act cool despite the fact that I was shaking from the cold, the bennies and fear.

"You were driving erratically. Have you been drinking?" "No."

He couldn't help but notice that I shook. "Why are you so nervous?"

"I've been driving for three days. I guess my nerves are just shot."

"Do you mind if we look in your trunk?"

I fucking well did mind but I didn't dare say so. "No, not at all."

I opened the trunk. They started looking around, but not seeing anything suspicious, allowed me to close the hood. My sweet innocent looking baby face did nothing to hurt my cause!

"There's been gun smuggling going on around here, that's why we're checking. OK, you can go on. Try to drive better."

"Thank you officer. I'll do that."

41

DO YOU JUST BLOW ON IT?

It was a little past midnight when I got to Boston and I knew that being MIT men, some of the brothers at my former fraternity would still be up studying. So hoping they had a bed for Delta 576, I stopped in. A few of the brothers who had been freshman when I left, were now seniors and leaving out any mention of drug dealing, I easily fascinated them with a few stories about my rebellious life style in Berkeley. They were more than happy to reward me with a bed.

The next morning I got in touch with Rolf, who was pleased to hear that I was in town. Being sure to avoid any mention of the words grass or pot in case the phones were being tapped, I assured him I had brought the merchandise. A half-hour later I was at his pad just off of Harvard Square. Garrulous as always, he grabbed his hash pipe and filled the bowl to the top, all the while expounding how much healthier it was to smoke pot from a pipe. After a few tokes, a look of satisfaction crossed his face. He didn't seem to mind the feint taste of rubber and paid me the three hundred bucks that we had agreed upon. I was quite the businessman, only losing seventy percent of what I had sold the Cabale for.

The three hundred bucks would have to do me until I found some kind of work. When I drove over to Pembroke Street to say hi to Bernie Goldhirsh, I found that appearance wise he hadn't changed much, still wearing sandals and shorts and sporting a floppy mop of black hair that looked like it had been styled with a soup bowl. But his appearance was misleading. By selling the lesser of his two townhouses, and using the profit to both restore the one he still owned, and launch his first magazine, Sailboat Directory, he was well on his way to building a publishing empire that would become one of the biggest in America. Sailboat Directory was only a catalogue of virtually every mass marketed sailboat available to consumers, but its immediate success was propelling him towards much bigger things. In contrast, I had no goal and was being propelled to nowhere but had no doubt that I would not stay there.

I saw an opportunity for myself. He still had lots of work to do in his townhouse and I offered to do some of it in exchange for lodging. It would allow him to devote all his time to his publication. He had plenty of spare room and liked the idea. The townhouse had three stories above street level and three basements below. I moved into the upper basement apartment. Below me lived a dour family of three that Bernie referred to as the mole people and below them a single man who had the gross habit of not reporting when his toilet overflowed, preferring to wade around in ankle deep water for a day or so. He was known as submole man.

For the time being I was set. A skid row diner five blocks north on Tremont Street offered home cooked meals for a buck fifty and a little ten inch black and white TV, which I shamelessly lifted off the desk of one of the fraternity's freshman who had carelessly left it sitting next to an open alley window at the annex, provided me entertainment during the evenings. I rationalized that I was doing the student a favor by keeping him from wasting his time watching television.

Due to the fact that the city's powerbrokers wanted to redevelop Scollay Square, my beloved Old Howard was no longer. To get their way, they snuck someone into a show during a performance by Irma the Body, whose real name was Irma Goodneighbor, and filmed her with a 16mm movie camera doing some nasty stuff while the red light was off. That was enough to have the theatre closed down and while efforts were being made to preserve it as an historic site, it mysteriously; "ha ha," burned down. Adult entertainment in Boston was now only to be found on Washington Street in a section known as the "war zone." The erotic shows that could be seen at the Old Howard were replaced by all night movie houses that showed triple features of nudist camp films. Several Go Go and Bikini bars promised amazing sexual thrills in a back room if you were willing to shell out forty bucks for a bottle of champagne. I was sure that it was a hustle and couldn't afford it anyway, nor could I afford any of the five or six hookers who worked the corner of Washington and Copley late at night. My sex life was now seriously stressed.

Bernie wasn't the only hip entrepreneur who saw a future in South End real estate. Being liberal didn't preclude making money and quite a few artists had bought townhouses in the area and were rehabbing them. Many of them would stop by each evening to congregate around Bernie's long English dining room table to sit in high back chairs and smoke pot, drink wine and have conversation. They were all talented and interesting people: Allen West, a gangly trust fund baby, specialized in large abstract paintings, Richard Stroud, a handsome powerfully built light skinned black man, was a master sculptor, John Ashworth was a modernist who painted multicolored narrow straight lines on very large canvases and Jeff Spence, who, if not for his pot-belly, could pass for James Dean, was a master painter. Also included was an ex school teacher who suffered from schizophrenia but was nevertheless extremely intelligent and Al McGoo, whose balding head, stocky build and psychotic eyes, made his living by rummaging during the wee hours of the night through abandoned buildings around the area.

Much of the conversation concerned the Vietnam War. All agreed it was mindless and avoiding the draft was imperative. Bernie, had gone to a shrink known to be sympathetic to draft evaders and as they talked, he took from his briefcase a toothbrush he had invented; its handle was a pressurized hollow tube filled with toothpaste that would ooze a dab onto the bristles when a small button was pushed. "That's it" the shrink exclaimed, "Men like you should be home thinking and not fighting," and wrote him out a special 4W deferment given to those who were making important alternate contributions to the national welfare. We were all having a good laugh when someone asked if anyone had tried the 'rubber grass' that was floating around town. I thought it best to stay silent about my involvement with that.

After a few months, my usefulness to Bernie began to dwindle, as did the money I had made from the rubber grass deal. Thankfully, Jeff Spence offered to let me partner up with him doing small carpentry jobs around the area. It not only provided me money for food, but enough to rent a basement room at Stroud's house, just one street over from Pembroke. Jeff and I were both novice carpenters and sometimes got fired for doing lousy work, but our skewed senses of humor led to us becoming close friends.

Getting laid in Boston wasn't anywhere as easy as it had been in Berkeley. No longer a club owner, I was just some wild looking dude living in Stroud's basement apartment. An opportunity arose when one of the delightfully cute twin sisters who lived two doors up the street from Bernie's place, let it be known that she was interested in me. Her twin already had sex, but she was still a virgin. Recalling the trouble I had staying hard with the virgin bar maid who visited me before I finally got laid, I couldn't help being anxious and tried to make myself extra horny by paging through a skin magazine while I waited for her to arrive. Because she was at home excessively washing herself to make sure she didn't smell dirty, she showed up over two hours late. I understood her fear; society goes out of its way to make girls feel that way, but I spent my load on one of the magazine's fantasy girls and had nothing left when she arrived. Trying to explain that to a virgin who had no clue how the male physiology worked, was futile and she left the room feeling rejected and disappointed and me feeling like a worthless shit. Virgins were not going to be my thing.

My best sexual experiences had been with girls who were anything but and the vision of Bridgitte Bardot with long blond hair and pert breasts posing near naked on a movie set wearing nothing but a 'cache sexe' had become my idea of the perfect woman. I was killing time at Bernie's townhouse, listening to Al McGoon give a detailed description of the booty he had uncovered the previous night and not wanting to take any chance to make him angry, I was feigning interest when Bernie came bursting into the room, excitedly proclaiming that he had just found me "my perfect girl!" He had been at the Boston Museum Art School taking a class in drawing the human figure—his way of admiring the female body—when just as he was about to leave the campus, he spotted a nymph like beauty with long blond hair strolling across the campus lawn. Knowing that was the image of the ideal female that I had described to him; he ran after her and with elfin-like enthusiasm, managed to extract her name and phone number, which he now handed to me.

Her name was Rita Fogelis. It took me a few days to build up enough courage to call her, but after Bernie's heroic effort, I had no choice. She worked at Mass General in a lab and agreed to meet me over a cup of coffee at the hospital's cafeteria. She asked that I wait outside the lab until she could join me. When I saw a young nymphette with small features, long blond hair, rosy cheeks and laughing eyes that peeked out from beneath her bangs dressed in a lab coat, I knew it had to be her.

She looked like a loveable little kitten hiding beneath a bed. Our mutual shyness gave neither of us a reason to be intimidated and we began to date frequently.

Her parents were Latvian immigrants, but her father had died a few years earlier and she now lived in a second floor flat in Dorchester with her mother, whom she affectionately and aptly called Tubby. Though her mother suspected that I was a ne'er-do-well, she tolerated me—though with indifference.

Rita was still a virgin, and considering my less than stellar record with uninitiated females, I didn't push her. Most of our dates were typical; movies or a dinner, but some were special like attending a Mom's Mabley concert to celebrate the recent civil rights victories in the Supreme Court. Little Richard and The Coasters were the featured acts. Only a few specks of white faces were among the black audience. I was aware that blacks had little tolerance for homosexuality and found it ironic that most of the crowd had no clue that when Little Richard came sashaying onto the stage in a gaudy effeminate costume, that he was gay. Mom's Mabley ended the concert by telling the crowd; "Now that you have your civil rights, its time to use them."

Rita and I were frequently asked by Bernie to go sailing. On one particular day trip, we were forced to anchor at a private yacht club when a sudden storm blew in. Water was coming in over the sides and we needed shelter. The stuffy yacht club only belatedly allowed him to tie up to one of their buoys until the storm blew over. The experience was Bernie's motivation for starting Sail Magazine, as a poor man's option to "Yachting," which was geared to appeal to the super rich.

As the sixties era began, having sex before marriage, was more than just for the pleasure. It was certainly that, but couples also wanted to know they were compatible in bed before making a serious legal commitment. This was not the case with Rita. We had not done anything even close to having sex, least of all spending a night together. I was becoming frustrated. I didn't fault her for avoiding sex; attitudes about it were unsettled at best.

When Bernie asked us to join him in sailing a small yacht from Cape Cod to Boston, meaning that we would be thrust into an intimate situation, I saw it as my best opportunity to loosen her up. The night voyage across Cape Cod Bay would be a romantic adventure and I looked forward to it.

Bernie also had his 'dream girl," a sexy Jewish spitfire named, Phyllis Santos, but she had recently and unceremoniously dumped him for a successful heroine dealer who she was living with in a luxurious high-rise pad overlooking the Boston wharf. Thinking Bernie could use some company, Rita offered to ask one of her Latvian girl friends to join us for the sailing trip. He loved the idea.

Tanya was a gorgeous strawberry blond with the kind of soft body that begged to be pawed. A fun loving girl, she offered to drive the four of us to the Cape in her red convertible. After the sail, Bernie would drive her back to retrieve her car. As Rita and I sat quietly in the back seat, she and Bernie laughed and joked all the way to the Cape, portending the good time that they were about to share. Once at the Cape, we settled on a deserted windswept stretch of beach among some grassy dunes, to spend the day before the evening's sail.

I removed my pants and shirt and gave everyone a moment to react to the small black bikini I was wearing. It was the same one I had purchased from a gay oriented store in San Francisco, but this was Boston and I wasn't sure how it would be looked upon. I knew my thin body looked good and didn't care that it was outré and shocking; it made me feel sexy. Rita seemed to like it. She then surprised the hell out of me, when after disappearing behind the dune to change into her swimsuit, she reappeared in an Itsy bitsy teeny-weeny polka dot bikini; just like the one described in the hit song by Brian Holland. She looked like a little Bridget Bardot and it made me hot. An American girl wearing a bikini was quite bold. Things were beginning to look promising. After we all got a bit tipsy on a couple of bottles of wine, Bernie and Tanya started making out, so I took Rita by the hand and led her behind a nearby dune where we could be by ourselves.

We placed a large towel against the slope of the dune just above its base so we wouldn't have to lay completely flat and could enjoy the views of the oncoming waves. She looked sensual, but apprehensive. I began kissing her on her neck and ears and slowly worked my way down her thin tanned body until my head was by her bikini bottom. Edging my head between her legs,

I pulled the bikini's crotch to the side and began sucking on her pussy. She didn't resist. Nor did she moan or move to show that she was enjoying what I was doing to her. But she let me continue. This was good.

Noticing how much I was enjoying myself she asked, somewhat in disbelief: "You really like doing that . . . huh?"

"Yeah it tastes nice" I assured her as I continued sucking away.

My body was glistening from the sun induced perspiration and my dick had hardened enough that I had to furtively move it to the side to give it room to expand. She couldn't help but notice how she was exciting me and nature's powerful sexual forces began to unleash her from the societal restraints that heretofore had kept her captive. She reached beneath my bikini and pulled my hardened dick out so she could fondle it.

"What am I supposed to do?" she asked with sincere honesty. "Just put it in your mouth and suck on it."

"I'm not supposed to blow on it?"

In an age of sexual naiveté, it was an honest question.

"No, you suck on it. It's just called a blowjob. You don't really blow."
"Ahem" came from ten yards away.

It was Tanya peeking around the side of the dune. She had a pleasant smile on her face that showed she was pleased to see what we were up to; but told us that Bernie wanted to leave so we could make preparations for the sailing trip.

A short time later I was pulling hard on the halyard to raise the mainsail of the forty-foot yawl that we would be sailing across the bay. A light breeze began to fill the sail and under a clear black sky, dotted with millions of stars, we began to move out into the open sea. An hour later the wind died and we were locked in irons. Without wind there was no sailing to do, so Bernie took Tanya below and the sounds of sexual rustlings were soon to be heard. Rita had several hours to sober up and think about how close she had come to losing her virginity. Her fear of sexual intimacy returned and she rebuffed my advances. When Bernie and Tanya came back on deck, the satisfied smiles on their faces made my mood even sulkier. Having to finish the trip under motor power, because of a lack of wind, was the appropriate metaphor for the evening.

Rita and I still continued to date. She was my first serious girl friend, or at least I thought so. Be that as it may, I wasn't interested in getting married and she wasn't into sex so why was I hanging around Boston? I didn't have a good answer. Equally disconcerting was that I still had no direction as to where my life was going. Out of MIT, out of the Cabale and a financial bust as a marijuana smuggler, I began to seriously consider a proposal Bernie had made to me.

42

THE BIG FOX

He was well on his way to a career in publishing and was now contemplating starting a business in sailboat manufacturing, more specifically, trimarans. A few years earlier, he had built a twenty-footer out of plywood and loved the fact that it was fast and stable. He speculated that a mass-produced twelve-foot trimaran made out of fiberglass that could be poured from a single mold, could be a market success. It would have great appeal for people who were only into day sailing and wanted something that was easy to sail and difficult to capsize and most importantly; inexpensive.

The father of the modern trimaran was Arthur Piver, who lived in Mill Valley, California. I had already begun to toy with the idea of boat building, going so far as to read a text on the subject. The fact that I didn't really like sailing, finding the best part of the trip to be pulling up to the wharf, didn't get in the way of my reasoning. Bernie suggested that I travel to California to see what I could learn from Piver, and if things panned out, we could go into business together building twelve-foot trimarans. Half lured by the idea of Bernie's business offer and half by the lure of the road, I found myself standing at the edge of Cambridge with my thumb out looking to catch a ride heading west. Bernie had given me a few hundred dollars to cover my basics during the trip.

Halfway down the Mass Turnpike, I decided to make a little adjustment to my plans to help answer a question that had long been bugging me. What was my real birth father like? Was I a chip off the old block or someone completely different? I had heard nothing from him or his side of the family since the incident at Fort Knox. A side trip to Milwaukee could clear up those questions. Two days after leaving Boston, I was outside of Chicago, standing in a noisy section of grass that sat in the midst of a cloverleaf intersection. Cars traveling in every direction, sped around me. My last ride had dropped me off in this hectic lea, and as it was already dark, not wanting to chance being killed crossing the lanes of traffic at night, I tossed my sleeping bag on the ground and slept sound as a baby until the morning.

The labyrinth of twisting expressway roads, none of which I had any clue as to where they led, was not a reasonable place to hitch a ride, so after getting across the expressway during a lull in traffic, I hiked a short distance to where I could catch a bus into the city. Eventually I made my way to Chicago's behemoth Union Station, where I purchased a one-way ticket to Milwaukee.

The tracks of the Milwaukee road faded into infinity and the metropolis of Chicago quickly disappeared under the horizon as I peered out the back window of the Hiawatha's club car. I had little time to have second thoughts about what I was doing, since the hundred-mile trip would be completed in less than two hours. Moments after arriving at Milwaukee's Union station, I was in a telephone booth looking for a Dittman listed in Wauwautosa. I came across only one; an Edward Dittman. Could that be my father's brother? I placed a call to the number and was almost not sure what to say when someone answered:

"Hello, Dis iss Eddie Dittman."

His voice was high pitched with a German accent—a good sign. "Hello, I'm not sure if this is the right number or not. I'm looking for a Howard Dittman."

"Howard Dittman doesn't live in Milwaukee anymore, but I'm his brother Eddie."

Damned if it wasn't the uncle Eddie who used to sit me on his knee and tell me ghost stories when I lived with Grandma Dittman. I told him I was Howard Dittman's son, Howard. He was shocked.

"Little Howie?" "Yaah, that's me."

I had always wondered why people asked me where I was from as if I wasn't an American. But hearing Eddie talk made me realize that it was the way I pronounced "yeah." I pronounced the word drawn out as "yaaah" the way a German would. Already I was learning something about myself.

I told him I was in Milwaukee at the train station, and without hesitation, he offered to pick me up. Within an hour I was at his home. He was a bit of an odd character, but had a heart of gold. Both he and his wife, Mary, who loved to talk, were overjoyed to see me. I was getting celebrity status and couldn't help but think that my arrival was the most exciting thing that had happened to them in decades.

Being around my relatives was comfortable; like coming home. I reminded Eddie how he used to sit me on his knee and tell me ghost stories when he stopped in at grandma's house. He then repeated the one about the train being driven by skeletons, that used to make me hide my head under the covers when I went to bed. When I asked about my grandparents, he said with a very slow cadence and macabre timbre in his voice: "Grandpa died several years ago and grandma's grave is waiting for her right next to him."

There was more to his fascination with ghost stories than met the eye, but I wasn't there to psychoanalyze him. He hadn't heard from my father for many years, but told me my grandmother may still be in touch with him. She was in a home for the aged located just outside Chicago. "We will all drive down there tomorrow. She will be thrilled to see you," he exclaimed.

The next morning, before we left to see grandma, he drove me by their old house in Wauwatosa where I had spent so much time when I was little. It was exactly as I had remembered except for one feature: it had shrunk in size by at least seventy-five percent. What had seemed to my young eyes to be a large mansion, was actually a modest middle class mid-western home. The two huge vases that sat like sentries at the front door, were only two feet tall. The long walkway was only a few steps before it reached the house. One window on each side of the front door was the extent of the visage. A small window on the second floor was the room where I romped in my crib while wearing my grandmother's silk slip. Without going to see the backyard, I could see from the street that it was quite modest. The grandiose existence of my youth had just come down several notches.

Taking two lane country roads, we snailed our way to Chicago at twenty-five miles an hour—the speed uncle Eddie felt comfortable maintaining. Aunt Mary kept us entertained with idle chatter for the entire four hour trip, only breaking long enough for uncle Eddie to tell me about his idea to build mini-Cadillacs—an idea I laughed about to myself at the time but maybe I shouldn't have—fifty years later they came into vogue.

The home for the aged where grandma Dittman was being kept, was a few single storied dormitories nestled comfortably under large elm trees surrounded by large fields of yellow wheat. A few scattered farmhouses could be seen in the distance. It was a warehouse for people nearing death and made me feel queasy.

Grandma's room was near the end of the hall where she was lying in a bed half asleep as we walked in. She had little energy and it was obvious she didn't have a long time to live. As I stood in front of her, flanked by my uncle and aunt, Eddie blurted out:

"You're never going to guess who this is. This is Howard's son . . . Howard!"

She looked at me with eyes that didn't really see. After a moments silence she said to me in a voice that had lost its strength from age:

"I don't remember you . . . all I remember is little Howie."

"This is little Howie!" my uncle excitedly blurted out as he held my arm to put me on display.

"I don't remember you . . . I just remember little Howie" she feebly repeated. "This is little Howie, he's big now!!" Eddie yelled.

He told her I was looking to find my father Howard. Did she know where he was? Still unable to acknowledge that I was the long lost "little Howie" she volunteered that she had gotten some letters from my father who was in Los Angeles, but hadn't heard anything from him in several months. "He hates the blacks so much that I hope nothing has happened to him with all those riots going on," referring to the Watts riots which were in the national news. She took out a little black book from the night table next to her bed and copied down the address she had for my father and still not sure who I was—handed it to me.

Our goodbyes were said with little ceremony and at my request; Eddie drove me to a spot at the side of the road where I could catch a ride headed west to Hollywood, California; the address listed on the paper my grandmother had given me. The trip to see Piver would have to wait. As I watched him disappear into the distance at twenty-five miles an hour, I could only imagine what he and aunt Mary were talking about. I hadn't revealed much about myself and even though I knew I would never see them again, there was something heartwarming about the hospitality they had shown me.

Las Vegas 1965

Two days later, I was heading across a large expanse of Texas with a young twenty five year old cowboy, who had lost the use of his legs after being bucked off a horse. He drove a specially modified pickup, so he could operate it using only his arms. His plight left me a bit depressed when he dropped me off. My blues had all but dissipated when a cool looking guy in a red Corvette stopped to pick me up about a hundred miles outside of Las Vegas. The little cock of curled hair that hung above his forehead, made him the spitting image of Ed 'Kookie' Byrnes, the star of the hit TV show, '77 Sunset Strip.' We were having a typical hitchhiker/ driver conversation about nothing, when just as we began to descend a long three-mile incline into Vegas, Kookie said, "Let me show you what this baby can do." He floored the accelerator and the engine revved as the car began to pick up speed. Going downhill made the car go even faster. My eyes were bulging out from my head when 'Kookie' casually poked my shoulder and pointed at the speedometer. It was pegging at one hundred twenty five. It was all I could do to hold my stomach down. Nat King Cole had said in song: "Get Your Kicks on Route 66," and I was doing that and more.

A bit pissed that the cat had scared the shit out of me; I knew he was just thrilled with his Corvette and silently forgave him when he redeemed himself by treating me to breakfast at a truck stop on the western edge of town. After filling my gut at his expense, I approached several truckers parked outside and quickly found one who would carry me all the way to LA.

I took a long look up and down Main Street to get a sense of where I was. It had taken over six hours to get to LA, and though the sun had begun to retreat behind the tall buildings, the August air was still hot and smoggy. I relaxed a bit when I saw no evidence of the Watts riots, which had taken place two weeks earlier. A spasm of excitement pulsed through my groin, when I noticed The Burbank Follies just up the street. After I found a place to stay, I would be paying them a visit. For two bucks, I rented a room in a funky, but reasonably clean flop house nearby. After splashing some water on my face, I went back outside and followed the aroma coming from a little outdoor stand on the cornor. A buck got me six deep fried shrimps on rice covered with brown gravy. I left feeling sated and my dick was already hardening, as I walked towards the Burbank Follies. Peaches O'Day was the feature of the week and despite not being familiar with her act, my heart pounded with anticipation as I took my seat. It was a hot show—not as good as the Old Howard—but a hell of a lot better than the ones at the President Follies in Frisco. I stayed for two shows and a couple of orgasms and then headed to another burlesque house at the other end of Main Street called the New Follies. Its marquee advertised the Latin bombshell, Lillian Gamont, and daring strippers, but after watching a few of the over-the-hill daring strippers, I called it a night and a little past midnight returned to my hotel room. I had a big day planned for tomorrow.

The air was already hot and unpleasant when I awoke. I refreshed myself quickly in the room's funky shower (I hated dirty bathrooms) and then hopped a city bus to begin my quest to locate my biological father. The driver looked at the address my grandmother had given me, and after several transfers, I found myself standing at the busy corner of Santa Monica Blvd. and Western Avenue. Telephone poles and overhanging wires cluttered the area where an ethnic mixture of working class Latinos and whites scurried about the sidewalks. The address I had been given, 5245 Santa Monica Blvd., was only a block east from where I was standing, so I decided to case it out and clarify the situation before I proceeded. It was a seven-story brick apartment building that looked like it had seen better days. In the building's small foyer, I ran my finger down to 614, and there it was; Dittman and two other names! I needed to compose myself before what could be a traumatic scene, so I retreated back to the corner where I had noticed a little donut shop. I hadn't eaten anything yet, and as I filled my stomach with several sugary glazed donuts washed down by a cup of black coffee. My energy returned and, though nervous, I felt I was composed enough to return to the apartment and introduce myself. I pushed the button labeled six in the small worn out elevator which after lumbering up several floors, its doors opened to let me out in a dingy dark hallway redolent with the musty smell of a carpet that had been shampooed way too many times. Near the middle of the hall, I came to a worn looking door with paint chipped metal numerals that read: 614. Taking a deep breath, I lightly knocked three times. No one answered so I knocked again, this time a bit harder. I heard rustling inside and waited almost a minute for the door to open. Keeping the chain lock in place, a face peeked out through the crack.

"Are you Howard Dittman?" I asked. "Yaah" was the gruff response.

"I'm Howard Dittman too." "So what." I was taken aback.

"I'm your son, Howard Dittman."

Briefly stunned, he took a hard look at me.

. . . Howie?

"Yaah . . . I got your address from Grandma."

It took him a moment to digest the situation before he loosened the security-bolt to let me in. Despite it being the middle of the day, the room was completely dark. Shades covered the two windows looking out to the street. I noticed someone was asleep beneath them in a single bed. As my eyes adjusted to the dark, I noticed someone else was sleeping against the wall on a single bed across the room. My father was dressed only in a T-shirt, black ankle socks and loose fitting jockey briefs. His legs looked spindly and the crotch of his underwear sagged halfway down to his knees. I had obviously woken him up. His round face was worn, but not weather beaten. It reminded me of Lloyd Bridges, star of the TV series 'Sea Hunt.'

As his shock began to ebb, he realized he was not a pretty sight and ushered me back out the door, whispering, so as not to wake his roommates, about how amazed he was to see me. I had caught him off guard and it was understandable he needed time to process what had just taken place. "Give me your address and we'll get together in a couple of hours. I can't believe you're here. This could be what I need to turn things around." were his parting words.

His joy in seeing me had seemed legitimate. Since I had neglected to note its address, I could only give him the name of my hotel and that it was on Main Street. Another hour and a half bus ride got me back to the hotel where, exhausted from the emotional ordeal I had just been through, I plopped down on the bed and took a nap. A knocking on my door interrupted my slumber. Clueless who it could be, I was surprised to discover that it was half of my gene pool, all spruced up and covered in enough perfume to make a whore happy. It pleased me that he had shown up so quickly.

For the third time that day I was drinking coffee, this time while listening to my father tell me his story. He was always good with numbers and loved strippers. "Jesus Christ" I thought, "That's me to a tee." After he and my mother split-up, he took over my grandfather's business. He had high aspirations—was going to expand it into something really big—but things didn't work out and the business went under. I could see from his red face and large gut that he liked to drink and speculated that probably had something to do with his demise. He told me my grandparents really thought a lot of me; that the old man always said he "could make something out of that boy." But after the experience at Fort Knox, he gave up seeing me again. He had gotten remarried and had several other kids and then divorced again. He didn't mention whether he was still in touch with any of them. For that matter, I didn't really care that I had more half-siblings hanging about. He was full of himself: very confident—not like me—shy to a fault. I barely told him anything about myself and he didn't push to find out.

When the bill arrived, he picked it up and told me he didn't have a lot of time to spend with me; he worked a night shift driving cabs and had to report to work, but was anxious that I meet his roommates, who were also cab drivers. So I drove back to Hollywood with him in an old Chevy that he told me the three of them shared.

His two roommates were up when we walked in, but the shades were still drawn. I wondered if they remained that way all the time. I was introduced to Gene, whose dark complexion and dour-mood fit someone who was brought up in a trailer park, and Karl, a Belgian with a blond crew cut. Both were in their mid twenties. My father proudly stated that they called themselves "the three amigo's" and all had girl friends in Tijuana whom they visited at least once a month. Gene's 'T. J. girlfriend' had given him the moniker; 'Genie with the long weenie.'

He said he would like for us to spend some quality time together if it was all right by me. Of course I told him yes. When he came by the next day, he was in high spirits. He wanted to show me around and after nodding to Gene and Karl, who were already sitting in the back seat of the old Chevy. I took a seat next to my father. "Howie, this is the best thing that's happened to me in years, kid." He was in a celebratory mood and told me we were going to a great little club where he was going to show me how "the Big Fox" operated. Gene and Karl sat silent, doing nothing to contradict my father's claim, that he was "quite the lady's man." With a little chuckle, he added that it was the reason why he got into trouble with my mother.

The "great little club" was located about a mile from downtown on Temple Street in a poor, mostly Latino, area of town. The façade of the club, which was actually just a bar, had a small signboard on the outside where eight inch red letters advertised: 'Bikini Dancers.' As soon as a Mexican woman followed by her brood of three niños pushed her baby stroller past the doorway, we entered the club. The two or three patrons already inside sat in near darkness at a row of small tables placed against the back wall. We took seats at the bar where the dancers would perform behind the barmaid on a narrow counter against a mirrored wall. It didn't fail to astonish me that my father preferred—just as I would have—seats that were closest to where the action was. A sour faced waitress served us up three beers and while we worked on them and my father went on bragging about what an operator he was, a lethargic looking dancer with less than average body, climbed up on the counter and began moving to the beat of the juke box music, just enough to let it be known that she was alive.

She wore a full-bottomed white bikini and a little white bra that had no trouble covering her modest sized tits. California laws at the time, prevented tipping bar dancers, so there was no point in her making any attempt to acknowledge our existence. As she danced with a "when-is-my-shift-over look," my father gave me a friendly bump on the shoulder and with a cocky smile said; "Now Howie . . . your going to get to see the Big Fox operate."

Plaintively he called to the dancer: "Miss . . . miss!"

Irritated that she had been interrupted from admiring herself in the mirror, she turned her head slightly with a look that said: "What the fuck do you want?"

With a sincere look of concern, my father asked: "What's that little brown stain on your bottom?"

Initially I didn't grasp what he was asking. But when the girl twisted to check to see if there was indeed a brown stain on her bikini bottom, possibly because she hadn't wiped her ass clean or had diarrhea, I realized what the "Big Fox" was up to. Unable to see anything, she strained to twist her neck as far back as she could to see what he was talking about.

"No . . . no, a little bit lower" my father advised.

Just as she realized that she was being had, the 'Big Fox' burst out with a hardy chuckle. I don't need to describe the look the girl shot back at him. I did my best to manage a stupid smile only because I felt obligated to make him feel cool. Inwardly I was thinking; "Jesus holy fucking Christ!! My father is an idiot."

I was thinking it was time for me to head north to San Francisco to look up the trimaran master, Allen Piver, when my father threw me a screwball. After we had left the club and returned to his apartment, he asked me what my plans were. I told him I was thinking of going into boat building, but didn't have anything concrete.

"Look Howie, I've been thinking. You and I could go into business. Before I ran into problems, I was the best estimator in the business. We could go into remodeling. I have a connection here in town that lives in a mansion who can turn us on to good jobs to help us get started. And some people owe me money that we can use to buy tools."

It was an appealing idea—a blood related partnership. I mentioned that I had carpentry experience and would be willing to do the physical work. I thought to myself that if he could sell the jobs, something that I wasn't comfortable doing, it could work out well. He suggested we call ourselves "Howard Dittman and Son" and added, "Why don't you stay here with me until we get something going?"

The next day I moved in with the *Three Amigos*. My father slept in the apartment's one bedroom and I would sleep on a couch in the living room along with Karl and Genie with his long weenie. Food played second fiddle to whisky on my dad's priority list, and each night when he came home from his nightly shift, he had a pint of whisky, but never any groceries. I had no clue what he ate, maybe donuts? With the few bucks I had left to my name, I went to a market just up the street and bought a big bag of potatoes, eggs, ketchup and cooking oil. For the next couple of weeks, morning, noon and night, I subsisted on a cholesterol laden diet of fried eggs and French-fries with ketchup. It helped that no one knew much about cholesterol at that time.

Needing to make a few bucks until my dad and I got our business going, I headed downtown to the state employment office and after registering took a seat among the unemployed in the waiting area. A woman behind the window shouted: "Can anyone here do painting?" I and about ten other guys raised our hands. We were given instructions to go downtown to a large old office building. Its owner was a foreigner with an eastern European accent and wanted all the windows painted before he covered the floor with linoleum. Around noon, he stopped by and wandered over to where I was painting. Noticing a few specs of paint on the floor, he shouted: "you are no painter. Don't bother to come back this afternoon." The vehemence with which I was fired, made me suspect that there was more than just bad painting. Maybe he had been in a concentration camp during the war? My blond hair and name labeled me German. Nevertheless, I had made a half-day's pay, enough to buy more eggs and potatoes.

The money that my father claimed was due him from a former business associate, turned out to be bullshit. After I called Bernie to tell him I had found my long lost father and was going to go into business, he agreed to help me out with a couple of hundred bucks. As soon as the money arrived, the 'Big Fox' suggested we go to where the pros went for their tools; Union

Hardware. It was indeed a magnificent hardware store, situated in a three story architectural building with thirty-foot high colonnades in front. In my eyes, that he knew the store, gave him credibility.

On the way home I was about to see why my grandmother had said he hates blacks so much. A month after the riots, the air was still thick with racial tension and we were stopped at a red light, when two blacks pulled alongside us. Because of the hot day our windows were rolled down. Our eyes stayed focused straight ahead and when we heard a mumbled, "White mother fuckers" they stayed a bit straighter. When the light changed, the two blacks sped off and my father turned to me and said: "Now you see why I hate niggers so much, Howie." Was I now in business with a racist or was he just of a generation that was stuck in the past? I had many good experiences with black people and could understand the pent up anger that was now bursting forth. You can only push people down so long. Nothing more came of it and I just let it pass. I knew he wasn't the only one with those feelings.

Of more concern to me than my father seemingly to be an idiot, a bull shitter, an alcoholic and a racist, was that he was a procrastinator. I got sick of hearing his constant excuses about why we couldn't meet the guy he said would be able to steer us towards some jobs. And sharing a room with the three amigos and eating oily French fries was becoming more than even I could take. So I took some of the money left over from Bernie and rented a cheap apartment on Melrose Ave near Vermont. The backend of the building abutted the Hollywood Freeway. It was only a few blocks from Los Angeles City College, which meant that there were plenty of young people around as well as a couple of fast food joints and a pool hall.

My new neighbors were a little old lady who never came out of her room, a freckle faced Irish kid named Colm Gallagher, a telephone operator named Phyllis Solomon and a taciturn young guy whose eerie blank stare suggested that he had mental issues. Though Phyllis wasn't a beauty, she made up for it with a bubbly personality and a love of fucking. Her vagina was not very pleasant smelling but it was always available for me to bury my face and dick into.

I still held hope that my partnership with my father would come to fruition. I was beginning to enjoy LA with its varied culture and perpetual warm weather. After much cajoling, my father finally took me to the connection that could find us some jobs. He turned out to be a blind man and his mansion was a very ordinary house in the south of Pico section of Beverly Hills. The job referral only came after obsequious pleading from my father. The blind man gave us a lead to a job at a small convalescent hospital in Encino that needed some work done. 'Procrastinate' was my father's middle name and even checking that referral out took two days: "Don't want to appear too anxious." he said. When we drove out we were told by the owner that all he needed was a small shed to shelter their garbage cans. On the way back to Hollywood, the 'Big Fox' spoke as though we had just been offered a chance to remodel the Taj Mahal. "We should be able to get seven-hundred dollars," he exclaimed. I was dumbfounded, even more so when he said: "We should make them wait a few days before giving them our bid; don't want to let him think we're desperate." I would have asked about one hundred fifty, but then I didn't know anything about bidding and he had worked as a professional estimator. "I'll give him a call the day after tomorrow around 11AM. That'll be the perfect time." was the last thing he told me.

With nothing to do in the two-day interim before we submitted our bid, after dressing up in what I thought was a cool looking outfit, Levis, cowboy boots and a big Stetson cowboy hat, I decided to explore the town. I walked up to Hollywood Boulevard and began sauntering down the walk of stars. Along the way I passed a carnival of shops that hawked everything from Hollywood souvenirs, magic tricks, hot dogs and exotic lingerie. Looking at the brazen window displays of mannequins dressed in erotic and scanty lingerie at Playmates and Fredrick's of Hollywood, was almost like going to a burlesque show. I paused for a few moments to tease myself by playing pocket pool while speculating about the hot sluts who shopped there and wore those naughty outfits. Not wanting to make the store manager suspicious that I was a pervert, I limited my ogling to five minutes.

Ever since going to the Follies Bergere, I had fantasized about how exciting it must be to parade around in a little male g-string like those I had seen the male dancers in the show wearing. I had no idea where to buy one until I saw a window display in a little shop next to the Hollywood Warner theatre. They had little silk ones in pink, blue, black and white; sheer and knitted ones, and even gold and silver ones made of a metallic fabric. I didn't have money to immediately purchase a few, but the thought of my junk snuggled provocatively in a g-string, was making me hard. I speculated that a lot of girls might also enjoy seeing a guy wearing a g-string. They all liked my bikini swimsuit, but compared to this, that was prosaic. I knew I would soon be returning to buy as many as I could.

I was walking home going east on Hollywood boulevard, when I vaguely became aware that a young blond male was coming towards me from the opposite direction. He was wearing tight jeans and a white tank top that showed off his well-toned biceps and shoulders. As we were about to pass, he abruptly stepped in front of me and blocked my path:

"AC or DC?"

"Huh?" was all I could manage.

"Never mind" he shot back derisively as he got out of my way and continued down the street. "What the fuck was that all about? What's AC or DC?"

On the day the 'Big Fox' promised to call in the bid, I knocked on his door at three in the afternoon to see how it had gone. No one answered, but the muffled voices inside told me he was at home so I continued knocking. Three minutes later he opened the door. He was hung over and began bullshitting me about how tomorrow would be the perfect time: "Don't let the guy think you're hungry." Unbelievably I allowed the same scenario to be repeated two more times before I admitted that Howard Dittman & Son was going nowhere. When he eventually got sober enough to call in his seven hundred dollar bid, the guy laughed and told him he had hired someone for two hundred bucks and the job was already done.

43

ITS TIME TO GET MY ACT TOGETHER?

Enough! It was my good fortune that I had not got more involved but it was not entirely a waste of time. I realized that if I drank alcohol like he was inclined to do; I would physically deteriorate until I looked like him by the time I turned fifty; pot bellied and slovenly. The thought terrified me. I gave up alcohol immediately: nothing more than a glass of wine on special occasions and one or two beers a year. I would never waiver.

I didn't think I could go back to Bernie and ask if he still wanted to continue with the trimaran idea. Even if he did, it was more groveling than I was willing to do. I had blown that deal. While thinking about what my next move should be, I decided to hitch hike up to Berkeley and see what some of my old friends were up to. The adventure would help clear my mind. Thumbing out of busy LA, where traffic was mostly local, was not easy. It took me several rides just to get to the Pacific Coast highway. From there a young blond in a convertible pulled over and told me to jump into the back seat that was already filled with her three cute girls friends and a young guy. They could take me as far as Zuma beach, wherever that was. To make room, one of the bikini clad cuties offered to sit on my lap, which made the hour-and-a half bumper-to-bumper ride to Zuma, if nothing else, stimulating. The whole day was almost blown and I took the next ride that came my way without really knowing where it was taking me. What a mistake! At seven in the evening I found myself in downtown LA on Main Street, almost exactly where I first arrived several months earlier. I had spent the entire day going around in a circle! Was this a metaphor for my life or what?

The sun was beginning to set and rather than go back to my apartment, which I could have reached by city bus, I decided to do the burlesque house routine. So after a quick bite at my favorite jumbo fried shrimp stand, I took in the shows at the two burlesque houses and then, rather than rent a hotel room, bought a ticket to a ninety-nine cent all night theatre that showed sex exploitation and nudie camp movies. Catching a few winks during the likely boring movies should not be a problem.

That assumption was amazingly wrong. It was true that the movies were boring, but the theatre turned out to be an all-night-beehive of homosexual activity. Seconds after I took a seat, a guy took the vacant seat next to me. He kept glancing my way, showing no interest in what was on the screen. Since I paid him no attention, he jumped up seconds later and scampered off to take a seat next to someone else. Moments later, the same scenario was repeated with another guy. As my eyes adjusted to the darkness, I could see that there were scampering guys all over the place, like little mice hunting for cheese. The theatre was a gay pickup center. It eventually became known among the scampering mice that they weren't going to get a nibble from me and traffic eventually subsided enough for me to grab a few winks before returning to the road in the morning.

At five AM I began to make my situation worse when I jumped into a car about to enter the freeway. I had told him I was "heading up towards San Francisco," and he told me, "I can take you to Riverside." I assumed Riverside was on the way to San Francisco, but as it turned out, Riverside was sixty miles in the opposite direction! Jesus Christ! At the rate I was going, it would take me a month to get to Berkeley. After checking out a map hanging on the wall at a gas station, I saw that from where I now was, there were no direct roads to the bay area. I would have to go north through the Mojave desert and then take US 99 up the San Joaquin valley to Tracy, and from there west on US 50 into the bay area. By the evening, I had hitched all the way to the small farming town of Modesto.

Exhausted and needing sleep, I noticed a railroad yard a hundred yards away from the side of the road. Some boxcars had been assembled as though they were to be part of a train about to leave the yard. Although an engine had yet to be attached, I figured it was an even chance that the train would be heading north, so I traversed the small field of dry waist high grass and climbed over a low chain link fence and within minutes found an open boxcar. Remembering what Perry had taught me, I placed a piece of wood so the door couldn't slam shut on me. I had stuck my head out the open crack to see what was going on when a sudden jolt from an additional boxcar being added caused it to smash against the side of the doorjamb. I was momentarily stunned. The jolt didn't draw blood but left me feeling feint so I laid down atop my sleeping bag to give myself time to recuperate.

Moments later the train began to slowly move. I wasn't sure which direction we were going, but I was too discombobulated to care and dozed off. Throughout the night, the train made repeated stops, possibly to yield to other trains sharing the same track. I slept like a log and didn't awake until mid morning. The train was at rest. I got up and looked out the door to see where I was. Good luck! A highway where I could hitch a ride was just a short distance from the tracks. I was marveling at how similar the area looked to what it was in Modesto where I had first boarded when: "yikes! It was Modesto!!" I was only a hundred yards up the tracks from where I had started! The stopping and starting was just cars being added and subtracted.

Back on the highway and looking like shit, I still managed to catch a ride with a guy in his early thirties who was actually heading to the bay area. My juvenile look and dirty unshaven appearance seemed to be at odds and made him curious.

"How old are you?" "Twenty six." After a moments pause:

"Do you have any plans for yourself?"

I responded in a diffident voice, "Nothing special right now." He glanced at me with a look of pity.

"Don't you think you better get yourself together?"

I didn't have a good answer. I wasn't feeling any urgency to change my life-style, but I knew this complete stranger was right. He didn't give me any crap about finding god; he was just a good guy. I also knew that getting myself together wasn't what it meant for most people. But what it was: I knew not.

44

I'M A PHONY WANNABE

Before driving off after we got to Berkeley, he handed me a couple of bucks. It was appreciated. The first thing I noticed was how much Telegraph Avenue had changed. Free love and drugs had attracted dealers and bikers. The warm zeitgeist created by naïve idealists and folkies seemed to have disappeared. Dave Cleveland was still listed in the phone book and I gave him a call. He told me our old friend, Sidney Locker, was now living in Frisco near the Height Ashbury district and offered to drive me across the bay so the three of us could reminisce about old times. Sidney was glad to see me and offered to let me stay at his place while I was in town.

We made plans to go to the Cabale when it opened that evening. He hoped to sell a few lids and I hoped to collect the five hundred dollars Peery still owed me. In the meantime, I entertained myself by sitting on his front porch ogling at the scantily dressed black hookers who were plying their trade right out side his front door. When they bent over to stick their heads into a car window to negotiate a trick, their panties and round butts were a titillating sight to behold. The free show lasted until one of them realized what I was doing and marched up the steps to tell me right-to-my-face that I was screwing up her business by intimidating potential customers. She had a point, so I went back inside and ogled through a crack in the window blinds.

Lightning Hopkins

Carol Peery pretended to be delighted to see me, but I knew he wasn't, especially when I brought up the money I was owed. He gave me a long line of bullshit and I knew the money was history. Lightning Hopkins was booked for the weekend and I wandered to the back room to say hello. He was seated on a chair, sipping apricot brandy and holding court for a few admirers. He beckoned for me to come forward so he could whisper something in my ear. He quietly asked if I was looking to buy some grass. "Lighning was dealing grass?" I wasn't sure what the fuck he was talking about and I responded to his question in perfect black wanna-be English: "You be jivin' me Lightnin', you be jivin' me." His unfriendly pissed off reaction surprised me more than the fact that he was dealing grass: "I ain't jivin' you Howard." I realized that I had no real clue what *"jivin'"* meant. Thinking it was just the cool way to talk to a down-home Negro, I couldn't understand why he seemed pissed but began to realize that I had unintentionally called him a liar; being that "jiving" meant lying. The conversation ended there. It was another little lesson. Don't be a phony, talk the way you normally talk, not in some patronizing dialect that's not you.

The Cabale Creamery closed down a few months later. Maybe after I left, there was no one around to do the grunt work. Forty years later, Tony Glover, a reviewer for "Blues On Stage," wrote in a write up about Arhoolie's CD release of, "Mance Lipscomp At The Cabale." "The Cabale was a Berkeley institution." For me it had been one hell of an adventure.

Back in L. A. I began thinking what the guy had said: "Don't you think its time to get yourself together." I had returned from Berkeley with Kenny Marshal, a light skinned Creole with arms and chest like Popeye the Sailor Man, who had offered to let me tag along with him while he delivered a ten-speed truck to LA. I could help with the driving which entailed a quick lesson in ten-speed gear shifting that I mastered easily. Kenny's sense of humor made him one of my favorite friends from the Cabale days. He didn't have a violent bone in his muscular body but liked to toss out phrases like "jacking that boy's jaw" if he thought someone had dissed him or "That damn fool done near muh . . . dged all over me" when some damn fool nearly sideswiped us as we were trying to merge onto the freeway from an access ramp. Much of the trip was spent teaching me how to speak Creole which Kenny pointed out was done by pretending your mouth is full of marbles. "We laughed all the way to L. A.

Kenny decided to stay in LA after he delivered the truck and rented an available one-bedroom apartment that was adjacent to Phyliss's apartment in my building. As soon as he could make some money, he planned on bringing his "squeeze" down from Berkeley. While pondering how I could get my act together, Kenny and I teamed up to do a few painting jobs around the neighborhood, including the Campus bookstore. Time working with Kenny passed quickly since we bantered back and forth with inane Creole talk all day. But like my father, Kenny was an alcoholic and I usually wound up doing most of the work since he spent much of each morning sleeping off last nights binge.

Painting was certainly not the career I was envisioning to "get my act together." When I discovered that my Irish neighbor, Colm Gallagher, also played guitar and loved rock music and was as much a delusional dreamer as I was, I embarked on a far-out dream that only befitted a pot smoking LSD user. I suggested the two of us write rock and roll songs. Sans the pot smoking and LSD tripping, Colm was as delusional as I was. But then again, Hollywood was the Mecca for those with far-out dreams. Why not us? We became a song writing team. I had overcome my tin ear and had become fairly adept at putting a melody together, essentially by constructing a series of chord changes and then adding a melody over them. He, being more cerebral, would write the lyrics. We weren't modest and set our sights high, aiming to become another Burt Bacahrach—Hal David team. Each evening after he came home from his job as a waiter, we began writing songs in his room and within a few weeks had several in the bag.

But dreams don't make money, at least not immediately, so I took the full set of carpentry tools that I had purchased to go into business with my father, and went down to the local carpenter's union and signed up as an apprentice. It meant taking classes once a week and finding jobs in the various disciplines of carpentry: i. e. foundation work, framing, finish carpentry etc. It made sense to have a backup career in case my fantasy career didn't pan out.

The union referred me to a job at the Forest Lawn Cemetery in Burbank, where a large auditorium was being built. To get to work, I arose at 5:30 AM in order to catch the first bus of the day that ran down Melrose. It dropped me off at Highland, where in order to catch my transfer to Burbank, I had to run a good mile up to Hollywood Blvd., lugging my twenty-five pound tool belt, so I could make the Burbank connection before it departed. That bus left me off on Forest Lawn Road, where I then walked the half-mile to the entrance of the Cemetery and trudged up the hill past graves and stone statues that were all "John Birch Society" inspired. One labeled 'Liberty,' was of a woman with a snake wrapped around her neck labeled, 'Communism.' Though it bugged me that Forest Lawn was obviously a big supporter of The Vietnam War, it was not my concern. I was just happy to have a job.

Over the next seven months, I helped the carpenters assemble an assortment of metal units, called pans, to make the desired forms that after they were filled with vast amounts of concrete, would become the huge beams that would support the walls and roof of the auditorium. Burbank was usually scorching hot and the supervisor would order the concrete trucks a little before the forms were completed to make us work double speed so they would be ready when the concrete arrived. If I wasn't lugging pans up and down the scaffolds, I was building and tearing the scaffolds down. Some were fifty feet high and I was forced to overcome my fear of heights.

As was the case at the Cabale, where I recognized that I didn't fit in with the "Folk" crowd, here I recognized that I didn't really fit in with the white carpenters, and since my work was mainly working aside the "black" labor workers, I sat with them when we broke for lunch. The disapproving looks made me feel that it would be wise to join "my kind" or else risk being ostracized. However, one of the laborers, a black man in his mid fifties, named Jessie, lived in Watts and offered to drop me off at my apartment on his way home when our day was done. It saved me suffering an hour-long bus ride after a hard days work. As soon as I walked into my pad, all I could do was crash. When I awoke, usually two hours later, Colm had come home from his job and the two of us would work on our music for a couple of hours.

It wasn't long after I had started working at Forest Lawn, that my father dropped by my apartment on a weekend afternoon to ask if he could borrow my tools. He and his roommate, Karl, needed them to do a job together. I had to hand it to him, he didn't lack for audacity. Phyllis stopped in for a moment and I introduced her to him. After she left he commented: "She sure ain't a looker." What an asshole. It felt good to tell him I wouldn't be loaning him the tools: "I needed them for my work." That would be the last time I would ever see or hear from him. Good riddance! I had no idea what had possibly attracted my mother to him in the first place? Only many years later, when I was arguing with her about abortion, I would learn that I was an accidental baby. She argued that my existence was predicated on the fact that she was pro life. It was no secret to me, that most women at that time, still in the clutches of the church, chose pro life over damnation in hell. In reality, it made no difference to me. If I had been aborted, I would not have known. But at least I eventually found out that being pregnant was why she married a jerk like my father.

The apprentice school instructor couldn't help but notice that I had an aptitude for math and told me I had what it would take to become a supervisor; a position and career that paid well. As encouraging as that was, the difficulty I found melding with the union crowd made me doubt that I had a future in construction. My long hair and free association with the black workers, typed me as being a liberal as did the '67 Volvo I bought when I had enough money to make a down payment. When I drove it on to the work site, my foreman remarked: "I see you bought yourself a little foreigner." It wasn't meant to be complementary.

While a journeyman carpenter and I teetered at the top of the tallest scaffold on the site, over fifty feet, he told me we would be fired once we finished disassembling it and reached the ground. Obviously it made sense for the supervisor to give that dangerous job to someone who was expendable and when we hit the ground I got my walking papers. I went to the union hall to see if they could give me some help finding another job. Behind the hall, I noticed the cars of the union bosses, all large black Cadillac's with tinted windows. Inside I spoke to a faceless voice behind a tinted window that told me I was on my own. While I roamed the area looking for another job that would advance me along the apprentice program, I began to reassess what I was getting into. The work was brutally hard and tough on the body. Guys who I thought were sixty were only in their early forties; their skin wrinkled by the constant exposure to the sun and their bodies aching from stooping all day. Some were driving a hundred miles just to get to the job site. This was definitely not the answer to: "getting myself together," and I decided to call it quits. My brief career taught me the meaning of hard work and also left me with a well-toned muscular body. My days of being 'fragile' were over!

45

A SCHEME TO MY MADNESS

While checking out the want ads looking for a job that might appeal to me, I noticed: 'Looking for photographers, No Experience Necessary—Will Train—Must Have Car.' Somewhere, deep in my grey matter, neurons were firing that were telling me this job would provide essential elements that would lead to the inchoate career that would "get my act together." I was still pondering when someone knocked on my door. It was Kenny. His 'squeeze's' father, an ex-circus barker, who was temporarily living with them, had scored some acid and he wanted to know if I would like to join them. Both Kenny's 'squeeze' and her father looked like distant relatives of W. C. Fields. Neither struck me as psychic adventurers but the father had a street-smart élan that made him amusing. I had completely recovered from my first acid trip and thinking that a mind expanding mental experience may be fun and even musically beneficial; I put down the want ads and joined him in the hall. Kenny noticed the mental guy standing alone, as he often did, outside his door, and Kenny, always good-natured, decided to invite him to join us for the trip. Without much emotion, he followed us into the apartment. Other than an old lady who no one ever saw, there was no one home in any of the other apartments.

After making ourselves comfortable on the soft chairs in the living room, the circus man handed each of us a sugar cube doctored with LSD. Kenny's squeeze gave everyone a glass of water to wash it down. It was my understanding that the dosage was about 150 micrograms, so it would be twice as strong as what I had taken before.

By now, taking acid had become fairly commonplace, and 150 mics was considered very conservative, so I had no anxiety about flying off the planet.

I should have. Fifteen minutes later all hell broke loose. I was just beginning to hallucinate when the mental guy jumped up out of his chair and ran out into the hall screaming: "Is it real? . . . No it's not real . . . Nothing's real." Continuing to scream and shout his rhetorical question, he zigzagged down the hall until he reached the glass window at its end. Still only tripping mildly, the rest of us peered out into the hallway where we saw him smashing his hands through the pane glass window. From the distance, I could see that blood was flowing profusely from the cuts on his hands. The little old lady peeked out her door and instantly retreated as the mental guy came running back down the hall, flinging his gushing blood all over walls. He was screaming something about Jesus.

Hallucinating and clueless what to do, Kenny, his squeeze, her father and I stood mortified. Phyllis was at work and as far as I knew her apartment was empty; so I was surprised when I heard her door open and even more surprised when her former boy friend, Don, stepped out into the hallway. I had met him a few days earlier and learned that he had been walking around the country over the last year looking for the meaning of life. He was a bit odd—a guru type—but was a master wood carver, as witnessed by the magnificent hand-carved cane he had whittled for himself. His claim to be a devout Zen Buddhist and his long straggly auburn hair and beard and my cynical view of religion prompted me to give him the sobriquet—albeit not to his face—'Messiah Don.'

My facetious nickname would prove to be well chosen. For him, the mental guy's freak out was a scenario made in heaven or in 'Tushita,' being that he was a Buddhist. It gave him an opportunity to justify his philosophy—to use it to spiritually conquer the situation. As soon as he saw what was happening, he ran down the hall until he reached the screaming kid. He grabbed the boy's hands and pressed them into his lap, adroitly managing to stop the bleeding and calm the fellow down as well as could be expected. I still had enough control of my mental faculties to be able to call the telephone company and reach Phyllis. I pleaded with her to believe me when I said a disaster was taking place at the apartment and she needed to come home immediately. She arrived fifteen minutes later and called the medics who came and took the kid to the hospital.

My trip would continue as I listened to Don relive the whole bloody scene over and over. Saving a lost soul had made him feel like a real Messiah, not just an ersatz one. Maybe he was? Phyllis had to go back to work, but Don, still dressed in his bloody clothing, sat on the floor in lotus position with an angelic smile on his face and chaperoned us travelers back to planet earth. Despite the horrific disturbance, the rest of us had good voyages. Nonetheless, there was no way to think of the day as anything but tragic. If not for 'Messiah Don,' something horrible could have happened. LSD was not to be taken lightly.

Kenny and I were both given immediate eviction notices. I never was given a chance to find out if the mental kid was able to return to his apartment or what happened to him. Kenny got lost in the shuffle, but as one used to moving, I found a great little bungalow in Santa Monica on Strand Street between Main and Second. It was only two blocks from the beach. A little restaurant owned by a large black woman, called Olivia's, offered two pork chops, mashed potatoes with gravy and a vegetable for a couple of bucks.

To keep our song writing team intact, Colm followed me to Santa Monica, taking a bungalow next to mine. A month later Phyllis followed suit, moving into a small house just around the corner on Fourth Street, meaning I still had access to easy pussy. A couple of days after moving, I answered the ad looking for photographers and got the job. All was cool.

The small photography studio was in a predominantly Spanish neighborhood, just south of Sunset on Alvarado Street, It specialized in photos of babies and young children. The bulk of their business, however, was generated outside the studio by a sales force that canvassed low-income areas of LA and Orange County; selling ten-dollar coupons to mothers that entitled them to one 8x10 and three 4x5 photos of their child. A photographer would then come to their house to take the pictures followed by a salesman a few days later with the prepaid pictures as well as other shots that were taken during the session. He would then try, usually successfully, to convince the mother to buy more pictures of her precious child, often increasing her outlay of cash tenfold. I was hired to be one of the photographers.

My new bosses, a balding Jewish guy named Earl, and a staunch wasp Republican, named Larry, were both in their early forties and all about making money. When I mentioned that I was thinking of taking a class in photography, they strongly urged me not to. "We don't want a photographer who is going to fidget with lighting and camera angles," Earl told me. He just wanted me to hang a backdrop on a stand behind the subject, place two lights and my camera at preset positions, and then snap pictures of the mother's little dear. My camera had to be a Rolleiflex, because it used a large format film that would render bright sharp prints. I had to purchase it on my own dime. The only training I got was a short list of standard poses, like the hand under the chin or against the side of the cheek. These were proven to endear a mother's heart. "Get a smile, that's the most important thing," Earl told me. I would be booked at three houses every hour, which meant I had to work fast. Paid by commission, I would earn one dollar fifty cents for every session that resulted in photos of smiling tots.

Getting a kid to smile was usually pretty easy, a few peek-a-boos or cootchie coos on the tummy would usually do the trick. There were times when getting a smile was near impossible. I had entered a Mexican woman's house in Silverlake and was stunned when I saw that there was no furniture, rugs on the floor, or pictures on the wall. The light coming into the room had to pass through the drawn yellow shades. She was likely a single mom. Her child, about three years old, just looked at me with a blank expression as though he had rarely seen another human. I don't think he knew how to smile. "Why was she spending money on pictures and not on furniture or toys?" I failed to get a smile. I wouldn't be getting paid for my visit but was more depressed thinking about that kid.

As I discovered from my father, it was in my genes to be attracted to strippers. Despite while living in Berkeley having enjoyed more than my share of sexual encounters with "free love" girls, nothing excited me more than the thought of having sex with sleazy sluts—the ones who liked to tease and flaunt their sexuality, and I had yet to have that experience. Sex with that kind of girl would result in the ultimate orgasmic experience. Paying for peeks at strip shows was very satisfying as was looking at girls in the skin magazines, however, as much as I wanted to meet some of those girls, the thought was terrifying. They would see me as a nerd, as someone who couldn't possibly satisfy them. I had no "pick up" skills to speak of, so how could I possibly ever meet such a slut. It was a twisted mental conundrum. When Bernie's ex girl friend, Phyliss Santis came to LA and gave me a call, I sensed an opportunity had arrived. She had left her heroine junky boy friend and Bernie had given her my number to call when she got to LA. I wasn't sure what her long-range goals were, but I had met her several times while I lived with Bernie and strongly suspected that she was a "slut in the making." I began to form a plan.

In Hollywood's Fairfax area, there were several small Model Studios that advertised with signs out front: "Nude Models Available." All of them also had a smaller sign that read: "Models needed." A couple of these studios were located in small bungalow sized homes that had been converted into studios by blocking out their windows with plywood. A little red light outside made them appear to be whorehouses, but I doubted if that kind of business could operate so blatantly in Los Angeles. I had not been able to muster up the courage to check them out. It would require having direct contact with the model and I didn't know if I could handle that. Watching strippers on stage was one thing. There I could sit in the dark in anonymity, the dancer would barely-if at all—know I was there. I didn't want girls to see me as a pervert, which I was convinced was how the girls in the modeling studios probably saw their customers. So despite my burning curiosity, the glowing red lights didn't lure me in, but acted as a barrier to keep me from entering. Nonetheless, my curiosity about what went on inside was killing me.

Phyliss was a spirited and zesty Jewish girl with an overt personality. She came off as a sexpot, but I sensed it was a bit of an act and she struggled to believe it. I speculated that she might be willing to do something risqué or naughty to prove to herself that she was indeed hot. That's why she was in Hollywood; to be discovered. When she asked if I could help her get on her feet, I saw a chance that might benefit both of us, a way for her to prove to herself how hot she was and for me to see what went on in those modeling studios without appearing to be a pervert. I suggested that she apply for a job at one of them. I would be happy to accompany her to the interview. My hunch turned out to be right. She liked the idea and we arranged to meet the next day for what should be an exciting experience for both of us.

I drove the little trumpet to a studio a half-block south of Santa Monica Blvd. near Fairfax. Its windows were boarded up and a red light hung over the door. Being that I was just Phyliss's chaperone, I had no fear of being seen as a pervert and the two of us entered without anxiety. A seedy looking slob sat at a little desk just inside the entryway. A curtain behind him prevented anyone from getting a free peek inside. Phyllis told him she was looking to be a model and after a few perfunctory questions, we were both taken past the curtain into the reception room. I was told to wait there while she was taken to a room in the back, so the guy could check out her body.

My ears flushed as I realized that three sluts, wearing only panties, stockings and see-thru negligees, were sitting on couches against the opposite wall. I wanted to stare, but knowing it would look creepy, managed to keep my eyes down; allowing myself only a few furtive glances. Since I wasn't a potential paying customer, there was no reason for any of them to erase the ennui registered on their faces. But on one of my furtive glances, I recognized a girl that I had recently seen in 'Black Nylons.' She had posed lying on her back with her legs spread wide wearing only black diaphanous panties. While masturbating to her pictures, I had imagined rubbing my nose across her soft sexy crotch. But now, all I could do was sit silently with my eyes downward and hope to steal a few more peeks while I waited for Phyliss.

She came out a few minutes later and after we were outside, excitedly told me that she got the job. If she were chosen for a session, the patron would pay her thirty-five dollars to take nude pictures. She got half the fee: no touching, masturbation or sex was allowed. The patron was supplied with a camera and film by the studio.

Being that Phyliss was a bit flat-chested, she didn't get booked very often. Frustrated and disappointed that she wasn't making the grade as a Hollywood sex-object, she returned to Boston after a few weeks. I never attempted to have sex with her; it was enough that she provided the vehicle that allowed me a brief peek into the sex industry. I now knew it was my calling. How to get there; I had no idea.

46

CALIFORNIA SUNSHINE

In a down mood, I inched down the crowded San Bernardino Freeway, as I headed home from Rancho Cucamonga, a small town south of downtown Los Angeles that is close to the El Toro Marine base. It was already past six-thirty and I had just finished a "failed-to-get-a-smile" shooting at a Marine's house. The family was already eating dinner when I arrived and after the wife showed me where I could set up, she returned to the table to rejoin her burly husband and their child. They ate in silence and an undeniable vibe told me that the Marine was not a fan of my long unruly hair. Maybe he thought I was a pinko commie? When I was ready to shoot, the mother brought her little four-year old over and placed him on the stool in front of the backdrop. He was cute; dressed in a nice jacket and tie and short pants. He starred at me with a look of terror as though I had just arrived from Mars. My peek-a-boo and coochie-coo routine was having no effect and I was in the middle of a stretched-mouth Bozo-the-Clown bit, when a menacing voice came from the dinner table: "Are you going to smile or do I have to get the good-be stick?" A pathetic strained smile followed and I snapped my pictures: click-click-click; and hastened out of there. I couldn't erase the kid's look for the entire trip back to Santa Monica.

When I got home I looked into Colm's bungalow to see if he wanted to work on our music. His kitchen light was on and the front door left open, which was unusual. Not having anything better to do, I walked around the corner to Phyllis's house, where unexpectedly I found Colm. He was freaking out! A few weeks prior, he had bought a tab of acid and placed it in his refrigerator where it had sat unused—evidently until today. He was by nature, very cerebral and my experience with acid was that it overwhelmed one's mental capacities. That's why it was called a trip. It was not something you thought your way through. You just went along for the ride—looked out the window and enjoyed the scenery. I knew about the acid in his refrigerator and had warned him several times not to use it unless he felt very comfortable and was in a secure environment and in the company of someone he trusted. I could see he hadn't taken my advice.

Poor Phyllis, she seemed to be the dumping ground for everyone's bad trip. Colm was running around the room like he was about to go zonkers, not too different than the way the mental guy had gone off. Thinking that I would make his experience even worse if I got excited, I played it real cool, barely acknowledging him, hoping my calm demeanor would calm him. But he kept getting more and more panicked.

And then, as though by magic, 'Don the Messiah,' arrived. He had just come by to say hello to Phyliss and as much as I liked to joke about the guy's mystic persona, he knew how to deal with anxiety—especially the acid type. He wrapped his arms around Colm and hugged him. After a few minutes, Colm's sobbing slowly subsided. Don consoled him for the next several hours until the effects of the drug began to wear off. When the trip had run its course, he walked him back to his bungalow and put him to bed.

The next day, Colm was livid, insisting that I should have wrapped my arms around him like Don had done. I tried to explain that just wasn't my style, I wasn't a touchy-feely guy. "You would have felt tension from me if I tried to be something I wasn't and things would have gotten worse." I told him. He didn't want to hear it and accused me of being cold and unfeeling. We would remain friends, but he said he would always see me in a different light. There wasn't much to say. I knew I wasn't a guru or had any interest in becoming one. I was trying to exorcize my own demons. That we continued to work on our music was a relief to me. I still harbored dreams of a music career, even though a career in the sex business was now also in the back of my mind. I hoped time would heal his bad experience and his bad feelings towards me would drift into the past.

As panicked as Colm was during his LSD trip, he was as panicked about the prospect of being drafted. He was desperate to do something about it.

He couldn't be blamed. By late 1967, the Vietnam War was out of control and it had become next to impossible to avoid the draft. If you claimed you were gay, they shot back that you would be put in a gay platoon or if you had a bad back it was; "So what, lots of guys do." Colm was worried that if he refused to serve, it would preclude him from becoming a U. S. citizen.

Psychosis was one of the few sure fire ways of getting a deferment. A rumor had spread that it was possible to be hypnotized to react psychotically when being inspected by the draft board doctors. Through the grapevine, Colm learned that Pat Collins, a hypnotist who performed on weekends at Gazzarri's, a club on Sunset Strip, was sympathetic to boys trying to evade the draft. He arranged to have a session with her at her home in the Hollywood hills. Wanting to show that I supported him, I came along. Pat Collins was an attractive middle-aged woman with neatly coiffed hair. She was not the hippy type that most people associated with the anti war effort. What she was doing was admirable and gutsy. She risked serious repercussions if she was caught abetting draft dodgers.

Before the session began, she made it clear that not everyone could be hypnotized. A degree of trust between the subject and the hypnotizer and a willingness to be put under was necessary for the process to be successful. After she had both of us close our eyes, she began slowly counting backwards from ten. As she counted, she made suggestions to relax, to go into a deep sleep. I listened but didn't feel anything happening. When she reached zero, she told us to open our eyes. I didn't feel a thing. I looked at Colm and it looked like he didn't feel a thing either.

"You're not hypnotized," she told me. "Colm, you are."

"I don't think so." Colm answered. "Colm—SLEEP!" she commanded.

Like a popped soap bubble, he instantly collapsed into a deep sleep. His willingness to obey her command to turn his body into an iron bar so it could traverse the space between two chairs; convinced me he was in a trance. Before releasing him from his spell, she gave him some suggestive actions to perform at the draft board, such as pretending to be catatonic. Then she told him that she was going to count backward from ten and he would awake and remember nothing that had happened. When he awoke, it was as she had said; he remembered nothing. Before we left, she warned him that there was no way to be sure that a post-hypnotic suggestion would activate at a later date. It was only a possibility, not a guarantee.

On the ride home, I asked Colm what he had felt. "Nothing special. I just wanted to do what she asked. I could see no reason to resist." That would explain why I wasn't affected; my persona resisted being controlled by anyone. My mother always insisted that I was a stubborn ox.

Pat Collins final remarks had Colm worried. If the post hypnotic suggestion didn't kick in, he would be screwed. He began to panic again. He had heard a rumor that psychiatric deferments were easily obtained from hospitals in Massachusetts and decided it was worth traveling east to find out. He asked me if I would be interested in joining him. I was looking for an excuse to get out of LA. After the Marine complained to the studio about my long hair, they took me off the photography gig and put me to work building them another studio in Anaheim. My Republican boss thought by paying me a minimum wage to do carpentry work, he was getting a good deal, but since I was not supervised during the job, I worked so slow, that at the end of the day it actually cost him more than if he had hired a regular carpenter and paid a fair wage. I had my fill of the photo studio and told Colm I would go back east with him. A few days later we had our guitars and amps piled into the back seat of my '67 Volvo and headed out for Boston.

The South End of Boston was experiencing a real estate boom; everyone was getting rich. Yuppies were buying everything they could get their hands on. But we weren't in town to get rich. Bernie let us move into his vacant basement apartment and the day after we arrived, Colm went right to work on his draft evasion project. He walked over to Mass General, only a few blocks away, and tried to convince the admitting clerk that he should be institutionalized. His persistent arguing got him nowhere: "Only the police or an immediate relative can have you committed." he was told. Back at the apartment, he was dejected, but not defeated.

Two days later, a blustery wind and light rain made for an unpleasant chilly morning. If one would have driven past the Back Bay Police station at the intersection of Tremont and Dartmouth around ten in the morning, they would have seen a red headed Irish guy standing out front, seemingly without the sense to get out of the rain. He was not properly dressed, wearing only jeans and a tee shirt rendered soaking wet by the rain. The beads of water that ran down his forehead and dripping over his eyes seemed not to have the least affect on him. The cold did not make him shiver. He stood motionless, impervious to the elements and the world around him. It was Colm Gallager playing the role of a Schizophrenic Catatonic.

The police parked their cars diagonally along the sidewalk in front of the old red brick station. At the top of a wide swath of concrete steps, a worn double door with glass portals opened to the station's front desk. Any officer, checking in or out, had to pass through these doors. Very little pedestrian traffic passed in front of the station, especially on rainy days, so Colm, standing like a statue, stood out like a sore thumb. His glassy stare seemed not to have any focus or awareness. The few cops who bothered to ask what he was doing, scurried up the stairs to get out of the rain when they got no response. This was not how Colm had hoped the day would go, but he had made his move and had to stick with it. Suffering in the rain was better than going to Vietnam. Things started to look promising, when one of the cops came out of the station and removed his wallet from his pocket to check his I. D. But several more hours passed without anything happening. Then Colm overheard a conversation bleeding out to the street from the front desk that gave him a ray of hope.

"What's going on with the guy standing outside?"

"I don't know. It's just some fucking California Sunshine," the cop who had checked his I. D. said.

"Shouldn't we take him in.?"

"What the fuck for? Leave the fucker alone. He'll go away eventually."

But Colm, stubborn Irishman that he was, stood his ground until finally, around five o'clock, two cops came out, grabbed him by the arms, and dragged him to their patrol car. Success at last! After the cops made a quick stop at their personal cars to transfer some of the booty confiscated during the day's patrolling, he was on the way to the nut house.

By the time they arrived at Mass General, it was dark, and rather than take him in to the admitting desk and have him committed, they just pulled him out of the car and left him standing on the sidewalk in front of the entry door. His day of misery was now appearing to be all for naught. Fortunately, a sympathetic hospital worker couldn't handle looking at the pathetic looking man standing outside in the rain, and decided to bring him in. His non-responsive answers to a fifteen-minute interview he was given, combined with his deteriorated physical condition, convinced the hospital staff that the unknown stranger needed to be admitted to the psychiatric ward!!!

All that was left to do was to stay in the hospital long enough to obtain a report that described him as unable to function normally in society, and therefore unfit for the military. Within a few days, one of the nurses began to suspect that he was a malingerer, but notwithstanding, he was allowed to remain in the hospital. However, pretending to be a mental case became stressful and two weeks later Colm cracked. A real mental patient in the bed next to him, saw through his ruse and told him point blank that he didn't think he was crazy. Colm screamed for the nurse and fessed up.

The hospital staff, not unsympathetic to his plight, reminded him that as a non-citizen he could refuse the draft. It may affect his ability to get citizenship if he was so disposed, but that was something he could deal with when the time came.

He decided to take their advice and made plans to go back to LA and move in with his cousin, Florence, and her two daughters. Because my romance with Rita had been reignited, albeit still platonic, I decided to remain in Boston for a while to see how things developed. Both Colm and I felt that some of the songs we had written had potential, so we agreed to put our music careers on hold until such time that I returned. His cousin would always know how to get in touch with him. He would take his guitar and one of the amps back with him and leave my guitar and the other amp with me.

The guitars and equipment almost didn't make the trip. Without them, our musical fantasy would likely have ended. Like naive fools, a couple of days before he was to fly back to LA, we had left the window of our basement apartment open and someone had reached in and taken all our equipment, including my treasured old Martin and the electric guitar I had bought from Willie Chambers. Colm was livid and determined to get the equipment back. We started asking around if anyone knew anything. That's when a young black kid of high school age whom I was casual friends with, told us he knew where the guitars were. He led us to an apartment building five blocks away in a tough ghetto-neighborhood; the type of hood where getting shot or stabbed was a real possibility. Colm raced inside and pounded on the door until a young black woman opened it a crack. Impervious to any danger, he shoved the door open and marched into the room demanding the return of our equipment. I meekly followed behind. A shirtless male in his twenties came out of the bedroom to join her rebuttal, claiming they had no clue what he was talking about. Colm's face was flushed with Irish rage and he stormed right by him into the apartment's bedroom and opened its closet door. Both the shirtless male and I stood speechless by his audacity, but there, in the closet, was all of our equipment.

47

RACE WAR BREWING

I often though about the young black kid who helped us out by ratting a brother out to whitey. He told me he played football at the high school and hoped to go on to college, but that the learning environment at his school was so poor, he wasn't sure he would get the opportunity. Racism in Boston had been kept under wraps, but was there none-the-less. A demonstration led by a woman named Louise Day Hicks, to resist desegregating some of Boston's schools, had made the entire city tense. When Debbie and her now, fiancé, Erick Anderson, dropped by to say hello a few weeks after the Hicks demonstration, we went around the corner to have a drink at a little bar that catered to blacks. We thought as liberal folkie liberals, we would be welcomed. Three minutes after we were seated, a black dude came up and told us nicely, if we valued our safety, we would be wise to leave. Racial tension was engulfing the city. Bluesman, Otis Redding, whose resonant soulful voice had captured the hearts of blacks and whites alike, was giving a concert in Boston and along with Bernie and his date, Rita and I had tickets to attend. Throughout the week, a rumor circulated that there was going to be a riot during the performance. Two minutes after we took our seats, the two young black males sitting in front of us, intentionally made an overtly loud remark about "white mother fuckers," and then turned and spit at one of the empty seats next to Bernie. The riot never materialized, but someone popping a paper bag, caused a lot of people to scurry to the exits.

I was beginning to think staying in Boston had been a mistake. But Rita's coquettish eyes, long blond hair and thin delicate body had me thinking irrationally. The fact that some day she would look like her mother, fat and grumpy, mattered not. We had yet to have sex and yet, implausibly, we broached the subject of marriage. Her mother wasn't too pleased when she heard what we were planning; even more so when my car was repossessed right outside her house for failure to keep up with the payments. Rita had cajoled her mother to let me sleep on the living room couch after I brought her home from the Otis Redding debacle. The next morning, Tubby cooked me breakfast and served it with a: "You're not good enough for my daughter" look. When I finished, I walked outside to get my car, parked a half block up the street, and drive back to my place. My stomach sank when I saw that it was gone. Thinking it had been towed, I ran back to Rita's house and called the cops, but they had no report of any cars being towed. I didn't have to spend anytime thinking about what had happened. I was three months behind in my car payments and hoping to appease the bank, had sent a payment to them using Rita's mother's address as a return. The bank had a repo guy stake out the house and when I stayed over for the night, he hit pay dirt. Pleads to the bank fell on deaf ears.

"You get a yob" Rita's mother demanded in her thick Latvian accent. She even got me a job with her cousin who did remodeling work, but I only lasted one hour. I fit in with his Latvian crew like a square peg going into a round hole. Goeff Spence, always the good buddy, was glad to have me work with him again, doing odd carpentry jobs. The small income was enough to rent a funky room on Bartoloph Street, just a few doors away from his apartment. I was feeling like a character in a Tchaikovsky novel. My room had a single bulb hanging from the ceiling and a small funky sink in its corner that looked like it had noxious organisms festering in its drain. However, Spence's apartment was immaculately clean and cheerful. It even had a red Louis the XIV velvet couch that I could lounge on when I paid him frequent visits.

During the winter months, work was sparse, and when available, in harsh conditions; like the job we checked out at Logan Airport, where icy artic winds whipped across the terrain all day long. Thinking that I would at least be out of the cold, I hired on to a night shift job at the A&P warehouse in Sommerville, loading flats with boxes of groceries that were to be delivered to their various outlets by early morning. The warehouse wasn't heated and the cold concrete floor was like standing on blocks of ice for eight hours. Still convinced that I had the innate ability to "get-my-act-together," I soldered on and made the best of my situation until better days arrived. Listening to the stories my co-workers —all from the tough neighborhood of Charleston-brag about the fights they had been in over the weekend, where chairs were busted over their heads, made each week begin with laughter. Each morning, at 2AM when I got off, I trekked back to my cold room past the black hookers huddled in doorways along Tremont Street, knowing all was well because in the morning I would be walking over to Spence's apartment to share with him the half-dozen four ounce cans of lobster that I had pilfered from the warehouse. When you're down and out, small rewards can make one feel like a king.

On New Year's Eve of 1967, I sat on Spence's red velvet couch strumming my guitar while waiting for Rita to come by so we could welcome in the New Year together. Jeff enjoyed my guitar music and as I played for him, he began an oil painting of me .As midnight approached, it became clear that I was being stood up. The portrait reflected my saturnine mood. The next day Rita called to tell me she had fallen asleep.

Without a car or much money, I began to wonder why I was staying in the dead end that was Boston. Why I had broached the topic of marriage was even more perplexing. I was not interested in having kids and had no clue if I was in love or even if I knew what love was. I was acting out of blind desperation. She was as clueless as I was and fortunately for the good of both of us, the idea of marriage silently fell away. I decided that night that I would continue working at A & P until spring, and then, to make a little adventure out of it, hitch my way across the Canadian highway back to the west coast. If I was going to be a grocery packer, it might as well be in sunny California.

In the spring of 1968, I hitched up to Sudbury, a small town a few hundred miles to the north of Toronto, where the copper mining industry had left its environs looking like a grey moonscape. From there, since Canadian cities were far apart and the rides all tended to be long hauls, it took me only three days to reach the incomparable majestic beauty of Canada's Glacier National Park in British Columbia. On one all night ride, I was asked to help with the driving. We were going to cross the monotonous grain fields of Manitoba, but since the guy who picked me up had just had a brake job, he pumped them every ten minutes to convince himself that they would hold. Except when he was sleeping and I was driving, we lurched every five minutes when he hit the brakes. It was unlikely he had told me the whole story, because ten miles outside of Alberta the brakes failed. Miraculously the road was level and we were able to limp into town at five miles an hour without an accident.

48

RITA BECOMES A GANGSTER MOLL

A few days later, after my discombobulated stomach had settled from the all night lurching trip, I was in LA knocking on the door of Colm's cousin. She lived in a Spanish style duplex close to Los Angeles City College and only a few blocks from where the "mental kid" nightmare had taken place. Florence was a middle aged Irish woman, lively and still attractive but very business like. She told me Colm was no longer living with her and had moved in with the lady who owned the duplex next door. It turned out the lady was a sexy Latino single mom who I suspected had introduced him to the joy of blowjobs and possibly more. This worked out well for me, since Florence now had a bed available and as a favor to a friend of Colm's, offered to let me use it until I found my own place. As a trusting good-natured Irish divorcee she had to be worldly, yet was oblivious that putting me in the same room where her two daughters slept; Evelyn, age nine and Charlotte, age fifteen, had the potential for trouble.

Florence worked as a waitress and was out of the house until after midnight, during which time I was left alone with the girls. Naturally I was horny and would have liked to get laid, but Evelyn wasn't an option and though hormone charged Charlotte kept flirting with me, she wasn't an option either. I was crazy but not insane. Then one night, with Evelyn sleeping fifteen feet away, I was surreptitiously jacking off to some pictures in a girlie magazine I had secreted under my covers, when Charlotte came into the room with her gorgeous seventeen-year old friend, Tanya. Tanya worked at the Foster's Freeze just up the street on Santa Monica Blvd. and had served me up generous hot-fudge Sundaes from time-to-time. Charlotte had coyly intimated that Tanya found me to be cute. It had been passed on to me that she was desperate to lose her virginity. Now, here she was, standing at my bedside and it didn't take a genius to guess why.

I had let the girlie magazine drop out sight next to the wall and while I debated what I should do, Tanya had no such conflict and climbed on top of me; expecting to be ravished. Charlotte stood besides the bed hoping to watch the action and Evelyn, who I assume didn't know about sex—but probably did—pretended to be asleep. Fucking in front of Florence's daughters could put me in jail. It was a messy and tension filled situation and I didn't have a rapist type mentality that could just fuck through trauma, besides, virgins intimidated me. But not wanting to disappoint Tanya, I whispered in her ear that I would love to suck her pussy. She liked that idea and took off her panties and climbed under the covers where she spread her legs and whispered: "Let's see what you got." As I fluttered my tongue across her hard clit, I could hear Evelyn giggling from across the room. Tanya left a happy girl an hour later and when Florence came home all remmanats of the sex charged energy had dissipated and we were all sound asleep.

I was sitting on a powder keg and knew it. One of the girls would likely spill the beans, so before that happened I needed to find a job and rent my own place. A day later I was wearing the silly little costume of a Weiner Hut employee, scooping beans over Chili Dogs. Not only did it provide me money to rent a cheap room in a boarding house a block away from Florence's house, but all the Chili Dogs I could eat. There was also a silver lining I hadn't expected. A dozen or so leggy hookers, dressed in high heels and little short minis, plied their trade in front of Schwab's famous drug store just across the street. When I wasn't serving up a Chili Dogs, I could arouse myself by massaging my crotch as I watched the girls bend over at car windows and strut their stuff on the sidewalk.

Later in the evening I was to find the area was an equal opportunity sexual marketplace. When my shift ended, at two in the morning, because the buses stopped running at one AM, I had to hitchhike home. This was not a problem. Within seconds after sticking my thumb out, I would have a ride, but one that would never take me more than three blocks for the simple fact that all the cars cruising down the street were on the hunt for young gay hookers and when it was revealed that I wasn't a working boy, I was discarded. Repeating the scenario six or seven times was usually enough to get me within easy walking distance of my pad.

Either Colm's Latin honey got tired of giving him blow jobs, or he got overwhelmed being a father to her child, because he moved out of her apartment and took a room at the same boarding house where I was now staying. This meant that we could now get back to writing songs and within short order we had a half dozen in the bag. But neither of us had a clue how to sell a song and while we pondered, I continued to look for a way to make some decent money. Making chili dogs wasn't my idea of getting my act together. A solution would come from the unlikeliest of sources.

I had stayed in touch with Rita Fogelis and had called just to see how she was doing. After a few "How are you doing" exchanges, she launched a shocker. "Can you still score kilos of marijuana?" I wasn't sure I was hearing right. She went on to elaborate. A friend of hers in Boston was willing to pay a hundred and fifty bucks a key. He was looking to buy large amounts. Could I provide that? I had no intention of doing the Mexican thing anymore, but I knew kilos went for fifty bucks or less in LA, meaning I could make at least a C profit on each Kilo I moved to Boston. This wasn't heavy-duty math. After a few trips across the country, I would have a nice bankroll. The thought that Rita had become a gangster moll gave me a little chuckle.

I had enough money on hand to score three Kilos. That would net me four hundred fifty dollars after one trip to Boston, which could be parlayed into at least seven or eight kilos for the next trip. It wouldn't take long before I had enough money to score a hundred kilos, which would net me fifteen grand; a lot of money in 1968. That would be enough to stake myself in some kind of business adventure. Bottom line, it couldn't hurt. Having a stake couldn't be a bad thing.

The Campus Pool Hall, across the street from Los Angeles City College, was frequented by a small group of young disparate and open minded fringe characters. Though all were intelligent, they had little in common other than none had established careers and smoked pot. I had easily found a place among them. There was Pat Breheny, an alcoholic aspiring screenplay writer, Arnie, a lanky kid of Scandinavian heritage, who supported his pretty black wife and child by stealing hub-caps each evening, Martin, a rail thin chess whiz who looked like a chicken and supported himself by pilfering items out of unlocked cars and Eliot, a short portly Jewish kid, with curly reddish blond hair and the confident demeanor of a Rabbi. My hope was that one of them might be able to turn me on to someone who had a connection for scoring keys.

I knew Pat Breheny subsidized his struggling writing career by selling lids, so it was the logical place to start. I stopped by his apartment on Virgil and broached the subject with him. After making sure there was a way for him to get a taste if a deal went through, he told me Eliot the Rabbi had a connection. Later in the day we went to the pool hall to hook up with the Rabbi, who usually came by in the afternoon.

He was already there when we arrived. Over a game of pool, Pat told him what I was looking for. There was always a bit of paranoia among dealers, and though the Rabbi knew me, it made him feel more comfortable that Pat, whom he already had dealt with, was there to vouch for me. I sweetened the deal by telling him that as long as my price was fifty bucks per, I didn't care what he paid.

And I made it clear, I didn't want to meet his supplier—I wanted my operation to be clean; one contact in LA and one in Boston, namely Rita's friend. That would keep the risk of getting busted near impossible. There was always the chance of someone in a long chain getting popped and making a deal to save their ass by fingering someone else, but my scheme would prevent that possibility. Eliot agreed to the terms and conditions. He had no interest in turning me on to his source anyway.

After I double-checked with Rita that her buyer was for real, Pat called the Rabbi to tell him the deal was on and that he should come to his apartment so I could give him the money. The Rabbi didn't know where I lived and I wanted to keep it that way, so after giving him the hundred fifty dollars, I waited at Pat's place until he returned. Being Irish, Pat loved to drink, or as they say in Ireland, have a pint, and he got a bit tipsy while we wiled away the time. Eliot was not the type to burn me, so I had no worry about being ripped off. Two hours later he showed up with three nicely wrapped cellophane bricks. I tore open a corner of one of them and shredded off a half-ounce to pay Pat for his troubles and rewrapped the package. My Boston buyer would never notice such a small quantity missing. Eliot had already made his share on the front end and Pat, in a mild stupor, was more than happy with his. I split back to my pad and called Rita to tell her in coded language that I would be in Boston tomorrow with the three pieces we had talked about. "Tell your buyer so he has the cash on hand."

The next morning I was at LAX to purchase a youth fare ticket on American Airlines. To encourage young people under twenty one to fly with them, they were offering a half price youth fare. They didn't ask for I. Ds and since my baby face didn't look a day past seventeen, I quickly had a ticket in hand. Being slow to mature had its benefits. Knowing that my illicit merchandise was safely stashed in the cargo bay of the plane, I sat back and enjoyed a delightful flight across the USA; dinning on a small steak diner and a free movie supplied by the airline to help make the trip more pleasant. Life was good.

49

WHAT ARE 'BEAVERS?

I had arranged with Jeff Spence to stay at his pad while I was in town, so after collecting my three kilos from the luggage conveyor at Logan airport, I took a cab to his apartment where he had left a key on top of the doorframe in case he wasn't home when I arrived. He always made me feel welcome and took nothing in return. I placed a call to Rita to let her know I was in town with the goodies. An hour later she showed up, her eyes peeking out from beneath her bangs and being that she was now a criminal, looking a bit mischievous. I had no clue what was in it for her other than the excitement of abetting a crime and didn't ask. I told her I wanted to meet her friend before I showed the product, so she drove me to the current hip hangout for the young Back Bay crowd, a busy coffee house operating out of a below street level location on the corner of Mass Ave and Newbury Street. The buyer, a young, hotshot named Jimmy, was about five-five with thick black hair and a friendly round face. After talking to him for a short time, I felt confident he was not a cop. He showed me the money and I told him I would be back within a half hour to make the delivery.

Everything went smooth. Jimmy said he could handle all I could bring. He hung at the coffee house every night so I would have no trouble finding him. The next morning, I flew youth fare back to LA in a plane that was only a third full, allowing me to stretch my long frame across four seats in the center aisle and have a pleasant sleep. When I awoke we were already descending into the LA basin. I had finally pulled off a drug deal that made a profit.

Because of the time zones, it was only noon when I arrived back in LA, so I went directly to Pat's apartment and had him set up another meeting with the Rabbi. By three in the afternoon he came by and since I was buying more quantity, I negotiated a better price; Four hundred bucks for ten kilos. The fifty bucks that I would save would pay for my youth fair plane ticket back to Boston. Eliot assured me that wouldn't be a problem. But when he returned later in the day, I was told nothing was available until a shipment came up from Mexico; probably in about a week.

I had time to kill, but sadly both the Burbank and New Follies burlesque theatres had closed their doors. However, on the cab ride back from the airport, I had noticed that a nearby theatre, called the Vista, was advertising, "Direct from San Francisco, two continuous hours of all color 16mm Beaver films." What was a 'Beaver' Film? The Vista was just a few blocks from my apartment so I took a walk to check it out. The theatre sat on the north side of the busy trisection of Sunset, Santa Monica and Virgil Boulevards. LA was experiencing one of those blazing hot days where the heat can be seen rising off the pavement. Because of traffic coming in six different directions, I was having a lengthy stay at the intersection, waiting for the lights to change so I could cross over to the theatre. While wondering what these "Beaver" movies could be, an old man sidled up next to me:

"You interested in making a little money?"

He looked to be in his mid fifties. His grey hair that was closely trimmed in a crew cut was not much longer that the stubble on his fleshy face. Wearing a white dress shirt and a tie, both loose around the neck because of the heat, and an unbuttoned gray sports coat, he could have been a traveling salesman or maybe someone's grandpa out for a stroll.

Not wanting to be rude I asked: "Doing what?"

"Oh nothing hard, just a little spanking—that's all."

His nonchalance made it seem like a totally normal request. "A spanking?"

"Yeah, nothing big . . . just a little warming up, that's all. I'll pay you twenty-five bucks."

I stood silent for a few seconds, hoping the light would quickly change. Spending the afternoon paddling a flabby old butt was not my idea of a good time—even for twenty-five bucks. I left the old fellow standing rejected after the light changed and dashed across the street to check out these "Beaver" movies.

However, before going into the theatre, I noticed a magazine store just around the corner and went in to see if they carried girlie magazines. To my ecstatic delight, not only did they carry the normal selection of American smut, but several issues of two Danish publi-cations that I had never seen before; *'Cover Girl'* and *'Exciting.'* Each 4x6 inch magazine, had a high gloss color cover of the featured model who posed in and black and white pictures inside wearing panties, nylons, garter belts, half bras and diaphanous lingerie; and unlike any American girlie magazine, in the nude doing poses that showed the girls pussy in graphic detail. One of the 'Cover Girl' magazines featured a beautiful oriental girl with long black hair and a shaved pussy. She was lying sideways on her hip with her legs drawn forward so that the lips of her hairless pussy pouted out from between her thighs. My dick was so hard that it was hurting as it strained against my pants. Before leaving to go to the Vista to see 'beaver' movies, I had paged through all ten issues the store carried of each magazine. When I left to go to the Vista, I knew I would definitely be returning on a later date, dressed in proper attire so I could pilfer the entire collection for my personal enjoyment. The hours of stimulation they would provide for masturbation was endless.

Each of the eight silent 'beaver' films, all in color, were of a girl sensually stripping off her cloths while rolling around and undulating on a bed as though she were sexually aroused. A generic music track, supplied by the theatre, added to the sleazy ambiance. Many of the girls wore nylons and garter belts and though they willingly spread their legs while still wearing panties, they were required to keep them closed once the panty was taken off. However, as a last bit of titillation, they were allowed to let a little triangle of pubic hair to peek out from above their closed legs, evidently what was now being called a "beaver." My favorite was a baby-faced black girl wearing a page-boy wig, black nylons, panties and bra. When she opened her legs, the bulge her pussy made against the wide crotch of her red panties, made me shoot my load.

I left the theatre sexually drained and walked back to Pat's place to see if there was any word from the Rabbi. He had good and bad news. A shipment was due in from Mexico but had yet to arrive. It would probably be a week at most.

While I killed time diddling on my guitar and waiting for my merchandise to arrive, I got up enough nerve to embark on another escapade that I had been contemplating for a long time. My interest had been piqued for over a year by ads that ran weekly in the LA Free Press: *Models Needed for Nude Photography, female and male, no experience needed.* I had never had the nerve to respond to one. "Damn it, just do it!" I told myself and called a number listed in one of the ads that didn't seem intimidating. A man answered the phone and after I answered a few questions regarding age, general appearance and whether I had any problems with nudity, gave me his address and told me to come right over.

The address was in west Hollywood and after getting off a bus near Grauman's famous Chinese theatre, I walked a half block up Orange Street and found myself standing in front of a typical two story fifty's style California apartment building. Two palm trees and a few small cacti in a bed of white gravel were planted in front of a high concrete lattice that hid the stairwell to the apartments on the second level. The sound of traffic on Hollywood boulevard could be heard in the distance. It seemed an odd place for a nude photo shoot. After a deep breath to boost my resolve, I walked around the concrete lattice and up the stairs to the door of the apartment I had been given; and after a brief pause . . . knocked.

Rather than a dirty old man or a mobster, I was surprised that the door was opened by a friendly, thirty-something guy, wearing army issue kakis and tank top. He had a receding hairline and well-toned arms. He introduced himself as Stan Grossman, which seemed ironically appropriate for a nude model photographer. His eyes had a twinkle to them and after quickly deciding that I fit his needs, he invited me in and directed me to take a seat at a table against the wall while he finished working with the models he was already shooting.

The girls, a blond and a brunette, both young and pretty, were on their haunches sitting atop a mattress in the middle of the room. They had barely acknowledged my entry and I forced myself not to gawk at them, but out of the side of my eye I could see that both were wearing sexy bikini panties and high heels. The blond was topless while the brunette was wearing a satin push-up bra, nylons and a garter belt. Stan was shooting a layout for a girlie magazine!! Cool!!

I understood, as a professional, I needed to appear nonchalant. Managing not to ogle, I watched Stan snap the girls in various simulated lesbian poses. Both girls happily followed his directions. Short of touching pussies, they shamelessly ran their hands over each other's bodies. After the blond took off her panties, he took shots of them with their beavers exposed, but none with their legs spread. Like a humming bird, he moved around the room, taking a hundred different shots from every conceivable angle, all the time uttering "good-good-good" to let the girls know he was happy with their work.

After he shot several rolls of film, I was told to take my cloths off and join the girls on the mattress. At first I felt a little weird standing in someone's living room butt naked, but I was in good shape from my stint as a construction worker and soon relaxed. The girl's demeanor made it clear that everything was strictly professional. We were there to do a job. They were the stars and I was little more than a prop. American law didn't allow for any genital touching. Even though I was naked, my genitals had to remain hidden, so obviously a boner was verboten. In any case, the pressure of being filmed made getting a hard on next to impossible. Grossman's directions were explicit, "honey, arch your back, Howard put your hand on her hip and move a bit to the right." None of the poses feigned sexual activity, just nude bodies cavorting, albeit in an erotic manner. When we finished, Stan gave each of the girls thirty-five dollars and me twenty-five. In some ways, I considered being paid a bonus.

The blond quickly left the apartment after being compensated for her work and the tall brunette disappeared into a bedroom. As I finished putting my bikini underwear back on, Grossman invited me to hang around for a while. I had no idea what he had in mind, but felt privileged to be asked. Seconds later, the brunette came back into the living room wearing only sexy panties and a push up bra. Stan and her began making out on the mattress and he singled for me to join in. She parted her legs so I could pull her panties to the side and suck on her cunt while she blew Stan.

Obviously she was Stan's girl friend, however, her vibe said she was participating in our little orgy more to please him than herself. Stan was content in just getting a blowjob and suggested that I should fuck his lady. It turned him on to see her getting screwed by a stranger. It was more than I could handle on my first shoot and I lost my hard-on as I tried to penetrate her. That brought the orgy to an end. A pallor of failure filled the room: Stan's girl friend wondering why she wasn't sexy enough to get me hot and my ego deflated by my inability to perform. But Stan didn't seem too upset and we parted amicably. Despite the poor finale, it had been a hell of a day and I had every intention of doing more nude modeling in the future.

50

ERIC IN A MUDDY POND

A few days later, the kilos from Mexico arrived. Dawning upon me that the thirty-five kilos that Eliot handed over to me weighed almost eighty pounds, I reconsidered how I would transport them back to Boston. Checking in at the airport with that much pot could be dangerous. I decided I would take the train. That would allow me to never let the bags leave my hands. By placing them on the luggage rack above my seat, I would be assured that no one else would have access to them.

For that matter, I enjoyed travel by train. The service from Los Angeles to Chicago was quite luxurious and relaxing. The seats were large and soft and reclined enough to offer a reasonable night of sleep. On the second day out of LA, I was feeling quite secure about how things were going. My illicit cargo sat innocuously above my head and it was unthinkable that anyone would tamper with it, so I walked back to the lounge car to have a coke. My hair was neatly trimmed and I wore a nice blue pin striped suite that I had purposely purchased to make myself look conservative. To encourage rapport between fellow travelers, the seating arrangement in the club car was arranged in a horseshoe, but I had no intention of talking to anyone, so after the black attendant brought me my drink, I just sunk back in my chair and with a bored look on my face, watched the scenery go by.

Maybe because I looked so young and professional, I piqued the interest of an elderly gentleman sitting across from me. He had a professional demeanor and lured me into a conversation with a bit of small talk. I didn't want to appear standoffish, as that could look suspicious, so I humored him by trading a lot of meaningless badinage. But the conversation soon became more probing: "Where are you from? Where are you going? Who are you going to visit?" My radar went up and seeing no benefit in providing accurate information considering what I was doing, I provided evasive answers. When I learned that he was the head of the American Psychiatric Association, red lights flashed and sirens screamed in my head. Could he see through me? Did he know I was lying? I couldn't just walk away—then he would really know I was up to something. I had to control my paranoia and calmly continued the conversation, sipping on my coke with a look of ennui on my face. Finishing the coke finally gave me a pretext to politely excuse myself and leave to go back to my seat. It didn't help that he gave me a knowing smile as I left. "He knows, but why would he turn me in? Freud was a cocaine addict," I thought to myself as I walked away.

From Chicago's La Salle Street Station, where all the west coast routes ended, I lugged my two forty pound suite cases to a cab and had him take me to Union Station from where trains headed to the east departed. I avoided letting the cabbie lift my unreasonably heavy bags which he appreciated. The comfort level on the east coast train diminished sharply, small hard seats and many stops waiting for freight trains to pass or mail to be dropped off slowed us to a snails pace; but twenty-four hours later we were approaching Bean Town.

Jimmy and I were now trusted partners in crime and there was no reason to involve Rita anymore. I had called him from Chicago and had given him the specifics of when to meet me at Boston's Back Bay Station, which was just a quay alongside the tracks. It was near desolate and we could make our deal right on the spot, rather than me first lugging the heavy bags to Spence's before I called him. His smiling face was a welcome sight as I stepped off the train. We looked like two fraternity brothers coming back to school. He helped me carry the bags to his car, where after a quick check of the merchandise, he handed me five grand and split. It was more money than I had ever seen-what an MIT grad would make in a year. With my pockets full of hundred dollar bills, I walked the short distance from the Back Bay Station to Spence's pad. The next day I was flying youth fare back to L. A.

A hundred keys was the biggest deal the Rabbi had ever handled and his sources couldn't guarantee when a shipment of that size would be coming into town. At best it might be available in three weeks. He would stay on top of it and get back to me as soon as he knew something. In the meantime, I continued working with Colm writing songs and modeling.

Another ad in the Free Press led me to Orman Longstreet, a grandfatherly gray haired man with a bit of a paunch, who not only shot naughty pictures of sexy girls for Parliament Publications but also volunteered his time as a boy-scout master. He had a professionally set up studio on the little street that ran directly behind the apartment where my father lived. The Big Fox had no clue! My interview went well and I was told to show up at nine the next morning.

My heart skipped several beats when I took a seat on the floor in the back of Orman's van and saw, sitting in the front seat, the gorgeous blond flower child that I would be posing with. "Man would I like to score with her." Alas, during the long ride to a secluded bubbling creek in Angles National Forest, I learned the bad news that she had a steady boy friend. But I still looked forward to seeing her model.

That fantasy was struck a blow when I was told to wait in the truck while the gorgeous flower child changed into her modeling outfit. When she emerged, dressed in small yellow silk panties, matching bra, black nylons with seams, frilly garter belt and high heels; all provided by the scoutmaster: she had been transformed into a lascivious bedroom whore. Christ was she sexy! I immediately got a boner, but lost it when Orman told me to wait in the van while he led her off to where the shooting would take place. "I don't want an extra set of eyes to intimidate her," he told me. Later I was brought onto the scene to appear in a few poses where I was hiding in the trees spying on her. None of the poses were particularly raunchy, so maybe I hadn't missed much. But then: a few months later, while browsing girlie magazines, I saw her layout in 'Nylon Jungle.' She was lying in the stream on some rocks in a way that allowed the water to flow over her tummy and down her crotch; making the yellow silk of her panties become near transparent. As my hard-on pushed against my pants, all I could think was: "Damn you Orman Longstreet, Damn you!"

The hundred kilo score was proving to be next to impossible. If I had a brain, which I didn't, I would have realized that it would weigh almost two hundred and fifty pounds and be very difficult to move across the country. Nevertheless, I didn't let messy details like that bother me and continued to take modeling jobs while I waited. Not every interview led to a job. On one I was asked to show what I had and was given a humiliating: "nothing special" rating.

Obviously there were fewer jobs for male models than female, so if you wanted to work you couldn't be fussy or prudish. I wasn't bisexual, but I no longer had any qualms about gays and didn't mind appearing in a gay magazine, so I answered an ad placed by Pat Rocco, the reputed crème de la crème of gay photography. I let him know I was straight and was only interested in posing for a solo layout. He liked my look and had no problem with that. He took me up in the hills of Griffith Park, not far from the famed observatory, and to the end of a dirt fire road that branched off of Mt Hollywood Drive. It was an area I would learn the gay community affectionately referred to as the *'Swish Alps.'* While I enjoyed the spectacular panoramic view of the city that could be seen through the trees from where we were going to shoot, Pat made a quick survey of the area to make sure it was deserted.

He then asked me to strip naked and put on a two-inch black leather belt around my waist, a leather peak cap and some knee high black leather boots topped off with a sexy white g-string that held my genitals in a provocative little package. I felt quite sexy. We would first shoot a short black and white 8mm film and then a roll of black and white stills.

With his back to the city panorama, Pat mounted his camera on a tripod at the end of the dirt road and just at the edge of a shallow puddle that remained from the prior day's rainstorm. As soon as he was ready to shoot, he directed me to slowly saunter down the path towards the camera and stop at the edge of the little puddle and then look around as though I were an Adonis just enjoying nature. I hadn't taken fifteen steps, when I noticed an unexpected observer standing behind Pat. Neither of us had seen the dirt trail that ran just below the crest of the hill where a bicycle rider now stood gaping at the odd scene he had just stumbled upon. But Angelinos are not easily shocked by the shenanigans of the film industry and, after a brief look, the man pedaled on as though nothing had happened.

Once the scene was clear of unwanted eyes, I went back and repeated my sexy stroll, stopping as I had been directed, just short of the puddle to let my eyes take in the amazing nature surrounding me. Pat slowly paned down to the muddy puddle where a light breeze was causing the water to ripple, and filmed the denouement of the film, a shot of my slightly distorted reflection. Laws about male nudity were quite a bit more liberal for gays than what they were for straights and he then shot a roll of stills on me sans the g-string. A few months later, I found myself being marketed in the gay section of a sex shop as: what else? *'Eric in a Muddy Pond.'*

The Rabbi finally told me he had a connection that could score a hundred kilos. I would be trusting Eliot with five thousand bucks in one hundred dollar bills which was going to make me nervous, but it was the price I was willing to pay to maintain my anonymity. Pat was his normal half-snookered self while I sat with him at his apartment waiting for the Rabbi to arrive. He came by about four in the afternoon and told me the score was set to go down that night around ten in the evening. I made it strictly understood that he was not to part with the money until he saw the weed. After he left I tried to remain as stoic as possible.

Only then did it begin to dawn on me how difficult it would be to transport that much grass across LA, let alone the country. For that matter, how was Eliot going to transport it back to Pat's place. A few tokes of the joint I was sharing with Pat helped to relegate those discomforting details to the foggy recesses of my mind. When the Rabbi hadn't returned by eleven, the fog lifted and I started to get a queasy feeling in my stomach. Why was it taking so long? About midnight, he called to say that he was in the valley with the two dealers at the home of one of their parents. They were adamant about not letting him accompany them to the drug warehouse. Doing so would require them to reveal their source. "Did I want him to give them the money?" He felt they were cool. The parents were an elderly couple and they had no problem of him remaining at their place until their boys returned.

The San Fernando Valley was a blue-collar area and I pictured a typical one-story two-bedroom house with a pick-up truck sitting out front on a yellow unwatered lawn. The parents were probably two over weight losers sitting on a funky worn out velvet couch, but I was getting frustrated and despite this negative image, told myself it was not unreasonable that everyone wanted to remain anonymous—just as I did—so I said OK.

By two AM Eliot still hadn't returned. Stressed out and exhausted, I tried to convince myself not to worry. "What could go wrong? He was with the fucker's parents for Christ sakes." I fell asleep on Pat's couch and woke back up around six AM. Eliot finally called about 9AM. He was still at the parent's place, but the dudes still had not come back. He told me the parents were in there fifties and didn't seem to know what was going on. An image of Valley trailer scum popped into my head. The dealers were probably long hair biker types. My nerves were on edge. Five grand was a lot of bread. I told him to stick it out and he agreed. Maybe they would still show up. Who would put their parents in a dangerous situation like that? A stupid question being that Eliot was anything but dangerous.

A full twenty hours passed and Eliot was still at the parents. There was no sign of the dealers. No call, no nothing! It was obvious that we had been had. Like when I had been burned previously by the space dude, I wasn't in to beating the shit out of anyone. That wasn't my game. It would only lead to something really bad. "Fuck!!" I told Eliot to come back. I had no reason to suspect him; he was just a fat little Jewish kid who had the same kind of personality I had—laid back. Maybe that was the problem.

I took my loss like a big boy and figured I could start again from the bottom and rebuild my nut back to five grand. Everything had gone smoothly up to the big deal. It was just one bad deal that fucked everything up. Scoring large quantities of weed, even five or ten kilos, could sometimes be difficult, so building my nut back up was taking longer than the first go around had. But because I had become known as a dependable model for nude photographs, I was getting hired on a regular basis. It was more about having fun than making money, but the money didn't hurt.

Bill Rotsler had become my favorite photographer to work for and he hired me and four other models, a guy and three girls, to go down to San Felipe, a small fishing village on the east coast of the Mexican Baja peninsula. He planed to shoot a nude Sherlock Holmes spoof for Adam Film Quarterly. After shooting all day on a large desolate beach just south of the town, we slept on the beach overnight. One of the models was a cute oriental girl and I had hopes she would like to share my sleeping bag, but she didn't share my fantasy and I slept alone. When the layout was published, I would appear wearing nothing but a safari hat and using a stick to tease—or more likely irritate—the cute oriental girl who I was poking as I walked behind her. I had a bit more luck on the ride back to LA when one of the other models, a bosomy black chick, was happy to let me eat her pussy while we sat in the back of the van.

At the time, I had no reason to believe that I would ever direct a scene, but I was still able to appreciate how comfortably Rotsler handled his actors and crew. He kept his sets relaxed. Standards in the adult magazine world were changing rapidly and male genitals were now cool, as long as they weren't erect On another shoot that Rostler had hired me for, I was standing under the large doorway that connected the living and dining rooms of the house next to a model in her panties and bra. We were watching Bill shoot a simulated lesbian scene on top of the dinning room table when I felt my dick getting hard. I had a towel wrapped around my waist but became worried that Rotsler would call me to the set where my hard-on would be problematical and embarrassing. I was supposed to be a pro. I tried to psyche myself down and when I couldn't, turned to the side to hide my bulging tent. But the girl standing next to me had noticed my infraction and I didn't want her to think that I was a pervert and began to offer an explanation, half expecting her to be offended:

"Well, at least you can get a hard-on, that's better than a lot of the guys" she told me.

That was surprising; a lot of guys can't get hard? And that she found my hard on a plus was equally surprising. Some of the attitudes in the sex business were confusing. Most girls, strippers and models, didn't appreciate guys getting free erections at their expense. Many of them saw male models as losers, who weren't able to get dates the regular way. When a model I was posing with in the spoon position felt me getting hard she turned her head to give me a "what the fuck do you think you're doing look." The girl I had been standing next to was an exception and if I had been more secure about myself, I might have offered to take her out on a date, but I wasn't and didn't. Other than a three day affair with a Latina who had a shaved pussy, I had no dates with models

Between modeling gigs, I managed to make a few flights back to Boston and was once again transporting two suitcases filled with kilo bricks across the country that would result in another five K payday. American Airlines had become aware that their "youth fare" program was being abused and were now asking for I. D.s, so I opted to try a new mode of transportation; Greyhound Bus. My bags would be in the bins beneath the bus where no one could mess with them and it would be highly unlikely that I would encounter any psychiatrists like I had on the train. Each time the bus made a stop, I got out to make sure no one accidentally unloaded my merchandise.

We had just finished making a twenty-minute layover at a roadside café somewhere in the middle of the Ozarks, where after gobbling down a burger and a coke, I had returned to my seat for the next leg of the trip. Ten minutes after we were back on the road, I was about to take a nap when I felt something smelly bumping against my head. I turned and found that a hillbilly, who had just got on at the last stop, had put his two big smelly clodhoppers up on my headrest. In a somewhat indignant voice, I turned and asked:

"Do you mind taking your feet down?" "How come?"

"Cause they smell!"

Grudgingly, he removed them from my headrest and I again closed my eyes so I could resume my nap. But just as I was about to nod off the stench returned. The fucker must not have washed his feet in a month. They were back on my headrest and after directing a glowering look his way; I took my hand and knocked them down to the floor; confident that my six foot two construction-hardened body was enough to make my point clear. Thank god he got off at the next stop to head up into the hills to his bootleg still.

The Greyhound bus is a regular social club. You never know whom you're going to meet. Sometimes the encounters were irritating, like the one I just described, and sometimes were very helpful. A light skinned, freckle-faced, redheaded black kid, took the vacant seat next to me when he boarded the bus at Harrisburg, Pennsylvania. We hit it off, and in the course of the conversation I mentioned that I was taking the bus because my youth fare card had expired. I was surprised when he offered to give me his youth fare card, which he said he had no intention of using again. Understandably, I made no mention why I traveled across the country so frequently, but gladly accepted his generous gift. Despite it only having about nine months remaining, I would use it for my return trip to LA.

The delivery to Jimmy went smooth as usual and with five grand in my pockets, I walked over to Spence's pad. I phoned Rita to tell her I was in town and staying at Jeff's. When I told her about my new youth card, which pictured a negro with reddish black hair, she offered to come by in the morning and give me a dye job so my appearance could match the picture on the I. D. It was nothing that a normal gangster moll wouldn't do.

That afternoon, the attractive young female ticket agent at the airport did a double take when I presented my youth card and my cosmetically altered self.

"This doesn't look like you," she said incredulously. "Well, it is," I shot back.

She noticed that the dye job hadn't completely covered my blond roots. "Your hair's not black."

Sounding a bit plaintive, "It just looks blacker in the picture." "And your eyes are blue and you don't have freckles."

I was out of retorts when she had a paroxysm of sympathy and issued the ticket. Unbelievably I was twenty-eight and still flying youth fare!

Maybe pot and LSD had impaired my ability to reason, because if I had been smart, I would have scored the hundred kilos in several smaller amounts; like thirty or so at a time. But oblivious to what had happened the last time, I asked the Rabbi to score a hundred kilos, and once again he told me that no one he knew could get their hands on that many at a time.

The news made me depressed so I drove out to Santa Monica in the two hundred dollar pile of junk I had recently purchased from a used car dealer, to hook up with Phyllis and have some guaranteed sex. On the way, the pile of junk began sputtering half way through Beverly Hills and I knew it was going to die, so I turned onto the residential side of Rodeo Drive and abandoned it in front of some la-de-da's house. It had yet to be registered and there was no way to trace it to me. I caught a bus out to Santa Monica and after Phyliss took me to her parent's house for a disgusting gefilte fish lunch, I was in her bed smoking an after-sex joint, when I mentioned that I was having trouble finding a hundred kilos. The long wait was making me a little sloppy about letting people know what I was up to, but Phyllis was like family and I needed to blow off some tension. I had no intention of getting her involved.

To my surprise, she called a few days later to say that she might have a supplier. Was I interested? The irony didn't escape me that my girl friends, Rita, and now Phyllis, seemed to have more big time connections than I had. At first I was skeptical and passed, but when the Rabbi still couldn't come up with anything over the next two weeks, I called Phyllis to see if her connection was still operative. Once again making it clear that I would not hand over any money until I had seen the merchandise, she got back to me later in the day. The grass was still available and the dealer had no problem with my conditions. We could do the deal the next day if I wanted. I told her I'd be at her place around ten in the morning.

Don the Messiah was there when I arrived, so it was obvious that he had set up the deal. I had no reason to mistrust him—he was a guru, not a thug—and if his connection didn't show the merchandise, I wouldn't hand over the money. That I was violating my principle of not having any direct contact with dealers didn't go unnoticed, but this would be my last score and what were the chances of it being a set up by the narcs? Not much. So everything was cool as far as I was concerned.

The three of us jumped into my latest cheap car and Don directed me to drive to a neighborhood just north of Lincoln and west of Venice Boulevard. It was an area of many small single story homes built in the fifties. Most were painted a muted yellow color and sat on small lots with a concrete driveway that ran alongside to a one-car garage that was located in the rear. The sunny day and bland neighborhood was not a setting where one would expect a large drug score to take place; but then again, maybe it was the perfect setting.

Don told me to park the car in the middle of the block and we had only waited for a few minutes when a scrawny young hippy with a scraggly beard came walking from across the street to the passenger side of the car. Don said it was our guy and rolled down his window to see what he wanted us to do. We were told the kilos were in a garage behind a nearby house just up the street. We should get out of the car and follow him there. After a wet-fish handshake, the scrawny guy led us to a house a few paces up the street and down its driveway until we all stood before a single car garage with a paddle locked door.

He turned to me and said, "The hundred kilos are inside."

The padlock secured a sliding latch bolt at the bottom of the doors left side. I was waiting for the guy to unlock it but instead we all just looked at each other. The scrawny guy had sidled up to Don who was standing at the rear and whispered something into his ear. Don then approached me and said: "He wants to hold the money before handing you the key."

It didn't seem unreasonable. He didn't know me. I didn't know him. He was standing right there—he couldn't run away—so I handed him the five grand and took the key. I got down on my knees so I could insert it into the lock. Phyllis, Don and the scrawny hippie stood just behind me, watching as I attempted to open it. I was having a bit of trouble getting the key inserted, so I twisted the lock into a more accessible position, but after a few seconds of finagling, I still couldn't get the key to fit. I looked up to ask the guy what the problem was.

HE WASN'T THERE!!

I looked down the driveway. HE WAS NOWHERE!! I jumped up.

My heart was beating hard and my stomach had dropped to the ground. Phyllis and Don looked at me dumbfounded. While all of our eyes had been glued on me inserting the key, the hippie fuck had disappeared like a poltergeist. I ran out to the street, sweating more from panic than the hot sun. The street was deserted. GOD DAMN MOTHER FUCK!!

Maybe I was just overreacting—maybe my hands had been too nervous to insert the key. I went back to the door and got on my knees again to make another attempt but before I could even try, a strange voice came from a few feet away:

"Can I help you?"

A straight-laced older man was standing on the stoop outside the back door of the house. He was glarring at me with a humorless look on his face. I muttered that we had some of our stuff inside and couldn't get the lock to open.

"That's my garage pal and I'd like you to leave or I'll call the police."

"BURNED BY A FUCKING HIPPIE LOVE CHILD!!" How could I be such a stupid fuck? A stupid ass!! I knew Phyllis wasn't involved, but I couldn't be sure about Don. After all, I was fucking his girl friend. He claimed complete surprise. What was I going to do—beat the shit out of him? Kill him? I doubted if he was complicit. I was just a lousy dealer and worse—stupid.

My problems were mounting; no money, no car and no career other than nude modeling. Even that was drying up because photographers were always looking for new faces and I had been around too long.

51

JUST A PUSSY SUCKING BEATNIK

My recent obsession with making money probably meant I was bull shitting myself by claiming it didn't matter to me. I just didn't want to work for someone else or be bored doing something mundane. Smuggling grass was exiting, but obviously I wasn't very good at it. I decided to work harder to find a spot in the music world. I took a couple of guitar lessons from a studio musician and even signed up for a piano course at LACC. But then a couple of weeks after my last smuggling fiasco, I got a call from Bruce Campbell, a preppy trust-fund baby, who I had previously met through Bernie Goldhirsh. Somehow word had gotten out around Boston that I had access to kilos. Bruce said he was willing to front me five hundred bucks if I could bring three of them back to Boston. Maybe he wanted to sell lids to the kids at Amherst; grass was becoming popular everywhere. With the five bills I could score six keys, give Bruce his three, and sell the other three to Jimmy, making myself five hundred in the process. I told him to wire me the money.

Until I wrapped up Campbell's deal, I was very low on funds and knowing I would soon be on my way to Boston, decided to save money by moving out of the rooming house and sleep on Pat Breheny's couch until Eliot delivered the product. Six kilos was no big deal and I assumed it would only be for a couple of days at most. But Eliot had some bad news. A big trafficker had been busted and kilos could not be found anywhere in LA. He had no idea when things would get back to normal. It put me in a bit of a funk. I wasn't getting a lot of modeling jobs anymore and hanging at Pat's pad listening to his half soused ramblings was hard to take.

Don Quixote had his ideal woman, 'Dulcinea of Tobosco,' who he irrationally fixated on for his entire life; mine was Debbie Green. This fixation is a flaw in the male gene and has no rational explanation that I know of. She had never given me any indication that the feeling was reciprocal. Other than a few sexual encounters, there was not much of a bond. Nevertheless, in my funk, I placed a call to her at the last number she had given me, supposedly at her mother's house somewhere back east in New York state. I didn't expect the call to be successful so was very surprised to hear her voice when the phone was picked up. Its alluring and soothing quality melted me like butter on a hot day. When she addressed me as "Howie" made me feel warm.

She told me her mother's house was in a little town called Patchoque on the south coast of Long Island near West Hampton Beach. Eric was off promoting his career and she had the whole place to herself for the summer. It was idyllic; but with no one around, she was lonely and needed company. I told her, as though I were a knight errant, that I would be there to rescue her as soon as I could.

Eliot said things were beginning to look up, so I fronted him the money and left Pat with a suitcase and Jeff Spence's address and told him as soon as my weed came in, to send it to me by UPS. I was going to hitchhike back east to rescue Debbie and then continue on to Boston thereafter. Thinking the grass might arrive in Boston before I did, I told him to send it *hold-for-pick-up*. I gave him one key to lock the suitcase and kept another so I could open it when it arrived.

Like a little puppy beckoning to his mistress's call, I hit the road. I was at a rest stop five days later on the Pennsylvania Turnpike, where I had been dropped off after declining to have sex with my last ride. The guy wasn't too happy and I wondered what he might have done if he knew I was none other than: 'Eric in a Muddy Pond.' Within a half hour, I had another ride, this time with a young priest who had just graduated from Seminary School. He was on his way to his first assignment at a diocese in Manhattan and was willing to take me all the way to Manhattan. I half expected to hear him speak of the glories of the Lord, but instead he spent most of the trip lauding the ancillary benefits he expected from his new gig; tickets to the

Knicks, the Yankee and Broadway shows as well as invites to art openings; all delivered gratis by his new parishioners.

He was a decent guy though and went out of his way to drop me off in Greenwich Village where I hoped to find a cheap hotel to spend the night. A phone call might have hooked me up with someone in the folk scene, but it seemed more apropos to stay at one of the flophouses on Bleaker Street mentioned by Kerouac in his beat bible 'On the Road.' After all, to be a songwriter, one had to be close to the hoi polloi. So after the priest dropped me off, I went right over to Bleaker Street to check it out. Just like Jack had described, there were several cheap hotels up and down the street with rooms for rent. Most looked like run down townhouses that had been converted into over-night sleeping quarters for derelicts and winos. Not particular which one I chose, I walked up the three steps off the street and through the once elegant, but now ratty, Victorian door, and found myself in a dimly lit foyer where to behind a half opened Dutch door to my left, sat a rough looking desk attendant.

When he finally deigned to look up from his newspaper I told him: "I need a room for the night"

He took one look at my baby face and said: "You don't want to stay here son. They'll steal everything you've got, including your shoes, while you're sleeping."

I knew he was right and shelved my "On the Road fantasy," and rented a cheap room at a civilized third class hotel in the village. The next day I took the Long Island Railroad and was in Patchoque by midday. I called Debbie to tell her I was at the little station by the stop and ten minutes later she arrived to pick me up. We were both excited to see each other. She looked as beautiful and sexy as ever.

After a few typical exchanges she asked: "Did you hear what happened to Janis?"

I wasn't sure what she was talking about since I had lost touch with the folk scene. I told her; "no."

"She's the biggest thing going!" Debbie exulted.

Janis Joplin, who was now the lead singer for Big Brother and The Holding Company, and brought down the house at the Monterey Pop Festival with her gut wrenching rendition of, *"Ball and Chain."* Who would have thought it? I felt good for her. I hadn't realized how strong her drive and ambition was. It was a lesson never to be too quick to judge a person's potential; something I should have known after all the doubters while in high school about my drive to be accepted to MIT.

Debbie's mother's modest single story seashore house, sat on several acres of land that abutted Patchoque Bay. Its aged white wood exterior blended comfortably with the surrounding gentle slopes and wispy sea blown grass. Later in the afternoon, she suggested we go sailing. Her mother kept a dingy tied to a small wharf a short walk from house. The libidinous side of my personality, always at odds with the introverted, had led me to bring along the small black bikini that could be very helpful in the seduction that I hoped to achieve. As we walked to the wharf, I knew that my lean body, glistening with perspiration, was looking very sexy. In the dingy, she took the tiller and I reclined facing her on the bow as we pushed off from the wharf. Knowing that I was teasing her turned me on, and my cock became half turgid with anticipation. Its outline couldn't but help to make her excited. An hour later we were in her mother's bedroom fucking.

Being that she had told me that she and Eric Anderson were planning to get married in the near future, led me to think she was having a last fling as a single woman. She blew my mind when she asked after we had finished having sex, if I wanted to pop some acid. I was not there to question her decision—on getting married or taking acid—so I agreed.

The trip was a mellow visual experience. We were both stable individuals and trusted each other; enough that she handed me the keys to her mother's car so we could take a drive. There was almost no traffic as we headed north on Sunrise highway that skirted several miles of links land before reaching town. The world seemed like a Renoir painting—slow and idyllic. When we began to approach a populated area, I turned the car around and we headed back to her house. No reason to take a chance that the town folks might fuck up our trip. We laughed and giggled as though we were attending the Mad Hatter's tea party—a world distorted and crazy. Driving at ten miles an hour, it took some time to get home safely, but we did so without any problems. It had been an unforgettable day.

It was hard to step away from the pleasure I was having, but staying longer wasn't an option; I had business to take care of. The next morning I thumbed my way to the north end of the island and caught the ferry to New Haven and from there took a bus to Boston. I expected that my kilos would be waiting for me at the UPS terminal. When they weren't, I called back to LA to ask Pat if there were any problems. There weren't. He had shipped them a day after I had left LA.

Spence suggested we walk over to Bernie Goldhirch's town house, to see how he was doing. I wanted to see Bernie anyway and it might help to subdue my paranoia about what was going on at the UPS warehouse. As usual, he was headed towards big things. His publishing business had grown to the point where he wanted to set up permanent offices on Commercial Wharf, which was controlled by a Mafioso tub of lard that he affectionately called, "Big Tuna." Everything that happened at the docks went through 'Big Tuna.' Bernie had been instructed to meet him at ten at night on his private yacht to close the deal. Tuna's yacht was tied up at the end of an unlit pier; a scene right out of 'On the Waterfront.' After Bernie left, Spence and I hung around smoking some righteous weed and when Bernie hadn't returned by eleven, our imaginations began to get the better of us. Why was the meeting taking so long and why was it held so late in the first place? Was Bernie going to be shot and dumped into the harbor? Spence, very moral at heart, convinced me it was our duty to go down to the wharf and be available if Bernie needed assistance.

We were too scared to walk to the end of the wharf where Tuna's yacht was tied, but crouched down behind a boxcar that was parked next to a warehouse that ran alongside. From there we could keep our ears pealed for any screams that might signal trouble. What we would do if anything happened, neither of us had a clue. After a half hour, our high had waned and we went back to Bernie's place to wait for him, feeling much like the idiots that we were. Bernie returned shortly after, unharmed, and with a deal in hand! When we told him what we had done, we all had a good laugh over a glass of wine.

For the rest of the following week, I was not in a laughing mood. A notification that my suitcase had arrived had yet to come. "Could Pat have fucked me over? Did Eliot even score the Kilos?' I wasn't sure about anything anymore. When I called, he continued to insist that he had sent it. Then, on a Friday, ten days after I had arrived in Boston, a notice finally showed up in Jeff's mailbox, that a parcel was waiting for me at the UPS warehouse. My paranoia exploded like a supernova. 'Why had it taken so long? Had the narcs opened the package and discovered what was inside? If

I went down and picked it up, would they be waiting there to arrest me on a federal interstate transportation of narcotics rap? If I didn't pick it up, the suitcase, it, would eventually be opened and I would be in trouble anyway." If ever there was a 'catch twenty two' this was it.

I had no choice but to bite the bullet and on Monday morning Jeff drove me to the warehouse. I told him to remain outside. There was no reason for him to be put at risk in case a bust was about to take place. I felt some relief when I saw that only a single shipping clerk was working behind the desk. He took my receipt and disappeared for a moment before coming back with my suitcase. It had a loosely tied rope wrapped around its outside. I was very happy that I hadn't just been arrested, but as I carried it out to Jeff's car, I became concerned that it felt very light.

In the security of Jeff's apartment, I removed the loosely tied rope and began to fiddle with the latch so I could insert the key. Oh oh! I didn't need a key. The latch sprung open as soon as I touched it. "What the fuck?" I touched the other latch and found it sprung open as well. Inside were two crumpled up burlap bags. My stomach dropped; something it had been doing a lot over the past few months.

Pat's explanation was beyond stupid. He hadn't actually taken the suitcase down to the UPS office himself, but had paid a cab driver to do it instead. The rest of the scenario was obvious. Whether he had locked it or not didn't matter. When the cabbie took one look at Pat, likely soused, it had to be obvious what was going on. If anyone knew the streets, it was cabbies. The rest need not be said.

One would think that I had reached the final act of this stupid play that I found myself performing in. But there was yet a short epilogue to play out. Knowing Bruce Campbell would be furious when I told him he had lost all his money, I decided to hitch back to LA before calling him. A young friend of Bernie's asked to accompany me so I could teach him the tricks of the road, something I was glad to do. Knowing most cars wouldn't stop to pick up two hitchhikers, I devised a few tricks, like saying one of us was taking a piss to explain why one of us was seemingly hiding after the ride had stopped and we had already piled in. Only a few told us to get out.

Back in LA, I rented a forty-dollar a month room in another boarding house. The room was actually a small sunroom, just big enough to accommodate a bed and little more. It was only a block away from where

I had formerly lived so I was still close to Colm. The tiny room was quite cheerful, its French windows allowed abundant light to shine in. To make some quick cash, I signed on with a door-to-door sales crew selling martinizing coupons. I hated the job. It made me feel guilty selling a woman something that she didn't need and consequently I didn't sell many coupons. I was never much of a salesman anyway. Nonetheless, the job gave me enough money for a little breathing space. Somewhat settled, I faced the music and called Bruce Campbell to tell him I had lost all his money. He was pissed and a bit hysterical. He told me he would be flying to LA tomorrow so he could take charge of things himself. All he wanted from me was to set up a deal as quickly as possible. Some bizarre innate sense of morality told me I owed it to him. I said I would see what I could do. I left him Colm's phone number so he could get in touch with me when he got into town.

The Rabbi hadn't been seen in awhile, but I was still able to stir up some action at the Campus Pool Hall. This was going to be my last grass deal and I didn't feel the need to be overly careful with whom I dealt. Not that I was going to approach strangers, but if someone could make a quick score for Bruce, I was willing to deal. I often played pool with a young articulate spade dude with slender Somalian features, named Ronnie, and asked him if he had any sources for kilos. He didn't, but told me he would look around.

Bruce called the next morning to say that he was in town and was booked into the downtown Hilton. "He sure isn't on a tight budget," I thought to myself. As a "swell," he was accustomed to be demanding and wanted to know if I had anything set up yet. I told him I was working on it, but it would probably take a few days. He pushed me to act quickly.

Later in the week, Ronnie informed me that he had found a connection. We all could meet when he came by the pool hall at two in the afternoon. I was apprehensive about meeting a stranger, but Ronnie's connection turned out to be a harmless looking twenty year-old white kid and I let myself relax. His name was Eddie. With a nice full head of hair and a clean face, he came off as a young guy just looking to make a little money dealing grass. Campbell was getting on my nerves, calling me several times a day I just wanted to get the deal done so I didn't bother asking Eddie how it was that he had bulk connections. After a bit of negotiation that would leave a small taste for everyone involved, Bruce's five hundred would score eight kilos. I gave Bruce a call to bring him up to date. He was cool with the deal. I told him to be available. The score was going to go down later in the evening.

Eddie was back at the pool hall at five in the afternoon. He had checked with his supplier and everything was copacetic. It was a go. I called Bruce and told him to be at the pool hall at one AM. "Bring your money!"

In the wee hours of the morning, Bruce and I climbed into the back of Ronnie's Ford van and took seats on a couple of the mats covering the metal floor. Eddy rode shotgun so he could give directions to the rendezvous point. Typical of the early hour, the air was cool with a slight mist. We pulled out onto Vermont Avenue and headed south towards Wilshire. From my vantage point on the floor, all I could see were the glowing streetlights passing across the front window. They looked like small flying saucers streaking across LA. Eddy quietly directed Ronny to make turns without naming streets. I got the sense that we had turned west on Wilshire and then turned south on Crenshaw, but I wasn't sure. I didn't think it would be cool to ask where we were going. After what seemed like about a half mile, Eddie told Ronnie to make a turn to the right at the upcoming street. As we did, the inside of the van was briefly lit by neon light coming from an elevated Mobile gas station sign. Eddie said to slow down and we proceeded very slowly down a sparsely lit residential street. Two . . . maybe three blocks later, Eddie told Ronnie to pull to the side and park.

After we stopped, Eddie surveyed the street for a few moments. I raised myself on my haunches so I could get a better view. The area was unlit and near black. I couldn't tell much. A small pool of light coming from a lamppost spilled onto the corner across from where we had parked. The homes appeared to be substantial—upper middle class at least.

Then Eddie announced that everything looked good. A cigarette being lit in the distance was the signal he had been waiting for. It was time for him to go alone with the money. I couldn't help thinking, "Oh man, here we go again!" The whole scene was eerie. After Bruce handed Eddie the cash, he left the van and headed up the street, disappearing within a few steps into the total darkness. The silence in the van only added to the eldritch air. Suddenly a loud bang jolted our karma. We all looked at each other; barely able to speak.

"Was that a gun shot?" Bruce asked, his eyes wide open.

Ronnie and I just looked at each other, too scared to respond. Five minutes passed and Eddie still hadn't returned. Something had gone wrong.

"Maybe Eddie's in trouble?" Ronnie mumbled.

"I don't know. Maybe we should drive down the block?" was all I could offer.

Ronnie started up the van and began to tenuously drive up the dark street. I climbed into the passenger seat to add another set of eyes. We had only driven a hundred yards when we came to an intersection with a small circular island in the center—very unusual in LA. Something was lying on the ground at the far side. Our mouths drooped as we approached. It was Eddie, lying face down on the cold cement sidewalk. The hazy light from the street lamp was enough to reveal a small stream of blood trickling from his mouth.

We weren't street hardened thugs, just little city boys fucking around with drugs. After checking to make sure the shooter wasn't around, we overcame our fear and jumped out of the van to run to Eddie's side. None of the neighbors had turned on their lights. Maybe they hadn't heard the shot or didn't care. Eddie was bleeding profusely; but still alive.

We lifted him into the van and because Ronnie knew where a nearby hospital was, were able to get him into an emergency room within fifteen minutes. We had no idea if he was critical or not. He had been unconscious from when we first found him.

A gun shooting required the hospital to notify the police. In short order, all three of us had been taken into custody and brought to the brightly lit local precinct station. With a few lip-read whispers, we made it clear to each other to say as little as possible. Each of us was put into separate rooms to be interviewed. My evasive answers prompted the cop to look at me with disdain: "We know what's going on here." He walked out of the room and left me to my own thoughts. I didn't know if someone had broke or he was just making an obvious assumption. The bottom line was that there was nothing to charge us with. No drugs because the deal never happened—and we didn't do the murder. Around five in the morning, we were released.

Bruce was pissed about losing his money. "Fuck him!" So what if he went back to Boston unhappy. Eddie died the next day. A few days later his parents flew out from Michigan and showed up at the pool hall looking for answers. Who was involved? What was Eddie doing? Ronnie wasn't in the hall at the time they came by and no one else knew I was involved; so I drifted out of the hall to avoid any contact. There was little I could have told them that would make them feel better. Their son had been killed for a measly five hundred bucks!

I was done with the drug business. It was a business for sociopaths. Because I had not been busted and only lost money, I could claim that my unique adventure had certainly not been boring, but after the murder, I knew it was not a business for a pussy-sucking beatnik like myself.

My resolve was made even stronger when Colm dropped by my small sunroom a week after the murder. A visitor had come by his room. He was from the FBI and wanted to know if he had any information about a guy, supposedly out of Boston, who was dealing drugs. Of course Colm told him he didn't. How they knew where I was living and doing deals in Boston, I had no clue. Someone was ratting big time. Maybe Jimmy had been busted? "But who knew I rented a room in the same house that Colm lived? Who knew I was going to Boston? And how did they know all this without knowing my name?" I had no clue. Apparently I had been close to getting busted. Muddy Water's blues line, "If I didn't have bad luck I wouldn't have no luck at all" certainly applied here. The bad luck—the murder—turned out to be the good luck—getting out of the drug business before going to jail.

52

HYPOLETTA AND PERVERTO

The FBI's visit frayed Colm's nerves and by week's end he moved out of his room and rented an available room in the house where I was living. For us, moving was almost like playing musical chairs. His room, at the front of the house, had formerly been the living room and came with a fireplace. He and I were now sole occupants of the entire first floor. Noise was not a problem in the house. The two tenants who lived upstairs, were a biker, who came home each morning at 3AM with a hot looking blond straddled behind him and revved his engine several times to announce his arrival and an old lady who must have been hard of hearing, because she never complained. Colm and I were free to play our electric guitars without any fear of upsetting anyone.

However, our biggest obstacle still remained. How do you sell a song? Colm had an idea. Let's form a band; that was how the Beatles had done it. If people liked your songs, it was only a small step from making a sale.

Why not? We ran an ad in the LA Free Press for a drummer and a keyboard player and within a week we became a band. Our drummer, Fred Heupol, born inArkansas, came with a perpetual shit-eating grin that exposed his brown eyetooth and our keyboard player, Tim McCarver, was fresh in town from Carbondale, Illinois. He was an eighteen-year old with a big mop of curly black hair and was far and away our group's best musical talent. I would play lead guitar and Colm; red hair, glasses and Irish accent, would play bass guitar and be the group's lead singer. What he lacked in having a great voice he made up for with a complete lack of self-doubt. For absolutely no good reason, we decided to call ourselves; 'Lucifer's Cellar.'

We wasted no time putting a repertoire together. To get a gig we needed to be able to play top-forty material and my ear had developed enough that I could work out the chord changes for most songs. By two o'clock in the afternoon of our third day we were in Colm's room rehearsing. We had put together rough versions of six songs; among them Wilson Pickett's 'Midnight Hour,' Chuck Berry's 'Memphis Tennessee' and the Beatle's 'Hey Jude.' As we took a short break, Colm picked up a copy of the new weekly edition of the Free Press that he had sitting on his desk and opened it to the help wanted section where he gleefully pointed to an ad by a club looking for a small band. He averred that since this was the first day the paper was on the street, there was a good chance that if we called for an audition, we might be able to get the gig.

We barely knew the words and chords to any of the songs we were working on and Colm didn't have a natural feeling for chord changes as it was. We would sound like crap. I thought the idea was nuts, but I was in the minority and Colm placed a call to the club. It was now a little after three and when the owner asked if we could be at his club, located in West LA, by four; Colm told him: "No problem." Minutes later, we were speeding and weaving through the jammed streets in Fred's funky Ford convertible, to make the audition on time.

The club was in a circular one story building on Pico near Bundy. The area had almost no walk-by traffic. The front door was open, so we walked in. It took our eyes a moment to make the adjustment from bright sunlight to near darkness. The sound of clanking dishes came from the back of the room where someone was working behind the bar. Fred shouted that we were the band who was supposed to audition. A guy in his late forties, wearing a partially buttoned white shirt with the sleeves rolled up, making him look like a beer delivery-man, came out and introduced himself as the owner. He told us to set up and then returned to the back of the room to finish washing dishes.

His last words were: "Start playing as soon as you're ready." So while dishes clanked in the background, Colm counted down: "three-two-one" and we began belting out Wilson Picket's 'Midnight Hour,' the only song we sort-of knew. We were halfway through mangling Chuck Berry's 'Memphis

Tennessee,' the only song I sung, when the owner came from behind the bar and just as I was about to sing the line: "Her home is on the south side, high upon . . ." he cut me off. I was sure we were about to be told: "Thanks but no thanks;" but instead he surprised the shit out of all of us: "I can't use you fellas for this club, but I have another club on Hollywood Blvd where I think if I put a little music in, it might help to pick up business. Could you start on Saturday night?"

"Was the guy tone deaf?" That had to be the only explanation! Saturday was only two days away! How could we possibly learn enough songs to be able to carry an evening? On the other hand, how could we turn down a gig on Hollywood Blvd—the street whose sidewalk is imbedded with stars commemorating the legends-of-entertainment. It was unbelievable. Bands worked for years to get a break like this—we did it in three days!

By Friday night we had managed to build our repertoire to ten songs, enough material to do two complete sets without repeats. The Hollywood Boulevard club where we would be performing, a half-block east of Highland Avenue, turned out to be only a bar—and not an impressive one. It was sandwiched between a parking lot and a small stand that hawked cheap souvenirs. Because Grauman's Chinese theatre was just two blocks to the west of Highland, there were plenty of tourists about. But on our side of Highland, there were mostly, runaways, winos, hookers and druggies.

The bartender's bored saggy looking eyes showed little excitement when we walked in and asked him where he wanted us to set up. The club was about twelve feet wide and sixty feet long. A few booths that could seat four people lined the wall opposite the bar. Two tired looking patrons sat sipping beers and wondering what the fuck we were doing. It was an effort to cram our band onto the small makeshift stage that had been thrown together earlier in the day; but regardless, we were all thrilled to be there. Once accomplished, Colm commandeered about two square feet of the stage and counted down from three to begin belting out; "In the Midnight Hour." The world had just been introduced to *'Lucifer's Cellar.'*

After fifteen minutes, before our first set ended, the two patrons that had been sipping beers, walked out. When it came time to take a break, we sat down at one of the sidewall tables, half elated that we had got through the first set and half wondering why the two guys at the bar walked out. Fred, who had a bit of previous experience working in bars, hit the bartender up for a free beer; his gloating smile indicating how proud he was of that accomplishment. For him, it made the evening a success.

As Fred nursed his beer, we all agreed that Tim and I, battling to be the dominant sound, had to stop turning the volumes of our amps up. It was what had driven the two customers away. After 15 minutes, we ended our break and went back on stage, vowing to be more restrained. The bar was still empty.

That was to quickly change. Our music was carrying out onto Hollywood Boulevard and evidently it was having a seductive effect, because halfway through our second set, four beautiful girls came prancing in the front door and sat down at one of the booths. They weren't just beautiful; they were sexy as hell! All of them were in tight mini skirts and skimpy sleeveless tops that showed a lot of cleavage. As we played they gyrated in their seats to the beat of our music. "Man . . . this is amazing! These babes are completely grooved to our sound." Even more amazing, was that they seemed to be hot for our bodies, smiling at us with promiscuous eyes. "So this was what being a rock star was all about!"

During our next break, they nodded for Fred and I to come join them at their table. Two of them sat their hot little butts on our laps so we could all fit in at the booth. I had never met girls like these. Unlike the girls on the photo shoots, that never wanted to make out, these babes were hot to go. Within minutes, Fred and I were not only French kissing, but also coping feels of their tits and asses. Fred's little brown tooth seemed to glow brightly as he smiled with delight at our good fortune. My cock began to react to the gentle teasing it was getting from the buns of the honey sitting on my lap. Fred and I smiled at each other. We were just a couple of wild and crazy rock dudes.

Then, without warning, all the girls jumped up, and as quickly as they had come in the front door, they dashed back out onto the street. Fred and I sat with our mouths agape. "What had just happened?" Like dogs in heat, we got up and followed them out onto Hollywood Blvd. About twenty yards up the street, they were cavorting with some other equally hot babes. Fred and I did a double take as the truth hit us. Out honeys were transvestites!! Yikes! There were transvestites all over the place, a literal sea of them— all dancing and prancing about. Our bar was located in the epicenter of Hollywood Boulevard's, *'Trannie Nation!'*

Fred and I, feeling a little weird, wandered back into the bar and joined Tim and Colm who had kept to themselves during the break. For the rest of the evening, a few patrons dropped in for a drink, but it was obvious that it was not because of our music since our last set was to an empty house. It didn't discourage us. Not in the least. We were now a working band with a future. Fred even took an empty room on the second floor at the house where Colm and I were living, so we could all bond better. Two attractive girls, in their late twenties, who lived a block away, took Tim under their wings so he not only had a place to stay, but was probably getting laid as well. He kept it to himself.

But it would not be a surprise that the rest of the band, three dudes at the height of their hormone years with no girl friends, would resort to mischief to entertain themselves. Fred let it be known that he was a practical joker and all hell soon followed. Dylan had warned the older generation: "don't criticize What you can't understand; Your sons and your daughters Are beyond your command; Your old road is Rapidly agin." There was anger against the older generation. Whether it be the war or civil rights abuses, they just seemed to go along with the program. Fred had a fertile mind for finding ways to freak people out, to shock them out of their apathy and at times just shock them for the fun of it, and I was happy to become a willing partner. He facetiously pointed out to me that since he and I had just made out with transsexuals, we were technically gay, and like other gay trannies, we should adopt names that were apropos to the sexual culture we now belonged. He would become 'Hypoletta' and I, 'Perverto.' While we were at it, we gave Tim the name, 'Little Extremo,' reflecting his big mop of hair and propensity to turn up the volume control of his amp. Only Colm was spared, as we weren't sure he could handle a nickname.

Knowing that the average American had no use for homosexuals, Fred and I would entertain each other by using our alter egos to engender disgusted looks from nearby straights. Pretending that we were a couple of swish faggots, Fred would hold up a pair of women's panties that he had pulled off the rack at a JC Penny's or similar store, and with one hand akimbo, hips tilted, and other hand, 'sissy style,' i. e. his pinky extended and his thumb pressed against his cheek; would shout across the room in a whinny effeminate voice:

"Honey cakes, I'm so confused which I should buy, the blushing pink ones or the pretty twinkle blue? They're both so darling."

I would respond in similar pose and swish style with:

"Oh Hypoletta, you damn queen, you know how much I prefer you to wear twinkle blue." "Oh god baby . . . you always make things so right. I just luuuv you."

He would throw me a kiss and to our great joy, everyone nearby would cringe and gape in shock. Then we would rush towards each other and join our hands by the pinkies and swish out of the place, laughing how shocked we had made everyone.

Fred also had another little prank up his sleeve that got us free meals from time-to-time. He was not a big guy, and to protect himself, he carried a little pocket canister of mace, a noxious chemical that he bought through a mail order company. When breathed in, it caused severe eye burning and coughing. With the promise that we would be eating for free, we joined him at a Norm's restaurant on the corner of Sunset and Vermont. He insisted we each order a full course meal with all the trimmings. "Don't worry about the bill, I have it covered," he told us. After desert and coffee, he politely excused himself and went to the men's room. When he returned, he told us that when no one was looking, he had sprayed a few hits of mace into the air-vent system. He promised that havoc would shortly ensue. The first whiff of mace began pouring out of the air vents just as I was finishing my coffee. A few people began to cough, and within minutes the entire place was coughing and rubbing their eyes. Patrons and staff alike poured out onto the street, everyone wondering what had happened. In the confusion, we casually walked away, leaving our unpaid bill sitting on the table. We called our petty crime: "dining and dashing."

Business at the bar didn't improve—it actually went down—and we were let go after three weeks. Without any idea how to find another gig, we spent our evenings on the floor in Colm's room, playing Monopoly. We got so good at it that we could go through an entire game in about a half-hour. Each of us knew where every roll of the dice would lead and what it would cost. While one of us was completing his turn, the next was already halfway through his. Then one night a stranger walked in on our Monopoly orgy. Colm's door had been left open and he now stood to the side without uttering a word, just watching us as we frantically rolled the dice and bought and sold property at a speed that would have made a Wall Street trader proud. When I looked up, I recognized it was the motorcycle guy with the hot looking blond girl friend. He had a Clint Eastwood like air about him: a man of few words, strong and confident. He told us his name was Bill Osco, and not much more, other than he came to LA from Akron, Ohio to play baseball.

He looked to be about twenty-five and had movie star looks, hindered however, by a nervous tic of rapidly blinking his eyes. He didn't lack for self-assurance. After watching us play for a bit, he suggested that what our band needed was a manager and he would like to provide that service. He acknowledged that he had no prior experience, but since, after losing the Hollywood Boulevard gig, we had no prospects in mind, there was nothing to lose. A handshake closed the deal. He would earn ten percent of any gig he could book for us.

The next day he dropped in with good news. "You guys have got an audition tonight at Gazzarri's." He had to be kidding! Gazzari's and the Whiskey A Go Go, both on the Sunset strip and within a block of each other, were the best clubs in LA. The best bands in the country played there.

In the late 60's, the atmosphere on Sunset Strip was electric. Thousands of kids, walking six abreast, meandered up and down both sides of the street; all the way from Doheney on the North to La Cienaga on the south. Eateries, head shops, strip joints and bars lined the boulevard that overflowed with traffic. 'Flower Child' drug dealers brazenly hawked their products shouting out: "Thai stick, Panama Red, LSD, uppers, downers" as they strolled through the crowd. One could get stoned a thousand different ways. The 'Iron Butterfly' had a steady gig at one of the small clubs, their music bleeding out over the passing crowds. A few cop cars were interspersed in the bumper-to-bumper five mile per hour traffic on the street, keeping their eyes peeled for trouble makers and occasionally entertaining themselves by blaring some obscenity over their loud speaker at a drug fogged hippie or in some cases taking one of them out of view down a side street to be roughed up for some sundry infraction.

I felt our chances of getting booked at Gazzari's were slim, but it would at least give us a chance to play in front of a teenage audience. It would go a long way in showing what we were. When we arrived, Bill went in first and took charge of the logistics while we waited outside in the car. He returned shortly and told us to set our equipment up on the stage and wait to be called. The club was packed and vibrant. This was the real deal! Just to be carrying equipment onto the stage was a thrill, although scary at the same time.

Five other bands—all of them good—did their thing before we got our chance. The emcee's request: "Let's hear a nice hand for *'Lucifer's Cellar,'*" was met with much the same perfunctory applause that all the bands got. Colm, showing no fear, took the mike and gave a one-two-three count to initiate the 'Midnight Hour,' which he sung with all the zeal he was capable of. Still suffering from stage fright, I was happy to be playing guitar in the background. We finished with a performance of the Door's 'Light My Fire,' Little Extremo doing a more than adequate job on the keyboard.

While we were walking off the stage, Bill was in the back of the room talking with Mr. Gazzarri. Not wanting to interrupt, I only approached close enough to overhear the conversation.

Bill: "Where do you want my guys to leave their equipment?" Gazzarri: "What do you mean?"

Bill: "Well, you're going to hire them aren't you?"

Gazzarri gave Bill an incredulous look and politely told him to have his boys take their equipment off the stage. But I was impressed as hell with Bill's balls. I would have just slunk out into the alley, but he made Gazzarri say no.

One week later he had us booked at a stripper bar in Lenox, a small blue-collar neighborhood near the LA airport. I looked forward with heightened anticipation to the job. It would be like working at the Old Howard in Boston. Being around strippers was a dream come true. But the place, much like the bar the 'Big fox' had taken me to, had only one dead-eyed stripper whose facial expression clearly stated: "stay away." It was to our good fortune, however, that a nearby all-you-can-eat for three bucks restaurant made the twenty bucks we made for performing, more than enough to keep us happy. And of course, Fred got a few free beers each night.

The feedback we were getting at the club was anything but inspirational and even less when we included a song or two that Colm and I had written. There was little to motivate us to practice harder so we spent most of our free time driving around town shocking people and acting silly. On one torridly hot day, we were piled into Fred's convertible and amusing ourselves by shooting old people standing on the corners with a squirt gun or shouting loudly to make them jump out of their shoes. They were reactionary pawns of the government who could use a little shaking up.

We had just come to a stop at a traffic light on the cornor of Sunset and Vermont when all of our eyes popped out their sockets as we noticed, standing on the curb, two beautiful and practically naked girls. One was black and the other white. It could only happen in Hollywood. They each wore tight mini skirts and cut-off tops. The black girl's top was see-thru and her large firm breasts and nipples were clearly visible. They had their thumbs out and it was hard to believe they hadn't already been picked up. This was indeed a lucky day and of course we offered them a ride. Both Colm and Tim were in the back seat and I was sitting next to Fred in the front so they jumped in and joined Fred and me in the front seat, the white girl squeezing between us and the black girl taking a seat on my lap. Before the light turned green, the white girl exclaimed:

"God it's hot. Do you mind if I cool off?" and lifted her top exposing her large firm breasts and protruding nipples.

Then turning to Fred she said: "You can suck on this one if you like."

Hypoletta didn't need a second invitation and quick as a wink, latched his mouth around her nipple, only briefly taking it off so he could make the turn onto Sunset Boulevard. As we ambled along, Fred took every opportunity to nurse himself on the young lady's nipples. Meanwhile, the tall black tart placed my hand on her tits and began to sensually gyrate her hips. I became aroused and tried to reciprocate the pleasure by reaching inside her panties so I could finger her clit. But she was a bit more restrained than her friend and pulled my hand away: "Uh uh honey . . . I don't want to get too hot"

We were now under the spell of the feminine mystique. There was nothing more important than making these young girls happy. Fred dutifully followed their directions down Sunset, not caring in the least where we were going. Drivers in adjacent cars were doing double takes when they saw Fred's mouth sucking on a big bare titty.

The girls said they were on their way to visit some friends and needed to stop at their apartment to change into something more comfortable—if that was possible . . . ha ha. I wondered if Fred and I might be invited up for a quickie before we continued on. Just before we turned off Sunset and approached their apartment building, I finally managed to get my hand into the black hottie's panties . . . where I discovered a wee surprise . . . a growing wee surprise. She had a dick and it was getting hard!!

Too embarrassed to register shock or outrage, I slowly withdrew my hand. I just sat as though nothing had happened. Fred, unaware of my discovery, continued to suck the white girls tits until we arrived at their apartment. Like a taxi service, we were ordered to wait outside while they went in to change.

With my fantasy of having sex already dispelled, I looked at Fred: "Uh . . . you're not going to believe this."

His beaming smile was the look of someone who didn't want to hear bad news:

What? "They're guys."

After a moment to ponder what I had just said: "How do you know that?"

"I felt his dick getting hard."

"No shit!" was all Fred could manage.

Our brains somewhat stunned, we waited in silence for the girls to return. In the back seat, Colm and Tim were having a good snicker at our expense as Fred and I wondered what to do. Moments later, the hybrid girls came bounding out of the apartment building and took their former positions in the car. Fred obediently obeyed when he was told to drive to another apartment a mile away, where they said they needed to make a quick stop. This time I kept my hands to myself and Fred did likewise with his mouth. If the two hybrid girls knew they had been outed, they gave no indication. Again we sat silent while we waited. It was only a short wait until they were back in the car. Fred was told to drive back to their apartment. I felt weird having a guy sitting on my lap, but when I glanced in Fred's direction, I found him once again sucking on the white tranny's titties at every chance he got.

After we dropped them off and said goodbye, I asked Fred; "Why did you suck on those tits when you knew they were guys?"

He looked at me as though I had just asked a patently stupid question: "When I see titties like that, I'm going to suck on them no matter who owns them!"

53

LUCIFER GOES TO HELL

Our gig at the stripper bar ended as unceremoniously as it had at the Hollywood bar. Since the All-You-Can-Eat restaurant was too far away, we reverted to "Dining and Dashing," while Bill looked to find us another gig. That didn't work out too well. Norm's had gotten hip to what was going on and passed the word around to its mangers to call the cops if caustic fumes started coming through their vents. No sooner had we finished pulling our antic at one of their restaurants on Ventura Boulevard in Encino, when a cop car came rushing onto the scene. The four of us scattered helter-skelter. I crawled beneath a house and sweating like a pig, managed to remain unseen until the cops stopped searching the neighborhood with their flashlights.

My modeling career was on the downside. When I did get a gig, the photographer often hooked me up with a girl who didn't turn me on or who wanted to dig her fingernails into my back or worse when Tom Parker booked me for a gay session, he wanted me to embrace my partner sexually. When I provided him only with Greek wrestling poses he was not too pleased. I was liberal, but not being gay, his request was more than I could handle.

Fred still had a lot of Mace left, but with the restaurant incident precluding using it that way again, we began using it on each other. I awoke one evening from a good nights sleep, coughing and my eyes burning; and ran out into the kitchen, where I found Fred, Bill and Colm all having a laugh at my expense. It was the first salvo in an internecine Mace war. Only

Fred and Tim were safe; Fred since he possessed the Mace and Tim, because he was still living with the Cougars up the street. Over the next two weeks, we each teamed up to retaliate against the odd guy out. Colm would get hit, then Bill, then me and on and on.

That the days of Lucifer's Cellar were numbered was made evident when Bill brought a promoter to the house to hear us play. First thing out of his mouth was; "You need a better lead guitar player." Even though I bristled, I knew he was right. You either have it or you don't and in my heart, I knew I didn't. But Colm and I had started the band and my ego wasn't about to let me step aside. So the mace wars continued and it was Bill's turn to be attacked. It was time to punch a hole in his cool 'Mr. Clint Eastwood' image.

While he was out and about during the day, Fred and I loosened the latches on his bedroom door, so even if it was locked or blocked with a chair, it could be pushed open enough to squirt Mace through the crack. When he returned home around 2AM and locked it so he could go to sleep, Fred and I crept up the stairs and tied one end of a rope to the door's knob and the other end to a newel at the top of the stairs. Enough slack was left so the door could be slightly pushed ajar, but not enough for him to be able to escape. A few good squirts of mace got him hoping out of bed like a jumping jack and after he discovered he couldn't escape through the door, he ran to his front window and climbed out onto the portico over the house's entry door. Just as quickly, Fred and I ran outside and began drenching him with water from a hose connected to a spigot. Lights came on around the neighborhood and a small crowd gathered to watch the show.

Walter, our landlord, a nice establishment type guy in his mid fifties, was alerted by a neighbor and on the scene within minutes. We were already under his radar, when the phone company came to the house a week before to empty the pay phone in the hallway. It should have been full with about fifty dollars of quarters, since several long distance calls had been made from it to Ireland. Instead, they found the coin box to be empty. In those days, an operator had to verify the amount of money being deposited by listening to the distinct sound each coin made when it was deposited. I had prerecorded a tape of the sounds of quarters being deposited, and Colm had used it to fool the operator. When Walter saw that night what was taking place in front on his house, he justifiably screamed; "I want all of you out of here first thing in the morning. Is that clear!!"

The next night we all found ourselves living in a single room of a fifteen-dollar a week flophouse, a few blocks away on Melrose Ave. There was only one bed, so two of us slept together on the mattresses and the other two on the box springs. It was a home for losers so we fit right in. However, despite the future not looking bright, Bill managed to get us a new gig at a small club on Virgil Street, eponymously called, "The Virgil." Its patrons, mostly Latino, liked to dance and they seemed to enjoy our music. To get a fresh start, we changed the band's name to *'Father Flotsky and the Umbilical Chord.'*

Though it was only a weekend gig, it paid enough for us to rent a very cheap three-bedroom apartment above a three-car garage just around the corner on Lockwood Street. There was a good reason the apartment came so cheap. The hollow cheeked couple that owned the property had a young male child suffering from a horrific brain condition that caused him to scream out in terror almost every evening. They called him their "little handicapper." It was very unsettling and only a group of desperados—like us, would want to live there. Our entire band, including Tim, who had recently been expelled from the Cougar den, was now together.

On one of the rare occasions when I scored a model during a gig, I had brought a pretty bright-eyed girl with jet-black "Betty Page" bangs back to the apartment and after introducing her to my roommates and "Little Beasty," the starving alley cat that I had nursed back to health, we went to my bedroom and screwed each other's brains out. She enjoyed it enough that she decided to stay.

Delia had a fleshy, yet not fat, body, and attractive small firm breasts. Her dark eyes gave her a wild and exciting look and she enjoyed sex. Having a woman in the apartment felt good. Contrary to popular opinion, female models weren't sluts, even though it turned me on to think of them as such. They were girls trying to find their sexual identities, much as I was doing. Delia was a perfect example. She had been raised in a strong Catholic family and was rebelling against her upbringing by doing something they told her was sinful and wrong. She was discovering that sex was enjoyable and fun.

Then one afternoon, it all came crashing in on her. Bob Mantel, a still photographer who I had met several times on shoots, dropped by the

Lockwood apartment to share a joint and a bottle of wine with Fred, Delia and me. Bob was a loner and I suspected an S&M (sadomasochist) freak. If not, his wire rim glasses, half-bald head and stern round face, sure gave him that appearance. The fact that he and I shared an engineering background had led to our casual friendship. Delia was in a playful mood and I began feeling her up while Fred and Bob watched. She was enjoying the feeling of having three pairs of male eyes lusting upon her.

The "little handicapper" was having one of his hallucinatory attacks, but because they happened so often, we were all inured to his screams. Delia was in an agreeable mood and after she let me pull her panties off, I easily coaxed her to come down on the floor and get on her hands and knees so I could suck on her pussy. Without being invited, Mantel quickly joined in and began to aggressively push his penis into her mouth. His eyes had the look of a sadist, but Delia didn't protest and seconds later, Fred, with his omnipresent silly grin, had his dick out and was asking Delia to pleasure it as well. Her cunt had become soaking wet and I was engrossed in putting as much of my face into it as possible, when suddenly Mantel appeared at my side. He began using his head to ram mine to the side so he could have Deliah's pussy for himself. Naturally I fought back. For a few seconds it was like two alpha dogs, vying for the rights to be the dominant pussy sucker.

Suddenly—without warning—Delia began screaming hysterically. At first I thought she was having an orgasm; but when she jumped up and ran into my bedroom and slammed the door, I knew something was wrong. I could hear her sobs coming through the door. Fred and I looked at each other; wondering if we were guilty for what was happening. Mantel didn't seem to give a shit one way or the other. Over the next hour, she didn't calm down and appeared to be hallucinating. Our landlord and his wife came in to see what the racket was about. Because of their experience with the 'little handicapper,' they knew a mental breakdown when they saw one and called for an ambulance. I felt helpless and guilt ridden as she was driven away. "Why had the orgy turned so ugly? Was it Mantel and I bucking heads behind her as though she were a bitch in heat or had all the negative indoctrination about the evils of sex that she had been exposed to by the church suddenly burst forth like lava out of a volcano." The next day she was released from the hospital into the care of her mother. I was too guilt ridden to even attempt to see her again.

The inevitable news came from the Virgil Club that our services would no longer be needed. The reality that "Father Flotsky's" umbilical chord was about to be unraveled was not a rude shock. A week later, Tim moved back to Carbondale, Illinois and Fred went back to Arkansas. None of the songs that Colm and I had written had raised any eyebrows. It was all a dream going nowhere. He moved back in with his Latino girl friend and quickly found work performing solo at Irish bars, where everyone was too drunk to know that he never changed chords during a song. I was left staring at Bill wondering what to do. I still had no doubts that I could "get my act together."

54

WE CAN ALL HAVE SOME FUN

Bill had come to Hollywood with the dream of becoming a movie star. As he and I looked at each other wondering what futures lie ahead for us, he suggested that he and I make a movie. He wanted to make a Biker movie starring him. We only had forty dollars between us and were too stupid to know that wasn't enough to make a movie, but the idea was intriguing and I said; "Why not?" But even as I spoke, I was already scheming how I could manipulate the idea towards making 'Beaver' movies which I harbored as a secret passion.

But dreams aside, I needed to get a job to pay my bills and when I saw an ad in the Free Press for a job that was too good to be true, I jumped on it. Continental Adult Bookstores was looking for someone to work the swing shift at one of their adult magazine stores. When I called to apply, it was explained to me that working the swing shift meant working from four to midnight for two days, mid-night to eight AM for two days, and finally, eight AM to four PM for two days. After telling them it was no problem, I was hired. Not only would I earn a regular salary, but I would be wallowing in a sea of girlie magazines. Chances were that I could pilfer as many as I desired to add to my collection. And the fact that my schedule would allow me to have both a day and night life was also pretty cool.

The store, located on Park Avenue, was in the heart of a Latino neighborhood near Echo Park. Outside, there was a constant din of traffic, street merchants, large families taking strolls and people shopping. Adjacent to the store was the Park theatre, also owned by Continental. It specialized in films exclusively for the gay market.

Thus, much to my dismay, the bookstore's stock was primarily for the gay crowd and there was only a smattering of girlie magazines on its shelves.

The store's manager was a very good-looking young gay guy in his late twenties, named David. We got along very well, and understanding that I was not a homosexual, he made no advances toward me. During my late night shifts, as I suspected, I was the sole employee in the store and was able to take home a few of the girlie magazines that turned me on.

A month after working swing shift, I realized that I had grossly underestimated the strain it would have on me. Having no regular sleeping schedule began to render me a zombie and unable to converse coherently. About five A. M, near the end of my early morning shift, I sat on a stool behind the counter, struggling to keep my eyes open. Standing in front of me was a neatly dressed and well-groomed customer, who appeared to be about forty years old. He seemed intelligent, so with my elbow propped on the counter holding my head up so it wouldn't keel over from fatigue, I pretended to listen to what he was rambling on about. By now I was use to having gay guys hit on me and had learned how to shine them off. But I didn't sense this guy was putting a move on me, so in my stupor, and feeling obligated to be courteous, I just agreed with nods and uh huhs to everything he said. He had been talking for about fifteen minutes when I became cognizant of a few phrases that he kept repeating; "it's actually very hygienic" and "my doctor even says it's cleaner than regular sex." My interest began to pique and when I forced myself to listen a bit more carefully, I suddenly realized that the guy was talking about how much he enjoyed having people piss in his mouth. "Yuk! Holy shit!" I didn't know weird stuff like that even existed and I had been agreeing with him that I also thought it was cool. "And who the hell was his doctor?"

It was obvious that working swing shift was deleterious to my health, so I asked David if I could be put on a normal schedule. He was sympathetic to my plight and was able to pull some strings at the main office to accommodate me. It took a full week before I regained a normal sleeping cycle. Fucking up my sleeping pattern and teaching me about pissing sex put aside, the job allowed me to significantly raise my standard of living. I used my first paycheck to rent a one-bedroom apartment on Romaine Street, just south of Santa Monica Blvd. Like many of LA's residential streets, it was verdant with lots of trees. The wings of the two-story apartment building surrounded a swimming pool and its patio was landscaped with a few palm trees and large ferns. Each unit had a view of the pool, and since my place was on the second floor and in the rear, it had a bit of privacy. It was the nicest pad I had ever lived in. Little Beastie liked it as well and discovered that he could leap out of the kitchen window onto a nearby tree and go hunting for most of the day and then return in the evening to be petted and, if hunting hadn't gone well, have a can of cat food.

Bill saw himself starring in another "Easy Rider,' but had to come down from the clouds when it became obvious that it took more than forty dollars to make a feature film. The opportunity to get into the sex movie business was at hand. Osco had demonstrated that he was a salesman and I knew that I understood sexuality, especially the sleazy type. We were perfect partners. I suggested we make a silent 'beaver' film; like the ones that played at the Vista. Bill just wanted to make movies and didn't really care what kind. He liked the idea. It would be a start. However, we didn't even have enough money to do that. We discovered that after buying one 400' roll of 16mm film, renting a camera and lights and hiring a model, we were looking at a minimum of two hundred dollars. So I made another suggestion. Adult bookstores sold packaged sets of eight 4x5 color stills of a single girl posing in sexy lingerie. Each set sold for five dollars. I still had my Rollieflex camera and if we shot outdoors, where we could use natural light, we had enough money to produce a set of these pictures. All we needed was a model and I told him I thought there was a good chance I could convince my new girl friend to pose. We could sell the negatives to a store or a chain like Continental and parlay the money into another shoot. It would get us launched.

I had met my new girl friend, Josie Catalin, several months earlier at Los Angeles City College when I was taking the beginners piano class I had enrolled in. It always amazed me when a girl accepted my offer to go out on a date, but she did and we hit it off. She liked my free spirited swashbuckling style mixed with an artistic bent and moved in with Little Beasty and me. She was a physical knockout; five foot seven, long-blond hair and nicely formed breasts—cover girl material. She had never posed before, but the idea excited her. I was actually surprised how little convincing it took to get her to agree to model for me. My baby face and quiet artistic nature made it all sound like fun. I was ecstatic that she had agreed.

Site of our first shoot

Being that it was wintertime, it was too cold to shoot outdoors in LA, so on a Saturday morning, Josie and I piled into Bill's blue Pontiac GTO convertible and headed to Palm Springs. Bill had a knack for always having a nice set of wheels. Despite having no set location in mind and that this was a first time adventure for all of us, we were in an elated and confident mood. Palm Springs sits in the umbra of the San Jacinto Mountains, which rise majestically from the sagebrush and cacti covered desert floor to the meadows and pine forests that exist at the higher elevations. Summer temperatures on the desert floor rise as high as one hundred twenty degrees and winter temperatures rarely go below a comfortable eighty, even on a slightly overcast day, as was the current condition. Hundreds of tourists and college kids were strolling up and down Palm Canyon drive, enjoying the balmy weather as we drove through town. The main drag is little more than a mile long and upon reaching the edge of downtown, Bill noticed a secluded bluff atop one of the foothills. His guess that a dirt road that pealed off to the right led up to the bluff turned out to be correct and within two minutes we were parked on a perfect spot to shoot. The view from the bluff looked out over a beautiful vista of the valley and the town below; but most important, it was isolated. Years later it would become the site of Bob Hope's gymnasium sized home, but for now it was about to become the launching pad for my career in pornography, or euphemistically speaking, adult entertainment.

As a life long aficionado of girlie book erotica, I had, in essence, a degree in cheesecake photography. My modeling experience had taught me how to conduct a shoot and my experience as a baby photographer taught me how to make my subject relaxed. It didn't hurt that I knew where to shop for sexy lingerie and undergarments, which I would now ask Josie to don to make her look like a hot whore hanging out in the desert. Purchasing the garments had been a thrill in itself. Since I was now a professional, I didn't have to feel like a pervert when I browsed the sexy undergarments and lingerie for sale at Fredrick's of Hollywood. I was just doing my job.

Josie took the red satin half-bra trimmed with black lace, black see-thru bikini panties, a frilly red garter belt and most importantly, black nylons with seams, and stepped out of the car and went around to its front so she could have a bit of privacy while she changed into her modeling outfit. The seamed nylons were a touch I learned from famed leg photographer, Elmer Batters. Not wanting to upset or make her nervous in any way, I resisted my urge to stare while she dressed. I had enough to do anyway. My prior experience doing baby pictures had all been done by the numbers, so this would be the first time I would have to determine what camera settings should be used and I busied myself taking light readings. Bill was also all business; acting as a lookout in case anyone came up the road. After Jose finished dressing, she slipped on a pair of red high heels that she owned and then used the rear view mirror on Bill's car to do her make-up. Looking at her bent over and her butt thrust toward me left little doubt that the shoot would be a success—provided I didn't screw up the photography.

With a cactus in the background, I placed a blanket on the ground and began with some simple standing poses that would put us both at ease. "Place your hands on your hips and cock your head to the side," I told her. "Good. Now arch your back a bit and give me a what-are-you-looking-at-big-boy look." I quickly snapped a picture and had her do a few variations on the same pose. Then I had her kneel on the blanket and did a series of shots that accented her curves. She was a natural. She arched her back and let her long blond hair partially hide her nipples that peeked teasingly over the top of her little red bra. When I asked her to lie on her back, she didn't have to be asked twice to spread her legs. She knew instinctively to give me a smile that said: "let's fuck." If I had been religious, I would have believed god had sent her from heaven to be my first model.

Our small budget could only afford four rolls of film, which provided for a total of forty-eight shots. By three in the afternoon, we were finished and I was exhausted. Being behind the camera was hard work. It was literally ball draining and gave me no time to get aroused. Josie was relaxed and smiling and looking very proud of herself. Whether Bill had become aroused, I had no idea. He had stayed far off to the side, which I wasn't sure was because he didn't want to interfere or had a hang up about watching a girl act like a slut. American religious and sexual taboos had left us all with hang-ups.

Leaving Palm Springs without indulging oneself with a piece of Dolores' incredible banana cream pie, would be imbecilic. So before heading back to LA, we waited in the omnipresent line in front her famous coffee shop on Palm Canyon Drive, to have lunch and celebrate the day's success. Many a celebrity had visited Dolores's coffee shop, and Josie, wearing a long fur coat, was drawing lots of furtive looks from admirers thinking she might be a Hollywood actress. If they had known that she had nothing on underneath the coat except the trashy outfit she had posed in, she would have raised something more than attention.

It was still warm enough to keep the top down on the trip back to LA. When I glanced back at Josie, sitting in the rear seat, the wisps of her long blond hair blowing across her face was like looking at a page in a men's magazine. There was little doubt that being an object of men's desire had turned her on. It certainly excited me and I asked her to open her coat up so I could look at her sexy body. She gladly granted my wish and went a step further by reclining across the back seat and straddling the backs of the front and rear seats so her legs were spread. What a sight she was, her nipples erect and her pussy teasingly visible through the crotch of her black see-thru panties.

Bill was in a playful mood as well. He pulled alongside a big semi rig and adjusted his speed so the driver would get a quick glance of what we had in our back seat. The trucker's perfunctory glance to the side was followed by a near neck-breaking jerk when he spotted Josie with her crotch staring him in the face. Bill floored the accelerator of the GTO and the disbelieving trucker fell fifty yards behind, but a moment later he was rolling along aside us at eighty miles an hour and shouting out his window: "Pull over so we can all have some fun!" The grin on his face showed he thought we might oblige. Over the next few miles, Bill played a cat and mouse game with him, speeding up and slowing down, leaving him in the dust and then allowing him to catch up. Josie gave him a few new poses to drool over each time he pulled alongside. Being a sex object was exciting. It made her feel good to see how desirable she was. I could only imagine what the conversation would be later in the day when the trucker pulled into a stop.

The next morning the film came back from the lab and I anxiously waited to see the results. "Were they exposed correctly? Did I get the framing right? Were they sexy?" Not only did they look great, they were much better than any of the girls currently being pedaled in picture sets that I had seen in the stores. Josie photographed like a juicy peach, a bombshell. We had a bit of luck as well. My knowledge of photography was in its incipiency and I had no idea that shadows had to be lit with fill light to prevent high contrast. If not for Mother Nature providing the slight overcast that had diffused the light, the shoot probably would have been a disaster. Bottom line; we had pictures that should be easy to sell.

Bill made an appointment with Continental adult bookstore's buyer to see if he could sell him our pictures. The meeting was set for three in the afternoon and by five he was back with a cocky smile on his face. He had sold the negatives for one hundred and sixty bucks. We had quadrupled our forty dollars. Wow! Bill laughed when he told me the buyer, Monroe Bealer, was as gay as a fruitcake and couldn't take his eyes off of him as they negotiated. By letting him think he might be available, he was able to get top dollar for our pictures. We both laughed. Play the cards your dealt. Right?

My affair with Josie lasted only a couple of more weeks. She left me to move in with a black guy involved with the civil rights movement. It was just as well, because I was about to turn my apartment into a full time smut studio.

For most men, letting your dick dominate your brain, leads to a bad place, but in my case it had led me into the business that I knew I was meant for and would have a hell of a lot of fun at the same time. I had found my niche; I had got-my-act-together. I was well aware that I had to improve my knowledge about photography and began reading books on lighting and camera techniques. I was essentially starting from the bottom. For the time being, it made no sense to leave my bookstore job. Bill and I agreed that the money we had just made should be poured back into our new business. I used some of it to buy a couple of halogen lights so my next shooting could be done indoors at my apartment.

To procure more models, I placed an ad in the Free Press but failed to mention "females only." That omission would earn me endless calls from gays looking to get laid. It was not uncommon for my phone to ring at three in the morning; "I'm answering your ad for models." I had read John Retchy's 'City of Night,' which was a riveting expose of the gay scene and their fanatical pursuit of sex and now I was part of it. It was ridiculous.

But a few girls called as well and were delighted to pose for twenty-five bucks. I hired a cutie with short amber colored hair and a trim dancer's body for my next shoot. I dressed her in tiny little orange bikini panties and light orange nylons held up by a satin garter belt. Nylons and garter belts were to become my signature; there was something super sexy about them: it was that peek up a woman's dress that I had coveted since childhood.

After we finished shooting, she was happy to let me eat her out and fuck her on the floor. Man this was the life! No expensive dinners, stupid conversations or pretending to be in love. I gave her a ride home and dropped the film off at the lab.

My quick study of lighting had paid off. All the shots looked good; well lit and nicely composed and most importantly—sexy as hell. Monroe Bealer was delighted to see that Bill had returned and again happy to purchase our negative.

55

SHE PISSED IN MY BED

Our goal was to make movies, but with the small profit each still shooting was producing, it would take forever. We needed an intrusion of cash and Continental, unknowingly, helped us to get bankrolled. They had opened a reading room upstairs in the bookstore for gays to peruse the magazines before making a purchase. I became the sole employee assigned to that room. It didn't take me long to realize that after I had rung up a few sales on the cash register, I could steal a few bucks out of the till and reenter the sales data so the money wouldn't be missed when the store's manager rang me out at the end of my shift. Then two weeks later, Bill also got a job at the store. Monroe Bealer continued to harbor hopes of someday mounting Bill's buns and was more than happy to arrange for Bill's employment. At times, we were the only two employees at the store, Bill downstairs and me upstairs. We were like two rats in a pantry. Bill carted out boxes of magazines from the storage room and put them in the trunk of his car so he could pedal them the next day to other bookstores at a discount they couldn't refuse. We were both careful to take only enough so that it wouldn't be noticed. No need to kill a good thing in the bud.

From the start, Bill pushed our business forward. I was totally happy shooting stills and getting fucked from time to time. His dream was to make money and he pointed out that movies were where the money was. He assured me, if I made one, he could market it. Even though I had never made a film in my life, I had a good idea how it was done since I had worked for filmmakers during my modeling jobs. I was confident I could pull it off. With the money we had after he sold our last set of stills and the money we had looted out of the book store, we felt we had enough cash to finally make a film; nothing big, just a silent 16mm 'beaver' movie. If it had taken a little criminal activity to get started; so be it. We wouldn't have been the first business to get started that way.

The ban against showing pubic hair had been broken by the Swedish magazines now available in the magazine stores and 'Beaver' films made in San Francisco by shooters like Alex DeRenzy, were already showing pubes. That was why if a film was labeled as being from San Francisco, it meant that it was guaranteed to be hot. Hotter films meant more patrons so naturally LA adult theatres were buying all the films they could get with the San Francisco moniker. By the time Bill and I were ready to make our first loop, the name given to one 400 foot role of 16mm film, girls were allowed to spread their legs as long as they didn't spread their lips or penetrate themselves. In other words, as long as 'Beavers' didn't get too rambunctious, they were being allowed to run free and show themselves in their natural state.

When it came time to make our first loop, our goal was to put LA films back on the map as the hottest in the business. The only source I had for models, were from responses to the Free Press ad. To make sure they were attractive enough to shoot, I asked them to come by my apartment for an interview. Not all girls were comfortable doing movies, it required emoting rather than just posing. A girl named Arlene, had come by on a Saturday afternoon for an interview, and though not beautiful, she was pretty.

Standing at five feet six, her shoulder length brown hair looked sexy and she had a nice body and tits that didn't sag. When she learned she could earn thirty-five dollars for doing a film rather than the twenty-five I paid for doing a still shoot, she was more than thrilled. She assured me that spreading her legs would not be a problem. Since I needed time to gather the equipment and give myself a crash course on how to operate a motion picture camera, I scheduled the shoot for the following Friday.

Lloyd Berman, an avuncular WWII vet, owned and operated Lloyd's Camera Exchange on Cahuenga Blvd. His store, just a short block south of Hollywood Blvd., had the ambiance of a pawnshop. It was stocked with everything from vintage to modern projectors, still and movie cameras, rewinds, Moviolas, splicers and anything else that pertained to the movie business. He sold and rented equipment and since I had purchased my Rolleiflex still camera from him, I was hoping he would remember me and be willing to work out some kind of easy arrangement to allow me to rent a 16mm movie camera. As I had hoped, he had a big heart, and seeing that Bill and I were struggling to get off the ground, agreed to rent us an Ariflex camera, a tripod and a small light kit for a hundred bucks. He would need a two hundred dollar deposit, which could be a check that he wouldn't cash. That worked out just fine, because if he was going to cash the check, there weren't sufficient funds in our bank to cover it. Equally important was that he said I could pick up the equipment late Thursday and return it by Saturday noon for the one-day fee. That would give me plenty of time to get familiarized with it before the shoot.

The Ariflex was the camera of choice in the adult film business. I had watched carefully how Bill Rotsler and Tom Parker used it when I shot for them, so it made sense to just mimic what they had done. I would place the camera with a zoom lens mounted on a tripod and do all the shooting from one position.

Loading film into the camera was a bit complicated, since it had to be done in total darkness so that it wouldn't be exposed to light during the procedure. This required putting the camera and film inside a black, light proof bag, and do all the threading by feel. During the entire week before the shoot, I read and reread the descriptions in the Cinematographer's manual on how to load an Ariflex. Lighting for a motion picture, even a 'beaver' film, was much more involved than lighting for a still photograph. I struggled to understand the concepts of contrast, back light, fill light, key light and soft light, but as some one pointed out, light is light, so I tried not to become overly technical.

On Thursday evening, I was in my apartment preparing for my 'Cecil B. DeMille' moment. Being that my bedroom was very small, I would shoot in the living room where I had taken my mattress off my bed and placed it on the floor next to the wall. To give it a little erotic flair, I covered it with a large red satin sheet that I had purchased from a yardage store. To add some character and color to my set, I added a couple of colorful knickknacks around the mattress and pinned a decorative Indian cotton bedspread to the wall, all purchased for a couple of bucks from the Asian superstore, Pier

One. Also from Pier One, I bought two ten-dollar sheepskins that would provide my model a nice soft surface to writhe and hump on. Satisfied that my set looked appropriately sleazy, I turned to the camera.

Lloyd had provided me with a small roll of exposed film so I could practice loading the camera's magazine in the daylight. After I felt confident that I knew what I was doing, I placed its magazine and an unopened 400 foot roll of 16mm film inside the black cloth loading bag, and then carefully sealed it with the double zipper system that made it impervious to light. Through the bag's long black sleeves, I inserted my arms so I could open the can of film and load the magazine. A few feet of the unexposed film ran from the feed reel through several sprockets to the take up reel. Once the magazine was closed and the unexposed film safely inside, the magazine could be taken out of the black bag and the small loop of film that was exposed on the outside, threaded through the camera's film gate. If that sounded complicated, it was; especially to one doing it for the first time. If the film was incorrectly loaded it would spell disaster. We didn't have money to buy another roll. There was no room for error.

Arlene would be arriving on Friday morning to do the shoot. At mid night on Thursday, I was still taking light meter readings. Before going to bed, I plugged the camera's battery charger into a wall receptacle to make sure it would be fully charged by the morning. I tossed and turned for an hour before falling asleep; reviewing everything to make sure it had been done right.

An infrequent light rain was falling on Friday morning. Not a sanguine day for Bill and I to produce our first film, but we would be shooting inside, so it mattered not. Bill found me still checking and rechecking everything when he came by around ten AM. Arlene was scheduled to show up between 11:30 and 12 and we made idle talk while waiting for her. Models were notoriously unpredictable and when noon approached, she still hadn't shown. We began to get nervous. All our money was tied up in the shoot and depended on her showing up.

Just before noon, my phone rang. It was Arlene! We both expired a sigh of relief. She had gotten off the bus a couple of stops too early and was at the corner of Santa Monica and Western Ave and needed a ride. I wanted to go through one last check-up and since Bill had come on his motorcycle, I suggested he take my car to pick her up. I was driving a run-down white,

'57 Cadillac, which I had purchased for a hundred fifty bucks, and like so many of the cars I had owned, it had a few flaws. Its brakes needed to be pumped three times before they would catch. Before Bill left, he assured me he understood what I had told him; "Pump the brakes three times when you need to stop."

Forty-five minutes later, they hadn't returned. Western and Santa Monica was only five minutes away. What was taking them? Then the phone rang. It was Bill. He was with Arlene but had just had a minor accident. After picking her up, he had just begun to move out into the street, when an old lady who had yet to complete crossing the intersection from the far side, walked in front of him. He forgot to hit the brakes three times and lightly bumped into her. She had been knocked down but not hurt. He told me everything was cool. He would explain when he got back.

That was to be an hour later. Bill explained that when the cops arrived on the scene, he was able to play the roll of a nice young man and argue that since the little old lady wasn't injured, pressing charges should not be necessary. Both the little old lady and the cops agreed. "Fucking Bill was the best!" It was already late in the afternoon and all of us were pretty shook up. We all agreed that the best thing to do was to put the whole thing off until tomorrow morning. We could still get the camera back to Lloyd's by noon, and even if we were a bit late, I was sure he would let it slide.

The next day went a whole lot smoother. Arlene showed up around 9:30 and we went right to work. I noticed that Bill seemed a bit uncomfortable being around the set and worried that his vibe might make the girl feel uncomfortable, so reminiscent of how Orman Longstreet had asked me to stay in the van while he shot pictures, I suggested Bill leave the room while I did the filming. He had no problem with it and said he'd be back in a couple of hours.

I asked Arlene to take off her dress and seeing that her under garments were prosaic, replaced them with one of my gauche nylon and garter belt creations that would make any whore proud. I made sure she wore her panties on top of the garters so she could remove them without taking off the garter belt and stockings. Very important! After she put her soft silky dress back on, I asked her to recline on the mattress with her head resting on her hand, so I could frame her in a wide shot. It was time to roll. I hit the switch so juice would flow from the battery to the camera and as soon as the meter indicated it was traveling through the gate at 24 frames per second—the speed necessary to make motion look natural—I called action. She began to undulate and sensually move her hands across her body as only a woman can do. She was loving every minute of it! Being a slut was turning her on! Not recording sound, allowed me to give her directions and encouragement as the film rolled: "That's it, move your hands real slow. Get on your hands and knees . . . slow . . . good." I couldn't help but notice that her hirsute flesh pie had become sopping wet. The smell of urine was undeniable. She had gotten so excited that she was pissing all over my mattress! I kept shooting, delighted that I was getting such a good performance from my first star.

The sound of rapid spinning from the pickup side of the camera's magazine, indicated that all the film had been exposed, so I turned off the motor. Arlene was still gyrating, even though she knew we were done filming. A needy look in her eyes told me what she wanted and I joined her on the damp mattress. Oblivious to the sweet smell of urine, I began by eating her pussy. Sex is not a time to be prudish. After she sucked my cock I was inside her and we were humping away. It only came to an end when Bill knocked on the door.

After pulling my pants up, I went to the door to let him in. I told him everything went great. He didn't ask why the room smelled like piss, but reminded me that we needed to return the camera to avoid a late fee. While I packed up the equipment, Bill took care of business by having Arlene sign a release and giving her thirty-five bucks. We gave her a ride to the bus stop on our way back to Lloyds and before she got out, I thanked her for a job well done and gave her a little kiss to let her know I enjoyed the nice fuck as well.

None of the mainstream labs would process 'beaver' films and some, thinking it was their right to protect society from smut, would even confiscate them. A lot of the independents would process 'beaver' films, but some would pirate a few prints to sell on the side. It wasn't as though you could go to the cops to complain that someone was stealing your smut. Bill had gotten wind of a small independent lab on Highland Avenue, owned by an Egyptian immigrant name Marty Rustin, who was happy to process our film at a very reasonable price and had an honest reputation to boot. When our seminal epic finished running the gauntlet of developing chemicals, I was relieved to find that the lighting and exposure were fine and the camera work, although conservative, was made moot by Arlene's strong performance.

Not having the finances to strike prints, our only option was to sell the negative. Mike Henderson, who was one of the top producers in Hollywood of silent 'beaver' loops liked what he saw and paid us two hundred bucks. We got robbed, but it earned us a small profit and the ability to make another loop. Only six weeks after shooting Josie in Palm Springs, we had our foot in the movie business! And incredibly, the very first footage we shot made a profit!

Henderson would strike prints off of the negative from the "pissing girl" loop, and within a month would probably make a five hundred or more percent profit for himself. Until we could grow our cash reserves, we had no option but to sell the negative and shoot one loop at a time.

56

TEASING DOESN'T MEAN FUCKING

The advent of "spread beaver" was drawing more and more men to the theatres. I wasn't the only guy who was desperate to examine that delightful little morsel lying between a lady's legs. Business was so good, that Alex DeRenzy opened his own theatre on Larsen Street in San Francisco to show his own loops. It was called 'The Screening Room.' He had made a brilliant discovery. By converting a storefront into a theatre that had less than fifty seats, he wasn't required to obtain a theatre license from the city. Other entrepreneurs quickly recognized that a lot of money could be made by doing the same thing, and forty-nine seat mini theatres that exclusively showed 'beaver' loops began to pop up all over, including in Los Angeles. There seemed to be no limit to the number of men willing to pay five bucks for two hours of dick stiffening entertainment. Each mini theatre needed ten films a week to comprise a show, and unlike DeRenzy's Screening Room, needed shooters to provide them product.

Bill and I both realized that the opportunity to make big money was at hand. But we had to be able to sell prints if we wanted to get in on the action. Our meager bankroll was an obstacle and wasn't helped when I got fired from my job at the Continental Bookstore. I had been working on the night that Continental was premiering Pat Rocco's new gay movie, 'Let There be Boys,' at the adjacent Park Street Theatre. Shan Sales, one of the two owners of Continental and overtly gay -Bill and I affectionately called him Miss Sales—wanted this to be a flamboyant affair, and sent word out that everyone, including those working at the bookstore, were to be nattily attired and on their best behavior. For the occasion, I wore my blue pin-striped-drug-smuggler suit, the only natty attire I owned.

On the night of the event, hundreds of gays of all shapes and sizes meandered under the bright keg lights in front of the theatre. Many of them wandered into the bookstore and came upstairs to where I was working; to massage their libidos by browsing through a few gay magazines before the premier began. When an announcement outside the theatre was made that the screening was about to begin, everyone scampered out of the bookstore and dashed into the theatre to take a seat.

I took the opportunity to pocket a little bonus for myself out of the cash register, but for no particular good reason, decided rather than waiting to the end of my shift to reconcile the cash register, to do it immediately. Maybe it was a subliminal premonition, because fifteen minutes later, 'Miss' Sales came into the store and after taking a quick look around, bolted up the stairs to the reading room. He had money on his mind and opened the cash register to do a quick verification that everything was copasetic. If not for the fact that I had reconciled the sales tape with the amount of cash in the drawer, I would have been busted. But everything was copasetic, and without saying a word to me, dashed down the stairs and left the store to attend the premier.

Continental's managers met each Monday morning at the home office, which was above the Paris Theatre on Santa Monica Blvd. High on the agenda was that Sean Sales wanted me fired. My manager, David, told me what happened. Sales 's first question to him was:

"Who was that guy working upstairs?" "That's Howard Ziehm" he replied.

"I want him fired. He looked repulsive in that blue suit. Get rid of him tomorrow."

David was taken aback by Sales's demand and was upset when he told me that I had been fired. He gave me his card and said if I needed anything to give him a call, not as a gay come on, but just as a friend. In passing, since he knew that Bill and I were dabbling in the movie business, he mentioned that his lover, Mike Naismith, was a professional cinematographer.

There was no reason for Bill to quit, he needed the money as much as me, and he stayed on. Two days later, Continental got what they had coming. David, still upset how everything had gone down, called them to say that he was resigning and unexpectedly on the same day, another employee resigned. Continental had a big problem—not enough employees to operate the store.

A call begging me to stay on for another week quickly followed. Of course I happily agreed; chuckling to myself how I would make them pay dearly. By the end of the week, Bill and I had carted off several hundred dollars worth of gay magazines from the supply room, which he fenced to bookstores around town. Thanks to Continental, we now had enough money to start striking prints!

Not one to do things the standard way, I had already done things to make my loops more interesting and sexier. I took the camera off the tripod so I could take low angle shots that reminded me of looking up grandma's dress. Since I didn't understand that the camera had to be held very steady, some of my early attempts were a bit shaky, especially when the zoom was racked out, but I quickly fixed that problem by bracing myself against a wall or placing the camera on my knee. I also included a little opening tease to each loop. I would have the model walking down the sidewalk in a short tight skirt with the top of her stockings showing or straddling the trunk of the statuette of a mammoth at the La Brea Tar Pits like she was humping it. We would then go to a residential neighborhood where I could have her walk up to to the door of a random house as though it was her home and she was about to enter it. From there we would go back to my apartment and finish the sexy parts of the loop.

I relied on my own voyeuristic sense to decide when to change positions and angles; in essence, editing the film as I shot. From atop a ladder, a high angle full shot of the girl writhing on the bed for twelve seconds would be followed by a low angle pan from the floor for fifteen seconds coming to a stop on her hands massaging her breasts. I always included ample closeup shots of the model's facial expressions to show how much she was enjoying herself. Unlike the twelve minutes it took to shoot a loop with the camera mounted on a tripod, my technique usually required more than an hour. When I was finished I would be drenched with perspiration.

Since I was constantly stopping and starting the camera to move to another angle, several black frames would result between each shot. They had to be edited out and then the loose ends reattached to make the loop continuous again That required a hot splicer and being that they cost over three hundred dollars, we didn't have the money to buy one. Lloyd had one sitting in a showcase at the front of his store that was begging to be stolen. Of course, we could have approached him to let us buy it on time, but if he refused, we would grind to a halt. That wasn't an option. So while Bill kept him distracted on the far side of the room, I reached over the top of the glass case and took the splicer out, and after putting it under my loosely fitting sweat shirt walked out the front door with my arm casually across my stomach so it wouldn't fall out onto the floor, much as I had removed cans of lobster from A&P. It was a shitty thing to do, but this wasn't the time to have guilt feelings.

Bill took prints of the recent films I had shot and had no trouble selling them. Even better; they became such a success with the patrons, that Doug, the young owner of The Flick, a mini house on Western Avenue just a few doors south of Santa Monica Boulevard, asked Bill if we could supply his entire weekly show; meaning nine films each week. It got better! He was willing to pay a premium price of one hundred twenty five bucks per loop for having exclusive rights for one week. The going price paid for a print was seventy-five dollars. We would be making fifty dollars more per print than anyone else in town. After the one week run at The Flick, Bill was free to sell prints around town to other theatres and bars who were now also showing 'beaver' movies on screens tacked up on their side walls.

To produce nine loops a week, I booked two girls for each session. Each would do a single girl loop and then a simulated lesbian scene, which meant tongues could touch nipples but had to remain at least one cunt-hair away from touching a vaginal lip. The girls rarely objected to working with each other, in fact most seemed to enjoy it. For a stage for the girls to perform on, I purchased a round bed and had a red satin sheet made for it. Nothing spelled sex more than the color red and a round bed!

I was soon to discover that if I wanted to maintain a rapport with my models, not to expect them to have sex with me. Two sexy Los Angeles City College students had answered my Free Press ad and I booked them to do singles and a lesbian scene. I had previously seen one of them sauntering across the campus where she always wore tight pants and had a way of walking that spelled S-E-X. I was too chicken shit to approach her when I saw her on campus, but here she was running around my pad naked and doing a loop for me. After she and her friend completed their girl-girl loop, they continued to make out. One was kneeling on the floor with her butt and pussy facing me as she licked her girl friend's twat. Putting the camera down, I knelt on the floor and nuzzled up so I could join in. My interloping was not well received. An icy pallor filled the room that told me to back the fuck off.

The message was clear. If I wanted to succeed in the smut business, I couldn't get involved personally unless it was made explicitly clear that it was wanted. A photographer with a bad reputation would find it hard to procure models. Unwanted aggressive behavior could even be fatal. A shooter named Jack Richardson, was recently found murdered in his apartment. His loops were first rate and I considered him to be my main competition. He had evidently come on too strong to one of his models and her biker boy friend showed up at 3AM at his apartment and whacked him. Ironically, his bad break was a blessing for us. With Jack out of the way, theatres were even more likely to buy from us.

That I was totally self-taught, turned out to be another blessing. To stay abreast of recent developments and techniques, I had become a regular reader of American Cinematographer. An article in a 1970 issue, described a new Kodak film that was just becoming available. It was a 16mm color negative film, technically referred to as 7252. Even though it was more expensive on the front end to buy and develop, it drastically cut the cost of making prints. I immediately recognized that Bill and I would blow our competitors out of the water if we began using the new film. Prints were costing them forty-five dollars a pop to strike off the old film and we could make prints for twenty dollars off the new film. We could undersell everyone.

The premium price The Flick was paying us for first run rights easily covered the extra expense of developing and editing the new film. Bill scoured every corner of LA County and even flew up to San Francisco to look for new customers; two of them would be the Mitchell brothers, Jim and Artie, who had begun showing 'beaver' movies at a theatre they were renting on Van Ness Avenue.

Making nine films a week left me no time to do anything else. My day began early in the morning and ended late at night. After a quick breakfast of doughnuts and coffee, I dressed my apartment for each loop to make it look like a different whorehouse. I paid a seamstress two make me two large velvet pillows, one red and one yellow, that I placed on the bed or the floor and I made sure to have abundant furry sheep skins for the girls to slither across as they caressed their sexy bodies. After shooting the days loops, I would rush the film to the lab and pick up the previous days footage so I could take it back to the house and edit out the black frames. I usually ate dinner as I worked. Around midnight I was finished, just in time to feed 'Little Beasty' his nightly dinner before I crashed.

The demand for girls to model for films and magazines had grown large enough to support two talent agencies that catered exclusively to the adult industry. Pretty Girl International, owned by Reb Sawitz, an erstwhile biker, and another run by a transplant from New York, named, Irv Sofsky. It was a relief to not have to advertise in the Free Press anymore. There were also a few people I paid a small fee if they found girls for me to shoot. One was my neighbor, Doreen, a Scientologist, who lived in the apartment just across from my front door. The other, Larry Lamont, was a likeable Italian ne'er do well street hustler who was adept at picking up girls off the street. Between the four of them, I had more than enough girls available to never have to use the same face twice.

There were still loops coming out of San Francisco, but our product had a huge advantage over them: no one could match the beauty of Southern California girls. Their sun warmed faces were cheerful and healthy. Their bodies were toned and shapely. And their personalities were upbeat and playful. They enjoyed being beautiful and were happy to show it off. That's why the Beach Boys were inspired to write; "I Wish They Could All Be California Girls."

Word went around that I was someone easy to work for. That I was young and innocent looking and didn't push myself on them to have sex, made it easier for them to flout their sexuality around me. I made them feel that being sexy was natural. And it was! Millions of years of evolution had endowed them with curves and attributes that were pleasing to the male eye. I understood that they enjoyed that power but didn't necessarily want to romp in the bed. However, I still managed to treat myself to a little thrill by rubbing a little baby oil on their pussy lips to make it look like they were aroused. I overheard one girl telling her friend: "When he rubbed oil on my lips I almost came!" Naturally, all that being said, there were still plenty of girls, who after the shooting was finished, let me know they were available to fuck.

57

A MOST DISGUSTING THING

The complexes that I had developed while growing up, were still an integral part of my personality. I tended to be shy around girls, not expressing myself forcefully. I was to learn that didn't work when I was wearing my director's hat. There were a few girls who, because of my baby face, felt that I could be intimidated. One girl, in her mid-twenties, even asked me: "Aren't you a little young to be doing this?" I had no choice but to adopt an assertive directorial persona. There was no point in beating around the bush—no pun intended—when directing a sex scene. "Spread your legs wide; stick your butt up in the air so I can see your pussy; suck on your nipples," got results when said firmly but in a nice way. I was a natural. When commanded, my models were more than happy to oblige. That I had a soft veneer helped to remove the "dirty old man stigma" and flaunting their sexuality in front of me came easy.

There was tremendous competition among the mini theatres. Those that showed the hottest films got the business. Only hours after the new shows opened on Friday, the raincoat underground had passed the word around the city letting everyone know who had a hot show and who didn't. No theatre wanted to get busted by the vice for going too far, but they also wanted to stay as close to the edge as possible.

Zoco films, the combination of Ziehm and Osco, became the trendsetter. I used special attachments, called diopters to shoot extreme close-ups of erect nipples and clits that made them appear ten feet high on screen. I also began asking my models to pull the lips of their pussies open, showing pink as it would eventually became known. One of the girls I was shooting got so excited that a gush of juices flowed profusely onto her thighs. At the end of each silent loop, I had my model look directly into the camera and clearly mouth words such as: "I want to fuck you" or "Can I blow you?"

Bill was always looking for ways to increase our profits and thought he had found one when a lab offered to do our processing for a substantial discount. But instead of saving us money; they almost threw a major wrench into our business, which was still fragile at best. We had grown so rapidly, that our profits were always a half step behind our overhead. We knew that situation would eventually turn around, but as we were not the kind of business that could go to the bank for a loan; we kited checks. When Bill picked up the prints on Thursday evening to deliver to the Flick and the other theatres we were supplying, he would pay the lab bill with a check he knew would bounce, but would be covered on Monday after he deposited the money he was about to collect from our customers.

The new lab had got wind that we kited checks and refused to hand over the prints we had ordered when Bill showed up on Thursday evening. Our customers were expecting them for their Friday openings, the biggest grossing day of the week. From eleven in the morning on, customers in raincoats or holding newspapers to the side of their faces to hide their identities, streamed into the various theatres around town to see the new line-up of fresh 'Beavers.' A packed house was not uncommon. If the theatre didn't have a new show, they would walk and go elsewhere. The theatre would lose money and possibly a steady customer. But the lab wouldn't listen to Bill's pleas unless he paid them in cash. We had always made good on our kited checks, but the new lab was adamant and wouldn't budge.

It was not time to panic and Bill showed his mettle under fire. He came by my apartment at one in the morning, to tell me he had been able to get the Flick and our bar customer to advance a thousand dollars each so we could get our product released. He was down at the lab first thing in the morning and picked up the weeks show just in time to get it to the Flick before their doors opened. To add insult to injury, when the prints were projected, they all had a green hue. The fucking lab had done shoddy work. None of our customers or their patrons was too happy. Green girls were not a turn-on. There was nothing to be done except chalk it up as a bad experience.

It didn't stop our juggernaut. Two months later, our loops were showing at sixty percent of the forty-nine seat theatres in LA. They were so in demand, that after the Flick's one hundred twenty five dollar per loop first run, second run buyers were paying us one hundred per loop, and subsequent buyers willingly paid seventy-five to fifty per loop. In less than three months, we had become the 'Beaver loop' kings of L. A.

It was time to go national. Bill packed a suitcase full of our loops and took a two-week sales trip to introduce Zoco to the New York market. Shelly Wilson, an elderly Greek woman who owned The Eros Theatre located on 8th Ave in the middle of New York's Hell's Kitchen, was charmed by Bill's good looks and also so delighted with our product, that she agreed to buy everything we produced. Other trips to Cleveland, Chicago, Dallas, Portland, Saint Louis and any other city where 'Beavers' were permitted, gained us more customers.

Just seeing a pussy soon was not enough to keep audiences happy. Even showing 'pink' became blaze'. The fact that nobody got busted; emboldened 'Beaver' theatres to request more brazen footage. The Flick asked Bill if we could add a few feet of insertion footage, like dildos or bananas. I was fairly certain that if I offered an extra ten bucks, my models wouldn't object. It was little different than inserting a Tampax. But some of our customers weren't willing to take the risk of getting busted if the loop showed penetration, so to get around that problem, I began shooting an extra hundred feet of each model inserting a finger, dildo or some other interesting object into her pussy. That gave the theatres the option of using the extra footage or not. Again, when nobody who added the hundred feet of insertions got busted; I just began including penetration as an integral part of each loop.

I had been using my apartment as a studio for several months

without any problems. No one in the complex, other than my Scientologist neighbor, Doreen, knew that I was using it to shoot 'beaver' loops. Conveniently, the little old lady who resided on the opposite side of the pool; kept her blinds shut all day and the other residents were at work. And most propitious, was that the apartment's manager, Jay, who was a purblind elderly overweight man from Oklahoma, never ventured out of his first floor apartment adjacent to the complex's entryway.

As much as possible, I kept my models inside the apartment, and if one wondered out on the stoop to have a cigarette, although not a big deal, not wanting to press my luck, I would hustle her back inside. There was nothing to be gained if it became known what I was up to. Being that August days in LA are stifling hot, my non air conditioned apartment would become unbearable; especially if halogen lights were on while I was shooting. I was set up next to the entry door, which I had left open with the screen door closed, so a breeze could blow through the room while I was hard at work shooting a loop that featured a girl doing herself with a coke bottle. My model was sitting in a lounge chair adjacent to the open door, with her legs jacked up and her ankles almost behind her head, so she could slowly work the coke bottle in and out of her pussy. The slight breeze that flowed into the room was doing little to keep us cool and though I was shirtless, I still sweated like a pig.

I was kneeling on the floor in front of the young lady. The camera was resting on one knee to keep it steady and my eye was glued to its eyepiece so I could focus on the action and give her directions.

"Ok, slide it in as far as you can."

"Yeah, that's good. Move your hands to the side a bit so I can see it going in better."

"Nice . . . nice. Slide it back and forth a little faster. Oh yeah . . . nice."

We had been shooting for a little over a minute, when suddenly the screen door slammed shut. From halfway down the stairs, I heard Jay's Oklahoma drawl screaming as though he had just seen Satan:

"Oh god . . . That's the most disgusting thing I've ever seen in my life."

Knowing it wasn't meant to be a complement, I got up and

stepped out onto the stoop just in time to see him waddling below along the edge of the pool. Because of his visual handicap, he probably only saw my shadow as he looked up:

"Oh god . . . what kind of filth . . . Oh god. I want you out of here!" he screamed as he stumbled along, desperate to return to the sanctuary of his own apartment.

When I stepped back into the apartment, my model was still in the position when I had left; her legs spread and her cunt plugged with the coke bottle. She told me she had seen him standing at the door:

"I thought it was cool with you cause he just stood there and you didn't say anything."

I had been so focused on getting the shot that the world around me had disappeared which it always did when I shot. I didn't hear the screen door open or sense Jay's presence. I told her it was OK and got back on my knees to finish the shot, which I knew was going to be the highlight loop of the week.

After I paid her forty-five dollars, and sent her on her way, I went downstairs to try and pacify Jay. He would have none of it and gave me to the end of the month to move out. I was forbidden to do any more shooting in the apartment. It was time we moved into a proper studio anyway, and within two days, Bill had found an office on Sunset Boulevard at "The Crossroads of the World" that would be perfect for our operation.

The Crossroads

The Crossroads was a collection of European style buildings arranged along a wide free flowing walkway that gave the feeling of strolling through an English village. The entry on Sunset was a moderne building, made to look like a cruise ship. It had a huge globe of the world sitting on a pedestal atop it that could be seen by traffic driving by. Halfway, between Sunset Blvd. and Selma, was a water fountain that spilled into a little pool surrounded by a seating ledge. The village was originally built in 1936 to be a shopping mall—some say LA's first—but was now converted into artsy offices, many of them occupied by other people in the skin trade; including Mike Henderson, Dave Auerbach and Johnny Castanno, who shot for Adam magazine. Our new studio was the first office at its entrance, just to the left of the world globe. It had three rooms; the front would be my studio and the other two for operating our distribution side of the business.

There was tremendous confusion about what were the limits of acceptability as far as explicitness was concerned. The vice and courts had failed to define what the limits should be -one way or the other—and producers and exhibitors were left with the choice of pushing the limits themselves and risk getting busted, or staying put and losing ground to competitors who chose to go forward. Single girl penetration and simulated lesbian loops hadn't brought on the heat and DeRenzy was already showing simulated boy girl films at the Screening Room. One of The Flick's competitors began buying a few of his loops to show in LA, so I had no choice but to follow suit.

Not that I had any compunction about doing so. It gave me a thrill to put the establishment on the spot as far as defining what was hardcore. If a girl appeared to be giving a blowjob, but her long hair hid the action in such a way that it was impossible to say with certainty that the dick was actually in her mouth; could it be called hardcore? Or if her mouth was over a stiff cock that was covered by a silk or a chiffon scarf, meaning her mouth was not in actual contact with the penis, was that hardcore? Maybe it was just a zucchini or carrot beneath the scarf. Another deception I liked to use was to put whipped cream on the tip of a dick or a pussy and then shoot the action from an angle which did not reveal genital contact being made, but when the fellator lifted their head, the shot would reveal that the whipped cream was now all over their face. One couldn't say with certainty what had transpired.

But the public still wanted more. The silent beaver loop was quickly disappearing into the dustbin and being replaced by sound loops or even cheap one-hour features with a storyline. Shooting sound was a lot more difficult. To muffle the chattering noise that the Arriflex made while film ran through its gate, a sound muffling cover, called a barney, had to be placed around it. A tape recorder and a microphone also had to be operated to record the sound. At first I tried doing the whole thing by myself. Since some of our market still wanted silent films, I had to add two additional days of shooting just to supply sound films for those who wanted them. Both Bill and I were working hectic schedules. Delivering and shipping films to all out customers was beginning to overwhelm both of us. We needed an assistant.

Bill had become friendly with a rail-thin Vietnam vet with scraggly red hair and beard who ran the developing machines at Crest Film Labs, the small independent film lab where we were now doing all of our processing. His name was Lynn Rogers and when offered a chance to get away from the smelly chemicals and become our boy everything, he was happy to accept the offer. Helping me shoot beaver loops and assisting Bill in delivering the product around town, was a lot more exciting then running miles and miles of film through chemical solutions all day. If Murray Stein, the lab's owner, was perturbed that we hired Rogers away from him, he never said anything, probably because we had become his largest customer and were one of the prime reasons for the lab's financial success.

Rogers became my grip, gaffer, assistant cameraman and soundman; all at the same time. Neither of us had any formal training so to say that we were self-made would be an understatement. Lynn didn't talk much, but was a pleasure to work with. He had energy to burn and never uttered the slightest complaint. I was also pleased that he wasn't a pussy hound, or at least didn't show it. I didn't need any competition when I flirted with a girl that might offer me a quick fuck. The specter still remained that we could be busted, but being a Vietnam vet, he showed no fear of working in an environment that was at the edge of the law.

I had continued to keep abreast of new innovations and equipment available to 16mm filmmakers and convinced Bill we should purchase a French camera called an Éclair. It was beautifully balanced for hand-held work and even without a barney, almost silent. We would also need a tape recorder that accurately matched the speed of the film going through the camera's gate. The industry standard was a machine made in Switzerland called a Nagra. We didn't have the cash on hand, but Bill negotiated a deal with one of the equipment supply companies, F&B Ceco, to allow us to put five grand down and pay off the balance over the next six months. He was proving to be deft as a deal maker.

58

STUD FLAME

From the start, my goal was to satisfy my need for sexy women, whether it was getting laid or just being teased, it didn't matter. Bill's dream was to be a movie star or at the least; a big time producer. I didn't consider myself to be a great artist, but when it came to making 'beaver' movies, I was more than adequate. Bill, on the other hand, didn't appear to have much artistic talent, but he had an innate sense for business. He liked the process and the money that came along with it. I couldn't fault him with that. The thought of making big money appealed to me as well, but at the time, almost all of our money was being plowed back into the business so there was little personal benefit. Being that Bill was out in the field making sales; he was aware what the public, and therefore the theatres, were looking for. When he saw that a mini house on La Cienaga, called The Po No, was doing good business by showing a one-hour feature, he insisted that we needed to make a feature. It was the future. The PoNo was rumored to be mob-connected and were closed down within a month. Since the Mickey Cohen days, LA vice had no use for organized crime. But Bills observations had been on target up to this point so there was no reason to disagree with him.

I had never written a story of any kind and had no clue how to write a script, so when he suggested he could handle it, I was not in a position to doubt him. He still had dreams of making another Easy Rider and maybe he could write. Two days later he showed me his six-page script. It was a simple story. There was no need of being too critical of its artistic merits, almost anything would work as long as it could be produced for almost no money. After reading it, I felt that was the case.

But it offered a look into his mind that struck me as strange. A gorgeous girl picks up a hitchhiker and after noticing that he has a nice bulge in his pants, takes him home to have an orgy with her and three of her friends. Unbeknownst to the frolickers, a window peeper is outside the house, masturbating as he watches the action. In an attempt to get a better view, he loses his balance and falls through the window. He is easily captured and tied up. But his punishment is what gave me the cause to wonder. The window peeper's penis is cut off with a knife and left lying on the ground. The end calls for a stray dog to pick it up and scamper away to eat it.

Thinking it would be smart to have a mentor show me the ins and outs of making a feature, I recalled that David, my gay manager from the bookstore, had told me that his lover, Mike Naismith, was an accomplished cinematographer. When I called he was delighted to accept my offer. I didn't ask for any references, David's recommendation was enough. When we met, I found him to be typical of many gays, very handsome with an agreeable friendly personality. I would direct the action; he would do the cinematography and Lynn Rogers would do sound and everything else. Our budget was fifteen hundred dollars.

I was still in touch with my voluptuous ex girl friend, Josie Catalin, and was happy when she agreed to accept the starring role. I also booked a busty blond cutie named, Niola, who was one of the current stars of the skin business, to take part in the simulated orgy. Jeff and Susan Patterson, who had shot a simulated loop for me a few months prior, would comprise the rest of the orgy members. Jeff, who worked as a juvenile probation officer during the day, would be the hitchhiker. We had become very friendly mostly because whenever I stopped at their apartment; he offered me a joint and Susan would take me into their bedroom for a fuck.

In the course of his work at the probation department, Jeff had come to know Lenny Goodman, a New Yorker who had a tendency to get into minor trouble. He suggested that he would be perfect for the window peeper. Lenny, when he came in to read for the part, insisted that he was the second coming of Dustin Hoffman. He proudly lifted his shirt to show off the long scar that ran across his abdomen, the result of a drunk slashing him during a recent argument down on Main Street. I had no doubt that he was a character and Bill was enamored by his neurotic persona, so we gave him the part. He promised our decision would make us all famous.

The filming began with the very simple scene of the girl picking up the hitchhiker. I had assumed we would shoot the whole film in one day. The script only had three scenes, the longest one being the orgy, which was essentially a loop. But after my mentor, Mike Naismith, spent the whole morning and part of the afternoon, adjusting lights, flags and scrims, to eliminate a reflection on the windshield of Bill's GTO that Josie was driving as she approached the hitch hiker, my assumption began to look doubtful. By the time we arrived at our next location, a house in Silverlake where the orgy would be shot, it was three in the afternoon. The sun was setting before Mike was ready to shoot so we had to rent some big keg lights to shine through the windows from the outside to give the impression that it was still daytime. Everyone was becoming hungry and irritable, so Bill had to go out for food, an expense that was not included in the budget. Naismith seemed oblivious to the actors; his photography was paramount. Lenny Goodman kept bugging me about what a great actor he was and I had to admit he did put his all into it while doing his 'yanking off' scene. At 3 AM, I awoke Jeff, Susan and Niola from their slumber to perform in the orgy scene. Not surprisingly, they didn't display a lot of energy. We finally wrapped at 5AM. The dog scene would have to be shot later in the day.

We reconvened in the afternoon to shoot the finale. Being as it was the dramatic crescendo of Bill's script, he was quite excited to see it pulled off in its full glory. He made sure that the ersatz penis, a hot dog, was the right size and had the foresight to bring a bottle of ketchup to serve as blood.

Goodman's stage name was 'Stud Flame,' so we decided to title the film, *'Whatever Happened to Stud Flame.'* He was convinced it would make him a star. As I watched Naismith film the final shot, a dog running off into the distance with a penis in its mouth, I had learned what I needed to know: that I would be totally capable of shooting our next feature by myself and in half the time.

Despite my misgivings about the amount of time Naismith had taken to shoot six pages of script, I agreed to hire him to edit the film. I didn't know any of the subtleties of stringing shots and scenes together to make a coherent feature and since I still had to produce a full schedule of loops, I didn't have the time, even if I did.

Because Bill's work required him going in and out of the Crossroad's office, which disturbed my filming sessions, we rented another office in an older two story Spanish style building on Hollywood Blvd near Gower. The building and area lacked the historic charm that our studio had, but its three room suite on the second floor not only gave Bill space to work in, but made him feel more like an executive businessman. And the space that was freed up at the Crossroads would provide for an editing room. After renting a Moviola and the other sundry equipment that Naismith said he would need, he was ready to go to work. That he preferred to work in the evening meant he wouldn't interfere with my shooting schedule.

Zoco was now producing both silent and sound loops and a feature, at the same time. It was paying off handsomely. Though we took little out as salaries, in less than a year we had gone from forty dollars between us; to a viable production company with an office, a studio and owners of our own equipment.

59

BROWN GRAVEY

"French fries with brown gravy?" That's what she wanted as I drove her home after we finished shooting. When the model I had scheduled for a four O'clock shoot had yet to show up, I gave her a call to see what the problem was. A very soft-spoken girl answered the phone and told me the girl I was planning to shoot was out of town. It was nothing unusual to be stood up by a model, but I needed to shoot a single girl loop to fill my weekly commitment. Thinking the girl on the phone must know what kind of work her roommate was doing; I asked her if she would be interested in filling in. Without hesitation she said yes, and assured me she would be at my studio within a half hour. Two hours later she showed up.

Though I was a bit pissed-off by her tardy arrival, it was not my style to get riled; especially when I saw how beautiful she was. Her name was Judy Callender. She had soft brownish-blond hair that hung to her shoulders. Her face was round and very soft and her voice even softer. She wore a white see-through chiffon top with no bra and though her breasts weren't large, they were attractive. I tried not to ogle her, but her ass that was jacked up by high heels filled out the tight gray cotton mini skirt she was wearing so that my eyes kept looking at it like a fish going for bait.

It was late in the day and I needed to shoot the loop, so as soon as she donned the trashy lingerie I provided her, I explained what I wanted her to do—essentially act like a slutty whore—and we got to work. Because the day was stifling hot, I had removed my shirt and sweat was soon rolling down my back, causing my bell-bottom jeans to slide below my hips and expose the crack of my ass. Only after she told me years later, did I know that I was turning her on. The loop, including one hundred feet of dildo work, went well and after I packed up and paid her, I prepared to leave.

When she told me she didn't have a car and had hitchhiked to my studio, I realized why she had been so late and offered to give her a ride back to where she was staying. On the way she asked if I knew a restaurant that served french-fries with brown gravy, a dish popular in her hometown of Dover, New Hampshire. Knowing that the Norm's on Sunset Boulevard would probably be happy to satisfy her somewhat unusual request, I pulled into its parking lot.

While we ate, she told me in a voice so quiet it was hard to hear, what had brought her to California. Her mother, with whom she had been very close, had suffered an aneurism that left her partially paralyzed and only able to speak with difficulty. Unable to deal with the loss, or her father, who was dealing with his own strain, she became rebellious and in a fit of anger during an argument yelled: "She isn't my mother." That got her thrown against the wall and the next day she moved out to live with a girl friend in nearby Hampton Beach where she took a job as a waitress. As she continued, she told me that Frank Delano, the owner of the Hampton Beach Casino, where her father had played trumpet in its band, had asked her to represent the Casino in the upcoming Miss Hampton Beach beauty contest. She didn't think she had what it took and declined his offer, but at the last moment, entered the contest anyway by representing another establishment. She took runner up honors. Delano's Casino had sponsored the contest, and he couldn't help but give her a little ribbing: "See, if you would have taken my offer you would have won".

Her picture appeared in the local paper as the contest's runner up. A month later it would reappear for something less flattering. She had been busted for transporting a carton of cigarettes from Massachusetts, where they were legal, to New Hampshire, where they were illegal. The stupidity of the act was that she didn't smoke and was just bringing them across the state border for a friend who was going to pay ten bucks for her taking the risk.

I easily commiserated with her story and encouraged her to go on. The picture in the paper garnered the attention of a Mafioso from nearby Worchester, Mass, who tried to coax her into becoming one of his gang molls. But waking up to the fact that she was heading towards big trouble, she split to Boston and fell in with a group of young kids; mostly hippies and runaways, where free love and drugs were part of the culture. Peer pressure led to using grass and uppers like crystal meth. She had another bad habit that I could also commiserate with: shoplifting. Removing a dress from Filene's department store got her busted and put on probation. She was to report to an officer each week, but when her boy friend, just flush with four hundred bucks from a grass deal, offered to fly the two of them to Los Angeles, she was naïve enough to think she was leaving her legal problems behind.

After she finished mopping up the last drop of brown gravy with the remaining French fry, I drove her to where she was staying. It turned out to be a closet with a mattress on the floor in a house that was only a half block down the hill from the Whiskey A-Go-Go. She was cohabitating there with several other girls, including Marty, the girl who was supposed to model for me earlier that day. Our life stories shared a lot in common and I liked that she was sexy, a bit rebellious, and not an intellectual snob. Communicating with a girl on a personal basis was still very difficult for me, but I managed to quietly ask if she would like to go to the 'Artists and Models Ball' with me. I was almost surprised when she said yes. I told her to wear something wild and I would pick her up around seven the next evening.

The Ball was a Hollywood happening, put on yearly by Gary Berwin, a successful car dealer. Although I had never attended, I had seen photos in magazines of the near naked participants, so I knew it was a racy affair. When I picked Judy up the next evening, she didn't disappoint. She wore high heels, black fish net stocking and a red and black merry widow from a production of Guys and Dolls. Her breasts, covered with a bit of see-thru chiffon, peeked over the bottom half of the bra. I wore a black satin cape that I could pull aside to reveal my body, naked except for the small red G-string that held my genitals in a provocative little pouch. We were a sexy looking couple. As it would turn out, compared to some at the ball, we looked like puritans.

The ball, held in the conference room at the Beverly Hills Wilshire Hilton, was the apotheosis of Hollywood exhibitionism and weirdness. Photographers scampered around the room shooting anyone who was willing to pose for a few shots. Despite my recent rise to success in the adult film world, I remained an unknown because of my low-key profile, so Judy and I garnered little attention, spending the evening dancing and observing. Though a few girls posed near nude for interested photographers, no one could compete against the gay crowd for flamboyance, creativity and debauchery. One young gay hopped up on the stage and removed his G-string and then swiveled his pelvis so that his cock and balls gyrated to the beat of the music. Other gays roamed the floor in stunning costumes hoping to attract the attention of the judges who were handing out invitations to enter the various contests. The best men's costume was a toss up. A very handsome guy wore a Little Bo Peep dress with a pole running up his back supporting a four by six foot canopy that was rimed with flowers and a sign atop made of roses that spelled CARASOL. Another gay, with a sinewy physique, had painted his entire body gold to match the color of his miniscule G-string. His headdress was a three-foot high birdcage, complete with live birds. A gold satin train hung from his shoulders, its ten-foot length attended by two G-string clad slave boys. The costumes must have taken months to put together.

After the Ball, Judy agreed to stay over night at my place on Romaine. My landlord had calmed down a bit after the coke bottle incident and had yet to force me out. The fact that I paid my rent on time helped him to forget the incident. I introduced her to 'Little Beasty' and was pleased to see that she sincerely liked animals. She seemed to have a lot on her mind and after we had sex, which if not exceptional, was good, we both fell asleep from exhaustion.

Though my wild hallucinating nightmares had become rare, they still occurred, and probably due to the fact that my unconscious mind was still wound up from the evening's excitement; I jumped out of bed just after we dozed off, screaming that there was an alligator in our bed. What it was about alligators I had not the slightest idea. Naturally Judy was shocked, but still held me as I calmed down. Embarrassed, I tried to explain myself to her, assuring her I wasn't nuts and it was no big deal. The next morning, after I made her breakfast, I took her back to her place near the Whiskey. She mentioned that she was broke; having spent the money I had paid her for the modeling job to put her costume for the Ball together. I played the daddy role—after all she had played the mommy role after my nightmare—and gave her twenty-dollars to tide her over for a few days.

Before we parted, she asked if I would like to take her to a free concert in Griffith Park where Gracie Slick of the Jefferson Air Plane would be playing. Without hesitation, I said yes. The next day, when we arrived, thousands of kids had already taken their spots on the large open meadow where the concert would take place. Along with one of Judy's housemates and her boy friend, we sat down on the grass near the back of the field where it wasn't so crowded, but still had a good view of the stage. I was looking forward to an afternoon of listening to music and getting to know her better, but she wanted to move close to the stage.

I had a hard time dealing with that. Maybe because my mother idolized the popular singers and movie stars of her day and I saw them as a threat to my relationship with her, they intimidated me. My early unsettled childhood had left me with a fear that I would be deserted. I wanted my mommy to think of me as number one. So when Judy insisted on moving close to the stage, it gave me the feeling that I was being relegated to a second position. As we drove home from the concert, I didn't have much to say. When I dropped her off, I told her that I wouldn't be seeing her again. She was surprised and protested; saying she really liked me. I was taken aback and my mood lightened. By the time our contretemps was settled, she had asked me if I would be interested in renting a house with her and Marty, the roommate I had yet to meet. I was still under orders to move out of my apartment and "what could be cooler than living in a house with, not one, but two 'beaver' models.

Marty, I would learn, was out of town recuperating from a medical problem which I figured was an abortion. Judy assured me that she would be in on the deal when she returned, so to get things moving, she and I took it upon ourselves to find a place for the three of us to cohabitate. We both fell in love with a little Hansel and Gretel cottage we found in Marina Del Rey on Anchorage Street, one of the several one block long walkways that ran between Pacific Avenue and theVenice beach. Pamela, the seventy-year old lady who owned the property, lived just across the walkway and was 'Venice' hip, so had no problem with a man living with two young women. I felt it best not to mention that 'Little Beasty' would also be an occupant.

The house's décor was little-old-lady gauche; lots of gold leaf and ornate decoration, ersatz fireplace set against a gold laced mirrored wall, gold shag rug and a gold chandelier hanging from the ceiling in the dining room. The single room upstairs was a small bedroom where Judy and I would sleep and Marty would have another small bedroom on the ground floor. A small garage and a yard planted with colorful flowers made the place charming as hell. It would also be a great location for me to shoot some of my loops. I signed the lease and Judy and I moved in immediately.

Other than having to purchase a used aluminum kitchen table, the three large colored velvet pillows that I used as props, was all that was needed to furnish the living room. Getting the large round bed up the stairs was a struggle, but once in place we were set to move in. Marty could arrange for her own bed when she got back in town. Having a beautiful house near the beach, two hot roommates, and thanks to Bill giving me his GTO after he traded up for a classier car—something he seemed to do often—I was feeling pretty good about myself.

A week later, a bit of reality would set in. First, Judy informed me that she was pregnant, not by me—thank god—but by Bernie Campie, the lead singer for the rock group, Black Pearl. She wanted to get an abortion but didn't have the money to pay for the procedure. The next day, after giving her two hundred bucks, I dropped her off at the nearby family planning clinic in Venice, to take care of the problem. Being a responsible daddy to my new girl friend made me feel manly.

She didn't ask me to wait at the clinic, so I returned to our new house. Who should walk in while Judy was away, but Marty? She was an attractive girl, tall with a trim body and happy Irish face. I was surprised to learn that she had not committed herself to move in with Judy and me. She was just now stopping by to check things out. I told her Judy was at the clinic taking care of her problem. While we waited, she remarked that my hair was flying all over the place, which was not unusual, and offered to give me a haircut. As she clipped away, I learned that the real reason she hadn't shown up for her shoot that day was because she had the clap. I assured her that everything had worked out fine and not to worry about it.

Just as Marty was finishing my haircut, Judy returned. Not surprisingly, she was upset; she had a tough emotional day. Without a single word or any acknowledgement to either Marty or me, she went straight up the stairs to our bedroom. Not really knowing what to say, Marty and I continued to banter, periodically laughing about meaningless nothings. Suddenly, like a wild cat left out of the cage, Judy came down the stairs and went off on Marty in a jealous rage.

That was the end of Marty. My ego was flattered that I had deserved so much attention, but by signing the lease, I had committed myself to live at the Anchorage house for at least a year. Unless Judy moved out, I was as good as married, something I had vowed never to do.

60

THE ALLIGATOR HAS TO GO

Naismith was to have a major hissy fit before he finished editing 'Stud Flame.' As I should have anticipated, he had gone at it as though he were editing, 'Gone With The Wind' and after it dawned upon him that he was bumping his head against a brick wall, he went ballistic one night and threw all the little yellow spools which had each shot wrapped around them, helter skelter about the editing room. Since he was the only one who could put 'Humpty Dumpty' back together again, I had to remain calm and not get too upset. It took him three days to reconstitute the film and he finished the cut as well as could be expected within a week.

My patience was to be rewarded in an unsuspected way. We still needed to shoot titles for the film and he offered to do that free of charge. Bill and I felt that our first feature should be produced by a more distinguishable name than 'Zoco Films,' but neither of us could come up with an idea. In a moment of gay creativity, Naismith suggested: "Graffitti Productions." At the time, graffiti was not a household word and I asked: "What does that mean?" He explained it was the trashy and sometimes poetic writing often seen in public bathrooms above the urinals or inside the stalls like: "Here I sit, broken hearted, tried to shit, but only farted," or public service announcements like: "4 best blow jobs, call Lois 456-2322." It was perfect and Graffitti Productions was born. Naismith went on to shoot the titles and credits written on sheets of toilet paper as they were flushed down our studio's funky toilet bowl.

'Whatever Happened to Stud Flame' was more perverse than sexual, but as usual, Bill managed to sell it. He also showed good business sense by finding a CPA to handle our books. Up to this point we had been operating unregistered and had paid no taxes. Even though our product was on the edges of the law, cheating the IRS was playing with fire. Our new accountant, Sy Katz, was an affable Jewish man in his early fifties. He had an easy going demeanor, a pleasant face and a hoary head of hair. He was just what we needed, someone who was grounded but not rigorous to the point where he would be stultifying. His vice was fine wine and fine food and now keeping the books for a sex film company seemed to exhilarate him. On his advice, we became a Corporation to protect ourselves against legal liabilities. Bill and I would each own fifty percent of the stock and when Bill argued that since he dealt with the public he should be President, I saw no reason to object.

The IRS asked for a meeting as soon as they became aware of our existence. Worried that Bill's nervous eye tic could be interpreted as being deceitful; I felt I would be better at explaining our situation. When I met at their downtown offices and the agent asked me to explain why we hadn't filed, I told him the truth. In our wildest dreams we never thought we would make so much money. "It was like a kid opening up a street side lemonade stand and discovering that there's a hundred thousand bucks in the box at the end of the day." I explained we now had a CPA filing our taxes in a timely manner. The agent was happy with my explanation. We were now a legitimate company, even in the eyes of the IRS.

I had to admit that I was enjoying living with Judy. She was sexy and open-minded and like me, not a goody-two-shoe. She didn't smoke, wasn't religious and didn't seem to have any interest in having kids or getting married. It was the first time I felt like I was in a relationship that would last. But once again, the alligators attacked me, this time in our little bedroom at the Hansel and Gretel house. To save Judy, I jumped out of bed and dragged the poor girl down the narrow stairs, almost twisting her ankle in the process. Breathing hard and sweating profusely, I began to explain the situation, but only got halfway through before I regained rationality. She was dumbstruck. It was 3AM in the morning. Living with me could be dangerous. She told me if I was going to continue flipping out like that she would have to leave. Miraculously, the threat was all that was needed to flip off the switch that resided deep in the recesses of my brain. The frightening nightmares suddenly ceased. For a while, I expected them to return, but when over the next few months, they didn't, I steadily became confident that the demon had been exorcised.

That we both came to each other with demons; might have explained why we were attracted to each other. Even so, I was a bit miffed that she had yet to tell me that when she first arrived in LA, she had gotten busted again for shoplifting. When it was discovered that she had skipped out on her parole obligations in Boston, she was given a thirty-day stay in Sybil Brand, the county prison for women. Nevertheless, that didn't erase the Boston problem. I was discovering that I was good at playing 'Big Daddy,' and hired her a lawyer. He cleared the whole thing up with a small fine.

It was not lost on me that not every girl could handle a relationship with someone like me, even with my alligator problem exorcised. Judy had no such problem. She was as much a sex freak as me, only in a feminine way. Understanding that Bill and I were pouring everything into making 'Graffitti' grow, to help pay for our personal expenses, she got a job as a stripper at a private men's club in Santa Monica, called 'The Ball.' She had learned about it when one of her former roommates who had worked there, brought Jim Morrison of The Doors back to the house for a fuck after her shift ended. That was a nice little bonus that I'm sure she didn't discount.

Whitey Locker, the son of a former Santa Monica police chief, owned the private club that featured nudity and alcohol. A small membership fee kept the riff raff out and assured that the clientele would be primarily professionals and even an occasional rock star. Since it served liquor, dancers needed to be twenty-one to work there, so Judy, only nineteen, got a phony I. D. that identified her as twenty-one year old Elizabeth Johnson. Her stage name became Becky. She was a damn good stripper—a natural, and quickly became a club favorite. The money she earned was a big help to us. Because we only had one car, she took a cab back and

Judy, a.k.a. Becky

forth to work each day and never complained. Other than insisting I put my large collection of girlie books in a box and stash them in the garage, from where they were stolen, she put no restraints on me. While she was at work, I occasionally shot a loop at our house and even had a fuck on the round bed with a willing model from time to time. How many guys had a relationship like that? Even Little Beasty found happiness at the Hansel and Gretel house, roaming the neighborhood during the day and returning in the evening with a mouse in his mouth.

61

WAS IT PENETRATION?

When the United States Supreme Court overturned a lower court ruling that banned a controversial black and white Swedish art film called 'I Am Curious Yellow,' from playing in the United States, a major challenge to anti pornography laws in the United States was about to begin. CarlosTobilina, who owned 'The World Theatre' located on Hollywood Boulevard near Vine, booked the film for its exclusive engagement in Los Angeles.

Previously, his theatre exclusively showed 35mm sexual exploitation films that he produced, shot and directed. None of them showed sexual penetration. On an early evening, in April of 1970, an eclectic crowd of everything from raincoat clad perverts to nattily dressed middle class couples, old and young, waited for hours in a long line outside the World Theatre to witness a scene in the film where the protagonist, Lena Nyman, kisses a penis before having sex with her lover. Putatively, the scene had a shot that showed actual penetration. The anticipatory tension was as thick as syrup as the entire audience, including Judy and I, kept its eyes riveted on the screen so as not to miss the controversial penetration scene, which was said to be very short. Few in the audience cared about the film's underlying political and social messages. A noticeable buzz was heard throughout the audience when the pornographic footage came on the screen. It was grainy and Nyman's kiss of a flaccid penis passed in a blink-of-an-eye. The shot of her being penetrated rolled by so quickly, that afterwards, outside the theatre, debates could be heard over whether actual sex had been seen or not. However, the promise of that putative little glimpse was enough to lure in big audiences around the country and make big dollars for any exhibitor who played the film.

The door was now open to show scenes of actual sex as long as they were cloaked in serious artistic content. A few weeks after '*I Am Curious Yellow*' opened at the World, the Pussycat theatre on Santa Monica Blvd. played a documentary called, '*Man and Wife.*' Matt Cimber, who was sex bombshell Jane Mansfield's husband, produced the film. A documentary could claim to be a scientific or historical chronicle of a subject. Simber's documentary, presented in a medical fashion; various techniques and positions of love making between married people. Though the claim was that its intent was not to be construed as erotic, and it was anything but, viewers flocked to the Pussycat theatre hoping to be erotically aroused. Like 'I am Curious Yellow,' it did big box office.

There were no busts and it became clear that documentaries were the key to showing live sex on American theatre screens. 'Sexual Freedom in Denmark,' 'Adam and Eve' and Alex DeRenzy's, 'History of the Blue Movie,' quickly followed. Each of them was a financial success. Bill averred that we needed to move fast or we would be left out of the market. After a bit of brainstorming, we came up with an idea that seemed like a winner. There were persistent rumors that many Hollywood stars had performed in underground porno films before finding fame. A documentary chronicling these films couldn't miss. We would call it 'Hollywood Blue.'

I had no experience making a documentary and spread the word around that I was looking for an editor to help with the project. When I dropped by to say hello to Jeff Patterson and fuck his wife, Susan, I mentioned my problem. He said he knew a young film enthusiast whom he though might be able to help me. The next day, Mike Benveniste came by our office on Hollywood Boulevard for an interview. He was about five foot seven and had curly black hair and a perpetual elfin like grin that spelled mischievousness. He loved movies and had a good knowledge of classic and underground films. When I described the 'Hollywood Blue' concept he wasted no time convincing Bill and I that he was the guy for the job. I was sold and Bill had no objections, so he was hired on the spot. His energetic demeanor left me with the feeling that Graffitti would have a documentary in the theatres in short order.

The Moviola had been the editing room workhorse from the first days of Hollywood, but I had recently read an article in American Cinematographer touting the benefits of a new German editing machine called a KEM table. Unlike the Moviola, the KEM facilitated viewing the footage on a large screen as it was transported between two metal plates, lying flat atop a desk-sized table. The speed and direction that the film moved could be controlled at the editor's discretion. I convinced Bill that we should spend fifteen grand to buy the machine. It would make editing Hollywood Blue and our future films much more efficient. We could turn one of the extra rooms in the Hollywood Blvd. office into an editing room. He agreed and I set up a meeting with KEM the next day. Their agent agreed to allow us to pay for the table over a three-month period. He told me we were only the second company in Hollywood to purchase the machine. Graffitti Productions was about to have one of the most modern editing rooms in the United States.

Marilyn Monroe

While we waited for the machine to be delivered from Germany, Bill began asking around the various theatres, bars and sex shops that we sold our films to, if they were aware of any celebrity porn footage and Benveniste began by rummaging through stacks of discarded vintage films that could be found at second hand shops around Hollywood. He also browsed all the public domain catalogues to see if there was any footage that he could incorporate into our documentary. Initially it looked like we would soon have enough film to do the job.

Bill came up with an 8mm film that featured two sailors sneaking behind a couple of bushes for a bit of gay oral and anal sex. One of the sailors had the undeniable chiseled face of TV star, Chuck Connors, who was currently the star of the TV hit; *'The Rifleman.'* Connors was also working hard to get Ronald Regan elected as California's governor. Benveniste came up with footage, shot at a press conference dinner attended by Ronald Regan and busty blond siren, Jane Mansfield, where Reagan, sitting only two seats away, can be seen repeatedly straining his neck to steal furtive glimpses of Mansfield's ample cleavage bubbling out of her low cut dress. Mike also dug up a short five-minute black and white 16mm film of Marilyn Monroe, at the time still known as Ailene Hunter, called *The Apple knockers and the Coke*, that showed no pubic hair or penetration, but did show her caressing her naked body with an apple and a coke bottle.

We had hoped to use an 8mm film that was rumored to be of Natalie Wood doing hardcore, but the identity of the girl was too dubious and we decided not to include it. We also used a short clip of the 'Candy Barr' 8mm film made before she became a stripper and a Texas legend, where she gets fucked but refuses to give a blow job because its too dirty.

Despite the promising start, when I checked in with Mike to see how the documentary was progressing, it was clear that we were woefully short of having enough footage to make a feature length film. To obtain more footage we decided to shoot some of the current borderline sex shows that had recently sprouted up in Hollywood. The 'Bat Cave,' on Hollywood Blvd. near Vermont, was by far the most controversial. It had become the talk of the town overnight. Guys were willing to pay ten bucks at the door just to get in; a lot of money at a time when the minimum wage was a buck sixty. Patrons lucky enough to get a seat around the oval shaped bar, could give a buck to a dancer who would then hand them a flashlight which they could use to illuminate her pussy after she squatted down and pulled her g-string to the side. Its owner was acting on the theory that if spread beavers could be seen in films, why couldn't they be seen alive and in person.

The place was being raided almost nightly, but the Bat Cave's clever lawyers kept getting it immediately reopened.

That they weren't about to let anyone in with a camera to make a movie was obvious, so it had to be done covertly. Fortunately, I had a willing partner in Judy to carry out my deceptive plan. She and I would pay to attend the show as just interested observers who liked to see women dance in the nude. Knowing the club's ubiquitous bouncers would have their eyes on us, we couldn't just pull out a camera and start shooting. The camera had to remain hidden. Judy's white vinyl purse with big black dots on it would have a small camera inside. One of the dots would be the face of the zoom lens attached to the camera. By choosing a spot against the wall that was directly across from where the girls were performing on the bar, we could rest her purse on the chest high counter for placing drinks that ran along the wall and I could operate the camera with a pushbutton cable that exited the purse By setting the zoom at wide angle and the f-stop open to full aperture, focus and lighting would not an issue. It came off like a charm. By the time the hundred-foot roll had run out, I had plenty of footage of the happy patron with the flashlight closely inspecting the pussy that was squatting inches away from his face and Judy and I packed up and split, no one the wiser of what we had just done. The vice finally managed to close the 'Bat Cave down' two weeks later. What we had shot would be very rare footage.

Loops continued to be the mainstay of our source of income, and I continued to shoot ten a week. Sometimes to change the ambience, I would shoot at locations other than my studio or my own home. Late in the afternoon after I had finished shooting at a location, I loaded my equipment into the trunk of my GTO and called The Ball to ask Judy if she would like to take in a movie. I suggested Franco's, 'Romeo and Juliet,' which was playing at a theatre in Beverly Hills. She liked the idea and I raced over to The Ball to pick her up so we could get to the theatre before the film started.

I felt lucky to find a parking space just around the corner from the theatre on Linden Drive and we got a seat just as the film was beginning. Two hours later, we were chatting about how much we had enjoyed it as we walked back to the car. Half way down Linden, I failed to see it. Holding back the paroxysm of fear that was bubbling up, I ran up and down the block to make sure I hadn't misjudged where I had hastily parked. It wasn't there! My first thought was that the cops had towed it, but I didn't see any signs indicating restricted parking. A call to the Beverly Hills station revealed that no cars had been towed around the area.

Not only had the car been stolen, but all of our camera equipment that was in the trunk! Nothing was insured; the car or the equipment! Somewhat hysterical, I unsuccessfully tried to cry, not knowing what else to do. Judy,

usually on the quiet side, snapped me back to my senses: "Act like a man."
It startled me for a moment. She was right. I stopped my whining and called
a cab to take us to the police station so I could file a report. There wasn't
anything else to do.

When I hooked up with Bill the next day, he was his usual cool self
as I related what had gone down. We could only hope that the car had
been taken on a joy ride and the cops would find it intact, but after three
days and hearing nothing, I called the station to see what the status of the
situation was. The pricks had found the car the next morning, but couldn't
be bothered to notify me. At the impound lot, I starred glumly at my once
hot GTO, stripped down to almost nothing. The trunk was barren.

It wasn't as bad as it seemed at first. Because we had been punctual on
our payments, F & B Ceco agreed to sell us another camera at the same
terms. Money was rolling in so fast that we had both the stolen camera and
the new one paid off in a few months. We also purchased a Chevy van to
cart my models and equipment around when shooting on location. I had a
metal security cage installed inside its bay and the van's windows secured
with heavy wire mesh. After all the stealing I had done, it didn't escape me
that having it the other way, wasn't very pleasant.

Benveniste was taking forever to finish 'Hollywood Blue' and it was
beginning to look like hiring him had been a mistake. Sex documentaries
were becoming less and less controversial and making less money. If we
didn't finish soon we would miss whatever remained of the fad. He kept
asking Bill for more money to buy rolls of footage from various Hollywood
shops that specialized in discarded short films and out takes. At his request,
we hired a writer, David Feller, to help him define a direction for the project.
Hoping it might encourage him to speed up, we also threw in five percent
of the net profits.

The two of them began to broaden the theme of the documentary
beyond Hollywood sex. Most notably, they inserted a short clip from a
16mm Catholic educational series presented by an asexual priest named
'Father Filas.' In a droning voice he claims that when it comes to discussing
sex: "for years the ball has been bouncing back and forth."

Father Filas "sex expert"

Mike cleverly intercut into the lecture, a couple of two second, black and white clips from a vintage art film that showed the naked backsides of two young girls skipping down the beach; their buns bouncing, "back and forth."

Despite Bill's concern that Benveniste was too cavalier about how he spent our money, it was that kind of artistic imagination that I saw in him that led me to continue to support him. Bill was seeing himself behind the wheel of a Rolls Royce, and Benveniste was getting in the way of that. To include me in his dream, he suggested that I could be driving a 'Rolls' as well as soon as we stopped spending so much money on 'Hollywood Blue.' I told him I would lean on Benveniste as best I could, but if we fired him, the whole project would be a loss. I remained optimistic that it would eventually work out to all of our benefits.

However, the demise of the 'sex documentary' came faster than I expected. Word was traveling around the 'raincoat' underground that the Drake, a fifty-seat mini house competitor of the Flick, was sneaking in a few unannounced hardcore porno loops to their weekly show. No one would pay to see a porn documentary when they could see a porn loop sans all the socially redeeming bullshit attached. Sitting on Benveniste's shoulder did little to hurry him up. He was an artist. Meanwhile, the Drake was packing the house around the clock. After three weeks, when the vice failed to raid them, they gave up with the sneak strategy and went porno full bore. They were buying films from San Francisco, where a more tolerant vice squad was already allowing mini theatres to go porn.

Doug, the Flick's young owner, told Bill he needed porn and he needed it fast and Bill passed the message on to me. Reb Sawitz had moved his Pretty Girl agency to an office just south of Hollywood Boulevard on Las Palmes. I was there as soon as it opened on Monday morning to ask him and his wild-eyed red headed assistant, Bill Marigold, if they had any girls willing to have sex on screen. I was willing to bump the modeling fee up to fifty dollars. The guys, lucky enough to get hired, would still get twenty-five.

As expected, every girl who had previously been doing 'beaver' films, didn't jump at the chance to do porn. Some decided to drop out of the business, but enough were more than happy to make the extra fifteen bucks and by the end of the week, I had a few hardcore loops in the can. My first efforts were pretty prosaic: just standard sucking and fucking. Some of the males were surprised that getting a bonner and keeping it up under the hot lights while taking direction, was not as easy as they had imagined. When I saw that they were intimidated, I would turn off the lights and leave the room to give them some space to overcome their anxiety. When they were ready, I would rush back onto the set and finish shooting as quickly as possible before they got nervous again and lost their wood. Since the ladies could just fake it, they didn't have to deal with the intimidation factor. Nobody would know if their pussies were soaking wet or bone dry. I also found that when the girls were asked to have lesbian sex with each other, few had a problem with it even if they were putatively straight. Some even seemed to prefer it, not having to deal with a male partner's anxieties made for a much easier day. It was obvious from the outset of hardcore porn, that even though the males put on more airs about their virility, the females were the more reliable performers.

Over the next few weeks, the films coming out of San Francisco continued to be the leaders in porn innovation. When The Drake screened a porn loop that showed the male pulling out just before reaching orgasm and spewing his jism all over the ladies stomach, it became an instant rage. Over time it would be termed the 'money shot.' Proving that an actual orgasm had taken place vicariously satisfied the libido of the viewer and this unnatural act became the required denouement of every loop. Sitting quietly in the theatre, almost every guy there imagined he had just shot his load or timed his own orgasm to the screen orgasm. They could face the rest of the day with smiles on their faces.

The explosion of explicit pornographic films got no unwanted response from the vice. They remained silent and no one got busted; yet no theatre was quite confident enough to blurt out that they were showing hardcore. Tom Parker, the same who I had once modeled for, was now the eponymous owner of the "Tom Cat" mini theatre on Hollywood Boulevard. His ad in the LA Times read in couched language: 'NOTHING IS LEFT OUT—YOU KNOW WHAT WE MEAN.'

Even though San Francisco porn production preceded that in Los Angeles by a few weeks, Bill and I quickly caught up and surpassed them. Our ace in the hole: the oodles of beautiful and sexy southern Californian girls. It was more than anyone could compete against. San Francisco girls were still doing the hippy thing and didn't want to shave their legs or wear sexy lingerie and New York girls were pasty and pudgy from not getting much sun or excercise through the cold winter months. No one could hold a candle to LA's porn pussy.

My freestyle camera technique and abundant use of diopter close-ups, that showed lips sliding down a hard shaft or tips of tongues titillating a clit, made my work a favorite with the audiences. I also became bolder when shooting my intro scenes. I would lie down on Hollywood Boulevard's walk of stars and have my model walk over me so I could shoot a shot looking up her miniskirt. If pedestrians were shocked, so be it; we were gone before anyone could call the cops. On one loop, my male model leaned against the one sheet display case outside Grauman's Chinese theatre and the girl knelt in front of him with her head pressed against his crotch as though she was giving him a blowjob. We then went to a more secluded location, where I could frame the explicit details so it looked like the whole thing was taking place in front of Grauman's.

The success of Graffitti Productions didn't go unnoticed by the Press. A reporter from the Los Angeles Times called to ask if I would agree to an interview. She was doing a story about the burgeoning pornography business and wanted to talk to someone with inside information. I was assured that the story would give an unbiased account of the scene. I naïvely believed her. The interview was conducted at Reb's office. She asked a few questions about the social and moral implications of showing explicit sex on film and then turned to questions about the financial side of the business. I had been punked. The headline of her story read: "His Camera Cost Ten Thousand

Dollars." She had nothing positive to say about the industry. It wasn't that we were challenging repressive sexual mores; it was that we were making too much money. After the article came out, I decided it was best to stay in the background and let Bill garner the publicity. For that matter, because the exhibitors only knew him and already referred to our films as Osco films, he was getting most of the credit anyway.

62

PEDOPHILEA ISN'T SEX

As exciting as explicit sex was, it didn't take long before requests were made for films showing acts that took place at the outer boundaries. Straight porn was becoming blazé. Only eight weeks after we had begun supplying The Flick with porn loops, Doug asked Bill if he could provide a dog loop. It wasn't that bestiality was unheard of; 'Donkey' shows in Tijuana were legendary, but this was the States; American girls were principled and would never do something like that. They had values . . . Some models would tell me when I interviewed them: "I don't do anal and I don't do niggers," so I told Bill that it was unlikely that I would be able to find a girl who would fuck a dog. I knew lies about the Vietnam war and marijuana had made the foundations of those values suspect; but fucking a dog? How wrong I was!

A day after I went to Reb's agency and told him I would pay one-hundred and fifty bucks to a girl willing to do a loop with a canine, he called back two days later to tell me he had ten girls who had expressed interest. One was in his office as we spoke and I rushed over to check her out. She was a six-foot Amazon, named Linda. Her attractive face, short light brown hair, small firm breasts and a nicely proportioned body, made her the kind of girl I would have been thrilled to fuck myself. After making sure she knew what she was getting into, I told her she could have the gig.

All I needed now was a dog to perform with my Amazon lady. To my surprise, that turned out to be the more difficult proposition. People would say: "No, I don't want my dog doing something like that" or "It'll screw up his head." It didn't cross my mind that they might be right, but I was being swept along with the flow and after three weeks of searching, found someone willing to allow their year old German Shepard to take the job.

As soon as he heard what I had in mind, Mike offered to let me shoot at his place in Silverlake. He lived in the downstairs half of a Victorian house that had been converted into a duplex. It was set off the street on a hillside lot shored up by a stone buttress and surrounded by large shedding Eucalyptus trees. The evening I arrived with my crew and actors, human and animal, the gothic ambiance seemed perfect for the perverse act we were about to film.

As we set up, Mike's wife, Susan, gaunt and pregnant, watched with cold eyes as she stood in the corner of the room against its dark oak wainscoting. Mike, bubbly as ever, had taken the mattress off of their bed and brought it into the living room where he placed it on the floor, and was now enthusiastically helping me set up the lights. I didn't get the impression that he had consulted her about doing a dog loop at their apartment.

Once I was ready to film, I had Linda take off her panties and assume— what else—the doggie position. By being on her knees with her back arched so that the scent of her feminine fluids would waft towards our canine stud, I hoped he would be enticed to begin to hump her. That would not be the case. He showed absolutely no interest in having sex with Linda. Maybe she wasn't his type? His owner pushed his nose against her slit to show him what he was missing, but he just turned his head with a look on his face that said; "What's the big deal?" Linda tried to help by reaching back between her legs so she could massage his cock with her hand, but that had little effect as well.

I wondered what was going through her mind; did she feel any revulsion in touching an animal's penis? Was it really that much different then grabbing a human's dick and putting it in her mouth; something that I and most men would find repulsive? I had no clue. I had often seen how cavalierly women would run their hands over their pet dog's cock. Females were thought to be prissy, had seemed to have far fewer hang-ups about sex than men, who I was beginning to believe were more mouth than action.

It was time to try a different approach. Linda rolled over on her side so she could pull back the foreskin of the young German Shepard's penis and lick the exposed pink protrusion with the tip of her tongue. I would have liked to see her wrap her lips around it and start sucking, but figured it was best to be happy with what I was getting. But still the dog's libido stayed idled. Mike had an idea and ran to the kitchen to get some hamburger meat out of the refrigerator. He came back with a little handful and rubbed it on Linda's pussy, who was again in the doggy position. That began to do the trick. Slowly the young dog began licking the meat off of her cunt and his cock began to stiffen. It was understandable, that as a virgin having sex for the very first time; he was nervous.

Mike's wife retreated to a back room, not to be seen for the rest of the evening. The young Shepard had become hard enough to attempt penetration and his owner mounted him on Linda's back so she could reach between her legs and guide the canine cock to its target. Instinct caused him to begin humping. Getting good camera angles was difficult and after ten minutes, I had shot about as much as I was going to get. It wasn't a great dog film, but it was a dog film. The Flick would have to be happy with it.

As I drove Linda home, I imagined her to be a woman who loved cock—any cock—even dog cock. I felt myself attracted to her and thought of asking her if she would like to fuck, but it was two in the morning and when she told me she was living with a guy, I decided to pass. Truth be told, it would have been a blow to my ego if she had declined.

Reb would tell me a few weeks later, that Linda had done a loop with a couple of midgets for another shooter. She was quite the horny girl! I had missed my shot at her but my fantasy of having sex with a girl who would fuck a dog was satisfied a week later at Irv Sofsky's agency. While waiting for a second model to show up, I was getting a vibe from the girl who was already there, that she was in heat and would like to fuck while we waited. We went to Irv's back room where he kept a bed for girls to pose on. She had an especially hot and juicy pussy and was a great fuck. When she proudly boasted that she had fucked a dog the week before, it added to the excitement. Being around ladies who were that horny was thrilling.

I knew the dog loop had to be close to the limit, but still the vice remained silent. Two weeks after I had shot Linda, I got a call from Reb who asked me to come to his office and take a look at something unusual. When I asked him what it was, he said he'd rather not divulge it over the phone. Reb was already being watched by the vice and moved out of his office on Las Palmes. It had been identified as the hub of the porn business. Drawing even more attention; the Red Wine Barn was just across the street. It was a favorite and convenient location for porn producers to film because they could book a model at Reb's and begin shooting a few minutes later. Near naked girls were often seen running out of his office to get to the Red Barn. He had wisely moved his agency to a less public location to get out of the eyes of the heat. It was now on the second floor of a nearby office building on Hollywood Boulevard.

I had already made up my mind not to do any more dog, or similar loops. It was like begging to be busted and I would have assumed he felt the same way. So I couldn't imagine what he had in mind that required such secrecy. His new office, though very large, was dark and devoid of much furniture or decoration. As I entered, Reb got up from behind his desk at the far side of the room and signaled for me to follow him into a back room. As I crossed over I briefly noticed, sitting on a brown leather couch in a dimly lit corner of the room, a family of 'Grapes of Wrath' Oakies. The father appeared gaunt and weather-beaten and his wife looked worn and haggard. The two children, a boy, who looked to be about eight and a girl, around six, sat dutifully silent between them.

After Reb closed the door, he told me in a hushed voice, that the family on the couch was into incest. "The girl will suck the father's dick and the boy will eat the mother. The children will then eat each other and the father will finger fuck the little girl." He said it didn't matter to him, one way or the other, if I decided to shoot them. He just wanted me to see it in case I did. Polite by nature, I told him it wasn't for me but: "Thanks for thinking of me."

When I got back to my studio, I thought about it some more. Somehow the wrong synapses were firing and I thought: "Fuck, if I don't shoot them, someone else will and it will be an outrageous novelty film." Despite the fact that only a couple of theatres had bought the 'dog' film and this was much more taboo, I called Reb and told him I would shoot the family tomorrow. I would pick them up at his office at ten in the morning.

That night, I tossed and turned in my bed as my brain struggled with the decision I had made. I didn't approve of incest or find it erotic. The only such film I had seen, a black and white low quality 8mm loop, featured a young girl who looked about twelve years old. She had a heavily bandaged arm, probably the result of being punched hard. The 'dog' film had been with a consenting adult. If a woman wanted to stimulate her pussy with a canine dick it was her business. There were still laws that prevented an adult white woman from having her vagina stimulated by a 'negro' dick. But this involved two kids who had no choice in the matter. They were being forced; by their own parents no less. When I awoke, I couldn't wait to call Reb to cancel the shoot.

The 'red line' finally got crossed. Two weeks after my secret meeting with Reb, a book store located near the Santa Monica Western Avenue area, what had become a de facto porn zone, ran an ad in the LA Free press for a live show that would feature a girl doing herself with a dildo, another fucking a dog and then audience participation with both girls. Despite the fifty-dollar price of admission, I heard the place was packed. But minutes after the show began, a couple of vice, sitting in the audience, stood up and arrested the owner of the bookstore and the performers. The bust made it clear that there would be limits and crossing them would have consequences.

Dave Auerbach, a shooter who had a studio in the Crossroads a few doors away from mine, would pay a big price for not knowing that. He had shot the Oakie family and got busted when the lab that processed the film called the police when they saw what was on the film. He was fortunate that his stupidity only earned him six months in jail.

Questions of morality were being debated on many fronts, not just sexual behavior. Was war murder, especially when the reasons for fighting it were specious as was the case in Vietnam? Were the atrocities taking place there and the collateral damage justified because we disagreed with their political system? Was killing or torture justified to make someone abide by a religion's tenets? After shooting the dog loop, I had come to the conclusion that it was immoral to force an animal to have sex when it wasn't a willing participant. I regretted having made the film, not for the girl's sake, but for the animal's. Nevertheless, rather than removing it from our vault, I kept it, even knowing that we would never sell prints struck from it. That it was perverse still made it exciting.

I now understood that fetishism was a part of human sexuality. Repression had made us that way. There were just degrees that were too extreme, but most were not harmful and made sex more exciting.

My own personal fetish of dressing my models in nylons and garter belts or Hefner's fetish of augmenting his girl friend's breasts with silicon, didn't hurt anyone. But in the course of my work, I would discover fetishes that I knew of, but weren't as rare as I had thought. I was in the midst of a hardcore boy girl loop when the young lady asked if we could take a break so she could urinate. After uncoupling from her mate, she started to head to the bathroom when he interrupted:

"Wait a minute, would you like her to piss on me?"

A bit taken back, I replied with a wry smile: "I don't know? Do you want her to piss on you?"

"I don't mind, but it'll cost you extra; twenty-five dollars for on my chest and fifty dollars in my mouth."

I looked at the girl: "Is that OK with you?"

She was indifferent: "I don't care."

She didn't even ask for bonus money. Evidently there were more piss drinkers than I had thought. That it was still repulsive to me, I went for the milder option.

"Ok, let's just go for the chest scene."

After laying down a plastic sheet so as not to ruin the couch, my pretty young model climbed on top of the young fellow and pissed all over his chest. He seemed happy as piss. I gave all my loops titles, and appropriately called this one 'The Pee Wee Kid;' a title that would come back to haunt me some day.

Candy Barr—wouldn't suck a dick

The days of a 'Candy Barr' refusing to give a blowjob were history. All porn actresses willingly sucked dicks and many had developed innovative techniques to enhance the pleasure. Unfortunately, males lagged far behind when it came time to reciprocate. Maybe this was in part because feminine juices can have an unpleasant odor, but most modern girls douched and even when they didn't, I found that once a tongue begins to lap on a slit, all initial unpleasantness disappears.

Nonetheless, I rarely found males that ate pussy with gusto and in one case I came across a situation where my stud refused to do it at all for what seemed like a bizarre reason. The girl was clean and very pretty. He was a big strapping guy who was in great shape and had boasted about having some bouts as a professional boxer. We were doing a bit of foreplay before getting to the nitty-gritty and after the young lady had given him an excellent blowjob, I requested that he reciprocate by sucking on her pussy for a few minutes.

"I can't do that," he respectfully protested. Flummoxed, I asked, "Why? What do you mean?" "Yeah, why not?" the girl, feeling insulted, chirped in. "Because I'm a boxer."

"So what. What does that matter?" she asked. "What the fuck was he talking about?" I wondered.

"Cause if the guys at the gym found out that I ate pussy, I'd be the laughing stock of the whole fucking place. I wouldn't be able to show my face in the gym again!"

As bizarre as his explanation was, it probably was true—a testament to the absurd and confused male ego when it came to sex.

When it came to gay sex, I had mixed feelings. Female gay sex was exciting. Part of the attraction was the thought that the girls would still like to have a nice dick if it was offered, they were just doing each other until that time came. Of course, that wasn't true, but a lot of guys thought that way. And a female child is nursed on her mother's breasts just like a male. There is, in fact, a natural bond.

Male gay sex was not so easy to process in my mind. I had long ago accepted its existence, but the thought of a guy sucking on another guys dick was hard to accept. Young males suck on mom's tits but never on dad's dick. There is no reason to do so. And guys sticking their dicks into each other's anuses was even harder to fathom. So when Bill said to me: "We can make a thousand bucks if you're willing to shoot a gay loop," I had to think a bit before I told him I'd do it. Benveniste was still spending lots of money on 'Hollywood Blue,' and the thousand bucks was not to be sneezed at.

Bill told me I would be shooting the loop for a gay magazine publisher, named Mr. Green. How Bill had come to know him, I had no clue. In his ambling around Hollywood to sell our films, I knew he came into contact with a lot of gays and after 'Stud Flame,' I knew he had some unusual fantasies. He drove me over to meet Mr. Green, who lived in a tony neighborhood just above Franklin Avenue, a bit west of Highland. The house was a large two-story home typical of early Hollywood. As we waited on its porch after ringing the bell for the door to open, the sound of playful frolicking could be heard inside. A short moment later, a lean, shirtless-young man in cut-off Jeans opened the door and invited us in. We were asked to wait in the foyer while he skipped upstairs to find the boss.

We were at what could be called, 'a gay Playboy mansion'. Scantily dressed young gay men flitted up and down the stairs and through the rooms. After a short wait, Mr. Green made a regal entrance deserving of a queen. He sashayed down the stairs to give Bill and I an effusive welcome. His full head of puffed up blond hair gave him a remarkable resemblance to the famous author, Truman Capote.

Once we got past the niceties, he explained, that similar to the heterosexual community, the gay community was excited about the expanded freedom to view hardcore sex. He had just made a small killing with a niche gay magazine and now wanted to branch out into film, but didn't have the equipment or know-how. Could I put the whole thing together, including casting? He was doing much as I had done; hire a mentor to show him the ropes. I agreed to do the best I could.

Reb's Pretty Girl agency had several pretty boys stocked in his stall and arranged for me to interview several of them. I was surprised that I had previously shot one of the candidates, a guy named Rick, with his girl friend, Nora, in a boy girl film. She was one of my favorite models, a tall raven-haired beauty. I hadn't realized that he was bisexual, but I was learning something new almost every day. I gave him the job and for his partner, cast a dark skinned well-built mixed race kid, named Juan. I had no idea what look attracted guys to each other, but thought that Juan's straight jet-black-hair, attractive face and lean physique would turn them on.

Bill rarely came around when I was shooting loops, so I was a bit surprised when he mentioned that he planned to be on the set to watch "the faggots in action." There was notable excitement at 'Miss' Green's house, as Bill and I had come to call him, when I arrived with my assistant, Lynn Rogers, to begin shooting. After setting up in a small bedroom at the back of the house, I called Rick and Juan to the set and told them to take positions on the bed. I let them both select their own wardrobes, which turned out to be tight jeans and T-shirts.

I assumed a kiss would be as good a way to begin a homosexual love scene as it was for a heterosexual one. They responded with tongue tangling French kisses that left little doubt that they found it enjoyable. Sparse additional direction was necessary. Rick pulled Juan's T-shirt up over his head and began caressing his chest. Slowly he slid his hand downward until it was beneath Juan's Jeans and massaging his penis. As he did, the dark-skinned lad quickly unbuttoned his fly and slid his pants down to expose what was now a brown steel rod. It quickly found its way into Rick's mouth.

I feigned professional indifference as I positioned myself to get the best angles, just as I would have done if shooting a heterosexual scene. A small crowd of the boys of the house stole peeks through the open door as I filmed. Amidst them, were 'Miss' Green and Bill, whose little smirk gave no indication if it was because he was enraptured or grossed out.

Rick had taken the lead in orchestrating the action and got on his hands and knees so Juan could penetrate his anus from behind. As the brown bratwurst moved rhythmically in and out of the orifice, Rick reached back and stroked his own cock, being careful to keep it hard but not letting it climax. As soon as he sensed he was about to cum, he disconnected from Juan, stood up and spun around so he could cradle Juan's head with one hand and furiously masturbate with the other. When the inevitable jizim shot arrived, he directed it into Juan's gaping mouth where it was swallowed as if it were a milkshake. Spent, the two of them fell back down onto the mattress and cuddled in a warm embrace.

Ironically, it had been a lot easier than directing a heterosexual porn scene. There was no anxiety: None of the, "I don't do this or I don't do that," that I often got from the straights. It wasn't for me; but I could see that they loved every minute of it. Afterwards we chatted as though it was just another day at the office. I wondered a bit how Rick's girl friend, Nora, felt about fucking a man who also did guys? Obviously, she didn't have a problem with it.

Before leaving, I unloaded the magazine and gave the negative to 'Miss' Green who was going to do the editing himself. The next day he complained to Bill about the 'nigger' whom he didn't find at all attractive. It was an interesting experience, but I had no intention of doing any more gay films so I didn't really care one way or the other about his racist problem.

63

GRAFFITTI'S A PORN EMPIRE

Bill avered that despite Graffitti's loops being the most popular in the business, the big money was made by the theatres that screened them. Continental Theatres had put a for sale sign outside one of their properties, the Eros on Beverly Boulevard near La Brea. Shawn Sales

the same who had unceremoniously fired me at the bookstore—was primarily interested in gay films and didn't want it to compete with the exclusively gay Park Theatre. The straight porn that they were showing at the Eros wasn't pulling in much of an audience. Bill was convinced we could turn it into a winner with our own product. The asking price was one hundred and sixty thousand dollars. Bill, as usual, continued to impress me as a businessman, and got them to agree to carry a ninety thousand dollar loan if we could come up with the seventy thousand dollar balance on our own. He assured me, even with the money that 'Hollywood Blue' was draining from our coffers, we had enough cash to pull the deal off. Our accountant, Sy Katz, concurred and Bill and I were soon at Continental's office, sitting across from Sayles and his partner Alex Cooperman, to sign the papers.

I couldn't resist wearing my blue pin stripped suit to the meeting. I hoped to have a little chuckle if Sales recognized who was buying his theatre. If he did recognize me, he didn't say anything. He wasn't about to let a blue pin striped suit get in the way of dumping, what he thought was a turkey.

Before it became a theatre, the Eros was a nightclub called Shorsy's, owned by Mickey Cohen, the legendary Hollywood gangster.

Converted into a movie theatre sometime in the fifties, it only had room for a little over three hundred seats. The floor had been reformed so it was slightly sloped to allow for reasonable views of its twelve by twenty foot screen. In the small front lobby, an eight-foot long concession stand came complete with a popcorn machine. A three by three ticket booth sat next to the glass entry door. The marquee was of moderate size, but its blinking lights that ran around its perimeter were visible to traffic traveling in both directions on Beverly Boulevard and La Brea Avenue. Because the building had not been intended to screen films, there was not a straight shot from the projection room to the screen in the auditorium, so a periscope was necessary to reflect the image down from the projector and then out onto the screen. We intended to project 16mm films, so even though the theatre included two Peerless carbon arc projectors, at least initially, they would not be of any use to us. We would have to purchase a 16mm projector.

That the Eros had more than fifty seats, meant an operator's license from the city would be required. Although no porn theatres, other than the PONO, had been busted for showing hardcore films, its legality was anything but settled. There were powerful forces in the city, and for that matter in the country, that would love to stop the sex revolution in its tracks. More than likely, arrests were on the horizon. For that reason, neither Bill nor I were comfortable about putting our names on the license. Bill had a solution. He offered Danny Tafoya, a Mexican American who worked at a small adult bookstore on Santa Monica Blvd., the opportunity to substantially make more money if he was willing to put the license in his name and manage the theatre. With nothing to lose, he agreed. He was in his thirties, affable, with a good sense of humor. He had a clean record so his application for a license sailed through without a problem. Within a few weeks, we were screening our own porn films at the Eros and making more money than ever.

The market for 'beaver' loops, both sound and silent, remained strong, but the better theatres were turning more and more to features. That meant I would have to begin turning out features on a regular basis. I had gone to school on 'Stud Flame' and felt I was ready. To help with the extra load, I hired a sandy-haired John Denver look-a-like named Walter Cichy, to be my production manager for our feature department. He was given the task of writing a script and making all arrangements, other than casting, which I would still do, to set up a feature ready to shoot whose budget would not exceed five thousand dollars, including post-production.

To add an inch to his height, Walter wore elevator shoes, but what he lacked in vertical inches had no bearing on his tenacity to get things done. In less than a week, he showed me the ten-page opus he wrote called 'The Virgin Runaway.' While he worked on finding a location and assembling all the props, I put a cast together. There were still areas of the country that hadn't gone hardcore, so Bill and I agreed that only one scene would show explicit sex so it could be cut out at a theatre's discretion. Rene Bond, a sweet looking cutie with perky tits, was cast to do the hardcore scene. She had worked for me the prior week in a hardcore loop. I also cast Sheryl Powell, one of my favorite models who had opted not to do hard sex on film, but whose beautiful face and graceful body still enticed me. Walter arranged for the shoot to take place at a house in Marina Del Rey that was only a few blocks from where I lived. Similar to how I shot loops, I did the camera work and directing simultaneously. Lynn Rogers handled the sound, and he and Walter did everything else. Unlike *'Stud Flame,'* the whole film was in the can by the end of the day; a style that would become known in the business as a *'one-day wonder.'*

'TheVirgin Runaway' was of no great consequence other than proving to myself that I could string scenes together into a coherent feature. It also solidified my crew; Lynn Rogers, who because of his mountain man look, would be known as 'Buffalo,' and Walter, because of his tenaciousness, would be known as 'Gator.' They both understood we weren't trying to make 'Gone With The Wind' and, for what we were doing, I couldn't have asked for a better crew.

64

MICKEY AND JUNE AND MONA

Benveniste and Feller asked me to sit down so they could pitch their great new idea for 'Hollywood Blue:' interviews with Mickey Rooney and June Wilkerson! The justification was that Mickey had been close to Marylyn Monroe, Hollywood's quintessential sex goddess and June Wilkerson, a British actress who was now Hollywood's reigning big bosom queen, a title she inherited after Mansfield's untimely death in a car accident. They may have a few interesting insights or stories to tell about the Hollywood sex scene and it would add star value to the credits. Though it was going to be expensive, Bill and I both loved the idea.

After a little white lie about what we were making, Bill got both Mickey and June's agents to agree to let their clients to do interviews. I was not privy to how he spun the project, but I'm sure he left out a lot of the detail, including the title. Mickey was on Cape Cod doing a play and June was performing in Cleveland, which meant we would have to travel back east to hear what they had to say.

Bill and I, along with Benveniste, Cichy and Rogers, rendezvoused with Mickey on Cape Cod where he was staying in a charming weather beaten rooming house typical of the area. It was nestled against a small grass knoll close to the water and as soon as he heard us pull up on the gravel driveway, he came out to greet us. More than amiable, he did most of the talking as he led us into his room. He was very excited and had something he wanted us to see. Inside, he went to his desk drawer and pulled out a picture. It was of a very handsome dark-haired young man who resembled Rock Hudson.

As we all looked at the picture, feigning interest, Mickey expounded:

"I call him the rock. Isn't he amazing? He's one of the actors in the play I'm performing in."

We all nodded approvingly. I wondered, "Was Mickey gay or bi?" After he put the picture back in the drawer for safe keeping, Mike gave him a brief idea of what we were looking for, being careful to stay away from any words that might suggest pornography. He was Okay with everything, but said nothing to hint that he might have some earth shattering revelations about Marylyn to pass our way. We agreed to pick him up the following morning, and take him to a nearby wharf, where the boats moored in the bay would serve as an interesting background to conduct the interview.

Interviewing a Hollywood legend made us all, and especially me, a bit nervous. As we set up on the wharf Mike talked guardedly with Mickey as I finagled with the equipment and took light readings. I couldn't help but think that surely Mickey recognized that we were little more than rank amateurs. As soon as Lynn finished loading the magazine and mounting it on the camera, I told Mike I was ready to roll. Walter would operate the Nagra tape recorder and Lynn the sound boom. Bill stood aside looking very producer like. Mike and Mickey were sitting on a rail overlooking the harbor. I called for a sound test to set the levels. Mickey called out; "testing, one, two, three." The recorder didn't respond! My angst had made me brain dead and I began to panic. I had no idea what was wrong. I could sense Mickey asking: "What the fuck is this?" I juggled the cables trying to solve the problem. The cool ocean air did little to keep the sweat flowing off my forehead. I was beginning to think we might have to call the interview off and hope Mickey would agree to return the next day. Fuck! What a disaster! But suddenly it dawned upon me to check the little on/off switch on the Nagra. I toggled it to the on: Eureka!!

Mickey now had no doubt that we were amateurs and took over the direction. I was told to begin with a slow pan across the harbor coming to rest on him as he began speaking. As the camera came up to speed, Mickey cried out: "Testing, one—two—three. Testing one—two—three." He then called action and I did as he had directed, panning across the harbor and stopping on him as he began to respond to Mike's questions. The interview lasted about fifteen minutes, finishing with a bit of non-controversial talk about his relationship with Marlin Monroe. It wasn't a whole lot for the thousand bucks we paid him.

June Wilkerson—no crotch shots

The interview with June Wilkinson at the theatre in Cleveland went no better. To show off her stunning figure, we had asked her to wear a bikini. It was met with a clear-cut, "no." She did condescend to wear a one-piece bathing suit, but it would have limits as well. Filming her stunning feminine attributes were to be limited to her massive chest and any shots that managed to get a sneaky peek of her completely covered crotch, wouldn't be tolerated. She seemed to suspect what we were about. The highlight of the interview came when she protectively covered her breasts with her arms when Mike asked her to comment about the many racy pictorials she had done for men's magazines. We returned to LA with a lot of boring, *'star power,'* footage.

I was back to shooting loops and Walter was finishing the editing of *'TheVirgin Runnaway'* before he began making arrangements for our next feature. The situation with Benveniste had become ridiculous

and I began stopping by every day to see how he was progressing with 'Hollywood Blue.' As I got to the top of the stairs, Bill's office door was open and I noticed he was in the midst of a conversation with a short cherubic faced guy who appeared to be in his early 30's. Bill signaled for me to come in and handed me a thirty-page script that the guy had written. He suggested I take a quick look at it. He said he thought it was pretty good. In light of his 'Stud Flame' script, I was not inclined to respect his judgment about literary matters, but I began to read it nonetheless.

The script chronicled the adventures of a young girl who had no qualms about giving blowjobs, but assiduously insisted on defending her virginity until she became married. After I finished reading it, I concurred with Bill's assessment and told him I thought it would be perfect for our next feature production. Bucky Searles Irish eyes smiled as he realized his opus was about to earn him a hundred bucks. It was titled: *'Mona, the Virgin Nymph.'*

Mona with her boy friend

Benveniste knew he was probably out the door if he didn't complete 'Hollywood Blue' in short order. Bill was palpably upset that his Rolls Royce was on hold and while trying not to stilt Mike's creativity, I let it be known that I wasn't too happy as well. We already had over thirty thousand dollars tied up in the project and it was becoming questionable whether it could ever turn a profit or even break even. Regardless, when Mike learned that we were about to do a feature, he pleaded on hands and knees to be allowed to direct it; promising to come in during the evenings to complete 'Hollywood Blue.' He assured me that he was working as hard as he could and only needed a few more clips and some music and sound effects to finish. "Directing *'Mona'* will only take a few days and the editing, which I will do, will go much smoother if I am allowed to direct," he averred. He had a point. I was at best a novice when it came to directing a feature and Mike had been a film buff for many years. His enthusiasm won me over.

Since I would be doing the camera work, selecting all the angles and directing the sex scenes, I would still be able to assure that the film had good erotic content and Benveniste would add artistic touches that probably would escape me. We would complement each other in a positive way and I would still have enough control to insure that the filming moved quickly and we stay within our five thousand dollar budget.

Cichy went to work finding locations and I met with Reb to line up a cast. The next morning he sent a young girl fresh in from Phoenix Arizona, over to our Hollywood Boulevard office to audition for the lead. Her name was Fifi Watson. She was tall and slender, nice figure, more cute than glamorous, and a spunky face and personality that looked like she knew how to get her way. As soon as we saw her, both Mike and I knew she was perfect. The twinkle in her eye betrayed a rebellious spirit. That she was from Phoenix, and likely brought up in a Mormon family, made me think that might have had something to do with that. A lot of girls from religious backgrounds were willing to do porn.

We began shooting two days later behind our office in a little alley that ran along the back of the brick building. Mona, walking along and minding her own business; is accosted by a pretty blond hooker standing in a doorway recess. The hooker was played by Susan Stuart who had shot many softcore loops for me but had decided to opt out of boy/ girl porno but would still do lesbian scenes. The hooker finds Mona attractive and suggests they have a quickie together. Mona is hesitant, until she realizes having sex with a woman doesn't violate her vow of virginity. As Mona and the hooker make love, her boyfriend is cheating on her by having sex with her mother, played by Judy Angel, a glamorous fifty-year old and possibly the first MILF (Mom's I'd like to Fuck) to work in the porn business. Bucky's script called for both the boyfriend and mother to feign guilt as they cheat on Mona. At that time in porn history, no one cared about the identity of male actors. They were just some lucky guys that got to fuck the girls. Mona's mother, disappointed that the boyfriend can't satisfy her, does herself with a vibrator that had a little shredded plastic umbrella on its tip. As she lies on her back with spread legs, she has an orgasm and pulls the vibrator out of her sopping wet vagina. The umbrella's tip was covered with a thick white glob of pussy juice, a bonus that couldn't be ignored, and I directed her to stick it in her mouth and lick it clean.

My purient touch was counter balanced by one of Mike's sensual touches where he posed Mona sitting on a blanket with her boyfriend in grassy meadow amidst many wild flowers, repeatedly denying his requests to have intercourse. But to console him and maintain her virginity, she offers him a blowjob. Her fixation for oral sex is explained in a flashback scene that we shot in Mike's living room. Mona is made up to look like a little girl. To make it surreal and nostalgic, I lit the room with blue lights that cast high contrast shadows. Mona sits on the floor playing with her doll while her father, played by Bob Mantel, reads the newspaper in the background. Without putting the paper down to reveal his face, he coldly coaxes her to crawl across the room to fellate him. Mantel, the same who participated in the disastrous orgy with my girl friend Delia, was also doubling as the film's soundman. He wanted to do the part because it offered a solicitous blowjob, but worried that it might ruin his professional career, insisted that his face not be shown. Mike obliged by letting him keep the paper raised to cover his face, a fortuitous directorial touch that added immeasurably to the psychological implications of the scene. As Mona fellates her father, Mike gave the scene an artsy touch by calling for a shot of a scratchy LP playing on a vintage record player in the background.

The finale has Mona being forced into a bondage orgy with all the people she had left unsatisfied by refusing to go beyond oral sex.

All express their deep displeasure with the poor girl, tying her hands and legs to the bedposts so she has no way of resisting penetration.

'Mona, the Virgin Nymph' was shot in three days and within budget. Mike began editing it immediately, putting 'Hollywood Blue' on a side burner. We all sensed that the film was going to be a winner, but to what degree we were all clueless. The days of porn documentaries were over and Bill and I resigned ourselves to write 'Hollywood Blue' off as a loss; or modest success at best. I encouraged Benveniste to build the music tracks for 'Mona' as quickly as possible so the tracks could be mixed and we could open the film at our new theatre, currently named the 'Eros." By lifting various cuts of music from LP's he picked up at used record shops: i. e. baroque music for the scene in the meadow, a scratchy old time thirties piece for the molestation scene and the sound of a rocket taking off as the mother reaches orgasm, he built a sound track far in advance of what the common porn film had.

As the soundman, Bob Mantel was present when we mixed the film at Scott Sound, a small studio on Melrose owned by 300 pound Bruce Scott that was friendly to porn producers. The sound of a rocket taking off was meant as metaphor for the intensity of the mother's orgasm, and Benveniste kept pushing the levels higher and higher. When the meter began pegging into the red, Mantel began screaming that it would distort the sound and when Benveniste refused to back down, he stormed out of the studio; his last words were that he didn't want his name to be associated with the film. I didn't know enough about sound mixing to understand what his point was, but I was always for pushing the envelope so I let Mike do his thing. Fortunately, Mantel was wrong and the sound didn't distort and it made the scene riveting .

As prints of Mona were being struck at the lab, Benveniste finally finished Hollywood Blue. It had wandered miles away from what its original intent was. A clip from an industrial film showing a surrealistic animation of a piston pounding into a cylinder, what Mike explained was symbolic of sex in the future, was its denouement. The documentary had some interesting moments, but it lacked clarity. It was hard to understand what message was being delivered; or if it even had a message.

Our plans were to premier both films at the Eros, but being that documentaries were no longer a draw, we played *'Mona, The Virgin Nymph,'* first. I was very happy the way it turned out and considered it to probably be the best porn feature made up to that time. But it was still just a low budget porno, so after it ran for a week at the Eros, I was surprised as hell when the iconic Hollywood weekly, 'Variety,' called it: ***"A landmark, the long awaited link between the stag loops and conventional theatrical fare."*** 'Variety' had only recently begun to recognize that porn features were even films, so this was something special. But even after that accolade, I still saw it as a little five thousand dollar porn film and wondered what it was that the reviewer saw.

Hollywood Blue played a week later and got a plug in Joyce Haber's weekly column in the LA Times, specifically mentioning the "chiseled face TV actor known for his rifle work;" a non libelous way to refer to Chuck Connors. The Regan for governor campaign quickly pulled all the commercials they were running in which Connors was appearing as an endorser. The Republican Party had no use for homosexuals and Connors instantly disappeared from the political stage.

'Hollywood Blue' did modest box office for a few weeks, until word-of-mouth caught up with it and it died. To mislead out of town theatres into thinking it was a box office hit, Bill fed inflated box office reports to Variety and the Hollywood Reporter; a not uncommon practice in the film industry. In reality, it didn't earn enough revenue to offset its thirty-five thousand dollar cost. When poor Mickey Rooney was questioned about his appearance in a porn documentary, he responded: "It was the worst moment of my life." If that was true, he had led an incredibly blessed life.

I couldn't handle rejection—not that I didn't have to face it from time to time—but if I could, I avoided it. It was an aspect of my inferiority complex that I tried to keep concealed. Bill had no such problem. He was brazen and assured; at least he pretended to be and was convincing if he wasn't. I thought he was nuts when he told me he had set up a meeting with Lew Shere to screen 'Hollywood Blue' and 'Mona' to see if he could make an outright sale. Shere owned the Cinema on Western Avenue, The North Beach Movie House in San Francisco and forty other theatres across the country. Shere would certainly be outraged that Bill had the audacity to waste his time to try and pawn our cheap little movies off on him. My doubt fell on deaf ears and Bill headed over to the Cinema about one in the afternoon to take his meeting with Shere. He returned four hours later and practically caused me to shit in my pants when he told me he had just sold both films, in a package, for ONE HUNDRED GRAND!!

Both of us flew to New York to collect the check and hand over the negatives. It was surrealistic. Bill and I sat quietly on straight back chairs in Shere's small office, just off of Times Square. While, Manny, Shere's partner, sat to the side, Lew sat near invisible behind a desk piled high to the ceiling with paper, showbiz periodicals and film cans, writing out a check made payable to Graffitti Productions for a hundred grand. When he passed it over to Bill, I could see it was real and I became a believer. The deal was done! To celebrate the transaction, Lou invited Bill and I to join him and Manny for lunch. As it was only ten o'clock, we spent the next two hours making small talk as we peeked at each other around and between the stacks of papers and film cans.

The check was, of course, the apotheosis of our day, but for Shere, it was about going to lunch. We were to leave his office at precisely twelve O'clock and for the next hour and a half, he would look at the clock on the wall every ten minutes and announce the latest countdown figure: "Only one hour twenty to lunch time; one-hour ten," etc., until for the final five minutes he made the countdown by the minute as though we were launching a rocketship. At the stroke of twelve, he and Manny jumped up with the energy of ten year olds, and bounded down the stairs and up Broadway to their favorite deli. Bill and I huffed and puffed to keep up with the two septuagenarians on their way to the feeding trough. It didn't dawn upon me that maybe they were exhilarated because they had just made a real steal. Mona would make them a fortune; playing for two years at their north beach theatre alone. But not to complain, it would work out nicely for us as well.

65

I TIE THE KNOT AND HARLOT

Until I could complete another feature, Bill booked a film out of San Francisco to play the Eros. It was called *Confiscated* and actually had been confiscated by that cities vice. The Nixon regime was beginning to put pressure on local police forces to control pornography, possibly as a way of taking the public's eye off of his endless mess in Vietnam. Near the end of the film's first week's run, the vice arrived at the Eros unannounced, and confiscated *Confiscated*. It was deemed to be too prurient for American tastes. In fact, the film had little going for it other than it had been confiscated. Its producer immediately flew down a replacement copy, but the vice retuned the next evening and confiscated *Confiscated's* replacement.

The porn wars had begun. We hired the renowned first amendment lawyer, Stanley Fleishman, to try to get both of the confiscated films back. Stanley was crippled by polio at age one, but his handicap did not prevent him from becoming a giant in the defense of first amendment rights. His first victory was when he won a case defending an 8mm film of a naked girl walking up a stairs, that had been confiscated by the postal service. He won national fame after he successfully defended Henry Miller's Tropic of Cancer against obscenity charges. He was now known as the lawyer to see if pornography was at issue. Stanley was able to get an injunction against any further confiscations of *Confiscated*, but the film didn't have legs and it became even more imperative that I quickly get another feature in the can.

For good reason, the actions of the police were making us

nervous, and though there was no indication that we were being targeted beyond the theatre, Bill and I felt it would be prudent to move our editing room to another more secure location; somewhere where the cops couldn't just bust in and confiscate our films or equipment. The First Federal Bank building on the corner of Highland and Hollywood Boulevard provided just such a spot. It was a fifteen story corporate tower. The large letters that spanned across the top of the building's sidewall that read FIRST FEDERAL boasted who owned it. The cops wouldn't be fucking with them. We rented an office on the sixth floor, one of the many behind identical non-descript doors, and as an added precaution, didn't list our company name on the building's directory.

Cichy, Benveniste and I collaborated on writing our next script, to be called Harlot. It was a story about a young high school girl working as a streetwalker to pay for college. What would become my trademark, I worked scenes into the script that included straight, lesbian and fetish sex. That allowed me ways to use a variety of different girls doing different sexual acts. I didn't want the audience to become bored if they found one scene or one girl uninspiring. Kindling hardons and possibly orgasms, was the goal. I also wanted to include something in the film that was unique. For Harlot it would be a streaking scene in broad daylight at a shopping center and a helicopter shot of a couple fucking atop a corporate monolith, specifically on the roof of The First Federal Bank building.

Benveniste and I would work as we had done on Mona; he would direct nonsexual live action and I would determine camera angles and direct the sex scenes. He would handle the editing, including choosing the music being how pleased I was with what he had done on 'Mona.' Fran Spector, one of the new porn cuties who oozed sexuality, would play the lead role. Pretty Girl agent, Reb Sawitz, would play the role of a biker in the film; the fact that he had a bike and was a biker made it an easy choice. He, Fran and a girl from his agency, Patty Axel, would be the performers on top of the First Federal Building and he and Patty would also do the streaking scene. Porn was about being brazen and we weren't about to be intimidated by the police or the Nixon administration.

Gaining access to the roof of the First Federal Tower; became the first logistical problem that had to be solved. To keep Benveniste busy until we were ready to shoot 'Harlot,' I had him editing the loops that I shot each day which since he liked to work in the evenings, gave us a way to solve our "roof" problem. He often left the office to take a break, but on one occasion forgot to take his keys and locked himself out. He found the night janitor a few floors below and asked him to follow him back up to his office and let him back in with his master key. How to get that master key was the answer to our problem. For the next two weeks, Mike feigned that he was just an absent minded pest, and kept hitting on the janitor to leave his chores and follow him back to the office to open the door. As hoped, the janitor eventually tired of wasting his time, and just gave Mike the key, telling him to bring it back as soon as he unlocked his door. Two days later, he pulled the same stunt again, but this time Walter and I were waiting at the top of the stairwell leading to the roof. As soon as Mike had the key in his possession, he sprinted up the stairs and unlocked the door that accessed the roof. While he was zipping back down to return the key, Walter and I applied duct tape across the latch so the lock wouldn't close. It was unlikely that anyone would discover that it had been compromised before we were ready to shoot.

Fucking on top of First Federal

I was at theVan Nuys airport two days later, hopping into a helicopter specially rigged to do aerial shots. I had never flown in a helicopter, let alone shoot a scene from one. The pilot was a young dude and cool with what we were about to photograph. At a hundred twenty five bucks an hour, I hoped to pull the shot off in an hour or less. After strapping me into the special rig that would allow me to dangle my feet out the open side door and maneuver my camera so I could point the zoom lens at the fornicators on the roof, we took off and headed towards the Hollywood Hills. The pilot informed me as we approached Hollywood, that it was illegal to fly over the city without a permit, but since we would be in and out with one or two passes, he didn't think there would be a problem. Within minutes we were approaching our target—*The First Federal Building.*

So not to draw any undue attention from a passing news or police helicopter, I had instructed my cast and crew to remain hidden until I approached. When they saw the helicopter with a guy strapped into a swivel chair with his feet hanging out of the open side door, they knew it was me and ran into position. Reb laid on his back, Fran mounted his cock, and Patty covered his face with her pussy. The rest of my crew hid behind a large air duct so they wouldn't be seen in the shot. The distance that the shot would be taken from meant actual penetration didn't need to take place, making everything much easier. After one pass to make sure everything was set up, my pilot looped around so I could begin filming the first helicopter shot in porn history. I had no time to have fear. I swiveled my chair around to ask the pilot to bank in as closely as possible and then swiveled back and hung out as far as possible to be ready to shoot. The engine of the helicopter momentarily started missing. I assumed it was normal. As we approached, I began with the zoom racked back to wide so the shot clearly showed the entire building and the FIRST FEDERAL sign and then zoomed in tight to show the fornicators hard at work atop an American corporate giant. Confident that I had got the shot I needed on the first pass and not wanting to go over budget, I told the pilot to head back to Van Nuys.

On the way he told me that when I had swiveled my camera chair, I had inadvertently hit one of the two magneto switches into the off position, which was why the engine had sputtered. Chuckling, he admitted that he had a momentary panic when he couldn't remember if they should both be up or down. We both chuckled. When developed, the shot turned out to be a bit shaky and a bit grainy, but it was unique.

Porn sex wasn't always a joy for the male performer. As we drove out to our next location, a nude beach near Malibu, Reb leaned over and whispered in my ear that Patty's pussy reeked. I took it that he was just one of those guys that didn't like eating pussy. But once we began shooting at the secluded section of the beach where nude sunbathers could often be found, he kept glancing at me with a pained grimace as Patty sat on his face. I was becoming irritated and didn't want to upset Patty, but when he took a swipe of her vagina juice and extended his hand out so I could take a whiff, damned if he wasn't right. I needed for the two of them to have good rapport the next day when they would be doing the streaking scene and didn't want to hurt Patty's feelings, so I directed the rest of the action to spare Reb any more discomfort.

Many girls had yet to realize that if they wanted guys to eat them, they had to douche. Women were only beginning to feel emboldened to demand that men reciprocate with the same oral pleasure that they were now providing to them, but many had yet to learn how to keep their pussies smelling nice and it was unlikely that many mothers from the previous generations had taught them how to do that. There was much to learn by all about how to enjoy sex to its fullest.

I had hoped that there would be screaming, weeping and wailing when my "streakers" ran through a crowd of little old ladies at a busy shopping mall. At two in the afternoon, we arrived at a large busy outdoor mall located at the conjunction of Sunset, Hollywood and Vermont Avenues. Two vans were needed to pull off the shot. We began by parking the van from which Reb and Patty would jump out of to begin their naked dash, at the center of the strip mall with its rear doors facing the sidewalk that ran in front of the shops. The second van was parked seventy five yards away at the end of the sidewalk where Lynn and I quickly jumped out and set up the high-speed camera that we were going to use to film the streakers in slow motion. Walter remained behind the wheel with the motor running and in case something went awry and we got busted, Osco was parked a few blocks away to bail us out of jail if necessary. Benveniste stood by the rear doors of the first van, and when it appeared that the walkway was full of little old ladies waiting to be shocked, I hit the switch of the high-speed camera and signaled for him to open the doors to let Reb and Patty out so they could dash down the sidewalk. As soon as they had passed the camera and jumped into the back of the van and Lynn and I followed with the camera, Walter sped off the parking lot as did Benveniste in the other van. A minute later we were several blocks away and laughing our heads off.

It came off like a charm except that the people on the sidewalk were too stunned to be shocked and just stood and gaped. However, when we drove by to take a peek shortly after, a large crowd was gathered to share their stories about what they had just seen.

Knowing our brazen stunt atop the First Federal would draw the attention of the building's owners and possibly the vice, we stayed one step ahead of them by moving once again. A two story building on Melrose, directly across from Fairfax High School, was large enough to accommodate our entire operation. Bill and I could once again be under the same roof. We would both have an office on the first floor and the large open space of the second floor was perfect for our editing room. The high school across the street would certainly not be happy that a porn company was operating just across the way, so to eliminate any suspicions about what kind of business we were, I silvered the big plate glass display windows that looked out onto the street and put steel bars over the front entry doors. No models would be coming to the new office since I would continue to use the Crossroads studio or rented locations for shooting.

We added a bosomy secretary, named Patty, to handle phone calls and other office business. Though she came to work in tight hot pants, she was all business and kept our office operating that way. Benveniste was now consumed with editing 'Harlot' and Lynn Rogers took over the mundane job of editing the loops we shot each week. 'Hollywood Blue' was no longer leaching money and the deal with Lew Shere had put Graffitti on solid footing. Considering, that in little more than a year, we had gone from two guys who barely knew how to shoot a silent loop to a solid production company, was a lot to be proud of.

The money allowed for both Bill and me to raise our standards-of-living. Though I remained content with what I had, at least for the time being, Bill rented a ranch style house set on the cliffs overlooking Malibu and began shopping for the vintage Rolls Royce he craved. To keep me from being envious, he mentioned that he was looking for one for me as well.

Judy and I were both feeling good about ourselves. She had cleaned up her life: no drugs or pending legal problems and wanting to show her mom and dad how well she was doing, flew back east to visit them. It was the first time she had seen them since being busted in Boston. When she returned I was given an ultimatum: "Either we get married or I'm moving out." Her father had given her a bit of sage advice: "A stiff dick has no conscience."

It caught me by surprise. There was a lot of truth in that adage and evidently it had been nagging at her for some time. Marriage was not in my plans—mostly because I wanted to avoid a life of nagging like my parents had. But I couldn't deny that I was enjoying living with her. My 'alligator' nightmares had disappeared and she didn't complain about my free-spirited life-style. We had good sex and her pussy never smelled. She had willingly pitched in to help pay our bills with the money she made at the Ball. I thought about her proposal and began to think that like so many of life's clichés, the ones about the pitfalls of marriage were probably overstated. "How do you know if you haven't tried?" Living alone forever was not an attractive thought. She was sexy, not pushy, smart without being overly intellectual, and was of Scottish heritage, which I somehow equated with being level headed. Within minutes I told her OK; but with my own caveat: "I was in the porno business and she should not expect me never to have sex with my models. It would be unrealistic to think that naked girls could surround me all day and I would never succumb to their lure. I also told her, I understood, that as a stripper, she might get a little on the side as well, which I would be cool with. We were both in the sex business. Our marriage would have to be open. She said she didn't have a problem with it.

When I told Bill I was going to marry Judy, he offered to be best man. I explained we weren't going to make a big deal out of it—just go to Vegas for a quickie. The following day he told me, Danny Tafoya, our theatre manager, was planning to marry a polish girl named Judy who coincidentally, was also from Milwaukee. Bill said he would pay for the double wedding out of his own pocket. How cool was that?

In the next few weeks, Judy began to have second thoughts about getting married, suggesting that we call it off. But by this time, I was sold on the idea and convinced her to go forward. She got her nerve back and arranged for a fellow stripper at the Ball to knit her a wedding dress. Neither of us were 'ring' people and I wasn't asked to go through the charade instituted by the DeBeers mining company of buying her a diamond engagement ring, but we did have a jeweler make us custom designed gold wedding rings that we would exchange during the ceremony.

It went down quickly, like swallowing baby food. Judy and I stood with Danny and his Judy in front of the altar at The Little White Chapel located on the west end of the Las Vegas Strip. Bill, still with Kathy, the hot blond that rode on the back of his motorcycle, stood on the side as witnesses. The portly, non-denominational pastor, had already collected his hundred-dollar fee in advance, but with the quiet reverence that the occasion demanded, asked one last question:

"Do you want the ceremony with or without music?" Without a second thought I said: "With music." "That'll be five dollars extra."

Bill handed over a 'Lincoln' and the pastor asked us soon to-be-weds to take a few steps back down the short aisle. He then stepped to the side and dropped a needle on a 45rpm record that was preloaded on a turntable. A scratchy version of 'Here Comes the Bride' began to play and the pastor, standing on an altar livened up with several vases of plastic flowers and a plastic backlit facsimile of a stained glass window, beckoned for Judy and I and Judy and Danny to walk forward. Judy's face looked very virginal as she walked down the aisle in her all white tight fitting crocheted wedding dress with peek-a-boo holes as big as quarters that revealed she wore no bra and only a tiny white-crochet g-string beneath. Her trashy taste was one of the main things I loved about her. And of course, I wore my blue pin-stripe suit.

The pastor pried his eyes off of Judy and began reading the vows: "Do you Howard and Danny take Judy and Judy to be your wives?" We all said I do and he pronounced us man and wife. Later, Judy told me she almost didn't say yes because the way the question was phrased could have been interpreted as meaning she was taking both Danny and me for her husband. It was a valid point.

Necks twisted from all directions as Judy paraded around the MGM Casino in her wedding dress. After the ceremony we were in line at the casino to see the 'Ike and Tina Turner' show. Management, unhappy that she was distracting the gamblers, hustled us out of the line and gave us VIP treatment, a table in the front row. Before we returned to LA the next morning, Judy and I were in a small shop in the hotel lobby just looking over some of the merchandise, when she pulled a pair of men's slacks off the rack and asked me if I would like them. They were made of sheer black see-thru material with thin opaque stripes running vertically to partially obstruct the view. I told her yes and put them on before leaving the store. It gave me an erotic thrill knowing that the little red pouch that cupped my cock and balls was now teasingly visible. We left Vegas as two happily married sluts!

Put another way, we were two people who enjoyed showing that we liked sex and weren't ashamed to let it be known.

The Eros, even after the brief hassle we had with the vice over 'The Confiscated,' continued to do well as a venue to show feature length porn films. However, we still had a large market around the country for our porn loops, including the Artex chain in Texas. Having a chain made sense. If I was shooting loops, Bill argued, why not build our own theatre chain. Within weeks we opened a mini house on Melrose near La Brea to strictly show loops. To make it unique, I had found a way to shoot cinemascope on 16mm. Wide screen porn with open pussies projected across the width of the theatre would be sure to draw in horny patrons.

Bob Thetford and his partner, Larry Jones, who owned the Artex chain inTexas, were looking to expand into Los Angeles. They asked us to partner up with them in another mini house somewhere in Hollywood. Running porn theatres in 'right wing' States like Texas was risky, and Thetford kept a bodyguard, a big strapping six foot two simple-minded Texan boy, named Carl, in his employ.

My'beaver' loops had madeArtex number one in the'Lone Star State' and they depended on a shipment coming to them every week. That the feds had begun to fight pornography by using interstate commerce laws; made that a dangerous task. Pornography was considered illegal and shipping it across state boarders could lead to big trouble. At first Bill had hand delivered loops to Artex on his own, but not wanting to continue to take the risk of getting busted, hired a courier to make the deliveries for us. Mike D'gostin, a young curly haired New Yorker who had a vague connection to the mafia, was willing to take the risk for a fee.

By now I knew Bill well enough to recognize that he had a latent desire to be thought of as gangster. After all, he was Italian. D'gostin wasn't actually a gangster, but having him work for us helped to feed Bill's fantasy as did the strong-arm persona of the Texas boys. I was somewhat leery of teaming up with them, but Bill seemed thrilled and taking a chance of killing a relationship with a major customer was not an option, so we agreed to the partnership. Bill found a location for the new mini house on Hollywood Boulevard near Western Avenue and Bob and Larry, along with their bodyguard, flew to LA to put their seal of approval on it.

When they returned to Dallas, they left Charles 'Carl' Musick, the bodyguard's full name, behind to watch over their interests while it was under construction. I found it a strange way to start a partnership, but these were Bill's people so I kept my mouth shut. Carl kept his blond hair closely cropped in a neat marine type crew cut and although quiet and not unfriendly, he impressed me as someone, if crossed, was capable of violence. With that in the back of my mind, when he asked if I would use him in a porn loop, I assented. When he pulled down his underwear and exposed the smallest dick I had ever laid my eyes on—it looked like a pawn from a chess set—I wisely made no noticeable reaction. Though I kept my chuckles to myself, not so for Bob and Larry, who gave him a good ribbing when they saw the loop after it had been delivered to Texas.

As funny as Carl's mini dick was, John Holmes's gargantuan cock was amazing but problematical. It was so long and thick that his heart had trouble pumping enough blood in it to make it hard. The female models came with their share of problems as well. When one who was a former Marine opened her pussy lips and revealed a thick garden of vaginal warts inside, I almost threw up. As I made a slow pan up another girl's torso who was riding a guy in reverse cowboy position, I found her sound asleep. But all in all, my days at The Crossroads studio were often full of surprises. I never knew when a girl, or girls, would stay around to have sex with me after we finished shooting. Two blonds fresh in from Minnesota treated me to a threesome while their boyfriend waited outside in the car. But things began happening that weren't good and there was reason to be concerned. Not only had Dave Auerbach been busted for shooting the Oakie pedophiles, but a naked girl had recently run out of Mike Henderson's studio in the middle of the day, screaming for her life; claiming he had tried to force himself on her. I could see trouble in the horizon. I decided I needed to move, preferably to a larger studio where I could set up several sets.

I found what I needed beneath a nightclub inVenice, called the Beach House, that sat at the entrance to the now closed down pier that was formerly Pacific Ocean Amusement Park. The club was no longer in business and the area beneath was big enough for me to be able to set up ten permanent sets. The many props that had been left lying around from the arcades were perfect for dressing them.

It would be only a few miles from where Judy and I were about to live. We had been asked by our landlord to vacate the Hansel and Gretel house and had signed a lease at Edgewood Towers, a luxury high-rise apartment at the end of Sunset Blvd that overlooked the ocean. Since they didn't tolerate pets, I moved Little Beasty into the new studio where she could hunt wharf rats all day.

Time had come to meet the man who had warned Judy about my 'stiff dick.' We were traveling, thanks to an insurance settlement she had collected for being a passenger in a car that had an accident when she was still living in Boston, in the new 240Z that she had just purchased on the New York Turnpike just south of Buffalo. The road was being made white by a blinding snowstorm. I was fighting to keep the car on the road but was more nervous about how her parents, who we were going to stay with over the Christmas holiday, were going to react to me.

Snow kicked up by a passing semi forced me off the road, but once the worst of the storm abated, we pulled into the driveway of her parents' modest two-story house in Dover a few hours later. My fear of receiving a snowy reception passed as soon as we stepped inside. Judy's father, an ex navy man who was now working as a typesetter for the Manchester Union, greeted me warmly. Her mother, Connie, despite having difficulty speaking because of the aneurism, laughed at almost anything I said. I suspected Judy's dad was just relieved that someone had stepped up to take the 'little troublemaker' off his hands. Both her brother, Danny, and sister, Pamela, made me feel like I was now part of their family. But after a week, I was glad that family issues were now warm and we could leave cold and dreary New Hampshire to return to warm and sunny California.

Because the Datsun 240Z had had its side window smashed by a thief stealing the camera I had left in the car while it was parked outside the hotel we stayed at on Park Avenue in New York, we had to drive back to California with the window covered by a plastic sheet that chattered like a 'New Year's Eve' toy all the way across the country.

We were emotional wrecks by the time we got back to LA. But being that Bill and I were on such a good roll, the experience was soon forgotten. Our second feature, 'Harlot' was almost ready to be released and we were also adding theatres to our chain as soon as Bill could find cities and locations that were amenable to a porn theatre. Phoenix was such a city and on the cold foggy morning of February 9, 1971, I said goodbye to Judy and went down to the parking lot so I could drive to the airport to meet Benveniste, so he could accompany me to Phoenix and assist setting up the screen so we could show cinemascope loops. As I tried to start the engine, the van began shaking violently. When it was still shaking thirty seconds later, I began to think a tire was going flat so I climbed out to take a look. The tires looked fine and the van had stopped shaking, so I climbed back in and headed for the airport. On the way, I turned on the radio and found the airwaves to be full of frantic reports that a major earthquake had just hit LA. Unknown to me, Judy had been thrown out of our bed and onto the floor and was screaming out the window as I drove away. Benveniste was equally hysterical when we rendezvoused. From his house he had seen electrical power lines sparking and fires breaking out across the basin. It was as though the biblical predictions in Revelations were coming true and Mike, prone to be emotional, wondered if he should make the trip. I eased his anxiety with a bit of fatherly calm. It was a roll I was becoming more and more accustomed to. Our work in Phoenix went well and I returned with the pleasant thought that my loops would soon be causing little earthquakes in that conservative 'Mormon' city.

Bill Nancy Judy Me at the premier of Harlot

The Eros had not suffered any physical damage and Bill had gone ahead with his plans to stage a gala 'World Premier' for the opening of 'Harlot.' A damper was put on the celebration when the Fleishman office called to warn us that our premier was going to be disrupted by a process server showing up to hand us a lawsuit from Father Filas. He was claiming his appearance in 'Hollywood Blue' damaged his reputation. We decided to treat it like a grain of salt. It was just part of doing business, accept it and move on. There was a lot of media interest in our newest release. Bill had sent out invites to the local press and the Hollywood trade papers and arranged for searchlights to streak across the evening sky from in front of the theatre.

Close to three hundred people gathered that night to see what Graffitti Productions was about to unveil. Would it be another 'landmark' film? Bill had rented a mock army tank used for promotional events so we could arrive at the theatre with a flair. All eyes were upon us as we pulled up in front of the Eros. A barrage of blinding flash bulbs greeted Bill and my sister Nancy, who he was now dating, and then Judy, who came dressed in her risqué wedding dress and finally myself, dressed as usual in my blue pin-stripped suit. Bill, played the role of a major producer by acknowledging the crowd, and I, somewhat disbelieving of all the attention, walked into the lobby to pose for pictures—and to be served with our forewarned lawsuit.

The marshal was a cool guy and agreed to join in the festivities by posing for a picture with Bill and I as we accepted the suit. We placed our arms around the server's shoulders and smiled as though we were life long friends. It was a great picture: Bill and I looking like two young rebels; long hair with mutton chops and smiles that sneered at the norms of society.

The next morning, Stanley Fleishman explained to us as we sat with him in his office, that Father Filas was claiming we had damaged his career as a teacher of sexual education by making a joke out of him. The 'Holy Father,' backed by the church, thought we had violated copyright laws by taking a clip out of his educational film without permission. I knew absolutely nothing about copyrights and had assumed, that because the clip was in black and white, the priest was probably already dead. "Don't old people just get out of the way and disappear?" was how I naively looked at it. "And what do priests know about sex anyway? Aren't they supposed to be celibate?" The suit was nothing but a joke and Stanley told us not to worry. Bill and I assured him we had no intention of spending any time fretting about it.

Both the Hollywood Reporter and Variety reviewed 'Harlot.' We had doubled the budget to ten thousand dollars from what we had spent on Mona, still a miniscule amount when compared to mainstream films. The reviewers and other commentators took into account its low budget and gave it favorable comments, even complementing the photography. When it opened in New York, Woody Allen was said to have remarked: "it taught you everything you wanted to know about sex". When the First Federal Bank people were asked how they felt about porn being shot on top of their building, their response was: "none of our customers would go to see that kind of thing." Ha ha!

Our notoriety continued to grow. Variety ran a one-column piece about Bill titled:'The Boy King of Porno.' I didn't let it bother me that I was not included in the article. I accepted that it was reasonable for him to get the press and was content with being the creative force behind the scene. We shared our profits equally, so why should I care? And was it really a big deal to be recognized as a 'Porno King?'

"Not exactly like you're going to be invited to the 'White House' to receive an award for cinematic achievement!"

What the notoriety did bring was two more lawsuits for copyright infringement. Mike had embellished 'Harlot's' music track with a cut off of an I. P. by sitar master Ravi Shankar. And for good measure, he also lifted a cut off a record he found in a used record shop made by a band I had never heard of and probably few other people did as well since their record was already showing up in second had shops. There was no argument that these works were copyrighted, but low budget filmmakers often used copyrighted music without paying for it. Acclaimed and award winning experimental filmmaker, Kenneth Anger, was notorious for the practice, and according to some, pioneered the use of popular music into movie scores by using tracks he lifted without paying for the rights. But porn movies ruffled feathers. Whether we beat the lawsuits or not, it was going to cost us; Stanley didn't come cheap.

66

IT'LL BE THE BIGGEST PORN EVER

With the lawsuits in the hands of the lawyers, it was time to get back to making films. That meant shooting loops and 'one day wonders.' But to move forward we needed a major production that would surpass *'Mona' and 'Harlot.'* Benveniste came into my office and handed me a six-page outline for a script that his upstairs neighbor, Bill Hunt, had asked him to show me. It was called 'Flesh Gordon.' Much of its humor derived from the use of double entendres appropriate for a porn film. Emperor Ming would become Emperor Wang, Dr Zarkoff would become Dr. Flexi Jerkoff, etc. Mike enthusiastically promoted the idea. The film would require special effects, including miniatures and animation that he, or some of his friends, could easily handle. He assured me it wouldn't cost much money. Hunt performed with a theatre group called 'The Company Theatre' and if we made the film, he and some of his fellow actors would be willing to take some of the non-pornographic roles. Hunt wanted the role of Emperor Wang for himself.

I barely knew what a special effect was; let alone how to film them. Did it make sense for Graffitti to attempt something that would require specialists? To mitigate my doubts, Benveniste brought Mike Hyatt, a USC film student, to my office to talk to me about animation. His sandy red hair, glasses and seeming disinterest in sex made him look a bit nerdy, but as we talked I found him to be quite likeable. From the brown paper bag he had brought along, he removed a foam rubber puppet monster that he had built as one of his student projects. He explained it was inspired by

410

one of the creatures that the great Ray Harryhausen had animated for 'In that it had goat's hooves, it resembled a Satyr, but the comparison ended there considering its head and skin were lizard like and as Hyatt proudly demonstrated, its eyes were wired so they could glow bright red by adjusting a dimmer switch. He explained that when animated, the monster would appear on film to be thirty feet tall.

Over the next hour, Hyatt and Benveniste proceeded to give me a crash course in puppet animation. The creature's skeleton, called an armature, had little ball joints that allowed its limbs to be minutely moved into various positions. During filming, it would be placed on a sturdy table in front of a special screen that would have live action rear projected on it. The animator would then make tiny adjustments to each joint in the monster's limbs, so the creature's actions correlated to what was being projected on the background screen. A single frame of film would then be exposed and the background rolled forward one frame, the process repeated twenty-four times to achieve one second of action.

Oozing with confidence, Benveniste said he could build all the miniature sets the script called for, like Emperor Wang's castle, by just purchasing four-dollar hobby shop kits. Moreover, he went on to explain that if we hired Hyatt, we would not only get an animator, but a monster ready to go. And by doing the animation on 16mm film, the cost would be insignificant. Notwithstanding the fact that Hyatt admitted that he had yet to animate anything, it all sounded good to me.

I ran the project past Bill, who knew even less about special effects than I did; but we both wanted to do something big to follow on the heels of *'Mona'* and *'Harlot'* and *'Flesh Gordon'* would certainly do that. We told Mike we would do the film and assigned it a budget of twenty-five grand, which would make it the most expensive porn film yet to be made. Hunt wanted to write the full script, but I felt by looking at his promo piece, that he really was not attuned to what made a porn film work, so I told Benveniste to take a month off from his editing chores to put a script together.

Meanwhile, loops and one hour features would continue to be Graffitti's bread and butter. Cichy had quickly grasped how I wanted each feature to incorporate a variety of different sex scenes: boy girl, girl girl and something kinky. His fifteen-page scripts were all capable of being shot in no more than two days. They only needed to provide a theme to hook each sex scene together which I would adlib as I shot.

I needed to hire another editor for the one-day-wonders because I wanted Benveniste to work full-time on Flesh Gordon. We couldn't afford another endless 'Hollywood Blue' fiasco. Marty Rustin, the Egyptian owner of the small independent lab where we had formerly processed our film, knew of an editor with substantial experience who was looking for work. Being that he was from a Muslim country, I had some doubts, but after meeting Abbas Amin, in his mid 30's and single, he assured me he was not religious and had no qualms about working on porn movies. That he was fully acquainted with working on a KEM table and would be the first truly professional person to come to work for Graffitti, made it an easy decision to hire him.

Walter already had a script, called 'Tijuana Blue,' ready to go and after I put a cast together, it was in the can a few days later. Several shots were taken in Tijuana to add production value by giving the impression that the action took place south of the border when in fact all the sex scenes were shot States side. Abass claimed he would work much more efficiently if he had an assistant editor to work with him, so I assigned Rogers to the task. I quickly saw that his claim was true. He now could simply use a grease pencil to mark the beginning and end of the shots he wanted to use and label them with a number where he wanted them to appear in the rough cut and Lynn could come in later and physically cut them out and reassemble them in the order that he had requested. It now only took one day to make a first rough cut. I still wanted these features to look as good as possible, but as long as the sex scenes were hot, the theatres and customers would be happy. Many porn fans went to at least one movie each week to get their fix of erotic stimulation and it was the theatre's job, and consequently Grafitti's, to supply them something new.

That I had never been busted for any of my assorted petty crimes, made me contemptuous of the legal establishment and Bill was much the same. It was hard to have much respect for an establishment that the Vietnam War was exposing to be a bunch of liars and even less respect for the church who was seeking twenty-five grand to settle the Father Filas lawsuit. Somehow money would make the Holy Father pure again. Bill and I thought their claim was ridiculous and told Fleishman to resist. He assigned the case to one of his associates, Dave Brown who, as a good lawyer, told us not to worry; he could tie it up for a long time and hopefully they would back down in their demands. It was just the price of being successful.

Ravi Shankar, not wanting to be left out of the gravy train, also wanted twenty-five grand, claiming his reputation had been soiled by his music being associated with a porn movie. Frankly, I doubted that anyone watching a porn film would even be aware what music was on the sound track. Thought Ravi didn't have the Catholic church to help fight his battle, he had something better: George Harrison, guitarist for the 'Beatles,' who had been studying sitar with him and was ready to testify in court about the deleterious affect *'Harlot'* was having on his idol. The unknown band was only looking for six thousand dollars, probably the biggest payday they would ever see. I supposed they were doing what most people would do. The legality of porn movies was questionable and as such, we were easy punching bags. They probably thought Bill and I would crumble after the first punch. They were wrong! At the end of the day, the worse that could happen was that we would have to settle, but at least we wanted them to work for their money.

67

THE PIGGY SHUFFLE

But another warning came from Fleischman's office that was much more ominous. He had heard rumors that the vice were about to make some busts and that Graffitti was under surveillance. Being that I was the one who made the films; that meant me.

It was actually amazing that it had taken them so long; nevertheless, it made my ire rise. I found it repugnant that they thought they had the right to regulate what adults viewed. It seemed patently unconstitutional. "Weren't we a free country?" I was too rebellious and maybe too callow and stupid to know that in many ways we were not, but in my ignorance, I was not about to be intimidated and had every intention of continuing to make porn movies. I knew, in my heart, that a large part of the American population was glad to see sex come out of the dark and don't the good guys always win at the end?

That didn't mean that I wasn't going to take Fleishman's warning seriously. Abbas was just completing 'Tijuana Blue' and I told him to credit me as 'Harry Hopper.' No point of making it easier for the vice to make their case by signing my work. And if it was true that the vice had a tail on me; I would from now on use evasive action when traveling to a location. Cocky little bastards that we were; Cichy, Rogers and I named our vice shaking exercise: *'The Piggy Shuffle.'* After loading our equipment into the van at the Melrose office, I drove a zigzag route to the various rendezvous points where I had arranged to pickup my cast. Often it was a Norms or Bob's Big Boy restaurant. Hopefully by the time I arrived, if the vice were following me I would have ditched them. But knowing they were pros and I couldn't always be sure that was the case and it could be likely that if they saw me pull into a restaurant's parking lot, they would hang back until I continued with my cast to the location. Of course they couldn't just stop in the street blocking traffic, they would probably zip around the block and hope to loop around it in time to resume the tail as I drove back out onto the street.

After a few weeks of doing the 'Shuffle,' I had almost begun to think I was just having silly paranoia. "Why waste valuable time doing the 'Piggy Shuffle' if it wasn't needed?" But when on multiple occasions I noticed in my rear view mirror the same unmarked Ford sedan pulling back out into traffic as I got back on the road, I became convinced that Fleishman's warning had been correct. Lynn also saw the same car when he looked out the back window. The appearance of the same white Ford couldn't be explained just by random chance. To fuck up their plan, I began just pulling into the parking lot and leave the engine running so Cichy could dash into the reastaurants and hustle my cast back out so we could be back into traffic before the vice completed their loop around the block. In case I still hadn't ditched them, I would then continue the 'Piggy Shuffle' for another fifteen minutes, using more extreme techniques such as making U-turns in heavy traffic, going down one-way alleys and running yellow lights so that they turned red just as I finished crossing. It was a lot of extra work, but it was worth not getting busted. I still looked at it as more funny than serious.

Even with the tails nothing came of it and I shot a few more one-day-wonders without any problems. I continued to credit myself as 'Harry Hopper' or sometimes not to be too repetetive 'Ned Johnson,' and Walter wisely became 'Linus Gator' for the same reason. Why use real names on films that would be unlikely to get acclaim.

Benveniste finally showed up with the Flesh Gordon script. Not unexpected, he had taken two weeks longer than I had allotted him. Despite it only being sixty pages long, I thought it was quite clever. It had a lot of fun stuff. The beginning was similar to the serial *'Flash Gordon's Trip to Mars,'* which I had only briefly seen onece, but then quickly veered away by introducing a sex ray and a monster called a *'Penisaurus.'* Benveniste continued to assure me that our twenty five thousand dollar budget was more than enough to produce the film. He had been a big reason for the success of 'Mona' and I liked his devil-may-care attitude. We were similar in that way. I had confidence in him and after running it by Bill; the project was green lighted.

Mike Hyatt would animate his own monster. It was a big break for him—working on a feature length film—and a big break for us in more ways than one. As a USC student, he was in contact with some of the young up-and-coming talent who were into science fiction and fantasy, most significantly, an art director named Mike Minor. He arranged for Minor to come by the office for an interview. As I sat at my desk and Benveniste stood at my side, Minor sat opposite us with an open sketchbook. As quickly as Benveniste described some of the props and characters, he drew roughs that perfectly reflected what we had in mind. By the end of the hour-long meeting, we had a workable drawing for the Flying Phallus, the Penisaurus and costumes for Flesh and Wang. They were delightful and I told him he could have the job. Talented along with infectious energy, it was clear to me he had leadership qualities that would make things happen.

Minor said we would need a sound stage to build the sets in and suggested we check out Producer's Studio, located directly across from Paramount Studios on Melrose Avenue. It was one of the oldest in Hollywood and catered to independents. Bill was going to handle all the financial concerns of the film and began by negotiating a deal with the studio. He got us the eight thousand square foot stage 8, for fifty dollars a day while we were prepping and building sets and a hundred dollars a day when we were shooting. The deal also included a suite of offices on the lot for no extra money. Whether the studio knew that we were porn moviemakers, they didn't say or probably care. Our money was green and that's what they liked.

My head couldn't help but swell when I realized we were about to make a film at the same studio where 'In the Heat of the Night' with Rod Steiger and 'Whatever Happened to Baby Jane' with Betty Davis had been shot. To get onto the lot, you had to be cleared by a guard before he raised the gate. It was amazingly cool. We were real moviemakers and Bill was now a real Hollywood producer. He was not only driving a Rolls Royce Silver Shadow, which he explained he finagled his way into with a sweetheart lease deal that was costing him next to nothing, but had also bought an expensive house on Tower Road in the Hollywood Hills section of Beverly Hills. He explained that he was able to buy the house by putting almost no money down. That he and my sister, Nancy, were now going steady and living together, made him almost family. I accepted that when it came to business, he was just quicker and more clever than I and considered myself lucky to have him for a partner.

As I stood with Mike Minor and surveyed the stage, he explained where each set would be located and how some sets could be quickly converted from one use to another by simply using a little paint and moving a few props around. The biggest set, which would be built in the back corner of the stage and take up a fourth of it's space, would be Wang's throne-room.

Several of Bill Hunt's compatriots at the Company Theatre, hired on as Minor's construction crew. The first set constructed was the 'Penisauraus' cave. It would sit in the front corner of the stage just inside its large entry door. Everyone fed off of Minor's passion. Like the mad Disney comic book inventor, 'Gyro Gearloose,' he turned chicken wire, aerogel foam and some spray paint into the 'Penisauraus' cave. With energy and imagination that had no limits, stage eight began to fill up with the interior of the 'Flying Phallus,' 'Chief Nellie's underground cavern,' 'Jerkoff's laboratory' and the 'tickle girl torture room.' The set for Ronald McDonald's Land was in the stage directly across from Stage 8, and when they came over to see what we were doing, they said they liked our sets better than theirs.

Nothing of this grandeur had ever been attempted in a porno movie. Minor's creations were making something much bigger than any of us, including Benveniste, had anticipated. Bill and I both realized we were on to something big and both concurred, that despite its small budget, 'Flesh Gordon' should target the broader art house market rather than the strictly 'porno' market. We would shoot in 16mm, but then blow the film up to 35mm. Consensus opinion still held, that within a year the U. S. Supreme Court would rule that consenting adults would have the right to view what they pleased, so it still made sense to include some tasteful hardcore. We wanted 'Flesh Gordon' to be in the forefront when the more liberal standards became law. 'Flesh's' seduction by 'Queen Amora' and 'Prince Precious,' would still be shot hardcore, but artistically and without any 'porn house' close-ups. Other hardcore action would be limited to background scenes, like 'Wang's' subjects fornicating in front of him on his throne room floor. I would also shoot a hardcore gay orgy on the grounds of 'Prince Precious's

Merry kingdom.' The focus would be to make light of sexual fears and taboos rather than erotic stimulation.

Minor spread the word among his friends about the film he was working on as its art director. Several were up and coming special effects artists. Suddenly Flesh Gordon became a project they all wanted in on. Greg Jein, a quiet Oriental in his early twenties, signed on to build the miniature space ships, including the Flying Phallus, Wang's alligator ships, Queen Amora's Swan ship and Prince Precious's Beetle ship. Rather than build Wang's castle from a four-dollar hobby kit, Tom Sherman was hired to build it and all the other miniatures we would need. Tom, looking every bit his hero, 'Captain Nemo of Twenty Thousand Leagues Beneath the Sea,' wore a closely cropped beard and long sideburns that along with the stern mien he kept on his face, made him appear a bit eccentric; but when I went to his apartment and saw that he had remodeled it to look like the interior of 'Captain Nemo's' submarine, it was obvious that he was a master at his craft. Rick Baker, destined to become Hollywood's premier special effects make-up man, was hired to build a full scale 'Penisauraus' head to be used for close up shots when the creature attacks Dale. He wanted the job as our makeup man but his mother protested.

Mike Hyatt was already on board to animate his Satyr monster and Bill Hedge, who had just finished doing the animation for the 'Pillsbury Dough Boy,' came on to animate the 'Penisauraus.' It seemed unlikely that a talent like Jim Danforth, who had been nominated by the Academy for his work on 'When Dinosaurs Ruled the Earth,' would be interested in working for a little upstart like Graffitti, but I got word that he was interested in doing our Matt paintings. He had a reputation for being difficult to work with, so I was nervous, but pleased, when he came to my office for an interview. Benveniste knew Danforth's work and told me many experts considered him to be as skilled as Ray Harryhausen, the god father of puppet animation. The interview went easier than I had expected and after I wholeheartedly agreed to let him do our Matt paintings, he mentioned that he had a 'Beetle Man' puppet creature that he had built for another film that had been aborted and would be willing to donate and animate it if we had a scene in which it could fit. Without a moment's hesitation, both Benveniste and I said we did. We actually didn't, but a little rewrite of the script would take care of that problem. This was a major coup.

68

A MOST AMAZING CAST AND CREW

Jason William, Cindy Stokes, Joe Hudgins

Regardless that the film was not going to be a porn film per se, I did most of the casting through Reb's Pretty Girl Agency. I felt I owed it to him for supplying me models from day one. It was a big deal to him as well. He ran an ad in the Free Press that found us Jason Williams, a tall athletic blond and former 'little All American' wide receiver from San Diego State, to play Flesh Gordon. Although he had never done any porn work, he was far and away our best choice for the lead role. Happy to get the part, he agreed to do the two brief hardcore scenes as long as they weren't too graphic.

There were many physically attractive girls doing porn, but none could match the vibrant personality of Cindy Stokes. She was a bubble-butted teen, who I had first used in one of my early silent porn loops. Her cute perky face and sparkling personality had exhibitors begging for repeat performances.

Though I didn't know it at that time, since we didn't always check I. D.s, she was only sixteen when I first shot her. Rumor had it that she was the rebellious daughter of a Mormon Bishop. However, she was now eighteen and legal and the perfect choice to be Flesh's girl friend, 'Dale Ardor.'

Along with Bill Hunt to play 'Emperor Wang,' the Company theatre provided us with Joe Hudgins, to play the role of 'Dr. Flexi Jerkoff.' Beyond being a damn good actor, his soft eyes and friendly voice, ensured that the film would have an endearing and loveable quality that would make it appealing to the audience.

Nora Wiedernick, a Rubenesque German sexpot, was cast as 'Queen Amora.' I knew from personal experience when she did a porn loop for me, that her pussy was juicy and that she would help ease any anxieties that Jason might have while doing his first filmatic sex scene. Jason's other sex scene would be with Michael Brandy, a handsome bisexual who had also done a few loops for me.

'Chief Nellie,' leader of the Amazon porno underground, "an organization devoted solely to the overthrow of 'Wang' and his corrupt male chauvinist regime;" was inspired by a character from one of Mike O'Donoghue's graphic novels; 'The Adventures of Phoebe Zeitgeist.' Mary Gavin, a thirty-some buxom stripper, whose stage name was 'Candy Samples,' was cast to take the role. She would be seen as a cigar smoking invalid with a prosthetic leg and fore arm complete with a hook.

Thanks to Mike Hyatt, we were able to cast John Hoyt, a top-drawer Hollywood character actor who had played roles in classics like 'Julius Ceasar' and 'The Blackboard Jungle.' Mike had befriended him after attending a lecture he gave at USC and was now able to get him to agree to play the role of 'Professor Gordon,' Flesh's father.

Two members of the 'Hollywood Trekie Club,' Ruth Glunt and B. Jo Trimble, had gotten wind of 'Flesh Gordon' and offered to come on to head up our costume and make-up crew. What had started as the "biggest porn ever," was now a full blown Hollywood production.

Within three weeks, Minor had the stage filled with sets. I, along with Lynn Rogers, had pre-lit everything as much as possible, so shooting wouldn't have to be delayed for lighting. Sky pans were hung from the rafters and baby and senior key lights fitted with fresnel lenses were placed in positions to provide back and accent light. I used lots of colored gels to give ambiance to nooks and crannies. That I was a novice when it came to lighting a large set, gave me a sensible amount of anxiety about everything working out. To ensure the 35mm blowup would have good density, I planned on using a fine grain film, which meant that a lot more light needed to be poured onto the set than I normally shot under. It would mean that the sets would be very warm.

The day before shooting, we were all nervous as hell and doing our best to stay optimistic. That's why I had a hard time understanding why Benveniste, without any fear of being impolitic, suggested that he was worried that I might not be capable of doing the camera work. Cichy came to my defense by saying he thought I was the best in the business, (as far as porn films went) not unwarranted since the reviews of Graffitti's films in Daily Variety and The Hollywood Reporter, always made complementary mention of the photography. Benveniste countered that he considered San Francisco's Alex DeRenzy to be the best. It was a strange discussion to be having at this time, so I just let it slide. I considered that Mike might have been smarting a bit over the fact that after Minor was hired, he had lost some of his influence. But as our director, I was still relying on his vision. Not to be a complete special effects neophyte, I had given myself a crash course on the subject by reading several books on the subject. With all the money we were spending, I couldn't afford to be over my head!

On Labor day, 1971, just a little more than two years from when I shot my first silent 'beaver' film, we were ready to roll. For the first shot, the camera was mounted on a tripod and the zoom lens set at wide angle, when Minor rushed up with a block of Styrofoam that had a hole carved in it that was painted to make it look like a passageway in a cave. He quickly mounted it on a 'C' stand, one foot in front of the lens, telling me the 'forced perspective' would give the illusion that I was shooting from deep within a cavern. I knew then that we were making something far beyond what we had originally imagined. Once Minor finished, I nodded to our soundman, John Brasher, and when he signaled that the tape was rolling and I confirmed that camera speed was at 24fps (frames per second), I shouted out speed and Benveniste called "action." Flesh, Jerkoff and Dale poked their heads out from a passageway to see if it was safe to continue into the mysterious cave. They gingerly proceeded forward and exited the camera frame to the right. Benveniste called "cut" and everyone took a big breath. The first shot was completed.

Standing to the side, wearing a big black fur coat and sporting large dark sunglasses, Bill was doing his best to play the role of a big time Hollywood producer watching his baby come to fruition. There were a lot of shots to pull off that first day so we had to work quickly. Lynn stayed at my side, ready to move the camera to a new position or change the magazine when the film ran out. Since Graffitti now owned two Éclair cameras, when I didn't need his assistance, he operated the second one from a position that didn't interfere with the primary camera. Between setups, Benveniste rehearsed the actors to have them ready as soon as I was ready to shoot. Cichy, as production still photographer, busied himself snapping pictures. For a bunch of novices, we were working like a well-oiled machine.

Money and time constraints limited us to two takes of any set up and even then it was two only if there was an obvious problem with the first take, like a stumbled line of dialogue. As I did when shooting loops, I repeatedly switched between a zoom lens and a fixed wide-angle lens. It was simply a matter of loosening a turret knob on the camera's body and rotating the desired lens into place and then tightening the turret down. After one of the shots was completed, I took a little gulp when I noticed that the turret had been left slightly ajar while I had been shooting. The thick cloth barney that muted the sound of the film going through the gate, made locking down the turret cumbersome and evidently it hadn't been done correctly. I wasn't quite sure what kind of problem, if any, could have resulted from the oversight, but since the day was moving so well, I convinced myself that no serious damage had been done and didn't say anything. I would be a bit more careful in the future. Benveniste's snide remarks were still in mind, and it would have been humiliating to announce that I had already fucked up in the first hour.

Not only did we shoot all the live action that took place in the 'Penisauraus' cave on day one, but because Rick Baker had arrived just after lunch break with the full scale foam rubber 'Penisauraus' head, we were able to attach it to the end of a pole and use it to attack Dale while she lay helplessly on the floor. I also found time to shoot the 35mm 'plates' (the name given to the film that would be rear projected for animation or matt painting purposes) that Bill Hedge would need to animate the 'Penisauraus.' It required using a special 'Mitchell' 35mm camera that had double registration pins that locked each exposure precisely into place. Benveniste made it clear that it was essential that the camera didn't vibrate during shooting. To stabilize it, we mounted in on a heavy tripod secured tightly to the ground with sandbags. Eventually the 'plates' would be scrutinized by our special effects people when they were needed for animation or a matt painting, so I kept my fingers crossed that my first attempt was going to make everyone happy.

By five-thirty, Osco was rushing the first day's footage to Crest Film Lab to be developed and a print, known as a daily, struck. Normally, dailies were viewed before a set was torn down, but even as Bill was driving off the lot, Minor was taking down the cave set and moving the pieces to the far side of the stage where they would eventually be reconstituted into other sets. Tearing down a set before seeing the dailies was risky, because if something needed to be reshot, the set would not be there. Thinking about the loose turret was making me uncomfortable.

As cast and crew were leaving the stage, our prop man, Tom Reamy, was arriving with a set of rattan chairs with flower-print cushions that had once been the actual seats used in America's first passenger plane, the Ford Trimotor. fondly knick-named, 'The Tin Goose.' Minor would work into the night so the set would be ready to shoot in the morning. As promised, it was ready when I arrived. The chairs were in place and cloth curtains hung on the plane's windows, just how it would have looked in its hay day. By ten

I was shooting Dale stumbling down the plane's narrow aisle with a drink in hand. Being that the plane was in stormy weather and I had to simulate a rough flight, I crammed my six foot two frame into a shopping cart and had Lynn slowly dolly it down the aisle as I did a handheld shot just ahead of 'Dale,' bouncing the camera and tilting it left or right to keep it in sync with the passengers who were being cued by Benveniste to sway in unison as though the plane was yawing wildly left and right.

Before 'Dale' manages to reach her seat, the plane takes a sudden lurch and while trying not to fall, she not only spills her drink on the lap of the gentleman sitting next to the aisle, but loses her balance and finds herself sitting on it as well. Assuring her not to worry about the faux pas, 'Flesh Gordon' introduces himself: "Oh Professor Gordon's son?" she exclaims. Like a big kid, Flesh turns to the camera and blows a big balloon with the bubble gum he has been chomping on and it begins to fill the frame until it pops. This would eventually segue into the yet to be designed title sequence.

The rest of day two was spent filming the soft-core orgy that ensued after the plane runs into a mysterious ray that causes sexual havoc. When 'Flesh,' who is the only one who seems immune to the sexual madness taking place around him, realizes that even the pilots have fallen victim and the plane has no one at its controls, he ties 'Dale's' hands to her seat to save her from being debauched and then makes his way through the orgy in the aisle to get to the cockpit and attempt to bring the plane back under control. But 'Dale' has found 'Flesh's' allure to be overwhelming and manages to free herself and crawl down the aisle of groping hands, to join him in the cockpit, where he is too busy struggling with the controls to even notice that she is on her knees with her face buried in his crotch, to ackowledge her. In his overzealous panic, he only manages to rip the controls from their mounting and is left with no other option but to pick Dale up in his arms and parachute out of the plane to an unknown fate below.

It had been another long and successful day and after shooting ended, I joined everyone at Crest Film labs where Murray Stein had kept his screening room open so we could view the dailies from the previous day. As we waited for the film to roll, I prayed that there were no problems because of the loose turret. My prayers were not answered. The opening shot of Flesh and gang entering the cave was slightly out of focus. Possibly because I was the producer, no one else seemed to notice—or at least say anything.

Eternally optimistic and maybe naïve, I hoped there would be a way of fixing the problem when we blew the film up, but how, I had no idea.

The good news was that the 35mm plates came out perfect and could be handed to Bill Hedge so he could begin animating the 'Penisauraus.' He had already built the puppet, which since it was only a large penis without any joints; its armature was just a length of stiff wire. Hedge had his own studio and equipment, so was able to get right to work. He said that he would have the first finished cut completed in a week.

With the jitters behind us, shooting proceeded smoothly for the rest of the week as we moved from set to set. I was somewhat miffed when Mike Minor sidled up to me to let me know that he didn't think much of Benveniste as a director. He was upset that not enough shots were being taken to show off the detail of the sets, especially Dr. Jerkoff's lab. That it was primarily the creation of our prop master, Tom Reamy, who I now realized was Mike's partner and lover, I surmised that he was just being protective of his mate and let it pass as just a small fit of 'gay' bitchiness.

Halfway through the second week, Osco advised me that we had already surpassed our original twenty five thousand dollar budget. Neither of us saw it as a problem. In the coming days, scene after scene was put to bed, including: the 'hermaphrodite battle,' a naked girl being tickled to death in 'Wang's' lab and the 'Royal Flush.' When Bill Hedge showed up with an animated cut of the 'Penisauraus' monster, it enforced everyone's faith that we were making something special and that it was progressing smoothly. Minor was indefatigable and I kept driving everyone hard, especially myself, to keep up with him. The film was going to be more expensive than originally anticipated, but we would easily make our money back after it was released.

Word had gone around Producer's Studio, that exciting things were happening on stage eight, so it was not unusual for people on the lot to stop by and take a peek. But there seemed to be no rational explanation why two guys from the phone company suddenly appeared; saying they needed to install a line. When they kept straining their necks to see what was going on, I suspected they were vice. The fuckers never gave up. Since no filming was going on during their visit, they left disappointed.

The shooting schedule called for twenty uninterrupted days, and by the twelfth day, many of them sixteen hours long, all of us were exhausted. I could see that enthusiasm and creativity were suffering, so I announced a two-day break over the weekend to recuperate. A sigh of gratitude could be heard throughout the stage.

During the break, Greg Jein came into the office to show me the miniature 'Flying Phallus' that he had just completed. It was super cool! Scaled to look like it was thirty feet long with a skin made to appear like metallic panels held together by rivets, it was every bit the large flying dick we had envisioned. Several windows and a door along its shaft, make it look like a sci-fi space ship. It had exhaust pipes protruding from its rear where a sparkler could be inserted and spews of magnesium flecks would shoot out as the ship was in flight. A rear license plate made the ship legal. I returned to the stage two days later with renewed vigor.

Amazon guards capture Dale

The final push after the break began by shooting the scenes in the Amazon underground. Stage 8 was empty when I arrived early in the morning, but moments later one of the Amazon girls arrived fifteen minutes before her morning call and treated me to a quickie atop Queen Amora's bed. It was nice way to start the day. My wife, Judy, was to play one of the Amazon warriors and when she arrived shortly after, I noticed she had bright red bikini lines on her butt. She had fretted all week long about her part and wanted to look good, so had spent some time -obviously a bit too much—in the sun the day before. That she had agreed to shave her pubic hair, a prerequisite for the part, caused me to hold my criticism. Shaved pussies were yet to be in vogue and not all girls were willing, but it was a fetish I knew many would find exciting.

The day was spent celebrating lesbian lechery. 'Dale' had been rescued from a forced marriage to 'Wang' and had been dragged to 'Chief Nellie's' underground kingdom where she was told that she would be inducted into their organization, but first must endure an initiation ceremony. After she is strapped to a gurney, an exotic black 'Amazon,' played by Dee Dee Daily, climbs onto the gurney and slowly slithers across her body until she can rise on her haunches and submerge 'Dale's' face with her pulsating warm black pussy. Cindy would tell me later, that Dee Dee was method acting, enjoying every minute as she whispered trash into her ear.

The Amazon cave scene took two days to shoot and culminated when 'Flesh' and 'Jerkoff' burst through a wall of the cave to save her. Aghast at what they see upon entering, Jerkoff yelps: "Egads 'Flesh.'

They're dikes!"

'Flesh,' beyond disbelief: "DIKES?"

The 'Amazons' scurry as 'Flesh' rushes forth to save 'Dale' who is still tied to the gurney. Thanks to the largess of 'Queen Amora,' he and 'Jerkoff' are in possession of the 'power pasties,' its ray the only force strong enough to destroy 'Wang's' evil sex ray. But as 'Jerkoff' uses it to keep the ladies at bay, one of them sneaks to the side and grabs a mallet to strike a gong next to a large wood planked double door. Before 'Jerkoff' can regain control of the girls, the damage has been done.

The balance of the scene was the attack of the 'Beetleman.' A day was spent shooting the plates Danforth would need to do the animation. Between Benveniste and Danforth and Jason's athletic performance, an exceptional scene was choreographed that would be a challenge for any animator to pull off. The 'Beetleman' appears to be victorious, until a mysterious arrow kills him.

The arrow, shot by 'Prince Precious,' was "A poisoned tipped arrow" and after he explains to 'Flesh' that he is: "the rightful ruler of porno, but was overthrown by Wang, a maniacal botanist who became crazed when his organ was destroyed by a Penis fly trap," Flesh agrees to his request to fellate him as a gesture of appreciation. Over the next few days I shot that scene as well as Flesh's love scene with Queen Amora. As promised, neither scene showed any sexual detail. The Prince Precious shot was taken from an from an overhead angle and the Queen Amora scene was shot under blue high contrast light with diffusion filters on the lens. Nora Wiedernik had no difficulty seducing Flesh and moans: "fuck me . . . you huge blond giant," as her pendulous breasts swing across his face. He gave no indication if he enjoyed it.

I didn't think Bill was gay, or for that matter care, but still found it interesting that he only showed up on the stage when gay sex was being shot. Jason and Bill had become buddy buddy and had taken to cruising around Hollywood in Bill's Rolls Royce almost every evening after we wrapped for the day. An air of secrecy had begun to surround Bill. Of course I had some questions about how he had afforded a house and a Rolls Royce, but his explanations always sounded plausible and the fact that he was living with my sister prevented me from delving deeper. To keep the peace it was just better to not go there.

After the various scenes that held the thread of the plot together were put in the can, we set up in Wang's throne room to spend our final days of live action shooting in stage Eight. A nonstop orgy, a nice gig for the extras, would take place on its floor. Day by day, we knocked off all the scenes. Tom Sherman's 'Rapist Robots' had everyone in stitches. Each tube shaped robot had its own persona and came with a rotating corkscrew metal penis.

A short balding man named Bob Costa, a friend of Tom Sherman's, had come by to watch the shooting of the robot scene. After we wrapped, he approached me to offer a proposition. He was willing to set up all the special effects people with the equipment they would need, such as Mitchell cameras and rear screen projectors. He just wanted to be part of the production. All he would require was that we pay to rent the equipment, which he would offer at a big discount from what the other equipment houses charged. He also claimed that he was capable of building an optical printer and if we paid for the few parts that would have to be machined, it would save us a ton of money when it came time to do the optical effects, like adding rays and compositing the matt paintings, and most of all the blowup.

I hadn't even thought about the services he was offering, but it was intriguing and I liked his energy. Bill had already let me know that we had already spent close to seventy grand, but since the live shoot was nearing an end, I didn't see a problem. I was still thinking that, as Benveniste had explained, the special effects would cost next to nothing. Flesh Gordon seemed to have an aura that attracted people who could provide the perfect solution when needed. If Costa could save us money and relieve some of the pressure that was building, it made sense to hire him. I told him to consider himself hired.

After twenty-two days, shooting at stage 8 was finally completed. It was a good thing too. Benveniste seemed to be losing focus; disappearing from time to time with a few cast members to snort cocaine, a drug that was just beginning to gain popularity. In one instance he showed up ten minutes late with a wild grin on his face and began throwing out "great new ideas" that he had just come up with; like 'Jerkoff' threatening to commit suicide with a butter knife. He seemed shocked to have his suggestions rejected. Minor started giving me a, *"I told you so look,"* but I still felt accepting Benveniste's indiscretions was a fair exchange for his creativity. If not for him, we wouldn't even be making 'Flesh Gordon.'

A week of doing a few exterior and outside location shots, including, thanks to Minor's inroads with the staff at the Griffith Park Observatory, a scene of 'Professor Gordon' discovering the sex ray as he peers through the eyepiece of its iconic telescope. The observatory's art deco architecture was also used to shoot all the background plates that Hyatt would need to animate his 'Satyr' monster.

A light hearted respite took place at Lake Sherwood, unpopulated at the time and eventually to become the site of Tiger Woods' annual golf tournament, but now to be used to shoot the 'Prince Precious' orgy scene. Of all the scenes that were shot during filming, it would prove to be the easiest to direct. After action was called, it was near impossible to get the lads to stop.

A few shots at the Bronson Canyon caves, where the original

'Flash Gordon' serials were shot in 1938, was the end of live action shooting. With a friendly squeeze of 'Flesh's' balls, 'Precious' bids him goodbye with profound parting words: "The universe is once again safe for freedom and democracy." The halcyon words gave me no clue to the nightmare that was about to begin.

69

OUIJA BOARD GHOST, GUNS
AND HELICOPTERS

Mike Minor announced that he was leaving the production to work on a film being shot in Jamaica. I was sad to see him go, his creative energy would be missed, but I didn't envision any problems ahead. Work on all the effects, including the blow-up was accounted for and Bill Hedge was already at work animating the 'Penisaurus' which I expected to be completed shortly. With Costa's help, Hyatt could be set up to begin animating the 'Satyr' monster and Benveniste could now devote his full time to editing the film. Despite having gone way over budget; Graffitti's stressed bank account could quickly be replenished as soon as I got back to knocking out loops and 'Harry Hopper' features.

Danforth painting Flying Phallus matte

Costa recommended that I hire Dennis Muren, to be our director of special effects. As a teenager, he had made a short 8mm science fiction film and knew all the young, up and coming talent, including the ones I had already hired,. "Why can't the model makers just shoot their own scenes?" I asked. But Costa was adamant that hiring him would move things along at a faster pace and save lots of money in the long run. What did I know anyway, so I acquiesced and put Muren

on the payroll. I had no idea at the time, what a wise decision I had just made. The two of them took charge of our effects department, beginning by scouring the industrial sections of the San Fernando Valley to find a place to set up shop. They found a vacated venetian blind factory in a two thousand square foot building in Eagle Rock. Its high ceiling and wide bay entry door would allow air to flow through during the hot summer months. A fenced in paved lot on the side could be used to shoot effects that required daylight. Located close to where all the crew lived, made it convenient. As soon as Bill drove out to Eagle Rock in his Rolls Royce and handed the landlord a three hundred fifty dollar check, we were almost ready to go full bore.

Only Danforth and Hyatt needed to be provided with space to work. Producer's Studio agreed to let me wall off a few feet of the back end of stage 8 with a large sheet of black plastic to make a space for Danforth and after I rented a Quonset hut in the industrial section of Santa Monica for Hyatt there was little left to do. Costa set everyone up with the equipment they would need and when Danforth came into my office with his first completed matt painting; an enhancement of Bronson Canyon where Wang's three soldiers scurry down the cliff to pursue Flesh and friends into the Penisauraus cave, a few days later. Beyond the painting looking spectacular, it showed me that it wouldn't be long before all the effects were completed.

Everything was pointing towards a happy ending. Hyatt had moved a mattress into the Quonset hut so he could work around the clock and I was impressed by his commitment. He and Benveniste were still adamant that the 'Satyr' scene could be animated in 16mm and since animation is a tedious process, Hyatt was running a lot of tests before actually beginning. It made sense that all the technical issues were resolved before beginning work.

Now that Flesh was more or less out of the way, I was back to shooting porn movies and having a little sex whenever the opportunity arose; which was often. My studio at the amusement pier had gone the way of the wrecking ball—resulting in Little Beasty going feral—so I had to do all my shooting at locations, including my own apartment at Edgewater Towers. Lynn Rogers' time was taken up assisting me and he no longer had time to work with Abass, so I offered Judy's brother, Danny, the job. The magical attraction that is Hollywood, made it easy for him to put his business degree from Bowdoin College to the side and after cleaning up a few lose ends, drove his MG across the country and arrived two weeks later. I was back to churning out ten loops a week and a one-day-wonder every ten days. At times, I just let Lynn shoot the loops. They lacked pizzazz but most wanted features now anyway. Bill did his part by opening another mini house in Tucson, Arizona.

Hyatt had come to my office to show me a one second test he had made to check his lighting. The final composite of an animated shot is several generations away from the original and when I saw how grainy the 16mm test was, I knew we had to switch to 35mm. All the other effects were being shot in 35mm and if we continued to use 16mm for the 'Satyr' monster, it would not blend smoothly with the rest of the film. Though he and Benveniste argued, I arranged for Costa to set Hyatt up with 35mm equipment so he could get back to work.

Then strange things began to happen. At first he claimed it was just a technical problem. When Hyatt came into the office two days later, I expected to see another test, this time on 35mm film. But he didn't have one. He claimed he was having voltage problems at his studio and the lights would flicker every time he began to shoot a scene. It didn't sound like a serious obstacle, but when he made the same claim two more times, the last with a very serious look on his face. He told me he may have a ghost in his studio. I just took it as a dry humor joke and told him to give it another try. Three days later he was still insisting that the flickering lights were making it impossible for him to animate. He was now positive: a ghost was in his studio that for some reason didn't want the scene to be shot. I was learning that a lot of the people in the special effects scene were a bit quirky, but this was absurd. I told him to just go back and try again.

It got weirder. Another two days passed before he came in, this time with a frustrated look because not only was the ghost not allowing him to proceed but he had consulted his Ouija board and was told that the ethereal forces in the beyond didn't want the film to be completed. "WHAT THE FUCK ? ? ?"

He pleaded that I come out to the studio and see for myself what was happening. He insisted I come at night so the ambient light that bled into his studio during the day wouldn't interfere with his artificial lighting. At 9PM that evening, I stood with Benveniste and Cichy, who I had brought along to be rational witnesses, to observe the paranormal events that Hyatt had been describing.

It was the first time I had been to the Quonset hut since we had rented it for him. There was a single 75-Watt light hanging by a chord from the ceiling and a mattress tossed on the ground in the corner. It was haphazardly covered by a dirty sheet and a blanket. What appeared to be a men's magazine peeked out from under the pillow. It reminded me of my days in the backroom of the Cabale. The camera and rear screen projector was set up in the middle of the room. To begin the demonstration, Hyatt turned on his filming lights and pulled the plug on the overhead light.

"OK, watch closely and you'll see the lights flicker"

I watched carefully for a minute. Nothing happened. Hyatt assured me the lights would start to flicker. Nothing happened.

"It doesn't seem you have any problem," I said.

"He won't do it while you're here" was his explanation, expecting me to accept that as being rational.

I maintained my calm but my mind was racing. I speculated that he was having some kind of mental problem brought on by anxiety or possibly drugs; though he didn't seem to be into the latter. It didn't matter. I knew I had to get him off the project, but I couldn't risk alarming him; the possibility existed that he might run off with or destroy the 'Satyr' monster or damage the equipment we were renting. I left the hut about eleven in the evening, telling him to give it another try, knowing full well that nothing would be forthcoming.

First thing the next morning, I drove out to Eagle Rock. When I walked in I saw Tom Sherman had already completed the miniature landscape of the exterior of Jerkoff's lab. A little wooden launching ramp that looked somewhat like a ski jump, sat just outside the lab's garage door. He explained that when the Flying Phallus blasted off, the ramp would guide it upward and on its way to the planet 'Porno.' Denis Muren was already busy setting up the camera and lighting so the scene could be shot later in the day. It was plain why Costa had pushed me to hire him. He had the whole place operating professionally.

Ton Sherman hard at work

I explained the Hyatt situation to him, hoping he could take over the 'Satyr' animation. He was familiar with Hyatt and didn't seem to be surprised. He assured me he could get started as soon as I delivered the puppet.

When I got back to the office, I consulted with Bill and we laid out a plan to get the puppet away from Hyatt. We would have Patty, our buxom secretary, give Hyatt a call and tell him he needed to come into the office tomorrow to sign some papers for his taxes. It didn't come as a surprise that he told her it wouldn't be convenient for him to come by until two in the afternoon. That was actually to our benefit, as it gave us plenty of time to coordinate the rest of the raid we were planning.

Bill arranged for a locksmith to accompany us the following day to Hyatt's Quonset hut. We arrived around noon, wanting to make sure we were ready to spring into action as soon as he left to go see Patty. While Lynn Rogers and the locksmith waited in a rented moving van in a nearby lot, Bill, Cichy and I crouched behind some bushes on Olympic Avenue that allowed us a view of the Quonset hut. Every ten minutes, Hyatt would come out of the studio, look up at the sky and glance at his watch, before returning inside to do who knows what. It sure wasn't trying to animate. Finally, around twenty to two, he came out, locked the door to the studio, and left to go into town for his appointment with Patty.

The minute he was out of sight, we sprang into action. Within minutes the locksmith had the lock picked. Nothing much had changed since I was in the room two nights earlier other than the men's magazine was now on top of the blanket, evidence that he was at least a normal "nutty" guy. I gingerly took the 'Satyr' monster off the animation stand and packed it in a small box. Rogers and Cichy loaded the film equipment into the rented truck. An hour later everything was in Eagle Rock. I told Muren to be mindful that Hyatt may try to get the monster back, so be careful.

To no ones surprise, Hyatt was already at my office when I arrived the next morning. Of course he knew what had transpired and was understandably distraught, pleading between tears to be put back on the project. We had spent a bundle shooting the live action on Flesh and contrary to what Benveniste kept saying, I was becoming aware that the effects were not going to be cheap. And then there were still the legal expenses due to the copyright infringement cases. Despite the fact that Mike Hyatt had done so much to help launch the film, there was no way I could humor him. He left the office muttering something about what the 'Ouiga' board had said to him about the film never being finished.

I didn't let the lawsuits, the Hyatt debacle and the piggy shuffle become anything more than irritations. Finances bored me. I didn't even like to look at our books and never did. I continued to make loops and features at a prodigious pace and have lots of fun while doing it. Recently, after wrapping a scene for the Harry Hopper movie we were shooting, both Walter and I fucked the two girls who had just finished doing a butt-to-butt scene sharing a double-ended eighteen-inch rubber dildo. Bill was having fun too. He continued to expand our distribution network and theatre empire. The latest addition was another mini house in Portland.

Graffitti had separated into two cliques: Bill, Jason and the theatre managers being one and my production crew and I, the other. All companies have cliques and it seemed harmless. So when Bill and I were going to fly to Caldwell, Idaho to check out a full sized theatre we were thinking of buying, Bill said he was going to bring Jason along. To maintain a balance, I added Walter. I still didn't question how Bill had bought a home and was driving a Rolls Royce; accepting that he knew how to work the financial system, but I didn't want myself to become thought of as a minor player in our company. One of our clients had been in Bill's office sucking up to him by asking him about his Rolls Royce, when I unexpectedly walked in. The guy looked at me and turned to Bill: "Who's this?" Bill had no choice but to say: "He's the one who makes the films."

Caldwell was a small one-horse town, so the plane landed us in Boise, only ten miles to the west. After renting a car, it was only minutes until we were entering Caldwell's town square. The Top Theatre stood prominently to the right, the biggest building in town. I was puzzled how it had ever managed to survive in such a small environment. Filling its four hundred seats had to be difficult. But for whatever reasons, it had now fallen on hard times and its owners were only asking forty grand and more than happy to accept a small down payment and carry a low monthly mortgage, to dump it on two young idiots from LA.

Bill believed sex would sell anywhere and he was right. Two weeks after we opened, we were doing good business. Thanks to Boise's city fathers who had banned pornography in their fair city, hundreds of its citizens who yearned for adult entertainment, gladly drove the ten miles to Caldwell to get it. And the little town of Caldwell was more than happy with the infusion of money that thanks to us, was coming their way.

Coming from a conservative Christian family, I was a bit stunned when Bill told me his parents had agreed to move out from Ohio to run the Top theatre. It would have been incomprehensible for me to ask my parents to work in a porno house. I couldn't even imagine having the gall to ask them. But indeed; his family did move out and the arrangement worked out fine. His dad ran the projectors and his mom sold the tickets.

Although I didn't have the strong hankering for a big house and fancy car like Bill had, I wasn't averse to it. I just need a little kick in the butt to get moving and appreciated Bill telling me we were doing well enough for me to look to buy a house. With his connections at our bank—he had become personal friends with its manager—he promised he could set something up to make it possible. It was hard for me to admit that I had a fear of authoritative figures, something I knew was there for reasons I didn't understand. I put bankers on pedestals and was ignorant of what they do. I was brought up to think they were doing me a favor by accepting my money, not the other way around. It was part of my German heritage: "obey your leaders" So why they would want to associate with Bill made no sense? But I liked the idea of owning a house and Judy and I began to look for something in Malibu.

As the weeks passed, I began to think that the vice had given up on tailing me. I had shot several films after finishing 'Flesh' and hadn't noticed any cars following behind for the last few weeks. Maybe I didn't have to 'piggy shuffle' anymore. But when Rogers noticed that a car, equipped with standard no-frill hubcaps—a dead give away that it was government owned—seemed to be following us, I came back to my senses and even began adding a bit more time to the shuffle. Then I began to notice, on more than one occasion, that a helicopter seemed to be hovering high overhead when I was on my way to a location. My paranoia bumped up a notch. It was probably nothing, but I decided to be prudent, so to make my van blend in with the thousands of other white vans on the street, repainted it from orange to white.

I liked a breeze blowing in my face when I drove, so I always kept the window down. Walter had run into Bob's Big Boy to fetch the models as Lynn and I waited outside in the parking lot, when the omni present sound of a helicopter about a half mile away hovering high above caught my attention. When I spotted it, I could see that it was holding its position. That struck me as odd. As soon as Cichy jumped in with the cast, we pulled out on to La Brea Avenue and with my hackles up, I made a point of keeping my eye on the side window mirror for a few seconds. Fifty yards behind me, a white, indistinct car pulled out from the curb and joined the flow of traffic. It made me nervous enough to go into a full 'piggy shuffle.' After doing the regular routine of alleys, amber lights and one-way streets, I hopped on to the eight lane 101 freeway and headed north. Our final location was to the south in Silver Lake, but I sensed the extra effort was advisable. Maintaining a tail on a busy freeway would be difficult for the vice and I became convinced that I had lost them. But then, in disbelief, I saw high above and a half-mile to the side, the same fucking helicopter. "This is ridiculous," I said to myself. The police department would never dedicate such extreme resources to follow a porn crew. It had to just be my imagination playing tricks on me." So after weaving around freeway traffic for ten more minutes, I was confident that no one could have possibly followed us and doubled back to Silver Lake.

Exiting the 101 at Glendale Boulevard, I traveled east over the Hollywood hills towards the San Fernando Valley. Our shoot was at one of Walter's ex Army buddies who had an apartment in the hills. As we waited at a stop sign at the corner of Glendale and Ventura Boulevard where I would be making a sharp right onto the street that went up the hill; a white car with two straight looking dudes pulled alongside. I looked over and we exchanged quick glances, but when they drove on straight down the road, I relaxed. It was nothing; I was smoking too much pot. I made the sharp right turn and headed up the hill to our location, but still took a few diversionary turns on the way up.

Cichy's army buddy lived in a house cantilevered on the downhill side of a narrow one-way street, so I parked in front as close as I could to the road's edge. I got out of the car, glanced down the street, and seeing no cars whatsoever, followed Cichy along with my cast down a short flight of stairs into the house. While Walter introduced me to his buddy who began to show me around, Lynn got busy unloading the van. On his third trip up and down the stairs he told me in an apprehensive voice: "the guys in the white car just drove past." I was incredulous!

I walked out to the street and looked up and down, but saw nothing. Opposite our location and further up the hill, were a lot of trees and bushes where someone could hide. I looked hard but didn't see anything. The whole thing was probably nothing, but I decided to walk down the street where I saw a cul-de-sac was carved into the side of the hill. When I got there I saw a single white car parked in the far right corner. It looked similar to the one that had pulled alongside us. It was unoccupied, so I moved closer to quickly inspect it. The first thing I noticed was the plain hubcaps. But then, when I peered through the side window, I saw radio equipment and other law enforcement items sitting on the front seat. The **"fucking cops"** were up on the hill spying on us with binoculars!

We would have to call the shoot off! My blood was boiling. It was a hot day and I don't handle heat well; it makes me irritable. When I got back to the front of the house, I turned and looked up the hill. With a menacing stare on my face, I shouted as loud as I could at the bushes: "Why don't you fucking piggies leave us alone?"

I stormed inside and told Lynn to pack everything up and told the cast that I would reschedule them in a day or two.

Serious problems with the law in regards to producing and distributing porn, had yet to materialize in California, but in Texas, things were already happening. Mike d'Gostin almost got caught in a federal sting operation when he was on his way to drop off a shipment of our films to the Artex theatre in Dallas. Only hours before he arrived, there had been a raid by the FBI. Bob Thetford was on the phone a few days later, bragging to Bill, how his lawyer, 'Super Jew,' had the theatre back up and running within hours.

During the phone call, Bill had made a casual mention that we were thinking of shooting in 35mm. Bill saw it as a bridge to making mainstream films. His remark earned him an unexpected and unpleasant visit. Thetford and his goon, 'mini dick' Carl Musik, were in Bill's office two days later, holding a gun to his mouth as Bob explained that Artex relied on getting our 16mm product and we would therefore keep supplying it to them or there would be consequences.

Bill related the story to me when I got back to the office. He seemed to be as much thrilled as frightened. It was a little taste of a real gangster experience. It wasn't surprising to me when he added, that after pulling the gun away from his mouth, Bob told him that as punishment, we should no longer consider ourselves partners in the Cine Arts theatre on Hollywood Blvd. The idea that we had been strong-armed didn't sit well with me, but I was a pussy lover and a pussy when it came to violence. We would do just fine without The Cine Arts theatre and while 'Flesh' was still being worked on, I couldn't see any chance of shooting in 35mm anyway.

Porn kingpin arraigned in death plot

Probably to make sure Bill was sufficiently intimidated, Thetford called Bill a few weeks later to brag how he had shoved 'Super Jew' out of a helicopter for allowing the raid. I doubted that the story was true, but when I read an article several years later, that appeared in the Dallas Morning News on May 9, 1980, there was little doubt that Thetford was a dangerous psychopath. An investigation by the IRS, that exposed that the Arex theatres were grossing multimillion dollars during the period we were supplying it with product, explained why he was so set on when Bill suggested we might be getting out of 16mm. It was making him a fortune. The article went on to say, that when Thetford realized he was being investigated, he had Carl and a hired hitman known as the 'Arm,' take a troublesome employee who he was afraid couldn't handle the heat, and after strangling him with piano wire dumping him off a bridge along Interstate 10 in St. Charles Parish, Louisiana.

70

BUSTED

I took Bill's advice and found a beautiful home for Judy and me. Douglas Trumble, the effects genius behind, '2001, A Space Odyssey,' had built a beautiful modest sized A-frame that sat atop the Santa Monica Mountains on Fernwood Drive above Topanga Canyon. It had a 360-degree view of the ocean, valley and downtown LA. It even came with a small free form swimming pool. It was an exceptional find for eighty thousand dollars. Bill said with his connection at the bank, there would be no problem getting the mortgage approved when we went to the bank on Monday; so I had Rogers help me move some of our furniture out of the Edgewood Towers apartment and into our new house so Judy and I could sleep there over the weekend. I didn't bother getting permission from Trumble, the house was going to be ours by the end of the week, so who cared. We threw down sleeping bags on the lush thick carpet in the living room and gazed out the all glass front wall at the myriad stars twinkling brightly against the jet-black sky. Not even the remotest sound of civilization could be heard. It was Nirvana.

On Monday I went into the office expecting to go to the bank, but got some distressing news instead. Fleishman had called to tell Bill that we were about to be arrested within a day. My little out-burst outside the Silver Lake location had spurred them to action. It was only because of Fleishman's mole in the Los Angeles Police department, that we were able to get a heads up.

The thought of being cuffed and hauled off to jail didn't sit well with either of us. But if they couldn't find us, they couldn't bust us, so we decided to split town and mull over our options. Early in the evening, Bill and I rendezvoused at my parent's small apartment at the Oakwood apartment complex on 2nd and Virgil, where they had lived ever since my father retired from the army and had taken a job teaching dentistry at USC. Since he started dating my sister, Bill was a familiar visitor to the apartment.

Not wanting to leave Judy alone to have to deal with the cops if they came to pick me up, I brought her along, hoping my parents would agree to let her stay for a few days while I was on the lamb. They were both in their late fifties and had no clue what was going on; no one in our family had ever been busted for anything. My mother had grown to like Bill, who was treating her favorite daughter very generously, so I sensed rather than jeopardize Nancy's relationship with him, she grudgingly agreed to let Judy, who she had never given any indication that she was overly fond of, stay for a day or two.

Bill and I left immediately and drove to Palm Springs, arriving there around eleven in the evening. After checking into a motel, we were too tired and stressed to do anything but crash. In the morning we got in touch with Stanley Fleishman. As would be expected, he told us not to worry. He was going to have one of his hot young attorney's, John Weston, handle our case. He then passed the phone over to John who informed us that the warrant would stay in effect until we were arrested. We would have to turn ourselves in, but he would try to have us booked in front of a judge and thereby avoid the humiliation of a police booking.

We were so cocky and self-assured, that playing the role of gangsters was actually fun. After checking in with Weston after we returned to LA, we were prepared to go downtown to give ourselves up in front of a judge. But John had more bad news. Somehow the vice had found out what we were trying to do and would have plain cloths cops stationed in front of the courthouse ready to intercept us when we tried to enter.

This was becoming comical and we decided to play along with their little cat and mouse game. Before going to the courthouse, we stopped at Western Costumes, a three-story warehouse on Melrose Avenue near Paramount Studios, and rented two priest's frocks. Once downtown near the courthouse, we donned the frocks and were ready to rumble. No cop would dare to stop a priest without strong evidence. Sure enough, as we approached, standing at the base of the steps on Temple Street were two plainclothes cops struggling to look casual. Bill and I, hunched over in typical holy postures, passed right by them and trudged up the long rise of stairs so we could enter the courthouse through its gargantuan doors that were meant to make the common man feel like a bug in the presence of the justice system. It was serious but laughable at the same time; all this effort to stamp out the thrill of watching someone fuck or masturbate on film. We took the elevator to the third floor and when we stepped out; there was John Weston standing down the hall in front of the courtroom where we would be arraigned. He had more bad news.

Weston, a very good looking and vibrant young man, who was only a couple of years out of Berkeley law school, told us the cops had already got to the judge who was now refusing to accept our plea. We would have to go to the police station and be booked but would be spared some of the more unpleasant indignities such as the ass-hole inspection (not his term). Our bail had been set at twenty thousand each; a lot of money in a year when the average income was less than eleven thousand and a gallon of gas cost forty cents.

Before submitting ourselves to the cops, who were inside the courtroom awaiting our arrival, Bill went to a pay phone down the hall and by using the Beverly Cinema (the formerly named Eros) as collateral, arranged for bail with the Glassman Brothers Bail Bond Company. As far as I knew, Bill had never been arrested, so I was impressed that he seemed to have an innate knowledge of how to handle these things. The bond, which we would not recoup, would cost us ten percent, or four grand.

It was time to meet the two *"fucking piggies."* Martin, tall and cocky, was an oakie from Arkansas, and Brust, several inches shorter with a graying crew cut, was a straight arrow marine type. Sarcastically, he joked how smart I had been to repaint my van from orange to white: "It made it a whole lot harder for us to follow you." Bill and I were then handcuffed behind the back and taken to the nearby Parker Center Police Station to be booked. After two hours in a small holding cell, thanks to Bill's foresight, we were back on the street.

The charges against us were pandering and conspiracy to commit oral copulation. The theory for pandering was based on the claim that we were soliciting girls to commit prostitution. The mundane charge of committing oral copulation; a misdemeanor punishable by a fifty-dollar fine, was enhanced by making it a conspiracy; a felony punishable by fifteen years in prison. Conspiracy, 288A in the penal code, states that telling someone to commit a misdemeanor is a felony. Since I told girls to give blowjobs, I was being charged as a conspirator.

Conspiracy was the tactic du jour to put an end to pornography. Previous attempts to have porn films proclaimed obscene and outside the community standard, consistently failed when juries ruled that they were more offended by the effort to overturn the First Amendment than they were of the depiction of sex on screen. The average American held free speech to be sacrosanct.

As soon as I got out of jail, I had to move my furniture out of the Trumble house and back into Edgewater Towers. Between bail, lawyer's fees and 'Flesh Gordon,' it was not going to be possible to go forward with buying a house. Having the cops know where I lived was making me feel uncomfortable and since I had already notified Edgewater Towers that I was going to vacate, Judy and I looked for a new place to live. We found a modest two-bedroom house at the end of Monument Street in Pacific Palisades. The street ran along the north edge of the city and the house's back yard abutted the wilderness of the Temescal Gateway Park. Howls from packs of coyotes were a nightly occurrence. It wasn't that much of a step down from where we would have lived if I hadn't been busted.

There was no need for the Eagle Rock crew to know about the bust, it might freak them out and affect their work. Under Muren's guidance, progress was being made on many fronts. He had replaced Hyatt with Dave Allen, a very respected young animator. But for unknown reasons, Allen quit on him after one week and he had to replace him with Bob Maine and Jim Auppearl. They were already turning out shots when I dropped in. Muren asked for my approval to hire Joe Musso to design and animate a computerized scene of Amora's Swan ship sailing through the astrological constellations. I had no idea, at the time, that it would be the first use of computer animation in a film. 'Flesh Gordon' was about to be a pioneer. He also wanted to hire a twenty year old named, Joe Viskocil, to handle the pyrotechnic work. His job would be to provide fiery exhausts coming out of the various rocket ships and blowing up Wang's castle. I told him to go ahead.

Despite being busted, it was imperative that I keep producing loops and features and that Bill keep our theatres open and operating profitably. I kept pushing Benveniste to show me his rough cut so we could get a read on how much more work needed to be done. He steadfastly resisted. I didn't want to push too hard, but I was disturbed by the fact that when I dropped in he often seemed to be screening films or playing with Terren, his two year old kid, who he often brought to work. He insisted; "not to worry, things were going fine, he did most of his work late at night."

Two weeks after the bust, Joseph P. Bush, the Los Angeles District Attorney, dropped Bill from the case since he wasn't directly involved in the production of our films. I would be facing the charges alone, which wasn't bad in the sense that it would save Graffitti some legal costs. Weston was confident that he could tie the case up in the courts for a long time and hope things would have cooled down by then. I couldn't get myself too bent-out-of-shape over the situation, since in my heart, I felt I had done nothing wrong. I may have been naive, but I just couldn't imagine that in the era of free love, I could go to jail for making sex movies. I put the bust out of my mind and went right back to work shooting another Harry Hopper feature.

Bill and I were a successful partnership, but not close personally, even that he was living with my sister. Our ultimate goals were different. He wanted to become a movie tycoon and a star and I wanted to maintain the sexual 'Garden of Eden' I had created for myself. When he asked me to come to a new club called the 'Comedy Store' to talk with it's owner, Sammy Shore, about shooting some of the acts for a TV pilot, I was against the idea even before I got there. I wanted to stay emerged in the sex business and the 'Comedy Store' idea could threaten that. In fact, it was a damn good idea and may well have led to something very lucrative, but keeping my dick happy was more important to me than money.

Bill became a regular at the Comedy Store and befriended many of the Comedians. While still living with my sister, who was as clueless about him as I was, he started dating Sammy Shore's daughter, Mitzi, and also finagled his way into a date with Rachel Welch, who was probably impressed by the fact that he drove a Rolls Royce. In an interview he gave to a magazine, he boasted how he took her to a 'McDonald's' for dinner, where according to him, she jumped out of the car and called a cab to take her home.

The success of our films and Bill's hobnobbing with the Hollywood crowd, caught the attention of the entertainment industry's current gossip diva, Joyce Haber, who wrote a weekly column for the LA Times. She called our office to request an interview with Bill. He was more than thrilled with the prospect of gaining notoriety in a nationally renowned newspaper. The interview was conducted over a period of three weeks.

Haber's interview, that included a headshot of Bill, appeared on August 27, 1972 in the LA Times under the headline, "DISHING THE DIRT WITH THE BOY KING OF PORNO." It began with a quote from Bill expressing his disdain for Welch:

"Raquel Welch is the most untalented actress on the screen. I wouldn't even use her in skin flicks, she's so bad. I've been hung up on Barbra Streisand for years. I'm nothing right now. She wouldn't look at me. Do you know her? Do you think you can help me meet her?"

Haber followed the quote with her opening commentary:

"Much as it may seem so, this is not a case history from Henry Havelock Ellis' pioneering "Studies in the Psychology of Sex," It is rather the declamation of a neurotic, eager young film-maker who is reluctant to wear the title of filmdom's once and present King of Pornography. Bill Osco would have delighted Ellis as he would delight any student of shrink today."

Throughout the rest of the interview, Bill waxed about the millions of dollars our films had grossed and how his inevitable rise to the pinnacle of Hollywood's elite could not be stopped. Haber had no way of knowing that all of the numbers Bill quoted her were exaggerated at least ten fold. But for that matter, Bill understood that was what she wanted to hear so he gave it to her. When she called back a week later, to ask if he had something really controversial he could toss her way, he gave her:

"Hitler is one of my idols. He came closet to conquering the whole world. He had more power than anyone."

Haber probably didn't even know I existed. For that matter, it was just as well that I didn't provide the DA with any more information than he didn't already have. Other than having to explain to our Jewish lawyers that Bill's comments about Hitler were meaningless babble (he had no clue about the atrocities committed under Hitler) we were both pleased with his interview: all publicity is good publicity.

Judy's brother, Danny, had become bored doing the mundane tasks required of an assistant editor, so he asked if I would mind if he went to work as Bill's assistant where his college degree in business could be put to better use than what I had him doing. I smarted a bit that he was changing loyalties, but told him to go for it.

A perk of the job was an invite to join Bill and Jason on their frequent nightly cruises around the streets of Beverly Hills and Hollywood in his Silver Shadow. It would provide me a glimpse into Bill's private, and somewhat secret, personal life. As Danny told it; Bill would pull up next to a girl standing on the curb, roll down his window and ask: "Do you want to take a ride? "If the girl hesitated, which was more often than not, he followed with: "Do you know who I am?" On one occasion he happened upon his dream girl, Barbara Streisand, who was stopped at a light on Rodeo Drive. His pick-up line was rebuffed with a rude: "Go fuck yourself!"

Whether Bill had an actual 'sex life,' I wasn't sure. It seemed that he was more of a stalker than a Romeo. I wasn't even sure he actually liked girls. To be sure, mine and Judy's was way out there as well. An open marriage allowed for an abundance of sexual experiences with different partners, but it also required foregoing any deep romantic attachment. We were both teenagers at heart, but as a female, she sometimes didn't realize that a sexual affair was not a romance. I knew it was an ego trip for a guy to have sex with a stripper and at times I had to deal with her emotional trauma when an affair broke up. My affairs had no such problem. They were about having strange sex. She was my real partner and I expected to stay with her.

My goal, if I had one, was difficult to describe because I didn't know what it was. I needed a mental challenge and for that I had 'Flesh Gordon,' and I also needed to sate myself with hedonistic pleasure for which I had the loops and 'Harry Hopper' movies. They embedded me in an exciting sexual environment that quite often paid physical rewards. Of course I needed to make money and for that I had Bill. Where it would lead at the end of the day, I had no idea. For now, I would just keep making porn films and stay on Benveniste to finish Flesh Gordon and hopefully escape my legal problems at the end of the day.

That is not to say that I didn't see a nice payday at the end of the rainbow. It would come in due time. Bill and I were a perfect fit. I loved making the movies and he loved selling them. He was good at it. He had built a client list of twenty-five theatres that bought every 'Harry Hopper' I produced for a thousand dollars. For the time being, that was only one every ten days, but since the theatres changed their shows every week, they bought features from other producers when ours weren't available. When I could get to the point where I had one film in preproduction, another in production, a third in the editing room and a fourth coming out of the lab ready to be sold, Graffitti could provide them all their films. We would have a guaranteed gross of twenty-five grand a week. With the expected bonanza once Flesh Gordon was released, even with our legal problems, the future looked sterling.

71

TIME TO GET TOUGH

Under Denis Muren's supervision, effects were being completed in a timely manner and Danforth had almost completed all the matt paintings that we needed. My pestering Benveniste to show me what progress he had made on the rough cut, couldn't get him to budge. I would be told that he was getting close but just needed a few more weeks before it would be ready. The credibility points he had earned with 'Mona' earned him some leeway so I didn't aggressively push him even though I was becoming irritated that he often spent his time watching movies or playing with his son who he averred "should never hear the word no."

At her husband's insistance, a very attractive girl with long black hair and a trim sexy body took the starring role in a 'Harry Hopper' film to be called 'Miss Erotica.' It excited husbands to know that they were married to a woman who was a desired sex object. I was guilty of this myself. It was understood that the two of them would perform together but as was often the case, husbands found it more difficult to perform than they had imagined. Linda's husband, Derek, was such a case. I wasn't disappointed. His wife turned me on and I suggested I stand in for him just to do a few insertion close ups. After pondering for a moment, he turned to his wife and asked how she felt about that. He seemed to be a bit shocked when she said she was OK with it. Before any minds changed, I was going down on her to get myself aroused. Her pussy remained dry. She was just doing a job. As soon as I was ready, I entered her and was ready to cum within two minutes. Lynn filmed the money shot as I pulled out. Her husband, though not appearing to be angry, remained dour for the rest of the day. Having to explain to his wife why he couldn't get it up had to be troubling. Not all women understood that hardons didn't happen automatically. It was embarrassing for a man to explain that to them.

For the upcoming Christmas season, I asked Cichy to write a 'Harry Hopper' script with a holiday theme. He came up with one of his oddball stories that involved Santa Clause and a sex scene in the snow. I decided to shoot the film in Big Bear, a nearby ski resort in the San Bernardino Mountains. Driving the hundred miles, back and forth each day, between LA and Big Bear would be impractical, so we rented a small house in Big Bear to lodge the crew and cast. It would assure that we got an early start each morning and hopefully an orgy with the girls in the evening.

I was at Irv Sofsky's agency paging through his book of models, when Linda and her husband walked in. He had a request. He begged me to book the two of them again; promising me that he had overcome his anxiety problem and that they had successfully done several scenes together without a problem. She was a doll and feeling somewhat bad that I had fucked his wife when I knew he really didn't want me to, I booked them to make up for his bad day.

The 'Big Bear' shoot didn't start off well. I had hired Howard Neil, one of the more dependable studs in the business, to have sex in the snow with an attractive girl who had a natural two-tone bush, light brown with a tuff of white thrown in. She was on her knees in the doggy position waiting for Howard to fuck her, but for some unknown reason he was having an attitude problem and whispered for me to step in and do his insertion shots. She couldn't be faulted for having a bone dry pussy after being so rudely rejected and since everyone wanted to get out of the cold, I didn't prolong the scene any longer than necessary, ejaculating after a few thrusts.

The overnight orgy never materialized, the two-toned pubic hair girl, still upset by Howard Neil's rejection, made short work of my overtures and I was left to sleep alone in the bunk beneath her, where I quietly jacked off before falling asleep. The next morning there were more problems. One of the girls I had booked couldn't stay in Big Bear overnight and was going to drive up in the morning, but Irv Sofsky called to let me know she had canceled. "Don't worry," he told me. He had another girl who would fit the part perfectly and his assistant would drive her to Big Bear. She would be on the set within two hours. I had no choice but to trust his judgment and told him to bring her up.

Meanwhile, I shot the scene with Linda and her hubby, who, true to his word, was able to perform, if not with zest, at least adequately. I was relieved, because suggesting another stand-in scene would not be an option. Shortly after they finished, my new girl arrived. Her name, Patty, perfectly fitted her cute spunky Irish face and big perky tits. She reminded me of a bar maid that you might expect to find in a pub. Her scene called for her to be fucked on the staircase leading to the beds in the loft. For some reason, finding stiff dicks on this shoot was becoming a problem; so not being all that unhappy about it, I had her spread her legs so I could warm her up with my tongue and push my dick into her vagina. Again, I was in and out quickly, depositing the money shot on her tits.

After one final scene shot late in the evening in a small hot closet that made erections near impossible and only a substitution shot provided by Lynn 'Buffalo' Rogers, brought the scene to a climax, it was time to wrap. Though the last model said she enjoyed all those guys trying to fuck her, I didn't feel very good about the film; too many substitution scenes do not make for a convincing porn movie. Maybe the fact that it was the 13th 'Harry Hopper' movie had something to do with it.

The deluge of invoices pouring in from LA Scientific for the parts Costa was having machined for his optical printer and Benveniste continuing to refuse to show anyone the rough cut of 'Flesh Gordon,' was causing friction between Bill and I. Benveniste was already on his shit list for 'Hollywood Blue' and Costa was close to being added as well. The invoices weren't cheap. Bill had plans for the money that he felt he was being deprived of by their cavalier use of Graffitti's bank account. He didn't say anything to me, but I could feel he felt I was somewhat responsible.

Finally, on a Monday morning in mid March of 1973, Benveniste had some very good news. He told me that his rough cut was ready for screening. It had been one and a half years since we had begun the project and this was indeed good news. He warned me that there was a lot of special effects footage still missing, which he had inserted black slugs to delineate the places where they would eventually be cut in, but enough of the film was assembled to give us a good idea of what we had. Bill set up a screening for Friday evening in the auditorium of the Pacific Film lab on La Brea.

It was shaping up to be an excellent week. Thanks to another faltering penis, I had the opportunity to do stand in work with an oriental girl whose wet pussy made me so hot, that after the money shot, I reinserted and could barely force myself to withdraw so we could get back to work. The little smile she gave me as I pulled out let me know she had enjoyed being appreciated. And just as thrilling, when her film was ready for release, Graffitti would have reached its goal of producing a feature each week. I even mentioned to Judy that we could start shopping for a house again.

Over two hundred people showed up on Friday for the screening. I was pleasantly surprised to see how much interest there was in 'Flesh Gordon.' Sy Katz, had been talking it up and many of his clients were in the audience. He even brought a PR agent along so work could begin promoting the film. Several of the lawyers from Fleishman's office came. Of course all the effects people, including Mike Minor, who was now back in LA, were in attendance. Much of the cast and their friends were on hand. The room was buzzing with excitement. I took a seat with Judy and Cichy in the last row so I could judge the audience's reaction. Seated a few rows ahead was Bill, wearing his large black fur coat and sunglasses, accompanied by my sister and Jason.

Each segment of action in a rough cut is held together with tape perforated on its edges so the projector can feed the film through its gate. The sound track is similarly constructed, but on an independent reel. A special projector is required that can run both reels simultaneously and in sync. We could only hope that none of the taped joints would break and screw up the screening. Benveniste skirted in and out of the projection room like a water bug to make sure everything was in order. I had no idea what to expect. Not withstanding the law suites incurred by his illegal use of copyrighted material, he had always come through. Finally the lights dimmed, the murmur in the audience quieted, and the film began to roll.

Within a minute, a pall hung over the room. There was dead silence, not even a cough or a snicker. A cold sweat began to collect across my brow. Benveniste, seated a few seats to my left, seemed to be oblivious to it all, his perpetual impish grin still plastered on his face. The editing lacked continuity and drama; there were few close-ups or reaction shots, the editing was amateurish and clumsy. The effects that had been completed were impressive, but the number of black slugs was overwhelming. Not one animation scene was even close to completion.

When the lights came up, most people filed out without saying much. Sy Katz tried to be optimistic, but I knew it was just his nature. Mike Minor made a snide, "I told you so," remark. Bill didn't say much. What was there to say? After a year and a half and the expenditure of most of our money, there was little to show. I didn't say much either, but I knew what I had to do. When the crowd emptied the auditorium, I told Benveniste we should meet tomorrow for breakfast at the Old World Restaurant up on Sunset Boulevard. He agreed. He seemed to think there was not much of a problem.

The Old World was located across the street from Tower Records and within sight of the Whiskey a Go Go. Its European theme with wood floors and beamed ceilings made it popular with the Hollywood crowd and one of my favorite restaurants. Their mouth-watering one-pound cheeseburger on a wheat bun had no match. But I wasn't there for gastronomic pleasure. It was 8:30 in the morning and Benveniste was not due to show up until nine. I needed time to get my thoughts together before he arrived. The restaurant was sparsely occupied when Jim Brown, the hall-of-fame football player, came in and took a table not far from where I was sitting. After taking a quick look at the menu, he bellowed "waiter" in a stentorian voice that made it clear he didn't want to wait. I used it as inspiration for the commanding presence that I would need for my upcoming task.

Almost to be expected, Benveniste showed up fifteen minutes late. As he sat down, I thought to myself what a cocky little prick he had become. He ordered a couple of eggs over -easy and started to nonchalantly discuss last night's screening. He was clueless that it was a disaster. We talked in vague generalities until our food arrived. He had begun to think of himself as indispensable, but I was no longer asleep at the wheel. I had let the 'Hollywood Blue' situation and the law suits slide, but no more. 'Flesh Gordon' had become too big for him; the complexity of the special effects and editing more than he could handle. Maybe it was the cocaine he was using or the time he spent doting over his kid. I didn't care.

As he was about to shovel a fork full of eggs into his mouth, I broke the news to him that he was being fired. The fork dropped to his plate and he gaped at me with an incredulous look. His mouth remained open and a bit of egg yolk dripped onto his chin. When he regained his composure, he tried to convince me that the film was almost finished. He had to think I was stupid. I told him at best it was months away, and likely more. Finally realizing his pleas were falling on deaf ears, he got up and left the restaurant, his cold uneaten eggs still on the table. I felt relieved that my unpleasant task was behind me and while I mulled over what my next steps should be, calmly finished my breakfast. After I paid the bill, I headed down to our office, just a mile away.

Five minutes later I was parking my van on Genoa Street, which ran alongside our office building. I wanted to make sure that there was nothing Benveniste could do to spite us. The early morning meant there were no pedestrians and only sparse traffic on Melrose as I walked around the corner and took the few steps to my office's front door. I fumbled for a moment looking for the right key to open the mirrored glass doors. Just as I found it, I noticed a car being reflected behind me pulling up to the curb.

About to insert the key I heard: "Howie Ziehm?"

I turned to see two men stepping out of the car, neither of who I instantly recognized. Since they had used my nickname, I thought it was a friend, but the moment I saw the cheap tell-tale hubcaps, I knew differently. Brust stepped out of the car and onto the sidewalk. A split second later, Martin's head popped up from the driver's side. He hustled around the rear of the car to join his officious looking partner. The two stood menacingly in front of me.

With a deadpan look and hard voice Brust spoke: "We have a warrant here for your arrest and a search warrant to search your office and vaults."

My pulse shot up and I felt sick.

I meekly stammered: "Let me look at the warrant."

He stuffed it into my hands and before I could read it said sternly: "Are you gonna open the door or do we have to smash it in?"

I could see they were almost biting at the bit to have an excuse to be violent, so rather that affording them more of a thrill than they were already enjoying, I handed Brust the keys so he could open the door. A black and white suddenly pulled up and two officers jumped out to assist in the raid. While Martin and Brust were fiddling with the keys, I was able to quickly scan the warrant. Along with myself; Cichy, Rogers and our soundman, John Saundersm were also listed. Osco was not named. As soon as the door was opened, Brust turned to me and cuffed my wrists tightly behind my back and then put me in the back of their car. The warrant only made a vague reference to a girl with large breasts, so as I sat there, it was unclear to me what they hoped to find.

I tried to inventory in my mind what was inside. Unfortunately, the double walls with a foot and a half space between them that I had built, both upstairs and down stairs, to be used as a secret storage area for our films, had rarely been used. The cops were going to find a lot. Upstairs in the editing room they would find the features we were currently working on, including the one with the hot oriental, and downstairs, in Bill's office, they would find the prints that he was about to ship. Because of the screening the night before, I had the work print of Flesh Gordon still in the van, but all the out takes remained on the second floor by the editing table.

Forty-five minutes later, Martin and Brust came out of our office and got back into their car. As we drove away, I could see the uniformed cops coming out of the office with boxes full of film. In an attempt to irritate me, the two pigs chuckled as they badgered me with snide remarks as we drove downtown. Their efforts had little effect, as my mind was racing to analyze the situation. What were the charges this time? Did they know the van was parked on Genoa and that it was loaded with our expensive film equipment? What if they found the 'dog' film stored in the vault? It had been shot in the heat of the fervor that anything goes, but despite knowing it was a mistake to keep the negative, I had done just that. It could possibly lead to a charge of conspiracy to commit bestiality and I didn't need that! And of course, how was I was going to get bailed out?

Just before noon, we pulled into the underground parking lot beneath the eight-story Parker Center police department, located in downtown LA. I was removed from the car and taken by elevator several floors up to a brightly lit room painted in a color that was a blend of piss yellow and vomit green. The fluorescent lighting gave the room a mind-numbing haze. A cop was sitting behind the single desk in the room and after Martin and Brust signed me in, I was taken down the hall and placed in a small eight by ten foot holding cell, where to my surprise; Lynn Rogers and Walter Cichy were already incarcerated.

They were both stressed out. Martin and Brust had arrested them at their homes at five in the morning and then drove them around town for several hours with their wrists tightly cuffed behind their backs. They told me that the cops tried to entice them into turning states evidence against me, by offering to go light on them if they agreed. I wasn't surprised when they told me that they didn't give the cops anything. It didn't need to be said, but I assured them Graffiiti would cover all their legal expenses. Weird John Saunders, so called because he liked to set up in a closet and peek at the action through a crack in the door left ajar, had fortunately avoided arrest, because he was out of town. But the warrant for his arrest would remain active.

Our cage was unlocked a half hour later so we could be taken back to the front room and made to stand up against the wall for ass-hole inspections and photographs. There was a short waiting period until the ass-hole checker could come into the room and check our orifices for hidden weapons—or something. How humiliating. But I knew I would be in for some derisive laughs if they saw the little mesh g-string I was wearing when I lowered my pants. The cop sitting at the little table in front of us was busy doing paperwork, so it gave me time to surreptitiously work my hand beneath my pants and snap the g-string's waist band. Without him noticing, I managed to pull it up between my butt crack and drop it on the floor behind me. A little kick to the side made sure it wouldn't be noticed until we were taken back to our cell. I was in no mood to look sexy.

I use my constitutionally guaranteed phone call to try and reach Osco. It was just past Saturday noon and I hoped he would still be at home. Thankfully he was. Bail was again twenty grand each; sixty to spring the three of us and twenty more if they picked up Saunders. Again Bill knew just what to do. He headed downtown to Glasser Brothers Bail Bonds and wrote them a check from Graffitti for six thousand bucks, putting his house on Tower Road in Beverly Hills up as collateral. By mid afternoon we were back on the streets.

The cops had neglected to list on the warrant, our van and all the camera equipment inside. It was still parked on Genoa street and in case they still had plans to inflict more damage, I didn't want to lead them to it by showing up to drive it away. Instead, I had my brother-in-law, Danny, case the area and move it when he was sure no one was watching. The equipment had to be available to shoot another film after things calmed down. We still had to make money.

On Sunday morning, I dropped by the Seward Street vaults to see what damage, if any, had been done. The warrant was incredibly broad, a girl with "big breasts" could mean almost anything. Upon entering, I walked quietly down the hallway until I came to the middle corridor where our vault was. Its door was wide open but no one was standing guard outside. Then I heard voices coming from around the corner at the end of the hall. I suspected it was part of the search team taking a break. No one would see me if I walked down the hall and took a quick look into the vault. My assessment had to be quick. I didn't want to take a chance of being confronted by them. On top of my list was the negative to the *'dog'* loop. I gave a sigh of relief when I saw the shelf that held it hadn't been disturbed and nothing else for that matter. I was tempted to dash in and remove it, but thought better; if they caught me taking something out they would definitely want to see what it was and I could be charged with tampering with evidence. It was too risky.

I quickly split before anyone noticed me and drove over to Jason William's house, a modest duplex situated on the side of one of the steep ravines that empties into Laurel Canyon. He had generously agreed to let us use it as a temporary command center until we could get our feet back on the ground.

Jason had high-hopes that a successful 'Flesh Gordon' would launch his acting career, so he was willing to do all he could to keep Graffiitti above ground until we could finish the film. Despite the fiasco at the Friday night screening, he still had faith in the picture. After I related my experience at the vault, he offered to go back down with me and see if we could remove the *'dog'* loop. On the way we devised a plan. After we entered the vaults, he would keep out of sight while I went down the hall to keep the cops distracted by indulging them in conversation. The vaults were kept at a low temperature to help preserve the films in storage and I found the three cops huddled together like they were ice fishing. Just being beat cops, they weren't unfriendly and told me they were sitting in the corner because it was the warmest place they could find. I still didn't know what the specific film or action was that had led to the bust, but they didn't know either and probably wouldn't have told me anything even if they did. While I conversed with the officers, I saw Jason enter the vault and pop out a moment later, signaling that the mission had been accomplished. I gave the cops a sympathetic good-bye and left the building relieved that I might have just avoided one additional charge.

72

THEY WANTED TO KILL FLESH

John Weston had again been assigned by Stanley Fleishman to handle our case and when we met with him on Monday morning, explained that we were all being charged with pandering and conspiracy to commit oral copulation. The charges stemmed from the 'Big Bear' shoot. It was ridiculous to charge my crew, but the cops were well aware that it would cost us a pretty penny just to bail them out and pay for their legal expenses, even though in all likelihood, all charges against them would eventually be dropped. Much to my surprise and dismay, I was also being charged with statutory rape!

Little Irish Patty, the last minute substitution from Irv Sofsky's office, was only fifteen years old. As an agent, it had been Sofsky's responsibility to check her I. D. When I talked to him later, he claimed he had done so and it showed her to be eighteen. I believed him. No one was fool enough to book anyone under age on purpose. Moreover, she was married and had a mature looking face and demeanor. All of which gave no reason to doubt that she was legal. Because of Patty, Sofsky had also been busted, but in a separate case not associated with mine.

As usual, Weston assured me that he could beat the case, though hyperbole, it still felt good to hear it. I now personally had two pending felony cases and Graffitti still had three pending civil cases: 'Father Filas, Ravi Shankar and the defunct band.' We were already twenty grand in debt to the Fleishman law firm from the prior cases and it was now about to get much larger. Since we had been making payments on a regular basis, they were willing to handle the new case for several points in 'Flesh Gordon.' Evidently, even after the screening debacle, they saw the film as having a big potential. My freedom was in their hands. Options were not in the cards.

By Tuesday the cops had finished rummaging through our film vault and I went over to assess the damage. The situation had changed drastically from Sunday when I only had a chance to peek in. Footage was all over the floor. It took several minutes to get a sense of what had been confiscated. I saw that the negative and sound tracks of the last 'Harry Hopper,' the one with the beautiful oriental girl, was missing. We had five grand invested in that film and had yet to even strike a work print. But when I saw that the racks that held the negative to 'Flesh Gordon' had been cleaned off, my stomach fell to the floor. There was no warrant or justification to take that negative. I quickly scanned the room hoping that maybe the boxes had been placed somewhere else in the vault. They hadn't. Fucking pigs!! Their putative attempt to find footage pertaining to the girl with bit tits was just a ruse used to bring us down.

Martin and Brust were not dumb; they knew full well that the loss of the 'Flesh Gordon' negative could destroy Graffitti Productions and might even spell a ticket to jail for me. Bill was waiting at Jason's house for me to return and apprise him of the damage. There wasn't much to say other than we needed to get the 'Flesh Gordon' negative back or we were toast.

On Wednesday morning, Cichy, Rogers and I were to be arraigned. We

Judge Noah Canon

met Weston outside the courthouse and followed him into a courtroom presided over by one of the weirdest and most frightening people I had ever seen outside of a Halloween party. Judge Noah Canon looked like she had just come from an audition for a part in the 'Rocky Horror Picture Show.' Her long fingernails and lips were painted dark purple and a ring of equally dark mascara circled her eyes. Her cheeks were plastered with thick gaudy rouge.

When the bailiff called our case, we joined Weston, who was standing at the right side of a long table placed fifteen feet in front of the judge's bench. An assistant DA stood at the left side of the table. Weston began by stating: "Your honor, if you will agree, due to the nature of the charges, the DA and I have agreed to waive the reading of them to the court." A quick nod between Weston and the DA signaled that what had just been stated was true. This was highly unusual and several accused felons, who had been bussed in from county jail and were waiting in the docket for their turn to appear, asked in an incredulous whisper: "What'd you guys do?" I couldn't resist a cynical repost and whispered back: "A crime too heinous for human ears."

Judge Canon granted the request and Weston began to make a plea to have our bail reduced. Suddenly, a hot looking female, wearing a mini dress hiked halfway up her thighs, stepped forward. She said she was from the DA's office and was here to admonish the judge: "Your honor, our office strongly objects to any reduction of the bail and would like to point out that the witnesses have been threatened and are in fear of their lives."

Noah Cannon turned towards me and coldly stated; "Request for bail reduction denied." Continuing with a piercing stare: "If I hear one more mention of you intimidating witnesses, I'll send you away so long you won't see daylight again."

I was stunned and said nothing. At that time I had no clue whatsoever who the witnesses were and anyone who knew me understood that physically intimidating anyone was not my style. It was an absolute lie! The thought that this was the kind of game the city was going to play was unnerving.

That I had reason to be fearful of Judge Noah Canon was not an idle fantasy. An article that appeared on March 17, 1975 in Time Magazine, said it all:

Although her chambers at one time were done in shocking pink, Los Angeles Municipal Court Judge Noel Cannon often chose language that was decidedly blue. She once inquired in the vernacular whether guards conducting a search had looked up the rectum of a lawyer whom she had just jailed for contempt. On another occasion off the bench, she threatened to give a traffic policeman "a vasectomy with a .38." To round out her reputation, she sometimes heard cases with her pet Chihuahua in her lap, and for a while had a toy canary that punctuated lawyers' arguments with mechanical peeps. Few attorneys dared to pipe back publicly. So for twelve years Judge Cannon presided as a choice gossip topic in the L. A. bar.

But her increasing propensity to jail and dismiss defense attorneys for minor or nonexistent infractions led finally to an effort to spike Cannon. Last week a California judicial commission formally asked the state supreme court to remove the Stanford Law School graduate for willful misconduct and actions "prejudicial to the administration of justice."

Back at Weston's office, we discussed what had gone down. Again he told me not to worry. The next step would be a preliminary to be held in a few weeks, at which time the county would present its evidence, including its witnesses, to justify a trial. When I asked about getting our film back, especially 'Flesh Gordon,' he felt that he couldn't dedicate enough time right now to put sufficient pressure on the police to accomplish that task. He suggested that there were several attorneys around town who should be able to help us out. I could see that the Fleishman office felt we were into them far enough and didn't want to go any deeper. They couldn't be blamed.

The work on Flesh Gordon needed to continue. To halt the momentum that had been in place before the screening would be perilous. With Benveniste being fired, I approached Abbas Amin about taking his place. Could an Egyptian immigrant from a Muslim country understand the humor we were aiming for? His English was spotty at best. We all thought it was very funny when he asked Alice, our negative cutter out to lunch; "Alice . . . I think maybe I like invite you for sandwich beef?" I knew it would be a stretch, but he convinced me that it would not be a problem and equally important; agreed to work on deferment. In return, I gave him two points in the net profits of 'Flesh' and the right to act as our European agent when and if the film was completed. I knew absolutely nothing about foreign distribution and was actually miffed that he even wanted that. So he could make money while working for us on deferment, I also agreed, that on occasion, he could use our facility to edit other films. As a safety net, he would own the KEM Table if the film didn't get off the ground. Bill, who never liked Benveniste, was happy that I had made the decision to dump him and hire Abbas.

Our old office, now ravaged, was no longer a safe place to work. Until we could find another office, Jason Williams offered to let us move our editing equipment into his small apartment in Laurel Canyon. Another grand had to be spent just to hire an expert in moving KEM tables.

Word had leaked to the special effects crew about the bust and understandably Denis Muren had a look of concern when I drove out to Eagle Rock to make sure there were no problems. He and Tom Sherman wanted to know if their association with Graffitti put them in danger of being busted. I did my best to convince them that they had nothing to worry about. Not wanting to make matters worse, I made no mention that our negative was now in a property room at the Parker Center. I breathed a sigh of relief when I saw that their anxiety had waned by the time I left. They were a godsend for Graffitti, but I also knew that working for us was a godsend for them. The experience they were gaining would be invaluable later on in their careers.

Everything seemed to be copasetic when I left, but bottom line, if we didn't get the negative back from the police, 'Flesh Gordon' and Graffitti were finishied. Worse for me, jail might be in my future if my lawyers couldn't be paid. To get the negative back, we needed a lawyer who was a real bulldog. Bill spoke with several of our cohorts in the porn industry, and was told that Harry Hertzberg was the bulldog we were looking for. It was heartening that when Bill called him, he understood the exigency of our situatioGn. On the following day we were at his office, located in the Miracle Mile section of Wilshire Boulevard. He was in his early fifties, a bit portly and a fast talker. He got right to the point: "I can get your film back but it's going to be costly—five grand a week—up in front." There weren't any alternatives; we told him to get started.

Our bulldog attorney quickly got results. He called to let us know that he had hounded a judge into agreeing to hear our motion to have our confiscated film returned. At ten O'clock the following day, I sat with Harry in the courtroom waiting for the judge to come out of his chambers. Walter and Lynn, whose lives were also on the line, came along for support. Martin and Brust sat nearby with an attorney representing the city. Again, as seemed to be the sartorial standard for females working in the DA office, a cute babe wearing a short white mini dress and high heels came dancing into the room and began flirting with several male city attorneys who were also waiting for the judge. Surprise surprise, they liked sex too!

The judge arrived shortly after and the bailiff called the court to order. A few moments were used to deal with the extraneous matters that were before him, but then he turned his attention to our case.

Harry, dressed elegantly in a tailored gray suite with a vest that made him look very scholarly, began to make his arguments. But as the morning wore on, it seemed that they were falling on deaf ears. Judge Brown was a real ass-kisser when it came to the cops: they could do no wrong. It mattered not to him that the negative of 'Flesh Gordon' had nothing to do with "a girl with big breasts"—or that it was not even named in the warrant. He wasn't willing to give us the tiniest concession regarding its release.

After two weeks and ten thousand dollars, Harry's arguments continued to go nowhere. I tried to keep a positive attitude and believe at the end of the day we would prevail, but as the end of the third costly week began to approach, I couldn't help but wonder. The city seemed to have no problem paying for two cops, a city attorney and a judge, if it meant bringing us to our knees.

It was a Friday afternoon and the usual heat and smog was hanging over downtown as Harry, Walter, Lynn and I were slowly trudging up the Sixth Street hill to return to the courthouse, We had just had lunch at a small downtown café when for the first time, Harry expressed doubts that the city would budge. I was left totally depressed as we entered the large vacuous courtroom. Up by the bench, was the judge who was not in his robe, and Martin and Brust. They were just completing a discussion and without going through any formalities, the judge turned to us and stated that Martin and Brust were willing to release the 'Flesh Gordon' negative if they could remove any porno that was in the film. Evidently, the fact that we seemed ready and able to go to the wall had caught them by surprise. Possibly someone higher up had told them they had spent enough of taxpayer's money and it was time to make a deal.

Gleefully, I agreed. I had long abandoned the idea of releasing 'Flesh Gordon' as a porno film. The sets, costumes and special effects would be wasted on an audience just looking for prurient entertainment. It was an erotic science fantasy film and losing the hardcore footage mattered little. Even though the negative could be scratched while running through a viewer, it was a risk I had to take. It was the Easter weekend and the courts would be closed on Monday, so we would have to wait until Tuesday to begin screening the negative so porn clips could be identified and clipped out.

Rogers, Cichy and I couldn't help being giddy as we stood outside the courtroom on the elevated walkway that ran around the upper level of the courthouse. We profusely thanked Harry for saving the day. Behind us a custodian could be heard locking the courtroom's doors. It meant the machinery of justice, that had served us well, was now closed over the long Easter weekend. Harry headed north to the elevator that would take him to the underground parking area and we headed south along the walkway to the ramp that descended to Sixth Street. A quick glance to the north showed Harry stepping into the elevator. The courthouse was empty and still feeling giddy; we began to walk down the ramp. It was set up switchback style, doubling back on itself halfway down. Large architecturally attractive columns supported the whole structure.

Suddenly it felt like I was having a bad dream: that I was falling down a bottomless pit where an unknown horror always awaited me. Just as we were about to reach the switchback, Martin and Brust suddenly stepped out from behind one of the columns. A wry smile could not mask the supercilious look they had when they announced that they were in possession of a warrant for our arrest. Within seconds, our arms were thrust behind our backs and the two pigs had us cuffed. A couple of pushes encouraged us to walk faster down the ramp where a black and white was waiting next to the curb.

And pigs they were. By not serving the warrant that they had kept tucked away in their vest pocket all day while we were in court in front of a judge with our lawyer at our side, meant the judge would not have an opportunity to combine the new warrant with our prior case which he would have likely done since there were no new charges that differed significantly from the prior ones.

Once past the asshole check at the Parker Center jail and thrown into a small holding cell, I had to grudgingly admit, despite being unethical and possibly illegal, how clever their machinations were. Since it was a holiday, the court would not reopen until Tuesday and we would not be able to appear before a judge until then and possibly even later, depending on how many other cases had accumulated over the weekend. Bail was again set at twenty thousand dollars each, sixty grand total. Graffitti would have to fork up six grand or we would all do a half-week in the clink. Martin and Brust were going to win either way—jail time or money—our choice. It was already 8PM when I got a call through to Bill, who thankfully always seemed to have the where-with-all to pay for a bond. I got home about two in the morning, thoroughly exhausted. I went to sleep thinking, *"Fuck you-mother-fuckers, we're getting our negative back!"* Irony of ironies, years later Reb would tell me Martin had been kicked off the force and was working at an adult bookstore!

Tuesday morning I was back at the courthouse with a 16mm Moviescope, a simple viewing machine that wouldn't harm the negative, and a set of rewinds mounted on a board, so I could reel the film through the viewer for the pigs to look at. Ideally, negative is handled in a dust-free environment, since dust specks show up as little white marks when a print is struck but the cops wouldn't hear of any changes of venue. When I entered the back room in the courthouse, I could see it was quite clean, so I didn't see a problem. Martin and Brust were already in the room with all the boxes of 'Flesh Gordon' negative stacked on the table next to them. After donning white cotton gloves, I took a seat in front of the moviescope and took the first reel out of the box that Martin had handed me and loaded it onto a split reel. After gingerly running the film's leader beneath the viewer's film gate, I began to slowly draw footage through. Brust leaned his head over my right shoulder, keeping his eyes glued like a rapacious hawk to the small four-inch square screen. Martin stood to the side, doing nothing other than getting paid. When no footage of hard sex showed up, the snide smile on Brust's face relaxed. I knew only a few of the reels had anything questionable and began to reel the film through the viewer as quickly as possible, hoping Brust might blink and possibly miss something. My ploy had very limited success. When he thought he saw something, he would excitedly exclaim:

"Wait. What was that? Roll back a few feet." I would then roll back to the offending footage so Martin could peer across my other shoulder to verify Brust's discovery. When any offending footage was discovered, it was clipped out with a scissors and handed to Martin who would then wrap it around the 16mm film core that I had provided.

Despite being on opposite sides of the fence, we were quite cordial to each other. The whole thing was a game, like two football teams going at it on a Sunday afternoon: The LA Pigs against The Hollywood Pornographers. By getting me to remove the porn clips, they had scored a field goal, but I had the rest of the negative and a team of good lawyers on my offensive line and a trustworthy backfield of Bill, Walter and Lynn for support. I was the quarterback and confident that at the end of the day, I would toss a touchdown for the win. Let them enjoy their little momentary victory. Let them think that my future was going to be in the joint. I knew I was no ordinary opponent. They had no idea who they had picked a fight with.

At one point, during the second day of running negative through the Moviescope, Judge Brown came in to see how things were progressing. As luck would have it, I was reeling a role of footage of the gay orgy on the grounds of Prince Precious' Merry Kingdom, probably the most pornographic footage in the entire film. The judge took a brief look and gave a knowing nod, feeling confident that his ruling was helping to rid the world of vile filth. By the time I had finished running all forty four thousand feet of negative through the viewer, only three-hundred-eighty feet had been clipped out—less than one percent!

The LA porn scene was under siege. Irv Sofsky closed his agency after the "little" Patty debacle and Reb, of Pretty Girl, got busted for letting his kids appear in a nudist colony magazine. Two of my actors from 'Flesh Gordon,' Michael Brandy, aka Prince Precious and Nora Wiedernik, aka Queen Amora, were hassled out of town, Nora being deported back to Germany.

Graffitti was near broke. Our theatres were barely making enough money to keep 'Flesh Gordon' going, but not much more.

While tossing ideas around in Jason William's living room on how to dig out of the mess we found ourselves in, Bill suggested we do a straight film, a blood and guts bacchanal. It was a genre that he found fascinating. "Give me a bloodbath every ten minutes and I'll have no problem getting buyers" was the way he put it. Cichy, volunteered to do the screenplay. His 'Harry Hopper' scripts tended towards the cornball, so I had doubts about what he would produce, but Bill, who saw a chance for him to become the star he had always aspired to, pushed hard to give him a chance. Moreover, Bill claimed that he had a backer who would put twenty-five grand into the project. He had become very familiar with the area around Tucson because of the theatre we had there, and pointed out that the desert could provide endless free locations. We had been knocked in a corner and maybe this was a way out, so I agreed. If Bill was that confident that he could make sales, what was there to lose? Walter was told to write a script for that environment.

A week later he handed in 'Sweet, Mean and Deadly' a story about two coke dealers involved in a deal gone bad.

Bill would star and Jason Williams would co-star. Cichy would direct and I would do the cinematography. Bill was handsome, but had never acted in his life and then there was his neurotic blinking problem, nevertheless, we left for Tucson two days later and set up a production office in a motel. A local talent agent was able to supply us with a few actors and a reasonably attractive girl who was willing to do a nude soft-core love scene with Bill.

Not much went well. Bill's eye-fluttering love scene along with Cichy's unrealistic gun fight scene, where no one could hit their mark despite being separated by only ten feet, gave me serious doubts if anything was going to look believable. My mood didn't improve after I was driven into a jumping cholla cactus while I was filming Bill and Jason from a jury-rigged platform extending from the side of the car. Bill was driving down a narrow dirt road lined with cacti and inadvertenly drove me head long into the cactus. Its sharp needle like spindles jumped on to me in rapid fire and in less than a second almost half my body was punctured. I wound up on the ground screaming in pain, fighting not to black out. An hour later, I had recuperated enough to finish the day's shoot. Each day's footage was airmailed back to LA so it could be developed and Abbas could begin to put together a rough cut. Walter did his best, even taking the wheel of an ice cream truck and swerving back and forth across the road, that I thought for a moment would capsize, but despite Rick Baker's blood and guts make-up, which was so good it almost made me sick, my worst fears proved to be true when nobody wanted to touch the film. It was all blood and guts and nothing more. Bill failed to make a single sale—a first in his stellar run of successes.

We were still in desperate straits and because shooting a porn film anywhere in California was now out of the question, I drove my crew to Portland, Oregon where Bill had heard that its vice wasn't putting on any heat. Because I had become spoiled by having a large supply of pretty southern Californian girls willing to do porn; I naively thought that would also be the case in 'liberal' Portland. It definitely wasn't and over the next two days we drove to Salt Lake City and Denver, hoping to find willing sluts who wanted to be filmed, but in the end we had to bite the bullet and returned to Portland where we had found a local biker gang who was more than happy to let us use their house and mamas for a porn film. Though they guaranteed that as long as we "Just got them some coke they would fuck all day and night," that was not to be the case. But one of the girls took a shine to Walter and oblivious to the fact that it would cause havoc if his new girl friend, Viki, found out, he did a scene with her that was hot and sexy. Our soundman, weird John, joined us on the way up in Santa Barbara where due to his outstanding warrant he was still hiding out, did a scene with the gang's ugliest mama. John wasn't exactly a gem himself, but the scene turned out surprisingly hot. A masturbation and lesbian scene gave me enough footage to make a feature and I came back to LA with a film that I hoped would rekindle a small cash flow into our coiffers.

One of the few breaks we caught was when the police had failed to confiscate the 'Flesh Gordon' work print during the raid. By the time I had returned from the Portland trip, Abbas had already reassembled all the cut up clips that Benveniste had left scattered in disarray, and reconstituted them into several large thousand foot rolls that could be screened quickly on the KEM table. He planned a total reedit of the film. Playing office musical chairs once again, we moved out of Jason's apartment and now had all of our equipment set up in a three-room office in an older Spanish style office building on Argyle Street, just a block from the famed intersection of Hollywood and Vine. Two of the rooms would be for editing and the other for Bill's office.

73

COME ONE COME ALL, THERE'S A PORN TRIAL DOWN THE HALL

Two weeks after I returned from Portland, it was time for more courtroom drama. I felt like I was in a 'Perry Mason' movie. My codefendants and I stood in the hall outside the courtroom where our preliminary hearing would be held to determine if there was enough evidence to have a trial. At precisely 8:30 AM, the doors opened and a bailiff stuck his head out indicating the room was now open for business. A scurry of people came rushing from all directions and into the courtroom to get good seats. Word had gone out that a pornography case was about to be heard!

Weston was already at the defendant's table when we entered and we took seats next to him. An assistant DA named Samoyan, a rotund bespectacled slob, had been assigned to handle the case for the county. While we waited for the proceedings to begin, he sidled over to the edge of our table putatively to talk to one of the deputies working in the room. I couldn't help but giving him a contemptuous sneer. He countered with a chuckling: "I'm going to get you fifteen years."

The bailiff told all in the courtroom to rise while the judge entered the room and took his seat behind the bench. After we all were seated again, he asked Mr. Samoyan if he was ready to proceed. Looking very self-righteous, he began by calling Irish Patty to the witness stand. She wore a conservative flower dress and looked sweet and innocent, but also scared, as she climbed up and took a seat on the chair in the witness box. The judge, sitting just to her right, loomed over her from his seat on the bench. After Samoyan asked her to swear on a holy Bible that she wouldn't be telling any lies, he proceeded to ask a series of the usual "Please state your name." variety of questions. When he was satisfied with her answers, he asked the bailiff to dim the lights and then ordered a projectionist to begin running a film that had been preloaded on a 16mm projector sitting in the middle of the room. The screen was set up to the side so it was visible from the bench and most everyone else who was in the courtroom.

Samoyan took a position next to the small screen and told the projectionist to begin. As I expected, it was the film I had shot in Big Bear. All eyes were intently glued to the screen. The film in the projector had been cued so that within seconds a shot of Patty came on in which she was performing fellatio. It was the type of shot that made my films popular; a nice close up of her face with a big dick in her mouth.

Excitedly Samoyan shouted: "Stop the projector!"

He abruptly turned to Patty and asked with demanding authority: "Who is that on the screen?"

In a child-like voice that best could be described as resembling that of pop star, Michael Jackson, Patty responded: "That's me," with extra accent on the word *"That's."*

"And what are you doing?" Samoyan asked.

"I'm performing oral copulation," she retorted with obvious pride that she had not stumbled on her memorized line.

The judge leaned over from the bench and asked in a gentle grandfatherly voice:

"Do you know what oral copulation is, young lady?"

Showing not the slightest sign of intimidation Patty answered: "Yeath . . . That's when the girl sucks on the man's cock!" once again putting emphasis on the last word.

The entire room burst into laughter. The judge forced himself to stop smiling and brought order back to the courtroom with several pounds of his gavel. Samoyan, forcing himself not to see the humor, continued:

"And did anyone tell you to perform that act?"

Reminiscent of a scene from a Perry Mason movie, Patty scanned the courtroom and then stuck her arm straight out, pointing at me sitting next to my attorney at the perp table and said with conviction: "Yes . . . HE DID!"

It was hard for me to accept the seriousness of the situation, being that the morning proceedings were so laced with laughter. I had no way of knowing how my codefendants felt; neither looked too happy. My guess was that they were not in that much jeopardy. The case was about me.

As the morning's proceeding continued, Weston's calm manner was assuring. Then the time came when I was to discover who the witnesses were who were "in fear of their lives." Taking the stand was the husband of Linda, the pretty brunette I had done a substitution insertion with in 'Miss Erotica' and booked again in the 'Big Bear' film. Under questioning from Samoyan, he claimed that when Irish Patty showed up in Big Bear on Saturday morning, he warned me that she was under age. He went on to testify that I replied that I didn't care and intended on using her anyway.

It was all a categorical lie!! The pigs were willing to fabricate evidence to put me in the slammer. For good reason I became worried. But then John Weston went to work. By not being confrontational, he gained the respect of the court and put the witness off guard. John was much more than a charmer. He was smart and thorough. The DA had failed to mention that the hubby had been busted for robbery; stealing TV's from an apartment building. When John revealed that information, the witness began to falter. It soon became obvious that the cops and DA had made a deal to drop or reduce those charges if he would help nail me. It was clear why he had begged me to take him to Big Bear. He was willing to say anything to keep his ass out of jail.

My recent court experiences made me fearful that the judge would give the cops and the DA the total benefit of the doubt and rule against us. How wrong I was! After Linda's husband stepped off the witness stand, the judge made an incredible statement:

"Mr. Samoyan, I don't believe a single word that any of your witnesses have spoken this morning. Consequently I'm dismissing this entire matter."

Following the slam of his gavel, all of us, including weird John, who had yet to be booked, were off the hook. I was incredulous that the judge had seen through the whole charade. That I was impressed and grateful would be an understatement. I would have hugged the guy if I could have. Out in the hallway, I congratulated Weston for his brilliant work. He put a slight damper on the celebration by warning me that the DA could still re-file within ten days.

Which is exactly what he did. Weston assured me he would have no trouble stalling the new case from coming to trial for a long time, meaning that Graffitti would be paying legal fees for a long time. It also meant that Cichy, Rogers and Saunders would have to continue to live with that unwarranted cloud over their heads.

A few months later, I read a short article in the LA Times, that the judge had been demoted and reassigned to traffic court.

74

AM I GETTING SCREWED?

The twenty-five thousand a month we were planning on, was now a distant dream. Both Bill and I were forced to take big reductions in our pay. That he was able to keep his Rolls Royce and maintain his house on Tower Road, while Judy and I moved into a small house on Kirkwood Street in Laurel Canyon, seemed improbable. His home was surrounded by celebrity neighbors; Jill St. John lived just down the street. Our neighbors were a short stocky black dude named Jimmy who loved to get high and sit at the curb in the nude and a brash busty hooker, named Joyce, who lived across the street. But while Graffitti's finances were teetering on the precipice, it was not the time to make waves, especially when I had no proof that anything underhanded was taking place.

Besides, Judy and I felt very comfortable in our new digs. I, as a pornographer who wore tight hot pants and genital hugging cotton bell-bottoms, and she, as a stripper, who wore see-thru dresses that showed her skimpy g-string panties underneath, fit right in with the neighborhood's style. And the fact that the bail bonds that were keeping my crew and I out of jail that were being backed by Bill's house; precluded me from being too aggressive about challenging his stories. So I held my cool and didn't allow myself to become too upset and said nothing.

Moreover, once Flesh Gordon was finished and money began to roll in, it would all be resolved with a good laugh. In the meantime, Judy, who after trying to take a few normal low paying jobs, found that they didn't mesh well with her personality and returned to the Ball to work as a stripper. It wasn't a hard choice for her. She enjoyed the work and we were both pleased that she made enough money to cover most of our personal expenses.

Although I could still shoot loops, the raid had virtually destroyed my 'Harry Hopper' features factory. Bill attempted to transform the Beverly Cinema into a mainstream revival house by screening Spaghetti Westerns, but after a month of near empty seats, he gave up his Clint Eastwood fantasy and began renting adult product from other producers. The theatre quickly returned to profitability.

It was a good thing too. As Abbas began to assemble his new rough cut, major gaps caused by a poor script and lack of good directing began to show up. Much of my time was going to be needed to correct the problems. I hadn't taken Minor's criticism of Benveniste seriously while we were in production, but now I could clearly see what he was talking about. Missing were many shots that were necessary to make the various scenes work dramatically and coherently. They ranged from simple reaction shots, like when Flesh watches Wang fondle Dale's breasts to a whole scene missing inside the Flying Phallus as it crash-lands on the surface of porno. Because there was no live action footage of Flesh's daring rescue of Dale from the clutches of the Satyr monster, the scene fell flat. He had also overstated his knowledge of special effects and though I knew he hadn't deliberately misled me; some of the live footage that the effects people would need, had been shot incorrectly and would have to be redone.

I was beginning to think that maybe Hyatt's 'god of the Ouija board' was at work keeping Flesh Gordon from being completed. However, thanks to Bob Costa, partial pieces of some of the sets had been stored on the back lot of the Eagle Rock studio. Among them were the interior walls of the Flying Phallus. It was only by good luck that most of my cast, who tended to be transient, was still available. Not wanting to chance that any of them might soon disappear, I asked Mike Minor, now back from the Caribbean, to quickly reconstitute the interior of the Flying Phallus on the outside lot so I could shoot a slapstick scene inside the ship as it crash lands. The scene went well, but its color temperature didn't match with the shots that had previously been done on stage 8. As with the out of focus Penisauraus cave footage, all I could do was hope some corrections could be made during the blowup; but what I had no clue.

Having Minor's incredible energy and imagination back in the fold was a big plus. He built a thirty-foot high scaffold in the back lot and mounted a partial section of the underbelly of Wang's ship at the top, cantilevering it out so I could take low angle shots that would make it appear as though the ship was hovering above. From that setup, I was able to get all the shots I needed of Flesh rescuing Dale from the 'Satyr' monster.

Nonetheless, the 'Ouija board god' continued to wreak havoc. A week after getting all the shots I needed of Cindy Stokes, she disappeared for good. A vague rumor had it that she had married a supermarket tycoon. Now that the Beverly was making money again and I was back to shooting loops, Bill made no mention that our theatres were struggling. So it came as a surprise when I learned that several labs and suppliers were refusing to continue serving us because we had failed to pay our bills. Because I never checked the books, I had no idea what was going on. Bill handled paying the bills and I didn't want to interfere with his job much as I preferred him not interfere with mine.

The fact that he was still living large, should have raised my hackles, but I continued to accept his explanations of how he could afford a house and a Rolls Royce. It was only because we had a respected CPA in our corner that we were able to solve the problem. We had always kept our accounts current, and by the time our suppliers realized that we had fallen behind, they were caught flatfooted. Like a lot of people, Sy Katz still had faith in Graffitti and in particular 'Flesh Gordon.' We asked him to mediate a solution with the labs to keep them on board. Being that our debt was substantial worked to our favor. It basically came down that if they shut us off, 'Flesh Gordon' would go under and everyone would take a total loss. Sy explained that he was now in charge of paying the bills and would divvy out as much as possible and when the film was completed, everyone would get paid. We were too far in debt to be allowed to fail. They all agreed. Sy was now essential to our survival and we agreed to award him five points for his service.

Everyone had to chip in. Bill and I took big cuts in our salaries and Cichy and Rogers, agreed to defer a large part of theirs. They were still under indictment and couldn't afford to see 'Flesh Gordon' fail. For their continued support I gave them each a few points in the film. I also convinced the effects crew, who were only being paid two hundred a week, to take weekly deferments of fifty dollars. It wasn't lost on them, that if the film weren't completed, their outstanding work would never see the light of day. Producing 'Flesh Gordon' had now become a juggling act that required a lot of sacrifice and a high degree of blind optimism from everyone.

The tight money forced me to walk on a tight rope. Since everyone, to a large extent, was working for free, it limited my ability to be too demanding. When Danforth didn't want to animate one extra frame of the 'Beetleman' than was necessary and Abbas, also headstrong, insisted he wanted to have the luxury of snipping out bits and pieces of Danforth's work at his discretion, I had to beg Abbas to back down, which thankfully he did. Losing Danforth would have been devastating. Bill continued to bemoan the fact that Costa's optical printer was devouring money and even though I was fully aware that Bill Hedge was practically committing extortion by collecting a salary without showing any results—he hadn't animated a single segment over the last six weeks, I didn't know what to do about it. They both had us by the balls in one-way or the other. And Bill didn't make my job any easier when he would show up at the Eagle Rock studio from time-to-time driving his Silver Shadow Rolls Royce while I was pleading poverty with them. Bill seemed oblivious to how he was affecting everyone.

That included Judy and me as well. To her credit, she never complained about Bill and my sister living so much better then we were, but I knew it had to bother her. The two of us didn't see much of each other; she often got home from the Ball at two in the morning when I was already asleep. I was at a loss to explain how Bill had managed to send Nancy and my mother on a vacation to Hawaii and buy her a BMW. What was going on? My mother saw Bill as Nancy's knight in shinning armor who could do no wrong. A Thanksgiving dinner, which should have been a moment of family joy, felt more like a kick in the balls after my mother refused to serve anyone dinner until Bill and Nancy arrived. It was ready to eat at 1:30, but didn't get served until 5:30 when they finally walked in and we all, including my father, had lost our appetites. Adding to the insult, they split after a half hour.

Until Flesh Gordon was finished and my legal problems cleared, I had to resist entertaining any suspicions about Bill's finances. It was best to stay in the dark. Ignorance and an exciting sex life helped. 'Free Love' kept our open marriage from becoming bitter. We both got our share and neither of us smarted while the other was getting laid. She not only fucked the young musician living next door to us—though I wasn't happy that she also gave him my guitar amplifier—and also disappeared into a closet at a party we were attending to have a quickie with a young kid freshly arrived in Hollywood, named Jerry Bruchiemer. I got my turn at a party thrown by one of my favorite models, Howard Neal, where a dozen or so of his guests, including Judy and me, sat in a circle on his living room floor where a buxom stripper crawled around to tease each of us as she removed her cloths. Near the end of her act, she whispered in my ear if I would like to take her into the bedroom and fuck her as soon as she finished her performance. Judy wasn't a swinger per se, but patiently waited while I ate the girl's pussy for a half-hour before we fucked; a service that earned me thanks for providing a much better time than she had anticipated.

But was too much steam building up in the kettle for bad things not to happen. Bob Costa arrived panic stricken and shaking at my office early on a Monday morning to tell me someone had thrown a brick through his front living room window the previous night. It had barely missed his wife who was sitting on the couch watching television. I tried to calm him by assuring him we had nothing to do with it; maybe it was a gang or teen prank. Bill was conveniently out of the office but I had no doubt about what had happened. Costa's drain on our bank account was making Bill very irate. Our theatre manager, Danny Tafoya and his cousin Rick Espinoza, were making good money and if either were told by Bill to put a brick through Costa's window, it would be done. To no surprise, Bill denied any knowledge of the incident when I questioned him.

Surprisingly, there was no immediate indication at the Eagle Rock studio that the event had caused a problem. Work continued at a healthy pace. Using left over pieces of the 'Penisauraus' cave that Costa had stored in the side lot, Minor created a miniature canyon to stage Amora's Swan ship crash and ten days later he had another elaborate miniature fabricated outside as well, this time the surface of Porno, including a river and an extinct volcano.

And once Abbas supplied Danforth with the exact cuts he had requested, he put in long and lonely hours at the back of Stage 8 to complete the Beetleman sequence. It was an incredible piece of artistry. I was told by the head of Cinema Research, the lab where the footage was being developed, that it was as good as anything Ray Harryhausen had done.

Then the 'Ouija board god,' struck another blow. Danforth asked me to come by his apartment; he had something he wanted to discuss. He had recently turned out a lot of work, including the entire 'Royal Flush' scene and was about to start doing some of the especially difficult animation of the "Satyr" monster, so I assumed the meeting was about technical problems. Jim's temperamental nature kept me on edge, and not wanting to do anything to irritate him, I rushed out to Sherman Oaks where he lived. After he introduced me to his wife, a tall attractive lady with a Slavic look who I couldn't help but fantasize would look great in a dominatrix outfit; caught me speechless when he told me that he was quitting the film. I could only manage a gulp until I steadied myself enough to ask why. He said he was just tired of the project. I begged him to reconsider. I told him I understood how stressful his work was and asked if there was anything I could do to make things easier on him. But he was adamant. After a half-hour of begging, I could see I was getting nowhere.

My face was overcome with an unmistakable sad countenance. There wasn't anything I could think of to change his mind. In a barely audible voice I told him: "I guess this is it. I give up. I really don't know what to do." Suddenly his mood changed. In an understanding and consoling voice he said: "Don't give up. Look, I'll come back and finish the scenes." Evidently he couldn't stand to see a grown man cry, because I was close to doing so.

Bill had moved his office again, this time to a suite on the top floor of a two story building on Third Street just west of La Cienaga. From there he would handle distribution of our films and management of the theatres. I would have the entire Argyle office for editing. His move was propitious, because he was conveniently not around when I would have a confrontation with the effects crew that I had a hard time believing wasn't a delayed reaction to the "brick throwing" incident.

Mike Minor had made an unannounced visit to the Argyle office two days before to ask if he could see the rough cut. Editors are usually not wont to show rough cuts since they can easily be misinterpreted, but Minor was the film's production designer and in many ways its inspiration, so I told Abbas to run it for him. When he left, I felt he had liked what he had seen. But two days later, after Walter and I returned from having lunch at a nearbyThai restaurant, we found the entire effects crew, including Minor,

Muren and Danforth, standing in the room. The dour looks on their faces told me something bad was about to happen.

Minor did the talking. He was there to deliver an ultimatum: "they were not pleased the way the picture was going or how they were being paid. They would complete the shots that were necessary to finish the film, but from now on, they would retain the negative and only give us a work print of each shot they completed. We could have the negative only after we paid off our entire debt to them." It could have been a lot worse. Their position on holding the negative was totally reasonable, but I didn't understand where "they didn't like the way the film was going," was coming from. On second thought, it was clear that since Minor was the only one who had seen the rough cut, he had made that decision for the group. It was also possible that they were having second thoughts of being involved with what they might have still thought of as a porn movie, but being that they were already owed over ten grand, I knew they weren't going to walk away without finishing. I agreed to their demands, but was surprised that just before leaving, Minor, Muren and Danforth, threw in one more condition; they didn't want their names listed in the credits. I thought the request was absurd, but for now it was not something worth arguing.

75

FLESH DESERVES AN
ACADEMY AWARD7

The stories about Bill's star stalking were amusing but harmless. We were both audacious and irreverent in our own ways and its what had led to Graffitti's success so when he suggested an outrageous scheme to promote Flesh Gordon, I was all ears. According to him, it was an unwritten policy of the Motion Picture Academy to nominate at least three pictures each year for any particular category. The fact that there were only two main-stream films in 1973; *'Poseidon Adventure'* and *'Soylent Green,'* that had enough effects to be considered for the Best Special Effects category, left a slot open for a third candidate. He felt it was a spot we could fill. 'Flesh Gordon' had a lot of damn-good special effects, but the film wasn't even close to being finished.

There was more to his plan. All that was required by the academy to be considered as a candidate for the Special Effects Award, was that a reel of the effects be submitted to the committee and that the film screen for one week during the year under consideration. We could easily submit a reel of the effects; Danforth's Beetleman alone would catch the Academy's eye. Since we owned our own theatre, the one-week play-date requirement could also be easily satisfied. We could play a black and white dupe of the Flesh Gordon work print with slugs inserted to cover any uncompleted special effects, at the Beverly Cinema for one week; but rather than during normal hours, we would screen it at 3AM in the morning and charge fifty dollars for a ticket. It was unlikely anyone would show up at that hour and if they did, would turn away after they were told how much they would have to pay to go inside. It was insidious and clever.

I told him I loved the plan.

I arranged for a lab to strike a black and white copy of the rough cut and marry a sound track to it that consisted only of the dialogue. Since no one was expected to see or hear the film, a sound track without music or sound effects was not a concern. During the last week of December 1973, the smallest ad possible ran in the theatre listing section of the LA Times announcing that Flesh Gordon was now playing for one week only at the Beverly Cinema; showtime: 3AM. It was the time of year when most people in the industry would be gone for the holidays so who would notice.

Incredibly, a handful of people actually showed up; one of them being Bill Hedge. But all, including him, declined to shell out the fifty-dollar ticket price. After the week was over we pulled the film and delivered our reel of effects to the academy for their consideration and patiently waited for them to announce their selections.

Meanwhile, I knew some of my straight laced effects crew would have preferred to be making 'Flash' Gordon, so at times I had to push a bit to be sure that some of the shots were done with the kind of bad taste that would be appropriate for 'Flesh Gordon.' Muren didn't want to do the shot of Dale in the big 'Satyr' hand that we shot at the observatory because he felt it would look too hokey. After I pleaded that humor was more important than technical perfection, he gave in and did the shot. It was a winner. Rob Maine did his part by agreeing with my request to animate a few shots of the 'Satyr' to make him appear to be a "queen" and thus the world's first gay monster.

Light began to shine from the end of the tunnel when Joe Musso and Muren finished the computer animated scene of 'Amora's Swan Ship' traversing the Zodiac and Bill Hedge finally finished the 'Penisauraus' scene, which allowed me to remove him from the payroll. Danforth had totally mellowed out and was now totally committed to wrapping up all the segments of the 'Satyr' monster that I was counting on him to do. And after working on it for three months, Tom Sherman had completed 'Emperor Wang's' impressive miniature castle. It was to be blown up in a spectacular explosion, but before that happened, I used the forced perspective trick I had learned from Mike Minor on the first day of shooting to make it appear that Flesh and Jerkoff were approaching the castle from a half-mile away. Jason and my brother-in-law, Danny, who was standing in for Joe Hudgins who was no longer around, stood crouched over three feet in front of the camera's lens and pretended to run down a hill towards the miniature castle far away in the background.

Once that shot was out of the way, it was time to blow up the castle. A lot of nerves were on edge that day. Reshots were not an option. Muren had set up three cameras to record the action from different angles. Each had to run at high speed to slow down the expansion speed of the blast to make it appear to be much larger than it actually was. Joe Viskol, our young pyrotechnics man, had set up a string of various sized magnesium based explosions that were timed to go off sequentially and create a juggernaut of mayhem that would spell the end of the evil 'Wang.'

To make sure he had all the settings on the cameras correct, Muren made several last minute light readings. Tom Sherman, looking every bit Captain Nemo at his sternest, stood glaring quietly to the side, waiting for his masterpiece to be blown to smithereens. Cichy readied himself to snap stills of the entire event. After a quick nod to Viskol to make sure he was ready, Muren started the cameras rolling. The whirring sound of high speed cameras added to the tension. Muren's call for action brought Viskol's index finger down on the igniter button and a string of explosions of various intensities quickly reduced the castle to rubble. It was cool as hell. Everything came off to perfection. A major studio couldn't have done better.

Or so we thought. While smoke and the acrid smell of burned magnesium still hung in the air, all eyes turned to Muren for acknowledgement that the photography was successful. For a moment he didn't respond. When he quietly stated that the main camera had jammed after a short run of film had traveled through the gate, there was a deathly silence. Everyone stood stone-faced with mouths agape, looking at him in disbelief. If looks could kill, it would have happened that day.

Was it that damn 'Ouija board god?' For a few days it appeared so, but miraculously, after the film was developed, it was discovered that the main camera had caught enough of the explosion before it jammed to enable Abbas to cut an excellent scene together. Even so, Muren had to endure a week of peer shame because of his faux pas. Maybe the crew wouldn't have been so tough on him if they had known that in the coming years, he would put eight academy awards on his mantle and be given his own star on Hollywood Boulevard for his special effects work on Star Wars, Indiana Jones and Terminator, just to name a few. But that day, his name was Mud.

That 'Flesh Gordon' didn't get nominated when the Academy made their announcements in February, was not that surprising. But how they did it, was a cop out. Through some of Bill's friends at the Comedy Store, he learned that there was a lively discussion about whether we should be considered or not. The effects roll we had submitted impressed a lot of the members, but others were vehemently opposed to nominating an X-rated film. To avoid a controversy, the academy decided not to nominate any films for the Special Effects Award that year, but to instead endow, 'The Poseidon Adventure,' with a Special Achievement Award.

Recognition by the academy would have been nice, but thanks to Walter, we got a huge publicity boost anyway. Without my knowledge, he had submitted a set of slides to Penthouse Magazine for their consideration. At the time, Penthouse was still a fledging publication in a battle with Playboy to become the number one men's magazine. Walter could barely hide his excitement when he announced that they were going to publish a twelve-page layout in an upcoming issue. It was tremendous news. The layout appeared in February 1973 and was to be the first issue of Penthouse to sell out. Four million people were now aware of Flesh Gordon.

Bill didn't want to take the snub by the Academy sitting down. One of his Comedy Store friends gave him his Academy Award car pass that gave access to the queue of cars dropping celebrities off at the red carpet in front of the Dorothy Chandler Pavilion, where the 45th Annual Academy Awards would be presented. On the evening of March 27, 1973, Bill's Silver Shadow Rolls Royce looked very much in place among limos and other ritzy cars waiting to deposit their celebrated passengers at the carpet. Bill was at the wheel, I was in the front passenger seat and Walter and Lynn in the rear seats. Our adrenalin heightened as we approached the fabled carpet where the glare of the intense light was so blinding it was hard to see. A hoard of photographers and TV crews was gathered there to film the celebrants as they debarked. Seconds after the formally dressed couple from the previous car began scurrying up the stairs, Bill pulled up to the final stop. A team of valets ran in military precision to open each of our car doors in perfect unison.

Before anyone had a chance to react, we were out of the car and scampering up the stairs holding protest signs that said such things as: "Flesh Gordon Scorned by Academy" or "Academy Unfair to Flesh Gordon." Each of us scattered helter-skelter once we reached the patio above. Cameras bulbs were flashing and there was a noticeable murmur from the august guests: "What the fuck is going on?" I barely had any sense of where I was as I waved my sign while making my way through a throng of people. Just as I caught a glimpse of Gator across the patio near the theatre's entrance waving his sign, a strong hand grabbed my arm and thrust it up behind my back with a succinct warning: "make one move and I'll break your arm."

Needless to say I didn't make a move. The security guard marched me off to the side where I couldn't be a further disturbance. My cohorts quickly met the same fate. As we stood to the side, hidden by a pillar so we couldn't offend the legitimate guests, the security team held a brief meeting and decided not to "blemish" the Awards by giving us any more recognition. We were summarily told to get the hell off the premises.

All the evening and morning news coverage of the Awards carried a little clip of our demonstration. We garnered more attention than many of the stars. Between Penthouse magazine and the Academy Awards, 'Flesh Gordon' was now in the national eye. The question still remained, when would it be finished?

76

JUDY SAVES FLESH

A few weeks later, I was in bed and half asleep when Judy got home around 2AM from the Ball. When she mentioned that one of the patrons at the club had told her that he had just seen Deep Throat at a theatre in Caldwell, Idaho, I muttered he must have meant Boise. Graffitti owned the only movie house in Caldwell and I knew we weren't playing Deep Throat. Not thinking much more about it, I fell back to sleep. The next morning after relieving my throbbing hard on with a fuck, I asked her again about the 'Deep Throat' story. "Are you sure he said Caldwell? Maybe he was confused. Caldwell's only ten miles outside of Boise." She was positive he said Caldwell.

'Deep Throat' was a phenomenal hit for the sole reason that its star, Linda Lovelace, had the ability to perform a previously unheard of sex act; engulfing a ten-inch penis down her throat. The film was directed by a former hairdresser, Gerald Damiano, and had been financed with mafia money. The unique talent of Ms. Lovelace brought people from far and wide to see her amazing achievement. When the New York police department attempted to prevent the public from seeing the dirty deed by blocking off the street that ran in front of the theatre, 'Deep Throat' went stratospheric overnight. Something that forbidden had to be seen.

In Los Angeles, the powerful 'PussyCat' chain had the film locked up; The Beverly Cinema had no chance of outbidding them. Similarly, I assumed that in Idaho, there would be venues in Boise that could offer

'Deep Throat' a much better deal than we could in Caldwell. And if we were showing 'Deep Throat,' Bill would have certainly mentioned it. It would have meant a financial bonanza for Graffitti and help to greatly relieve the financial strain we were under. I was positive that the guy Judy had talked to had just made a mistake.

The next night, he happened to be in the club again, and Judy told him I thought he was mistaken; he had seen the film in Boise, not Caldwell. But the next morning she told me he was vehement about seeing it in Caldwell.

Maybe there was an explanation or as I was beginning to realize; I just didn't want to face the truth. If what Judy was telling me was true, there was a problem. I couldn't just let it slide as I had always done when I had questions about what was going on with Bill's finances. He had his family running the theatre and knowing I might not get a straight answer, I placed a call to the Top Theatre without identifying myself. His mother, who ran the ticket booth, picked up the phone.

Still expecting to hear that "Deep Throat" was not playing there, I asked: "What are you guys showing now?"

"Deep Throat" she replied.

My blood pressure went up. Maybe it just started showing this week and that's why Bill hadn't mentioned it yet.

"How long have you been playing the film?" "It's in its fourth week".

"Thank you." I said politely before hanging up.

What the fuck was going on? If we were showing Deep Throat, we were probably making ten grand a week. Before I confronted Bill, I went to a newsstand and picked up a copy of the Idaho Statesman, which served most of the state. Quickly turning to the entertainment section I was knocked over by a big display ad: 'DEEP THROAT now playing at the TOP THEATRE in Caldwell.'

It was time to stop being a dumb asshole! Why I hadn't confronted Bill before, was a mystery I couldn't answer. Being under indictment was part of the reason, but there was more. I was afraid of conflict. That's why I didn't like selling. I couldn't stand hearing "no."

But I couldn't let the situation go on any longer. Confident that I had the goods on Bill, I went over to his office on 3rd Street and with the Idaho Statesman in my hand, marched up the stairs and entered unannounced. A very skinny, but sexy oriental female, who bought our films for the

Japanese market, was standing next to him and pushing her body against his shoulder. She always wore satin hot pants and the way they looked at each other, it was obvious they were doing each other. Pushing aside my brief flash of envy, I asked her to leave the room for a minute, which she obliged; saying she was about to leave anyway.

As soon as she was out of the room, I dropped the Boise paper, already opened to the theatre section, onto Bill's desk. I expected him to crumble—embarrassed by the web of deceit I had just caught him in. The fucker didn't blink an eye—well maybe the blink he always had

but not a serious blink. With a smile akin to that of a child caught stealing from the cookie jar, he calmly explained that he didn't tell me about the 'Deep Throat' booking because he didn't want the effects crew to know that we had a lot of money coming in. It was better to keep them hungry—otherwise they might start demanding more. I stood speechless. It was like he knew I was on my way to confront him and had already concocted one of his seemingly rational explanations to counter my accusation. I was stymied and couldn't think of a response.

The next day I went to see Sy Katz, and filled him in with what had gone down. Sy had become a father figure and financial mentor to me and I trusted his advice. Although he didn't say so, I got the sense that he already had his own suspicions about Bill. Sy had great faith in 'Flesh Gordon's' potential and the future of Graffitti Productions. His outward conservative appearance belied his risk taking investor inside. He had points in the film and it wouldn't be to his benefit for us to go belly up. I told him it was now impossible for me to trust Bill with our money. I suggested a plan where checks drawn on the Graffitti bank account would require two signatures, one being his. That would enable Bill and I both to function without me having to worrying if money was being skimmed from the bank account.

When I presented the plan to Bill, to my relief, he accepted the proposal. I suggested that if things didn't improve between us, we could work out a way to dissolve the company after 'Flesh' was finished. I assumed he would play straight until that time. I knew he had big plans for himself. In an interview he had done for a foreign magazine, he waxed about what a wealthy celebrity producer he would become after 'Flesh' was released: "They're watching to see if we're gonna hit or not. And once we hit, the fucking doors are open all the way. And it's gonna happen, I see it happening. I feel it."

The contretemps between Bill and I was shattered only one week later. Fleishman's office called Sy Katz, to inform him that the IRS had found over fifty thousand dollars in Bill's personal account that didn't match up with Graffitti's tax returns. During a routine audit, which the government liked to conduct on companies associated with the pornography industry in the hopes of finding tax violations that could be used to close them down, they had hit pay dirt when they scrutinized Bill's personal bank records. It was similar to the technique used during the prohibition era to put Al Capone behind bars. Graffitti's corporate and my personal books were clean, but Bill had a problem—a big problem.

I had been a naïve jerk and I knew it. Bill was driving a Rolls, my sister a BMW and the two of them living in Beverly Hills, while Judy was stripping to help pay the rent on our modest one bedroom house in Laurel Canyon. Enough was enough.

Suspecting that I might learn something, I decided to make an unannounced visit to the Beverly Cinema. I had always considered it Bill's purview and hadn't been to the theatre for almost a year. Around ten that evening, I startled our manager, Rick Espinosa, when I showed up at the front door. After a friendly, but nervous greeting, he asked me if I needed some money. That stated loud and clear that Bill often took cash from the box office. Inwardly I bristled. Rick was only doing as he thought he was expected to do. With a smile, I told him I was OK. I didn't want him to think anything was amiss. I needed some time to think about how I was going to handle the situation.

Obviously Bill couldn't be trusted not to skim funds. I had to find a way to take over the operation of the Beverly Cinema. Hopefully, it could generate enough money to finish 'Flesh Gordon.' Bill had already signed the agreement that required Sy Katz to be a cosigner on all of Graffitti's checks and because of the situation with the IRS, Katz now agreed with my request to only co-sign checks that I had endorsed. Osco's situation with the IRS had put him in crisis mode. He was going to have to hire a lawyer to defend himself and could eventually face big fines and even jail. Unlike the legal problems I faced, his were personal and not related to our business. He would have to cover his own expenses. I had no intention of getting involved in a battle with the IRS on his account.

My quandary was how to keep the partnership intact until 'Flesh Gordon' was finished. As Graffitti's president, there was the distinct possibility that he might be able to use its assets to negotiate a settlement with the IRS. I needed to have him removed from that position. But my lack of understanding of corporate law dealt me a momentary blow. Steve Rhode, who handled civil issues at the Fleishman firm, seemed doubtful that Bill could be removed, explaining that despite Bill and I being equal shareholders, Osco, as president, held a dominant position. He could only be removed by a special act of the stockholders as for instance, being unfit to hold that office because of criminal behavior. I argued that was the case! Rhode pointed out that Bill and I were equal shareholders and a vote would result in a tie and thus he would remain in office.

I decided to play hardball and make Bill an offer that if he had an ounce of brains, he would accept. He would immediately relinquish the Presidency and any involvement with the Beverly Cinema and in return have the right to operate the Top Theatre and the two mini houses we still owned in Phoenix and Tucson to help him pay for his legal problems. When 'Flesh Gordon' was finished, I would pay him thirty-five thousand dollars for his shares in Graffitti, which would include the Beverly Cinema, 'Flesh Gordon', all the porn negatives in our vault, the company van and all the film equipment we owned. He would be given sole ownership of the Arizona theatres and The Top Theatre and could also have 'Sweet Mean and Deadly,' which he still loved, but I considered worthless. He would eventually rename it 'Cop Killers.'

Temperatures were hitting the low nineties on the day I walked into Bill's 3rd Street office to present my offer. I found him seated behind his desk bundled up in his black fur coat. The coat's collar was pulled half way up around his head and his large dark sunglasses covered what little of his face remained exposed. He was in some kind of cocoon mode—a ground squirrel taking a peek from his lair to see if it was safe to come out. Bill listened to my proposal but said nary a word. When I left, I had no idea what his thoughts were.

A week passed without the offer being accepted. In the meantime, Steve Rhode, on further analysis, felt that I could call a meeting and forcefully remove Bill from office on the grounds that because of the time he was going to have to spend on his legal problems, he would be too distracted to properly tend to the company's business. Rhode drafted a letter and sent it to Bill's attorney, announcing a corporate meeting to be held at Sy Katz's office for the express purpose of removing Osco as President of Graffitti.

The meeting was set for three O'clock on a Wednesday afternoon. I showed up a half hour early to discuss the proceeding with Rhode. None of us were sure if Osco would even show up. But just minutes before three O'clock, wearing his fur coat and shades, he marched in with his attorney at his side. They both had sour looks on their faces. Before either could say a thing, I began reading a statement Rhode had prepared for me, that in essence, announced that because of malfeasance, Osco was being removed from his office as President. I struggled to keep my voice from trembling. I did not enjoy this kind of confrontation. Before abruptly turning about face and storming out of the office, Bill's lawyer made a quick retort that what we were doing was unfounded and illegal. After they left, it took me a moment to quit shaking. Rhode assured me I was well within my rights. Two days later, Bill accepted the deal I had offered.

77

I TAKE THE BULL BY THE HORNS

To say that I knew very little of what Bill was doing behind my back would be more than an understatement. Only years later, did I learn, in conversations with my sister, Nancy, the extent of his machinations. On the day of the big bust, while Walter, Lynn and I were in jail, Bill, along with our theatre managers and Jason Williams, was busy moving a large library of prints and negatives that he had stored in the attic of his house, to a place that couldn't be traced to him. He had a thriving business on the side distributing our films for his own gain. That, along with the money directly pilfered from the theatres, was a substantial source of the money found by the IRS in his personal bank account.

She also told me that the bust had forced him to sell the Tower Road house and buy a more modest home in Beverly Hills on Beverly Glenn, a purchase that he made behind her back. But his secret dealings began to unravel when the IRS found my sister's name on the mortgage, which he had put there without telling her. The IRS, in an attempt to solicit information about Bill's finances, had requested an interview with her.

That she couldn't see, or worse didn't care, that Bill's wealth was coming out of my share of Graffitti's profits, was hard to accept. I eventually realized that faulting her for having loyalty to her lover and possible future husband, was something I might have done myself if I were in her shoes. She claimed to the FBI during her interview, that she wasn't married to Bill, but they refused to be totally convinced of her non-involvement and told her to stay in town. However, without an indictment, the Feds had no authority to restrict her travel, so Bill paid for her and my mother to take a trip to Hawaii—explaining the truth behind what my mother had thought was a wonderful generous gesture. He wanted Nancy out of town so the Feds couldn't ask any more questions.

When the Feds found out that she had ignored their request not to travel, they were pissed and called her downtown for a more extensive interview. As they began to see that they were getting nowhere, they pulled a surprise rabbit out of the hat and accused her of transporting girls across state lines for prostitution. That caused a light to go on in her head. She had taken a trip to Vegas with Karen Shick, a young woman living next door to her and Bill and was not aware that Shick was hooking. That the Feds knew about the Vegas trip, meant that Shick was cooperating with the investigation. It was also likely that she was the one who had tipped the Feds off about the Hawaiian trip. But my sister, like most people around Bill, had no idea what he was actually up to and could provide little information, so they backed off after she agreed to sign a paper stating that she was not married to him.

It was not a big deal. Her romance with Bill had already hit the rocks when she had come home early one day and found him in bed with Mitzi Shore, the daughter of the owner of The Comedy Store. Unlike Judy and I, Nancy didn't brook outside affairs and chased the still naked girl out of the house and onto Tower Road. When Nancy confronted Shick about her cooperation with the Feds, she broke down and owned up that she was also having an affair with Bill. At one time I had wondered if Bill even liked sex, but was now surprised to find that like many of my assumptions, to be far off base; another deep flaw in my personality.

Our breakup was not a moment of joy. We had done well for each other, but there was no going back. That my sister had cut her ties with him made things much cleaner. It would have been cumbersome if they were still together. As it was, my mother was never able to stop admiring Bill, simply because he had showered my sister with largess. She refused to admit that he had stolen money from me, justifying it by saying; "You couldn't have made it without him," conveniently leaving out that it worked two-ways, he couldn't have made it without me either. It left me feeling that, "family," was very overrated. There was no justification for what he had done; especially since I was still facing possible jail time for producing the films that had led to our success. But now I had only one concern— finishing 'Flesh Gordon.'

Anticipating that Osco would have to accept my deal, I had already taken steps to find a manager that I could trust to operate the Beverly Cinema. Walter Cichy's friend, Marvin Lawrence, was one of a kind. A non-religious Jew, in his mid thirties, six feet tall, reasonably good-looking and with a small paunch, he was every bit as addicted to sex as I was. But where I became a pornographer so I would have easy access to sexy women, he used his gift of gab, and a technique that was beyond bizarre to pick-up girls on a daily basis.

When seeing a lady on the street or elsewhere that he desired, he would sidle up to her and innocently stand a few feet away to ogle her for a moment and then as she became aware of his presence; mutter:

"Ooooh . . . Ooooh . . . are you really that beautiful or am I just seeing things . . . oooooh . . . oooooh . . . you can't be real.

His posture and demeanor made him look harmless, so girls would either just walk away or stay to enjoy the fact that they were having such a strong affect on him. For those who didn't run, he would continue to mutter and eventually throw in: . . . ooooh gotta have it . . . oooooh . . . how can you stand being so beautiful?

Many were charmed enough to agree to follow him up the street to his nearby modest one bedroom Hollywood apartment, where he encouraged them to take a shower and sometimes a nap, while he prepared dinner; which always consisted of a steak smothered in teriyaki sauce and a baked potato prepared on the hibachi barbecue that sat on the small porch off the dining area. His menu never varied and no date ever cost him more than ten dollars.

I had often used Marvin's apartment to shoot loops and even had him to do a stand in if my stud was having difficulty, so it was natural that our love of feminine sexuality caused us to become good friends. Dropping by Marvin's apartment never failed to be an experience. After I knocked, he would open the door a tiny crack to see who was there and then put his finger to his lips to make it clear that I should be very quiet before I entered. I would then be led tiptoe style to take a peek into the bathroom where his guest du jour was taking a shower or to the bedroom where she might only be wearing panties and bra while napping. Marvin never forced himself on a girl, he was more fixated about seeing them scantily dressed or nude than having sex, although he didn't refuse the later when offered.

But of more interest to me at the time were his other attributes; including that he was an excellent bridge player, very frugal and organized, and most of all—honest. He had mentioned that he was looking for something to do and I began thinking he might be a perfect fit to run The Beverly Cinema. That he had a modest income from stocks and a trust fund and knew my situation, I felt salary would not be an issue. He was delighted to accept my offer when I presented it to him. I was going to count on this unlikely person to generate the money I would need to finish 'Flesh Gordon.'

With Marvin waiting in the wings, I undertook the unpleasant task of going down to the theatre at ten in the evening and explain to Rick Espinoza, that I had to let him go because of his connection to Bill. He had to know that Bill was stealing from me. I actually liked Rick; unfortunately he was just another of Bill's victims. I was relieved that he understood without causing me grief. I handed Marvin the keys the next morning and told him to get started as quickly as possible.

It actually blew my mind how quickly Marvin took command of the situation. His first move was to involve Ed Muckerman, Lew Shere's adman who had designed the highly successful campaign for 'Mona' when it first opened at the Western Avenue Cinema. How Marvin was acquainted with Muckerman, I had no idea, but between the two of them, they were able to book and promote some of the best porn films available, and the grosses at the Beverly Cinema shot up overnight to ten grand a week.

The Beverly Cinema was providing me with enough money that I would be able to pay off the effects crew when they finished in the not to distant future so I could take control of the negative. But then legal hypocrisy struck again. George T. Trammell, a municipal judge running for reelection, decided to make anti pornography his campagn slogan. Each night he had the police chauffer him from porn theatre to porn theatre, where he would jump out of the car and take a perfunctory look inside so he could declare the film obscene and have the cops go in and confiscate it on the spot. His raids garnered him daily mention in the local media as a strong fighter against pornography—the kind of judge who deserved to be reelected!

The theatres, including ours, had to keep backup prints off the premises, so the confiscated print could be immediately replaced to allow the show to continue. To counteract that ploy, Trammell began confiscating the projectors along with the films; on the grounds that they were involved in an illegal act by being used to screen illegal obscene material. The raids continued unabated and in short order all our projectors had been removed, including the large six thousand dollar Norelco that weighed over a hundred fifty pounds. Marvin managed to keep replacing the films and I did my part by renting projectors to keep the theatre's doors open, but the free publicity the LA Times gave Trammwel was priceless, and he kept making raids. With good reason, the rental houses were not too thrilled that their equipment was landing in the police evidence room and told me not to ask for more. It had come to a breaking point where one more raid would have closed us down. Thankfully election night came and Trammell, on the basis of his unparalleled rectitude, won handily. As I suspected, his interest in regulating pornography ended the next day once he was again ensconced in a nice high paying government job.

Twenty-five years later, the following article appeared in the LA Times:

February 1, 2001 | DAVID ROSENZWEIG, TIMES STAFF WRITER

Former Superior Court Judge, George W. Trammell III was sentenced to 27 months in federal prison Wednesday for giving favored treatment to a criminal defendant with whom he had a clandestine sexual relationship. "This case is not about sex. It's about the betrayal of the public trust, "U. S. District Judge A.

Howard Matz told Trammell before handing down his sentence.

The fucking hypocrite!! Mysteriously, I could not find a single picture of him on the internet.

It was music to my ears and an anti acid tablet for my stomach, when Muren announced that his crew would have everything wrapped up in one more week sweetened by Danforth telling me he needed just a few more weeks to wrap up the 'Satyr' monster animation. To keep him happy, I had just spent an entire morning driving around to pick up a few items he needed, so I was surprised when I drove up to Stage 8 to see him bursting out the door with all his personal possessions tucked under his arms. When he saw me he turned to shout: "Graffitti's got the last drop of blood they're going to get out of Jim Danforth." Offering no further explanation before storming to his car and throwing everything into its back seat before driving off in high dudgeon. I hadn't the slightest idea what had gone wrong.

After consulting with Abbas, we determined that we could live without the shots he had failed to complete. It was a relief to know I wouldn't have to genuflect in front of him again; his last little outburst could go without a challenge. Because the work he had done for us was beyond priceless, I had no need to hold a grudge. It was just Jim being Jim.

The 'money-for-negative-exchange' was nothing less than a Keystone Kop comedy. Muren had insisted on a cashier's check, so at nine in the morning, I arrived at the Seward Street vault where he had asked me to come with it in hand. The whole effects gang was already assembled outside the vault. Mike Minor assumed the lead role for them. Until he had one hand on the sixteen-thousand dollar cashier's check, did he push the boxes of negative towards me; not taking his hands off the boxes until I had released my hand from the check. They seemed oblivious to the fact that I was the one taking the risk, since I had no way of checking what was in the boxes as we made the exchange. Nevertheless, all felt a sigh of relief as the deal was consummated.

Once Cichy and I returned to the editing room with all boxes, we took an inventory of what we had just been handed. All the basic footage was present, but I was disappointed to see that they had left me with a lot of work yet to be done. I had been given various shots of the 'Flying Phallus' that were intended to be combined with star backgrounds, or in one case with a moon with a blinking eye, but no direction was given as to which shots and backgrounds were intended for each other. Neither the sex or power pastry ray had been created. I would have to design them myself. The 'Moronosphere' lacked imagination and would have to be redone to make it more deserving of 'Flesh Gordon.'

There were at least a half-dozen other shots that needed to be worked on, but by now I knew enough about creating simple effects that I felt confident that Cichy, Rogers and I could shoot everything ourselves. I understood how to adjust camera speed to give body to miniatures and had already received critical approval from Danforth for some of the shots I had made for him that he needed to use as background plates. In a way, it was a relief not to have to be in the dark about what was being done. It was all in my control from here on.

Bob Costa had stayed out of the fray that I had with the effects team and I was still relying on him to do all the optical work. When he called to tell me he had something to show me, I was sure it must finally be the completed optical printer. I was right!! When I arrived at his house he took me down to his basement workshop and with a big prideful grin on his face; opened the door: "There it is, it's finished!"

Indeed it was. In the center of the room, sitting among a medley of mechanical junk strewn across the floor, was a black, four-foot high, rectangular, optical printer. I patted him on the back and exuberantly complemented him. Another piece of the puzzle was in place. We could immediately commence doing the substantial amount of optical work that remained. The endless drain of money to build the machine was no more.

My euphoria would last one fucking day. I dropped by Bob's place the next afternoon, to go over details of the work that I wanted him to begin. When we went down to his workshop; I gasped. The printer was gone! It had dissolved into the pile of junk spread across the floor. Bob turned to me and said with the same prideful grin I had seen only twenty-four hours earlier: "I'm going to make it even better!"

I was numb. It didn't register with him that the blank look on my face meant his printer was history. I called him a few hours later to let him know I wasn't going to be using his services anymore. He knew he had screwed up and didn't put up much of a fight. Bob had given a lot to the film, but I no longer had the luxury of indulgence.

Judy and I had been forced to rent another house when our landlord reclaimed the one we were living in. It was actually a blessing. I found another small house just a few blocks away that had a garage abutting the street and a backyard patio. I could use it to film the remaining effects that needed to be done in natural light. Over the next six months, Cichy, Rogers and I, spent countless hours filming the omissions and making improvements where needed. A road flare was used to create both the sex ray and the mystical aura that would surround Amora after her death. A rotating Budweiser beer display and a rheostat controlled light bulb attached to the end of a long pole became an onrushing fireball that would segue to the title credits. I dumped a box full of pills, marijuana joints, miniature bottles of booze, cigarettes and bags of tea and any other drug I could think of and shot them in slow motion as they cascaded over the miniature 'Flying Phallus' that had been mounted so it stood vertically and the shot would make it appear that the ship was flying through a sea of drugs—the 'Moronosphere.'

After Abbas completed cutting the destruction of Wang's miniature castle, it begged to have live people running away in a panic so I hired Bill Hansard to set up a large rear projection screen on stage 8, upon which various cuts of the castle exploding could be projected and I could have Wang's subjects run by the screen with looks of terror on their faces. As they did, I had pieces of Styrofoam tossed at them to make it look like falling debris from the explosion. It was also an opportunity to give a few people a chance to appear in cameo roles. Reb Sawitz, critic Bill Marigold and of course, Cichy, Rogers and myself took the opportunity to appear in what we all saw as a pending classic. To stay true to my character, I carried a girl with her hands on Reb's shoulders and her legs straddling my shoulders so I could be seen eating her pussy as we ran by.

The established optical houses, like Cinema Research, were expensive and only because of Marvin and Muckerman doing miracles at the Beverly Cinema, was I able to keep paying them for their work. But at least I was seeing something for it and it gave me motivation to keep pushing.

Rarely did a day go by when some unexpected problem didn't surface. Walter suggested I take a look at the original, 'Flash Gordon's Trip to Mars,' because he thought Benveniste's script came dangerously close to plagiarizing chapter one of the serial. After a hasty conference with my lawyer, John Weston, explaining my concern, he assured me that there was no problem, but just to be safe, he advised I put a buffer between us and King Features, the owners of the Flash Gordon franchise, by putting a disclaimer at the beginning of the film. It stated in part that: "in these troubled times, America was in need of a new superhero, and though Flesh Gordon was indeed inspired by the original Flash Gordon, our intent was to honor his memory with a comedic spoof."

Abbas, busy building an elaborate effects track, was cutting in growls for the 'Satyr' monster when I noticed how the creature's mouth opened and closed. It dawned upon me that it might be possible to dub in dialogue and give him a voice. If it could be done, it would make him cinema's first talking puppet monster. Despite my issues with Bill, he kept abreast of what was happening with the film and had even brought Frank Zappa by the editing room to take a look at the work print in hopes that he might be interested in doing the music, which he wasn't. But when I mentioned my idea to him about giving a voice to the monster, he came by the editing room a day later with Craig T. Nelson, at the time a struggling comedian he knew from the Comedy Store. It was around nine in the evening and I was ready to call it a day. My mind set about Bill was still angry and I had a hard time accepting that he could add anything positive, but I threaded up the scene on the KEM table anyway and ran it through so Craig could take a look. Craig began to adlib lines that sometimes matched the monster's mouth and at other times were off screen. They were incredibly simple and yet so funny, that not wanting to take a chance of losing the spontaneity of his first attempt, I immediately constructed a sound booth out of a few mover's blankets laying around the room and set Craig up inside with a microphone, leaving a little slit so he could see the picture on the KEM's screen.

The result was hilarious. As the monster plucks off the sheer shaw from Dale's breasts, he gave him a slow, lummox like voice, with lines like: "I just . . . want . . . to look . . . at your tits!" When the monster comes trudging out of the dark castle cavern to wreak havoc, Craig had him saying: "A monster's work . . . is never done." A few cuts later he gave what would be a belly laugh line when the monster just barely misses snatching our heroes, and plaintively cries: "oh . . . fuck!" and moments later when he gets shot in the butt, "My ass . . . the pain . . . the agony . . . the hemroids."

Word had gotten around that 'Flesh Gordon' was something special and despite having almost no money to pay for anything, I, with major help from Walter, was able to hire some top talent to do our titles and music. Walter found Corney Cole, who had recently won an award for his animated 'Flip Wilson TV special' to do our title sequence for a thousand dollars and also found Peter Tevis, a producer at Capital Records, who not only agreed to raise the money to have a score composed by, Ralph Ferraro, a top rated talent, but to pay for it to be recorded at TBS, (formerly Warner Bros.). Finally, Todd

A. O. agreed to mix the tracks and let me pay their fee of twenty grand over a three-month period. I had done it! Flesh was finished.!!

Then the 'Ouija board god hit us with another missle from outer space. I had given all the boxes of the 16mm negative that we had fought so hard to get back from the police, to a company in Burbank that specialized in cutting negative. They had only been working on the job for two days when they called to tell me several rolls of negative were missing. I insisted there had to be a mistake! Walter and I rushed out to Burbank so we could go through the boxes ourselves. Sequence numbers run along the edge of negatives which are transferred to any prints that are struck from them. I was shown a list of the numbers in the work print for which no corresponding negative could be found. After carefully going through every box, I realized they were right and we had a problem. A very very big problem!

My first thought was that the police had failed to return all of the footage—hopefully by mistake. All of the other non 'Flesh Gordon' footage they had confiscated during the raid was still in their evidence vault and possibly a box of 'Flesh Gordon' negative had gotten lost in the pile. I called, John Weston, to tell him I needed to get into the police vaults so I could go through the boxes to see if that was the case. The pigs weren't about to go out of their way to be cooperative. Days went by without an answer. In the meantime, Murray Stein let me check every corner of his lab where the film had originally been developed. I found nothing. After ten days, the cops finally agreed to let me come down and rummage through the boxes they were holding. If I found negatives of 'Flesh Gordon,' they would release them. The next morning, behind the wire mesh of the enclosed police locker room and under the watchful eyes of a police sergeant, I searched through the entire inventory and found nothing.

I had no way of proving that Martin and Brust had fucked me over by hiding or destroying some of the negative, but it was obvious that's what had happened. The shots that were missing were from disparate rolls shot on different days. It wasn't that somehow one roll got lost, it was several from different boxes. The two assholes knew that by throwing a couple of rolls of negative into the trash, they would destroy the whole film and Graffitti right along with it. It would make their day.

I was so depressed I couldn't think straight. I went back to the office and broke the news to Abbas, Walter and Lynn. Some of the missing footage was critical to the story; there was no way to cut around it. I felt like I had met my Waterloo and didn't bother to come to the editing room for a few days. I searched my mind for a solution, but for once, couldn't come up with one. I needed a miracle and atheists don't believe in miracles. It appeared the 'Ouiga board God' had won.

But I was wrong. A miracle did happen. Three days later, when I returned to the editing room, I found Walter running out takes— the shots that weren't used in the final cut—through a Moviescope. As he continued to roll film through the viewer, he told me he had found shots, many of them from the second camera operated by Lynn Rogers, that would cover almost all the shots that had missing negative. Abbas was in the room and concurred. Because Lynn was shooting from a secondary and sometimes unfavorable angle, some of the shots weren't ideally composed, but considering the situation, they were more than acceptable. When Walter finished screening all the outtakes, we were left with only three shots in two different scenes that couldn't be covered: the Ford Tri-motor pilots reacting to the sex ray, Dale walking down the aisle of the Ford Tri-motor as it flies through rough weather and Flesh rushing to reclaim the power pasty from the Jewel chic who is crouched on the floor in Wang's throne room.

I knew I could easily rebuild the Ford Tri-motor set in my back yard and by using a bit of trick photography, shoot the missing scene in 'Wang's' throne room. Martin and Brust's irrational hatred and illegal machinations were going to go for naught. Years later, my suspicions were confirmed, when I was told that Martin had mentioned to someone that giving me back the negative of 'Flesh Gordon' was a mistake he would always regret. The crazy fucker actually thought he was America's censor.

The little "Gator" had saved the day. By week's end, I was in my backyard building the sets necessary to do the re-shoots. I would film at night so I could match the artificial lighting originally used at stage

8. Costa still had the interior walls of the Ford Tri Motor, a piece of the black onyx floor of Wang's throne room, and two of its side walls, stored on the lot in Eagle Rock. Walter was able to relocate the Trimotor seats at a property house and I even outdid Minor, by building a much better set that looked across the hood of the Ford Trimotor so I could shoot a frontal shot of the pilots reacting to the sex ray. Cindy Stokes, aka, Susanne Fields, was long gone, so I had Judy, who was about the same size, to stand in for her in a shot I composed that kept her face out of the frame as she stumbles down the aisle to take her seat next to Flesh. Lynn Rogers, Abbas and several other friends became the passengers. Abbas, never failing to surprise me with his sense of humor, added a line in Arabic that translated into English as "fuck you" when his arm is accidentally bumped by the stumbling Dale.

The most difficult shot to replace was when Flesh rushes the Jewel chick to retrieve Queen Amora's Power Pasty. With only the two wall panels and one four by eight piece of the glazed Masonite flooring, a normal shot would have been impossible. But thanks to my knowledge of diopter lenses, I was able to design a shot that overcame that problem. I set the two wall panels as far in the background that my small yard allowed and put the one piece of Masonite at their base. I then had the 'Jewel Chic,' Marie Arnold, lay on her back with the side of her face only one foot from the front of the zoom lens which was racked out to telephoto so it would only include the two wall panels twenty feet away in the background. The side of her face coved the entire bottom half of the frame and Flesh, standing in the distance in front of the wall panels, the upper half. By using a split field diopter, I could keep them both in focus. When action was called, his run to the Jewel Chic appears to be from a distance. The comic book quality of the composition made it very 'Flesh Gordon.' As the evening came to a close, all I could think was; "Fuck you Martin and Brust."

There was to be one last problem. To my great humiliation, Benveniste had been right to worry about my photography. Due to a lack of a formal education in cinematography, I didn't understand that the aspect ratio of

35mm is different than 16mm. A 35mm frame is much more rectangular than a 16mm frame, which is almost square. It was explained to me at Cinema Research that the top and bottom of the 16mm frame would be lost when they did the blow-up. Heads might be chopped off in the middle and action important to the scene lost. There was a way to fix the problem, but it was going to cost me time and money. I would have to go through the entire film, approximately one hundred twenty thousand frames, with an eye glass, and write out explicit instructions what part of the frame I wanted to be favored; top, bottom, or in some cases, a pan, to ensure that the 35mm blowup frame looked as good as possible. It took three eye-straining weeks to complete the task.

On the bright side, the blow-up gave me an opportunity to repair other mistakes and problems that had occurred during shooting. Laying fog over all the shots in the 'Penisauraus' cave made everything fuzzy and masked the out-of-focus error I had made on the first day of shooting. I was also able to repair the lighting problem when I shot the interior shots of the 'Flying Phallus' outside at Eagle Rock. I shot a close up of a warning sign that was supposedly mounted on the ship's control panel that would blink on and off with a warning that said "trouble" or "double trouble" and then have Cinema Research put a red filter over alternating frames during the blowup to make it appear that light from the warning sign was bathing the scene in red light. It not only fixed the problem, but would get a big laugh from audiences as well.

My eyes teared up with pride as I stood at the back of a stage at The Burbank Studio with Peter Tevis to watch Ralph Ferraro conduct a twenty-piece orchestra to perform and record the score he had written for 'Flesh Gordon.' It was hard to believe that what had begun as a twenty five thousand dollar porn film, was now getting its final tune-up at a major studio. A week later, when we mixed all the sound tracks: dialogue, effects and music, together at Todd A. O; Jack Woltz, the head of the three man crew handling the pods, turned to me and said: "You've got a hit on your hands."

The MGM lab, after seeing the final product, happily extended us short-term credit to make a color corrected master and a first answer print, There wasn't an empty seat in the house on the night we screened the film at their plush two hundred-fifty seat theatre located on their lot. A standing ovation made Mike Hyatt's parting words and the curse of the 'Ouija board God, a distant memory. Three years of work and a half million in costs—much of it still owed -had been worth it!.

78

THE BOYS FROM SCREW

Bill approached me after the screening and asked if I would like to meet two guys from Screw magazine who were interested in distributing the picture. My radar went up! There was no way in hell I was going to let him run off with 'Flesh Gordon!' I already had indications that he might be thinking he could do that when I found the original piece of artwork George Barr had created for our one sheet pined crudely to his refrigerator door. It was a sign that he thought of it as his personal souvenir. I had intentionally listed his name in second position in the credits, but I knew if I let my guard down, he was capable of pushing me into the corner. Giving the film to a distributor with whom he was connected, would mean I never could be sure that no side deals had been made. I declined his offer. For that matter: it already pissed me off that the Screw guys had talked to him in the first place? Was I that invisible?

If I couldn't find a distributor that I felt comfortable with, my plan B was to open 'Flesh Gordon' at the Beverly Cinema and then drive from city to city and four wall it; rent a theatre for a flat price and not have to share any revenue beyond that. Recently, Tom Laughlin, who produced, directed and stared in 'Billy Jack,' reclaimed his distribution rights from Warner Brothers after they had botched its release and made millions by four walling it on his own.

After the reaction at the MGM theatre, finding a distributor should not be a problem. A day later, Randy Johnson, a young straggly haired music producer, called to tell me he had a producer at his place with a briefcase full of money who wanted to meet me. Randy liked to roam around town in a purple velvet gown that made him look like Merlin the Magician, so I wondered if he might be hallucinating, but I had longtime designs on his coquettish girlfriend, Mercy Lamont, who had choreographed and performed in the cheerleader bit at 'Wang's' wedding; so if nothing else, I could use the visit as an excuse to flirt with her.

They lived just four blocks away on Laurel Canyon Blvd in the attic of what had once been the Hollywood home of the 30's sex vamp, Jean Harlow. After parking my car in the spacious semi-circular driveway that fronted the aging white mansion with flaking plaster and scooting up a wide swath of stairs and across the roman villa patio so I could pass through the house's massive unlocked front door and climb a long narrow staircase for three flights to the open door of their attic apartment; before walking in I paused for a second to regain my breath. Mercy, attired in a sexy pink slip, noticed me first and peeked out from her bedroom down the hall to give me a flirty, "Hello Howard."

Randy led me down the hall where he introduced me to Maurice Smith, the producer with the suitcase full of money, who was sitting at a small wooden table in the apartment's dinning area. He was tall and trim and spoke with the kind of charming English accent that mesmerizes Americans. Randy insisted that he open his briefcase to show me that it was full of money, which indeed it was.

Maurice liked to gab and told me he was the son of an English coal miner and after making his way to Hollywood, got into the film business where he produced several films with Roger Corman, including Glory Stompers with Denis Hopper and a film he was currently working on, Cycle Savages with Bruce Dern. He had been at the apartment of a buxom lady (I would eventually learn that he was addicted to big tits) when Randy, who was a friend of hers, unexpectedly showed up. In the course of conversation, Randy mentioned that he was going to the 'Flesh Gordon' screenng and showed him one of my business cards that had George Barr's impressive one sheet art on its front side. Maurice mentioned it was the first time he had ever seen a Hollywood business card with the film's one sheet printed on it. He told me his initial mental response was: "This is a license to print money." When Randy mentioned he was going to the screening at MGM that night, Maurice invited himself along.

Smith didn't pretend to be a distributor, but wholeheartedly suggested that he may be able to set me up with someone who was. I made it clear that I would only deal with someone who had a track record and was willing to put up a minimum of twenty-five thousand dollars for a promotional advertising campaign. Maurice assured me that would not be a problem and arranged for me to meet John Lamb, who was flush with the money he had recently made from, 'Sexual Freedom in Denmark.' I met him the following day at his house, an impressive ranch style home that overlooked the Sunset Strip. My terms were not a problem and we might have signed a deal that day, except for the fear he had of being sued by King Features for infringing on their copyright of 'Flash Gordon.' Convincing him that that was not a problem, eventually gave me a migrain headache and any chance of a deal falling to the wayside.

After another failed attempt, this time set up by Peter Tevis with Warner Brothers, whose buyer liked the film but the upstairs bosses didn't think it appropriate for them to get into bed with an X-rated picture, I swallowed my pride and asked Bill to arrange a meeting for me with the guys from Screw Magazine who were still in Los Angeles.

Peter Locke and Jim Buckley, in association with Al Goldstein, had recently produced and directed 'It Happened in Hollywood,' a porn film that was more comedic than erotic. It had done very well at the box office. Buckley was Goldstein's unsung partner at Screw magazine, the controversial weekly paper that primarily ran ads for hookers and burlesque houses around Manhattan. To my surprise, the meeting turned out great! They had guts and were not afraid to buck the establishment. I made it abundantly clear that Graffitti Productions, not Bill Osco, owned the film and they would be dealing with me, not him. They had no problem with that. With Screw's financial resources to back them up, the minimum terms I set for a distribution launch was not a problem. As soon as I could get to New York, they would have a distribution deal drawn up and ready to sign.

It seemed that fate had meant for Peter and I to join forces. A year earlier, while he was standing in line to see a movie with his new girl friend, singer and actress Liz Torres, a friend came running up to him with a Penthouse magazine in his hand: "You've got to see this." He opened it to the twelve-page layout of 'Flesh Gordon.' Even more surreal, was that the movie he was in line to see was, 'Mona, the Virgin Nymph.' It was currently an art house sensation in New York.

At the Screw offices, just south of Broadway on 14th street, Locke, Buckley and I worked out the details. Goldstein was only a silent partner. Unlike the Lamb deal, there were no snags. They were willing to invest a minimum of twenty-five grand in advertising and had no worries about being sued by King Features. They were also in accord, that 'Flesh Gordon' should be treated as a cult film, not a porno. I wanted it released in mainstream theatres, not porn houses.

Peter had already formulated ideas about how to release and promote the film. He felt that it was essential that we open in New York. If it did well in the Big Apple, the national market would follow. "NewYork sets the trends for the country," he averred. Buckley nodded agreement, but it was obvious from the start that Peter was going to run the show.

"Oh shit, here we go again" Two days after returning to LA, I received a demand letter from King Features that I desist from distributing the picture. They claimed that the salacious nature of 'Flesh Gordon' would do harm to the wholesome image of 'Flash Gordon;' the exact issue that John Lamb had feared. I was feeling like a punching bag. Stunned back on my heels, I contacted the Fleishman office and was given a meeting with Steve Rhode, who handled their civil cases. After apprising him of the situation, he fired off a strong letter, warning King Features, that any attempt to stop the distribution of 'Flesh Gordon' would result in a multimillion-dollar lawsuit. He pointed out that the film had clearly been in the public eye ever since the release of the Penthouse Magazine article, a full year prior. If King Features had concerns, they had had ample time to make their case and there was no justification for them to silently wait while Graffitti continued to spend thousands of additional dollars to complete the film. King Features evidently felt that his argument had merit and backed down.

Peter and Buckley decided to call their 'Flesh Gordon' distribution company, Mammoth Films. At their request, I hired Don Ringe, a friend who had an advertising background, to cut several trailers and TV spots and sent them to New York two weeks later. I was finally free of Flesh Gordon. Mammoth ordered a single print from the MGM lab, and allowing for a couple of weeks for its delivery, scheduled a screening for the New York theatre owners.

Judy and I were both exhausted and in need of some R&D. Naturally, I wanted to be at the premier for 'Flesh Gordon's' opening night, but that would likely be a month away, so Judy and I embarked on a camping trip across the United States. Each day we planned to drive no more than a hundred miles and pitch a tent each night in a national or state park. By the end of our slow trek across the country, we should be arriving in New York close to 'Flesh Gordon's' debut in the *Big Apple*.

Smoking a joint while sitting atop a rock in Joshua Tree National Monument or hiking down a narrow trail in the Grand Canyon that edged past four billion years of geology, was exactly what I needed to mellow out. It felt amazingly good to know that Peter was busy setting up bookings for Flesh. I hadn't spoken with him for a week and after spending a day taking an exhilarating raft ride down the Colorado River rapids at Moab, Utah, I placed a call to see how things were progressing.

I was not expecting the words that came out of his mouth: "Nobody is interested in showing the film."

Trying to stay calm I asked; "Why? . . . You've got to be kidding." "The guy from the Rugoff chain asked me; "Who would want to see that?'"

He made sure I understood he wasn't giving up. The Rugoff chain was the largest in New York and getting booked with them would have been like hitting a homerun on your first trip to the plate. He hadn't lost his faith in the film and would continue with his efforts to get it a play date.

I didn't mention the 'Ouiga Board Monster" because after the standing ovations we got at the MGM theatre, I couldn't fathom the response Peter was getting in New York. For the moment, there was nothing I could do other than remain optimistic. After cooking for four days in one hundred degree temperatures at Utah's famous national parks, we spent a night in a motel at Colorado's Grand Tetons to clean up and get a solid night's sleep. In the morning I called Peter to see if things had improved.

This time the news was much better: "The 11th Street Theatre, an art house in the village, has agreed to let us screen 'Flesh Gordon' for its Saturday night midnight show. He had the first showing last night and there was a line around the block to get in. Evidently, the New York theatre owners had not been aware of the tremendous pre-publicity the film had received from the Penthouse layout."

After we talked a bit more about how excited we were, Peter mentioned that he thought the film was too long and should be cut down. I was in no mood to hear about any re-editing: "The length is fine. It only runs a bit over 90 minutes. How can it be too long? Everyone loved it in LA. Why a problem now?"

He didn't have an answer; just saying it seemed too long. I told myself it was just the hyper-tense New York go-go persona. They think the rest of the country is retarded. I had seen dozens of comedians at the Comedy store do bits on how slow LA is compared to New York: "In LA you step off the curb and expect the cars to stop, in New York they try to hit you to teach you a lesson." 'Flesh Gordon' would work fine once it was given a chance.

After visiting Mount Rushmore in South Dakota, we began crossing the long prosaic Nebraskan landscape. From an aluminum cigar tube, I tapped some flakes of grass onto a cigarette paper and rolled a joint with one hand as we flew down the highway at seventy miles an hour. The mellow high made the drive very pleasant. But since Judy didn't smoke grass, the monotony was making her irritable and we began sniping at each other. We avoided further snits by not speaking to each other and I just kept driving. Finally, in pitch darkness; we pulled into a park located on the edge of the Missouri River. Other than the sound of crickets, the air was still and silent. After quickly pitching our tent, we hurriedly climbed into our sleeping bags and tried to fall asleep. At three AM, I was taking down the tent and we were both dashing to the van to escape the most rapacious mosquitoes either of us had ever seen. The netting on the tent proved feckless to stop them and both of us were covered with itching welts as we sped away.

Daybreak found us at a Howard Johnson's, where we could have breakfast and use their restrooms to clean up and apply anti-itch lotion over our entire bodies. I called Peter and was told that the second weeks screening at the 11th Street Playhouse was again sold out but he also repeated his concern about the film being too long.

How could I not love a woman who not only didn't deny me my sexual indulgences, but also never complained when I needed to play a round of golf. Before continuing on to Leech Lake in Minnesota, I stopped to play eighteen holes at a course just off the highway while Judy entertained herself with a hike through the surrounding woods. By days end we were at the lake where cold artic winds were already creating white-capped waves. Though the night was chilly, harsh winter weather was yet upon us and we decided we had plenty of time to travel the last lap of the trip across Canada.

That was almost a big mistake. As we headed across the three-mile long International Bridge at Sault Ste. Marie into Canada, we were again snipping at each other over nothing. Upon entering the jurisdiction of our friendly northern neighbor, I pulled into one of the lanes at the customs checkpoint where a Canadian border agent began asking some routine questions: "Had either of us ever been convicted of a crime?" There was no need for either of us to say yes, but Judy did just that. Her minor shop lifting charges didn't warrant mentioning, but an ingrained fear of being untruthful to authorities, caused her to blurt out that she had been arrested in Boston for a minor charge. The agent told her she would have to come inside.

As I waited in the van for her to return, my brain became overwhelmed by paranoia. The remaining few flakes of grass in the aluminum cigar container could be a big problem if they were discovered. I had to get rid of it! I got out of the van and holding the cigar tube in my hand, casually sauntered to the edge of the adjacent lane and dropped it onto the ground, giving it a nudge with my foot to push it against the curb so it wouldn't be easily spotted.

Moments later, Judy returned and told me the Canadians had cleared us to enter their country. As we were climbing back into our van, a woman with a family that had just pulled into the adjacent lane was getting out of their car. When I heard her say: "Oh, what's this?" I knew she had spotted the cigar tube lying on the ground. As we pulled out, I could see in my rear view mirror that she was picking it up. I was already two hundred yards down the road when my paranoia got the better of me. The Canadian agents would put two and two together and deduce that it must have been put there by the "Californian van." I envisioned being pulled over down the road and subjected to a search and who knows what else, so I hung a U-turn and headed back over the bridge to the safety of the good old USA.

My unexplained U-turn was enough for them to alert the U. S. side of the bridge and as we pulled up, the American border agents were waiting for us. "Step out of the car and please come with us." An explanation wasn't necessary, but since I knew the van was clean, I didn't sweat it while they made a thorough search. After forty-five minutes, I was told that they had found some marijuana seeds on the floor. I knew it was bullshit, so acting innocent and not wanting to sound confrontational, I told them it was probably from a hitchhiker we had picked up a few days earlier. They had no choice but to buy my story, and we drove off to spend a beautiful night at Michigan's Lakeshore National Park.

"Get the fuck out of our face if you know what's good for you lady." It was one in the morning at Harrison Lake State Park, just inside the Ohio border, where we had stopped to camp two days later. A biker gang had announced earlier in the evening, that no one should try to sleep and reved up their big hog engines every fifteen minutes to make sure no one did. The naïve woman thought a reasoned request could get them to stop. This wasn't camping; it was a nightmare.

I was already contemplating calling a halt to our meandering trek across the country, when I called Peter:

"You've got to get to New York as soon as possible. We're opening up at the Plaza theatre in three days."

He went on to explain: The Plaza theatre, on 57th street, was dying with MGM's compilation picture, 'That's Entertainment,' and was willing to let us have the house for ten days until 'Harry and Tonto' would be opening. It was the only theatre he had been able to book and we had to take it. There was little time to promote the film and he needed all the help he could get. I assured him I'd be in New York by the morning. I fired every booster rocket I had in my van and Judy and I were soon rocketing our way towards the Big Apple.

By mid morning, I was at the Screw Magazine office with Locke and Buckley. Because he needed to get back to work on a porn film he was producing, that featured a girl from Missouri who could tie her labia into a knot, Buckley could only stay for a moment and left me to spend the next few hours with Peter listening to his ideas on how he planned to promote the film. He had a plan to overcome the fact that the booking at the Plaza Theatre had been given to us on such short notice, that there was no chance to run a traditional advertising campaign.

While we talked, Judy had left the Screw offices to take a trip downtown and check out Times Square. Peter had given her directions to the subway station just up the street on Broadway as well as where to get off. He made sure she had the phone number of his office in case she got lost. I appreciated the fact that he was concerned about her welfare.

He went on to say that he had already arranged for a thousand Flesh Gordon one sheets to be plastered all over the city by a midnight poster campaign crew. By early morning, 'Flesh Gordon' would be on the walls of subway stations, telephone poles, phone booths, construction walls and any place that could catch the public eye. The artwork was so alluring that he felt it couldn't help but be noticed.

"Did I still have the costume Flesh Gordon wore in the film?" he wanted to know. I told him I did and he asked if there was anyway of getting it flown out to New York by tomorrow. I told him I could call Cichy and have him go to my house where the costume was stored in a box in the closet. I kept a key hidden in the backyard that he could use to get inside. He could overnight it by FedEx to New York and it would be here by the morning.

Any doubts that I had about my decision to hire Peter to distribute the film, were dispelled as he elaborated on the publicity stunt he had in mind. As soon as we finished talking, he sent a news release to all the local media outlets, including TV, radio and newspapers that read as follows:

King Kong has been lately attacking women in front of the Plaza hotel. Fortunately, Flesh Gordon is in town and promises to put a stop to this menace at precisely three PM tomorrow afternoon.

Peter explained that by sending the announcement as a "News," rather than a "Press" release, significantly raised the chances of the event being covered. The News department was always looking for something interesting to report, whereas the entertainment department was inundated with promotions every day.

Our discussion was interrupted when a secretary came in and announced that Judy was on the phone. I took the phone and she started babbling that she got off at the wrong station and was on the platform at 116th street and wanted to know what she should do. I had no clue and told Peter where she was. He grabbed the phone out of my hand and told her: "Get the fuck out of there on the first train going back in the direction you just came from and don't talk to anyone. Definitely do not leave the station or you might get into a dangerous situation." She had inadvertently gotten off in Harlem and

Peter's admonishment, although well meaning, was probably over stated, but it was a time of high racial tensions, so maybe not.

After hanging up the phone, he went on to further explain the details of his PR stunt. He had already determined that he could get a parade permit for only one hundred fifty dollars, which would provide us a legal right to stage an event across from Central Park on the Grand Army Plaza and in front of the ritzy Plaza Hotel. The centerpiece of the plaza was the multi tiered Pulitzer Fountain, where water cascades from its top tier through a series of basins, until it falls into a large pool at ground level. Tourists flock to the site, not only to see the fountain and the hotel, but to rent horse driven surreys to take them on rides through the park.

We would pretend that we were there to shoot a scene for a low-budget film. Peter would act as director and I would mount a camera on a tripod and feign to be shooting an ape charging down from the top of the fountain, who after splashing through the several basins of the fountain and reaching the pool at the bottom, would climb out and run to a nearby surrey, where he would attack the two women sitting in it. Flesh Gordon, hanging from a wire attached to an arm of a large crane, would then be swung onto the plaza, where after being lowered to the ground, would run to the carriage and grab a cream pie from a nearby vendor and smash it into the uncouth ape's face. If the police challenged our right to film, we would be on our way by the time they figured out what was going on. It was a brazen plan; perfect for Flesh Gordon.

Judy walking back into the office provided a light-hearted moment. She always had a way of adding a little excitement to the day. Peter suggested that the three of us visit the Plaza theatre where 'Flesh Gordon' would make its debut. I fell in love with the theatre as soon as I saw it. A 'Flesh Gordon' one sheet with a large tag pasted onto it read: ***World Premier Friday night***, was already being displayed outside the theatre in its showcase. Located on 58th street, between Madison and Park Avenues, its Tudor style architecture, wood paneling and ornate molding, gave it an air of artistic sophistication. The five-hundred-seat auditorium had a friendly and intimate feeling. Playing 'The Plaza' would go a long way in establishing 'Flesh Gordon' as a sexy science fantasy film rather than a pornography film.

At three O'clock the next afternoon, Judy and Liz Torres, dressed like two antebellum southern belles, sat in a surrey on the edge of the Grand

Army Plaza. A traditionally dressed Italian vendor, selling cream pies from his pushcart, stood a few feet to the side. A large crane was parked on 58th street so its extended boom could reach into the plaza. I pretended to be making final adjustments to the camera while Peter directed a friend of his, outfitted in an ape costume, to climb to the top tier of the fountain. Within seconds, a large crowd had congregated around our faux movie production and several police officers dutifully joined to help with crowd control. On Peter's call for action, the ape came bounding down from the top of the fountain, frantically waving his arms as he splashed his way through the tiers of cascading water and then climbed out to lumber towards the carriage. The crowd screamed with laughter as the ape began his attack on the two damsels.

Seemingly out of nowhere, hanging by a cable attached to the end of the crane's boom, Flesh Gordon came flying onto the scene—a bit of theatrical privilege used to overlook the fact that Flesh didn't fly. Since Jason Williams wasn't in town, "Marc 10 1/2 inch Stevens," the well-endowed New York porn star, was hired to stunt double for him. After he had been gingerly placed on the ground and ineptly extricated himself from the harness, he rushed to the carriage to save the ladies. But finding that brute strength was no match for the ape, he grabbed a cream pie from the nearby vendor and smashed it into the hairy offender's face. The ape scampers away and Flesh Gordon had once again saved the day.

The crowd went ballistic and in true New York fashion, gave us a big hand to show their appreciation. But the real pay-off would come later that evening and the next morning when two TV stations who were piqued by Peter's news release, gave us three minutes on the six O'clock news ninety seconds on the morning news.

All of our futures, but none more than mine, hung on how the film performed on that mid May night of 1974. As we drove around Manhattan looking for the Flesh Gordon posters that had been hung during the night, Peter screamed; "faster, faster," to make me fly along at sixty miles per hour to catch all of the eight blocks of lights while they were set to green. 'Flesh Gordon' posters were everywhere, but when we returned later in the day, most had been torn down—a good sign according to Peter. Fans wanted them as souvenirs.

At six O'clock, when Judy and I got to the theatre, there was already a long line that stretched westward up 58th street until it almost reached Park Avenue, waiting for the ticket office to open. People of all stripes were lined up; couples, singles, hippies, professionals—even Elton John stood waiting. The first show was sold out within a few minutes.

79

A PANICED ALL NIGHT RE-EDIT

An excited buzz filled the theatre as the film began. When the line in the disclaimer: "America was in need of a new super hero to help relieve the tension of the modern world" got a big laugh, it portended good things. 'Flesh Gordon' was already lightening the mood of a stressed out war weary America. For the first twenty minutes it continued to deliver, even getting laughs that I didn't expect to get, but then I began to feel the energy in the room slowly ebbing. When the 'Beetleman' scene fell flat, I had to admit that there might be a problem. As I stood in the lobby and watched the audience file out, I couldn't help but feel the dull ennui that hung over them. After a similar response during the second showing, I knew that Peter had been right; the film was too long! My screenings in LA were for cast, crew and friends. The only meaningful critic is a paying customer and they were bored by the time the film ended.

In a panic, I told Peter I had to do something immediately. If the film continued to play as now cut, we would be dead in a week. He agreed. A friend of his, Shawn Cunningham, who had just produced a hit horror film called 'Friday the 13th,' had an editing room just two blocks away. Peter called him from the theatre's lobby and miraculously found him at home on a Friday night. After explaining the problem, Sean agreed to meet us at his editing room around 11PM. Peter and I grabbed the six reels of 35mm film out of the projection room and lugged them up the street to Sean's editing room to be there when he arrived.

Expecting to see a wild-eyed madman, Sean was quiet and unimposing, the antithesis of how one would think a horror filmmaker should look. He was the same age as Peter and I and as a fellow low budget filmmaker, understood our plight. After giving me a quick course on how to use the Steenbeck editing machine, wished us good luck and left the room. Peter stayed for an hour and then left to go home. I planed to work throughout the night and into the next day, whatever it took, to make cuts so the film would run at a crisper pace.

I had already identified quite a few places that could be trimmed when I watched the second screening at the Plaza. The difficulty was going to be making the cuts so that they didn't destroy the sound track. The optical sound track along the edge runs forty frames in front of the corresponding picture frame, so I had to be careful not to hack off dialogue when I made a cut. I had never done anything remotely close to what I was about to attempt. If I failed, the print would be ruined and spell the end of the play date at the Plaza.

My work was made much easier when I discovered that just by looking for a gap on the optical track that had no modulations, I could visually spot stretches where a cut could be made. If there were no peaks and valleys, it meant there was no sound and a cut at that point wouldn't affect anything. By morning, I had snipped out clips that were only six or seven frames and others that ran for over a minute. When I lugged the reels back to the Plaza Theatre, where it would play later that night; 'Flesh Gordon' had been reduced from ninety-minutes to seventy-eight minutes, an unusually short length for a feature.

But we weren't selling T-bone steaks where a few missing ounces would be an issue, we were selling entertainment, and seventy-eight minutes of brisk entertainment was a lot better than ninety minutes of dull entertainment. The proof in the pudding came after the first showing that evening. I expelled a sigh of relief when I saw that the audience had remained alert and entertained throughout the film. People were excited and upbeat as they filed out. They had enjoyed themselves!

A list of the cuts I had made was immediately forwarded to the MGM lab so they could conform a new negative to the shorter version and quickly strike a new print. It was just a matter of time before the tape-spliced print that the Plaza Theatre was now playing, would begin jamming in the projector's gate. MGM did a rush job to get a replacement print to New York within a few days. What a pleasure to work with real pros.

Nothing else could go wrong and for once it didn't. 'The Ouija board God' had been defeated! Over the next several days, reviews started coming in from sources as diverse as *The NY Daily News to Women's Wear Daily*. They were all surprisingly good, recognizing, that as a low budget independent film, it shouldn't be judged by the same standards that would be used to judge a major studio release. All, except for a few stuff shirts, agreed that the film was good campy fun. A humorous bad review came a month later after we went national, from a reviewer at the Cleveland Plain Dealer who wrote: "remember these names, Howard Ziehm, Bill Osco and Mike Benveniste, because if you see their names on the credits of any film in the future, avoid it at all costs." It was my favorite review. He was likely a distant relative of Martin and Brust.

Most telling and important was that word of mouth spread quickly around New York and people kept flocking to The Plaza Theatre. So much so, that they decided to bump *'Harry and Tonto'* and hold us over . . . and over . . . and over, for a total of thirteen weeks. We were a hit—in the Big Apple no less!

As Peter claimed, New York set the stage. A few large ads placed in Variety and some of the other industry trade papers, extolling the film's outstanding first week grosses at the Plaza theatre, brought in calls from around the country looking to book 'Flesh Gordon.' To deal with the surge of business, Peter hired Stan Gotleib, a septuagenarian who had worked with AIP (American International Pictures) and was savvy to all the nuances of national film distribution. Peter's secretary, Rosemarie, a cute feisty Italian, handled the phones and all the bookwork with aplomb. By mid October Mammoth had two hundred prints working around the country.

Jim Buckley helped the cause by doing a lengthy interview of me for Screw Magazine, but since he was not inclined to deal with the daily grind of distribution, Peter hired Barry Cahn, the friend who had showed him the Flesh Gordon Penthouse Magazine layout when he was standing in line waiting to see 'Mona;' to become his right hand man. Barry was running a shoe manufacturing company in Puerto Rico, but when Peter called, offering him a chance to get into the movie business, he dropped everything and flew to New York. Mammoth now had a small, but effective, distribution team in place and money began to flow in from all across the United States.

As exciting as the New York premier was, the film was made in LA and for all involved, the home turf opening had to get special treatment. Seymore Borde and his son Mark, was Mammoth's sub distributor for the west coast and booked Flesh Gordon simultaneously into the UA theatre complex in Westwood near the UCLA campus and the Vogue on Hollywood Boulevard. When The Society of Motion Picture Science Fiction and Fantasy learned of the LA premier, they offered to fly the original Flash Gordon, Buster Crabbe, in from Arizona to attend the gala event planned on opening night at the UA Westwood.

The steady rain that poured on the evening of October 11, 1974, was not enough to dampen anyone's high spirits. The police barricaded the street that ran in front of the theatre so interviews could be held by the LA press. Danny Elfman and The Mystic Nights of the Oingo Boingo snaked their way through the crowd. Elfman had yet to become a legendary composer of film scores, and was quite happy that his friend, Randy Johnson, had got him and his band a hundred dollar gig to play at the premier. Searchlights lit up the sky and a large crowd stood under umbrellas to watch the stars of 'Flesh Gordon' arrive. Many hoped to see a porn star.

After the film let out, a reporter from Channel 4, asked Buster Crabbe, who was in his eighties, how he felt about the film. Beyond saying that he was a bit discomfited by the sexuality, he was too nice to say anything negative. Notwithstanding, the crowd and the the local critics ate it up. Kevin Thomas, the esteemed movie critic for the LA Times wrote:

> **"Considering that such successful practitioners of parody as Mel Brooks and Woody Allen after all work on a hit-and-miss basis, Flesh Gordon's creators, Howard Ziehm, Michael Benveniste and Walter Cichy deserve much credit for sustaining their spoof pretty consistently from start to finish . . . Flesh Gordon may be utterly without any socially redeeming qualities— but it sure is lots of fun."**

The next morning, Bill and I were invited to appear on Channel 5 to do an interview. We waited in the green room with Vida Blue, the Oakland Athletics sensational rookie baseball pitcher, who seemed as nervous as we were about the sudden adulation. I took it upon myself to do most of the talking, but as I began responding to the first question: "Could you give a brief description of the picture?" I realized that the names of almost all of the characters, i. e. *Dr. Jerkoff, The Penisauraus* or *Emporer Wang*, would probably be bleeped out as being obscene. My adlib attempt to give a G-rated version was less than stellar. It didn't matter; like New York, Flesh Gordon ran at the UA for several months.

As Graffitti's coffers grew by thirty grand a week, I was most happy to be able to pay back all of our creditors and especially Walter, Lynn and Sy Katz, whose belief in the film when things didn't look good, had made it possible. Being able to continue to pay my lawyers to keep me out of prison, was an even greater relief. And not least was being able to make a clean severance from my ex partner, Bill Osco. There was no doubt in my mind that I would never have succeeded without him, but ironically it seemed impossible to succeed with him. If he could make an honest dollar or a dishonest dollar, he seemed to prefer the latter. Despite my best efforts, our names would always be intertwined and he would continue to get more than his share of the credit for much of the work I had done. That's just the way it was.

80

NEUVEAU RICHE

Hollywood is always looking for new talent and I had just made a hit picture. Katz's office received a call from a TV producer inquiring if I would be interested in directing a few episodes. I told Katz's secretary to decline the offers, telling them I only worked on my own projects. Truth was that I had my own way of directing and was sure they would be horrified when they saw me work. Despite my resistance, Peter Tevis twisted my arm to take a meeting with Bob Hagel, a friend of his and president of TBS (the Burbank Studios). Rather than pitch a project, I mostly sat silent during the meeting. Afterwards, Hagel told Tevis that I didn't seem interested in working with a studio. I didn't even know what working with a studio meant. That they financed projects was a mystery to me, but even if I knew that, working under watchful eyes would have been difficult for me. I was a loner at heart.

I was suddenly richer than I had ever envisioned—not super rich, but more than comfortable. I told Judy that we could start looking for a house. I wanted to be free of landlords and banks, so I hoped we could find something in Malibu that I could pay for with cash. A pretty young realtor spent the morning showing us homes all the way out to Zuma Beach, but when she took us to the last house on her list, a ranch style house two miles up Las Flores Canyon with a view all the way out to Catalina, that had large picture windows in every room, I knew it was exactly what I had envisioned. It sat on a half acre of land and had almost no nearby neighbors. Though the location gave the impression that it was isolated from the world, Santa

Monica was only twenty minutes away. The asking price, a hundred thirty-five thousand, was well within my budget and without quibbling; I told the realtor I would take it. The cute girl had just earned her first commission and Judy and I were about to own a home in Malibu, free and clear.

Fame and money was something new to me and I had to be careful how I handled it. I wasn't the kind of person who was going to go on a spending orgy, but there were nice things that I could now afford. Yet I was new to the experience and some saw me as gullible. Randy Johnson made a surprise visit with a friend who looked like the Disney cartoon character, Yosemite Sam. They had come to sell me some Nevada mining stocks at only ten percent of par value. Par value was ten thousand dollars and I could have them for only a grand each—if I bought ten. Did I really look that stupid? Maybe so . . . at least in their eyes. However, I used his visit to my advantage by getting the phone number of his ex, the lovely Mercy Lamont, who was now living in Paris. I had a premonition that I might be traveling abroad in the near future and her phone number might lead to some sexy fun.

My fame had spread around the country and even earned me a call from my former girl friend, Rita Fogelis, still single and still living in Boston. She had seen 'Flesh Gordon' at a theatre in Harvard Square and got my number from Bernie Goldhirsh to see if it could possibly be me. I was flattered that she had called and told her: "yes it was me." I mentioned that I was planning a trip back east and, if possible, would come up to Boston to see her. A bit full of myself, I couldn't resist the thought of showing her what a prize I had become.

The hectic situation that Judy and I had gotten married under, hadn't allowed time for a honeymoon. The one-month vacation we were about to take would be that and more. It would begin with a one-week stop in Sarasota, Florida, where her parents had moved to escape the freezing New England winters; and then on to the Virgin Islands for three weeks. While we were away, work would be in progress to turn our new home into an exotic paradise. A free form pool was being built that went into a room beneath the house and at its deep end would have water trickling out of a Jacuzzi over a stone waterfall. The barren dirt yard was being turned into a small urban park with a meandering free form lawn and a small redwood forest. There was to be an orchard with a variety of fruit trees at the back of the house.

The sand at Longboat key beach in Sarasota is so fine, that it squeaks. While Judy and I lie atop it on a blanket soaking up the suns rays, the thought of possibly screwing Rita was dancing in my head. There was something alluring about gaining access to a pussy that had previously been denied. The lure overwhelmed me. I knew Judy wouldn't be happy about me visiting an ex girl friend, so, I lied to her and said I had to fly to New York to take care of some business with Mammoth Films.

Once in New York, I gave Rita a call to make sure she still wanted to see me. She did and I was in Boston within a couple of hours. She picked me up at the airport and possibly to make myself feel better about my deception, we drove over to Bernie's new offices on the pier to say hello. With that out of the way, we dashed over to her apartment where she coyly asked: "Do you still like to do . . . you know what?" No need to say what the answer was. After we finished, she confided that she was thinking of marrying some guy she didn't really love. I advised against it: assuring her that she was a beautiful woman and good things would happen to her in time. Now that she enjoyed sex, she was in the driver's seat. Any man would be lucky to have her.

I returned to New York that evening so my flight back to Florida would originate from there and Judy wouldn't suspect that I had been in Boston. The next day, while Judy and I were having a mundane conversation as we soaked up more rays at the beach, I let it slip that I had seen Bernie. As the words were falling from my mouth, I knew I had fucked up big time. She was no fool and sat up immediately. Her piercing stare said it all. It was one thing to have quickies, another to see someone you had once been serious with. Our 'open' relationship wasn't supposed to include lying and I had broken the rule. She blurted out that she, "hated me and always would," which I didn't really believe, but didn't exactly enjoy hearing.

Judy's most endearing quality was that she didn't hold grudges and by the time we reached the peaceful and idyllic Virgin Islands, the incident had been washed away as if it was sand in an ebbing wave. The next two weeks were spent drinking daquaris, snorkling and golfing by myself on a fabulous Trent Jones golf course on St. Croix. Only a minor car accident on St Thomas and the discovery, which would explain why I was the only person on the golf course, that a massacre by a group of rebellious locals had occurred there ten years earlier, marred what was otherwise a perfect vacation. That unpleasantness would soon be replaced by an exciting experience we were to have on St John island, where we had moved to and were now living in a tent at the Buck Island National Park.

Judy was back to being her normal sexy self. After snorkeling among the giant brain coral and the barracudas who swim there, we were sipping Daiquiris and lemonades while talking with a young couple we had just met at an open air bar in the little town at the end of the island. When it became known by the soon-to-be-wed couple, that I was a pornographer and she a stripper, we were asked, in an off-handed way, if we would be willing to give the bride-to-be a lesson on how to give a blow-job. Without being sure they were actually serious, we still told them we would be happy to help out.

They were serious. An hour later, the bride-to-be dropped by our tent hoping to take a lesson. She was very attractive, had a nice personality and was intelligent; just one of the many girls who were brought up in the "sex is dirty environment," that is so American. It was obvious that she wanted to escape that curse. With a modicum of coaxing, she came closer to the open end of the tent so Judy and I could begin the watch-and-learn lesson. Judy was obviously going to be the instructor and I the willing sex object. After I took my position lying down on my back on the cot, she began by loosening the zipper of my hot pants. The thrill of sexual exhibitionism had already made me half erect and my cock was pushing hard against the little red pouch that was covering it. The young girl probably had no idea that she was going to get such a well-scripted show that included top of the line costuming. Judy knelt on the ground besides me and lowered my hot pants and the little red pouch down to my knees. Taking my three-quarter-husky in her hand, it only took a few passes of her mouth sliding up and down to make it rock hard. Playing the role of a teacher, she graciously took time to look up and explain to her student all the subtleties of the art of fellatio. The engrossed student, only a few feet away, stood transfixed and amazed at how easy it was for a female to make a male happy and helpless. I couldn't resist suggesting that she take a few practice sucks to make sure there were no questions, but she declined, wanting to stay pure for her soon-to-be hubby. The next morning, hubby-to-be, stopped by to thank us for our service and verified that wife-to-be had learned her lesson well.

81

A NAÏVE AMERICAN ABROAD

My vision of modern Europe, formed when I lived in Erlangen, was incredibly out of touch. I still imagined bombed-out-ruins to be everywhere and my idea of the foreign motion picture market was beyond callow. A typical foreign theatre was like the one in the classic Italian film, *'Cinema Paradisio:'* twenty five seats in a small shack set on the side of a dusty dirt road and run by a single man who after selling tickets cranked up his primitive projector to show a film. That was the vision I had in mind when I gave Abbas the rights to be my foreign representative for 'Flesh Gordon.'

There was not much for me to do while our house was still being worked on, so when he called from Italy to tell me he was about to make a deal with a former Egyptian army colonel named Frank Agrama, to help him make sales of 'Flesh Gordon' at the Caanes Film Festival, without giving it a second thought, I told him it was fine with me. Agrama had an office in Rome and according to Abbas, knew the foreign market inside and out.

He suggested that I come over and though he and Agrama would be very busy during the festival making sales, I would have a chance to see what was going on. After the festival, I could fly to Rome where we could all get together at Agrama's office and close the deals. I doubted that there was much money involved and other than Bridgett Bardot causing a sensation when she appeard on the Caanes beach wearing an outrageous bikini, I had no idea what the festival was about. It sounded fun and interesting and Judy and I packed our bags and flew to France.

I hooked up with Abbas in the lounge of the Hotel Carlton where he introduced me to Frank Agrama whose fit physique, domineering personality and half-bald head, comported well with his former position as an Egyptian colonel. My image of a bombed out Europe was grossly off the mark. It was now vibrant and had no resemblance to what it had been after the war. After the brief meeting, Judy and I spent the next few days strolling up and down the Boulevard de la Croisette, which fronted all the best hotels on the French Riviera. Greco style mansions peppered the verdant hills that overlooked the small provincial town that had begun eons earlier as a fishing village, but was now swarming with star hopefuls and onlookers as well as high-ranking executives from the studios. Harold Robbins, the prolific author, had his yacht moored a hundred yards off the shore. Word was out that he was throwing a party later that evening for invited guests only. It was the kind of event Osco would have wormed his way into but in my mind it certainly didn't include me.

Seeing film buyers from all over the world scurrying to small theatres and screening rooms up and down the cobble stoned streets of the little village, made it obvious that the festival was a busy market place, yet it still didn't register on me that there was a lot of money to be made. I was more taken by the sexy looking prostitutes dressed in trashy attire that had come into town from all over Europe and were now offering their services on some of the side streets. But after the Rita ordeal, even I wasn't about to desert Judy while I checked them out.

Subsequent to discovering that the beach in nearby St. Tropez, wasn't filled with lithe, near nude beauties wearing only a cache sexe, but was actually a small swath of sand at the end of a little dirt path just past the town's waterfront, where a few bored sun bathers didn't give me a second look as I walked past them wearing my small red nylon pouch, we boarded a plane and flew to Rome where I was to meet with Abbas and Agrama to vet the sales they had pending from the festival. A hustling cab driver whisked us past the ubiquitous soldiers carrying machine guns at Rome's Leonardo De Vinci airport into his cab and we were quickly on our way to the Grand Hotel on the Via Veneto where Abbas had reserved us a room.

The cab driver spoke a bit of English and asked what I did. I told him I was a filmmaker, not mentioning 'Flesh Gordon,' fearing that it could lead to a discussion about pornography. When he asked what I thought about

DeSeca, I had no idea who he was talking about. The only Italian filmmaker I knew was Enrico Felini. He proudly told me that DeSeca had made 'The Bicycle Thief; it was a very famous film.' I felt grossly stupid that I knew so little about film and vowed that when I got back to the states I would make a point of viewing 'The Bicycle Thief.' It would turn out be, as he said, a classic; a simple story of a young boy seeing his father wrongly accused by the police of stealing a bicycle.

Judy needed to take a nap once we got to our room, so I used the time to take a stroll around the area. A tall raven-haired hooker wearing tight black satin pants that clung tightly to her camel toe, stood in a doorway next to the hotel. It was a nice introduction to Rome. Two blocks up the street was the Villa Borghese, the largest park in the city, and almost directly across was Harry's Bar, made famous as a location in Felini's 1960 classic, 'La Dolce Vita.' I meandered serendipitously across one of Rome's seven hills and found myself starring at the Coliseum. It seemed that every alley had a piece of art that most American cities would be proud to have in their centers. When I returned to the room, Judy was awake and ready for dinner.

We dined at a wonderful little restaurant just around the corner from the hotel. Set slightly below street level, its entry was through a short arched red brick passageway where there were delicious looking bowls of salads sitting on a long linen covered table. We were new to fine dining and sated ourselves for two hours. I had a veal chop extraordinaire and she had an equally marvelous chicken dish. Unlike in America, there was no pressure to leave. After a couple of glasses of wine, I was ready to retire. I would be hooking up with Abbas in the morning and wanted to be fresh.

About ten in the morning, Abbas picked Judy and I up at the hotel and took us to Agrama's office. It was located on the first floor of an old two-story building, just a few blocks from the Via Veneto. Since Judy had no interest in the business we were about to conduct, Agrama suggested she take a tour of Rome on one of the busses parked nearby. Judy was not the kind of girl afraid to venture off by herself and happily took the suggestion. I told her to meet me back at the hotel about four.

Frank Agrama was a fast confident talker. Feeling somewhat like a country bumpkin; I realized I was no match for him and didn't particularly want to be. There was no reason to think I wasn't going to be treated fairly. He sat behind a dark hardwood desk that positioned him in front of a large window with its Venetian blinds drawn just enough to dimly light the room. Abbas and I sat across from him in comfortable leather chairs. Two indoor ferns gave the room a modicum of warmth. Needing some information for a press release, Agrama asked me to tell him a little bit about myself. When I began by blurting out that I was a 'free thinker' and into 'free love,' he quickly stifled the rest of my response. Shaking his head he said: "that will never fly in Catholic Italy." He assured me "he would take care of things." I was quite surprised to hear that King Features had contacted him as soon as they learned that he had obtained the Italian rights to 'Flesh Gordon' and were planning to sue in Italy over a claim of plagiarism. I mentioned their threat in the States and how we had forced them to back off, but he pointed out that Italian law stated that you could not even put a product into a bad light. However, he seemed not to be worried and assured me he could handle it.

Before getting down to business, Agrama drove us to the Technicolor Roma lab where all of our European prints would be made. They had invited us to have lunch and when we arrived, I was treated more like a foreign dignitary than the small time pornographer that I saw myself as. After a warm greeting by the head of the lab, we were taken to the executive's dinning room and joined there by several members of his staff. I was given the seat of honor at the head of a large, well-appointed round dinning table. The kitchen staff poured us drinks and served us freshly prepared salads as the various execs explained to me that Technicolor would provide top notch prints and dupe negatives and that my film would be completely secure in their hands. As we talked, the dinning staff placed a three-foot long sea bass in the center of the table for our consumption. The whole scene was Feliniesque.

Back at his office, Agrama presented me with the offers he had gotten from various territories: fifty thousand dollars for Germany, forty thousand for France, twenty thousand for Australia and twenty five thousand for England. Only the English contract was against a percentage of earnings, which meant it could be more if the film did good business. Agrama assured me they were all good offers; "the best he could do." The numbers, much more than I expected, didn't seem unreasonable for a low budget Indie film. The contracts showed that the English deal was with a company called Entertainment Film Distributors, but all the others were with a nameless company located in Lichtenstein, which struck me as strange. When I asked Agrama why that was, he suavely stated it was common for European companies to do business through Lichtenstein to avoid paying taxes. Gullible and overwhelmed by Agrama's persona, I bought his explanation and signed the contracts.

At the time, I had no clue what a sensation Flesh Gordon had been during the festival. Month's later, while visiting Los Angeles, Michael Green, the English distributor, told me how he had come to buy the rights for the United Kingdom. He and his wife, both in their fifties, were in Caanes looking to buy Independent films that might help them grow their small company. Michael was sitting on the patio of the Grand Hotel when his wife, Jean, came practically running down the street to tell him she had just seen a film that couldn't miss. She had just been at a screening of 'Flesh Gordon' and her enthusiasm was so convincing that the two of them rushed back to catch the next show. He immediately made an offer for the UK and its territories. I wouldn't know, until ten years later, that it would be the only legitimate offer that Agrama had presented to me, all the others were bogus, which I will explain later in this story.

But that day, I left his office happy as a lark and after killing a few hours in a theatre watching Tinto Brass's 'Madam Kitty' the current rage in Rome, I went back to the hotel to meet Judy. I had seen 'Madam Kitty' in the states at a fifty seat theatre where it had been presented as a porn film, but left after fifteen minutes because it was so boring. In Rome, it was playing at a theatre with well over a thousand seats to a near riotous audience. A guy a few seats from me rose to his feet and shook his fist at the screen as he yelled, "Facisti." I left thinking, "How was it that we Americans were so unaware?"

The explosive atmosphere in the theatre and the armed guards at the Rome airport made me reflect upon my own feelings about rebellion. I had been rebelling for a long time, but was still unclear why. After dodging the Vietnam War, I had avoided overtly becoming involved in any of America's political marches or demonstrations. And now, despite 'Mona' and 'Flesh Gordon' being heralded for being in the forefont of breaking down the barriers of sexual repression, I still didn't accept it as true or take credit for my role. A fog of doubt hung over me that went all the way back to my childhood.

As I walked back to the hotel, I pondered why I continued to allow myself to be so overwhelmed. I had sensed that Agrama might have just run over me, but did little to challenge him to determine if it was true or not. Was it just because my freedom was still on the line. Hardly anyone knew that I was facing prison time. Even after I had made a pointed effort to make it clear that I had made 'Flesh Gordon,' one reviewer wrote that; "Flesh Gordon was made by Bill Osco and some other guy." I only had myself to blame. I was paying a price for not being a good socializer. The Chinese adage says it best: "A wise man knows everything, a smart man knows everyone." But changing one's personality is easier said than done and I wasn't sure it was something I would ever do.

Maybe that's why my marriage to Judy worked. Our personalities were Yin and Yang. Where I was socially shy, she was anything but. Back at the hotel she told me about her wild day in Rome. She had met an Italian guy named Mario, who owned a hotel in Sicily. He had given her a personal tour of the city; the Coliseum, catacombs, aqueducts and a lunch in a fine café to boot. When they departed, he gave her his card and said that anytime she wanted, she could come to Sicily where he would put her up in his hotel. I assumed the offer didn't include me. I was happy that she had a nice day and understood it was a complement to her ego to be the object of pursuit by a hot—and given that his hotel was in Sicily—mafia connected Italian.

The next day we rented a little Fiat and after negotiating our way out of Rome's insane traffic, headed to Pisa, Florence and Venice. Judy was unusually silent and I started to think that her moodiness was because she was again romantically smitten, this time by her new Sicilian friend. I hoped that after climbing to the top of the Tower of Pisa and seeing Michelangelo's nude statue of David (it would have been banned in America) and gondoliering through the canals of Venice, the spell would have passed; but it didn't. Her sour mood and a waiter at an outdoor café in St Mark's Square attempting to overcharge me ten bucks for a cup of coffee; began to make my mood sour as well.

It came to a head when on the way to Paris, the train made a one-hour refueling stop at a small mountain village in Switzerland. It allowed us time to have dinner at a little restaurant in a chalet that sat across the street from the quaint railroad station. The Swiss aren't a lively lot and we fit right in with the other comatose diners, but Judy's continued brooding finally made me explode. She had a bad habit of thinking I was stupid and claimed her sour mood was about a sweater that she had left in our room at the Grand Hotel. But I had dealt with her irrational romantic fantasies before and knew what was happening. Her sweater story was absurd. I finally hit my wits end.

While we waited for our food, I made an offer. I would give her enough money to take the train back to Rome and she could do whatever she needed to do: I could care less. She could rejoin me in Paris ten days later when we were booked to fly back to the States. Our plans had already included hooking up with our friend, Mercy Lamont, so I told her when she arrived in Paris, I would have made sure Mercy knew where I was staying and could tell her how to find me. I was somewhat surprised when my offer was accepted. It was fine with me; I could use the ten days to seduce Mercy. As the other Swiss diners, we finished eating in silence. I reboarded the Paris bound train and as the train pulled out, waved goodbye to my wife standing alone on the platform. She had six hours to kill before her train back to Rome would arrive. I felt an irrational pang of pity for her as she disappeared in the distance.

By early morning I was in 'the city of light' or as some prefer, 'the city of love.' Frugal by nature, I booked myself into a modest three star hotel. After a breakfast of a *café leche* and a *croissant acec beurre*, I was pleased to catch Mercy at home when I gave her a jingle. Within an hour, I was at her small apartment on the third floor of a building near the Notre Dame Cathedral. She was her usual playful self. Her flashing eyes and coquettish smile left little doubt that we were going to have sex. Only moments after she excused herself to take a bath, I was invited in to wash her back. My soapy hands soon eased their way down to the soft crevice between her legs. A dash to her bed and a great wet fuck soon followed.

After we both recovered from our sexual paroxysms, she took me for a short walk around her neighborhood and knowing how much I enjoyed erotically dressed women, a tour of the Rue St. Denis. The street, located in the center of the garment district, was a sexual Shangri-La. Even in the middle of the day, it was a candy store of sexual delights. Prostitutes tricked out in every kind of sexy outfit imaginable, stood along the curb or in the recesses of the doorways. Many were young beauties, packed into everything from tight crotch-hugging hot pants or micro minis that offered a peek of their panties, to tall svelte dominatrixes in see thru negligees, naked except for the tiny g-strings they wore beneath. An endless stream of men, like ants seeking sugar, snaked up and down the Rue and its side alleys. There was a fuck-for-hire almost anywhere one turned.

My heart was racing as I walked Merci back to her apartment. As soon as we kissed goodbye, I rushed back to the Rue St. Denis where I planned to spend the rest of the day and night exploring all the nooks and crannies of the area I could. With my right hand in my pants pocket, I kept my cock bone hard, being careful not to let it ejaculate and ruin the day. Trying to be subtle, the looks of some of the ladies let me know they were hip to what I was doing. If they resented me getting pleasured for free, I didn't give a shit. A hard cock made me oblivious to everything.

After joining the ant line for two round trips of femme de jour ogling, I approached a beautiful blond with neatly coiffed hair who could have been a receptionist in a corporate office and asked in my limited High School French, "Combien?" She matter-of-factly replied, "deux cent." I quickly computed that to be about twenty bucks. I told her "D'accord" and she snatched my hand so I couldn't change my mind and pulled me up four flights of an uncomfortably narrow staircase and through a door at the top where a fifty-something madam sat behind a little desk. There I was asked for another hundred Francs for the use of a bedroom. As a hooker novice, I pondered for a split second; but my lovely blond sex-worker whose perfect breasts were pouring over the top of her small lace bra, nodded for me to cut the bull-shit and pay up so we could get down to business. I dutifully obeyed.

Once that messy detail was resolved, my charming young whore took me down the hall and into a room just large enough for a sink against the wall and a single bed fitted with a clean sheet. She told me to take off my pants and underwear and after inspecting my cock to make sure it was in good health, had me hang it over the edge of the sink so she could wash it off with warm soapy water. The gentle massaging was enough to get me excited and she wasted no time laying me down on the bed so she could begin to give me a blowjob. I indicated that I wanted to suck on her pussy, but was disappointed to learn that pleasure, at least with this girl, was not part of the deal. It only took her professional mouth five minutes of sucking to drain my balls of sperm. My attempt to thank her with a peck on the cheek was rebuffed with a look that said: "Are you nuts?" and before I knew it, I was being hustled down the stairs so she could get back to soliciting.

As day turned to night, I took a brief dinner break at a brasserie on the corner of Rues Reaumur and St. Denis, a location where I could sit at a window counter and watch the night girls arrive. I was enticed by a girl coming down Rue Reaumur carrying a small suitcase. She was dressed in baggy street clothes appropriate for a factory worker. I watched as she turned on to Rue St Denis and then disappeared into a doorway within my view. Ten minutes later she stepped out, dressed to kill in nylons and a short mini cut just below her crotch. Watching the transformation from street cloths to a fuck-me-slut was a thrill in itself.

Several more hours of roaming up and down the rue with my fellow pussy hounds, resulted, despite my best efforts, in accidentally shooting my load twice more. At one in the morning, I was finally spent and returned to my hotel where I slipped out of my damp trousers and fell asleep. I had visions of repeating the same routine tomorrow.

"Judy is going to arrive in Paris around three this afternoon," Mercy told me when I checked in with her in the morning. I had been thinking she might like to join me for breakfast and have a quick fuck, but that news changed my plans big time! With Judy in town, my trips to the Rue St Denis would be limited—we were . . . after all—married—so before having to meet my wife at the Gare St. Lazarre, rather than a fuck with Mercy, I opted for a few hours of pocket pool at the expense of the noontime girls working the Rue St. Denis. As three O'clock approached, I took my hand out of my damp pocket, and trekked the short distance up Rue Sebastopol to the train station.

While I lugged Judy's suitcase outside so we could catch a cab, she told me that after my train pulled out of the station, she had immediately canceled her plans to go to Rome, but had to stay overnight in Switzerland until the next train to Paris arrived in the morning. Amazingly, she still tried to convince me that she had just wanted to go back to Rome to get her sweater and realized it wasn't worth it. Not wanting to hurt her feelings, I resisted telling her that her story was pure bullshit.

Actually, I was glad to see her; but not enough to immediately look past her ridiculous behavior. As far as I was concerned, I was now in Paris with Mercy and, for a while, Judy was going to be the third member of the party.

I didn't intend to rub it in her face by hanging out on the Rue St Denis all day, but at least for a day or two, she would play second fiddle. On a scenic trip on the Seine the next day, I sat with my arm around Mercy while Judy sat by herself on the opposing bench. Paris being Paris, it really wasn't that strange. It was the city of lovers and trysts. That's why Americans, from Ben Franklin's time on, loved Paris.

All was forgiven and forgotten by our last day in Paris. Mercy suggested that we celebrate by having lunch at Lazarre, one of only five restaurants in the world with a three star rating from Michelan. High cuisine was a fitting way for a neuveau riche producer, whose film had been quite the success at the Caanes Film Festival, to celebrate. Because lunchtime seating ended at two, Merci had to prod our taxi to drive at maniac speeds so we could get in. We made it with only three minutes to spare and after the Maitre'd gave me a look down his long Gaelic nose and informed me I would have to rent a tie for fifty francs, we were shown to a table. It wasn't just about haute cuisine, it was about a dinning experience par excellent. The twenty-five foot high ceiling in the magnificent dinning room, slid open every ten minutes to let the smoke in the room ventilate. Our table was set with fine silver utensils and ornate condiment holders. Four waiters, under command of a captain, began attending to our needs. Mercy pointed to France's leading Rock and Roll star, Johnny Hallyday, seated only a few tables away, "France had Rock and Roll stars?"

Once we had finished our meals that were prepared and served beyond perfection, a little ashtray in the shape of a minature skillet sitting in the center of the table, caught Mercy's eye and her fancy. It begged to be taken and she did just that. When the waiter came with our bill he brought along a nicely wrapped little box:

"I am sure madam would like to exchange zee little ash trey she aaze in her purse with zis one wrapped in zee nice box?"

Red faced, Merci pulled the pilfered ash trey from her purse and exchanged it for the gift-wrapped one, it's twenty-five dollar cost already added to the bill. Oh those sneaky French, I'm sure every American who ate there fell victim to that con.

It had been one hell of a trip, a little of everything, travel, money, fraud, education, luxury and sex; not a boring moment. But it was good to be going home and I looked forward to the myriad opportunities I assumed I had in front of me.

82

THE DOG EAT DOG DAYS

Still believing that the Supreme Court would liberalize censorship laws affecting adults, I would waste the next two years trying to raise money for 'Mat Hari.' It was a true story that could blend hardcore sex with a serious plot. Mata Hari, the French spy, accused of soliciting secrets from high-ranking military men while she entertained them in her bed, only to be caught and convicted, some thought falsely, was executed by firing squad.

Cichy, working with me as co-producer, got busy developing a screenplay. Not about to put myself on the financial brink again, I began looking for investors. Sy Katz did his share by pitching the project to some of his clients, but I was soon to learn that raising money was much more difficult than I had expected. Once seen as a pornographer, always a pornographer. It was ingrained in the American psyche that producing sex oriented movies was not serious art. When Bernie Goldhirsh remarked that 'Flesh Gordon' wasn't his kind of movie and a girl at a party stormed away after I mentioned that I made 'Flesh Gordon' saying "Oh that porno thing," I became reticent to even bring it up unless I was sure the listner was open minded enough to deal with it. Of course the fact that I walked around town in see thru pants or sexy shorts, which I knew excited many girls and rewarded me accordingly, didn't make investors flock to my side. It was sex or money and I chose sex. Getting Mata Hari off the ground eventually proved to be a waste of my time and money and I shelved it as an idle fantasy. I knew sex, not drama.

There was no need for panic. Unlike most motion pictures that have a brief window of exposure, 'Flesh Gordon's' kept growing. Peter Locke averred that if we could get the film re-rated to an R, its earning power would increase multifold. There were still many states, most notably in the Bible Belt, that wouldn't touch anything rated beyond an R. Thanks to Martin and Brust, there was no hardcore footage left in 'Flesh Gordon' and only a few scenes had nudity, so with a few minor cuts we should be able to have an R rated film.

Peter submitted it to the MPAA review board and asked them for a detailed list of the footage they found offensive. The descriptions they described in the list they returned were surprising pointed, almost pornographic and definitely funny: Reel 2 . . . eighty-five feet . . . nude humping, Reel 2 . . . flash of phony erect penis, Girl bouncing up and down Reel 5 . . . Flesh attempts to remove stone from girl's vagina, and on and on. After snipping out all of the *"too naughty for American eyes"* footage, we were left with a seventy-one minute R-rated film that could play thousands of theatres around the country, including drive-ins.

Buckley had finished his twisted-labia porn film and now had time to help promote Flesh Gordon. He suggested it would be funny and good publicity to get the MPAA's prurient list of cuts published and so did Gallery Magazine. In their 1975 January issue, they not only printed the entire MPAA report, but also spoofed it with a three-page comic book satire.

The MPAA was Jack Valenti's baby. He was its president and had been personally responsible for making it a defacto government censorship agency. He was a Catholic and well connected to the upper echelons of government and not surprisingly, didn't take lightly that his organization was being made into a joke. I would have guessed that he would have withdrawn the R-rating if he could, but knowing that doing so would bring on even more bad press, he remained silent—at least for the foreseeable future. Fighting these Luddites was what the sexual freedom war was all about. How hypocritical it was to condone screen violence and at the same time be outraged over screen sex!

The R rating did indeed rejuvenate 'Flesh Gordon.' It was free to play almost everywhere in the country and more money then ever rolled in. To be expected, a lot didn't roll in because it was so easy to steal. Theatres could turn in fudged numbers or hold a print for an extra week without it being detected. A rumor had it that one sub in the southeast claimed he had stolen enough money to retire for life. There was no way of knowing how much I had been cheated out of, but even so, considering that theatre tickets went for two dollars or less, Graffitti's four million dollar share of the profits was pretty damn good.

I was now living comfortably and getting plenty of sex. I didn't

have a need to become super rich, it wasn't my style. Freedom was the most important thing to me and with my money concerns taken care of and if John Van de Kamp, won the upcoming election for the office of LA's District Attorney and kept his promise to drop pornograpy cases currently on the books, it was possible my legal concerns would finally be over as well.

And when Peter Locke suggested that he, Barry Cahn and I form a company to produce porn features, it was the opportunity I had been waiting for. He would produce, I would direct and co-produce when needed and he and Barry would take care of the distribution. They would take care of the things I hated to do and I would be back in my element with the sluts I loved. Equally important, wearing hot pants would not be a problem.

I only had one condition. I was not interested in making one or two day-wonders any more. Directing the same repetitive sex acts over and over was more than I could bear. I only wanted to make films that were well made and unique. Drawing inspiration from how the burlesque shows that I had so enjoyed at the Old Howard were structured, I suggested that each film have four different sex scenes that catered to the various fantasies, each with different performers. It would be like watching different strippers do their acts. If you didn't like one of the girls or her act, there was the promise that you might like the next girl and her act. The scenes would be tied together by a central erotic theme. If we only made one film a year, so be it. They were in agreement and we became, at Peter's suggestion, DOG EAT DOG Films.

Peter wasn't one to waste time and we were soon in production. I wrote a script based on the classic Faustian theme of making a deal with the devil. The Angel of Death makes an appearance while a young couple is in the midst of making love. He tells them he envies their enjoyment of sex, something he hasn't experienced in five hundred years, but unfortunately has arrived to take them to the other side. Their pleads appear to be falling on deaf ears until they entice him with a deal. If they can tell him some stories that gets him aroused, he will let them live. He agrees and each story is visualized of film as they tell it.

I flew to New York with my camera equipment and was picked up at the airport by the limo Peter had arranged for and taken to his apartment on the upper Westside. I liked his style. He had already cast the respected porn star Jamie Gillis and a beautiful new comer, Wendy Miller, a. k.a C. J. Lang, to play the young couple facing death.

After an early dinner at a nearby steakhouse, we worked into the evening tightening up the script. The next morning, while Peter continued to line up cast and locations, I went out shopping for trashy panties and lingerie to be used in the various scenes. Because on my previous trips to New York, I had already located shops that sold bedroom attire for sluts. Since my shopping was finished by noon, I had time to check out a rumor that the strippers at the Harmony Burlesque Theatre, just off Broadway on 49th street, were allowing their pussies to be fondled for a buck. If the rumor was true, I wanted to get there when the theatre opened at noon, to be sure to get a good seat. It didn't hurt to have an aroused libido when I began the shoot the next day. The rumor was true and I spent the rest of the afternoon fingering pussies of all shapes, colors and sizes.

We shot the seduction of the devil at Peter's apartment. Wendy was stunning and playful; allowing me a few licks of her pussy before we began shooting. The scene went well—Jamie, formerly a professional actor doing his lines without a hitch—and ended with him vigorously fucking Wendy from behind, culminating with his iconic butt slapping treatment during the money shot.

Over the next few days, we shot a lesbian scene that starred, Candy Love, a black stripper from Baltimore, who had a 'ten' body and a shaved pussy, which she allowed the Baltimore burlesque show patrons to penetrate with a dildo, a flasher scene in Central Park, a Lolita scene that starred an eighteen year old cutie named Jenny Lane who was leaving the city the next day to work in a whorehouse at a resort in upstate New York where she would be making twenty-five dollars a trick and an S&M scene starring doe-eyed Sue Rowan as a French maid working for two austere dominatrix lesbians. For failing to clean a spec of dirt off the carpet, she is punished by being strapped to a table with her legs pulled behind her head and then fucked by, Bruno, the lesbian's Aryan slave. He deposits a voluminous amount of cum on her delightful pink breasts and angelic face, all shot in slow motion.

Both Peter and I were convinced the scene was a winner and as Sue was wiping the sperm off of her face and tits he asked her:

"That was a pretty hot S&M scene, wasn't it?"

We were both surprised by her answer: "It was OK, but it wasn't very real."

It turned out that she was into S&M in her private life and participated on a regular basis in threesomes with a black guy and his girl friend. Peter, always the producer, wanted to know if she and her friends might be interested in doing a scene for us in our next picture. She said they might and agreed to look into it and get back to us with an answer.

The next morning, Peter arranged for a limo to take me and my equipement to Kennedy Airport so I could return to LA with it and the film which I had just shot for editing. Six weeks later the job was finished and I suggested calling the film 'Sexteen' with a tag line claiming "8 never before seen erotic beauties." Still nervous about using my own name, I took the alias, Lynn Metz, as my credit. Our forty thousand dollar investment was a solid success on the porn circuit, grossing over seven hundred thousand dollars.

While in LA editing Sexteen, Reb Sawitz invited me to have lunch with him at a sidewalk café on Melrose, called the Melting Pot. He said he had someone he wanted me to meet. The tall, beautiful strawberry blond he had brought with him was as juicy as the half-pound cheeseburger I was devouring. As we talked, I could see Sarena was a very bright young woman who wanted to make a career for herself in the porn industry. I was flattered when she said how much she admired my work and a bit shocked that any of the models actually knew of my work. I was still a bit slow to realize that porn was being accepted as an art and a chance to work for a good director was a way for a girl to advance her career. Liberal minded girls were beginning to recognize that if they were pretty and knew how to fuck on screen, they could be very sucessful in the industry. Even thought the mega salaries were a decade away, it was possible for a girl to make better money working in porn films than they could by sitting in an office typing all day where they would be hit upon by the male bosses or employees. In porn a girl would know what she was in for and if she was in the mood, have a lot more fun besides. I didn't hesitate to tell her that I would use her in my next film.

That happened quicker than I expected. Shortly after 'Sexteen' was released, Peter called from New York to say that Sue Rowan's S&M friends had agreed to let us shoot them doing their thing as long as they got to write the script for the scene. He also mentioned that Jennifer Wells, a gorgeous B movie actress, was willing to do a hardcore sex scene if we wrote a part for her into our next movie. He told me she was a glamorous blond with big breasts and a chorus girl face. Porn had mostly featured young girls, the kind men felt they could dominate, but horny older woman, who knew everything about sex and how to dominate men, were quickly finding their way into the adult film business. Using Jennifer in our next picture would be a real plus.

I told him about Sarena and about an idea I had to use her in a lesbian scene and an idea for a sex act that I had seen in a layout in my favorite Swedish porn magazine, Erotica, that showed a girl taking two dicks in her pussy at the same time and then one in her pussy while the other penetrated her ass. If we could find a beautiful girl willing to do a similar act, we would have something sensational that would guarantee mention around the porn circuit. He got back to me a few days later to say that he had a girl who was willing to do the double penetration scene. Her name was Teri Hall, and because she had recently dropped out of the New York Ballet Company so she could pursue a career in porn, she was getting a lot of press. We both agreed that I should come back to New York as quickly as possible to begin our new production. I would shoot all but the Sarena scene in New York, which I would shoot when I returned to California. I hastily wrote a script that had two writers for a Men's magazine pitching ideas to its editor. Al Goldstein offered to play the role of the editor and let us shoot the scene in his office at Screw, all he wanted for pay was a blowjob.

Peter was in an effusive mood when I arrived Saturday evening. To get our next film off to a good start, he took me to a whorehouse that he had previously frequented, but when we walked in unannounced and began to check out the girls, the establishment freaked out. The proprietor—probably a mafia guy—realized we hadn't called in to make an appointment and fearing that we might be the vice, quickly escorted us out the front door. Evidently, New York sex wasn't as open as it appeared in the ads that ran in Screw Magazine and "vice" still had to be done on the sly When we got back to Peter's apartment, he called an out call service that ran an ad in Screw Magazine and asked for a couple of girls to be sent over. When they arrived, at 3AM, I was near comatose and could only manage a half-hearted orgasm. Moments after she left I was fast asleep.

On Monday morning we met with Al Goldstein at the Screw office to talk about his upcoming role and blowjob. After going over a few minor details, Al showed me an article he was going to run in the upcoming issue of Screw, about a nearby bar on 8th Avenue that was allowing patrons to eat the dancer's pussy for a dollar. The bar was only three blocks away and he suggested that the three of us pay them a visit for a pussy lunch.

It was a little past noon, and the small neighborhood bar surprisingly only had a few patrons eating pussy when we arrived. The oval shaped race-track like bar, served as a stage where the girls could saunter around soliciting customers. One of the girls knew Al from when he had dropped in to do the article and joined us as we watched a cute little honey get eaten out on the far side. She allowed the patron about a minute for a buck and when he declined further service, she casually pulled her g-string back up and came our way. I felt blood rushing to both my head and penis as she stood in front of me with her legs slightly spread and hands on her hips to see if I was interested in parting with a buck.

A bit clumsy with excitement, I hurriedly stuffed a dollar in her garter. She dropped her g-string and left it hanging around one ankle and then plopped her butt down on the bar and wrapped her legs around my shoulders to give me full access to her waiting feminine delight. Drooling at the mouth, I began enthusiastically running my toungue across her gash, making sure I had a few dollars ready in my hand if she decided to leave. We were into the second dollar when she abruptly stood up and pulled a tissue from the little box she carried with her and wiped off her pussy, complaining with an anguished face to the dancer who had joined us, that I had made her all messy with my slobber. The girl reminded her fellow dancer that was the job that she was being paid for. It failed to mollify the succulent young slut and much to Al and Peter's dismay, she sauntered away in a huff without allowing them any licks.

Al Goldstein had a face that always looked like it needed a shave, but that, and the fact that he needed to shed a bunch of pounds, didn't seem to be a problem the next day for the girl under the desk who had been hired to suck his dick during his scene as an editor. Peter had told her that she was being hired as a performer and her role was to suck Al's dick under the desk, but we actually had no plans to film her, it was just a ruse to get Al his blowjob. Staying in character, he gave no indication how much he was enjoying himself as he listened to Alana Blue, a cheeky New York sexpot and Bobby Astyr, who were playing the roles of the magazine writers pitching him ideas. When I finished shooting Al's scene, the girl under the desk either didn't hear cut or was just enjoying herself, because when Al got up to walk away, she crawled out from beneath the desk with his dick still in her mouth. She seemed disappointed when I told her the scene was finished and offered herself to any of us who wanted to fuck her. I was just too busy to oblige, but if I had known it was soon to be megastar, Annie Sprinkle, I would have definitely found the time.

Jennifer Wells was even sexier than Peter had described. The scene I had written for her played on a mother son fantasy, an older woman seducing a young virgin boy. I lit the scene with soft light and used a soft focus filter to make it ethereal. She and Sammy Teen, the stage name for the actor who would be seduced by her, gave a gentle and believable performance that would stand in sharp contrast to the one that was to follow, the S&M scene by Sue Rowan's friends.

Mel White was a tall articulate African American, who, like me, liked to wear hot pants. The other member of their threesome was Mary Stuart, an attractive, but intense brunet in her mid to late twenties. The script that Mel had written was based on the sexual ritual they routinely performed in their private lives. Mel would direct, all I had to do was film the action. It was to be staged in a small windowless room with black walls at their apartment. Hooks, chains and other bondage paraphernalia were already securely attached to the walls. I knew once the halogen lights were turned on, the room would become stifling hot and anything but convenient for filming. Mel mentioned that normally they would not have sex during an S&M session, but as a concession to what we were about, they would do so.

The following is a full description of the scene as it unfolded. Without any hint of the pain that would come, Sue and Mel lure Mary, who they have just met at a neighborhood bar, back to their apartment. She has been seduced by the promise of having the most intense sexual experience she will ever have. Once inside the small black room, she is asked to sit on a mattress placed on the floor. Mel wastes no time to begin to prepare her psychologically for what is about to transpire. He assures her that he is not a sicko and makes it abundantly clear that though she is about to be subjected to pain, she will not be physically injured. Most important, is that she understands that she can stop the ritual any time she pleases; but that once the action is stopped, it won't—under any circumstances—be restarted. He promises that if she endures the pain, it will take her to a sexual nirvana. He pushes her to the point of begging, that she is clear about what is about to happen before he will begin.

Once there is no doubt that she wants to go forward, her wrists and ankles are bound with leather cuffs attached to the chains connected to the hooks on the wall. She is left with her arms incapacitated and her legs pulled back over her head so that her buttocks, asshole and shaved pussy are unabashedly exposed. Mel, wearing yellow hot pants, stands over her and asks in a voice with a touch of tension, if she would like Sue to spank her. After he insists that she plead "yes" several times, he rubs her buttocks with a skin cream and then directs Sue to begin using a small leather whip to lightly lash her buttocks. When Mel sees that her skin is only turning pink, he takes the whip from Sue and lashes her more intensely, repeatedly demanding that Mary beg him to continue:

"Do you want more?" "Yes." She gasps

"Louder, do you want more? Say please!"

"Yes, spank me more. Please."

Sue also demands: "Say please! Louder!"

Her flesh has now turned red, just short of bleeding, and she begins to sweat and writhe in anguish. Mel offers her a chance to stop. She refuses.

By this time the temperature in the room was at least a hundred and I stripped off my shirt. My chest glistened with perspiration and my tight white Felipe Salve cotton pants were soaked. I was conscious that they molded tightly around my crotch. It only added to the scenes ambiance and my excitement.

As he promised, Mel briefly sucked and fucked Mary's pussy, but after that messy detail was accomplished, he returned to an even harsher orgy of pain—one that I could not have imagined on my own.

From a nearby table, he grabbed a chain about two feet long with a pair of nipple clamps attached to each end.

"Are you ready for the nipple clamps?" he asks Mary in an austere voice."

She responds with a gasping but sincere; "Yes."

He makes her say it two more times and then without the slightest hint of viciousness, he and Sue begin to attach clamps to her nipples. Small rubber tips prevented any breaking of the skin when the clamps would be tightened. Once they were applied but only tightened enough so that they stay attached, Mel orders Sue to put the chain connecting the two clamps into Mary's mouth; its length just long enough so that if she tugs back with her head, the clamps will pull on her nipples.

Placing his hand on each clamp, Mel now asks in a stern and again—non-threatening voice: "Are you ready for the clamps to be tightened?"

"Yes" she gasps.

"Are you sure? Tell me to tighten the clamps."

Mary's face, drenched in sweat from a combination of the stifling heat in the room and the thought of the pain she is about to endure, replies in a weak, yet assertive voice, that leaves no doubt:

"Yes. Tighten them."

Each click of the ratchet begins to reflect the additional pressure that is being applied to Mary's nipples and the look on her face says that the excruciating pain she is enduring is not contrived. Understanding the duress Mary is under, Sue comes to her side and tenderly strokes her forehead and asks in a soft and compassionate voice:

"Are you OK?"

Her quivering voice responds; "Yes, I'm fine." "Do you want me to stop?" Mel asks.

Barely audible, "No, don't stop."

"Tell Sue you don't want us to stop. Say please don't stop."

To take her mind off of the pain caused by the clamps, Mel delivers a few harsh lashes from the whip across her buttocks. The only evidence that she is enjoying this torture is that she refuses to ask for it to be stopped. Unbelievable, the real pain is about to come. Mel orders her to tug on the chain she is holding in her mouth. Her nipples stretch to the point where they look as though they might be torn off. But she still willingly obeys his demands to pull harder. Her mouth grimaces and her eyes roll as she does so but the tips of the clamps refuse to release.

"Pull harder, pull harder," Mel commands as he continues whipping.

I moved quickly around the room. Using the fact that the wide angle 10mm lens had a wide depth of field, I could kneel next to Mary's face to shoot a close up of the contortions on her face and then race back by the door to catch a wide shot of the whole scene.

Mary's eyes had rolled back into her head. Only the whites were showing as she made a last concerted effort to pull the clamps free. She reminded me of a zombie in "Nights of the Living Dead." But then one of the clamps mercifully broke free. Her look quickly morphs to one of satisfaction and accomplishment. Mel quickly grabs the chain and tugs it until the clamp on the other nipple breaks free.

A smile appears on Mary's soaking wet face. Her ordeal is over and she shows no signs to indicate that she did not enjoy every minute of it. The three hug as Mary thanks them for her wonderful sexual experience.

I had to remind myself that this was not theatrical and Peter, who had been standing outside the open doorway, was left mouth agape and speechless. Hard to believe it was their normal sex routine. I was sweating profusely from shooting the all hand-held scene. The intensity didn't allow for any breaks, so I was dying of thirst and probably dropped ten pounds. When I joined Peter outside the room, he had a smile on his face. He knew we had just filmed a classic. A few months later, when the late Richard Corliss reviewed the picture for Playboy Magazine, he advised that the more squeamish might want to retire to the theatre's lobby until the scene was over.

Deep Throat had already established how Americans would flock to a porn film that showed acts previously not believed possible. Missionary sex, i. e. that which met with approval from the church, was not exciting. The multi penetration scene that I was about to shoot with ballerina Teri Hall would be. We filmed the scene at Barry's rustic vacation home in Woodstock. The script called for Teri to be left alone with two handsome young workers her husband had hired to chop wood. The sight of their shirtless bodies glistening in the sun, is enough to cause her to run upstairs to the house's small attic and masturbate as she watches them toil in the yard below. I shot the scene of her massaging her cunt from the floor to get full benefit of the sensuality of her long well toned legs.

A teasing smile and an offer of a couple of cool glasses of lemonade, was all it took to lure the boys inside, where she offers both of her love orifices so the boys can enjoy her at the same time.

Fantasizing about bizarre sex acts is much easier than actually performing them, especially while being filmed. One of my studs, Barry Christian, a handsome twenty five year old blond, had difficulty sharing Teri's pussy with Rocky. It took leaving the room repeatedly to allow him and Teri to get going before Rocky, who could get erect on command, and I could come back in and he could slide his cock into Teri so I could quickly shoot some footage before Barry went soft again. Teri, who enjoyed having multiple cocks inside of her, did her part by adlibbing lines expressing her pleasure: "a cock in my cunt and one in my ass" and "two cocks in my cunt." They gave me the cutaways I could use while doing the editing to make the scene look much more fluid than it actually was.

We spent the night at Barry's cottage so Teri could be dropped off at the set of another film that she had been cast for that was also shooting in Woodstock. You can imagine how stunned I was, when Teri who was sitting on my lap as we were taking her to her next gig, told me she was going to be working on a film produced by Bill Osco— an X-rated 'Alice in Wonderland' musical. I was still reticent to put my name on an X-rated film, but Bill didn't have that problem since he had never been charged. He was now piggybacking his fame as co-producer of 'Flesh Gordon' and had wisely hired a competent director, Bud Townsend and a two-time playboy cover girl, Christine DeBell, to be his star. When finished, it would be wildly successful. I had to hand it to him. It was time for me to get over him.

Peter and Barry flew out to San Francisco to be on the set when I shot my recent discovery, Sarena, in a lesbian scene. She would be working with one of Alex DeRenzy's favorites, Sharon Thorpe, a very pretty practicing lesbian. Sharon, in the role of a ballet teacher, convinces Sarena to stay after class for a baby oil massage. The two ladies slithering over each others golden bodies was hot. Porn reviewers, Jim Holiday and Bill Marigold, would both describe the performance as the best lesbian scene ever.

Jim and Artie Mitchell had helped us out by sending us a few girls to be extras in the Sarena scene. Afterwards, we headed over to the O'Farrell Theatre, to check out the sex emporium they had recently opened using the profits from their mega hit, 'Behind the Green Door.' It was the talk of the town. Jim was in an effusive mood when we arrived and brought out the Uzi he had just purchased on the underground market. I had little interest in their assault weapon, but was totally impressed with the club they had put together. It combined the best raunch of New York and Copenhagen under one roof. A twenty-dollar ticket got you an all day pass where you could watch strippers perform in the main room, called New York Live, where after dancing, they circulated through the room to offer lap dances for a dollar or grind their bodies against you if you were leaning against a side wall. More extreme stimulation was offered in the Copenhagen room where girls did themselves with dildos inches from your face and the Ultra room where the girls worked in a circular peep show room and if a patron paid for the little window to rise, a tip would allow you to fondle her tits and pussy. I knew I would return by myself in the near future, but a bizarre quirk in my personality made me feel embarrassed to tell that to anyone.

We named the film 'Honey Pie' and I used the alias, Hans Johnson. For the one sheet, Peter hired a top notch New York photographer to shoot Jennifer Wells in a pose reminiscent of the famous Marylyn Monroe playboy calendar pose. It was a knock out. Honey Pie had something sweet for everyone and grossed many times our sixty thousand dollar budget.

83

BEYOND THE HOUSE
THAT SMUT BUILT

When all the enhancements I had contracted for or installed myself, to improve the Malibu house were completed, it was a sex lover's Garden of Eden. A spiral staircase led from an oak planked game room to the kidney shaped pool in the room below. The walls of the cave room and surface of the outdoor patio; were all covered with a colorful slate rock from Bouguet Canyon. I had replaced the mundane outside plywood paneling with golden tongue and grove cedar and all the interior window trim with five dollar a foot Coco Bolo wood from the Amazon. As I stood on the lush lawn edged by red bougainvillea bushes, proudly looking at my magnificent home, I couldn't help but humorously name it; "The House that Smut Built."

Neither Judy or I wanted children, but we both loved animals, both the wild ones that surrounded us in the mountains and the tame ones that Judy rescued from shelters. Though I contributed, Judy was the social engine that brought life to the house. She was not one who wanted to stay home and do house keeping. She loved socializing and stripping and was soon back at The Ball. Thanks to her; we always had sexy guests, many who she worked with or met at the Ball. It could just be some of the girls and their boy friends coming by on the weekend to take a swim and enjoy the Jacuzzi or people who needed a place to stay for the night while they were in L. A.; like nine members of a pot smoking Rastafarian band or folk singer Jack Eliot among them. We never locked our doors (we didn't even know where the keys were) and the welcome mat was always down. There were few boring moments at "the house that smut built."

Our open marriage was our strength. We both continued to find new lovers. She had an affair with a charming Italian clothing merchant named Georgio, whose sexy accent tickled her libido and ego and I often dated Mercy, who had moved back to LA from Paris, sometimes having threesomes with her and her horny girl friend Yogi. We treated each other's lovers as friends. I even allowed Georgio to persuaded me to buy a couple of suits from him because he said they would make me look more like a movie producer, even though I knew I would never wear them.

Surprisingly—or maybe not—material wealth didn't erase the irrational self-worth battle that continued to haunt me. I never quite believed it when I learned that a girl found me to be attractive, even though there were countless examples that they did. On my last trip to New York, Peter had mentioned that Wendy Miller, the thought of my tongue ticklig her clit still in her head, had expressed interest in fucking me. Of course I was pleased, but didn't try to call her. Sometimes I tried to hide my inferiority complex with humor. I jokingly said to Peter that we were "rude, crude and socially unattractive; a phrase I first heard from Bruce Karnoff, my irreverent Theta Xi fraternity brother. Peter thought the remark to be strange and said not to include him in my assessment. He asked me why I would say something like that. I didn't have an answer.

My self-doubt was one of the main reasons I became friends with Marcial Coppolino. Not that he was a guru; he was anything but. He could sense weakness and knew how to exploit it in a way that didn't make you feel abused. He was adept at showing other people how to spend their money. This was not all a bad thing, Judy and I were still hicks and had little knowledge about what money could buy when it came to the finer things in life. I first met him when Judy and I attended a Halloween party thrown by her boss, Whitey Locker, for his strippers and staff and their beaus, Marcial was living with one of the dancers, a tall beautiful blond with a sylphlike body, named Catherine. He had chiseled features, a strong physique and a full head of reddish blond hair. Being that he and I were the only males at the party audacious enough to wear next to nothing, he in a black bikini and me in a cape and g-string; we couldn't help but notice each other.

His personality was both brash and charming, at least in my eyes. He claimed that his father was connected to the mob in Las Vegas and while living there and working as a waiter in one of the casinos, he had dated the most beautiful showgirls in town. He claimed to be a former Green Beret, but refused to give details. Shrouding himself with a veil of mystery, made his persona more engaging. If it was true that opposites attract, my attraction to him was its best evidence. I saw him as an alpha male and subconsciously felt that it would do me good to let some of his outward self-assurance rub off on me. By the end of the evening he had made me feel like I had known him forever and we became good friends.

He had dropped out of Stanford to spend the summer traveling around Europe with a trust-fund-baby friend of his, named Wilson Tait,. He liked to brag that they ate at the best restaurants and drank the finest wines, all on Wilson's tab. His stories about beating the shit out of *'niggers'* when he and his buddies were off base in Vietnam, didn't dampen my admiration for him. Many white men used that pejorative; rarely did it mean anything. Unbeknownst to me, he saw me as his new, "Wilson Tait."

Waiting tables in Vegas had made him somewhat expert in wines and fine dining and he began introducing Judy and I to some of LA's better dining experiences; which was good except that it was all at my expense. After an evening with Michael McCarty at the Overstreet Wine Cellar in Beverly Hills, where we all sat at long wooden tables with our own small gas stove and mimicked exactly how McCarty, fresh out of the Cordon Bleu School in Paris, chopped the vegetables and meats and then sautéed them to perfection to create a mouth watering gastronomical master piece, which hopefully ours were its equal, so that McCarty could come to each student and pour a glass of the perfect wine that would complement each dish.

I was delighted that he had brought Judy and me to that most enjoyable experience, but a short time later I would begin to learn that if not kept in check, he was capable of using me like a dish rag. He and Catherine had joined Judy and I for a weekend in Carmel, where I treated him to a round of golf at Pebble Beach as a way of thanking him for the dinning experience. We were all staying at the Old Del Monte Lodge and the next day, after Judy and I finished playing a round of golf at the adjacent course, we were climbing the stairs up the balcony as we headed back to our room, when I noticed that my recently purchased BMW 530i was missing from the parking lot. Thinking I had just forgotten where I had parked it, I raced around the lot but found nothing. BMW's were the hot new car and maybe it had been stolen? Panicked, I ran back to Marcial's room and knocked on his door. He wasn't in. I returned to my room and was about to make a stolen car report, when there was a knock on the door. It was Marcial; smiling broadly as he walked in and explained what a huge favor he had just done for me. As one, who, of course, knew everything about BMW's; he had taken the liberty to take the keys out of my room so he could take the car out for a spin to make sure it ran up to snuff. According to him, it was meant to run revved up into the red zone and while he was testing it, pegged to the limit, a mechanical problem developed. He waxed how fortunate I had been that he was able to identify the problem and got it to a local BMW garage to have it fixed; saving me much aggravation down the road. Stunned, but inexplicably wimpy, I accepted his more than likely apocryphal story.

Nevertheless, even after that and other equally insulting stories, we would remain long time friends. He offered stimulating company, both mentally and physically. We enjoyed playing racquetball and one on one basketball, which he usually won by a point or two due to his better conditioning. To keep our friendship on an equal keel required a bit of friendly masochism. His dream was to be a writer and like his idol, Ernest Hemmingway, he kept a daily journal that he made longhand entries into with his pride and joy—a Monte Blanc pen. Regrettably, he never sold anything and his income came from jobs as a waiter or insurance scams, which at the moment had left him near penniless. To help him out, I gave him a day of hard labor doing some work in my yard, which forced me to listen to his half-joking complaints about how I was exploiting him like a slave.

My financial success had blinded me to the fact that I was caught in my own bubble, one that I had no interest, or need for that matter, to break out of. Peter had previously asked me what I wanted to be in the film business and if I would be interested in joining him to make more serious films. I was unclear if my future was as a director, cinematographer, producer or what have you. Peter had no such confusion. While I was spending my time with Marcial doing nothing constructive, he knew he wanted to be a mainstream producer and had already made inroads to know some of the promising New York talent. Wes Craven had recently made a low budget horror film called

'Last House on the Left' and despite the films acclaim, had yet to get another project going. It was originally intended to be a hardcore porn film, but its potential as a horror film was so overwhelming, that its distributor decided to dump the hardcore and go for the fright-night crowd. To encourage and build his relationship with Wes, Peter was already producing a porn film with him to eventually be called; *"Angela, Fireworks Woman."* I declined Peter's offer, mostly because I valued my freedon and didn't want to be under anyone's control. There had been no reason to think that Peter wasn't going to be sucessful and it was patently clear that my relationship with him was on a per film basis.

Meanwhile, I had another taboo-busting idea for a Dog Eat Dog Film that would cause a sensation if we could produce it: two identical twin sisters having lesbian sex with each other. It had been almost a half-year since the release of 'Honey Pie' and I called Peter to toss my idea at him. Despite his involvement with Wes, he liked my idea and got back to me two weeks later to tell me that two identical twin sisters had just come to New York who were willing to do hardcore lesbian sex. They would do everything from finger fucking to pussy sucking. We both agreed they should be shot immediately before they changed their minds or left town. Wes had done some comedy writing for Peter's new wife, Liz Torres, and he suggested we let him do the dialogue. I was fine with that but still wanted to keep the structure of the story under my control and quickly put together an outline that detailed the sex acts and set ups that I wanted to use, and sent it to Peter so Wes could get started.

I was in New York a week later, just as Peter was wrapping up Wes's film. He showed me the rough cut which impressed me more for its cinematic qualities than its eroticism. A scene with a guy clubbing someone with a large fish was notable. Being that Jennifer Wells was such a big hit in 'Honey Pie,' we decided to cast her again; this time as a reporter interviewing a famous men's magazine photographer. During the interview, the photographer describes his favorite layouts. By the end of the interview she is so aroused that she can't resist disrobing and offering herself to him. It was a simple idea for a way to hook four porn loops together, which is why the films I would do with Dog Eat Dog, would eventually become known as 'loop carriers.'

The twins, Brooke and Taylor Young, were set to shoot for us the day after I got into town. Their scene would be a parody of the famous Double Mint chewing gum commercials where two twin sisters promote the gum and its tag line: "Double your pleasure, chew Double Mint Gum." Our story began with a behind the scene look where the girls are in the midst of the advertising photo session. Wes agreed to take the role of the photographer, which did not require nudity or sex. Because the girls find the photographer to be attractive, they play coy and disrupt the flow of the session. But he is all business and they return home frustrated with no other option but to relieve their pentup passion by making love to each other. I opted to forego my usual trashy cheesecake style and dressed the girls in soft beige colored panties, bras and stockings. Using slow hand held pan shots down their torsos allowed me to get the maximum exploitation of their sensual lithe bodies. When it came to the sex, they had no qualms about kissing each other and sucking on each other's tits and pussies. It was obvious to me that it was not their first time. Thinking back in time, I wondered if there was more to my infatuation with the twins who were in my first grade class then I knew about?

The next day was Saturday and I spent the morning picking up props for a teenager scene staring, Jeannie Dalton, a cherubic and cute little spitfire, that I was going to shoot on Monday. After buying a pair of saddle shoes, ankle sox, short plaid skirt and an assortment of sex toys, including a large cucumber, I dashed over to the Harmony theatre to catch the afternoon show. The place was packed and I soon saw why. For a buck, the dancers were getting down on their backs and sliding up to the edge of the stage with their legs spread so the guys in the front row could suck on their cunts. The New York vice had closed down the little bar Goldstein had taken me to—the owner was none to happy that the story in Screw had alerted the cops to what was going on—but evidently the Harmony had some kind of insider clout and was allowing them to get away with the same raunchy entertainment. Most of the girls were reasonably attractive and I spent the rest of the day gash gorging, hooking back up with Peter in the early evening. Deep-seated shame that I couldn't dislodge from my psyche, prevented me from telling him what a glorious day I had just had. Then again, keeping my private indulgences to myself actually made them more exciting.

After eating pussy all weekend at the Harmony, I was in high erotic spirits when I went back to work on Monday to shoot Jeanie playing the role of a young high school student. While walking home after school with, Billy, a male classmate who is in her sex education class, she discovers that not only is he a virgin, but also doesn't know how girls can masturbate. Since her parents are still at work, she offers to bring him home and show him how its done.

Billy is directed to take a seat on a chair next to the bed so she can begin the demonstration. From beneath her bed, she pulls out a bag that is filled with sex toys; vibrators of various sizes and shapes and an organic large fat cucumber. She drenches the crotch of her silk panties with baby oil so it becomes translucent and clings to the curves of her puffy pussy. Billy's eyes bulge as she slides her hand inside her panties and then, after covering herself with more baby oil, removes her little tank top and explains in a husky voice, the benefits of each sex toy as she inserts them into her vagina. The big green cucumber renders Billy awestruck and he can't resist inserting his own organic member into Jeanie's accommodating vagina, his virginity suddenly a thing of the past.

In an interview with Playboy, Jeanie mentioned that she enjoyed doing the scene, although she could have done without the large cucumber, which she described as painful. Most men are unaware that female porn actresses are not wont to complain, and willingly endure a lot of pain for the sake of giving a good performance; large cucumbers and anal as examples. Jeanie Dalton certainly did that and I considered her scene one of my best.

Before shooting the Jennifer Well's scene, I had a day off and headed over to the Harmony thinking I would be lapping on cunts all day. When the first dancer came out from behind the curtain, I put a dollar on the edge of the stage to lure her my way and no sooner did she have her legs spread wide and her g-string pulled to the side, when the near hysterical manager came running from the rear of the theatre waving his arms for her to stop. He nervously made it clear that pussy eating was not allowed during weekdays. To my great disappointment, the Harmony had some deal working with the New York vice that allowed for pussy eating only during the weekends. The day wasn't a total waste. He made it clear that finger fucking was still permissible, but only during a lap dance and not on the stage.

My stay in New York ended after shooting Jennifer Wells, who did her best to make a hot scene with Raz Keane, who was playing the role of the famous photographer. He arrived late to the set because his cab had been in a bad accident. He was shaken enough that it took him several hours to keep a hard on long enough to make a convincing scene. I hoped that when I got to the editing room, I would be able to do some magic to make it work.

A Civil War parody provided a setting to attack another social taboo, interacial sex. Sarena, a beautiful black girl named Deserai West, would be the stars in a civil war scene where Johnny, a rebel soldier, played by Sarena's new husband, a stonner named Thomas, returns on horse from a recent battle. It was mind boggling to me why Sarena had married such an uninspiring doper, but she would now only work with him in porn scenes. He arrived on the set after staying up all night getting high and after repeated failed attempts to get a boner, I had to reschedule the scene for the next day. It took place in a stable, where Sarena and her pretty black maid, reward her lover with a romp in the hay. Deserai was by far the prettiest black girl doing porn and I was fortunate enough to be able to go down on her the previous day when Thomas couldn't get a hard on. She had a big fan club, including my rock star friend, John Mayall.

The final vignette would be one of my all time favorites. Peter and Barry had again joined my crew and me in San Francisco to assist in the production of an oriental bondage scene starring Linda Wong. None of us had previously met her, having booked her on a recommendation from the Mitchell brothers. After we drove to her apartment to meet her, all I could say to myself was: "Wow." Beautiful Asian women are the most erotic on the planet and she was all of that. As we were all still ogling; she suggested, since her role was to play a hooker, that we take a tour of Oakland's McArthur Street currently a beehive of scantily clad street walkers prying their trade both day and night. It would give her some inspiration on how to play the part.

McArthur Street was not quite as good as the Rue St Denis, but not bad for America. We were at least on the way to catching up. As we drove around the block several times to admire the girls, a homely honey stood to the side in hot pants pulled on so tight that her slit bulged out. Paris had introduced me to the street hooker bug and so far, because of American laws, satisfying that fantasy had not been possible. I promised myself I would find my way back to McArthur Street before returning to LA.

Renting a room on the first floor of the luxurious Myako Hotel, located on Post Street just south of Van Ness, provided us a set at little cost. Its décor was perfect and even included a sauna. Knowing the hotel would never allow a porn film to be shot on its premises, we were forced to surreptitiously move all of our equipment, piece by piece, into the room the day before we filmed.

After Peter, Barry and my crew had a 6AM breakfast at a café on VanNess, we were back in the hotel room shooting Linda's scene where her 'john,' played by Ken Scudder, asks for some 'kinky' sex. She has no objections and he has her lie down on a thin bamboo cushion placed on the floor so he can bind her ankles to a bamboo pole. Once that is done, he pulls her legs behind her head and then ties her wrists to the pole so she is left helpless. Her exposed crotch, covered only by soft shear panties, begs to be touched. I lit the scene with low-key lighting so her curves would be highlighted and the room would feel erotically foreboding.

While uttering adlibbed lines that make him sound like a harmless pervert, Ken begins by using a Hitachi Magic Wand vibrator to gently stimulate the inside of her thighs with low frequency vibrations. As it begins to tiptoe its way across her crotch, her pelvis begins to rise. Her reactions were real and not simulated and as the vibrator is dialed up to a high frequency and pressed firmly against her clitoris, she twists and writhes violently. Her wimpers to be freed are ignored and she is forced to endure the pleasurable but masochistic torture he is subjecting her to.

I had studied Oriental rope binding techniques from several of the Oriental Bondage magazines I had in my private collection and understood that it was essential that the various wraps had to be made with clean thick white ropes and meticulously wound so no overlapping spaces appeared between each winding. The effect was to make it clear that the female had willingly subjected herself to be tied up, showing that the eroticism was mutually agreeable and not psychotic torture or rape.

The scene culminates in the sauna, where again, Linda's arms are bound tightly to her side and all the stimulation that she is about to give Scudder's nine-inch cock, must come from her mouth. The confined space made her face and body perspire and restricted me to using a 10mm lens. I judiciously took advantage of its wide angle and deep depth of field, by placing it right next to the base of Ken's penis, so I could capture Linda's face as she pumps her mouth up and down his stiff shaft. Saliva and cum ooze out of her mouth and slide down his cock, my camera angle making it appear to roll right down onto the lens. The frantic joy she shows as she drains every last drop of sperm from his testicles, made it the best blowjob scene of my career. She and her john were actually married, just fantasy playing to add a little fun to their sex lives.

Peter and Barry returned to New York and I had Cichy and Rogers drive the Graffitti van back to LA, so I could remain in Frisco for an extra day. I couldn't get Linda's hot dick-sucking face out of my mind and fantasized, after she agreed to let me take her out for dinner the next night, that I would soon be inside her. During the afternoon, as I waited for the evening to arrive, I couldn't resist massaging my cock as I thought about what lie ahead, but I was afraid I might be too primed by the time I got into the sack with her, so to try and cool myself down and avoid premature ejaculation, I drove over to Oakland about four in the afternoon to see if I could find the bursting-hot-pants honey that I had seen two days before. I would hire her for a quickie and limit myself to a controlled partial ejaculation, so that I would still have plenty of jisim available for Linda.

My honey wasn't on duty, but I found another trollop who was just as good. Within minutes she was sucking me off in her room that was conveniently just off the street. As planned, I managed to have a partial orgasm and still have plenty of juice left for Linda. When the young lady took my dick out of her mouth, I was surprised to find I had a condom on. That explained why it had been so easy to control myself. I was impressed with the girl's technique. It was something I hadn't seen before and asked her to show me how she did it. She explained, that before beginning the blowjob, she had put the rubber in her mouth and rolled it over my shaft as she went down the first time. After thanking her for her professional service, I drove to Sausalito to wine and dine and fuck Linda.

The evening didn't go as planned. The window table at a Sausalito restaurant overlooking the bay, wasn't romantic enough to overcome the dull and uninspiring conversation I was able to provide, possibly, because all I could think of was how beautiful she was and how good it was going to feel once I was inside her. I came off like a nerd. When I drove her home, she declined to invite me up to her place, giving me the suspect excuse that she was living with someone and it wouldn't be cool. Right! Thank god I had at least treated myself to a good time in Oakland!

I had become quite skilful as an erotic editor and cut all the scenes in the film so they worked to perfection, including the one with Ras Keane and Jennifer Wells. There was not even a hint of the struggle that took place to get the scene shot. Following up on the pastry theme, we called the film *'Sweet Cakes'* and again gave it the bi line "starring 8 never before seen erotic beauties." The gay incest scene with Brook and Taylor Young was the talk of the "adult" town and DOG EAT DOG had its third hit in a row.

Porno movies were lifting the veil that sex needed to be hidden and that women didn't enjoy sex. And what was the deal about private parts? Unless your sex organs are deformed, what is the argument that they should be hidden, made even more absurd considering that they all look, more-or-less, alike. The popularity of my porn films, as well as those of others, and the availability of more and more attractive and talented people willing to work in porn films, showed that many Americans were feeling the same. But those that wanted to repress sex; didn't seem to know this and continued to try to make arrests and send people to jail for natural behavior. They were given a rude shock. When federal anti pornography lawyers opted to try a case in the jurisdiction of Utah, because they felt a jury selected from that conservative State's citizens, would insure a conviction, they lost! The idea that community standards in Utah would deem pornography to be beyond the pale; was false. A survey showed that Utah had more fans of pornography than any state in the union.

84

I'M A HIT IN DRAG

It was not as though the people who visited our house expected an orgy; most came by to enjoy the Jacuzzi, smoke grass or play pool in the grotto room or a game of backgammon in the living room, but if someone wanted to fuck, it was no big deal. What a life! Judy didn't get jealous if I treated myself to a quickie on the living room couch with one of her stripper friends from the Ball or Susan Patterson and I performed an exhibitionist fuck atop the pool table in the grotto room. She had put her butt up to the edge of the table and her knees bent so I could fuck her standing up. Several people, including her husband, Jeff, stood to the side, watching. He couldn't resist asking: "Is he big enough for you?" She smiled and replied: "its just right." My reputation as a pussy sucking maven was growing steadily as well. When Judy and I visited one of her current lovers, a short young kid who had challenged me to an arm wrestling match, but then after humiliating me by slamming my arm to the table, suggested that if I would like to take his girl friend into the bedroom, there would be no problem. She liked the idea and when we finished and came back into the living room, the first words out of her mouth were: "Wow, does that guy know how to eat pussy or what!" It was music to my ears.

Not that Judy was being left out. Though she didn't share in my love of exhibitionist sex, she satisfied her fantasies in her own way. She loved hiking and camping and after she returned from a three day trek in Yosemite's Tuolumne Meadows, with Scott Carey, a friend's cute seventeen-year old virgin son, all, including the boy's father, were delighted to hear that the lad had been deflowered.

Halloween is a time to play fantasy roles, and what better place to throw a party than at "the house that smut built." Judy jumped on the idea and was delighted to put the whole thing together; if she knew how to do anything, it was how to throw a party! It would be our own version of the 'Artist's and Model's Ball' and more. As sexual extroverts, we would provide plenty of stimulation to make the party memorable. She was sober—almost to a fault—and it meant that she would be available to be a good host, making sure that there was plenty of food and continuous music. We both loved dressing up in sexy costumes so the mood of the party would be a given. If any girl arrived who wanted to look a bit more slutty, she could change into some of the scanty costumes that I kept for my film work in a portmanteau in the bedroom closet.

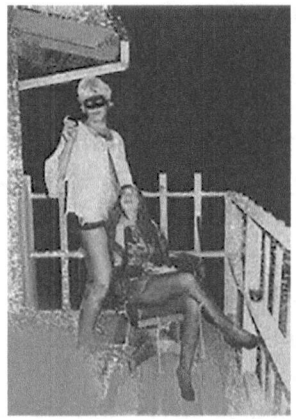

I was putting the finishing touches to my costume, when Mercy Lamont arrived and offered to help me out. A light-blue string bikini panty that I had borrowed from Judy's wardrobe barely covered my shaved cock and my long legs were sheathed in thigh high sheer black nylons purchased from Lily St. Cyr's lingerie shop. I had bought a pair of high heels I found at a thrift store that were strong enough to support my weight and elevate my six foot two frame another four inches. They made my buttocks look full and firm. The whole ensemble was covered with a babydoll negligee to keep it from being too indecent . . . just kidding. I knew my outrageous drag outfit was exciting her. She even volunteered to help me do my make-up. When she finished doing my lashes and applying rouge and lipstick, I donned a platinum wig so I could begin welcoming the guests. To steel myself against some of the reactions that I was sure were about to come, I focused my mind in a semi-trance of indifference.

Word spread that there was a party at our house. Over a hundred guests were soon in attendance; many whom Judy and I didn't know nor did they know us. Reactions to my drag costume were mixed and interesting. Our fifty-year old Swedish neighbors were straight-laced schoolteachers, but being from Sweden, they were just amused. Some of the girls at the party let me know it turned them on. Another, who I didn't know, grabbed her date's hand and ran screaming down the driveway in horror the moment she got a glimpse of me after they opened the door. Later, while I dirty danced in the living room with Merci, a guy dancing with his date next to us, kept giving us condescending glances. Probably not knowing that I was the host, he decided to voice his disapproval and with a glare said: "That's disgusting." Not missing a beat, Merci cocked her head and gave him her best coquettish and devilish smile: "You think that's disgusting? Get a load of this!" and dropped to her knees so she could whip out my cock and voraciously suck on it. I continued dancing as though what else should she be doing, making no effort to see how the guy was reacting.

The party was going strong when Judy wended her way through the jam-packed room redolent with marijuana, to answer a loud pounding knock at the front entry door. When she opened it, the room went silent. A cop with a stern look on his face stood in front of her. After a momentary panic, everyone relaxed. It was Peter Tevis in a rented costume! Not funny!

A few hours later, she opened the door again to a firm knock; but this time it was a couple of authentic cops responding to a call from neighbors who had complained about the noise. Being straight, she adroitly handled the situation and, to their satisfaction, assured them that we would keep the noise down. The bacchanal finally ended at two AM. Word spread around Malibu that the place to be on Halloween was at the "house-that-smut-built;" albeit that no one knew I had given it that appellation.

Even though we were twenty miles north of Santa Monica, there were always beautiful girls stopping by. Penthouse Pet, Helena Lang, a raven-haired Latino beauty with dark flashing eyes, danced with Judy at The Ball. She had been coming by the house from time to time, sometimes with a male friend and sometimes by herself. By some sixth sense that I had no clue from where it came, I knew that she liked to be spanked and after I took her by the arm on one of her visits, and bent her across my knee, all the time telling her what a naughty girl she had been, to administer a few firm harmless swats to her behind, we became good friends. Because I was the only one who recognized her need for discipline, she expected and was delighted when I accommodated her with a spanking when she visited. On occasion, she would offer me a blowjob if we were in my car together, but our relationship was more akin to that of a father and daughter—a very naughty daughter.

In the early spring of 1977, she came up to the house mid-week with Earl Miller; the photographer who had shot the Penthouse layout of her that appeared in July of 1976 that earned her *Pet of The Month*. Earl was always looking for locations to shoot at and her description of our house and the last Halloween party had peaked his interest. It would turn out that we had a lot in common.

We both had gone to college in Boston; he at Tufts and I at MIT.

He had been taking premed and like me, dropped out of school and came to Los Angeles. Like me, his obsession with sexy women led to a career in the adult entertainment business. By the time he left that day, we had become quite friendly and I told him to feel free to stop by on any Sunday afternoon when we spent time with friends around the pool.

The following Sunday he accepted my offer and came by with his girl friend, a quiet but stunning Penthouse Pet, named Viki. We spent the afternoon smoking grass and playing eight ball in the grotto room. Earl liked to analyze each shot to find its fullest potential and a game that would normally take five or ten minutes, took a half hour. I would come to realize that his patience was what made him such a good photographer.

When he returned the following week, he not only came with Vikki, but also with another Penthouse Pet, Moira Weiss. Her husband Barry and an eighteen year-old sister named Duane. The sexual energy at the house was already high, but it was about to explode big time.

The sisters, like my wife, were from conservative New Hampshire, which I now knew meant that they were probably anything but. Both were baby-faced, Moira very cute with freckles and Duane with a body that still carried some baby fat. Renowned photographer Ron Raffaelli, Jimmy Hendrix's personal photographer, had shot Moira in a hardcore lesbian layout for Puritan Magazine. In it she makes love with a beautiful eighteen-year old girl named Valerie. Her innocent face belied her willingness to embark on sexual adventures. I would eventually learn that while still in high school, her fantasy was to move to Boston as soon as she graduated so she could become a street hooker, working the beat in front of the State theatre at the south end of the 'war zone.' She gave up her street walker fantasy when she met Barry Weiss, who, as the black-sheep son of renowned composer George Weiss, famed for his many all time classics such as *"What a Wonderful Life"* and *"Lullaby of Birdland,"* was as wild and unusual as she was.

While I sat with Earl and Barry under an umbrella to shade us from the sun, Barry explained that, inspired by the French soft-core porn film 'Emmanuel,' he and the sisters had formed a sexual fantasy cult that he had named, *'The Magic Theatre.'* I had no idea what he was talking about. A few other people had dropped by to hang around the pool and I had lost sight of the sisters who had wondered off. I was in the midst of sharing a joint with Earl and Barry, who after exhaling the deep toke he had just taken; looked at me with an elfin like smile and nodded with his head for Earl and me to take a look towards the pool. The two sisters were sitting on the wide steps that led into its shallow end and taking turns eating each other out. Barry remarked nonchalantly: "that is so cool." 'The Magic Theatre' was indeed spellbinding.

Within the hour, I was in the house on my big round bed with my head comfortably resting between Duane's spread legs sucking her pussy until it was ready to be fucked. In the coming months, Earl and the 'MagicTheatre' arrived each Sunday around eleven A. M. Duane expected me to suck her pussy and have sex with her as soon as she got to the house; so until that time arrived, I waited atop my round bed wearing a small sexy bikini and watched the football game playing on the TV that sat on a wall shelf overlooking the bed. As soon as she walked into the room, without saying a word, she would hop up on the bed so I could begin stroking her slit with my tongue. Being a fanatic Cheesehead, I kept one eye peeled on the game until Big Benaldo, the name I had given my dick, became just firm enough to allow me to stuff him into her wet vagina. The warmth of her pussy finished the job of getting him hard. She liked that and told me the feeling of a cock growing hard inside of her was a turn on. We usually humped in the spoon position so I could continue to watch the game, which had the added benefit of drawing my concentration away from how good the sex felt and prevented me from cumming. After a half-hour, I would pull my still excited cock out of her and stuff it back into my bikini or minuscule g-string so the two of us, in a quasi stimulated state, could join the other guests for the rest of the afternoon. Word quickly spread that weekends at Howard and Judy's house were hot, and not because of the sun. More guests began to stop by.

85

LES 'BELLES DE NUITS'

While my iron was still in the fire with 'DOG EAT DOG,' I suggested we make another 'pastry film.' To find new talent and give it a non-American ambiance, I told him I wanted to shoot a few scenes in Europe. We had made a lot of money together and both Peter and Barry green-lighted the proposal.

An idea borrowed from a photo layout I had seen in an issue of the Swedish porn magazine, *Eros*, was to be the foundation of the loop carrier script. It would have a Rod Serling 'Twilight Zone' twist. A man browsing in a used bookstore is invited by the stores elderly owner to join him in a back room to see something very unusual. Thinking he is about to see illegal pornography, he accepts the offer. But upon entering the dimly lit room, he discovers that he has entered a small art gallery with several gilded framed paintings of handsome young couples hanging on the wall. At the far side of the room is an exotically attired statuesque woman kneeling on a small stage where she is masturbating with a two foot long silver pole. As the man is transfixed on what he is seeing, a strange aura suddenly envelops the room that causes the man to begin to hallucinate that the paintings are coming to life.

I had intended for one of the paintings to be a scene with a French whore on the Rue St Denis. Walter and I would fly there so we could shoot the sexy looking girls working their trade. Afterwards we would drive to Denmark to shoot a scene or two with some Danish porn actresses.

The Rue St. Denis idea fell flat on its ass immediately. When the girls recognized that we were trying to surreptitiously photograph them as we drove down the rue, all hell broke out. Walter was driving and I was in the back seat with the camera peeking out from the back window of the car we had rented. The rue, jamed with horn dogs eyeing the girls, was moving slowly. I hadn't rolled fifteen seconds of film when one of them noticed what I was up to and screamed "FOTOGRAPHIE! FOTOGRAPHIE!, FOTOGRAPHIE!" Like little

bunnies diving into their hutches, every girl ran with practiced efficiency for cover down any alley or doorway they could find. Because of the narrowness of the street and the fact that it was jammed with cars, there was no way for us to make a quick exit. I rolled up the back window, hoping the hooker's panic would subside; but as we slowly edged down the rue, the screams of rage continued. I was afraid that pimps would emerge from the shadows and beat the shit out of us or worse—take my ten thousand dollar camera. I told Walter we had to get the fuck out of there, but the *gator*, who didn't like to give in to anything, tried to convince me that we should give it another try. I would hear none of it. As soon as we reached Rue Reaumur, I told him to take a right turn and get us the fuck away. We had escaped unscathed and still had our camera. So much for the Rue St Denis shot.

We split Paris the next morning and headed for Copenhagen where Barry Cahn had arranged for me to meet with Milton, the publisher of the Swedish porn magazine, 'Private.' He had graciously agreed to give me some inroads to his talent.

On the way we made a stop in Hamburg, the German seaport city renown for it's brothels and prostitutes. Maybe I could get the footage I was looking for there. Once we checked into a hotel, I left Walter in the room to call his new wife, Vikki, to convince her that he was being a good boy, while I wondered down to the *Bunderstag* to see what the famed German sex market offered. When I couldn't find a single working girl on the street, I began to think that I was in the wrong area. But just as I was about to leave, I spotted a sign in the middle of the block that advertised a live sex show. The entry to the club was an open portal framed by red lights, the international symbol for sexual entertainment.

After pushing back a black curtain to take a peek inside, I was disappointed to find that there were no girls performing on the small stage at the back of the sparsely lit room and was about to leave when a plump girl grabbed my arm and ushered me into the darkness to a table near the stage. Before I could say Jackie Robinson, I was asked to buy the two of us a drink, which was understood not to be a request, but a demand. Against my better judgment, I obliged.

The equivalent of forty bucks in German Marks, got me two watered down drinks and the privilege of suffering through several minutes of inane conversation with my new plump friend. Since no entertainment had come to the stage, I was again about to leave when a stocky German emcee appeared on stage and called for us to give a big hand for 'Nadine.' I gave 'Big Benaldo' a few squeezes to alert him that he was about to be aroused. But the sight of Nadine quickly put that idea to rest. She was a thirty-some-year-old with stringy bleach blond hair and a small potbelly. After sitting down on a wooden chair that faced the audience, she pulled up her dress, pushed her pelvis forward and spread her legs to reveal her hairy snatch. With a look of ennui on her face, she proceeded to insert a run-of-the-mill dildo up her vaginal canal. For all the excitement she showed, she could have been shoveling coal. I pitied the poor dildo.

Then came the big finale. A scratchy LP provided a bit of fanfare music as the emcee welcomed 'Mr. X' to the stage. He was a barrel-bodied, balding German, wearing a silver mask over his eyes. If anyone could be less appealing than Nadine; it was he. I surmised the mask was to keep his reputation in the community safe from calumny. When the emcee announced: "Duh Nadine will now fuck duh Mr. X, I couldn't imagine who else would want to fuck either one of them, so resigning myself to the fact that I wasn't going to get my rocks off, and not wanting to risk having the repulsive vision of *"Mr. X fucking duh Nadine"* churning in my head for the next month, I scooted out of the place and rejoined the Gator at the hotel. He was fast asleep; an indication that he had convinced his nervous wife that he was not straying.

A short trip on the Autobahn, where eighty miles per hour is considered slow, found us in Copenhagen, the city where the sexual revolution had begun. The moisture in the air and the eternal dusk due to its proximity to the Artic Circle, made the city seem bleak and did nothing to lift my spirits from the fiascos I had recently experienced in Paris and Hamburg. It had been said that the reason Scandinavians are so sexual is because living in that kind of atmosphere leaves nothing else to do but fuck.

The Regency hotel was located in the town center and within sight of Old Town and the Tivoli, the cities famous amusement park. Walter, as usual, began by calling his wife and as usual I went out looking for pussy. A brochure in the hotel lobby led me to a club located in a nearby upscale business area. When I peeked in, I saw two beautiful girls on the stage and a sign that said the cover charge was a hundred-dollars. I peeked right out. I preferred cheap sluts, not high priced prima donnas. There was no street action that I could see and I began to fear that the entire European trip was going to be a waste.

It almost was. The sun which finally set at 11PM but came back up four hours later at 3AM, made sleeping difficult. Until we could meet with Milton, Walter and I took a walk around the area. As Americans, it was hard to feel comfortable. Anti war posters were everywhere. One bookstore had its entire front window plastered with *Nixon War Criminal* posters and a slew of books supporting that contention.

Milton greeted us with typical Scandinavian coolness. He was happy to help us out, but almost all of the girls I had seen in his magazines were no longer available. I had decided that shooting sex scenes in Europe would expose me to having the footage confiscated by American customs when I returned, so I told Milton I was looking for a couple of girls who would be willing to fly to LA and work for me there. He recommended two girls that he thought would be right for me.

The first, a Lithuanian girl named Barbo, turned out to be an expensive disaster. After paying for a round trip ticket for her to fly to the states, she wasn't off the plane for a half-hour before she was telling me what she wouldn't do and because I had failed to check out her body while in Copenhagen, I discovered when she went outside to tan herself by the pool, it had deteriorated to the point of being unattractive. I cut my losses by sending her back the next day on the first plane available.

Milton's top photographer was to introduce me to the second girl the next morning at a local coffee shop. The stunning young blond he brought along made my pulse rise. I had seen her in several hardcore layouts in PRIVATE; one with American porn model, Eric Edwards, playing the role of a priest receiving a blowjob. Her name was Anna Magle. When she told me that she had just turned eighteen, I realized, since her layout had been published two years earlier, that she had been doing porn since she was sixteen. She was obviously a wild girl.

At one point, the conversation turned to a discussion about a Pakistani girl that I had asked Milton about when I was at his office. It made him very upset and any discussion of her ended quickly. The reason was a very tragic story. She was not only Milton's favorite model, but also his lover. During a weekend sojourn in his Rolls Royce to northern Sweden, an argument had erupted and in a rage, he had shoved her out of the car while it was still moving. Her arm became tangled in the door and was so severely mangled that it had to be amputated.

After the thought of that depressing story subsided, I told Anna I would like to use her in my film. She was happy with the same offer I had given Barbo, so I told her to make arrangements to get a visa and I would send her a ticket in a few weeks. She was very excited about coming to the States and even invited Walter and I to join her at a local disco later that evening. It would be the beginning of a life long friendship and the start of an incredible adventure for her.

Deciding not to shoot in Europe had been wise. When we landed in Los Angeles, Walter and I were made to wait in a holding room while the U. S. customs searched my camera for contraband. If I had brought film back, more than likely, it would have been confiscated. After two hours, I was given back my equipment and we were released. In Europe we had crossed multiple borders without the slightest problem. Things were not so easy in the "land of the free."

Anna's scene was with newcomer Joey Salvera. It was hot so I was surprised to hear her tell me the next day that she wasn't turned on to him. She was going to remain in the States for three weeks and would be staying in my guesthouse. I wanted to fuck her in the worst way, but sensed that if I moved too fast it would blow my chances. I recognized that she had different standards for 'free sex' and 'paid sex.' Paid sex was a job and free sex was for enjoyment. I had lots of time. By the third week, my inclination had proved to be correct and we became good friends, sexually and otherwise. It helped that she was as much a junky for having her pussy sucked on as I was for sucking it.

When I saw her off at the airport, it was doubtful that I would ever see her again, so it came as a complete surprise when she called a month later to tell me she was back in LA. Even more surprising, was that she was now married to an American citizen and had plans to become a citizen herself. While in the lobby of the LA International airport, two middle-aged Iranian-Americans, Keon and Cyrus, sat nearby, waiting to board the same flight. Cyrus, nudged his friend, Keon: "Get a load of the one sitting over there." Though not physically dashing, he made up for any shortcomings with high-energy, resourcefulness and self-confidence. He went to the boarding counter and arranged for his seat to be changed so that he could sit next to Anna during the long transatlantic flight. By the time they landed in Denmark, he had fallen in love with her and being that she had already fallen in love with the United States, was able to get her to agree to marry him for one year, the time required to be granted a permanent green card. Much to my joy, she told me she would not be living with him during the year and would be available to date me if I liked.

Judy and I had already agreed to make Saturday night our independent night out on the town. Anna was too independent minded be become anyone's mistress, and I wasn't looking for one, but the relationship we would have was even better; sex and friendship without commitment. It came at a good time. My sex life with Judy was hitting the seven-year mark and the excitement was beginning to wane. The fact that Judy and Anna got along well, made adjusting to that, even easier.

Before traveling to Europe, I had already shot a very exciting scene with Gail Lawrence, whose stage name was Abigail Clayton.

She was a strikingly beautiful blond who played the role of a socialite who asks her date to sit up front with the limo driver and watch while she is driven around town and picks up strangers to have sex with her in the back seat. Gail had flown down from San Francisco with her husband and new born child to take the role and as we drove to our first location, she told me a story that was most amusing and indicative of the times.

As she suckled her newborn child on her still lactating breasts, she told me that a few months prior, she knew she was about to appear in a pictorial feature in Playboy magazine called; *'The Girls of Porn.'* It was creating a dilemma for her. Her folks were conservative Easterners—her father a successful doctor—and she knew that after the magazine came out it was only a matter of time before it was brought to their attention. Their daughter would be exposed as a porn star. To mitigate their shock, she began hinting that there was something she had to tell them. This went on for some time without her revealing what it was. But a week before the issue of Playboy was to hit the street, she called them to break the news and fess up about what she had to tell them. Rather than the gasps of dismay that she had expected, she got a huge sigh of relief. "Oh my god, we're so happy to hear that. We thought you had joined the SLA (the group headed by Cinque who had kidnapped Patty Hearst) or something like that." Just being a porn star was no longer shameful.

Mercy Lamont had been pining to have sex with Judy for well over a year. In fact, a lot of girls had crushes on Judy. After practically begging me to shoot a scene of the two of them making love, I agreed after Judy, though not overtly bisexual, agreed I staged an antebellum picnic where they join a gentleman for a picnic in the countryside. After he over imbibes and passes out, the girls are left with no other option but to entertain themselves. When I got home after the shoot, I caught hell from Judy. Part of the love making routine I staged called for her to be on her hands and knees with Mercy's head laying between her legs. I then had Mercy take a bottle of wine and reach up so she could pour some over Judy's butt crack and let it run down across her pussy and into her mouth. It was hot and painful. I had no clue that the wine made her sensitive skin burn like hell.

The man who has been hallucinating over each painting on the wall, regains his mental faculties just as Rocky Balboa, a fighter who had agreed to be trained by a female sports writer, who convinced him that lots of sex was key to being a winner, knocks out his opponent. The man suddenly realizes that all the paintings that had been making him so horny, were of young couples who had recently disappeared. But before he can question the bookstore owner, he is drawn to another wall of paintings, this time of living erogenous zones in gilded frames.

The masturbating erotic dancer, played by Sarena, turns up the heat by plunging the entire length of the two foot pole into her vagina. It is too much for the man and he rushes to indulge himself with each framed erogenous zone, sucking on the pierced pussy lips, fucking a pulsating ass hole and more. As he spends himself, a snapshot of the experience becomes itself a painting. The exotic comes off the stage to stand next to the bookstore owner, who it turns out is her father. They are aliens who have come to earth to take back documentation of human sexuality.

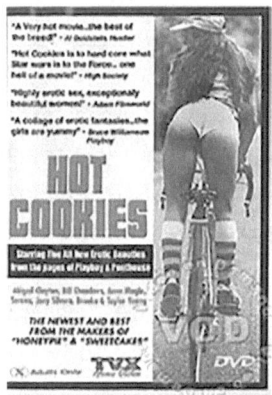

When Peter and Barry paid a visit to Mickey Zaffarano, a no-necked grey haired capo in the Bonanno family who once had done a solid stretch in the joint, to work out a deal for our new film, 'Hot Cookies,' to play in one of the adult theatres he controlled in Manhattan, it would not go well. His office was in Times Square above the 'Playland Emporium'; a facility where I had enjoyed good experiences when I had previously stopped in for some "peep show" fun. Peter and Barry wanted a deal where we would earn a percentage of the gross; New York was a large source of our potential profit. But Mickey didn't see it that way. He wasn't willing to consider any kind of revenue sharing deal and only willing to offer a flat fee; in essence, his deal would remove the lucrative New York market from our earnings potential. As Peter told me later, when he cut into Mickey's spiel to make a counterpoint, Mickey just glared at him and spoke slowly with a mobster like cadence:

"When I talk . . . you don't talk . . . Understand!"

We got around his obstinance by four-walling a theatre in Manhattan, where thanks to a strong word-of-mouth, *'Hot Cookies'* wound up doing very well. But the scenario in Zaffarano's office was a harbinger of where the theatrical porn business was headed. The free wheeling days were coming to an end! Each of the DOG EAT DOG films took up to three weeks to shoot and a couple of months to edit. If pictures didn't make a profit, there would be no money to produce another one. The days of big budget porn could not survive under Zaffarano's formula. He was too stupid to see that he was cutting his own throat.

Ironically, Mickey's façade was not as tough as he liked to pretend. In 2000, when Mayor Giuliani and the Feds made a concerted effort to destroy the porn industry around Times Square, Mickey was arrested and hauled out of his office in handcuffs. The thought of spending more time locked in a cage was more than the fat asshole could handle and he died of a heart attack on the way to the station.

86

SPIDER AND THE FLY

The Playboy and Penthouse strategy for selling magazines was so blatantly simple, that it was amazing that no one had tried it on film. They ran pictorals of beautiful women that were as racy as possible without going over the edge and then surrounded them with articles by prominent writers, interviews with celebrities and important politicians and cartoons. It gave the buyer a cover for why he was purchasing the magazine. The magazines were legal even in the 'bible belt.' Why not use the same formula for a film? I suggested to Peter that we hire Earl Miller to direct two 35mm glossy porn vignettes and surround them with an olio of comedic skits, short human-interest stories and possibly an interview with a controversial director. In essence it would be a cinematic 'Penthouse.' If the sex scenes were done tastefully, the comedic scenes and interviews would provide enough social redeeming value to overcome any suggestions that the film was pornographic. Having Earl involved would insure us free publicity in Penthouse. They liked the idea.

Thought it began well, it was, like Mata Hari another idea that eventually faltered. Thirty thousand dollars was spent to produce two scenes directed by Earl. They were both stunning and artistic. The first was an imaginative idea he came up with called; 'The Spider and the Fly.' Two Penthouse Pets, one costumed as a spider and the other as a  fly, would perform a lesbian sex scene on a giant web. The fly, caught in the web, escapes death by seducing the spider.

The second was a low key masturbation scene of a woman grieving her lost lover. Delia Cosner, brought up in Louisiana as a Catholic and currently one of the strippers at The Ball, overcame her fear that appearing in a film doing anything sexual might offend the Lord, when it was explained to her that she would be paid a thousand-dollar fee and another five-thousand if she became a Penthouse Centerfold. Earl felt my cinematography had too many rough edges for his taste, which was true, and he hired a Stephen Spielberg protégé, Alan Daviau to be his cinematographer. The result was a beautiful and inoffensive porn scene made all the more believable when Delia became overwhelmed by feelings of guilt and began to cry.

Delia would become a Penthouse Centerfold and earn her bonus and Daviau would go on to win an academy award for his work on Spielberg's *'Raiders of the Lost Arc.'* That Peter and I had trouble working together on anything other than pornography quickly became apparent when we tried to shoot our first comedy bit, an *'All in The Family'* spoof where Archie brings home a do-it-yourself S & M kit. The whole project was soon scrapped and the two Earl Miller scenes would up sitting idle in a film vault.

87

GIVE THEM THEIR POUND OF FLESH

News came from the Fleishman office that John Van de Kamp had dropped all the charges against my crew and me. Having to no longer face pandering and conspiracy to commit oral copulation and most importantly, relieved of the charge of statutory rape, was a big burden off my mind. Though the statuary rape was done without my knowledge, I knew I was lucky to have escaped. And of course I was glad for Cichy, Rogers and Saunders, who should never have been charged in the first place.

If not for the Father Filas case, I would finally be free of the judicial system. The Catholic Church remained adamant about getting their pound of flesh and the ashen-faced lawyer they had sent to LA from Mississippi, refused to budge from his demand for twenty-five thousand dollars. My lawyer fees were already nearing sixty thousand dollars and if I went to court, a pornographer against a priest, what chance would I stand? Probably none! They had me against a wall so I wrote a check to the goddamn holy hypocrites just to get them out of my hair. I had plenty of cash on hand and it was time to get on with my life; free of the courts.

But like the mythical Phoenix, new legal battles kept arising out of the ashes. Shortly after I settled with Filas, I was served with a civil suite from Mike Benveniste; claiming he was entitled to a percentage of the profits from 'Flesh Gordon' and 'Hollywood Blue.' I had, in fact, verbally promised him five percent of the net profits of 'Hollywood Blue,' but between the cost of the film and the Father Filas suit, it was a net loser. When it came to 'Flesh Gordon,' he was never promised anything. His incompetence had nearly bankrupted Graffitti Productions and making up for it had nearly exhausted me. Despite the fact that he had initiated the project, I was not in a mood to give him anything. He had no contracts to support his claims and after consulting with my lawyer, Fleishman partner, Stephen Rhode, I felt totally secure in rejecting his claims. He was now living in San Francisco and had hired a lawyer there to represent him. Over the next few months, I thought little about the case, thinking that it had such little merit that it would just go away.

And for good measure, Jason Williams also filled a suit, claiming he was promised a twenty five thousand dollar bonus for his part in the picture. It was not a stretch to speculate that Bill, while they cruised around town in his Rolls Royce, had promised that to him. Jason had done a lot of extra things to support the picture and it wasn't unreasonable for him to expect some financial benefit, but on the other hand, it was hard for me to believe that he wasn't aware that Bill was stealing money from me. Years later, my sister would tell me how Jason was at their house on the day of the big raid, helping Bill hide all the films he had stored in the attic. Knowing this, I felt giving in to him was giving in to Osco, so I instructed Rhode to fight that claim as well.

I was suddenly stranded on an island with nothing to do. Peter had already charged ahead and was doing a project with Wes Craven; a horror movie to be called, *'The Hills Have Eyes.'* I agreed to make a small investment in his project, partly because he had turned me onto an investment with a close friend of his, Dave Brown, that worked out very well, and also because he was going to use Walter Cichy as his production manager. I was happy to see Walter getting work, since at the time, I didn't have anything to offer him.

My assumption that Benvenite's law suite would just dry up proved to be naive. Thinking no lawyer would devote time to such a flimsy case, I was surprised when Steve Rhode told me that a court date had been set for a civil trial. Benveniste's San Francisco lawyer had passed the case onto a lawyer based in Los Angeles, which I assumed was a sign that he thought the chances of winning were so slim, that it didn't make sense to spend time and money on travel expenses.

But here I was, back in court again. I hadn't seen Mike since the day I had fired him. We traded guarded glances as he entered the room. His LA council was well into his sixties. A paunch, full bushy mustache and shock of hair that hung down just above his right eye, made him look more like a kindly grandfather than a lawyer. I didn't think I had much to fear.

Seniors comprised more than half of the jury pool. Who else had enough time on their hands that they could give that kind of near free service to the city. When asked, none claimed to have a problem dealing with issues that dealt with pornography. The dour look on one old lady's face, made her claim seem suspect. Only three, when asked by the judge, said they understood the difference between a criminal and a civil case. The judge took five minutes to explain the difference before voir dire began. That it takes only eight votes to reach a verdict in a civil trial, I had to trust that Rhode's picks for the jury would be fair.

Mike, at his lawyer's request, took the stand and mixed fact with fiction to describe the financial promises that I had made. His claim that he was promised a small percent of 'Hollywood Blue' was true, but his claim that a similar amount was promised from 'Flesh Gordon,' was false. Using a cajoling folksy manner, his lawyer asked him to elaborate. With a little smile on his face, Mike began by stating that he was promised a small percent of 'Flesh Gordon,' but then with a little more coaxing, he clarified that "small" meant a point and a half and after still more coaxing he said it meant five percent of the gross profit. He had no written contract backing up his claim. Rhode requested that the case be dismissed on the grounds that Benveniste's claims were vague; going from a "small" to a "defined five" percent. It was denied.

It was my turn to take the stand. Aware that speaking in public made me nervous, I drank water constantly to keep my mouth from going dry. I stated the honest facts; Benveniste had indeed been given a contract for 'Hollywood Blue,' but for reasons I have already stated, the film never made a profit. As far as 'Flesh Gordon' was concerned he was on salary and was never offered a percentage of the film.

I had been a fool to think that the old geezer was just a sweet little grandfather. He was a lawyer!! After a few perfunctory opening questions, he went right to character assassination. Benveniste had supplied him with a list of the loops that I had made when Bill and I were just getting started.

As I previously explained, each loop had been given a name to make it easy to identify. A lot of them weren't exactly G rated.

After studying the list for a moment he looked up at me and asked: "Did you make a loop called *'The Pee Wee Kid'* and did that title refer to someone being urinated on?"

Rhode jumped up and loudly objected: "Your honor, that is totally irrelevant."

The objection was sustained but before an eye could blink I was asked: "Did you make a loop called *'The Meat Eaters'* and what did that refer to?"

Again Rhode objected and was sustained, but Gramps was scoring points. He probably didn't bring up the 'dog' film because it was shot at Mike's house with his wife present and that would not have reflected well on the little angel. But by just getting the names mentioned in front of the jury, he had succeeded in making me look like a callous animal. To some eyes on the jury, I probably was.

I didn't have a large wardrobe, especially when it came to dress clothes, and each day wore a light brown camel hair sports jacket. I made a point of glancing towards the jury as often as I could but saw for the most part, blank stares. However, a few who were young professionals seemed to be listening attentively to the evidence. I didn't expect the trial to last more than one day, but when it did, seeing no reason to change my wardrobe, I wore the same camel hair sports jacket.

On the second day, Grandpa approached me with a copy of the Hollywood Reporter in his hand. He began by reading the reported grosses for Hollywood Blue: big numbers week after week. "How can you claim it lost money" he wanted to know? Taking a drink of water and struggling not to gulp as I spoke, I related how my ex-partner, Bill Osco, fabricated the grosses in order to give him leverage in selling the film to other theatres around the country; "Its common practice in the film industry to exaggerate box office grosses; since there is little likelihood that anyone would or could check their validity. Big grossing films get bookings, bombs don't." Of course I didn't tell the jury that I admired Bill's bravado and was admitting that we cheated. I could sense that some of them didn't see my explanation as sympathetic.

In his summation, Rhode pointed out that in all of Benveniste's dissembling, he had never once stated he had been given a written contract for 'Flesh Gordon' and since 'Hollywood Blue' had lost money, especially after the expensive lawsuit, nothing was due. More importantly, the fact that he went from claiming a few points to two points to five points made his claim unbelievable.

Before the jury retired to debate the case, the judge instructed them that they could not "make up a contract, verbal or otherwise. You have to believe that there is credible evidence that the claimant had been promised a contract with defined terms." After the jury had cleared the room the judge said to Steve: "It looks like you've won your case Mr. Rhode." It was good to hear. I felt Rhode had done a good job.

I assumed the jury would be out with a verdict after a few hours of deliberation. The judge had instructed them not to concoct a contract. But when they didn't come in by the end of the second day, I began to worry. What were they deliberating about? On the third day, I got a call from Rhode to come to the courthouse as quickly as I could; the jury was about to announce its verdict. They were brought in moments after I arrived. I was unable to get any sense from the somber faces sitting in the box as to what the verdict was. The judge took a few minutes to read it before handing it back to the bailiff to give to the jury foreman so it could be read aloud.

It took me a moment to catch my breath when I heard that they had ruled completely in Benveniste's favor. Contrary to the judge's instructions, they had made up a contract for 'Flesh Gordon,' giving him five percent of the gross. Five percent of the gross wasn't even part of the 'Hollywood Blue' contract! After all the costs of distributing a film: theatre's percentage, sub distributors percentage, distributor's percentage, cost of prints, advertising and more, the percentage back to the producer is not even ten percent!! In essence they had given Benveniste half ownership.

A sympathetic juror who had voted in my favor spoke with Rhode and me after the court cleared. She said more time was spent on discussing my camel hair sports jacket than on the merits of the case. One older woman couldn't stand it for some bizarre reason. Another juror argued that since I was drinking lots of water, I was lying. She told us that the deliberations took so long only because an oriental woman, who was an accountant, knew that Benveniste's claim was crap, but after three days, she threw in the towel. In a way I couldn't blame her.

Their ruling was devastating: it was possible that Benveniste would be owed hundreds of thousands of dollars and reports into perpetuity. Rhode said the fact that the jury had ignored the judge's instructions by making up a contract, made an appeal possible, but to do so would cost forty to fifty thousand dollars and there was no guarantee that we would win. After what I had just seen happen, I told him to offer fifty grand to settle. Two days later the offer was accepted.

Six months after receiving his fifty thousand dollar check; Benveniste committed suicide. I heard that he had slit his wrists while sitting in a bathtub full of water so the blood wouldn't coagulate as it went down the drain. That he would leave his wife and child without support, said a lot about him. He had been blessed with a lot of talent and contributed greatly to my success, but his detachment from reality and self-absorbance led to his demise. Mike couldn't see beyond himself. As long as he was having fun, not much else seemed to matter. It would be lying if I didn't admit that I wished he had slit his wrists before I wrote him the check. Hopefully, for the sake of his wife and kid, some of the money was still in the bank when he killed himself.

I had enough with lawsuits and agreed to give Jason Williams the twenty-five grand he was asking. It would probably cost me that much in lawyer fees to fight on. And discounting my dislike for Bill, he had done all that was asked of him and more. Despite the fact that I suspected that he, at Bill's request, was behind a burglary at my Laurel Canyon house where Graffitti's Nagra recorder and Judy's and my wedding rings were stolen, I had enough reasons to rationalize that he deserved the money. I was once again free of lawyers. I vowed to do everything in my power to keep things that way.

88

THE LEGEND OF ORAL ZIEHM

Now that I had no felonies hanging around my neck and had paid to get rid of the civil suites, I was left free to live a life that Nero would have been proud of. The Sunday parties became sexier, wilder and more interesting. I considered it my job to make sure they had a bacchanalian atmosphere and paraded around in a mini bikini or a g-string that barely covered what was underneath. I got off being a sex object. Because I took every opportunity to bury my head between a lady's legs, Earl tagged me with the moniker, *'Oral Ziehm'*

He not only brought beautiful models to the scene, but also friends of his from the music and entertainment industry. Lifting my head up momentarily as I ate a pussy, I held a delightful conversation with Chris Beard, an Englishman who was the creator of the super hit, *'The Gong Show.'* J. C Phillips, Earls next-door neighbor, who wrote the hit song *'Green Eyed Lady'* and *'By The Time I go to San Francisco,'* often came by with his small entourage of gay lovers. Bob Radnitz, Academy nominated director of 'Sounder' and James Poe, Academy Award screenplay winner for *'Around The World In Eighty Days'* and *'They Shoot Horses, Don't They,'* came by to ogle the wild women. Poe, the great grandson of Edgar Allen Poe, snorted more lines of powder than was healthy for a man of his age. Some celebs just dropped in to see if what they had heard was true including LeVar Burton and Kris Kristofferson.

It was an accepted fact that cocaine was non addictive. After all, it was Freud's favorite drug. Offering toots was the easiest way guys had of ingratiating themselves to females. Two lively 'cougars,' Elrica Cantor, who lived in the Malibu Colony and had an art gallery on La Cienaga and her friend, Cici Houston, director John Houston's ex wife came to the parties with their own drug dealer, a hyper and talkative Jewish kid, named Stephen Laufer. He liked to show everyone the lines on his hands, which, according to him, were the sign of the devil. His presence always guaranteed that cocaine would be available. Cici loved telling the story of when she walked in on Houston while he was in the kitchen getting a blowjob from the Spanish maid. Not wanting to interrupt his pleasure, he just ignored her and continued as though she weren't there; encouraging the girl in his deep resonate voice which she liked to mimic: "Suck it . . . ah yes . . . suck it more . . . yes that's good . . . more."

The sound of sex could sometimes be more exciting than the sight of it. Earl had come to the party with Teri Nunn, who he had shot, with her mother's permission, for a Penthouse layout when she was only sixteen years old. She was extraordinarily beautiful and sexual as well. After the sun went down she wound up in the Jacuzzi with Earl's assistant, her orgasmic screams that came cascading into the house made every guy there envious. It was at our house that a radio disc jockey discovered her which led to her becoming the lead singer for *'Berlin'* and their classic hit *'Take My Breath Away.'*

One of my favorite groups while I was in high school, was the *'The Diamonds.'* What a surprise when David Somerville and his beautiful wife, who kept her nee name, Gail Jensen, came to one of our weekend gatherings.

She was a beautiful tall blond and even though I knew she and David had an open marriage, my ingrained shyness prevented me from coming on to her. It turned out, I didn't have to. On her third weekend visit she came up to me and said in a sexy voice: "I wore this just for you Howie." She was referring to the miniscule light blue string bikini she was wearing. My skimpy bikinis and g-strings had caught her eye and she wanted to do more than just look. Our mutual love of cunnilingus led to a year-long relationship that only ended when she divorced David Summerville and married David "kung foo" Carradine.

The previous year's Halloween party had left an indelible impression on all who had attended, as well as those who hadn't and wished they had. Judy was constantly being asked if we intended to throw another party this year. Her answer was a definite yes.

Again, I was assisted by three of Judy's stripper friends to help do my drag queen makeup. Being in drag had gotten me laid so many times the previous year, that it would have been crazy not to do it again. As the girls worked on me, I hooked the garters to my sheer Lili St. Cyr thigh hugger nylons. My g-string was not quite large enough to hold my shaved cock and required that I lay it sideways to main some degree of respectable deportment. To keep it turgid throughout the evening, I had soaked it in copious amounts of baby oil. Unfortunately that cost me a blowjob. One of the girls said she had been thinking of sucking me off but was afraid the oil might get into her hair. Damn!

Judy was in a walk-in closet just outside the open bathroom door
, helping Shauna, a gorgeous five foot ten transsexual into a black leather corset I had brought back from Europe. Shana had been hired by Chevrolet to be their model in a print ad they had produced earlier in the year. Her body was larger than a normal female and I could see that the seams of the corset were straining as Judy tried to close the clasps. What the fuck! It was not the time to get pissed off.

By eight O'clock, the house was rocking. As usual, Judy made sure the music was non-stop. The eclectic collection of people attending included strippers and porn people. Sarena came with Reb who also brought a couple of his biker buddies. George Dent, the United Airlines pilot who shot the promo cards of the girls of 'The Ball' agreed to operate a projector to run my porn films in the bedroom.

Earl Miller had come with his girl friend Viki and Barry Weiss came with the magic theatre girls, Moira and Duane.

The two beauties whose pussies I ate on a weekly basis, Anna and Gail, came with their husbands, Keon and David Sommerville. Marcial and his girl friend Catherine, added to the sexy atmosphere when they both showed up wearing small bikinis.

When Ulrika Cantor and her friend Cici Houston showed up with their cocaine dealer, Stephen Laufer, Cici began by handing me the 'Penisauraus' puppet monster, which had been missing from its perch in my office for several weeks. I had been wondering what had happened to it. Cici explained that she had borrowed it to attach to the hood ornament of her Rolls Royce, so she and Steven could freak people out while they drove down Rodeo drive in Beverly Hills; high—of course—on coke.

Barry Weiss and The Magic Theatre planned to put on a hippy like theatrical show on the patio during the evening. Judy was given the role of a butterfly prancing idyllically through the crowd. She had attended Woodstock and for her, this would be a reprisal of that experience, so she was excited to participate. A pretty stripper named Patrice, whom I had first met at Marvin's pad where she was in his bedroom having lesbian sex with her girl friend, was now one of The Ball's sexiest strippers and was dating the Magic Castle's magician of the year, who she brought along and graciously roamed the crowd performing feats of prestidigitation.

I had tried to initiate an orgy by inviting Serena to lie down on the living room carpet and spread her legs so I could suck on her pussy, but even among the wild crowd that was in attendace, deep seated inhibitions kept anything from igniting. However, later in the evening, after Duane had finished performing in the rather mundane 'Magic Theatre' show, she joined me in the den to put on a live sex show. While she sat on a chair with her legs pulled up against her chest so I could fuck her while kneeling on the floor, twenty people came into the room to watch. A pretty Jewish girl, named Shelly, was sitting atop the library hutch cheering the action, so I invited her to join us. She declined but the gyrations of my thrusting bare butt were too much to resist. I felt a brief stinging pain of something being rammed up my asshole, but was unaware what it was. It happened so fast and because the initial stinging pain subsided so quickly, I didn't bother to look to see what had caused the sting. It actually felt good and added to the intensity of the sex so I just kept fucking Duane. Only after I finished, did I reach back to pull out a large rectal intruder. Wow—she had inserted a thick rubber penis dildo up my ass. I was totally amazed that it had gone in so easily without the benefit of a lubricant. Anal sex actually felt pretty good!

Since there was lots of pot and cocaine but little alcohol, there were no fights. The only threat of violence occurred when a friend of Marcial's, Chris Wilson, stuck a gun in his wife's face while they were standing outside at the bottom of the driveway because she had insisted on leaving. I would eventually become very good friends and a business partner with him and had to believe that being forced to leave what was probably the hottest party he had ever attended, just made him go bonkers. Sex can do that.

I was unaware that something else happened that night that would cause more devastation to my life than all the previous mishaps combined. Judy, in a see-through Kamali dress was looking her usual provocative self and getting lots of attention. So it was not unusual that a nice looking admirer would approach her while she was in the den reloading the tape recorder. He asked her if she was the hostess. When she replied yes, he took a vile of coke from his pocket and told her he'd like to give her something special. She had remained clean from drugs as long as we had been together. Even with all the temptations that were around her at the job and at home, she didn't indulge in anything, not pot or even an occasonal glass of wine. But the young stranger's calm demeanor made her feel comfortable. He told her it would give her energy; make her feel good; it was no big deal. Of course she was aware that half the people in the house were snorting coke, many of them her friends and as they continued to talk, he opened the vile and used a little silver spoon, just big enough to fit through its neck, to withdraw a little pile of white powder, which he then placed under one of her nostrils.

"Just close your other nostril with your finger and take a deep breath in," he told her.

She paused for a moment, debating in her mind whether she had become too cautious. Coke didn't seem to be causing anyone problems. "Why not?" she told herself and covered her nostril as the guy had suggested and took a deep breath As she related to me years later, she instantaneously got a feeling of energy and vibrato.

She liked the state of euphoria she found herself in when she returned to the party. Moments later the doorbell rang and when someone opened it;

two cops were standing in the entrance. They were real cops that a neighbor had called to complain about the loud music and the cars parked in the street. It was well known around our sparsely populated neighborhood, that I was a pornographer and though no one confronted me directly, there were some who wouldn't mind causing me problems. Several people slinked off to the bathroom to flush their drugs down the toilet in case a search was about to take place. In my little baby doll, I was in no position to deal with the police, but Judy, armored with a cocaine-induced sense of manipulative superiority, approached them with élan. When they told her there were complaints about the loud music, she asked them if they could hear it as they walked up the driveway. They admitted that they couldn't, and after a brief and friendly warning to try and keep it down, they left.

She was ecstatic about her ability to handle a tense situation with such panache. She was sold on cocaine! I had no idea, as I stood nearby in my hot baby doll, that the seeds of a living nightmare that would almost rip my life apart had just been sewn that Halloween evening.

89

THE GATOR IS STRUCK DOWN

It was obvious that I had made a mistake by not making a sequel to 'Flesh Gordon' while it was hot. Osco had benefited more from his co producer credit by tagging *'Alice in Wonderland'* with 'from the producer of Flesh Gordon' than I had as its primary producer. It was time to make a 'Flesh Gordon' sequel.

My assumption that the Supreme Court was going to liberalize the censorship laws was looking less likely, and even more troubling, was that a lot of theatre chains were refusing to play anything rated stronger than an R. Consequently, I set out to write a script that still had lot's of sexual parody and sexy sight gags, but its main theme would appeal to a much broader audience. I decided it would be a conflict between the world's elders and its youth over the corrupting influence of 'Rock and Roll.' From his radio station on a nearby planet, a crazy disc jockey who calls himself, 'Captain God,' was flooding the air waves with the pounding beat of a noisy music he called 'rock and roll.' Like drunk-monkeys, young people were spending their time dancing to it rather than paying attention to their schoolwork. and it needed to be stopped. An upright American is needed to stop the menace and Flesh is asked to take on the task.

I quickly had a script in hand and armed with a dozen colorful production drawings, set out to look for investors. A million and a half dollars would be all it would take to avoid any financial disasters like what I had encountered the first time around. Sy Katz and Cichy, who would be my co producer, both concurred that financing the picture would be a slam-dunk.

I was so wrong!! No one, including people who had made money off of the first 'Flesh Gordon,' wanted to invest money in a sequel. That the age of sequels was still a few years off may have contributed to the lack of interest, but me being seen as too wild and outré to be trusted, was also a big factor. Without a record of working in a structured environment, it was like getting credit from a bank when you've never previously taken out a loan and didn't have a job. The fact that I had a record of completing countless films within budget didn't seem to matter.

Then on a drab and drizzly November morning, my ringing phone awoke me from a sound sleep around 8AM. The 1977 rainy season was beginning early, a welcome sign, considering that Southern California always needs rain. It was Walter's estranged wife, Vicki. After she had discovered that Walter had begun an affair with Peter Locke's secretary, Rosemary, while he was working on 'The Hills Have Eyes,' they had broken up. She was crying. At first I thought it was about an argument or maybe that he had left for good; but through her sobs she managed to tell me that he had just been killed in an early morning traffic accident. It hit me like a sledgehammer. I was numb for a moment and couldn't say anything. They had met at a Denny's in the valley for an early breakfast to discuss getting back together. After the meeting, Walter had left in his VW Bug to return to his apartment in Sherman Oaks. Just as he passed over the crest of a small hill, he was confronted with a truck double-parked in his lane. He made a hard swerve to the left to avoid a collision, but that took him into oncoming traffic and before he could make a counter move, a car coming the other way crashed into him head on. It was the pre seatbelt age and he had little chance in his VW bug. He was killed instantly when his head crashed through the windshield.

Handling the death of a friend left me confused. He had been a big part of almost every film I had ever made. Without him, there likely would have never have been a Flesh Gordon. He found the shots to replace the missing negative and was responsible for Penthouse publishing the twelve page pictorial article. He was going to be a big part of the sequel. I was use to leaning on someone and now that tree was gone.

When his mother flew out from Far Rockaway two days later to wrap things up, she put things into perspective. When I stopped by Walter's apartment to see if I could be of assistance, Vicki and his mother were already there. The mother was running the show. She handled it as though she was cleaning out an apartment so a new renter could move in. Throw this out. Throw that out. If she saved anything, I didn't see it. What I thought should have been a lachrymose scene, didn't create a single tear. By the end of the day, she was on her way back to Far Rockaway. If there was a funeral I wasn't made aware of it. I wasn't big on funerals anyway and found myself agreeing how she had handled it. Walter was dead and gone and it was time to move on. I would have to make adjustments to deal with the hard reality that I would no longer have his support.

90

SUZE RANDALL PORN MOM
AND BROWN SUGAR

A propitious meeting of the flamboyant Suze Randall, got me on track to find a new assistant and make, what would be, my last porn movie. Earl Miller had brought me as his guest to a Penthouse New Year's eve party and while Judy was out on the floor dancing Mata Hari style by herself, I began talking to the couple sitting nearby. I found I had a lot in common with Humphrey Knipes, a scholarly looking South African and his English wife, Suze Randall, who had come dressed in a semi-transparent gauzy white dress. Suze and I soon took to the dance floor to engage in a bit of dirty dancing. By the time we returned to the table, we knew that we were soul sluts.

Suze didn't look like someone you would expect to find shooting soft porn for Hustler magazine, but she was one of the best. After meeting Humphrey while living in London, they got married and, at Humphey's request, gave up nursing and moved to the States to take up a career as a photographer. It took off like an SST when she landed a Playboy magazine cover with the cutie-faced Kristine DeBell, the same who had starred in Bill's, 'Alice in Wonderland.'

Suze was as blatantly unashamed of nudity as I was. She had appeared in a self-shot 'spread beaver' layout in Hustler magazine with her pussy made to look more lascivious by it being highlighted with a small key light.

Humphrey, who never opened his mouth very wide when he spoke, told me the light was his idea.

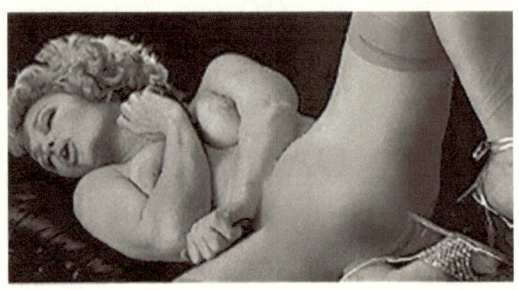

Cocaine was making Judy more and more independent and we began spending less time together, so I began spending a lot of time at Suze and Humphrey's house in Mar Vista. It always had a welcoming vibe and there were always a few models and other interesting people around, like Donald Cammel, the director of the Mick Jagger film, 'Performance.' At one of their afternoon garden parties, I struck up a conversation with another of their English guests, a skinny and somewhat awkward looking young man, named Jason Mayall. He was the son of blue's legend John Mayall, the leader of the British band, 'The Blues Breakers.' That he had come from London to get to better know his father who had separated from the family when he was still very young better made me feel an unstated sympathy for him. As we continued to talk, I mentioned I was looking for a new production assistant and he wasted no time in convincing me that he was what I was looking for. For a nineteen year old, he comported himself very well.

DOG EAT DOG still had a hundred grand in the bank that was just sitting idle. Peter, who had already teamed up with his old high school friend, David Debin, to produce a mainstream film that would star Debin's wife, Stockard Channing, no longer had the time or the interest to get involved with another porn film. I got the feeling that he would like to expunge it from his history. but it made no sense to let the money sit idle, so after I pitched an idea for a new film that he would not have to be involved with. I would produce and direct and Barry would handled distribution. We all agreed that I should go ahead and I began production in late 1979. The vice had relaxed for the time being so I could shoot in LA if I liked and the hundred grand would give me one of the highest budgets for a porn film up to that time.

'Star Virgin' was the story of a girl abducted by alien robots while she is still an infant and raised on their planet without the benefit of human contact. As she reaches her teen years, she becomes curious about the strange feelings she is having in her groin. Her robot overseer tells her it's all about a primitive earthling thing, something called sex.

Her persistent pestering leads him to pull up several digital examples of human sexuality on his viso screen. Rather than calming her down, each example gets her more excited and eventually leads to a gushing orgasm.

Jason's father, John, was delighted that his son had landed a job with me. He and I shared a lot in common. We both had large porn collections, although most of his was destroyed in a fire, including the film of a gerbil scampering down a Lucite tube inserted into a woman's vagina, and we both wore tight hot pants and unbeknownst to Jason, we both liked to wear women's panties on occasion. He proved to be everything I had hoped for, from building sets and finding locations and performing as a production manager. I liked the fact, that despite being a teenager, he didn't tolerate a lot of bullshit.

I asked Humphrey to write the dialogue for the script, I liked his dry sense of humor. I got an unexpected bonus when Suze suggested that I use Kari Klark, who she had recently shot for a Hustler centerfold, to play the lead role. The PR benefits were obvious. Kari was a biker chick, who looked anything but glamorous, but when dolled up by a makeup artist, she was a knock out Over the next three weeks, I shot the scenes that exemplified human sexuality: a high school hot rod scene in an amusement park called the Garden of Eden, a Rocky Horror spoof shot in black and white, a locker room scene where the cheerleaders revive the star quarterback after he is knocked unconscious during a football game, and a group sex scene in a backroom of a strip club that was inspired by the Copenhagen room at the Mitchell Brother's O'Farrell Theatre.

Porn was not the stigma that it once had been and several of the members of my cast had celebrity status. Songwriter, J. C. Phillips, played the snake in the Garden of Eden; Tom Poster, the son of New York Post columnist, Tom Poster Sr., did the sex scene in the garden with Tracy Walton, a cruise ship hostess. Character actor, Charlie Dierkop, who had roles in 'Butch Cassidy and the Sundance Kid' and 'The Sting,' played an ogre in the Dracula scene, although a Richard Nixon mask hid his identity.

I had hoped to film an extreme anal scene with Gene, "long dick" Carrier, whose shaft was second only to the legendary John Holmes, but my pretty blond actress freaked out when he tried to force his brobdignagian member into her liliput butt hole. It just wouldn't open up and she began to scream. As a favor to Suze, who I knew was thinking of making a porn movie herself, I had invited her on the set as an observer. When she saw that I was having problems pulling off the anal scene, she offered to help. She had boasted to me that she had taken football legend Jim Brown up her ass, so I knew she had expertise. But her efforts failed as well and not wanting to create an uptight vibe, I decided not to push it. If I would have left Suze continue, I'm sure she would have succeeded in getting the shot. "Maybe I was losing it."

The large budget allowed me to pay two girls enough that they were willing to do a 'gang bang' scene. Susan Song, a beautiful oriental stripper who performed under the name Zen Kitty when she danced at the Ivar Theatre, and Barbara Smith, a dancer at the Ball, agreed to take the parts for seven hundred dollars each. They would be asked to fuck thirteen guys and Barbara agreed to do a DP scene. "Gang bang" sex was new to porn and the fee I paid them was, as far as I knew, the most any porn actress had been paid up to that time. Barbara came up to my house the night before the shoot to give me a "thank you" fuck for giving her the role.

I had become friendly with Bruce David, Hustler's editor, while attending parties at Suze's house. When he told me he was naming 'Star

Virgin' best porn picture of 1979, it should have assured that the film would be a box office success. But good percentage deals with exhibitors were becoming more difficult to get and the rapidly growing video market was starting to make porn theaters obsolete. The gross was far less than I had hoped for.

The strength of an open marriage is that when the inevitable: "I don't want to have sex with you anymore" comes, it doesn't destroy the relationship. Ten years of having sex with the same person becomes boring. There were no more surprises. Each morning began by eating my wife out and once I was inside, I would hang my head over the side of the bed and pull out one of the girlie magazines secreted beneath the bed so I could stay hard by fantasizing about the models teasing me from the pages below. For her, feeling the same dick going in and out, was like Sysyphus pushing the rock. Nothing changes. It cums and then the day goes on just as it did the day before and the day before that. I had no need to be worshipped and she never demanded that I worship her. We had a good, although unusual life, and there was no reason to throw that out the window.

I had come to a point in life where I need change and variety to keep my libido stimulated. After I dropped off my favorite lovers; Anna, Gail and Mercy, I would make the rounds of the burlesque theatres and strip clubs to tease an orgasm or two out of myself before I returned home around 1:30 AM. However, it began to upset me that Judy would still be out, not so much that she was dancing, but that she was becoming a coke-head. And it made me even less happy to be awakened by the sound of her clanking high heels as she came walking through the breezeway an hour and a half later.

Crazy as I was, I couldn't help but see the madness that was begining to take place around me. When Judy came home from a date at two thirty after dancing with one of her lovers, a six foot five twenty-five year old, named Brian Mace, screaming like a banshee that he was going to come by and kill her, I knew trouble lie ahead. The coke had made her temporarily psychotic. Nevertheless, a day later, after she came down, she would be back hanging out with him, even joining him at the Marina where he had a small business painting boats.

As the temperature cooled down over the winter months, so did the weekend parties. But as the warm spring weather came back, the parties did as well. Backgammon had become a craze and there were always a few games going on around the house. Earl always insisted on an excruciating long game of eight ball and of course there was plenty of grass and toots of cocaine available. Although I did accept a toot from time-to-time, I didn't like the clogged up feeling that cocaine left in my nose and there was no way I was going to blow a bill on a gram; not to mention it hindered my ability to get a hard on.

I had just been asked by a spunky stripper with firm bullet breasts who I knew from the Ivar, to enjoy some sex with her out on the lawn when a bright eyed black girl who was just walking in said: "Hi, I'm Marsha Hunt. I knew you when you were at the Cabale." I remembered Marsha well. She was the eighteen year old who had ventured out of Philadelphia's German town and after coming to Berkeley had dropped into the Cabale because she had heard that it "was the real thing." She was now with her daughter, Karis, who looked to be about ten or eleven years old. Not wanting to keep my Ivar sweet heart waiting, I passed Marsha off to Judy so I could take care of our business outside on the lawn.

When I returned from doing my duty, I noticed that Marsha had closed the drapes to shelter her daughter's eyes. I wasn't use to having kids around and understood her concern. I was aware that Marsha had lost her virginity while in Berkeley, it was a celebrated story, but at the time, neither Debbie nor I had any idea that she had ambitions to become a singer. Over the next fifteen minutes, she told me the amazing story about what happened to her after she left Berkeley and moved to London to follow her dream.

On an overcast London day, she was walking to an audition for a new musical she saw advertised in the paper, when a sudden shower caught her without an umbrella. As her hair became wet, it blew up into a big round, what is now called, an Afro. She was worried that it might prevent her from getting a part, but as soon as she walked in the producers excitedly exclaimed: "that's exactly what we're looking for!" The new musical was called 'Hair' and she got the part immediately. Her part in the show led to a record deal with UK Track records. Needing songs for her to sing, they hooked her up with a budding, yet to be discovered songwriter, named, Elton John. Her career blossomed and the subsequent notoriety led to her becoming romantically involved with, Mick Jagger. An unplanned child—who was now standing in my living room—soon followed. Mick was smitten enough by her to memorialize her in the song, 'Brown Sugar,' but not enough to make it known publicly that her beautiful chocolate baby was his. Only after Marsha filed a law suite to force him to provide proper support, did the whole situation come to light.

Considering how shy I was when I ran the Cabale, Marsha must have been surprised to see that I had become such an exhibitionist when she dropped by that day. Unlike most American men, who were afraid of being thought of as gay, I knew who I was and also knew that erotic attire turned me and women on as well. Susan Birdahl gave me a soft-leather g-string that had a pouch to encase the balls and a shaft with a zipper to encase the penis. My cock got hard just putting it on. It was especially a turn on to wear it under my white silk hot pants where I had to tie the leather strings attached to its tip around my waist to keep it from popping out when I had an erection.

There was now a sex superstore in Hollywood, called The Pleasure Chest for uninhibited men to not only buy, but to try on sexy clothes and enhancements, in one of their private dressing rooms that came furnished with full length mirrors. To be expected, most of the customers were from the gay crowd who were way ahead of the curve when it came to erotic men's wear. The store, located in *"Gaywood,"* an area of Hollywood on Santa Monica Blvd that abutted Beverly Hills, stocked everything from male g-strings, bikinis, penis enhancements, sexy hot pants, lubricants, cock rings and every size and type of dildo imaginable, including the popular, 'Jack-Hammer Jesus.' On one visit, as I pondered which of several g-strings I should take into one of the dressing rooms to try on and admire myself in the full length mirror, two gay guys standing nearby were pondering which of the three-foot long, six inch in diameter, dildos they should take home for an afternoon of ass gaping fun, a popular fetish among the gay crowd long before it found its way into gonzo porn.

Anna Magle was not shy to admit that she loved the male sex organ and when I brought her to the Pleasure Chest, she insisted that I buy some black hot pants that came with a cod piece like pouch sewn in. I acquiesced to her wish and also threw in a cock ring that was held in place by a thin leather strap that could be snapped together behind the balls. After donning my new hot cod pants, we walked out of the store and took a stroll through the center of 'Gaywood.' Public exhibitionism made my dick stiffen, so afraid the gays on the street might get the wrong idea that I was available, I put my arm around Anna to let them know I was DC.

For a few short weeks in 1980, it looked like the future of open sex in LA was taking a giant step forward, when the controversial New York pay-to-go swing club, Plato's Retreat, opened a Hollywood branch. Anna was always a willing partner when it came time to check out a new sexual adventure. The club was a half block south of Hollywood Blvd on Ivar, just across from the theatre. It occupied two floors and the basement of a large three story industrial sized building. After I paid the thirty-dollar entry-fee, we were directed to go down to the basement where an attractive hostess gave us a friendly welcome and described what we would find upstairs after we changed into our togas. Anna and I were the only ones in the room, and after we put our cloths in the lockers the hostess had assigned to us and locked them with the keys we had been given, we left to go upstairs. On the way we passed a Jacuzzi room where several older and uninspiring swingers were frolicking.

The main room was a large open auditorium, lit throughout by small multi colored spotlights to make it sexy and mysterious. We were disappointed to see, rather than the wild orgy we anticipated, only a few couples in togas milling around a buffet table filled with fresh fruits and hors d'oeuvres and a few others at a bar beneath a Tahitian canopy that offered soft drinks and various punches. Alcohol and drugs were not allowed.

Among the dozen people in attendance, we didn't spot anyone appealing enough to swing with, so Anna and I decided to go up to the balcony where a row of small rooms separated by bed sheets, had been set up for couples who wanted to have sex. Each room had a clean, freshly made twin-sized bed. A diaphanous curtain over the door offered a combination of privacy for those inside and a titillating peek for those passing by.

A couple entered the adjacent room just as Anna and I were finishing having sex, which meant eating her pussy for ten minutes and then pounding her like a jack hammer until I came—she didn't like prolonged fucking. A bit of rustling took place on the bed in the room next to us, but no moans or groans ensued. We were about to leave and go back downstairs when a little argument between the couple broke out. We couldn't resist hanging around to eavesdrop.

"Why are you being so uptight?" a male voice asked. "I'm not being uptight" the female whined.

"If you don't want to be here, let's just get the hell out of here. I can't handle your bullshit much longer."

"I don't want to go," retorted the female as she began to sob. "Were getting the fuck out of here unless you stop being so

fucking up tight. Now are you going to get your act together, Jenny, or do we leave?"

After Jenny sobbed for a few moments, she calmed down and they left the room without having sex or further argument. Anna and I, quiet as church mice, waited a minute before leaving; to make sure they didn't know that their little squabble had entertained us.

When we returned to the main room, much to our delight, several more swingers had joined the party. A cute couple standing by the juice bar caught Anna's eye and she said she wouldn't mind fucking the guy. I felt the same about the girl, so we sidled up to them and introduced ourselves. When the girl said her name was Jenny, Anna and I did a quick double take. Apparently they had resolved their conflict. Within minutes, Anna and the guy left to go upstairs to the balcony to have sex in one of its little rooms.

I stood with Jenny for a moment, as we seized each other up. As soon as her husband was out of earshot, she almost bowled me over when she asked: "Would you mind sucking my pussy until it turns into a prune?" Did I give off some kind of mysterious vibe or what? She had no idea that she was talking to 'Oral Ziehm.' I took her by the hand and led her to the nearby, Arabian harem room, a tent like structure, fifteen feet square, with walls and ceiling made of see through cloth and a floor covered wall-to-wall by mattresses. It was meant for large orgies, but was unoccupied as we walked in.

We made ourselves comfortable in a corner of the harem tent just to the right of its entry flap. Knowing that she was probably nervous, I began with a little back massage, ear, neck and breast kissing and then slowly tongued my way down her tummy so I could gently spread her legs and honor her request. Within minutes, the sensual gyrations of her hips told me that she was thoroughly enjoying herself.

Evidently, Jenny's husband wasn't a pussy sucker and since Anna didn't like long drawn-out fucks, they finished quickly. He came by and peeked into the harem tent to see what was going on with his wife. I lifted my cunt-juice saturated face from between Jenny's legs just long enough to give him a perfunctory glance before plunging it back against her moist snatch to resume turning it into a prune. Before closing the entry flap, he let her know he was waiting outside. What a rude prick! We weren't even ready to fuck yet and neither of us was about to stop enjoying ourselves. Over the next fifteen minutes, he made periodic checks, noticeably becoming more irritated after each peek. It was pissing him off that his wife was having more fun than he had had. Maybe he should have learned how to suck pussy better! Jenny and I finally coupled and I came within a few minutes so he wouldn't blow a gasket. Later, Anna confirmed what I had suspected; the didn't like eating pussy and was a lousy lay.

Anna and I visited Plato's the next week and Jenny and her husband were there again. She said hi to me as she was being quickly wisped away by some guy to again have sex and hopefully have her pussy sucked into a prune. She was now a full-fledged swinger and was obviously enjoying it. Since Anna had no interest in her husband or any of the other "truckers" hanging around, we went up to the next floor and joined several couples on a couch to watch a porn movie. The girl sitting next to me was quite pretty, but the vibe in the room was cool and nothing happened. Three weeks later, the LA vice decided Plato's was too much for Los Angeles and closed it down.

Judy didn't concern herself with my sex life and gave no indication that she had any problems with it. She actually seemed closer to Anna than to me. We didn't consult much on anything anymore. Between the breast implants she had gotten and cocaine, her confidence had soared mightily from the quiet little waif that I had first married. She now spoke her mind—often loudly -and did what she pleased. I thought her implants were a bit too large, but they caught the eyes of plenty of admirers who she went dancing with. She didn't object to my behavior so I didn't object to hers. She had as much right to enjoy sex as I did. And as far as her usage of cocaine, everyone knew it was non addictive.

After Peter finished the The Kitty O'Neil Story, he quickly moved on to another project, again with another of his New York friends.

Donald Kushner had previously produced a film for Disney, called, 'TRON.' Their new project would also be with Disney. It spelled the end of our partnership. Paranoid that his association with porn could screw things up for him, Peter turned all the distribution responsibilities of 'Flesh Gordon,' which continued to have life, over to Barry Cahn. Peter was going to do whatever it took to succeed and his philosophy was to only have friends that could help him achieve that. It had merit even if it wasn't my philosophy Regardless, it was a waste to shelve the two Earl Miller scenes that sat in a vault. Earl was still anxious to get paid for his work and like many people, he was beginning to use a lot of cocaine: not a cheap habit. So I proposed doing another loop carrier feature that could incorporate the two scenes. The idea was for a TV network having rating problems; to call a meeting of its executives and ask them to pitch ideas for shows. Each idea would be a porn spoof of an actual TV show. The 'Spider and Fly' would be pitched as *'The Wild and Crazy Kingdom'* and the other Miller scene would become *'As the World Burns.'* I would shoot three new parodies: General Hospital would be *'Genital Hospital,'* Mash would be *'Trash,'* and, The Young and the Lonely, would be, *'The Young and the Horney.'* The obvious title for the film would be; *'Naughty Network.'* We all understood it was tp be our last production together.

Bob Vosse had made a ton of money with his 8mm 'Swedish Erotica' series that featured John Holmes fucking my 'Flesh Gordon' star, big busted Candy Samples. He now owned his own warehouse studio in South San Francisco and agreed to let me rent it from him. I had Jason and Lynn drive up a day early with the cast to prepare for the shoot.

Much like the Big Bear shoot, staying at a motel with my cast of porn girls, didn't result in an orgy. Jason and the girls had a little non sex party in one of the rooms and I wasn't included. I was of a different generation, like it or not. Earlier in the evening, Jason had complained to me that his dad liked to parade around the house in panties, a bra and nylons held up by a garter belt. Knowing I was wearing some of Judy's panties as we spoke, I feigned sympathy for his plight. We shot the 'Trash' scene at Vosse's studio the next morning and after he begged me to let his cameraman shoot a master shot from the rafters, I agreed. I would cover tighter shots from the ground with my second camera. Rene Blair, a soft looking blond stripper who I knew from the Ball, was cast to do a hardcore scene where she would by strapped into a leather hammock with her arms and legs bound. I knew her, from personal experience, to be a consumate tease, but since she was bound, she had no way of resisting. The results were incredible; a screaming writhing sexual paroxysm. She would tell me later that it was the best orgasm she ever had. Unfortunately, Vosse's cameraman had become so engrossed that he failed to hear that the camera had run out of film. Fucking idiot!

Despite the Earl Miller scenes, the 'gang bang scene and the teenage pussy shaving scene with Baby Sue Young who was momentarily blinded by the cum shot she took to her face, the film failed to make money. It would be the first and only porn movie I made that lost money. However, despite the film's failure, I managed to create a silver lining for myself. Being that it was my wont to stop for a game of golf when I traveled, I had planned to stop overnight in Monterey before continuing on to Frisco.

Not realizing that the Monterey Jazz festival was taking place when I got there at ten at night, I discovered that there was only one motel room available in the entire area. It was a room at a Seaside motel that would normally go for fifteen to twenty bucks, but was now asking a hundred. I was too tired to argue, so agreed to the price. The bathroom looked funky so I didn't bother to wash or brush my teeth and moments after climbing in bed, I began to itch. My prior days in Seaside told me that I was under attack by sand fleas possibly coming from the mattress and pillow which felt like they had been filled with sand.

My room was right next to the manager's office and through the paper-thin wall I could hear his shrill voice trying to explain to the owner who was on the phone why they were the only place on the peninsula that wasn't sold out.

"We're charging too much!" he shouted.

The owner evidently proffered that places in Carmel were charging the same thing and more.

"But this is Seaside, we can't get the same thing they're asking in Carmel!".

By four A. M., still itching and awake, I got up and stumbled across Freemont Street to an all-night Sambo's Pancake house. In between swilling down several jugs of coffee to wash down eggs and syrup-soaked pancakes, I killed time by reading every article in the morning edition of the San Francisco Chronicle while formulating a plan I intended to carry out.

At nine O'clock sharp, I was walking into the first, open for business, real estate office I could find in Carmel and said: "Show me the cheapest house you have available." Thanks to the only stock recommendation that Sy Katz had given me that paid off, a geothermal company called MAGMA, I was flush with thirty-five thousand dollars. I was going to use it to buy a second house.

The realtor drove me to a Charmer—the term Carmelites like to use for their little wood and brick storybook houses that are not marred by something so gauche as street numbers—and because the owner needed money fast to pay for his wife's cancer operation, I was able to get him to accept a forty-five thousand dollar down payment and agree to carry the balance, interest free, for three years. By late afternoon, I was back on the road, my sleepless nightmare turned into a dream.

Video was making theatrical porn films an anachronism and once again I wasn't sure where my future lie. Flesh Gordon 2 was doing no better than Mata Hari. I met with Russ Hampshire at his VCA office to see if he would commit to distribute any porn films I made if I decided to do so. He had purchased the video rights for several of the DOG EAT DOG films, so was familiar with my work. After he told me that VCA was now paying producers fifteen grand to make a film, which included the producer's profit, I declined. Going back to making one or two day wonders for the slim chance of getting laid, no longer had the same lure for me that it once had.

Marvin also saw that the future of porn movie houses was bleak and told me he had served his purpose and was going to quit. He had also discovered that cocaine was an easier way to pick up girls than his "oooh . . . I got to have it" technique, and after I gave him a two grand bonus for the good work he had done, he moved to Palm Springs where there were oodles of girls, especially during the spring break period, that could be coaxed into his apartment with an offer of a snort. Tragically, two years later, he would become one of the first to fall victim to cocaine's insidious clutches. The boy friend of one of the girl's he had given cocaine to, busted into his apartment late at night and murdered him.

Sy counseled that I sell the Beverly Cinema, but it was my security blanket and I decided to rent it out. After a few bad experiences, I signed a one-year lease with Sherman Torgan, a short scruffy looking thirty-year-old Jewish guy with an endearing personality, who wanted to turn it into a revival house. I had some doubts if he would succeed, but six weeks after he moved in he was well on the way to building a steady clientele who were fans of classic Hollywood and foreign films. Each week, his patrons had the choice of four or five different double features for the low price of five bucks and a big bag of popcorn for a buck. So that people would know that the Beverly was no longer a porn house, he renamed it, *'The New Beverly Cinema.'*

91

JUDY GETS BURIED IN SNOW

Other than the money I still owed for the Carmel house, which wasn't due for several years, I had no debt. Not about to let myself get in a funk about not being able to raise money for the Flesh Gordon sequel, I spent most of my time playing golf or indulging in hedonistic sexual pleasure. I loved golf and I loved being teased. To my relief, Judy seemed to recognize that cocaine was screwing up her life and started attending some of the AA meetings in Malibu. She even stared taking aerobic exercise classes and found a straight job as a salesperson in a dress shop.

I thought I was being smart when I suggested that if she could rent the Carmel house out; she could use the income for her own personal needs. She was not a lavish spender, not into expensive cloths or jewelry, but still always seemed to be broke. She liked the idea and headed up to Carmel in the new BMW 320i I had recently purchased for her.

When I didn't hear from her for a week, I began to wonder what was going on. It wasn't what I expected. She finally called to tell me, that rather than rent the house out; she was going to stay in Carmel and live in it. She claimed she needed to get out of LA and away from the drugs. There was little discussion; she had made up her mind. She had already found a job at 'Transitions,' the exercise studio owned by Clint Eastwood's wife, Maggie, and assured me she would be making enough money to support herself.

As usual, there was much more to the story than what I was told.

At a party during the Crosby golf tournament, she had met ex Cleveland Indian homerun hitter, Tony Conigliaro. His brilliant baseball career had come to an abrupt end after he got hit in the eye by a pitch and he now lived in Carmel. Judy suffered from ETGS—Endless Teenage Girl Syndrome—and it took the smallest spark to ignite one of her flighty love affairs.

Like all her affairs, they eventually passed as did this one. But now that I was living alone in my large Malibu home, I needed someone—preferably sexy—to fill the void. Lorna van Dorn, who had played a bit part in 'Naughty Network,' was temporarily staying at a friends trailer in the Valley and needed a place to stay. I suggested that she come and stay with me. She liked the idea and when I drove out to the Valley to pick her up, she stepped out from the bedroom only wearing tiny red bikini panties. It said: "Let's fuck right now." Having Lorna live with me made Judy's absence easy to handle. It had been awhile since I had a bed partner who wanted sex. I began each morning by lifting her hips up so I could suck on her asshole for ten minutes; not because I loved licking assholes; but because it was a way of letting her know that every square inch of her body drove me crazy.

The hot affair cooled quickly. The isolation of the hills of Malibu didn't suit Lorna's life style and three weeks after she moved in, I answered a knock on my door to be told: "I'm here to collect Lorna's things. She's living with me now." As I stood dumbstruck, the little fucker pushed past me and marched around my house as if he owned it, gathering up everything that he assumed belonged to her, including the trashy lingerie I had bought for her so she could dance at the Ball. When I made a mild protest, he said she needed the outfit for her dancing job and stormed out. It made me feel old.

When guys began coming to the weekend parties without a date, thinking they could pick up a girl at my place, spelled the end of the parties. Unlike Hefner, I didn't know enough to say: "unless you're a celebrity, single men not allowed." After Barry Weiss told me that Moira was pregnant and the 'Magic Theatre' would be focusing all its cult-like energy onto the soon-to-arrive newborn, I knew the days of the wild weekend pool parties were over.

There was no reason to hang out in Malibu just to entertain the stray person who might drop by, so I tried to cover up the sudden feeling of abandonment by spending more time at Suze and Humphrey's. Though there weren't any orgies, there was no lack of entertainment. It could be

Donald Cammell bragging with understated Scottish aplomb, that he had fucked Jane Fonda with his ten inch manhood behind the stage during one of the 'Rolling Stone's' concerts, Donald's sexy looking wife, China Kong, told me, much to my disbelief, that her sister, Jackie, was now married to Bill Osco. Grabbing a peek of porn star Veronica Hart's panties as she strutted around in a mini skirt and intellectual conversations with Humphrey topped off with suppers of Shepard's pie, made for a fulfilling day.

But for a lack of a better way to put it, like being attached to your old dog, I was still attached to Judy and began to miss her. So I called to see how she felt about me bringing Jason and Dr. Aaron, the black chiropractor who had an office next to mine, up to Carmel for Thanksgiving. She immediately said yes. She always had lots of sexy girl friends hanging around and as I expected, had invited them to the dinner. We all had a great time and when I returned to LA I was sure she would soon be returning to Malibu. I had become more delusional than I had realized, about her and about cocaine.

When I opened my telephone bill later in the month and discovered over two thousand dollars for calls to Brazil, all I could say was: "What the fuck?" Suspecting that Judy might have had a hand in this, I gave her a call. She claimed not to have anything to do with it. Fortunately, I was able to convince the phone company that I had no reason to call Brazil and they agreed to drop the charges. Judy's denial didn't ring true, there was the smell of cocaine about it, so to be safe, I closed the line and opened a new one.

If I had known the truth, which it seems I rarely did, about her or anything for that matter, I would have gone ballistic. She had been walking Buffy, her Golden Retriever, on the Carmel beach. A single girl with a dog was easy to approach and she found herself having a conversation with a good-looking, olive-skinned guy, who had been playing Volleyball with some friends. Roberto was from Brazil and she quickly fell victim to his Latin charm, letting him convince her to come to the "charmer" to cook a diner for her. One thing led to another, and despite having his own pad, he adroitly dropped his own place and moved in with her. He made it appear to be romantic. It was anything but.

Despite twelve years of marriage, Judy thought everyone except me, had her best interests at heart. She didn't bother to tell me she had some guy living in the house, especially the fact that he was a cocaine dealer! Having lots of coke available meant her previous efforts to clean up had been a waste of time.

Roberto was a snake; a cornered snake. He had a connection to a major supplier, a trained chemist named Olivio, who worked at one of the illicit labs in Brazil. Just a few weeks prior to meeting Judy, he had gone there to score a kilo with money fronted by a couple of students at San Diego State where he had once attended. As he was about to return to the states with the student's kilo, Olivio offered to front him another; arguing the risk would be the same whether he smuggled one or two. After he sold it in the States, Roberto could send Olivio his share of the money.

Roberto agreed and, without a hitch, smuggled the contraband into the States. He delivered the one kilo to his San Diego friends as promised, but before he could sell the other one, it slowly began to be used as trade bait for blow jobs and pussy or just a binge with friends from time-to-time. When Roberto kept giving Olivio excuses about why he had not been sent his share of the money for the fronted kilo, he became concerned. The excuses quickly became old and threats followed. Olivio said he would kill Roberto's family if he didn't get his money soon.

When Judy came lollygagging down the beach that day with her dog, he saw his salvation. All it took was an offer to cook her a meal and a little Latin panache and he soon had a quaint Carmel charmer to use as a hideout. Roberto knew, if necessary, Olivio would come to the States to collect his money. But for now he knew that Olivio had no clue where to find him, but just in case he somehow found out, he kept a fully loaded weapon in the charmer's small living room closet. A drug war shootout in Carmel was a possibility. The two thousand dollars worth of phone calls charged to my Malibu phone; were his desperate attempt to prevent that from happening.

His paranoia was not misguided. Olivio did come to the states and managed to get Roberto's phone number from the kids at San Diego State. It's area code told him that Roberto was in Monterey and hours later he was landing at the small Monterey airport. I would imagine that Roberto turned white when Olivio called to tell him he was in town at the airport. It was only a mile away, but too scared to pick him up himself, he convinced my gullible wife to drive there and take him to a hotel, telling her to pacify him by saying he would be taken to a party later in the evening where he would be introduced to someone who could distribute many kilos of coke for him around the entire Monterey Peninsula. It would make him millions.

Lots of money was music to a cocaine dealer's ears, and he calmed down a bit. That evening, still afraid to be alone with Olivio, Roberto had Judy pick him up at his hotel and bring him to the party. Back on coke, she was likely intoxicated by the excitement and oblivious to the danger she was exposing herself to. The party was being thrown at a house in Carmel Valley, owned by Lucien LeComte, a French Canadian and partner in the formula one driving school at Laguna Seca.

Things worked out well that evening for Roberto after he hooked Olivio up with the Monterey distributor. No longer in fear for his life, he started flirting with a young hotty. There was no longer any reason for him to waste time with Judy, an over thirty cougar. Judy's latent teen hormones kicked in. Feeling jilted, she responded by flirting with a short jovial kid who had accompanied the Monterey distributor. His name was Rick Palermo. He was the son of a wealthy local family who owned some nice real estate in Monterey, including the AM/PM market on the busy corner of Fremont and Carmel Hill. Rick couldn't help but notice Judy's new tit job, and offered her a few snorts of coke.

Roberto wasted no time moving back to his own apartment. Judy didn't take the loss too hard. Judy's new friend, Rick Palermo, had plenty of daddy's money and apparently needed a sexy mommy. Thirty three year old Judy with nice big silicon tits, was just perfect. They both loved to party, snort cocaine and I'm sure; fuck.

In Judy's cocaine addled mind, she was one step ahead of everyone, that is unless she got into trouble. When she did, I was once again her husband, friend and father: but not lover. A phone call came a short time after the Olivio episode ended. She informed me that she was going to jail if I didn't agree to cover some American Express bills she had rung up. She, and a twenty-nine year old girl friend, named Margie, who managed a motel in Pacific Grove owned by a wealthy widow, were being held for credit card fraud. Margie had stolen the widow's renewal American Express card when she noticed it sitting in a stack of mail that had been delivered to the motel. Needing a partner, she thought of Judy, and the two of them went on a shopping binge in Carmel.

Before they began robbing Carmel's boutiques, Margie had taught Judy all of the widow's particulars, and like a couple of pros, they soon had their arms full of ill-gotten gains. But one merchant got suspicious, and put them on the phone with American Express before allowing them to leave. They passed the exam, but American Express followed up with a call to the widow, who revealed that she was not the one making the recent charges.

The widow was no fool and had no trouble figuring out what had happened. She confronted Margie, who not only confessed, but also implicated Judy. The widow offered both of them a way out; pay American Express for what they had stolen and she would not press charges. It was time to talk to Daddy.

Why I would help her was a good question. The answer was complicated. I was not in a position to be judgmental. My past history included much worse. In our askew world, we depended on each other. She stuck with me through all my arrests. We weren't a: "Father Knows Best," family, playing bridge with the neighbors and going to church on Sunday. She had allowed and even contributed to my insatiable need for sexual pleasure. And having not pushed children onto me and all the accompanying responsibility and costs that they would have demanded, left a lot of room for compromise. I knew her rap sheet from Boston would put her in serious risk. I took care of the problem.

I hoped maybe her last experience with the American Express card would wake her up; make her see she was heading in a bad direction, and make her see we depended on each other. And not a small matter, was despite my cavalier attitude about money, I liked being rich. The few thousand dollars that her coke induced insanities were costing me was nothing compared to what a divorce would cost. Hopefully her close call with the law had made her realize she had to get off of cocaine, I called to tell her I was coming up to Carmel; I had something I wanted to throw at her.

We agreed to meet at a little French restaurant just a block south of Ocean Avenue on San Carlos. In case she decided to stand me up, I waited outside, but within a few minutes, she came walking down the street. Her see-thru black dress left the little red g-string she was wearing underneath clearly visible. It was totally out-of-place in staid Carmel, the irony striking me that it was the kind of outfit that had turned me on to her in the first place. Who was I to be judgmental—'Mr. Hot pants himself! I suggested we go inside and have lunch, but she wanted to go roller-skating on the bike path in Pacific Grove.

After stopping by the charmer so she could change, we drove the short distance to Lover's point, where the path began. I began to explain my idea. We would take a three-week trip to South America and hike up the Incan trail to Machu Picchu. Hiking was something we had always enjoyed doing together. I was surprised at how confrontational her demeanor was. There was no remorse for the phone bill or gratitude for paying off the American Express charges.

When I mentioned them, she shot back at me like a contumacious daughter: "you can handle it." The next day she agreed to take the trip.

A three-day hike along the Incan trail to the mystic ruins of Machu Picchu, would be an inspiration for us to rediscover each other and reunite. At least that was my hope. However, after a desk clerk at the Lima Sheridan convinced us that we might be robbed or killed if we hiked the Incan trail, our plans changed to now visiting Machu Picchu, by way of Lake Titicaca, and then on to a week in the heart of the Amazon at the Explorarama lodge down the river from Iquitos. It was a trip that would go from the highest lake in the world and its icy barren environs to one of the lowest places in the world where temperatures and humidity hung around ninety and more species remain to be discovered than have been discovered previously. Machu Pichu was all that it was said to be but I wasn't sure if Judy found it more impressive or the two-foot high pile of coca leaves we passed on the way to the Incan Sacsayhuam'an fortress. I had noticed her hypnotically starring at something out the window of the bus as it was wending its way around a switch-back curve. When I looked to see what she was transfixed on I saw it was a peasant at the side of the road sitting on a blanket with a stack of cocoa leaves next to him which he sold to the locals. They chew on them as pick-me-ups, much like we have a cup of coffee. It hadn't dawned upon me that by bringing her to Peru, I had in fact brought her to the very source of cocaine.

Before we left Cuzco to fly to the Amazon, I was treated to a couple of chuckles when I noticed how many souvenir peddlers sold various size onyx statues of Incan women sucking big thick Incan cocks. Some of the peddlers worked just outside the front door of a little catholic church we visited. In America they would have been arrested and taken to jail or sued by Father Filas.

The experience at the Explorarama Lodge, more than made up for what we had missed by not taking the hike. Iquitos, a small town built at the turn of the century during the rubber boom, was only reachable by boat or plane. It was so hot and humid when we arrived, that walking faster than a snail was insanity, but the light breeze that blew across us as we sat in an uncovered launch that motored us down the river to the lodge cooled us down enough so that we were in high spirits as we arrived. Judy loved nature and animals as much as me and neither of us would ever forget, despite the insufferable conditions, the five days we lived among colorful parrots, tarantulas, crocodiles, tapers, anacondas, bush masters and natives that hunted for game with blow-guns. But we sighed a breath of relief on the last day when we would soon be flying to the very cosmopolitan city of Rio de Janerio. That the Amazon is full of surprises should be expected, and a flash storm that came charging up the river like a herd of stampeding buffalo and forced the sea plane that was to take us to the Iquitos airport to retreat until the storm passed, which it did as quickly as it had appeared, was of much less consequence than our discovery at the Iquitos airport that all flights had been canceled because of a revolution that had just taken place in Lima. That we would miss our connection to Rio was more of a problem for me than for Judy. Her flirtatious nature and big tits had led to a conversation with a handsome Peruvian Air Force lieutenant, who was graciously offering to fly her out of Iquitos if the rumors proved to be true. She didn't mention if I was included in the offer. Mercifully, the rumor turned out to be false and by noon the next day we were checking into a small beachside hotel on the southern end of Rio de Janeiro's famed Copacabana Beach.

While Judy took a nap, I couldn't resist the urge to venture out onto the famous Copacabana to scope out the "hooker" action if there was indeed any. Though the famous tile embedded walkway was hard to enjoy, because one had to concentrate on not stepping into ubiquitous piles of dog poop and fight off scraggly hookers and urchins who tried to force their hands down my pant's pockets to remove whatever they could find, the action on the other side of the street was quite the opposite. There an ungodly plethora of beautiful olive skinned topless beauties wearing only miniscule thong bathing suits to cover their firm athletic bodies, swarmed on the broad beach.

"Wow."

When I returned to the hotel room, I was ready for a nap and Judy was ready for one of her quirky adventures. After being in the jungle for almost a week, she needed to dance and soon found a nearby nightclub that was open in the afternoon. After charming its owner, she took off her leather jacket and left it on a chair outside his office, and went out on the empty floor to perform a 'Dolce Vita' type exhibition for the few patrons who were in the club.

Few things upset Judy more than losing an item of clothing, and when she came off the floor and saw that her jacket was no longer on the chair, she ran to the owner in a panic-stricken furor to ask what had happened. Not bothering to appease her with words, he signaled two of his employees and Judy, to follow him to his Mercedes, parked just outside. All eyes were peeled as they cruised down the Copacabana. Suddenly the owner wielded his Mercedes sharply across the wide meridian that divided the street and cut directly in front of a car traveling on the other side. Even before coming to a complete stop, his two henchmen were jumping out from the back seat so they could quickly grab a couple of Uzis out of the trunk. The blocked thief was convinced, with little argument, to open the trunk. Voila! There was Judy's jacket. When she returned and told me her story, I was still half asleep and it took me a moment to realize that the story was real and not a dream.

There was no such thing as a boring day when Judy was around and I was happy to hear her tell me that she had decided to leave Carmel and come back home to Malibu. Like Abe Lincoln, I wanted to keep our imperfect union together and happily, she felt the same way.

92

WHITE BLIZZARD

Judy rented the Carmel house out to three young girls, who kiddingly I called the Wilnot sisters, because their cute round faces and sexy plump bodies reminded me of the 'Old Howard' stripper, Baby Lulu Wilnot. They were all delighted to be compared to a stripper, especially one who didn't give it up easily. In a renewed effort to sober up, she once again began attending the Malibu AA meetings. I accompanied her a few times; the speakers were terrific, especially those of entertainers who had risen from the depths of the gutter to reach the pinnacles of success. Nevertheless, it was disconcerting to see how many young teens were in attendance, many because of cocaine addiction. The whole drug thing was getting out of control. I shouldn't have been surprised, but I was.

She tried a few straight jobs again, but they didn't last long. The trendy Whale Watch restaurant at Zuma beach fired her when she came to work wearing her see-through dress and red g-string. The love of using her body to induce adulation from men and coax money out of them; soon had her back to The Ball. Whitey was glad to have her return. Her gregarious personality was good for business.

The Ball was in the midst of its own troubles. As a private club that catered to a professional clientele, it had never had any problems with bad behavior because of alcohol, but bazaar rules pushed by the right wing zealots at the new Alcohol and Beverage Commission, stated that hard liquor could not be served in establishments that offered nude entertainment. Why nudity encouraged crime was never explained. Whitey was not one to go down easily and let his patrons know that he would sell them full bottles of booze that he kept hidden behind the bar, as long as they agreed to hide them under the table after they had bought them. Eventually the ABC got wind of this ploy and began conducting raids, confiscating his hidden inventory. But Whitey stayed one step ahead of them, bringing up new booze from a stash he kept down below in the garage even as the ABC was going down the stairs with the booze they had just confiscated.

Though Whitey was hell bent on providing booze for his patrons, he was adamant that his girls didn't drink while on the job. Cocaine was a different matter and he not only liked to toot himself from time to time, but also offered a spoon full to his favorite girls when they asked. His fondness for a stunning tall Creole beauty, named Gootie, earned her the affectionate moniker around the club as 'Tootie,' because she could be seen repeatedly going to Whitey's office for hits during her shift.

Signs that Judy was fucking with cocaine again, soon began to appear. Her behavior became irrational; she would drive the seven hundred mile trip, back and forth to Carmel, just to collect the monthly rent from the Wilnot girls. At first I deluded myself into thinking it was just who she was; a little crazy when it came to money. When the Malibu Riding Club agreed to let her teach an exercise class in one of their spare rooms, I thought for a moment that she had had an epiphany and was going to get off coke. But after I spent two thousand dollars to buy mirrors for the studio and a couple days of work to set them up, she failed to show up for opening day classes. She had gone on a binge the night before. The club told her to forget it.

Coke explained why she was always broke as well as the snappy retorts I got when I asked her what she was up to: "I don't need to tell you everything I do." It made me stop asking. She and Helena, who loved coke as much as spankings, took off for a few days of skiing in Aspen. Maybe it would clear her mind. I had no clue that Aspen was known as a Mecca for celebrity cocaine users. A few days after she returned, my phone rang at one AM in the morning. Half asleep, I picked it up: "Is Judy there?" the caller wanted to know. I asked who was calling: "Tell her its Jack. We met in Aspen." The caller's voice was a national icon. It was Jack Nicholson looking for some pussy. She must have fucked him while she was on her ski trip. I couldn't fault him for that, but only a coke head would not think it a problem to call up in the wee hours of the night.

The late night phone calls became more and more common. Practically every night our phone would ring at some hour past midnight. My pleasant dreams, if I were lucky enough to have any, were broken up. It was irritating—even to a liberal, do-your-own-thing beatnik, like me. She wouldn't tell me who was on the phone, taking it into the other room to finish the call in a hushed voice. I eventually realized it was her Carmel boy friend, Rick Palermo. That explained why she was driving up to Carmel each month. It wasn't just about collecting the rent.

My fear of living alone or getting financially ruined in a divorce; put me in a tough spot. I couldn't imagine myself on the dating scene again. I wasn't even sure if I could conduct a normal conversation with a date if I had to. And though I would wind up with a fair amount of money after a divorce, my career in adult movies appeared to be over and I was at an age where finding a new one was not a given. I had made my own bed and had to live in it. I still had my freedom and I was going to have to deal with what else I faced.

Her cocaine-induced paranoia, led her to believe that I was hording all the money. I got the impression that she thought her money was hers and my money was hers too and began to clean out my wallet at night while I was sleeping. Of course the bills were all mine. I facetiously kidded her about complaining about the trials and tribulations of the struggling Malibu woman:

I got my Malibu House And one in Carmel Too Got a shiny new BMW But I'm still so blue

There wasn't enough money in making porn movies for the video market to interest me, but renting our house out, as a location for one-day shoots, seemed like a fun idea. Not only could I enjoy watching the hot porn chicks fuck, but also by splitting the thousand-dollar location fee with Judy, she wouldn't have to steal from me at night.

The "house that smut built" soon became the location for a porn movie almost every week, all one or two day wonders. As I should have expected, Judy didn't like sharing the fee and would intercept the producer before he drove up the driveway so she get the whole check and then split for the day. I was forced to insist that the various producers give us each a separate check. It wasn't all about ogling the girls. Having a porn cast and crew in the house and in the yard, required constant monitoring. The lighting crew would put their hot halogen lights so close to the cedar ceiling, that if I didn't insist that they be lowered, the wood would char. Some of the studs, oblivious to the neighbors, would stand in the front driveway having loud obscenity-laced conversations. When scenes were shot outside, the sounds of loud faux orgasms would cascade halfway down the canyon. If I didn't keep a cap on everything, it would just be a matter of time before complaints by the neighbors would bring on the police.

But watching the girls was exciting and there would be moments when I would have a passing fantasy that I should get back into the business, but then as the day continued, I would be reminded of all the downsides of dealing with porn people; like showing up late not knowing their lines and studs unable to get erections or just obnoxious behavior like ignoring the 'no smoking' signs that I had posted around the house. By the end of the day, I was quite happy to just be a voyeur while someone else dealt with the headaches.

Knowing what a sucker I was for sexual fantasy, Judy asked what I thought about renting our guesthouse to a strikingly beautiful dancer from The Ball, a Texan girl who went by the name *'Legs'* (although she could have also called herself *'Tits,'* being that they were of a quality that even a plastic surgeon couldn't replicate). Even as I said yes, I was already envisioning *'Legs'* cavorting around the house in her panties and maybe even available for a quickie from time to time. That she came accompanied by a boy friend, a short round biker, sans bike, named Ronnie, whose mustache seemed to always be partially in his mouth, was just a minor annoyance. If he had a girlfriend like 'Legs,' he was probably cool, although I couldn't help but wonder how she could be attracted to him.

Needless to say, that ingenuous fantasy never materialized. After she got home late at night from the Ball, she and Ronnie remained in the guesthouse with the shades drawn until she emerged in the early evening to go to work again. I never heard them talk or fuck. Ronnie seemed to live to sleep.

That's what I believed until I returned from a trip to London, where I had been invited by Michael Green, my English distributor, to discuss the feasibility of shooting the 'Flesh Gordon' sequel there. 'Flesh Gordon' had been instrumental in making Entertainment Film Distributors a major player in the U. K. So when Green indicated that he might be interested in backing a sequel, Sy Katz and I flew to London to see what he had in mind. I wanted Sy to come along to help negotiate a deal, if it got to that point.

The trip began oddly. Michael Green had booked us a room at the quaint Egerton House Hotel in Knightsbridge, just a stone's throw from 'Harrods,' the world's greatest department store. As we began to unpack, Sy started telling me his experiences during World War II. It led to him asking me about how I felt about him being Jewish. It was a strange question after all the years I had been doing business with him. I told him it wasn't an issue with me. "Why would it be?" Jews might have had good reasons for being paranoiac, but why he felt a threat from me, I had no idea. He then pulled out a document that when signed, would extend the contract I had with him to manage Graffitti's finances for another seven years. Michael Green and Peter Locke, both Jews, had previously questioned me why I stayed with Sy. Of course they had no way of knowing about how he had backed me during my battles with Osco nor that I still had a subconscious need for a father figure in my life, so I put it out of my mind that they saw something I was blind to. That didn't mean that I couldn't help but see that he was putting me in an awkward position. If I didn't sign the contract, it would put a pall over the rest of our trip. Was I being manipulated again? He was probably just trying to insure himself a piece of the action if a Flesh Gordon sequel came to fruition, so I signed it while wondering at the same time if I was making a mistake by locking myself in with him for seven more years.

The following day, Green chauffeured us around London in his Jaguar to check out several studios, including Bray Studios where the Rocky Horror picture was shot. As far as I was concerned, they were all fine. Bray was a bit small, but if the project went forward, I would make due, Sy was anxious for Green to have us in for a sit down and talk some business, but the invite never came. I would later wonder if it was my association with Sy that made him back off.

There was no need to waste a trip to Europe without going to Scotland to play a few days of golf followed by a couple of days of strolling the Rue St Denis to have a couple of romps with the Parisan ladies, so I let Sy fly home by himself why I took care of my personal needs. If I had known what was taking place in Malibu, I would have rushed home in all haste.

An hour after I returned home, I got a call from Marcial who had a strange story to tell me. Judy had come by his bungalow in Brentwood at one in the morning and banged on his door until he got out of bed. Standing alongside her were Ronnie and Legs. She wanted to know if he had some tools that they could use to break open a safe that they had in the van. He knew how insane she had become and told her he didn't. They had left disappointed and he had no idea what was in the safe or where they went.

I immediately thought of the ground safe that was hidden in the corner of my bedroom under the platform that the bed rested on. The platform had initially been built to discourage people from laying on my bed during parties but the space beneath was a convenient place to store some of my film equipment and an extra secure spot to imbed a safe into the ground. The floor beneath the platform was covered with a carpet making it almost impossible for Judy to know about the safe's existence. But addicts have an uncanny sixth sense where to find money. I kept a small stash of gold coins in the safe to be used only if there was a major financial disaster and a bag of silver coins that was too big to fit in the safe, hidden behind some of the film equipment.

When I crawled under the platform, I found the safe was undisturbed and began to wonder whose safe she had when she knocked on Marcial's door. As I began to crawl from beneath the platform, I checked to see if the bag of silver was still there. I didn't expect it to be missing, but when I looked, it was gone!

I racked my brain for an answer. Recently, one of Judy's favorite hangouts had become Bobby Hansen's house, about a mile further up the hill from our home. Bobby was a garrulous, short, portly twenty five year old, who was a plumber by trade. I called him 'Plumber Bob.' He shared his home with several other young guys, a Columbian named Jorge and a struggling actor named Andrew. The house sat on a little promontory off the side of Saddle Peak Road and had vista views of the entire city of Malibu and the Pacific Ocean out to the Channel Islands. I knew Judy liked to visit them frequently, not for the views, but because 'Plumber Bob' and his friends always had plenty of cocaine on hand.

Surprise, surprise! It would take several weeks before I learned the true story. With the bag of silver in hand, she had driven up to Plumber Bob's house and offered it to Jorge as collateral for a gram of coke. The value of the collateral far exceeded the value of the coke, but in her frenzied mental state, that really was not a consideration. "Just give me the coke," which he did. As she watched him put the bag of silver in a small safe, he told her she could have it back when she returned with the cash.

Her drug use unleashed other character flaws, and she quickly reverted to the kind of behavior that had gotten her into so much trouble when she had first left home as a teenager. It was near sociopathic and maybe worse. When she saw Jorge put the silver into the safe, she imagined that there was probably more money and cocaine inside. After leaving Plumber Bob's, she stopped a short distance down the hill at Olivia Newton John's house, which at the time, was being occupied by her manager, a scrawny Englishman in his early 30's. He had agreed to buy half the coke that Judy had just scored; the money, which she could then use to redeem the bag of silver. But the two of them started snorting and it didn't take long for the gram to wind up in their noses. Typical of a cokehead, the Englishman didn't have money on hand to pay for his half-gram, so he offered Judy his Rolex watch to hold as collateral. He claimed his mother had given it to him.

All the coke and money stashed in the safe began to grate on her psyche, and the following day, guessing that no one would be home early in the afternoon, she drove up the hill to Plumber Bob's house to see if she could steal it. The house was empty and as is common in laid-back Malibu, the windows were unlocked. She climbed in but found the safe to be too heavy for her to lift by herself, so she rushed back to our house and began telling 'hair mouth' Ronnie, about the big score that awaited if he could help her get the safe out of the house. For a fifty-fifty split, he was more than happy to be an abettor. When *Legs* heard what was going down, not wanting to take any chance of not getting her share from Ronnie, she jumped out of bed and insisted on coming along.

It took less than five minutes to lift the safe out of the house and throw it into the back of Ronnie's van. If by chance, Jorge came back and noticed it missing, he would likely guess that Judy was involved and come down to our house to confront her. So they rented a cheap room at a motel in Santa Monica, where they hoped to be able to pry it open. The Three Stooges themselves couldn't have orchestrated a more slapstick caper. After several hours, they realized that without the proper tools, there was no way to open the safe. That's when Judy got the bright idea of stopping by Marcial's bungalow to see if he could help.

Desperate, after he refused, they drove one hundred miles north to actor Stuart Whitman's ranch in Santa Barbara. Judy had met the rugged faced actor, purportedly worth close to a hundred million dollars, through Steven Laufer, who was his coke dealer. Enamored by Whitman's celebrity, the two had become friendly. In her addled state, she assumed he would be more than happy to help her crack open the safe for a little share of the white stuff.

Stuart wasn't home when they got to the ranch around three in the morning, but his handyman was; and got up out of bed and used a drill to open the safe in short order. Anticipating getting high, all mouths dropped when they discovered nothing inside but the bag of silver and an envelope. No coke, no money, just my bag of silver dimes and a fucking envelope! It didn't matter to 'hair mouth' that the bag of silver dimes belonged to me; he took half of them as his share for participating in the escapade.

The next day, Judy came to realize that the envelope contained diplomatic papers for Jorge, who was evidently the son of a Columbian diplomat. The papers, and their accompanying immunity, gave him free reign to smuggle coke into the United States. When he discovered the safe missing, he had no proof that Judy was involved, but he would have had to have been a moron not to think so. Word drifted down to her that he wanted his papers back—he didn't give a shit about the silver.

She was scared shitless. She had seen guns at Plumber Bob's place and was afraid if she went up and admitted what she had done, she might get beat up or worse. That night, at The Ball, she told Whitey, who was like a father figure to the girls, about her problem. Old Whitey knew how to deal with these things and gave some simple, but sage advice. Put the papers in an envelope with no return address and mail it to Plumber Bob's address from a post office as far outside of Malibu as was practical. She did as he advised and heard no more about the problem.

Judy, 'hair mouth' and Legs played innocent when I confronted them. The bag of silver was not the end of world and I let it go, but I was near my wits end. I began with a little house cleaning, telling 'hair mouth' and Legs to find someplace else to live. Judy, having a smidgen of guilt, gave me the Rolex watch Olivia Newton John's manager had given her to hold as collateral for his share of the score. The one my parents had given me as a graduation gift had been stolen out of my bedroom night table during one of our parties, so I was pleased to again have a Rolex. A week later, the manager was on the phone pleading with me to return his. It was a gift from his mother. Tough fucking shit!

I wasn't anti drugs per se, I still smoked grass when it was offered, but maybe I was just lucky that cocaine didn't have much of an appeal for me. I snorted a spoonful here or there, but that cocaine was dangerous was becoming clearer by the day. James Poe had recently died of a heart attack and I was strongly of the opinion that coke had a lot to do with it. A lot of my friends began having monetary problems, including Earl Miller, who needed to borrow seven hundred dollars from me to pay some bills.

A call from the Malibu fire department on a Sunday morning; opened my eyes to the fact that death was knocking on my door. I hadn't seen Judy for a few days and assumed she had been on a coke binge with some of her friends. I had no ability to control her. She did what she wanted and if I objected I was told to fuck off. The fire department officer told that my wife, apparently sick, was parked alongside the Pacific Coast Highway. He suggested I go down the hill and help her out. When I arrived, I found her sitting in her 320i, slumped over with her legs hanging out of the open door. Her hair was straggled, her bathing suit on backwards, and she was puking. She tried to say something, but her talk was so slurred and incoherent that I couldn't understand a word. I managed to get her home where she crashed on the bed, falling into a deep sleep. While she was asleep, a friend helped me go back down the hill and bring her car back up the hill to our house.

When she awoke and sobered up, she grudgingly told me that she had been at a party on a boat with Frank Carey—the father of the kid who lost his virginity with her in Yosemite. So much coke and pills was available, that after three days, she was close to OD'ing. Carey, worried about the trouble he could get into, refused to let her have any more snorts. She went ballistic when he told her he was going to put her ashore. While a small dingy was being prepared, she managed to steal some money out of his cabin. Back on shore, she headed directly to another cokehead's house and used the money to score another vile. To come down, they drank red wine and smoked some Mandrax, the trademark name for a pill containing methaqualone and diphenhydramine hydrochloride—pretty dangerous sounding stuff. The medical dictionary describes it as an addictive hypnotic-sedative linked to physical or psycho logic dependence, clinical delirium, headache, nausea, convulsion, renal and cardiac failure; used for anxiety and tension management. That pretty well explained the state I found her in at the side of the Pacific Coast Highway.

By the end of the day she was coherent, but without remorse. An innocuous remark I made, set her off and she stormed out of the house and headed for her car so she could go and binge some more. I was furious and grabbed her by the arm before she could get into her car and marched her back to the house. Enough was enough! In all our years together, I had never struck her and didn't this time, but she was so frightened that she shit in her pants and later would claim that I hit her. A small turd dropped to the ground as I walked her through the front door. It was ugly!

If I didn't do something, she was going to destroy both of us. The situation was becoming lethal. I drove up to Plumber Bob's house to tell him and his housemates, Andrew Varney and Jorge, that I didn't want them supplying Judy with drugs anymore. Varney and Jorge weren't present, so I told the Plumber to pass my message on to the others. Neither Plumber Bob nor Andrew Varney had dangerous demeanors, but I had heard rumors that Jorge could be. Columbian drug dealers had bad reps. I didn't give a shit.

My message didn't get taken seriously. A week later, Varney pulled up to the house in a limo to take Judy out for a night of binging. She stormed past me without saying anything. She was going whether I liked it or not. At four in the morning she returned, her high heels clanking on the walkway, as she stumbled into the house.

When I got up in the morning, I drove up to the Plumber's house. No one was home, so I took a walk along the side and peered into the window. I could see a substantial amount of grass lying around the room. More than likely, there were other drugs as well. I had dealt grass and didn't consider it a big deal, but I had warned them to stay clear of Judy. I was conflicted what to do. My old hippy moral code was against finking on someone using drugs, but my personal survival instincts said to shut these assholes down. Personal survival won. I went back to my house and made an anonymous call to the Malibu cops: telling them there were drugs at Plumber Bob's that could be clearly seen by just looking into the side window. A few days later they were busted. I was glad that Plumber Bob and Andrew Varney didn't get sent to jail, but I was relieved that they were removed from the neighborhood. Jorge couldn't be touched because of his father's diplomatic status, so he walked unscathed. As far as I knew, no one ever found out that I had blown the whistle, but if they had, I wouldn't have cared.

Sadly, nothing much changed. Judy kept using. I kept going to strip joints. She kept coming home late. I kept eating pussy and having lots of sex. She kept driving to Carmel to collect the rent and see her boy friend who kept calling in the wee hours when she was back in Malibu. Suze Randall advised me to be careful: I might get murdered while I slept. Marcial offered to kill her for twenty-five grand. It was not inconceivable that the offer was serious. Of course I said no.

The madness got more psychotic and she found friends who were equally so, some of them rock stars who she idolized. Keith Moon of 'The Who' was always available to get high and she went to his house on Point Dume at three in the morning and banged on the door for him to open up. She was surprised when Steve McQueen answered; she had banged on the wrong door. On another date with Moon; they had returned to his house after a night of binging when he discovered that he had lost his house key. No problem. He got out of the car and just placed a two by four between the grill of his Jaguar and the door of his house and rammed it open, smashing both door and grill.

By the time of our next Halloween party; the trauma had put me in a sour mood. Judy was her regular happy-go-lucky self, flirtatious and sociable. My mood, which bordered on anger, was concealed by my trashy costume. When I walked into my bedroom, I found the guy who someone told me did the music for 'Rocky,' lying atop my bed with the head of a pretty blond girl bobbing up and down on his dick. Possibly, because he was high on drugs, he was struggling to get a hard on. Next to them, but not participating in the sex, was a sexy brunette in her mid-twenties with her pantyhose pulled down below her hips so she could masturbate while she watched. Without saying a word, I pulled her pantyhose off so I could spread her legs and eat her. Of course she was fine with it. As soon as my cock was hard enough for penetration, I slid it into her like she was a piece of meat, giving her not the slightest indication that I knew she existed. The blond kneeling next to us continued to struggle with the uncooperative penis she was working on and I offered to suck on her cunt while I continued to pork the brunette. Though she appreciated the offer, she refused, suggesting maybe we could get together at a later date. I kept banging the brunette for another ten minutes and then unceremoniously pulled my cock out and shoved it into her asshole. She didn't resist or complain. As soon as I shot my load, I walked out of the room without saying a word. I wanted her to feel used.

It was the first time I had anal sex and, frankly, there was nothing special about it, the pussy was much more stimulating. To be honest, on that night, the angry sex was actually quite nice and I returned to the party in a better mood.

After everyone left, Marcial stayed on so he could fuck a girl on the living room floor that he had met earlier in the evening. She was a screamer and it was impossible to sleep while they were going at it. When they finally went silent, Judy and I would just start to fall asleep when they would start fucking again and the screaming would wake us up. By the third time, I yelled out for them to "shut the fuck up." I knew what he was doing, I had become a paradigm to measure his masculinity against and his performance was meant to send a statement; no different than male walruses battling on the beach over who is to be the top bull.

Nothing as drastic as the Pacific Coast Highway incident happened again, but the clanking of high heels and late night phone calls was more than I could handle. My complaints about the calls resulted in her moving into the guest bedroom and installing her own phone line. I sensed that she had been looking for an excuse to move out of my bed: Rick probably told her that the thought of her lying next to me made him jealous. His calls kept coming and even though she was in another room, they still woke me up. The whole thing was nuts. The fatigue was making me more hateful; but my fear of divorce and the inevitable upheaval, prevented me from taking that route.

I thought maybe I could wear her out by placing calls to her phone after she came home late at night and had fallen asleep. She would think the call was from Rick and would wake up to answer it. After treating her to a minute of hard breathing; as though some psycho was on the line: she would angrily scream; "Who is this?" Then after a few moments of silence, I would hang up; feeling good that I had fucked up her sleep as much as she was fucking up mine. That plan came to an end when she subscribed to Caller ID. It hadn't done much anyway; it's hard to wear down a coke addict.

93

WHY STAY IN THIS HELL?

It was the little things she had done, like taping a 'Wizard of Id' comic strip about golf to the refrigerator door. She knew I loved golf and taping the strip to the door would make me happy. The totally disorganized photo albums she kept, chronicled our adventures and friends, including some of my lovers. Our house was full of interesting items, including props from 'Flesh Gordon,' the little Incan blowjob statue from Peru and an Alaskan totem pole that some guy gave her simply because she was gregarious. And of course there were the pets, both cats and dogs. So despite the madness, I was heartbroken when she called from Carmel to tell me she had moved back there to live in the 'Charmer.' She didn't say, but I assumed Rick was included in the package.

Distraught, I walked out on the porch and tried to cry. I was never a crybaby and failed miserably, producing only dry tears; I just felt stupid. I was no longer a naïve young idiot. I had been around the block many times. I didn't believe in love in the sense that it's a form of mutual worship. It's a word that's impossible to define, using terms like endearment, passion or sexual attraction, to try to give it meaning. The Chinese don't even have it in their language. Judy and I had formed a partnership that afforded us a very comfortable and free wheeling existence. In California, she owned half of everything. It was as much her security as it was mine. I assumed she would eventually come back and since we didn't have children, no one would be hurt. In the meantime, I decided I was not going to sit up on the hill overlooking the ocean and mope.

A few weeks after she left, I was back to my old crazy playful self. There was nothing about cocaine madness that I missed. I soon had more female company than ever. My Penthouse spanking Pet, Helena, came by one evening with her date, an English travel writer. After a few glasses of wine and a joint, I did my best to entertain them. Knowing that he was English; I went to my closet and returned attired in a black leather thong held up by thin straps that ran between my butt crack and over my shoulders.

Helena was delighted, especially when I put her over my knee and doled out a playful spanking. Her English date thoroughly enjoyed the spectacle of discipline and even went so far as to take off his sports jacket and loosen his tie: "that wild maniac!"

Helena felt sorry for me living alone and set me up with a girl friend of hers so I could accompany Marcial to Yalapa. He had invited me to join him on the trip with the condition that I have a date. As was always the case with him, he had an ulterior motive. He was planning to put a move on a girl he had been trying to fuck and needed someone along to be a side act so he could come off as the dominant bull in comparison.

The girl Helena set me up with had recently broken up with her boyfriend and was told by Helena, that we would find each other mutually interesting. We actually did, but not for the reasons Helena imagined. Melanie was of Armenian descent and was very cute with a bright intellect and a nice firm feminine body. She lived nearby in the north end of Malibu in a little cottage just above the Pacific Coast Highway. Over our first dinner date at a local restaurant, I learned that she was a struggling singer/songwriter. My easy-going nature relaxed her enough to fill me in on the details of her recent breakup, which, as she did, explained why Helena thought of us as a perfect match.

A day after she had broken up with her boyfriend, he showed up at midnight standing outside her door in a pouring rainstorm. He was dressed in full feminine regalia and because of the rain, his hair was a matted mop and his makeup was streaking down his face. He pleaded for her to take him back, but she had caught him cheating and his begging and pitiful appearance were not enough to assuage her anger and she shut the door in his face. Like a scene in a French movie, he trudged back to his car through the rain and mud. I could see that Helena thought of me as a cross dresser because of my ostentatious outfits during the Halloween parties. Being that I liked to wear Judy's panties on occasion: maybe I was?

It excited me that Melanie was obviously kinky and since I wasn't looking for a long-term permanent relationship, her jealous side wasn't a big deal; so I described the trip I was contemplating with Marcial and asked her if she would like to join me. It didn't take much to convince her, albeit she said not to expect sex since she was still in a period of adjustment. I told her I was cool with that.

I appreciated Marcial for some of his insights—he got me to stop saying "you know" at the end of each of my sentences—and I admired his willingness to be outspoken on the current controversy beginning to brew over the rise of feminism. It was just beginning to be debated and opinions were all over the place. But I also knew he thought of himself as an alpha dog and me as a milquetoast. I intended to use the trip to let him know that he had judged me wrong. If I left his foot on the back of my neck, our friendship, which I enjoyed, would suffer.

Patty, the girl he was pursuing, wasn't an easy lay. His last effort to get into her panties had been clever, but fruitless. As she described it to me: they were at his little Brentwood bungalow, sitting on the edge of his bed, drinking wine; when he abruptly excused himself and left the room. After a few minutes had passed and he hadn't returned, she began to wonder what was going on. Suddenly, on the drawn shade of his bedroom window, his profile appeared as a silhouette, cast there by the light of the full moon. He was very proud of his strong chin and Roman nose, and held his head slightly tilted upward to give her the best view of those attributes. To add import to the display, he took a long draw from a cigarette and then slowly exhaled the smoke as though he were in the midst of some deep and profound thought. Rudolph Valentino would have been proud; Patty, not so much. It gave her a little chuckle, but not enough to give him some pussy. Marcial didn't brook failure with a woman easily, and thus the trip to Yalapa.

It had been a long struggle for me to overcome my sexual inferiority complex, and though I was still shy, I had a way about me that put girls at ease. By the time our plane landed in Puerto Vallarta, Melanie and I had become quite comfortable with each other. The fact that she had lived with a cross-dresser and I was a pornographer, made all false pretensions unnecessary. We were both sex freaks and it was becoming a given that her caveat was going to be forgotten.

Marcial had made all the arrangements and booked us into a delightful resort hotel in Puerto Vallarta, where, since the boat to Yalapa left only once a day, we would stay overnight. Each room was a little thatched cottage, set in a tropical garden crisscrossed with walking paths that crossed little ponds over quaint wooden bridges. It was very romantic. As soon as Melanie and I had the key to our room, we said goodbye and dashed to our room so we could fuck our brains out. So much for her caveat!

An hour later, with satisfied smiles on our faces, we rejoined Marcial and Patty at the hotel's restaurant for dinner. It was clear by the look on his face, but not hers, that his first hour in Mexico had not been as pleasurable as ours. A little sadistic side of me couldn't help but enjoy seeing him squirm. He was a lovable braggart, but not use to being second dog: "How could a quiet introvert get laid and he couldn't?"

The week in Yalapa had been incredible. Melanie and I would retire every four hours to our primitive thatched palapa, where we had to walk over the Gecko lizard that guarded its entrance, so we could have a fuck in the Palapa's hammock bed. Marcial's forlorn expression left no doubt that he hadn't even been treated to a blowjob. Patty was one of those girls saving herself for marriage or whatever and that was her prerogative. I just hoped he would have had some sense to recognize that this was a payback for his Halloween night episode.

Starting with a blowjob as our plane descended into Los Angeles, Melony made me forget Judy. We sucked and fucked and freaked people out all over the place: from parked in the car on Wilshire Blvd to the balcony of the Century City Theatre. I understoood that women saw men as support mechanisms, but times were changing. After parading around Palm Springs, where I had dressed her in yellow nylon hot pants that were jacked up by suspenders so the nape of her buns and cameltoe were lewdly exposed, we had gone to a sushi bar for dinner when she ordered me to double tip the sushi chef. My money had become her money. I already had that with Judy and when I called a few days later to let her know we were done; she slammed down the phone and shrieked: "Blow it out your asshole you fucking creep!"

That I was alone again didn't matter, I was about to have lots of sexy girls running around the house. Legendary porn star, Ron Jeremy, was now producing porn films and I had agreed to let him rent my house for a three-day shoot. He had become an instant sensation in the porn world when he demonstrated that he could bend over at the waist and suck his ten-inch pencil-thin dick. Because of the thinness of his penis, many upcoming porn actresses preferred to have their first anal experience with Ron. The three grand location fee he was to pay would come in handy to pay my upcoming property taxes.

On the morning of the scheduled production, I arose early and waited for him and his cast and crew to arrive. While downing my morning java, my ears perked up to a story being reported on the news. The L. A. vice was instituting a new tactic to stem pornography. They would now begin to confiscate homes that were used as locations for porn films!

Jesus Christ! The Christian fanatics are at it again! Why do they hate sex so much? It was a good reminder of why it wasn't a bad thing that I was out of the business. I sure as hell wasn't going to be the first test case to determine if this new tactic was legal, so when Ron showed up, I had to tell him I had to cancel. I appreciated the fact that he had heard the report as well and didn't try to twist my arm.

News was sparse about what my wife was doing. Her sister, Pamela, had come out from New Hampshire to visit her and told me all the windows of the 'charmer' had been covered with cardboard, a sure sign of cocaine use. She also had a redo on her tit job, blowing them up so she looked like a top-heavy cow. I would have bet a thousand dollars that it was done to make Rick happy. His mommy probably didn't breast-feed him properly. Pamela thought Judy needed to check into Hazeltine, a hospital in Minnesota that was in the forefront of drug rehabilitation. I told her that was just wishful thinking.

The more I learned about Rick, the less I liked him. He used his father's AM/PM market as a private piggy bank, snatching a few bucks from the till when he needed cash to pay for cocaine or just an evening of fun. He and Judy, along with race car driver Lucien Le Comte and his girl friend Monique, had taken a three-week jaunt to Jamaica and then on to Monaco. Money meant little to Rick. He won thirty grand at the tables in Monaco and gave it all back an hour later. What did he have to sweat? Dad was giving him money and he had my house to live in.

A month later Judy and Rick vacated the 'charmer' and moved in with his parents, probably to enjoy the home-cooked Italian dinners his mom cooked. The idea that the two of them were tooling around Monterey in the BMW 320i that I had bought for her, didn't sit well with me. I still paid all its insurance and fees. I felt used. It was in my name and I could legally take it. I began to scheme how.

It would be likely that the car would be parked outside the parent's house when Judy and Rick were home. I didn't know exactly where that was, but easily found out by checking the phone book. There were only two Palermos in Monterey, and only one lived in the upscale wooded area around the Del Monte Country Club.

Marcial had offered to help me repossess the car and we both had a good laugh about how easy it had gone after we got back to LA. While Judy and Rick were inside enjoying mom's spaghetti, I snuck onto the driveway and using a duplicate key I had, drove off without anyone seeing me! I handed the car to Marcial so he could drive it back to L. A.

My laughs were short lived. Judy knew in a minute what had happened and reported the car stolen and where in Malibu they would probably find it. Since I could show papers that proved I was the car's legal owner, didn't get her what she wanted, but the subsequent threats of divorce did and I returned it a week later.

I wasn't the only one having my fill with coke addicts. Rick's parents were probably realizing that having two cokeheads living with them was more than they could handle. Even a gregarious Italian family, loyal to a fault, had its limits. The easiest solution for them was to move their son and his coke whore out to Carmel Valley into another house the family owned. It abutted the eleventh fairway of the Rancho Canada South golf course where I often played when I was in town.

Judy had her fun with the 'charmer,' if you can call it that, and now that it was empty I would use it to have some fun as well. I asked Anna Magle to join me for a trip up the coast where we could take in some sex shows in San Francisco and then use the house for a couple of days so I could show her around Monterey. She liked sexy adventures and after checking into the classy Fairmont hotel across from Union Square, we headed out to enjoy some of the serious sexual entertainment that Frisco was famous for.

Anna enjoyed watching me run my hands over the bodies of several of the sexy strippers who I had tipped for lap dances at the O'Farrell Theater's New York Live room. We then shared an Ultra room booth to watch girls eating and doing each other with dildos and finally we went to the Copenhagen room, where we sat on a low cushioned seat that ran along the room's walls so girl working the small audience, could straddle our legs and bend over so she could put her pussy close enough to our noses that we could smell its sweet perfume.

Anna was a strong feminist and to be egalitarian, I was happy to agree to her request that I accompany her to a theatre just a few blocks away on Larkin Street to see a live gay sex show. It was our good luck to find two seats close to the stage that would give her a good view of the action. Unlike most things 'gay,' the theatre was on the drab side. Along with about twenty horny homos of various ages, sizes and shapes, we patiently waited for the show to begin. Anna was the only female in the audience. The ten-minute monotony was finally broken, when a scrawny young man, outfitted in a cowboy hat and chaffs, emerged from behind a worn red curtain and strutted to the end of the short runway. With little fan fare and after only a modicum of dancing, he plopped down on his haunches and dipped his hand into a jar of Vaseline that he had placed on the stage when he came out. With a big glob in his open palm, he wrapped it around his flacid cock and began to vigorously pump his fist up and down. For the first two minutes, his entire shaft remained hidden in his clenched fist: but he kept pumping until the tip of it finally peeked out over the top. The excitement in the audience was palpable. A few more piston-like strokes were all it took before a gush of sperm came shooting out. The sight of the creamy fluid slowly dripped over the back of his clenched fist brought satisfied smiles to all in the room. The dancer's wan smile reflected how proud he was of his accomplishment. Anna joined the audience to give the young fellow a standing ovation.

Being called; "You fucking asshole!" was getting to be a habit. As we prepared to vacate the hotel room the next morning, Anna busied herself scraping the last remaining powder from a vile of coke she had taken out of her purse onto the glass that covered the top of a chest of drawers. She managed to eke out only a small pile, but generous as she was, used a single edged razor blade to form two lines so we could each have a toot. Allowing me to go first, I was handed a little straw so I could snort the line up my nose. But being that I rarely used coke, after my line was sucked up my nose . . . I sneezed. She looked at me in horror as she saw her line go blowing up into the air. "You fucking asshole!"

But after a night at the 'charmer' where I softened her up with a half-hour of pussy sucking and one minute of jack-hammer sex, I was forgiven for my unfortunate sneeze. It was a beautiful day as we drove down the Big Sur highway on our way back to LA. Just as we passed the Hearst castle at San Simion she asked:

"Why don't we stop and have some sex?"

It still caught me off guard how overt women were becoming about their sexual cravings. It was a part of my traditional upbringing that died hard. The sexual revolution was changing things. Women were a horny lot and no longer ashamed or shy to admit it. On the other hand, I was still drained from the previous evening and tried to get out of it.

"You don't want to wait 'til were back in LA?" "How long is that?" she wanted to know. "About two hours."

With a look of disbelief: "Two hours ? ? ?"

We were in the middle of nowhere; there were nothing but large fallow fields on each side of the road. I succumbed to her wishes and pulled off the highway onto the first dirt road that I came upon. After bumping along for a few minutes at five miles an hour, we miraculously came upon a wide shallow stream that for some god unknown reason had a table sitting in the middle of it just waiting for someone to fuck on. Anna took off her panties and hopped up on the table and spread her legs so we could indulge in our usual sex routine. It made the day end on a high note and also made me wonder if women weren't more sex driven than men. Maybe that's why religions made a point of keeping them down.

I was learning but I really had no clue what women wanted. My little ad hominem snit to take Judy's car back, earned me what I had feared most, being served with divorce papers. I got out of bed on a 'June gloom' foggy morning to answere a loud knock on my front door. I stumbled, half asleep in my bathrobe to open the door. A plaintive "Howard Ziehm?" greeted me after I opened it a crack followed by a document being rudely shoved into my hand after I barely said "yes." By the time I looked up from taking a cursory glance to see what it was, the guy had disappeared into the fog. I had just been served with divorce papers!

It threw me for a loop. Our relationship, a marriage between a pornographer and a stripper, was crazy, but we were both crazy . . . and somehow it worked. We had both endured a healthy dose of legal problems and we both came with deep-seated emotional issues, so it was expected that there would be problems. But we had both helped each other. My sleepwalking nightmares were a distant memory and she had pitched in while I settled with Osco. Things had become good for us. She was my partner; the others were just sex toys. This couldn't be for real?

Not so much looking for advice, but just a shoulder to cry on, I called Marcial. But advice I got. Pamela Wells, an intelligent bookish looking girl, who had allowed herself to be drawn into Marcial's web to become his personal female pimp. He told me she worked for a killer divorce lawyer and strongly advised that I call her. She was happy to help and gave me her bosses phone number, who she added, had an obsession with elephants.

On Monday morning, with divorce papers in hand, I had been waiting for ten minutes in Robert Thaler's sterile lobby, when a sliding window opened and his secretary peeked her head out just long enough to give me a nod to pass through the double doors that led into the inner sanctuary. It took a moment for my eyes to adjust to the near dark room. Howard sat at the back of the room behind a large desk that had several elephant knick-knacks neatly arranged on top. Small accent lights spotted various pictures and statuettes of elephants placed around the room. The light coming off the wall behind him, backlit him so it was hard to discern his features. His voice was low and measured and his dark sunglasses made me feel like I was about to hire 'Dr. No' to handle my case. He had obviously put a lot of thought in designing an environment to make him appear intimidating. It worked—I was intimidated.

I was briefly queried to describe what my assets were and then advised to write him a check for five thousand dollars as a retainer. Hypnotically, I obeyed. As I turned to leave, he suggested I bring him the forty South African gold Krugerrands that I had mentioned I had at home in a safe; explaining: "they will be safer in my hands."

The next morning I woke up in a sweat. My mind had been churning all night. I was either going to get cleaned out by Judy or by Thaler. Voltaire's insightful quote came to mind: "I was only ruined twice in my life, once when I lost a law suite and once when I won one." I called Thaler to tell him that I wanted to hold off for a while until I heard more from my wife. I asked for my retainer to be returned. Two weeks later I got a check for sixteen hundred dollars. Thirty minutes with him had cost me thirty-four hundred bucks. I felt relieved that I had gotten off so cheap. Evidently Judy had come to the same conclusion, because I heard no more from her or her lawyer.

94

HALL OF FAME

Suze Randall droppped by my home one afternoon, accompanied by an attractive young women in her late twenties, named Dotty, and a pert little blond, just in from Chicago, named Ginger Lynn. Ginger was Suze's hot new discovery and she wanted to know what I thought of her. She had a cute, though a bit tough, looking face and a perfect female figure; firm breasts and a bubble butt.

Suze's work had pizzazz and a distinctive style that made it unique. It was always easy to recognize her layouts when they appeared in magazines. I admired the fact that she was succeeding in what had been a male dominated business. Her work was edgy and not watered down by being air brushed. But I would be a hypocrite not to say that it bothered me that I had been harassed out of the business by the police, while new people in the adult business, like Suze, were skirting along untouched. I knew the world was unfair, but it was hard not to be resentful. For various reasons, including my battles with Judy, I was developing a resentful attitude towards women. When Suze called later in the day to ask what I though about Ginger, my anger blinded me and I could only manage a perfunctory thumbs up. Both Ginger and Dotty would become two of the future mega stars of the porn industry; Dotty, aka Seka, as the first MILF superstar and Ginger as the first porn actress to earn six figures. She also woud become Charlie Sheen's live in porn girl friend. Having a porn star girl friend was now a status symbol.

Suze offered me a chance to reconnect with the adult business by asking me to play a small part in a to-be-shot-on-video porn feature that she was producing. It would star her recent discovery, Ginger Lynn as well as doll-faced Tracy Lords, another newcomer who was building a reputation as a wild fucking machine. Written by Humphrey Knipe, 'Miss Passion' was to be a space age fucking contest between four couples. Lisa De Leeuw, a big-breasted, freckle-faced porn star and I, would be the judges. Since the script had already determined the winner; we wouldn't judge anything, but hanging with sluts for a day couldn't be all bad.

In my role as 'Imin Ecstacy,' Suze had her make-up person give me a new-wave look by dyeing my hair bright red and punking it out so it stood straight up. I did my part to play a freak, by showing up on the set wearing my cock ring, which would constrict the blood in my penis so that it remained hard as a rock all day long. Hoping Suze might suggest I insert it into one or two of the girls she had cast as contestants, I paraded around the stage with my cock pointed to the ceiling. Not getting an offer to perform, I returned to my seat next to Lisa and gave her pussy a little licking. My ever-hard penis finally got noticed when porn star Lonnie Saunders, who was on the set helping the make-up artist, stopped by momentarily only to admire it:

"Oh what a nice cock" she said as she held it in her sexy littlehand.

Hoping maybe this was my chance: "Why don't you suck on it?" She smiled at me coquettishly: "I would like to, but I'm going steady with someone and were in love."

"What's love got to do with it?" Though I didn't get laid by her; I managed a quickie with my fellow judge, Lisa DeLeuuw, aka Watta Twat, and was most perversely proud that a shot of me sporting my flaming-red punk rocker hair and steely-hard cock appeared in 'Puritan Magazine' when the film was reviewed after its release.

But by the end of 1982, I had all but accepted that my career in the adult business was now reduced to a fond memory. Though 'Flesh Gordon' had played all around the world and along with my other films, earned me plenty of money, I was hesitant to boast about them. My golfing buddy, Mike Karg, had told me that the manager of a strip club who was familiar with my work, told him that I had pioneered almost all of the outrageous sex acts that were currently seen in films. Nice to hear, but it didn't mean much.

It was only when Suze invited me to join her and Humphrey to attend an adult film industry meeting, that was being held in the valley in a small convention hall, that I became aware that I wasn't as invisible as I thought. We had just wandered halfway down its entry hallway, when a short stocky man in his mid 30's greeted Suze. That I stood silently next to Humphrey with my hands in my pockets; clearly signaled with body language, that I was feeling out of place. Since I hadn't made a film in five years, I doubted if I would know any of the people in attendance.

After a moment, Suze turned toward me and as a normal courtesy, introduced us: "Jim, this is Howard Ziehm."

He took a step back and glared at me in disbelief: "You're Howard Ziehm? . . . The Howard Ziehm?"

I was taken aback for a moment, but nevertheless' felt my ears turning red as my ego swelled. His name was Jim Holiday. He went on to describe every film I had made from Mona to all the Dog Eat Dog productions and waxed effusively over the many scenes he loved. I would learn that he was the porn industry's top movie critic and historian. Until that moment, I was unaware that anyone was interested in the history of the porn industry. I was very dumb that way.

Six months later, the XRCO (X Rated Critics Organization) bestowed upon me two *"Hall of Fame"* awards during a ceremony held at Gazzari's on Sunset Strip, the same Gazzari's where my band had auditioned fifteen years prior. Again, I attended under Suze's wing and sat with her and Humphrey in the middle of the packed room, waiting nervously for the presentations to begin. Reb Sawitz came by to offer congratulations and introduce me to a striking young woman whom he said would like to meet me. I was overwhelmed and nervous about going up on the stage so I just smiled. She turned her back to me and bent over and pulled up her tight short skirt. Inches from my face was one of the finest mouth-watering asses I had ever seen! She scampered away before I could say much to her. I asked Reb who she was, and was told her name was Nina Hartley. Since I was no longer making porn films, the opportunity to shoot her didn't exist, but why I didn't at least make an effort to try and get her in bed, would never cease to perplex me—even now. She would eventually become a legendary star in the business and still works to this day. Many a mile of penises have found joy in her pussy and ass. Sadly I wasn't one of them.

'Honey Pie,' was given a 'Hall of Fame' award and I personally was inducted into the 'X-Rated Directors Hall of Fame'—being the second director to be given that honor; Gerald Damiano of Deep Throat and The Devil in Miss Jones, being the first. Fearing that I might freeze up when required to say something, I had written a few things on a sheet of paper. After giving my obligatory thanks, I pointed out that "when I entered the sex business, guys had to make sure not to get a hard-on," which managed to get a few chuckles throughout the room from those who understood the irony.

My fame was due in large part to 'Porn' historian, Sam Stetson, who had done work for the Kinsey foundation, and brought my work to the attention of Holiday. I was totally unaware of Holiday's book; 'The Hundred Best Porno Films of All Time,' published in 1983. In it, he placed *Mona* at the top of his list, describing it as *"the film that will always be regarded as the first classic from the explicit film era.* I couldn't help but be flattered that ll the films I had done with DOG EAT DOG were also included. Still, I left the ceremony unconvinced that the praise was noteworthy.

95

HARLOT HEAVEN

What can an erstwhile pornographer do who's living alone but still married to a cocaine addict whose not in a big rush to get his act back together because there is little demand on him to make a living. Although I dabbled with some success making 'Improve your Vocabulary,' audio tapes and wasting some money foolishly thinking I could build a golf course in Malibu, my top priority was still to have abundant orgasms, that magnificent paroxysm that makes all things good, the force that draws all bad thoughts into a black hole of irrelevancy. Jacking off was always available and I tried lots of ways to enhance the experience, like using baby oil or inserting an anal dildo up my ass. Strip shows were great, unless a girl got pissed off if she saw me massaging my rod instead of worshipping her. On the few times I dated, pretending to enjoy meaningless conversation when all I was looking for was to get laid, was excruciating, for me and the girl.

Cocaine was making girls disinterested in sex. Even getting a blowjob was difficult. Roger Mason, who had married the Penthouse spanking pet, Helena, was already discovering that the fantasy he imagined with her was a delusion, but since he and she had an open marriage, he had come up to my house after The Ball closed with his friend David Thayer, a dapperly dressed thirty year old whose well-trimmed goatee made him look like a UCLA humanities professor. They came accompanied by a couple of strippers from the Ball. We three guys looked forward to the sex party we were about to have. To insure its success, David had come with a full gram of cocaine. After several hours of tooting, no thighs had been parted and in the wee hours of the morning, Roger and David had resorted to putting toots of coke on the tips of their dicks just to get a nose job.

Not to say that there weren't sexy surprises that arrived at my door from time-to-time. Plucky Renee Blair, my Naughty Network actress, dropped by the house with a stripper called 'Humping Honey Bunny,' to ask me to show her the scene she had done in 'Naughty Network.' Both girls were looking very hot in silk hot pants that displayed half of their butt cheeks and I knew it was one of those special opportunities available only to a pornographer. I loaded the VHS I had of the movie and had the girls join me on my round bed, 'Humping Honey Bunny' lying with her backside nestled against my body and Renee in front of her. I had long admired, the 'humper,' when I had seen her perform at the Ivar and the Kit Kat Club, but never had the pleasure of meeting her. As Renee and Honey concentrated on the movie; Renee throwing in little bits and pieces of how excited she was while performing, I let my hard cock slide out the leg of my hot pants and into 'Honey Bunny's' pussy, which, despite Renee's harassing her to stay focused on the film, she seemed to enjoy.

Because Anna was now working for the 'Hollywood madam,' she and I saw less and less of each other, although when she needed to a proper pussy sucking, we would get together. One of her clients, famous for remarking that; "its good to be king" earned my respect when she told me he never paid more than a hundred bucks for a date. I totally agreed with his philosophy. A hundred dollar fuck is just as good as a thousand dollar fuck and a twenty-five dollar fuck is the best of all.

Like her famous client, I sensed my natural ability to attract girls was waning, but my need for sex was still strong. I needed lots of sex. I was a junky and didn't care. Like Anna's client, I felt no shame in paying for it, just as long as it wasn't too much.

So armed with a new phrase I learned from a French friend, Patrick Martin, "Je voudrais sucer votre chat," I hopped on a plane and flew to Paris to indulge myself for a few days on the Rue St Denis. "Shit, where are they?" Thanks to the new French socialist president, Francois Mitterrand, almost all the action on the rue had been closed down. The few belles who attempted to ply their trade, had to duck in and out of the shadows to keep from being arrested by the gendarmes.

I had heard rumors that Amsterdam had a red light district, so hoping I might be able to salvage the trip, I took the first train to Amsterdam out of the Gare du Nord and four hours later I was cursing myself for not having gone there sooner. Moments after stepping off the train at the city's Central Station, my uncanny radar guided me down Damrak Strade and across a little walking bridge that spanned the canal running aside. It led down a narrow alley and into a large plaza in front of the Oude Kerk church. As I began to look around, I saw beautiful red lights shinning all around the plaza and up and down the narrow walkways that ran off of it. An excited glow overcame me as I realized that I had serendipitously found whore heaven.

The variety was mind-boggling. Beautiful and exotically dressed women of all races and ages, stood behind windows or glass doors, waiting to offer their god given services. Most of the ladies were young, but for those who wanted something unusual, it was available. A sweet little gray haired granny, wearing a black negligee, small push-up bra, black panties, nylons, garter belt and red high heels, sat in a rocking chair doing her knitting as she waited for a customer who desired maternal care. A stunning tall blond, with a prosthetic leg, limped by me, and moments after entering her little room, a red light went on and she appeared in her window as a hot bedroom playmate sans one leg. Some of the girls would suggestively hump as I passed their windows, while others only smiled. I liked them all, even those that barely gave any acknowledgement.

And the price was right. "How much?" was always answered matter-of-factly with: "Fifty guilder. It was fifty guilder yesterday and it'll be fifty guilder tomorrow." Fifty Guilders was about twenty-five dollars. What a deal!

Over the next few days, I enjoyed three or four girls a day, sometimes just eating pussy. There was no pressure to hurry. A tall, fair-skinned young lady, who was working in her room a little after nine in the morning, suggested that I enjoy a cup of tea with her before we began. She told me she was a college girl and was paying her expenses by working in the sex trade. A bit later I passed the window of a slender Thai girl who began humping her hips so the top of her pubic hair peeked out over the top of the miniscule silver g-string she was wearing. It was more than I could resist and after she washed my dick and balls in the little sink in her room, she freely opened her legs so I could eat her out. When it came time to fuck, she equipped me with a condom and once I was in her, used her vaginal muscles to clamp down on my cock so that I came after five or six strokes. Unlike the French girls, I felt that she had enjoyed the experience, especially when it ended with a smile, a hug and a little kiss.

The next day I treated myself to a Chinese girl who had a shaved pussy and well-shaped firm body. I was planning on doing several girls during the day and didn't want to drain myself too early. When her hips began to undulate, I was pleased that my knowledgeable tongue was making her hot, but after doing her for twenty minutes, I indicated that I was going to leave so I could get on to the next girl. She would have none of it and grabbed me by the arm, insisting that I fuck her, which of course I did. In the safe environment of the Amsterdan Red Light district, there were many girls who enjoyed their profession.

96

THIS IS A FUN LOVING PERSON

The wild weekends at, "the house that smut built," had shrunk down to a few close friends dropping by to enjoy the ambiance, get high, and talk. Sex was becoming a thing of the past. Marcial had come by with Natasha, a stunning raven haired beauty from South Africa that he was pursuing so he could get his hands on her trust fund. Her brother had a business guiding Safaris in Kenya and Marcial had been pushing for me to sign up for one. By now I knew his ulterior motive was to get him a free trip if I did so. I was conspicuous as the only one without a female companion that day. How far things had changed! A few glasses of wine was all it took before Marcial began broaching a subject that most men, including myself, avoided bringing up: the rapidly rising feminist movement. He argued that women were becoming overly exploitive of men. As I was currently feeling threatened by the divorce laws, which in my mind seemed to be overly favorable to women, I silently agreed with him; silently, because I didn't want to offend Suze who I could see was taking umbrage at his ideas.

I understood why woman no longer were willing to be blindly dominated by men. Myths about their limitations, whether mental or physical, were quickly being dispelled and doing house chores and raising children, if they had any, no longer took all day. It was a conundrum. Money gave men power and sex did the same for women. It was an argument without a solution? The conversation became vociferous—just short of angry. Some of Marcial's comments about women could be though of as demeaning. But it crossed my mind that both Suze and I were pornographers who some were saying exploited women to make money; but weren't women using their bodies to extract money from hormone driven men, just as guilty. There was confusion everywhere. Recently, Sy Katz's secretary had told him she was perplexed about which side of the dispute between Judy and I, she should take. He had to remind her, I was paying the bills.

Nothing was being resolved that day and not wanting to end it in such an ill humored mood, I thought I could lighten things up by offering to give everyone a personality test that had come packaged with my new Mac 512K, the most powerful personal computer on the market; said to have more memory than anyone would ever have need for. Personality analysis was the rage in the mid 80's. The faux science of astrology was a popular way to get a conversation started. No matter how you answered: "What sign are you?" it could be twisted to describe who you or others thought you were. The personality profiler program that came with the Mac was developed at Stanford University and was primarily meant just for fun; but its readouts always seemed to be uncannily accurate.

After we all were profiled and laughing at how accurate it seemed, I couldn't resist filling out a profile for Judy. I ran down the list of questions and gave what I felt were honest answers: Is she honest?

—no. Does she care about others?—no. Can one rely on her doing what she says?—no. Does she lie?—yes. Is she punctual?—no, and on and on. When I finished checking the boxes, I clicked the mouse for an analysis. The readout came back within a second. It was one I had never -even remotely— seen before: "This is a fun loving person. If you have the opportunity to be with this person do not hesitate." WHAT THE FU . . . ? ? ?

I hadn't heard a word from her since being served with the divorce papers. I began thinking that maybe the Mac program was right. I had read an article in the LA Times in which a female psychologist at a school in St. Louis, stated that her studies indicated that the most stable relationships were those that were antagonistic. It made sense. If one person becomes too dominant in a relationship and becomes the unchallenged boss, resentment begins to fester. I was well aware by this time, that I couldn't dominate Judy and she knew she didn't dominate me. Maybe, despite all the insanity, that's why we had stayed together.

Thanksgiving was just around the corner, and thinking that she may be getting tired of Rick, I gave her a call to ask if she would like to join me for the holiday in San Francisco. We could spend the night at the Palace Hotel in San Francisco where presidents, Taft, Harding and both Roosevelts stayed while visiting the city. The hotel offered a sumptuous buffet-style Thanksgiving feast, served in one of the great rooms in the world; the Garden Court, where Austrian crystal chandeliers hung from its thirty-foot high stained glass ceiling. She said she would think about it. My fulsome description did its job and a few days later she called to say she would join me.

Regardless of what my main motivation was, a trip to San Francisco without visiting the O'Farrell was unthinkable, so after checking in at the hotel to make sure everything was kosher, I treated myself to several hours of lap dancing before hitting the sack in the one hundred eighty five dollar per night room that I had booked for the rendezvous.

Though the room was redolent from age and noise could be heard from the elevator shaft on the other side of the wall, I had a restful sleep and was in a good mood the next day as I waited in the Hotel's lobby for Judy to arrive. We had agreed to meet at noon, so reminding myself that not-being-punctual was a desirable trait, I didn't get upset when she didn't show up on time. But by one-thirty, I realized that I wasn't dealing with a lovable-late-to-the-party trait, but rather a go-fuck-yourself personality trait, and I said to myself: "Fuck her!" and went to the Garden Room where the maitre'd escorted me to a linen-covered table set with expensive silverware and so I could sate myself on the dinner fit for a king that I had already paid for.

A few good orgasms would erase any of the irritations that remained in my mind so after finishing eating, I headed back to the O'Farrell. Knowing that I would be lap dancing for many hours, I went to the men's room to put on my cock-ring and after pressing the snap shut on the thin black-leather strap that went beneath my balls, I stroked my penis a few times to get it slightly aroused, and then sauntered into the New York Live Room ready to rumble.

I was having a great time. One little darling who had danced on my lap several hours earlier, was most impressed when she returned for a repeat performance; "Oh you're still hard!" She was a rookie and wanted to know if it was best not to make guys cum so they would hang around longer. I assured her that her reasoning was correct. By ten in the evening, I had gone through both the day and night shift girls and my cock ring had rendered my penis blue; but despite it taking a full week to recuperate, I had no regrets. It was a reasonable sacrifice for the pleasure I had enjoyed.

Though I continued my dogged pursuit of sex; free, paid and voyeristic, I could feel changes in my body that made orgasms a little less exciting. That also was making my tolerance to be used by women a little bit shorter. Out of nowhere, Debbie Green, showed up at my house one afternoon. Now in her 40's, she still had beauty that melted me like cheddar cheese on toast and despite the fact that one of the first things out of her mouth was: "Gee . . . if I knew you had all this, I would have shown up sooner." I tried to rekindle a relationship by taking her up to Carmel that included a side trip to the O'Farrell. When we got back to the 'charmer' late at night, reflecting on the girl who had straddled her shoulders in the Ultra room she was still thinking of the show: "I've never seen my own pussy that close." It was now soaking wet and the source of much joy, but over the next few months I began to see that her life's experiences had made her dour, especially being left to bring up Eric's daughter on her own. The idea of me becoming a father to her daughter was ludicrous and after I drove her to Joanie Mitchell's house so she could drop something off where I was told: "Wait in the car, I could never bring you inside," I recognized the same 'in crowd' mentality that pervaded the folk scene at the Cabale and not needing more of that kind of humiliation, I called it quits.

97

YIKES

Judy wasn't a breeder and although she wouldn't say it, I knew Suze didn't think much of her. Suze, now with a child of her own, was championing Humphrey's philosophy that it was our duty to spread our genes. Hoping that I might spread mine with Martha, a girl friend of hers, an attractive single mom who needed a husband, she invited us to a small dinner party. Humphrey's philosophy had merit when there were few humans on earth, but not now when earth was struggling to deal with human over population, it was far off the mark. The dinner did nothing to make me want to team up with Martha, but it made me wonder who I was.

Sitting next to me at the table, was a thirty-something dominatrix, named Mistress Kat. During the badinage being tossed around the table, she averred that I was one of the most obvious cases of a submissive that she had ever seen. Humphrey responded; "I think he's very dominant." Martha chipped in: "I don't think hes dominant at all." I wasn't loud and boisterous, but in my own way I thought of myself as a dominant individual. Needless to say, other than a night in the sack, my relationship with Martha went nowhere.

I was still smarting from, what I considered, the insults that I had received from Judy, Debbie and Martha, when, in the accompanyment of Suze and Humphrey, I again stood in the lobby of the year's XROC award ceremonies before the event began. It had only been a year since my coming out and I expected to be treated with some respect as one of the industry's pioneers. A stunning American Indian beauty, Hypatia Lee, was telling Humphrey that she had just done her first D.

P. (double penetration) scene when Seka, the porn sensation of 1985, walked up and began talking to Suze. The sexual appeal of older women was just beginning to be recognized by the adult industry and with her short-coifed silver-blond hair, slim body and matriarchal face, she had become America's favorite MILF. She didn't seem to recognize me from when Suze had brought her and Ginger Lynn, to my house, so I offered her my hand: "We met when you were still little Dottie." Her face suddenly screwed up: "Don't you EVER call me that name again, do you UNDERSTAND!" She turned and abruptly stormed off. Humphrey commented; "It's the drugs," but Suze disagreed; "You patronized her." How differently males and females saw things. Unlike the previous year, I stood feeling humiliated.

Inside the auditorium, baby faced porn stud, Tom Byron, was adroitly emceeing the affair. He had once told me that he had come to LA hoping to work for me. Music was being supplied by porn star Herchel Savage's blues band. Traci Lords, who, at the time, no one knew was only fifteen when they had shot her, was named, the *Best Porn Actress of the Year*. When she took the dais she commented: "It's about time." It got a big laugh. These were all bright and talented people who also felt free to express themselves sexually, nothing like the craven moral degenerates that religious and right wing fanatics tried to paint them as. Despite my continued inner struggles, I felt proud that I had once been such a large force in the revolution.

On a pleasant Sunday afternoon, Marcial had again come by with Natasha, his sultry South African beauty. She wore a white string bikini that looked stunning against her sun tanned olive skin. Not wanting to hinder his plan to get control of her trust fund, I kept my furtive glances to a minimum. Wireless phones were still years away, and when I heard my phone ring; I had to run upstairs to answer it. J.

C. Phillips was on the line and wanted to know if I minded if he came by with a few friends. Being that he was gay meant that the few friends would be gay, so I tried to say no, but after a bit of cajoling, he got me to agree. A half hour later, my pool was filled with a harem of lean and tanned male bodies—wearing swim suits every bit as tiny as Natasha's. The scene didn't fit Marcial's agenda and I couldn't blame him for taking Natasha and leaving me with my gay frolickers.

I went into the house to get something out of the refrigerator and watch TV, but nothing was on that I wanted to watch and walked out on the deck where I witnessed JC, looking like an Orca, splashing around in the pool with a school of bronze skinned dolphins. There was plenty of kissing, hugging and ass grabbing. The "house that smut built" had become a playground for gay revelry. After they left I had to face the obvious. I was an island where people came ashore for brief stopovers when they had nothing better to do. It was a pit stop for cocaine whores, one who called at two AM to tell me in slurred speech that she and her friend would like to stop by where; "Howard Ziehm has his own private golf course and Jacuzzi." Malibu was no longer a paradise, maybe not hell, but at least purgatory. It was time to move.

I decided to make my life simpler. I rented the Malibu house out to a family of three and rented for myself a two-bedroom apartment in Brentwood, that was close to Sy Katz's office. Marcial lived a short distance away if I needed company. Tom Phelan and I could use the second bedroom to continue writing and producing the self-help vocabulary tapes that we made for Bantam Audio. I needed to prove to myself that I could do something other than make sex movies. If I needed to have meetings with investors interested in financing a 'Flesh Gordon' sequel, my deal with Sy Katz included using his office.

As it would turn out, Marcial was fully occupied with ingratiating himself to a very wealthy society lady named, Theo Gunn, the wife of philantropist George Gunn, who owned, among other things, the Cleveland Cavaliers. For erotic fun, he would have her dress up like a slut: short tight mini skirt, nylons and high heels, and then go to a porn theatre by herself where she was to take a seat where she could reach into her panties and masturbate in the dark without being noticed. He would then surreptitiously enter the theater and after he was sure her pussy was wet, take a seat behind her and reach over to finger fuck her. I was impressed. The clever skit would be rewarded with a thirty thousand dollar gift for him to start a business, which he used instead, to buy a new motorcycle.

I had little need for his company anyway, since thanks to some enterprising gangsters, at least that was my suspicion, several Amsterdam type whore houses, picture windows and all, were operating along a few blocks of Santa Monica Blvd near Crenshaw and on Hollywood Blvd near

Western Avenue. Attractive sluts wearing sexy lingerie or panties and bras, stood in the windows where a steady stream of cars could circle around the blocks to window shop for a young lady to enjoy or just masturbate for the free show.

For thirty-five dollars the price was right, but as I suspected the scene didn't last long. After some of the girls began running nearly naked into the street soliciting customers, the scene was closed down.

A dozen or so less pretentious massage parlors, quickly replaced the storefronts and though not all offered sex, I soon found several that did. One which I frequented on a regular basis, had an attractive black girl who enjoyed having her pussy eaten and having sex in unusual positions. But alas, after they got shut down, all that was left was a bevy of hot looking hookers who walked Sunset Blvd. between Highland and Cahunenga each day from two in the afternoon until two in the morning.

What little there was left of my sex life with Anna Magle, ended when Suze called to ask me if I thought she would like to become part of Henry Mudd's harem. Henry was the beneficiary of the incredible wealth left to him by his father, a principle owner of the Cyprus Mines Corporation, started in 1916 by the grandfather. The Mudd family had long been known for it's paternalistic attitude towards its workers; having used some of its money to fund the Harvey Mudd College of engineering, science and mathematics. Henry had always been a good boy when his father was alive, but once the old man died, he wasted no time in becoming a naughty boy; or more accurately, a naughty old man.

He was married with several children whom he treated very well, and they, including his wife, accepted his indulgence of having his own western version of a harem. He hired seven ladies of various ages—one being over fifty—to be his date for one day of each week.

The job paid three thousand dollars a month along with copious benefits. A date consisted of dinner at one of LA's finest restaurants, followed by some time in bed later in the evening. I told Suze I was sure the answer would be yes. Anna quickly became Henry's Saturday night date. She was aware that her career as a sex worker wouldn't last forever and had been exploring other venues to make money. After graduating from a truck driving school, she was now going after a much more ambitious goal; becoming a lawyer. Despite not having graduated from high school, she had already worked her way through Santa Monica City College and on to Cal State Long Beach with a straight "A" average and had been accepted to UCLA's law school. Her new position with Henry would mean she could drop the Hollywood madam, who had recently been busted, and concentrate on her studies.

Maybe or maybe not, Suze had felt quilty that she had caused me to lose my mistress, so she set me up with an attractive cougar who I called "Miz Lesslie," as a way of paying deference to her Virginian heritage. I paid deference to her pussy before we went out on a dinner dates, by lapping on it through the sexy chiffon panties she liked to wear. I had never had a screamer before and she was nothing less than spectacular. When we returned to my apartment and fucked, her shouts: "I love your cock;" would carry out the window and at least a block up the street.

I would have liked to think that it was my hot pants or obscene underwear that caught Stephanie's eye, but I knew my days of being an exhibitionist were coming to an end. More likely it was my skillful tongue that hadn't lost a beat. "Howie, you know what a girl likes," she would say as I lapped away like a mad dog. She was a single Latina mom who worked in Sy Katz's office and I would take her to lunch almost everyday, taking a brief stop at my apartment so we could fuck.

I considered it my duty to provide both ladies with what they needed. To extended the time so Miz Lesslie could ride my rod, I would focus my mind on some nonsexual subject that would keep me from cumming, like: "How do black holes form?" And though it was hard for me to accept, Stephanie's hot latina blood just wore me out. When I suggested that maybe we forego our lunchtime fuck and just go eat, she asked with a forelorn look; "You don't want to fuck?"

The time came to part ways with Miz Leslie when she unabashedly told me: "I love to spend money, especially other people's money," and when Stephanie, sensing that I was running out of juice, replaced me with a new beau who she called; "my little Guatemalan." He quickly got her pregnant.

I was learning that a call from Judy did not bode well. She called to tell me she would be in LA by five o'clock. Fear of loneliness does crazy things and I was happy to hear from her. By eight in the evening, she hadn't arrived and I reminded myself that it was: "one of her desirable traits." At eleven in the evening, I got a collect call. She was in jail in Santa Barbara for speeding; that minor charge being complicated by the fact that she had a suspended license. Could I drive up and bail her out? I immediately did what any submissive would do and agreed to come to her rescue. But I didn't have enough cash on hand and after an hour of trying to borrow the three hundred dollars needed for bail, I called her back to tell her she would have to stay in the slammer until the next day when I would wire the money up as soon as I got some out of the bank.

After she was bailed out, we agreed to meet for lunch at the Bicycle Shop. She arrived with a tall, beautiful black ex stripper named Enderi. Another of her endearing qualities was that she always associated with sexy women. That she had acquired a multitude of tickets, confirmed that she was still using cocaine. Over lunch she told me she had come to LA to rectify the situation. That sounded like good news. They each had ordered the escargot appetizer, followed with an entre' of poached salmon—the two most expensive items on the menu. After a flippant goodbye, the two pranced out of the Bicycle Shop and went on their merry way while I waited for the waiter to return with my credit card. Damn you Mistress Kat! You were right. I was not only a submissive but possibly a masochist as well. Rather than enjoying physical pain, I enjoyed mental pain. Was it just fear of losing my hard earned wealth? Deep down I knew I would never change. It was who I was.

The bane of drugs was becoming more and more bewildering. Even my family got into the act. When my youngest brother, Mike, who had never called me about anything, called at ten in the evening to ask for seventy-five dollars, I knew it was for drugs. I shouldn't have given it to him, but I did. My sister Nancy was more inventive. She told me my parents had blown all their money at the racetrack and could I loan her five hundred to buy them food. I told her if they were that stupid they should go hungry for a week. "You'd let your own parents starve?" she wanted to know. I knew both she and my brother were fucking with heroine and I wasn't about to help either of them get more fucked up.

After Humphrey treated several us, as he put it, "a little surprise" the current rage, Ecstacy, I began to rethink my relationship with drugs. The euphoric feeling of Ecstacy was overwhelming; it made your sphincter feel like honey. It also made you indifferent to how you were affecting those around you. Suze was still trying to find a husband for Martha and had invited her art director, who had a major crush on Martha, and me, to stay over and have dinner with them and Martha. After taking Humphrey's 'little surprise, I freaked the hapless art director out by fondling Martha with unctuous sweetness. I had no desire to have a future with her and I knew he did. It was a shitty thing to do, but knowing I was enjoying making him feel inferior, I continued.

I was already having serious doubts about using any drugs; period. Grass was harmless, but the experience was redundant; get high; have some inane observation about life or the universe; get the munchies; and finally doze off in a stupor. It was a prodigious waste of time. I was now in my mid forties and the final crash into the grave was not to far out on the horizon. I had no need to numb myself to enjoy life. It was one of humanities absurdities. Even Jesus turned water into wine. Why? Only a brain dead zealot could think that he somehow plucked a few nitrogen and carbon atoms out of nowhere to add to the two hydrogen and single oxygen atom constituting water to make a mind-numbing brew. Maybe that's how he conned people—with drugs. I had no need to numb my mind and vowed not to smoke grass again—and I didn't. I would deal with life on its own terms.

I admitted I was a happy sex addict, and as R. Crumb put it: why quit doing something that feels so good?" Not having a good answer for that I flew to Europe several times to play golf (which was becoming more and more like sex) and frequent the red light district in Amsterdam. It always provided me a variety of experiences, some thrilling and some not. After an English girl made the whole transaction like paying for a car wash, do you want a wax, do you want tire treatment, by adding a fee on top of the basic charge for each service, I put my pants back on and left her room in a huff. There were times when the action was sparse and this particular trip, that was the case. After a disappointing night of sex shopping, I noticed a tall blond standing in a dimly lit display window of a room several feet above street level just as I was about to call it quits. She was wearing a sheer baby doll, black bikini panties and nylons, the ensemble that renders me helpless. I succumbed to her beckoning finger and climbed the steps to join her for one last fling. She was pleasant and friendly and after going through the dick washing routine, she took me by the hand and coaxed me down onto the bed so she could begin to give me a blowjob. Her panties were still on when I reached down between her legs to warm her up. YIKES!! I WAS IN BED WITH A TRANNY!

I was open minded but not that open minded. I quickly got up, somewhat mortified and politely excused myself before scampering down the stairs and back to the street.

Sherman Torgan, my renter at the New Beverly Cinema, was as much a sex hound as I was and we kept each other abreast of where and when hot action was taking place, whether it be on the west or east coast, at a strip club or a massage parlor. We relied on each other to avoid wasting time or money.

On one of his visits to New York, he had brought his wife and son along for a visit to Times Square, but as they were about to enter a restaurant to have lunch, he noticed that a new storefront club, just a few doors up the block, was advertising a live sex show. As he sat in the restaurant with his family waiting to be served, the thought of the show was driving him mad. Finally, he told his wife and son that he had to excuse himself for ten minutes to make a business call back to LA. Once he turned the corner and was out of their sight, he sprinted out the front door and up the block and into the strip club to see the show. Ten minutes later, he returned to the restaurant to report to the wife and child that all was well.

Upon Sherman's recommendation, I flew to New York to indulge myself. My renter at Malibu had partially burned down my house—the guest house and half of the master bedroom—so while work was underway, having a few days of sexual fun seemed like a good idea. Patrick Martin, needed a place to stay and I was letting him sleep at my apartment until he found his own place.

The Times Square renewal project had forced the Harmony Burlesque theater to relocate to Church Street in the Soho district. The girls were offering lap dances facing forwards or backwards as you preferred and finger fucking their asses while on stage. But because of the current aids scare, pussy sucking was no more.

Upon my return, Patrick greeted me with a little smile and suggested I check out what's in my bedroom. Sound asleep was the curly blond haired French girl with laughing eyes that he had brought by my house the previous summer while I was still living in Malibu. At that time she had only been in the States for a visit to see if she could take courses at the UCLA film school and I doubted if I would see her again. Now she was back to begin classes in the fall and in my bed. Without any expectations of sex, I climbed in bed with her just to go to sleep, but when my hand found its way between her legs, I discovered a soaking wet pussy and nature took its course.

Her name was Florence and beyond being cute, she had a girlish mellifluous voice and French accent that was so disarming, that I felt myself doing something I thought I was incapable of: falling in love. Her glasses gave her an intellectual mien and her habit of puffing her cheeks full of air and blowing it out so that her lips fluttered, was her delightful way of saying; "no big deal." Patrick asked me to show her 'Flesh Gordon' which I was still unsure if it would impress or horrify, but somewhat belatedly, I set up my 16mm projector and a small screen and the three of us sat in silence for an hour and a half to watch the film. When it was finished, she got up and ran over to me and kissed me. A big smile of approval was on her face. It was beyond a five star review and my heart was captured.

"There's no fool like an old fool," and despite her repeatedly telling me she was passionately in love with her German 'uber mench' boy friend back home, and that she hated old skin, even that of her movie idol Robert Redford, and assuring me that the sex we had was just a one time accident, the result of being in a strange man's bed; I fell in love—goo goo gaa love. I got her a job with Barry Cahn's company that was producing a TV show called 'The Judge' and drove her the thirty miles back and forth to work each day, hoping to make her see that I was a better choice than the 'uber mensch.' A switch in my brain had opened a floodgate of hormones and I followed her like a love-sick puppy.

When she returned to France, I used a golf trip as an excuse to visit her in Paris. She was glad to see me, making arrangements for me to rent a nice room on the Left Bank and give me a guided tour of some of the sights of Paris not on the usual tourist maps. But when I offered to pick her up at her father's house, where she was staying, I got: "I could never bring you to meet my father."

Was I a damn fool or what ? ? ? Even though I shed a few tears as she disappeared around a corner into the Parisian environs, I felt more shame that I had been so fucking stupid than remorse that the imagined affair was over. "There's no fool like an old fool, especially one trying to act like a young idiot."

Thinking I could reclaim some of my ego, I took a train to Amsterdam but found disappointment there as well. Because of the Aids scare, few red lights were lit and those that were didn't offer pussy sucking. I came home dejected and a little wiser. Sex is not forever.

98

FLESH GORDON TWO AND MORE MADNESS

Disregarding that I didn't believe in lucky stars, it seemed that I was born under one. A bit of hard work didn't hurt either. When Anna told me she was thinking of buying a house, I suggested that we go into a partnership and buy one together. I had peeled off fifty grand from the insurance money to fix the fire damage at the Malibu house, and was looking for something to spend it on. Living in an apartment, with all its rules and restrictions, was not my style. By combining funds, we might be able to find a good buy in Venice, a colorful section of LA that was built in the early 20's by a real estate developer. It mimicked its Italian namesake by having canals rather than streets.

Venice was populated by arty-types and aging beatniks. From its heyday, property values had steadily declined but it seemed that now there was a lot of potential for growth. She liked the idea. We agreed we would need a house large enough for her to have her own room and me to have an office. She was currently in her second year at UCLA's Law School and needed privacy so she could do her homework and entertain Henry Mudd on her commitment day. Though we no longer had sex, in the back of my mind, I assumed she might like to be fucked once in awhile. It didn't hurt to hope.

Neither of us had good enough credit to qualify for a mortgage; in my case because I had always paid cash and never used a bank to make large purchases. However, Chris Wilson, the same who had pulled a gun on his wife after she wanted to split from one of my Halloween parties, had a thriving hardwood floor company and excellent credit. The Halloween incident was an alcohol caused anomaly and over time, being that we had a common bond as victims of Marcial's manipulations, we had developed a friendship. Chris was very handsome and athletic, but had a short man's complex; stroking his ego by deluding himself into thinking he was a world-class tennis player. He also had a condescending attitude towards women. I wasn't sure he would get along with Anna, who was becoming a pushy feminist, but without him, we had no way of getting credit, so we asked him to join the partnership. We agreed that we would each contribute ten thousand dollars. Anna and I would live in the house and pay rent.

Prospects didn't look exciting as we stood in the second floor bedroom of a rundown house on Horizon street that could be purchased for thirty grand down. It was a rattrap when the realtor noticed me looking out the window at a large two-story gable-roofed house across the alley. She mentioned it was for sale for two hundred sixty five thousand dollars. It was more than we could afford, but it didn't hurt to take a look. The ground floor consisted of a living room with hardwood floors and two sunrooms; one that looked out to Market Street that would be perfect for my office. Off to the side was a large kitchen that came with an old-fashioned six burner Wolf stove. Two large bedrooms upstairs would give both Anna and me private space. Market Street was at one time Venice's Grand Canal. Vintage pictures showed an arched wooden bridge crossing the canal just a short distance up the street from where the house sat.

It was perfect. I suggested we make a lowball offer of two hundred twenty five thousand and see if it would fly. It did. As it would turn out, the house's owner was another sex-mesmerized male who now found himself jilted by the woman he thought was his future. Rock star, Andy Summers, guitarist for 'The Police,' had, according to rumor, dumped his wife and kid and bought the house for him and his new girl friend to live. But a week after throwing a big party at the house to celebrate, the delusion was shattered when she unceremoniously dumped him. He couldn't be faulted for wanting to erase all vestiges of the memory and jumped on our offer. His misfortune was our good fortune.

I moved in immediately, but Anna wouldn't join me for a few weeks. Since I was by myself, I told Patrick he could sleep in the back sunroom until he found his own place. Word traveled quickly around the neighborhood and an attractive young girl showed up a few days later and asked if my French friend was home. When I told her he only stayed at the house on occasion, her expression became forlorn; "Oh, I had my heart set on fucking a Frenchman." Closing in on fifty, I was too slow to react and didn't ask before she left: "Would you consider a porn king?"

There was no shortage of street entertainment. Over the next few days, I noticed a nicely dressed black dude walked past the house every half hour with a baby in his arms. He was on his way to a phone booth at the end of the block outside the liquor store. I knew a drug dealer when I saw one. The baby was a prop. At three in the morning, it was not uncommon for someone out on the street to yell: "I'll kill you Mother-fucker."

I had been naïve to think that Anna would be interested in having sex, she wisely knew that mixing sex and business was a no no. Besides she was totally occupied by her law school studies and—as she put it— diddling octogenarian Henry Mudd's flaccid organ each Saturday night in her bedroom.

The move gave me an opportunity to do some housecleaning. The seven-year deal I had signed with Sy Katz was up and I felt I had repaid him many times over. The days of needing a mentor were long past. It was time for me to grow up and stand on my own two feet. I had learned a lot from him but by now he had to realize that his fantasy that I was going to become a big time producer and mine that he was a responsible manager had been dispelled. I almost lost the New Beverly Cinema because he twice had let its property taxes fall three years into arrears. Recently he asked me to give one of his other clients eight grand to do a breakdown of the Flesh Gordon 2 script, despite the fact that the chances of it being produced were still very remote and he also had convinced me to go into some bad investments, one to start an insurance company with a guy who had already served time for insurance fraud. It was obvious that the integrity of Graffitti's bank account was not high on his list. Money was no longer pouring in and I couldn't continue to be so cavalier as I had been in the past. It took me almost fifty years, but I no longer needed a father figure to cling to.

As soon as Judy heard that the Malibu house was repaired and I was looking for a renter; she wasted no time in trying to get her clutches on the money. A hot looking doll in a mini skirt with the hem just below the crotch, came by to negotiate a lease for a client in Carmel that she represented. I was assured they had lots of cash. I was also sure it was drug money and that the rent for the Malibu house would all wind up in Judy's hands.

The girl was almost insulted that her feminine wiles had failed to close the deal. Pussy was not the force it once had been. Thanks to my golfing partner, movie agent Mike Karg, I rented it to his client, Gerald McRaney, star of 'Simon and Simon' and 'Major Dad.' He moved in with his new love, Delta Burke, and moved out six weeks later to live at her house in Pasadena which was closer to the studios. The Malibu house just became his weekend retreat where he felt free to wear a bikini while he doted on Delta and a place to store his large gun locker. Men were overcoming their fear of looking sexy.

Once again, a desperate call for help came from Judy. Rick's crazy life style was finally wearing thin. It was also possible that it was vice versa. She was trying to get clean and couldn't do it around him. When she mentioned he was into some new chick; I knew what the real problem was. "Would you come up and help me move out?" She didn't want to return to LA or move back into the Carmel house, instead she had some hair-brained scheme to move into a house that she and two of her girl friends had rented on Carpenter Street in Carmel. I had become inured to her bullshit, but also was in no mood for a scene, including a divorce, so I told her I would be there the following day.

We hooked up at a local café in Carmel and then, since Rick was gone for the day, rented a trailer and hurriedly drove to the house. She told me another roommate might be home, but he wouldn't be a problem. Meeting Rick had the makings of a bad scene, so that was good news. I pulled up and parked outside the house on its large gravel driveway. The house was typical ranch style and notwithstanding that it abutted the eleventh hole of the Rancho Canada Golf Club, whatever greenery it once had was long gone from lack of care. After we entered the front door, I found myself facing in the far corner, a floor to ceiling temple to booze made of empty beer cans. The floor was littered with trash. A worn yellow couch faced the temple where I assumed Judy and the boys gained inspiration as they guzzled down six packs and snorted coke. I was at a loss to understand how, even with a drug-addled brain; she could have wanted to live in this depressing hovel.

The two of us went right to work, and soon had the trailer loaded with her belongings. The scraggy roommate she had mentioned, stood in the corner muttering to himself, but was too intimidated by my presence to speak loudly. Within fifteen minutes we were ready to drive away. As we did the muttering roommate gained courage and peered out the open door, shouting at the top of his lungs: "Get the fuck out of here you fucking coke whore!"

By late afternoon she was moved into her new house which I was surprised to learn was owned by one of Rick's cousins. It had been rented with a caveat that if there was any trouble they would be history. After Judy briefly introduced me to her roommates, we retired to her bedroom and climbed into bed together: the first time in over a decade and sans any sex or snuggling. My libido would not have been strong enough to put aside the abuse and rejection it had taken over the years. We soon fell fast asleep.

Loud pounding and screaming from someone at the door, woke us up at 3 A. M. It was obvious who it was. Judy got out of bed and walked up the hall to answer it. Keeping the screen door closed and latched, she partially opened the door to face Rick and his bruised ego. Profanities spewed forth like a skid row drunk. I was not about to play a knight in shinning armor by confronting the little jerk, this was Judy's own doing: so I let her do all the talking; but in case he went nuts, I moved down the hall and stood behind the door with a baseball bat in hand. Five minutes of cursing and pleading got him nowhere and he finally turned and walked out to Carpenter Street, shouting one last: "fuck you!" into the quiet Carmel night.

Judy showed her appreciation, the next day, by setting me up to have a quickie with one of her girl friends, who was enamored by the fact that I was a porno king. "If I can't have an orgy with Howard, *'Flesh Gordon,'* Ziehm, who can I have one with?" She was a willing fuck, but I would have enjoyed it more if her pussy hadn't smelled so bad. Why some girls didn't douche was beyond comprehension. Marcial, who I admired for his wisdom on subjects like this, told me when he ran into that situation, he would take a swipe with his hand and put it under the girl's nose and ask: "Would you like to lick that?" But considering that my sex life was no longer stellar, I just bucked up and enjoyed without complaint.

99

WILL IT EVER END?

At first I didn't believe it when Maurice Smith called from Canada to tell me he had investors willing to put up money for a Flesh Gordon sequel. "Could we do the project for a million and a half?" I assured him we could.

Despite being unhappy that he had missed an opportunity to be part of the domestic distribution of 'Flesh Gordon,' Maurice had stayed involved over the last ten years by reselling the rights to the foreign territories when the original contracts expired. Because of him, I would learn how extensively Frank Agrama had burned me on the original deals. His claim that the various companies operated out of Lichtenstein was a lie to prevent me from knowing who the real players were. France had actually paid seventy thousand, not forty; Australia, fifty, not twenty-five; Germany ninety, not fifty; and on and on. Agrama had not only pocketed the difference between the actual and reported sales, but took out his percentage from the phony numbers as well. How much Abbas Amin was complicit in this, I was never able to determine. It didn't matter. I was naïve and young and got used. But, so what? More important, 'Flesh Gordon' still had vitality around the world and I was excited to begin work on a sequel.

I asked a twenty three year old comedy writer, Doug Frisby, who worked at the Laff Factory in Hollywood to write with me. Having someone young with a good sense for teen humor would be a plus. To be sexy and R-Rated was going to be a challenge. Ronald Reagan's America was becoming less liberal by the minute. Anything rated beyond R could not expect to get playdates. People I knew who had testified at his 'Meese Commission on Pornography,' told me it was a sham and their views were barely listened to.

A 'Flesh Gordon II' without sex, wouldn't cut it. We came up with a story where Flesh is kidnapped by a group of cheerleaders from a nearby planet where for some unknown reason; all the men had become impotent. The villain would again be Emperor Wang, but because of the extensive damage he suffered at the end of the original 'Flesh Gordon;' he was now reconstructed with cosmetic surgery. The adventure wends its way through: *'Farting Assteroids'* and *'Mammary Mountains'* as well as confrontations with a *'Dick Head'* and *'Octopussy Eater'* monster that gave the script the same slap stick flavor of the original. It had scenes that I hoped would make people laugh at some of the phobias and obsessions they have about the human body and its functions. For big tit lovers, we wrote a scene that would take place in *'Babyland,'* where the *'Mother People'* would nourish the diapered denizens. Our first draft was completed in two months.

I was already working on a storyboard for 'Flesh II,' when I was treated to a big surprise. Judy called to tell me she was moving back in with me. She implied that I was her husband and thus had little to say about it. Crazy as it sounds, I still missed her energy, and along with my strong German sense of obligation, I restrained from arguing her point and told her to come back.

She arrived the next day with a little red ball of fluff, a Chow-chow puppy, named Sebastian. He was so docile and cute, it was impossible not to fall in love with him. Any anxiety I had about Judy, soon disappeared as Sebastian frantically wagged his tail to let me know how much he appreciated his new home. Judy's situation in Carmel had fallen apart after the cops had to be called to quiet a loud, late night party. Carmel was not a party town and Rick's cousin had enough and evicted her and her friends from his property. Where else to go, but home to Daddy?

Anna and Judy got along quite well, so it was not a problem. To keep busy, Judy got a job doing what she knew how to do best, stripping at the Wild Goose, a non nude club. She would have preferred working at The Ball, but it was no longer open. Whitey Locker had been busted for manufacturing Methamphetamine. To make matters worse, he jumped bail and screwed his brother who had put up his house to cover the bond. It won him a starring role on 20th Century Fox's popular show; 'America's Most Wanted.' His eventual capture and an eleven-year sentence in Chino, soon followed. Wow! Whitey was a great guy who pushed his luck one step too far. But eleven years?

I was delighted to be teased by three of Carmel's vixens who had flown down to LA to say hi to Judy and more importantly to be introduced to a rich doctor she knew. I couldn't fault the girls for looking for a sugar daddy and enjoyed watching them plan their strategies as they talked in front of me while I lay on my bed. Jennifer, a cute oriental who liked to wear a body hugging leotard to show off her sexy body, couldn't help but notice the effect she was having on my junk that was straining to get out from beneath the spandex pants I was wearing. I teased her by asking, "See what you're doing to big Benaldo," Henceforth, every time I saw her she would ask: "How is Big Benaldo doing?" Michelle Stevens, who stopped by on her way to the Caribbean where she had been paid ten grand to hang with some Saudis for a week and Madeline, who I had heard tell Judy that she often went to her doctor just to have her pussy sucked, would eventually score big with the doctor who had made a killing by cornering the market for Dialysis machines.

As much as I loved being teased by the girls and they loved teasing me, I dreaded the fact that Judy began associating with some of the stragglers who hung out in the back alley. She insisted that she was not into drugs anymore, but they reeked of cocaine and it made no sense why she would even want to know them. I couldn't see any overt signs of drug use but that she became angry when I asked questions was disquieting.

My suspicions grew stronger after she called to ask me to pick her up from a party she was at. The party was at Catya Sassoon's apartment in Beverly Hills. She was the daughter of the founder of the Sassoon hair care empire. The luxurious apartment he had provided for his daughter reminded me of an Opium den when I walked in. Through the thick smoke redolent of marijuana, I saw people snorting lines of coke on a table on the far side of the room. Being straight made me feel like a pariah. Yet I still deluded myself into thinking that Judy was not using.

Maurice and I were debating whether to shoot the film in LA or Vancouver. One of the considerations was to find a studio or warehouse large enough and cheap enough to fit our budget. After spending a morning with Maurice, looking at several facilities in the Valley, I returned home early after our search proved to be fruitless and found Judy in the back sunroom talking with Steven Laufer, the garrulous Malibu drug dealer. She hadn't mentioned that he was going to drop by, but his bubbly and ingratiating manner made him likeable. I just didn't want him giving or selling Judy any cocaine and told him so. He understood perfectly and assured me he I had nothing to worry about.

It was a hollow promise and I was a fool to have believed it, but why would that be unusual? A week later, I again found him at my home, this time on the back stoop on his knees hunched over a piece of newspaper chopping something up with a razor blade. Judy was standing aside intently watching him. They hadn't heard me enter through the front door and were surprised when I walked up to them. He was chopping up a little brown block of some kind of drug that I immediately thought to be cocaine. Stephen quickly allayed my fears by explaining in his most sycophantic voice, that it was just brown hash. Rather than challenging him, my neurotic aversion to confrontation led me to accept what he had told me. As far as I knew, Judy wasn't into smoking hash, so why make a big deal out of nothing.

Like the gullible idiot that I was; I learned a few days later that the little cube was brown heroine. I was a fucking wimp! An idiot that could be easily manipulated! When Laufer showed up later in the day, I told him not to come around anymore or there would be trouble. He tried to soft soap me but I didn't retreat . . . Finally! He slunk out of the house. Foolishly I thought I had seen the last of him.

The hookers had been swept off of Hollywood Blvd and my opportunities to have sex were becoming few and far between. Even the strip clubs were becoming mundane, the dancers doing the same three song routines over and over. What was becoming one of my rare fucks was with a baby faced German trollop, named Britta. She was a friend of Annas who also had a crush on Judy. Five years prior, she had modeled for Suze Randall in my Malibu backyard and the vision of her in yellow panties with her legs spread wide still lingered in my head. Heroine had led her to become borderline psychotic and occasionally turn to street walking to make a living. She was now homeless and as a courtesy to a fellow sex worker, Anna felt obligated to let her sleep beneath the Venice house. She liked to come upstairs into the house during the day to sit on the floor and make collages with snips out of magazines, which she never cleaned up. Despite her rough life, she was still sexy and attractive.

Hard as it was, I couldn't help but see that my sex life was drawing to an end. My body looked ridiculous in the sexy underwear I still paraded around in and tinitus kept a loud continuous ringing inside my ears, but since the herpes I had contracted years earlier had remained in remission for almost a decade, it was hard to say no when she asked me if I would like to fuck, I was surprised yet happy to oblige. *"I was actually going to have sex again."* Since Anna was at school and Judy was out roller-skating, we went to the rear sunroom where I took a seat on the couch that faced the French windows. She took off her panties and sat on my lap with her feet on my knees so she could watch my cock sliding in and out of her in the long mirror in front of us lying sideways beneath the windows on the floor. By using my 'contemplate-on-some-abstruse-subject' technique, we fucked for a full hour. If I had known that it would be my penultimate fuck, I would have gone another hour.

That evening, I was still feeling my oats, and after Judy came home, the three of us headed over to the big AA Halloween party at the Santa Monica Auditorium. It was a sign that Judy was trying to get clean. As we walked into the arena, I admired how nicely Britta's butt filled the tight white pants she was wearing and was glad I had fucked her earlier in the day. Judy quickly lost herself on the dance floor doing her Mata Hari routine and Britta disappeared elsewhere into the crowd. I stood with my hands in my pockets, watching Danny Elfman perform with his band, the Oingo

Boingos. His crazy red hair and make-up had put him in the forefront of the incipient punk rock movement.

I was feeling more like Judy's chaperone than her husband when she informed me a day later that she was moving in with Catya Sasoon. My skeptical looks that she was off of drugs wasn't sitting well with her. She called me as a control freak. Druggies delude themselves into thinking that they are smarter than everyone else. When I accompanied her on a late evening walk on the Venice walkway, a black gang-banger approached us and started talking to her. He gave me an indifferent look when she introduced us that said; "Who the fuck cares." Did she actually think that I couldn't see that he was a dealer?" Evidently yes.

Two weeks later she called, not from Catya's place . . . but from Sybil Brand, the women's jail just south of downtown LA. She had been arrested and needed to be bailed out. She rambled on telling me what happened. She had been caught climbing into Michelle Steven's apartment through a small bathroom window that was easily accessible from the little pathway that ran between her house and the next-door neighbor's. She was entering the apartment because she wanted to borrow one of Michelle's dresses. I knew for a fact that they both liked to wear 'fuck me' dresses, so the story rang true. The window was about six feet above ground level and Steven Laufer, who was along with her, gave her a foot boost so she could climb in. When a neighbor in the adjacent building heard a noise in the pathway, he called the police. She and Steven were still on the scene when the cops arrived. Judy tried to convince them that Michelle was cool with her going into her apartment—that they traded clothes all the time—but the cops thought the story sounded suspicious.

Judy gave them Michelle's phone number, hoping she would verify the story. However, while the cops were already doing their own checking, they discovered that Laufer had an outstanding warrant from Florida for drug dealing and when they finally were able to get in touch with Michelle, she denied that she had given Judy permission to enter her apartment. The two of them were promptly taken downtown to be booked for breaking and entry and the cops turned poor little Sebastian, who was out in the street sitting in Judy's car, was turned over to animal control and taken to the local pound.

The bust had taken place on a Friday, meaning that she wouldn't be arraigned until Monday when the courts opened. She would have to sit in jail unless I bailed her out. I had had it with her bullshit and decided to let her sit. She needed to get a taste of where she was headed. Sebastian's plight was more of an immediate concern to me. On Saturday morning, I found out where he was being held and went to spring him. Even before I entered the kennel room where he was being kept, he picked up my scent and began to bark. I recognized its distinctive sound immediately. His tail was wagging at a thousand miles an hour as he hopped up and down on the cold cement floor of the small cage that he had been confined in for almost twenty-four hours. His little butt wobbled back and forth as I led him down the hall and out to my car where he licked me from head to toe for three minutes. I gave him a hard hug to let him know he was now safe and sound. Anyone who claims dogs don't have emotions, is a fucking moron! The large number of weekend busts, meant that Judy wouldn't be arraigned until late in the afternoon. I felt a pang of irrational sympathy seeing her looking forlorn as she sat in the docket with two Columbian women and eight black men, all waiting their turn for the judge to hear their case. Laufer was not among them.

The legal system coddles its lawyers and not wanting to waste the time of the one who was representing the two Columbian women, the judge heard their case first. They had been driving a VW Beetle when stopped by the police for a traffic violation. It struck me as humorous that two short   fat unattractive women, had stuffed themselves into a little VW bug. During a cursory search, the cops found a large amount of cocaine stashed in the car. Their lawyer babbled away, suggesting that they had no idea there was cocaine in the car and that they should be released. He went on and on, the judge giving him every courtesy to continue with his nonsense. It was obvious that they were drug cartel mules, but after an hour of verbal diarhea, the judge agreed to set a nominal bail so they could be freed.

Because so much time had been allotted to hearing the Columbian women's case, not much was left in the day to hear the remaining ones and the judge dispensed them all with a perfunctory hearing at best. Judy, and all the remaining defendants, were being represented by public defenders who had no clue if there were any mitigating arguments for their clients or not. The judge gave her case two minutes of his time before dispensing it with nothing more than a date to return to the court for a preliminary hearing. She was quickly ushered out of the room and transported back to Sybil Brand.

After returning home from the depressing courtroom fiasco, I got a phone call around nine in the evening from some guy who claimed to be a friend of Laufer. By the sound of his voice and accent, I could tell he was 'barrio.' My mind pictured a fat pudgy 'homie' with a shaved head and tattoos. "How would you like to become the top producer in Hollywood?" he asked. *What the fuck was the dude talking about?* He went on: "If you would put up ten grand to spring Steven, I can make that possible." *Jesus Christ! What kind of a moron did they think I was?* Strictly for entertainment, I continued to talk to the beaner: "There's only one thing that can make someone a top producer and that's money—lots of it. We can provide that."

I started thinking that maybe it wasn't too cool to lead this guy on. He might be nuts and do who knows what. He could supply me with millions of dollars to make movies but he didn't have ten large to spring Laufer? I told him I wasn't interested in being a top producer. He wanted to know how it was I couldn't help my friend. "What?" I shinned him off and hung up. I heard no more from him or Steven. Eventually, I would learn that Laufer was extradited to Florida where he was given thirteen years in their big house.

Five days in jail was enough and after bailing Judy out, I drove to Sybil Brand bring her home. The single story complex sat on top of a hill overlooking south L. A. There were no high stonewalls or razor wire fences and at least from the vantage of the visitor's parking area, did not look that foreboding. I parked the car and was on my way walking towards the double glass doors that led to the prison's lobby, when she came running out the door and much like Sebastian, jumped into the car. There were no hugs and kisses. She looked haggard. Her only possession was a brown paper bag that held all her belongings.

She didn't have much good to say about Sybil Brand. Despite it's serene exterior, life inside was tense. A majority of the inmates were black and tough. A fight could break out over a pillow. It was the polar opposite to what she was accustomed to: Malibu and Carmel.

Midday traffic on the 101 was slow so she had plenty of time to fill me in with the details and the truth—or at least close to it—about what had happened. Michelle had been on coke for three days and needed something to help bring her down. Judy told her Steven Laufer could score a forty-dollar bag of brown heroine . . . no problem. Michelle liked that idea and gave her a hundred bucks, expecting her to bring back the change. Judy took the money and headed over to Laufer's pad and from there the two of them drove to his connection to make the score. When the dealer saw that Judy had a C note on her, he offered to make a bulk sale: 5 bags for the hundred. The deal was too good to pass up and she took it. When she dropped by to give Michelle her bag of heroine, she wasn't home. According to Judy, Michelle and her were always doing shit together, so she was sure there wouldn't be any problem about the sixty bucks she was due. She would give it to her later after she had sold the remaining bags for a nice profit.

I thought to myself: *"if you didn't use it yourself."* She went on to say that when she had stopped by Michelle's apartment to pick up the money for the score, Michelle had shown her the sexy black rubber mini dress that she had borrowed from Catya Sasoon and Judy, in turn, decided she would stop by and borrow it from her. I knew exactly what she was talking about; its hemline was just below the crotch and a zipper ran all the way up the front. Its back was totally bare. It said; *"I'm available but its not going to be cheap."* It was the kind of dress that suckered in guys like me.

The thought of the rubber dress sitting on the table was too much for her to resist. She and Michelle traded clothes all the time. But when the cops showed up, the dress wasn't the problem; it was the five bags of heroine in her fanny pack. She was looking at serious rock-busting time if they were discovered. Even though Michelle had no drugs in her apartment, there was a crack pipe and other paraphernalia sitting in plain sight on the coffee table. When the cops contacted her, to save her own skin, she let Judy hang.

As she stood next to the curb, still uncuffed, she saw that the cops were preoccupied doing warrant checks. She had to act fast to do something about the heroine in her fanny pack. A curbside drain was just in front of her, so as not to alert the cops, she slowly nudged her way towards the curb. Only moments before the cops got word that Laufer had a warrant out for him, she was able to reach around her back and drop the bags onto the street and with an innocuous step off the curb, quickly shove them into the city sewer system with her foot. They would now make their way to the Pacific Ocean where some poor fish would get fucked up.

I suspected it was going to be just another 'Perils of Pauline' story. Pauline always wiggled out from her plights. Not so! Three weeks later, I sat with her while we waited for the court to be called into session. There was a lot of confusion about what she was supposed to do. Lawyers were scurrying about and she had yet to meet the public defender assigned to her case. After twenty minutes, he suddenly leaned over from the row behind us, and in a hushed voice, asked Judy to accompany him outside so they could talk in the hall. Five minutes later she came back in tears.

Because of the prior she had for writing a bad check in Carmel, the DA was offering what was called a mid sentence—six years! Her public defender told her he thought he might be able to plead her down to four. He told her he thought it was a good deal, but as he had a lot of other clients he was representing that day, he needed to get an answer fast. American justice working at its best—one minute to decide if you want to be locked up for four years! She was fucking up her life with drugs, but this was about stealing a dress from a friend. It didn't warrant four years. If she had been a blue blood with a good lawyer, the case would have already been dismissed. It was obvious what we had to do.

We were both depressed as we left the court: she about the horrific future she was facing and me about how costly it was going to be to hire a lawyer. But we had been through a lot together and I felt it was my duty to back her up. If she went to prison for a long time, it would depress me no end. I consulted Mike Karg about what to do. Mike had had problems with cocaine in the past, even being a dealer for a while. He told me about making runs between LA and Vegas with a kilo of cocaine in his car, snorting lines off the dashboard as he flew down the road. Both his wife and his client, Gerald McRaney, stuck with him until he returned to sanity; so he understood where I was coming from. When I told him I needed a lawyer for Judy, he knew exactly whom I should call.

Looking at Mike Uritz would never lead one to believe that he was once an addict. Physically fit and financially successful, his battles with drugs were long in the past and he was now, not only a successful attorney, but also a founding partner in Gold's Gym. Both Judy and I began to feel better as he began to talk. He said he knew the judges who might be sympathetic if they saw that the offender was seriously trying to rehabilitate. It was important to get her case before one of those judges and he could do that. But saving Judy was going to be expensive. Ha-ha, what a surprise! He would need a five thousand dollar retainer to start with, and much more if the case went to trial. A personality profile would have to be prepared by a psychologist. When I asked how much that would cost I was told three thousand dollars. Judy would have to immediately check herself into a three-week detox program to show that she was serious about cleaning up. He recommended Brotman hospital, a facility in Culver City near the old MGM studios. After completing detox, she would have to enter a nine-month rehab program. Cry Help in the valley, was one of the best, but it's popularity made getting a bed there difficult. It was imperative that she be enrolled somewhere when a judge heard her case. The ringing from the tinnitus in my ears couldn't drown out the sound of a cash register ringing up a sale as he said Brotman would cost five grand and the rehab program about twelve hundred a month.

I had lots to worry about but it could have been worse. The days of Graffitti earning big bucks were over, but fortunately I had made prudent investments in various stocks and savings accounts. By the time Uritz finished talking, I had already figured out where the money would come from. And by shear serendipity, I had only recently bought into a health insurance plan for Judy and myself. It would cover most of the five grand for the three-week stay at Brotman.

Uritz had my five grand check in his hand as we walked out of his office. Judy took her first of several meetings with the psychological profiler the next day and by the end of the week she was enrolled at Brotman. No visitors and no phone calls, in or out, were allowed during the first week of detox. After that, outside contact was allowed only on three specific visiting days. Her time would be spent having sessions with a psychiatrist as well as group counseling with other people checked into the program.

Inadvertently, she got caught in a catch 22 situation: damned if you do and damned if you don't. The psychiatrist told her it was extremely important to be absolutely truthful. So she told him about the problems she had after she left home as a teenager and her use of crystal meth. Unknown to her, there was no doctor client privilege in detox and the information was passed on to the insurance company who was all too happy to be able to cancel our policy since Judy hadn't reported her prior drug use on the application. She had only been in treatment for five days when Brotman informed me that I would have to pay for her treatment up front, or she would be dismissed. There went another five grand, but since the insurance company refunded the balance of the years' premium, almost four thousand dollars, it was nearly a wash; we just didn't have health insurance anymore.

During the second week I was asked to attend a group healing session. The presence of family members or friends was meant to show support for those in the program fighting their addiction. I, along with about twenty other people, including patients and their supporters and a female therapist in her forties, gathered in a large circle: parents next to children, husbands next to wives, lovers next to lovers, me next to Judy.

Each patient in the circle was asked to give an opinion of the person who had come to support him or her and vice versa. I was taken aback when Judy claimed I didn't do much to support her. I had a hard time believing what she was saying, but could only manage a mild rebuke when I was asked by the therapist to respond. All the patients had someone supporting them except for a guy in his fifties who was confined to a wheelchair. He claimed to be a poet and was in fact, quite nimble with words. He instantly jumped to Judy's defense and called on the floridity of his words to describe me as an uncaring piece of shit. How he came to this conclusion based on the four or five sentences that I had uttered was beyond me. His handicap shielded him against counter-attack, so I just took it. I could feel the disdain from the others in the room. Judy said nothing in my defense.

Inside I was angry. Some might argue that we were both psychotic, her with her drugs and me with sex. What else could be expected when a porno king and a stripper unite? I recalled how my mother advised my sisters about men: "treat them like old shoes." Was this what it was all about? Strippers tease men just to get their money. Women get pregnant as a way of trapping a man into becoming a support mechanism for her and the child. That might have been the reality, but as crazy as it was, there was enough in my life that I enjoyed. Dealing with adversity was in many ways entertaining. It kept the juices flowing. Thank god we didn't have children, so the money wasn't really a problem. To some it may seem cold, but it had been a long time since I needed or expected any emotional rapport with her. Marriage had become a business relationship in America, and this was about keeping the company going by helping out my partner. She owned half the stock. Like dealing with Osco, it was just another storm to weather.

When it came time to check into Cry Help, there were no beds available but Soccoro, a rehab located in the heart of the Latino community in south L. A, had space available so I delivered her to their care on a Saturday afternoon, one day after her release from Brotman. We arrived there on a Saturday morning. A woman sitting at a desk in its dark foyer was friendly, but stern. Judy was only allowed to bring in a few clothes and a toothbrush. It was a voluntary prison and inmates were there because they recognized they needed stern help. Again no visitors and no calls, in or out.

Sebastian's joy in seeing me when I came home erased all vestiges of the dark mood I was in. He had been waiting on the porch off my bedroom that looked out onto Market Street and as soon as he caught sight of me parking my car, began to bark excitedly. As I entered the house, he was practically stumbling over his short legs as he raced down the stairs to get a hug. After he calmed down, I gave him his dinner and then tied his collar to a twenty-foot retractable leash so I could take him for a long walk around the canals. It was his wont to stop and smell something about every ten feet, making the nightly walk an hour-long routine. It was a joy to both of us.

100

IT'S A BIG FART

Flesh Gordon II would soon be making big bucks; so why worry. The money drain caused by Judy's situation was only temporary. When a bed opened in Cry Help, Judy transferred there from Soroco and I was able to give my full attention to *'Flesh Gordon Meets the Cosmic Cheerleaders.'* A few days later, I was on the road driving to Vancouver with Sebastian, where I would live until shooting was completed. After Canadian kick boxing champ Vince Murdocco and Robyn Kelly, two novice actors, were cast in the main roles, it looked like we were off to a good start. Our production designer, Al Benjamin, had energy similar to Mike Minor's. However, though I swore not to make the same mistakes that plagued the original Flesh Gordon, it proved easier said than done. Going topless suddenly made the strippers we hired to be the cheerleaders reluctant and one of them turned out to he a heroine user and was ready to fall asleep on the set by noon. Cocaine and alcohol also caused problems—a six-pack is considered light drinking in Canada. By the time we finished live shooting, Maurice was tearing his hair out, which I could only assume was about money because he refused to share the details with me, saying I didn't need that distraction. Despite all the problems, the live action looked great but unfortunately the effects team we had hired in Portland was a total disaster. Production had to be shut down until a new crew could be found.

Because Michelle Stevens had failed to show up at one of Judy's court dates, charges against her were dismissed and she was now back living in my room at the Venice house, along with another little dog that she had rescued from a homeless family who was camped at the base of the courthouse steps as she came out. Chris Wilson had been living in my room after his wife kicked him out of his house, and his son gave the little female dog the name of Rudy, but after a wrestling match on the floor with Anna—they were equally headstrong—he was back with his wife and family. It meant that we would soon be selling the house, which since real estate prices had risen dramatically, wasn't a bad thing.

Anna had just returned from a week in Hawaii where Henry had given 200 dollars to her and his other girls, along with wife and family, as a Christmas present, so she was in a happy mood when I arrived back home. Judy was happy to have her ordeal over, and was attending at least one AA meeting every day, spending the rest of her time roller skating and walking her dogs. Naturally there was a bevy of cute girls dropping by to say hello. She loved treating people to food and other than Anna's gross habit of digging the best strawberries out of the cream pie she brought home, the two of them got along famously.

What was it with special effects people? Much like what happened with the first 'Flesh Gordon', the team we had hired in Portland tried to extort ten grand from us or they wouldn't return the props they were holding. They changed their minds after Joe Garafalo, our Brooklyn born executive producer, threatened his best mafia intonation, to break their arms and burn down their house. I liked his style. This was not where any of us expected to be when the production began. After several fruitless weeks searching for a new effects crew, Garafalo found one in Detroit. Several of its members had worked with local filmmaker, Sam Rami, when he was making 'Evil Dead' and they were more than competent.

To direct our new crew, I soon found myself living in Lavonia, just south of Detroit. We were making good headway when another problem surfaced. Claiming Maurice had failed to send them their paychecks on time, they stopped work and my idle time was spent watching them do a food commercial—lots of spray to make things look tasty. Further investigation revealed that the crew's leader, Ed Wolman, had embezzled the last payments to pay personal bills. Ed, a devout Christian, acknowledged that he had sinned and made amends. Always something! Work continued and the effects began to be completed every bit as professionally as I could have hoped for.

I began shuttling between Detroit and LA so I could supervise both the effects work and editing that was being done simultaneously in LA by Joe Tornotore who Maurice had hired since he was skilled at video editing. Joe was a thick-necked Italian who could have worked as an enforcer for the mafia and was set on his ways about editing. Suggesting cuts to him was a waste of time, but Maurice wanted him on the job and he paid the bills.

Paying the bills didn't seem to be a problem until Maurice and Joe Garafalo came by the Venice house during one of my trips back from Detroit to have a meeting with me. It was put bluntly that we were out of money and unless I put a hundred grand into the project, it would have to be shut down. I wasn't sure what to say. Joe said he could get me a loan on my Malibu house at twelve and a half percent, the current rate at the time. Maurice started to get pissed as I pondered for a moment, saying he had mortgaged his house for much more. Joe had raised some of the money from people who wouldn't accept not getting repaid lightly—I assumed mafia. I had no way of knowing if anything that was being said was true. As usual, I had not insisted in seeing the books.

Joe Tornotore, not meaning to be complementary had said; "This is the kind of piece of shit that will make a lot of money." I owned twenty-five percent of the film. Did it make sense to not finish it? "No!" The Venice house was already in escrow and was going to make me a nice profit. I had invested almost two years of my time in 'Flesh Gordon Meets the Cosmic Cheerleaders' and didn't want it to be for nothing; so after conferring with Judy, who was more skeptical than me, I took out a loan on the house and handed Maurice a check for a hundred grand. There was no doubt in my mind that if not spectacular, the profits would be substantial.

We were under the gun to get the film finished so a print could be sent to France, where the distributor had paid a substantial advance for its rights, and had already booked a theatre in Paris for its world premier. I was now shuttling

between LA, Detroit and Toronto where the music, sound and lab work was being done. Because of problems with the music, the producer Maurice had hired was a complete incompetent, a print was shipped to France with nary a day to spare. When he reported that the results were terrible and he was going to lose money, I was sure it had to be an anomaly Why he chose to open the film in August, a time when the city is scorching hot and practically empty, made no sense.

For a moment, that seemed to be the case. Maurice announced that Universal, who had distributed one of his 'Screwball' movies, was interested in distributing 'Flesh Gordon Meets the Cosmic Cheerleaders.' That good news quickly fell to the wayside when one of their top executives nixed the idea with the pithy comment: "associating an upstanding company like Universal with a *'Flesh Gordon,'* is ridiculous."

Playboy liked the film but with a caveat: "Where's the sex?" So it came as a complete surprise when the MPAA refused to give us an R-rating. Countless decisions to tone down the content of the film had been made for the sole purpose of making them happy. When asked for specifics, they would only say it was because the general theme of the film was sexual. There was not a single scene in the film that was meant to arouse. All the sex was slapstick parody meant to encourage people to question their obsessions, anxieties and fears. It was on a par with Woody Allen's 'Everything you wanted to know about Sex but were Afraid to Ask.' Their reasoning was hard to comprehend. I had a deep suspicion that it was Jack Valenti's way of paying me back for having mocked his organization fifteen years earlier when we printed their review in Gallery magazine. After many cuts, including the lactating mammary mountain, we were finally granted an R-rating on the third submission.

Even so, we still felt we had a winner. Joe Bob Briggs, the iconic drive-in-movie critic, loved the film: "I wouldn't have believed the sequel could be as good as the original, but *'Flesh Gordon Meets the Cosmic Cheerleaders'* delivers everything the original had and more." As expected there were reviews that were not so glowing; "What kind of girl could possibly think that being in a picture like this would advance her career" or "the effects could have been produced with articles out of the top drawer of your desk," to quote a few.

Comments like those seemed to be more hateful than critical. I saw signs that the feminist movement, which I supported, was becoming so politically correct that they were unable to recognize humor that supported their cause. The jokes about large breasts were meant to be critical of silicon augmentation. Babyland and the Mammary Mountains was meant to be a commentary about men's neurotic infatuation with breasts; a fixation that probably goes back to being taken off the nipple too early. The modern woman no longer needed to think of herself as just a baby-making machine, but evidently as a director and writer, I had been unable to communicate that.

While we continued to look for a national distributor, we arranged to have our U. S. premier at the NuArt Theatre in West Los Angeles, known for showing avant-garde and controversial films. John Walters 's 'Devine,' in which Devine literally eats a dog turd, played the midnight show at the NuArt for years as did The Rocky Horror Picture Show. It was the perfect venue for our U. S. premier and they were delighted to have us.

But there were still more surprises to come. The LA Times went out of its way to suppress the film. We were told that they would not accept any ad for 'Flesh Gordon Meets the Cosmic Cheerleaders' that had a visual. They didn't stop there. They also would not allow us to use the word "Flesh" in the title. We could only advertise the film, as "Gordon" and that would be limited to the listing section of the entertainment page where the names of films are printed in tiny nine or ten point fonts. Our premier would be announced in a one-column quarter inch space that read under the theatre's name: "Gordon." In other words it was invisible. They called this the "free press?"

The "World Premier" at the NuArt was, as to be expected, a disaster. It didn't even get close to selling out. I had always been a big fan of the LA Times and thought of it as a liberal paper, but its recent decision to censor certain words had gone over the top. They had gone "politically correct" on steroids. To assuage their guilt, they gave me an opportunity to express my unhappiness in a column that appeared once a week in their entertainment section called 'Talk Back.' It was their way of trying to appear fair and balanced. Even that came with censorship. My letter was critical of its publisher, Otis Chandler, because he was the one who had the final say in what tone the paper would take. But before my letter was printed, I received a call from an editor who tried to convince me that I was wrong in holding Chandler responsible. I sensed that if I didn't pull his name, my letter wouldn't be published, so I took it out. Venting my frustration was cathartic, but was just crying over spilt milk. The damage had been done.

Reactions to the film were mixed. Those looking for hot sex were disappointed and the scatological humor, which would be a staple ten years later in the 'Beavis and Butthead' and 'South Park' movies, had yet to find an audience. A commentary to a review posted on BadMovies. com that ran on the Internet in 2006 said it best or at least made me feel better:

> *Flesh Gordon II was a great flick, Farrelly brothers were also big fans of this oddity and this film holds the first "Sperm" joke on screen long before There's Something About Mary. Why does everyone seem to think there'd be real sex in it? Granted, the*

cheerleaders are the homeliest chicks you'd ever want to see on screen, but the movie is a blast with so many fun scenes that you will NEVER see anywhere else. It's way ahead of its time. Lighten up people. It's one of the most original movies you'll ever watch

Roger Corman's, New Horizons, took on the distribution of the film but did little to promote it. Because of a dispute they had with Maurice over money they claimed he owed them, their box office reports didn't ring true. Equally disappointing, was when Morgan Fox, a. k.a 'Robunda Hooters' became Playboy's centerfold of the month in December 1990; she neglected to say that she had a starring role in the movie. It was time to face the facts. 'Flesh Gordon Meets the Cosmic Cheerleaders' was a bomb. I was left with a near empty bank account and a big mortgage on my house. Fortunately I still had my theatre and a second house free and clear. It was nothing that I couldn't deal with.

101

MY LIFE HAD BEEN A HOT TAMALE

Judy was crazy as ever, just sober. While I had been away in Detroit, she had moved back into the Malibu house which McRaney was happy to get out of the lease. Not only had she begun renting the house out for porn shoots again, but due to the ongoing discovery that older women are erotically attractive, got herself booked as a performer in a few videos, including one called 'Older and Anal' as well as shooting a layout for 'Over 40' magazine. I had no idea if the gigs were just for the money or, since we never had anal sex, a desire she had but failed to mention. I reminded myself that I was ten years older than her and that she was dealing with the autumn of her sexual days while I was entering my winter. As to be expected, Judy split after she took her half of the location fee Being a porn performer had become totally acceptable, both with females and males. It was no longer anything to be ashamed of. It was a job that paid good money. The girls enjoyed flaunting themselves and some were happy to give me a little thrill by teasing me. As I reclined in my sunken living room couch, Christie Canyon, completely naked, stood above me with her legs wide and asked in pretended innocence:

"What part of my body do you like best?" "I like your big pussy!"

"Yes, it is big, isn't it?" she proudly admitted.

The boldness of the girls didn't mean that they weren't sensitive to the fine line between flirting and harrasment. After watching a little tease named Madison suck on Tom Byron's cock all morning, I gave her butt a little squeeze when she walked by me after the scene was finished. She was wearing tight white hot pants and I couldn't resist. "What the fuck do you think you're doing?" was all I got for my effort. An hour later, she and one of the other models were outside on the lawn with their butts up to the sun so their pussies could be tanned. Chris Wilson had dropped by and we stood behind them admiring the view. Madison turned and said, "We like it when you look." The fine line between harrassment and flirting was not easily understood. Just because a woman needed to be desired and admired, didn't mean she wanted to be attacked. Males had a hard time understanding that.

Guys who could keep it up could make a solid living. They were no longer just props. Buck Adams, Peter North, Tom Byron, Randy West and Marc Wallace had no trouble doing multiple scenes a day. Peter North's ejaculations shot over a foot into the air.

Naturally the performers, both male and female, enjoyed themselves, but they also treated it as a job. After one of the shoots, I joined Marc Wallace, Tom Byron and Ginger Lynn for dinner at Alice's restaurant by the Malibu pier and listened as they argued about who had the harder job on a porn shoot. Ginger claimed having to suck on guy's cocks all day to get them stiff was hard work but Marc shot back "Yeah, but we gotta fuck you."

If a girl wanted a career in porn, she was now expected to do anal. Some, like Oriental porn sensation, Mimi Myagi, had no qualms and readily stuck her butt up to welcome a stiff cock into her anus.

But others only did it only for the money. I was watching a lovely girl having sex on my living room couch when it came time for her to do anal. She requested that only essential eyes be allowed. Doing anal embarrassed her. On another occasion, an Italian girl, brought over to the States to shoot several movies, protested when the director told her she would have to take it up her ass. "I wasn't told I would have to do that," she protested. I was standing nearby when I heard the director tell Marc Wallace, who would be working with her, that when she had her legs behind her head to; "Just stick it in her ass." "But she doesn't want it," Marc mildly protested. "Do it anyway," he was told. She got fucked in the ass!

I personally found anal much less satisfying than regular sex, so I never asked for it. If I accidentally seemed to be trying to put my cock into a girl's ass, a rejection would quickly follow. A finger was tolerated from time to time, but only for a short period before my hand was grabbed and the finger pulled out. Sometimes a "what the fuck do you think you're doing" look would be included. I had to believe that making a girl submit to pain had become a way of establishing domination; a symbolic way of males attempting to reinstate their traditional role of dominance in the face of the feminist revolution. Conversely, agreeing to anal sex was a way for a woman to signify that she was happy to accept the traditional role of being the submissive. I couldn't deny that scenes in my films had helped bring about this change and like many males, I found enjoyment in watching girls get fucked in the ass.

102

FIRE

As is the case for many American men, I replaced sex with golf. Hitting the sweet spot is truly orgasmic. To keep my mind active and celebrate my new raison d'etre, I began working on a coffee table book that was inspired by a Sunday 'Wizard of Id' that Judy had taped to the refrigerator door, her way of showing that she acknowledged that we shared the house. It inspired me to spend a few years of research at the UCLA micro film library, looking for comic strips that made fun or commented on golf. The result was a voluminous collection that ran from the Yellow Kid in 1897 to Dick Tracy and Peanuts today. I was busy weaning out the ones I wanted to include in the book I was assembling and left the house to take a lunch break in the Malibu center. It was early November of 1993, and a hot Santa Ana wind was blowing when I left Coogies, the Malibu restaurant that caters to the locals, to head back home.

I noticed a plume of dark smoke in the distance above the nearby mountains as I walked to my car. Santa Anas strike fear across Southern California, especially for those who live in the mountains. A downed power line, tossed cigarette or match from a psychotic arsonist can start a fire that can lead to a conflagration within an hour. My home sat in a canyon that hadn't seen a fire for over twenty years and was pregnant with plenty of fuel. A pungent odor had already drifted over the area and though not overly concerned that my house was in danger, I raced home to clear any branches that might be closer to the structure than was prudent. Reports on the radio were saying that the fire had begun several miles away in the foothills near Calabasas. If it made it to the top of the mountain and down the canyons into Malibu, my house could be in trouble. Fire-fighting helicopters were already in the air carrying water from the sea to the hot spots on the valley side of the mountain.

The wind was growing stronger by the minute and when I got home I began to work feverishly to clear any branches that hung too near my house. But then, flames that looked like little red-capped devils, began peeking over the top of the ridge. In a bit of a panic, I dragged a hose up a ladder and onto the roof so I could wet everything down. But the hot dry wind was so strong that the water evaporated as soon as it hit the surface. For all the good it was doing, I might just as well have been taking a piss.

The fire department had a good record of saving structures and my neighbor's tennis court, which abutted the back of my house, would serve as a firebreak. I was confident that my house was not in danger, but just in case the unthinkable happened, I began loading my car with my computer and non-replaceable items like George Barr's original 'Flesh Gordon' artwork and the boxes of comic strips that I had collected for my book, When Judy showed up, she began loading her car with our family photo albums and for some inexplicable reason

pillows. Most importantly, she got all five of our dogs: Rudy, Sebastian, One-eyed Popeye, Blind Canella and Kenja as well as one of our two Tabbies, and crammed them into her car. The flames were too close to search for the missing Tabby so hopefully he would be able to fend for himself if the fire hit the house. All the animals understood the situation and behaved flawlessly.

Orders to evacuate could be heard from police cars driving up Las Flores Canyon Road. I knew they could be ignored, but having heard stories about people, who thought they could survive by jumping into a swimming pool and then breath through a snorkel, had not been aware that the air heated to a thousand degrees would scorch their lungs.

After placing as many items as I could on the stone patio around the swimming pool, I carried the boxes containing the negative of Flesh Gordon and placed them on a strip of lawn behind the pool equipment pit. It should have been in a vault, but to save the six hundred dollar yearly rental fee, I kept it at home.

Judy's car was already packed to the hilt and I told her to leave with the dogs. I would meet her in front of her friend's house at the bottom of Las Flores and we could join up there to head into Santa Monica, where hopefully we could find lodging over night. Fire trucks had momentarily pulled up to the bottom of our driveway but had left to go to more critical locations. After one last attempt to find the missing cat, I headed down the hill, leaving the fate of the house in the hands of the professionals. They had the proper attire and equipment and knew what they were doing; taking refuge in the house as the flames blew across and running outside as soon as it passed so they could hose down any hot spots. There was no point for me to stay around.

Like swarms of fireflies, wind blown embers blew across my windshield as I backed down my driveway. Everyone had vacated except my Swedish neighbor's son, a big rugged kid who had opted to stay to help fight the fire. I thought he was nuts. Flames from a neighbor's burning Avocado tree orchard, leapt over my car as I started to descend down the hill. I was making my escape just in time. When I got to the bottom of Las Flores Canyon, a chaotic situation was already beginning to develop. Because of the bumper-to-bumper situation on Pacific Coast Highway, cars were backing up on Las Flores Canyon Road. "Damn!" Judy and the dogs weren't in her car when I spotted it parked on the side of the road across from her friend's house. "Where the fuck was she?" I got out and frantically ran to the back of the house. Stupidly, she had taken the dogs out so they could run in the backyard. I angrily told her to get her and the animal's asses back into her car so we could get the fuck out of Malibu!

My sense of urgency was justified. We managed to get to Santa Monica and find a room at the Holiday Inn before they were booked up. To that company's credit, they gave us a cut-rate fee and made no objection to us bringing all our pets into the room. From the room's balcony, we could see that the flames in the distance had worked all the way down the canyon and were now headed north to the center of Malibu. The entire hillside abutting the Pacific Coast Highway was on fire.

The next morning, television was reporting that the ferocious wind had blown flames across the Pacific Coast Highway and out over the ocean, where they were pushed back by the cold ocean air and set several beach houses on fire. It was also reported that Las Flores Canyon Road had become so gridlocked, that a lot of cars were unable to exit onto the Pacific Coast Highway and had burned. It could have been us.

For three days the winds continued to howl. No one was allowed into the area. An army of firefighters had gathered in Malibu, some coming from as far away as Idaho, Montana, Utah and Arizona. Water scoopers from Canada skimmed the surface of the Pacific Ocean and made drops on hot spots. A steady line of helicopters picked up water out of the little lake at Pepperdine University to make drops on the flames. Only after hundreds or maybe thousands of drops did the flames begin to be squelched.

But my stomach sank when I got a chance to go back. My home was gone. What was once 'the house that smut built' was now just ash. The fire had come through like a blowtorch, destroying what was in its path and leaving unharmed what wasn't. The two neighbors who had been complaining about porn movies being shot at our house, had survived. A pine tree had been burned vertically, black on one side and green on the other. A fire safe capable of standing seven hundred degree heat, which I had placed on the stone patio thirty feet from the house, was now a puddle of metal. Even water laden ice plant had burned. All the props from Flesh Gordon: the Flying Phallus, the Penisauraus and miniature ships from Flesh II, were gone. The hand made twenty foot long cabinet and book shelf that I had built out of thick ash planks and made hand crafted drawers out of walnut wood was gone. Judy's favorite burl wood armoire and a round coffee table with an acid etched picture of greek gods was history Even the small onyx statue of an Incan woman giving a blowjob, was gone.

There was one piece of good news. Other than a few burn spots from embers that had fallen on top of the boxes containing the 'Flesh Gordon' negative, there was no damage. 'Flesh Gordon' had survived! The wind blowing across the well that housed the pool equipment had caused the flames to leap over the boxes that were sitting on the grass and had not touched down until they were ten feet beyond. Beyond that, all the way down the canyon to the sea, everything was reduced to black ash. It felt like I had arrived somewhere in the Universe on a lifeless dead planet. I was not about to let the tragedy destroy me. Because I had taken my computer with me when I left the house on the day of the fire, I was able to use the time while we were domiciled in motels, aided by funds from FEMA and the Red Cross, to compile a list of every item I could possible think of that had been destroyed. The insurance company had no room to argue against granting me my full claim. Frank Nobato's brother in law was a contractor who had fallen on desperate times because of a bankruptcy and offered to guide me through the contracting process in return for letting him do the concrete work on the foundation. It was a good deal for both of us.

Because we had five dogs, I decided to buy a used mobile home and set it up on our burned out lot. Judy and I couldn't coexist sleeping in the same bed, so I had to shop until I found a sixty-five feet long one that fit the bill. As soon as damage to the roads was repaired, I had it towed up and placed on our property. A day later, the Tabby cat that I had been unable to coral, showed up. Though a bit dirty and feral, he had found a place to hide during the fire and quickly bonded with his former mate. Though now living in soot and dirty air, our family was still in tact.

My biggest challenge was to keep Judy's hands off of the rebuilding money; somehow she thought it was half hers to use as she liked. She was getting sober but still crazy; probably always would be. She actually got hold of the first check for fifty grand and tried to forge my signature so she could cash it, but the bank refused unless I was present. Nevertheless, putting that aside, she proved to be a good rummager and by using all available government assistance and a generous local Jewish charity, we were able to restock our basic needs for toiletries, furniture, dishes, appliances and clothes.

I was actually relieved that she found a young Mexican named Fernando to fill her feminine need for adulation while I rebuilt the house. Like most women, she was happy to trade blow jobs for flattery and all I needed was to be left alone so I could finish the house and my golf book which I worked on in my bedroom that I transformed each day into an office after I woke up. By late 1996, the "house that smut built," stood proud once again. Somehow tragedies seemed to do well for me. It was now a tile roofed Spanish style home that would withstand wild fires much better than the previous all-wood home could. After a year, nature was well on the way to restoring all its bounty to its former glory. Seeds that had lied dormant began to sprout new trees and trees that had remained stilted for years suddenly doubled in height.

Because of Coulson's help which allowed me to do the contracting myself, I was saving tens of thousands of dollars by negotiating my own deals with the sub contractors and suppliers and tens of thousands more by doing a lot of the work, like painting and hanging cabinets, myself. Jeff Spence showed up out of the blue and agreed to do all the finish work in return for feeding him and letting him park his van on my lot.

The savings had allowed me to pay off all the debt I had incurred from the 'Cosmic Cheerleader' fiasco and have a better house as well. The ceilings of the new house were all high and paneled with cedar. Windows everywhere made the rooms light and airy. The bathrooms and kitchen counters were made of granite and the young designer who drew up the plans provided us with an additional thousand feet of living space without adding more foundations. It allowed for both Judy and I to have our own TV rooms. I liked sports and she liked music and award shows. An office above the garage with hardwood floors and an arched window that looked down the driveway, gave me plenty of space to do my work. My living room sized bedroom had a large arched window that looked out to Catalina. Judy happily moved into the guest house with all her dogs and cats.

We booked a few porn shoots, but the two antagonistic neighbors began making complaints and along with the damage the crews caused to the new house, it was no longer worth the hassle. I was becoming less and less enthralled with watching the girls perform and scream faux orgasms and the money the producers were willing to pay for locations had dropped substantially. Both Judy and I agreed it was time to discontinue renting the house out.

Judy forced me to replace my credit card twenty times, but it wasn't something I couldn't handle; more of a cat and mouse game than anything else. I still found a lot to like about her. She never complained about my large girly book collection or complained that I privately masturbated at least once, and usually more, each day. And she didn't hold grudges. Even if during an argument, I called her the vilest names that popped into my mind like: "you dirty anal whore," it was forgotten an hour later and she was baking cookies later in the day. She wasn't bitchy and was always friendly to guests. Since we didn't have kids, our seven dogs were our family and absorbing the little body blows she threw my way were not enough for me to want to break it up. Many wondered in amazement how we continued to stay together. But they didn't know our history. She had allowed me the freedom to become who I was and without her there would not have been a Flesh Gordon. I owed her something for that. Seventy year old Michael Green, my English distributor who spoke with the wisdom of age, told me; if you've stayed together this long, you'll stay together till the end."

The golf book was eventually published by General Publishing Group and sold over thirty thousand copies around the country. The 'Augusta Constitution,' the local newspaper in Georgia where the Master's is played, devoted two full pages to give it a stellar review. However, General Publishing

Group went bankrupt before paying me my royalties and the book was a financial flop.

Money was becoming tight when an unexpected call from a guy in Fort Wayne was about to change my fortunes. Steve Newmark wanted to know if the video rights to 'Flesh Gordon' were available. I had totally misjudged the video market when it was first launched and had sold the rights for practically nothing. That distributor had long disappeared from the market and many people had told me that they had seen pirated copies of 'Flesh Gordon' in video stores. I didn't know what to do about it and didn't have the motivation even if I did. Having to deal with lawyers was anathema to me. As I listened to Steve give me his pitch I thought he had to be a quixotic dreamer, but still, if he was willing to run with it, why not.

He began by clearing up the various piracy issues with threatening letters and from there, his company, Hen's Tooth Video, which operated out of a small office in a Fort Wayne shopping mall, would manage over the years, to sell almost a million video and CD copies of 'Flesh Gordon' that continues up to this day. He also negotiated a deal with DirecTV where it proved to be a big winner. Flesh Gordon was back in the market. Twenty five years after its release it was still making ten grand a year

103

A BODY OF WORK TO BE PROUD OF

Along with age, came health problems which I don't need to dwell on because it's a rare bird who doesn't have more than they willing admit to. I didn't seek fame or fortune, but was happy to achieve a bit of each without being overburdened. I recognized that many people, including: my wife, Bill Osco, Mike Benveniste, Walter Cichy, Peter Loche, Maurice Smith and the entire 'Flesh Gordon' crew, contributed greatly to my financial success, but I also recognized that I was the driving force behind each film and the thread that that kept every project intact from beginning to end. I was the little kid who wouldn't stop what he was doing even if it meant shitting in his pants. I was a grinder. But I was slow to realize that the underpining of almost everything I did was to free myself from the chains of shame that were wrapped around me. The movies were a biproduct of that effort.

When I told Steve Newmark that I was still reluctant to admit that I had made 'Flesh Gordon,' he assured me that I shouldn't be because it was truly a cult classic. He was right. There were countless times when people enthusiastically told me it was one of their favorite films. Even strangers I met while golfing would exclaim: "You made Flesh Gordon, that's one of my favorite films!" Everyone remembered the 'Penisauraus!'

My false modesty was pointless. The Nuart theatre in west Los Angeles, a Mecca for revival cinema, posted a list of the hundred most popular films during the 80's; a period they referred to as the Repertory years. 'Flesh Gordon' was listed as number 13; ahead of such classics as *'China Town'* and the Beatle's *'Day for Night.'* How often does a low budget 16mm film get written up in a major paper twenty years after its release? But on March 22, 1996, Donald Liebenson wrote a lengthy story for The Chicago Tribune called "Flesh Gordon still offers a zany world". During a Jay Leno interview with actor Craig T. Nelson on the Tonight Show in 2004, Jay teased Craig by saying that his staff had found some footage of a porn film that Nelson had worked on years ago. When he ran a clip of Nelson doing the risqué voice-over for the Satyr monster, Craig broke up laughing and said: "When a producer (Bill Osco) driving a Rolls Royce offers you a part in a movie, you don't ask questions, you just get in the car and go!"

But the significance of 'Mona' would only begin to sink in after I met Bill Landis, a New York writer working for the Village Voice. He had called me in late 1999, to ask if I would be willing to do an interview for a book he was working on. His previous book, *'Anger,'* about pioneer low-budget filmmaker Kenneth Anger, had recently been published and he was now working on a similar book about the people who pioneered the porn industry. When he told me he had already interviewed Osco, I was slightly perturbed that Bill still seemed to get first credit for our films; but I got a little taste of schadenfreude when he told me that the interview was conducted over a pay phone at the California Men's Colony in San Luis Obispo. Bill was serving three years for again failing to pay his taxes. Stupid ass!

Osco had told him not to waste his time talking to me, that I was constantly zoned out on drugs, but after he realized that was a lie and found me to be amicable and coherent, we hit it off. At his request, I drove to San Francisco to join him and his wife, Michelle Clifford, also a writer, to be his guest at the Yeurba Buena Center for the Arts in San Francisco where he was giving a seminar on *"Sleazoid Cinema."* During a whirlwind tour of San Francisco I had given them the afternoon before the seminar, Bill showed off his ability to identify what kind of drug each hippy was hooked on as we drove through the Haight Ashbury district: "that one's on pot, that one's on meth, that a heroine junky, that one had a recent acid trip, that's a pill freak." That evening, as we were walking to the center he said: "You know, a lot of people consider *'Mona'* to be your best film." I had been told this once before by historian Sam Stetson, but never took it seriously and didn't now.

That evening, after watching two hours of Sleazoid classics, like the sadistic *'Fight for Your Life'* and the chilling, *'Henry, Diary of a Serial Murder,'*

I was feeling as though I was embodied in the terrifying Edvard Munch painting, *'The Scream.'* The black and white films were all cheaply made, but were as psychotically fascinating as any work by Kafka. When Bill broke for the intermission, he asked me to stand up and then introduced me as the producer and co-director of *'Mona.'* Most in attendance were academics and serious film buffs. I expected only a few stares and a smattering of applause, so was surprised when I was given a standing ovation. It made me think.

Richard Corliss, a respected author and staff writer for Time Magazine, wrote an article in 2005 titled, *"When Porn was Chic."* He listed the five most important porn movies of all time. 'Mona' was listed number one. He cogently stated why:

"Whether it was considered a real movie with explicit sex scenes, or a series of stag-reel exertions with a modicum of plot and characterization added, Mona created the blueprint for 70s porno chic."

The article ran the same week that Pope Benedict visited New York and drew five times more responses from readers than the pontiff's visit. It gave me a little chuckle to beat out his eminence in the polls after the battle his arrogant church had subjected me to over the Father Filas matter.

But there was more. An HBO documentary that aired in 2007, *"Katie Morgan's Porn 101,"* made my head swell when Katie, an intelligent and well-endowed porn actress narrating the documentary that traced the history of pornography from its prehistoric inception to the present had this to say:

"And then a film was released that was to change the whole porn business forever. No it wasn't *Deep Throat*, but a little film called *Mona the Virgin Nymph*. Because of Mona people like me are able to make a good living making porn films."

Ironically, Katie was yet to be born when 'Mona' first played, but that it had been in the vanguard of freeing her from the chains that would have prevented her from enjoying and exploiting her own body as she pleased, made me very proud. Her statement was the last little push I needed to expel the demon that had remained in my head telling me that sex was evil. I no longer had shame and neither did much of America.

Bill Landis died in 2008 from a heart attack. Only forty-nine, his death was probably made premature by his longtime use of drugs, something I repeatedly advised him to give up. Then a few months later, Jeff Rosen, the projectionist at the New Beverly Cinema, called to tell me that Sherman

Torgan had unexpectedly died from a heart attack while riding his bike on the Venice bike path. He was not yet sixty and seemed to be in good health. I was one of the few who knew how much he enjoyed sexual fantasy. His wife was shocked when she found a stash of girlie books under their bed. With Sherman out of the picture there was no reason to keep the theatre and I sold it to QuentinTarantino, a rabid fan of classic, cult and Grindhouse films who promised to continue it as the venue that Sherman had created for the Hollywood cinema affectionados. The money from the sale assured that Judy and I would be financially sound for the rest of our days.

104

THE ALBATROSS FLIES AWAY

Sexual freedom and pornography has benefited the mental health of countless people, both male and female. The days of having to get drunk or turn off the lights to enjoy sex are over. Women find the male penis exciting, not revolting. Nakedness is no longer shameful and eyes do not have to be closed and noses pinched at the sight of an anus. Blowjobs are no longer considered to be perverted—the best techniques can be learned by watching almost any porn film. Men are discovering that sucking on a pussy is not unmanly: learn how to do it right and the girls will love you.

We now know that our sexual orientations are determined by genes and porn films have shown that both sexes often enjoy participating in homosexual and bisexual acts. It is not rare. Porn films show that sexual arousal can be fickle, there is no need for either sex to be embarrassed. Thanks to porn, most people no longer have fear of seeing or participating in interracial sex, it is extremely exciting.

Society requiring us to cover our bodies is actually a blessing. It opens the door to fantasies about what is being hidden beneath. Thanks to porn; admitting to our various fetishes, many of them bizaare, is becoming less and less shameful "Betty Page," the 60's Fetish queen, is now heralded as a cultural icon and coffee table books of her photographs can be purchased in up-scale bookstores on Rodeo Drive. Many "normal" couples practice light spanking and bondage as part of their sex routine. One only has to look at the mega hit book and movie, "Fifty Shades of Gray" to see that this is true.

Recently, a young Malibu couple told me they enjoy using various sized egg plants as both vaginal and anal dildos.

Teasing is an important part of human's sexual dance. Females cover their sexual charms with skimpy material to draw attention and men are beginning to realize that women like to be teased as well. A physicall fit man wearing a little g-string drives women crazy. Male strip shows like the 'Dancing Bear' pack the girls in, many of them more than willing to take a cock in their mouth.

Trashy panties and bras are now sold in high-end boutiques. Victoria Secrets is a listed company on the stock exchange. Females are the roses on the bush, their beauty meant by nature to attract the male. Designers keep coming up with new and exciting ways to draw attention to the vagina, from cloth materials that pull into the crevice or just a string of pearls that somehow covers the slit. The advent of shaving pubic hair makes both female and male genitals more attractive and cleaner. Women who pierce their labia or clitorises show that they are cognizant of how attractive their vaginas are. The modern woman is discovering that the idea of private parts needs to go to the wayside.

Calling a woman who likes sex a slut while at the same time praising a man who seduces many women a stud is hypocritical. Neither men nor women can really understand the other's sexual needs or the pleasure derived; we are just different. Men's penis's are like heat seeking missiles filled with sperm bullets that yearn to be fired; women's pussies are passageways to the womb, which, like a candy store is full of tasty treats that wait to be fertilized.

Because the female understands that she can become burdened by a child makes her more discerning that the sperm donner will help support it if it comes. The male, on the other hand, can be so overwhelmed by the need to ejaculate that he is often unable to recognize the responsibility that could lie ahead. Abortion need not be a trauma. Religion tries to equate it with killing, but seems to turn a blind eye if a child is brought into a home that doesn't want it. Prisons are full of people who were raised without love.

But who would want to live in a world where this dance between the sexes doesn't exist. Sadly there are many. They are the ones who tied my sexual feelings into a knot. The emotions that sex elicits: joy, anger, jealousy, happiness, depression and on and on, are innumerable. Almost every, if not all, dramas, comedies and tragedies have an underlieing sexual element to them. Sexual attraction gives women a lot of power and men, endowed with big bones and large muscles struggle not to resent this. A sexy woman can turn a powerful man into a cooing idiot in a matter of minutes. Sane men, willing to control their urges without resorting to violence, are delighted to deal with this imposition, But those who use religious myths to teach that women are inferior and should be treated as possessions, deny the human race a huge resource. While these frightened men whorship imaginary spirits in the nether land, they auger their own superiority by forcing women to dull their appeal by wearing black dresses or burkas. How cowardly!

Even more twisted is how some religions can convince both male and female that their bodies are dirty and should not be touched. One of my wife's friends married to an Orthodox jew, told her that when they have sex a sheet has to be placed between them so their bodies won't touch. A little hole is cut out so the penis can get to the vagina and inject a shot of sperm. Christian women have for centuries been relegated to second level status, some even brought up in communes and forced to have sex and children for its leader.

Pornography is not evil—religion is. Sane men and women accept that in the battle of the sexes, there need not be a winner. They enjoy the delightful game for what it is, some pleasure, some disappointment. As Maurice Chevalier sang in the musical "Gigi," "Thank heaven for little girls . . . for without them, what would little boys do."

Pornography also serves another purpose, no less important. Nature intends that sex produce children, but nature had also arranged for diseases and wars to keep our population in harmony with the ability of the planet's resources to provide for it. We are a very clever little monkey, but not as smart as we like to think. The world is becoming so overpopulated, that we are now threatening the very ability of our planet to support life. Nature will eventually get the upper hand—one way or the other. Clear thinking people of both sexes are taking responsible measures to turn back the tide. In the face of religious zealotry, birth control and abortion is being championed around the world. To satisfy their maternal instincts, many women have replaced a brood of children with a dog or a cat and men, rather than fathering large family's that are beyond their means to support, have turned to spilling their seed with virtual girls on the internet. The recent explosion of 'cam girl' sex provides a safe way for the girls to make a safe living and the men to release tension without fear of disease or paying for expensive dinners.

Here I stand with Jason "Flesh Gordon" Williams who just released his new book, "I Fought The Sex Ray" and the beautiful porn star Ange Venus who is now producing and staring in her own vampire movies. We all smile because we enjoy life. How is that bad?

Like it or not, sex doesn't last forever, maybe it always remains in the mind, but surely not in the physical. I now fantasize more about the sex

I passed up than the sex I had. From five orgasms a day, I strain to get one teeny weenie one. Sex made life exciting and its loss doesn't have to leave one in a quandary. Men can golf or go fishing rather then becoming curmudgeons and women can garden or knit rather that become nags. Stimulants like Viagra are for old fools trying to pretend that they're still young. I had my fun. There is no need to be greedy. Sex was the strawberry on top of the cake but now that its been devoured time to move on.

My good fortunate was to live in the "golden age" of free love. Sexually transfrerred diseases have brought that era to an end and sex now comes with an element of danger. For the foreseeable future this unpleasant situation has become one of life's most puzzling conundrums.

All religions, in one form or the other, exploit the irrational fear of death by telling the same lie: that there is a perfect world where pain and suffering no longer exist. A sexual sop has been offered males for no other reason than to gain followers, Muslim radicals preach that seventy virgins await at the other side for male converts who agree to strap bombs to themselves to destroy infadels. No mention is made of what happens to the 'virgins' once they are deflowered. Less barbaric "western" men, who need more immediate gratificaton, only ask that they get at least one visit to the Playboy Mansion before they die so they can wallow in the bevy of surgically perfected beauties who are hired to roam Heffner's storied grounds. Are we really this nuts?. Yes!

But women have woken up and though males still somp on their fingers as they grasp at the top ledge to join in the benefits that life provides, they are proving that no man's foot is large enough to hold them back. Life has no "perfect" answers and there are no perfect relationships, but the options are simple. Live with someone and realize that tolerating each other's vicissitudes and insanities is what makes life interesting, or live by yourself and die from boredom. I always get a laugh when a "loner" stops by our house and can't stop talking. I opted for the first choice and have no regrets.

Ironically, the repression of sex allowed me to make millions of dollars and enjoy myself in the process. I was only one of the very few to be so lucky. I never had to suffer a life in a cubicle. It took a concerted effort to overcome my hang-ups and a lot of verve to do it in the face of societal forces that would have been delighted to lock me up, but all must admit that the path I chose was a unique and exciting adventure.

Judy and I are still together after forty-four years because she doesn't deny me the thrill of flirting with a sexy porn star like Ange Venus or keeping a well stocked library of porn magazines in my closet or enjoying a cam girl from time to time. The sexual part of our relationship ended years ago, but neither of us freaks out over each others harmless sexual fantasies. I always admired Hillary Clinton for doing the same with Bill.

Not many women could have handled living with a pornographer! Judy has been sober for almost twenty five years and can still put together a great party for our sober friends if we have the motivation to do so. She is now known as 'The Dog mother of Malibu' and can be seen walking her five rescue dogs around the rustic roads of Malibu. Together we have made a rather tumultuous, yet very comfortable, life for each other. Without her my life would have been very different and Flesh Gordon would never had been made.

My cradle to grave story is on the downside of the hill. If I were asked to impart one piece of wisdom it is to know that laughter can cancel all pain. A fellow I met on a golf course in New Hampshire mentioned that he had just come from visiting his ninety-two year old father who was on his deathbed. His father, still capable of a bit of sarcastic humor, took his hand and said: "Son . . . Growing feeeeble . . . isn't all that its cracked up to be." Shame is the ultimate hypocrisy. There's nothing to do in heaven except play harp music all day. Sex might not last forever, but enjoy it while you can and let laughter and humor make old age bearable. It has certainly worked for me.

I never thought of myself as a little angel, but unless I am deluded by hypocrisy and rationalizations, I am certainly not a little devil. I will let you decide.

ACKNOWLEDGEMENTS

Of course the book includes stories about most of the people who helped me make the adjustments to my life that were so needed. Below is a list of some of the people I want to thank who also meant much to me but there was not enough time to include them.

My wife Judy, who is half of this story, and knew better than anyone the crazy ride it took to make Flesh Gordon and my other films.

Sam Stetson, who unveieled my hidden identity to adult film historians and critics Bill Landis and Michelle Clifford who made me aware of the importance of my work Mark Grasso, whose constant prodding drove me to finish my book.

Ashley and April Spicer who not only gave me encouragement but spent hours helping me find a title and prepare a letter of introduction for a publisher.

My sister Nancy who critiqued the book and provided me with inside information about Osco.
Steve Newmark and Maurice Smith whose efforts kept Flesh Gordon alive in the public eye in the U. S. and abroad.

Christopher Chessnut who wizened me to some of the subleties of religion that I didn't know.

And of course, All the girls who dared to buck society's frowns to share their charms and sexuality.

I hope the book will make it clear how much is owed to all the technicans, my crew and all the people who supported me during difficult times. It is impossible to list them all but their contributions are no less appreciated.

www.ingramcontent.com/pod-product-compliance
Lightning Source LLC
Chambersburg PA
CBHW021655120626
46545CB00004B/1255